BOOK ON GOLPE

by Angelos Gialamas

BOOK ON GOLPE

by Angelos Gialamas

Graphic Design: Konstantakopoulou Panagiota

Copyright © 2019 by Angelos Gialamas. All rights reserved.

No part of this publication may be reproduced, stored in a retrieval system or transmitted in any form or by any means, electronic, mechanical, photocopying, recording or otherwise, without the prior written permission of the publisher.

Permissions may be sought directly from Angelos Gialamas. Brief quotations embodied in critical articles or reviews are permitted.

Part of this work is protected under USPTO application no. 62/326,830 *(Enhancing Stringed Instrument Learning With A Wearable Device)* and others.

Angelos Gialamas
3 Giannitson Street
Kalamata, 24100
Greece
https://www.guitartecnica.com

Sent feedback to feedback@guitartecnica.com
Visit online store at https://www.guitartecnica.com

Printed in United States of America
10 9 8 7 6 5 4 3 2 1

To place orders through Guitartecnica:
Tel: (0030) 27210 82838
Mob: (0030) 697 722 1180
E-mail: orders@guitartecnica.com

ISBN-10: 1-947596-05-5
ISBN-13: 978-1-947596-05-4

Significant discounts for bulk and educational institutions are available.
Please contact Angelos Gialamas at info@guitartecnica.com or (0030) 697 722 1180

Acknowledgments

This work would not have been possible without the loving support and contribution of many of you which I am very grateful. Your warmth and consistent encouragement throughout the years has truly been a lightning rod of creativity and hope for me and my music.

On this first ever publication endeavor, I would like to offer my sincere gratitude to my graphic designer Giota Konstantakopoulou for years of excellent collaboration and cooperation. Giota has been instrumental in organizing and presenting all graphical book elements since inception.

Special thanks to my dear friend, Niki Sakareli for her laborious translations. Eamonn Clerkin on his mechanical engineering contribution of the accompanied Rasgueados wearable device. Nikos Avraam for content curation. Petros Tsapralis, Christos Katsireas, Dimitra Margariti, Francesco Santini for their musical editorial review and assessment. Maria Baka, Gioula Nikitea and Kostantina Vraka for their positive attribution of book authoring. A heartfelt thank you to Giorgos Gialamas and Eleni Asproudi for teaching and instilling in me strong music foundations. Early introduced influences by Giorgos and Eleni resonate strongly in me. Their warmth and tenderness, their countless hours of instruction, commitment and dedication to their pupil, have inspired me to produce this volume of work. I am and always be indebted to them, for the love and consideration I have received.

I would like to also thank my loving spouse Amalia, daughters Christina and Fotini. Throughout the years, their discreet presence, patience and tolerance has cultivated an environment of tranquility and serenity for me to exist and work uninterrupted. Their consistent encouragement and attention is a true testament of selfless love.

Angelo Gialamas

Kalamata,
August 1, 2017

GOLPE

The present volume refers to the Golpe technique. Golpe is noted with letter **G** above the note. It is performed with a quick movement of the right hand ring finger on the guitar's body (front surface) while the nail and the finger also participate in this movement. Golpe can be played either in isolation or in combination with other fingers as it is shown in the present volume.

The usual finger to perform a Golpe is the ring finger and you are advised to perform the exercises of this volume with this finger. However the majority of the exercises can be performed with two fingers (middle and ring finger). The exercises where both fingers can be used are obvious.

The exercises of the present volume are based on:

a/ the chromatic scales of one string:

e.g: ‖ 1 4 2 3 4 3 2 4 ‖

b/ the ascending or descending rolling scales:

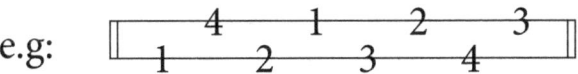

c/ the chromatic (or not) scales of two adjacent strings:

e.g:

For the interpretation of the exercises:

1./ The numbers indicate the fingers of the left hand:

    1 = index finger
    2 = middle finger
    3 = ring finger
    4 = little finger

2./ The lines indicate the guitar strings:

- the six (6) lines represent the strings and the vertical arrangement of the elements indicates simultaneous stroke.

```
1st ─────────────────
2nd ─────────────────
3rd ─────────────────
4th ─────────────────
5th ─────────────────
6th ─────────────────
```

3./ The fingers of the right hand are:

    p - thumb
    i - index finger
    m - middle finger
    a - ring finger
    x - little finger

- the arrows ↑ ↓ show the direction of the stroke:

↑ indicates direction of the stroke from the 6th to the 1st string.

↓ indicates direction of the stroke from the 1st to the 6th string.

TABLE OF CONTENTS
FIRST PART

CHAPTER 1.....page 3
GOLPE ONLY WITH THE THUMB.

UNIT 1.....p.9
THUMB STROKE TOWARDS ONE DIRECTION (↑).

UNIT 2.....p.19
THUMB STROKE TOWARDS TWO DIRECTION
DOWNWARDS (↑) AND UPWARDS (↓).

UNIT 3.....p.25
THUMB STROKE WITH GOLPE TOWARDS
ONE DIRECTION. TWO TRIPLETS IN THE FORMULA.

UNIT 4.....p.33
THUMB STROKE WITH GOLPE TOWARDS
TWO DIRECTION DOWNWARDS (↑) AND UPWARDS (↓).
TWO TRIPLETS WITHIN THE FORMULA.
ONE GOLPE WITHIN THE TRIPLET.

UNIT 5.....p.45
THUMB STROKE WITH GOLPE TOWARDS
TWO DIRECTION DOWNWARDS (↑) AND UPWARDS (↓).
TWO TRIPLETS WITHIN THE FORMULA.
TWO GOLPE WITHIN THE TRIPLET.

UNIT 6.....p.65
THUMB STROKE WITH GOLPE AND TRIPLETS.
1/. GOLPE ON EVERY THUMP STROKE.
2/. THUMP STROKE ON TWO OR
THREE STRINGS SIMULTANEOUSLY.

CHAPTER 2.....page 79
THUMB STROKE WITH GOLPE.

UNIT 1.....p.81
THUMB STROKE WITH GOLPE
AND FREE GOLPE
WITHOUT THE PARTICIPATION OF THE THUMB.

UNIT 2.....p.101
TWO OR THREE GOLPE WITHIN THE METER (ONE FREE).
THUMB STROKE ON ONE (↑) OR TWO (↑↓) DIRECTIONS.
STRIKE ONE, TWO OR THREE STRINGS
SIMULTANEOUSLY.

CHAPTER 3.....page 113
GOLPE WITH THUMB STROKE IN COMBINATION
WITH INDEX AND MIDDLE FINGER.

UNIT 1.....p.117
THUMB STROKE WITH GOLPE ON ONE, TWO OR
THREE STRINGS AND IN COMBINATION
WITH INDEX AND MIDDLE FINGER.

UNIT 2.....p.129
THUMB STROKE WITH GOLPE ON ONE STRING.
VARIATIONS WITH TRIPLETS.

UNIT 3.....p.149
THUMB STROKE WITH GOLPE ON ONE, TWO
OR THREE STRINGS SIMULTANEOUSLY.
VARIATIONS WITH TRIPLETS.

CHAPTER 4.....page 159

FREE GOLPE AND THUMB STROKE ON THE CHROMATIC SCALES OF ONE STRING (8 NOTES) WITH THE PARTICIPATION OF INDEX AND MIDDLE FINFER. ONE OR TWO GOLPE IN THE METER. VARIATIONS IN REGARD TO FINGERS INDEX AND RING FINGER, IN REGARD TO THUMB STROKE (DIRECTION OF STROKE). THE EXERCISES OF THIS CHAPTER SHAPED AS TRIPLETS.

UNIT 1.....p.161

FREE GOLPE AND THUMB STROKE IN COMBINATION WITH INDEX AND MIDDLE FINGER. ONE OR TWO DIRECTIONS OF THUMB STROKE.

UNIT 2.....p.183

THUMB STROKE WITH GOLPE ON TWO OR THREE STRINGS SIMULTANEOUSLY. FREE GOLPE WITHIN THE FORMULAS.

UNIT 3.....p.201

GOLPE EXERCISES IN COMBINATION WITH ARPEGIOS AND LIGADOS.

CHAPTER 5.....page 209
SIMULTANEOUSLY STROKE OF THUMB
WITH INDEX (i) OR MIDDLE FINGER (m) AND GOLPE.

UNIT 1.....p.211
THUMB STROKE SIMULTANEOUSLY
WITH INDEX OR MIDDLE FINGER.
TWO GOLPE WITHIN METER.

UNIT 2.....p.223
THUMB STROKE SIMULTANEOUSLY
WITH INDEX OR MIDDLE FINGER.
TWO TRIPLETS WITHIN THE FORMULA.

CHAPTER 6.....page 243
COMBINATION OF GOLPE AND SIMULTANEOUS STROKE
OF THUMB WITH INDEX AND MIDDLE FINGER.
TWO TRIPLETS WITHIN THE FORMULA.

UNIT 1.....p.245
COMBINATION OF GOLPE AND SIMULTANEOUS STROKE
OF THUMB AND RIGHT HAND FINGERS,
INDEX AND MIDDLE FINGER.

UNIT 2.....p.265
SIMULTANEOUS STROKE OF THUMB WITH INDEX,
MIDDLE FINGER AND GOLPE.
CONTINEOUS GOLPE IN EVERY STROKE.

TABLE OF CONTENTS
SECOND PART

CHAPTER 1.....page 275
THUMB STROKE AND GOLPE
ON SCALES OF TWO ADJACENT STRINGS.

UNIT 1.....p.277
VARIOUS EXERCISES OF GOLPE:
1/. ONLY THUMB GOLPE.
2/. THUMB GOLPE IN COMBINATION
WITH INDEX AND MIDDLE FINGER.
3/. EXERCISES WITH FREE GOLPE.

UNIT 2.....p.283
GOLPE EXERCISES
WITHOUT THE PARTICIPATION OF THE THUMB.
EXERCISES BASED ON THE ASCENDING
AND DESCENDING ROLLING SCALES.

UNIT 3.....p.291
GOLPE EXERCISES WITHOUT THUMB.
GOLPE EXERCISES WITH LIGADOS.

CHAPTER 2.....page 297
GOLPE EXERCISES BASED ON THE SCALES
OF TWO ADJACENT STRINGS.

UNIT 1.....p.299
FREE GOLPE OR GOLPE SIMULTANEOUS
WITH THUMB STROKE.

UNIT 2.....p.309
A/. GOLPE EXERCISES SHAPED IN TRIPLETS.
ONE OR TWO GOLPE WITHIN THE METER.
B/. GOLPE EXERCISES WITH LIGADO
WITHIN THE TRIPLET.

UNIT 3.....p.317
COMBINATION OF GOLPE WITH ARPEGIOS.

UNIT 4.....p.325
GOLPE EXERCISES ON THE ASCENDING AND
DESCENDING ROLLING FORMULAS.

CHAPTER 3.....page 333

UNIT 1.....p.335
COMBINATION OF GOLPE
WITH ACCORDS OF TWO NOTES ON ASCENDING
AND DESCENDING ROLLING FORMULAS,
AND ON SCALES OF TWO ADJACENT STRINGS.

UNIT 2.....p.345
SIMULTANEOUS STROKE OF THUMB WITH INDEX
AND MIDDLE FINGER WITH GOLPE ON THE
ROLLING (ASCENDING AND DESCENDING) FORMULAS
AND ON SCALES OF TWO ADJACENT CHORDS.

CHAPTER 4.....page 377
EXERCISES THAT REFER TO THUMB STROKE
WITH GOLPE IN COMBINATION
WITH INDEX AND MIDDLE FINGER.

UNIT 1.....p.379
EXERCISES THAT REFER TO THUMB STROKE
WITH GOLPE IN COMBINATION
WITH INDEX AND MIDDLE FINGER
ON THE VARIOUS FORMULAS OF THE LEFT HAND.

CHAPTER 5.....page 385
EXERCISES THAT REFER TO THUMB STROKE
WITH GOLPE.

UNIT 1.....p.387
THUMB STROKE WITH GOLPE IN COMBINATION
WITH INDEX AND MIDDLE FINGER.
SIMPLE FINGERING OF THE LEFT HAND.
TWELVE FORMULAS.

UNIT 2.....p.393
EXERCISES FOR STRENGTHENING THE THUMB.
THUMB STROKE ON TWO OR THREE STRINGS
SIMULTANEOUSLY WITH GOLPE.

.

CHAPTER 6.....page 403
EXERCISES THAT REFER TO THUMB STROKE WITH GOLPE
IN COMBINATION WITH INDEX AND MIDDLE FINGER
ON VARIOUS FORMULAS.

UNIT 1.....p.405

UNIT 2.....p.415

UNIT 3.....p.425

UNIT 4.....p.435

CHAPTER 7.....page 435
RASGUEADOS AND GOLPE.

BOOK ON GOLPE
FIRST PART

CHAPTER 1

Chapter 1 contains Golpe only with the thumb **p** without the use of the other fingers i, m and a.

1. The thumb strikes only downwards

2. The thumb strikes downwards - upwards

Stroke on the chromatic scales (8 notes) of:

one string

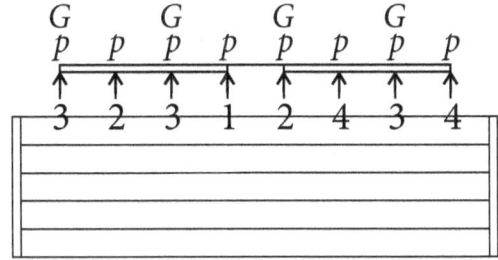

two strings

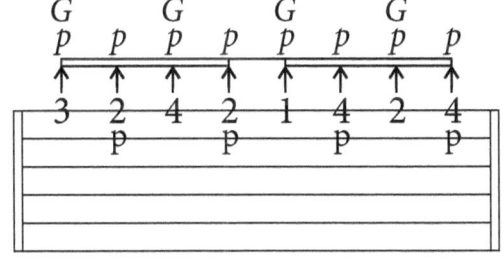

or three strings

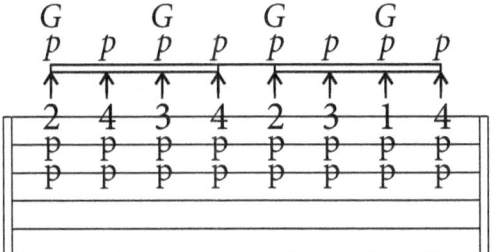

The chromatic scale apart from the above formation (with isochronous notes) can be also formed in three variations with the existence of two triplets:

VARIATION 1

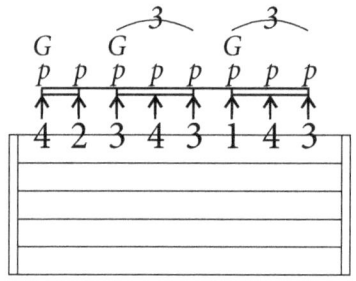

VARIATION 2

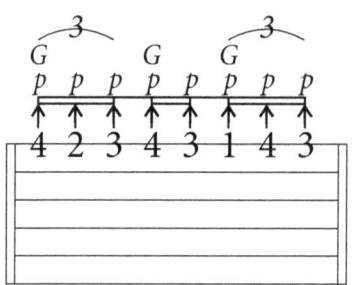

VARIATION 3

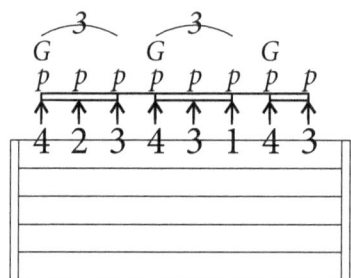

The two and three notes (triplet) have the same duration, the double and triple stroke in other words are isochronous.

In the whole book when the chromatic scale of 8 notes is on the 5th string, then the thumb can alternatively strike the 6th string at the same time. Eg:

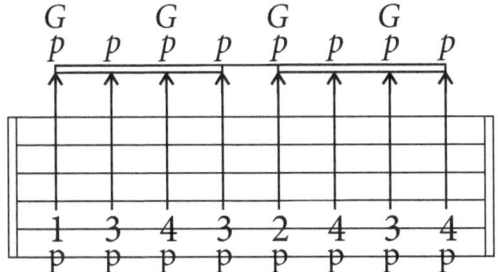 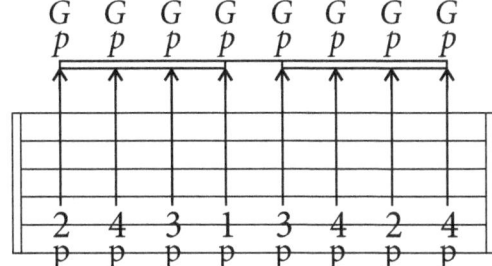

When the chromatic scale is on the 4th string, then the thumb can simultaneously strike the 5th and 6th string. Including the note on the 4th string we have simultaneous stroke of 3 strings.

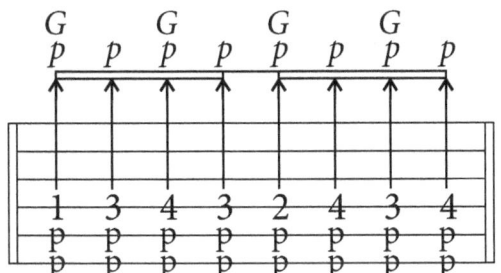 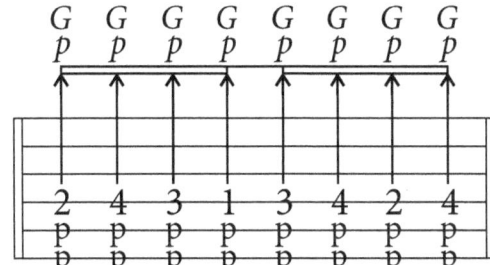

UNIT 1
Thumb stroke towards
one direction (downwards↑).

§I Thumb stroke with Golpe (two Golpe or four within the meter) on the chromatic scales of one string. The chromatic scales are played on the first, second, third, fourth, fifth and sixth string.

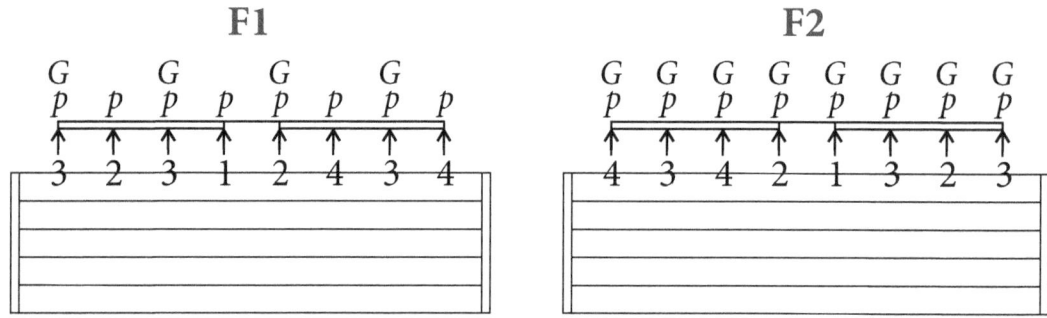

§II The chromatic scales move every two notes:

a/ from the first to the fourth string with return to the first.

b/ from the second to the fifth string with return to the second.

c/ from the third to the sixth string with return to the third.

The return takes place with the opposite chromatic scales.

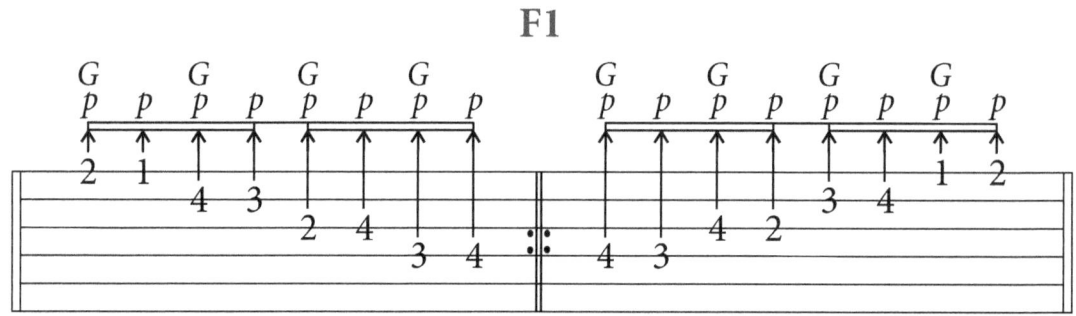

§III Thumb stroke of two strings simultaneously and one string within the meter (with two Golpe F1 or four F2 within the meter).

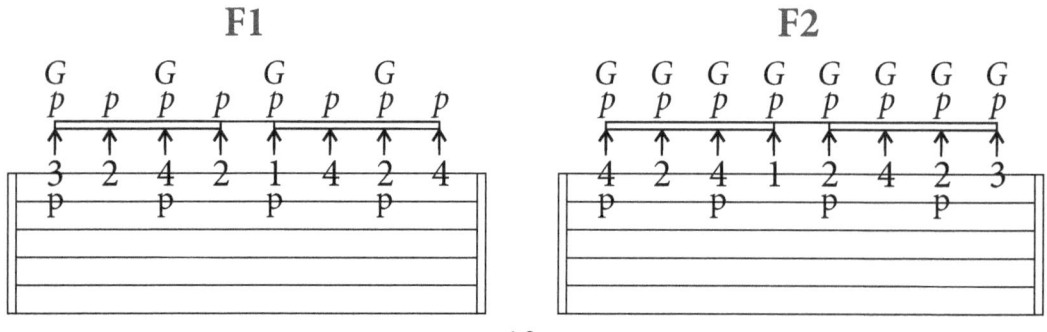

§IV Thumb stroke of two strings simultaneously (with two Golpe F1 or four F2 within the meter) in the whole Formula.

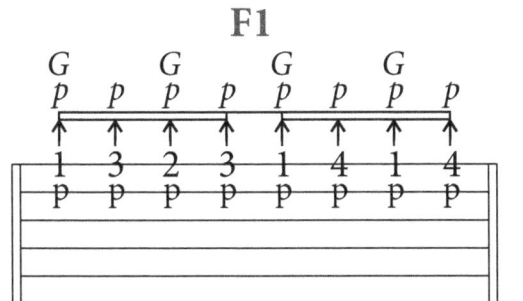
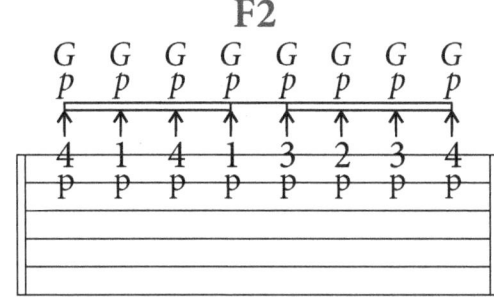

§V Thumb stroke of three strings simultaneously and one string (with two Golpe F1 or four F2 within the meter).

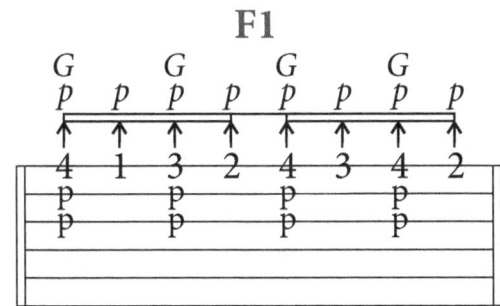
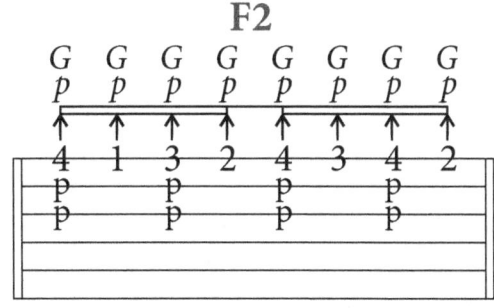

§VI Thumb stroke of three strings simultaneously and two strings simultaneously (with two Golpe F1 or four F2 within the meter).

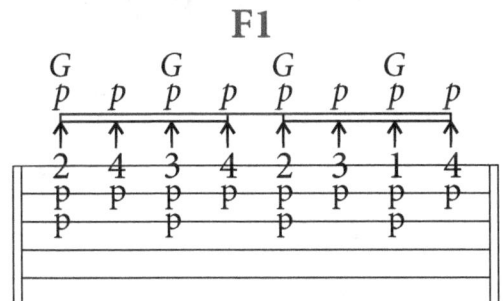
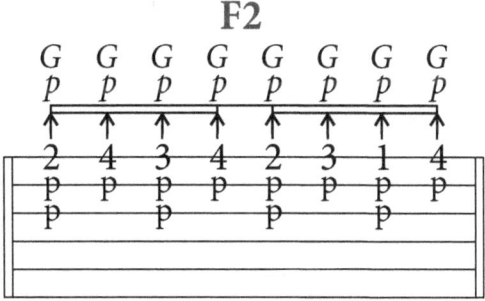

§VII Thumb stroke of three strings simultaneously (with two Golpe F1 or four F2 within the meter).

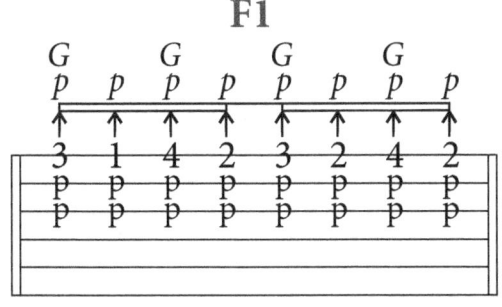
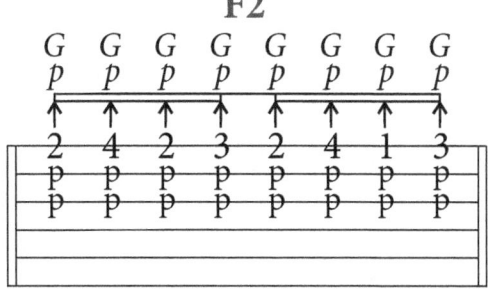

§ I

            F1   F2

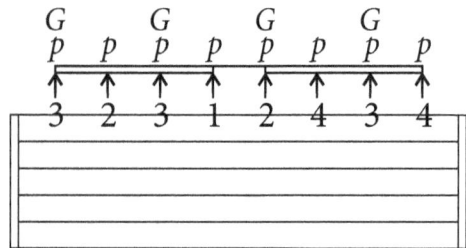 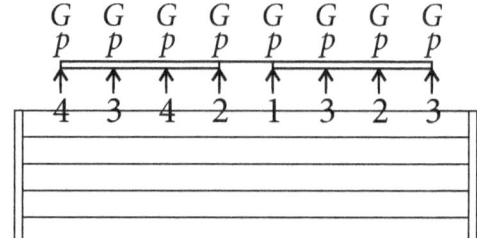

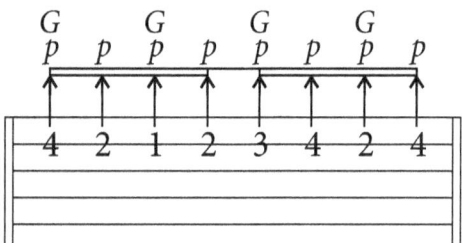 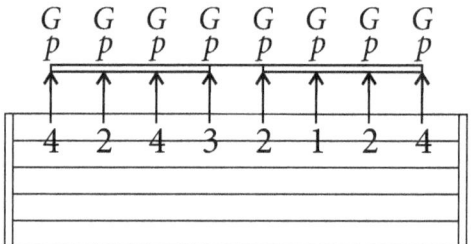

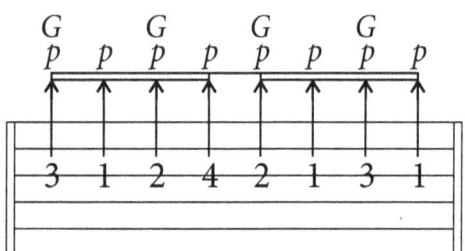 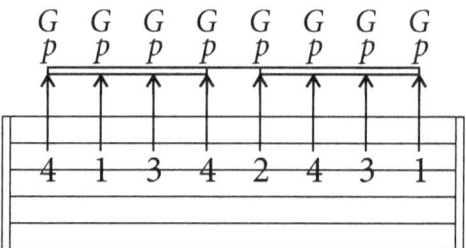

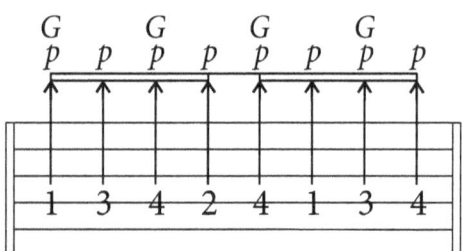 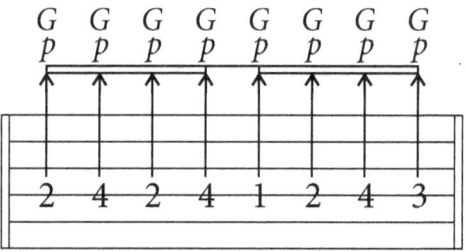

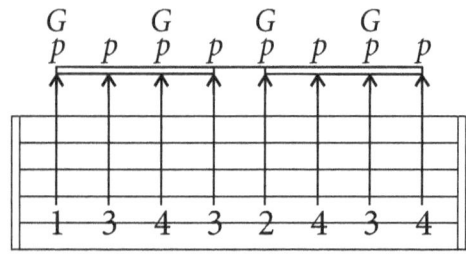 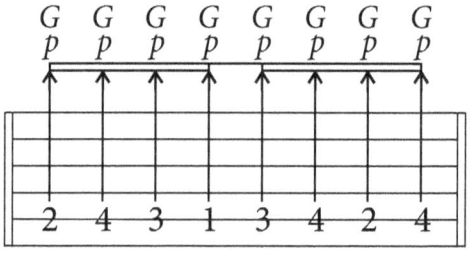

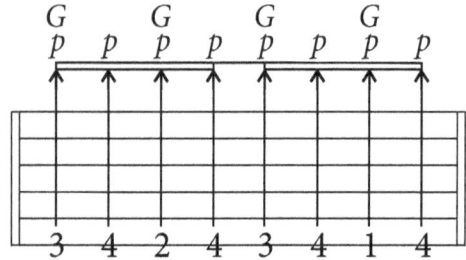 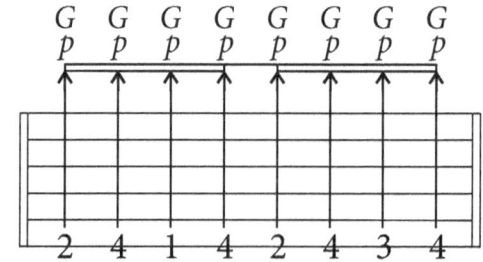

§ II

F1

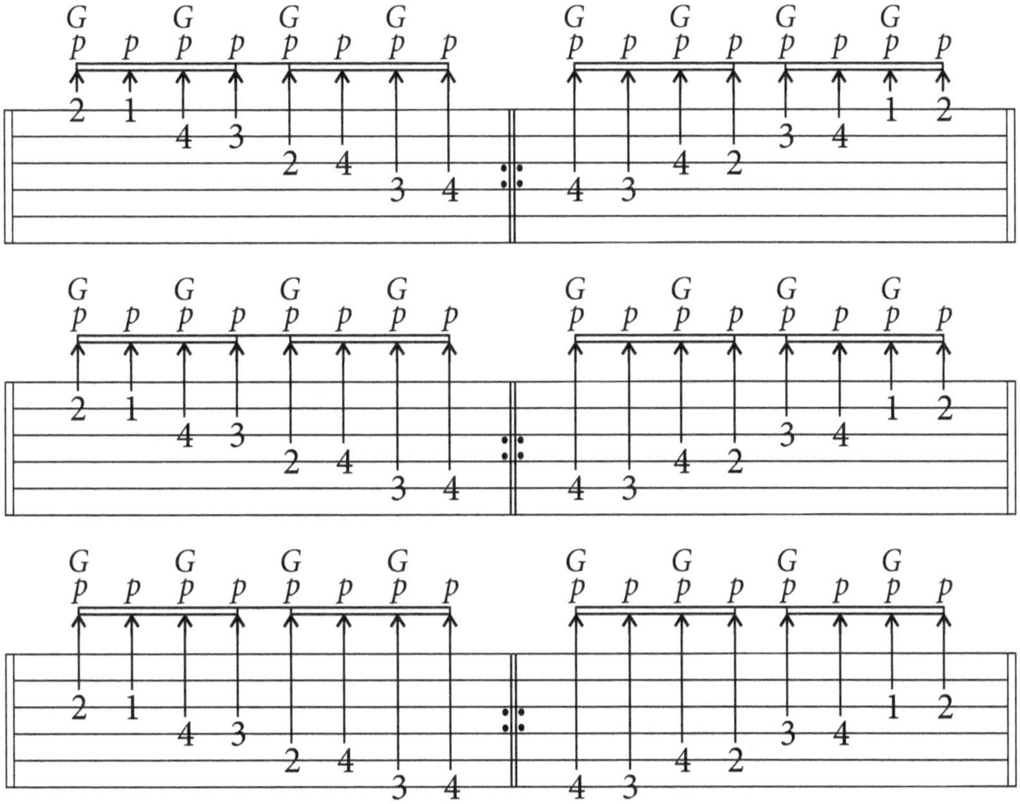

F2

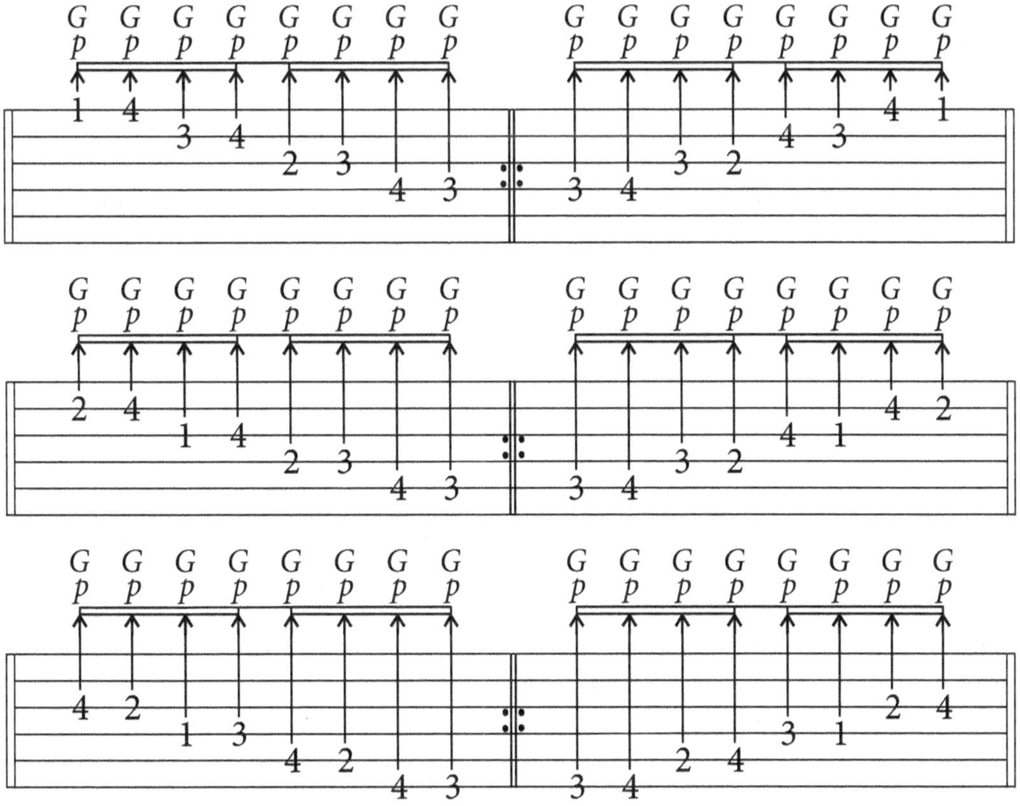

13

§ III

F1 F2

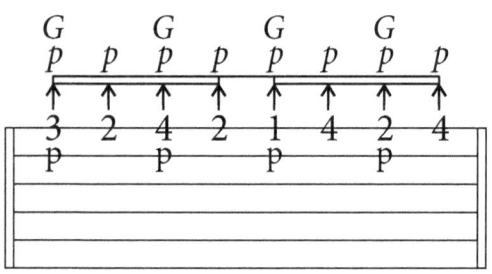 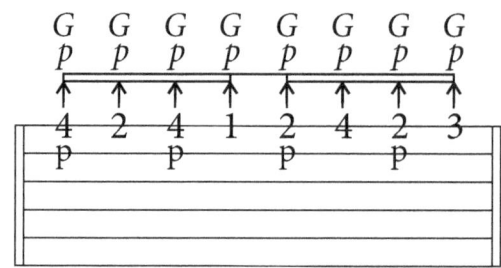
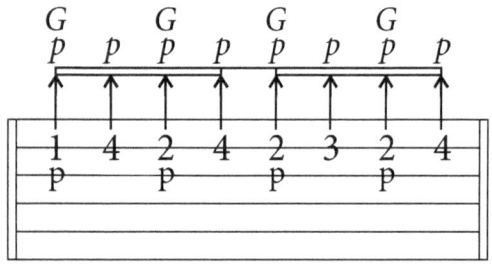 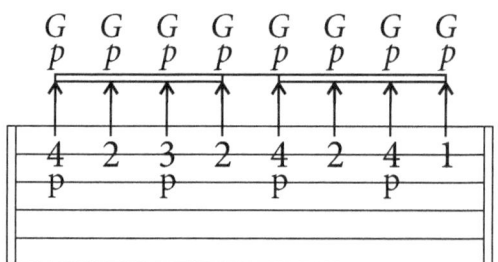
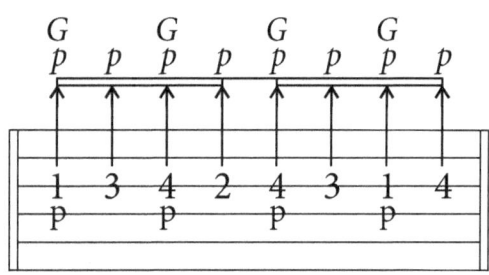 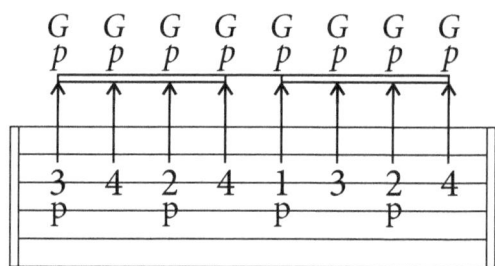
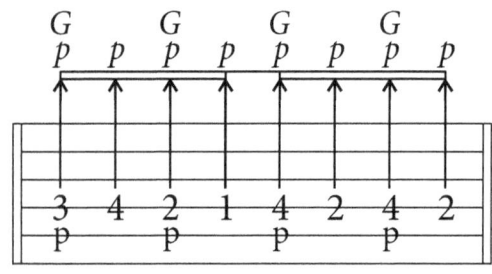 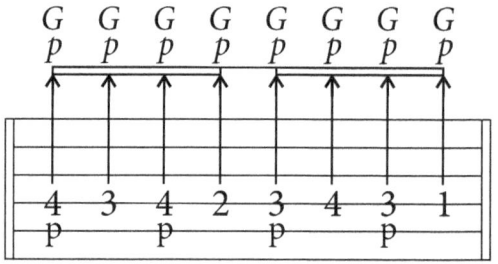
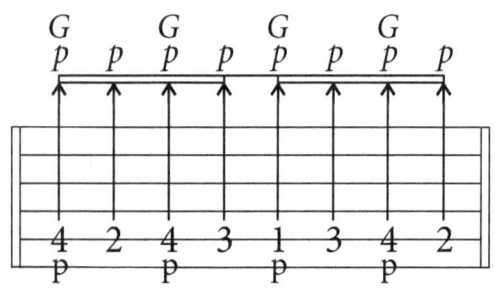 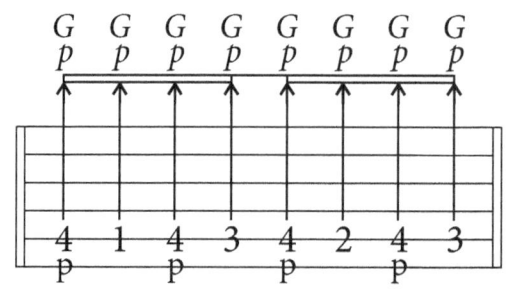

§ IV   **F1**   **F2**

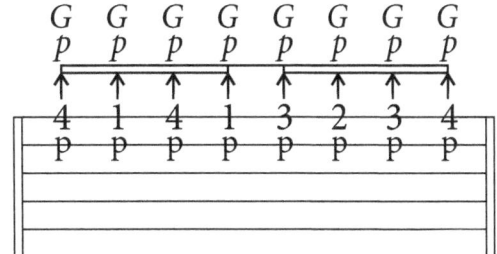
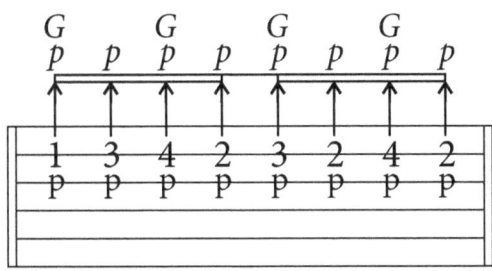
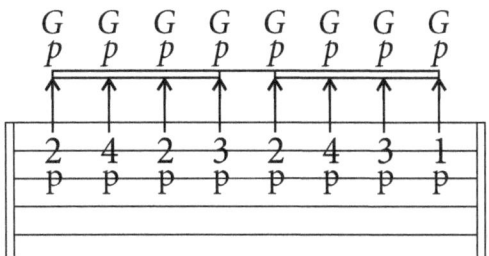
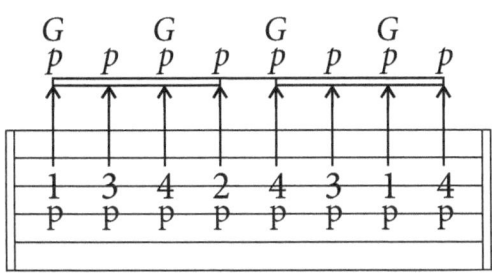
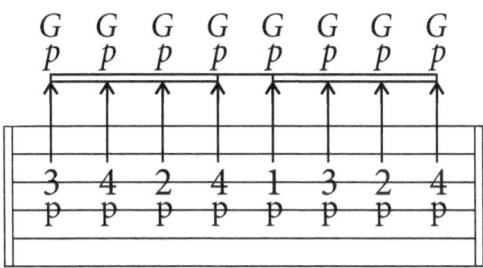
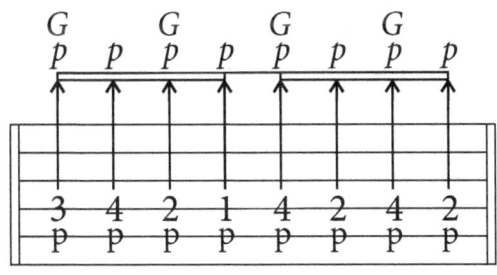
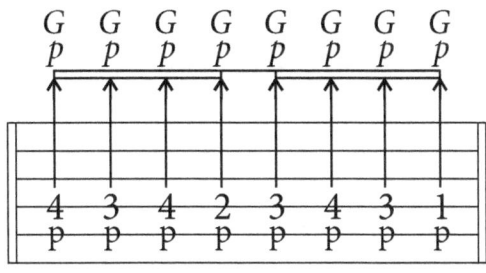
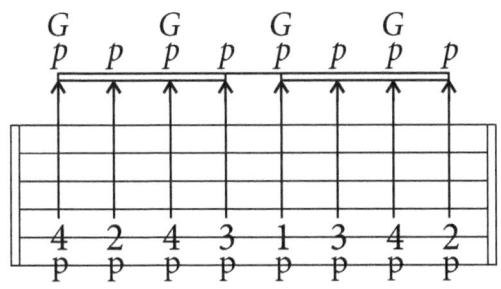
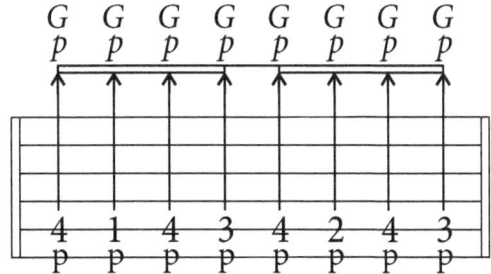

§ V

F1

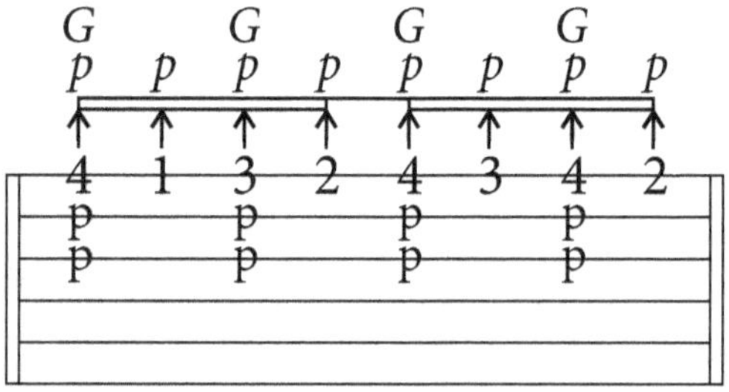

```
G   G   G   G   G   G   G   G
p   p   p   p   p   p   p   p
↑   ↑   ↑   ↑   ↑   ↑   ↑   ↑
4   1   3   2   4   3   4   2
p   p   p   p   p   p   p   p
p   p   p   p   p   p   p   p
```

```
G   G   G   G   G   G   G   G
p   p   p   p   p   p   p   p
↑   ↑   ↑   ↑   ↑   ↑   ↑   ↑
2   1   3   2   4   2   3   4
p   p   p   p   p   p   p   p
p   p   p   p   p   p   p   p
```

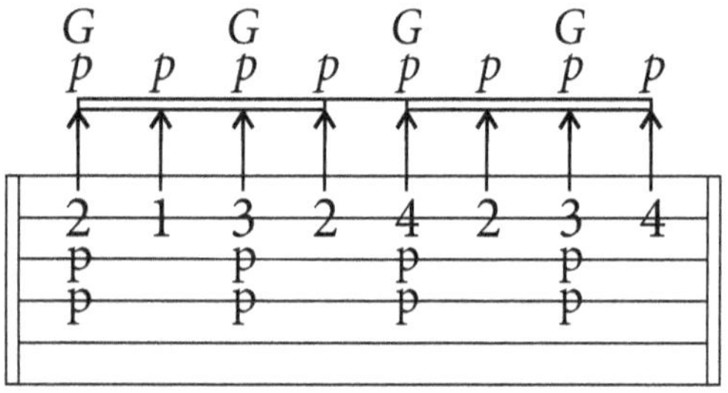

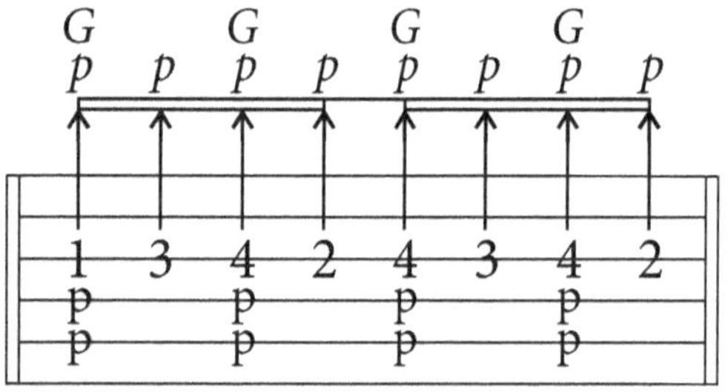

```
G   G   G   G   G   G   G   G
p   p   p   p   p   p   p   p
↑   ↑   ↑   ↑   ↑   ↑   ↑   ↑
1   3   4   2   4   3   4   2
p   p   p   p   p   p   p   p
p   p   p   p   p   p   p   p
```

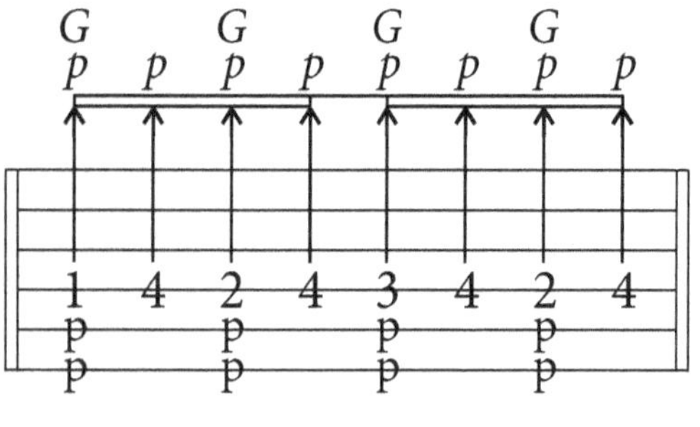

```
G   G   G   G   G   G   G   G
p   p   p   p   p   p   p   p
↑   ↑   ↑   ↑   ↑   ↑   ↑   ↑
1   4   2   4   3   4   2   4
p   p   p   p   p   p   p   p
p   p   p   p   p   p   p   p
```

F2

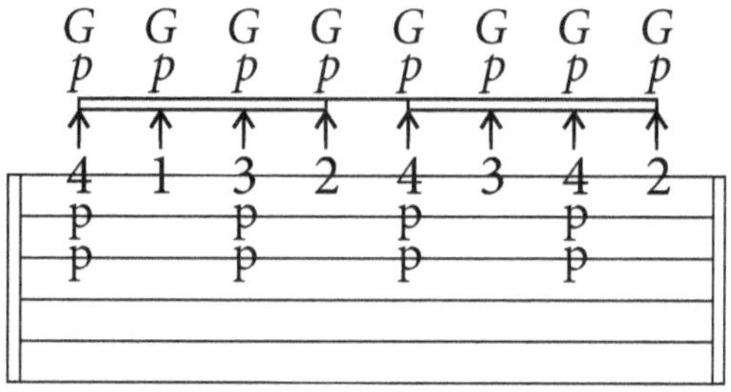

```
G   G   G   G   G   G   G   G
p   p   p   p   p   p   p   p
↑   ↑   ↑   ↑   ↑   ↑   ↑   ↑
4   1   3   2   4   3   4   2
p   p   p   p   p   p   p   p
p   p   p   p   p   p   p   p
```

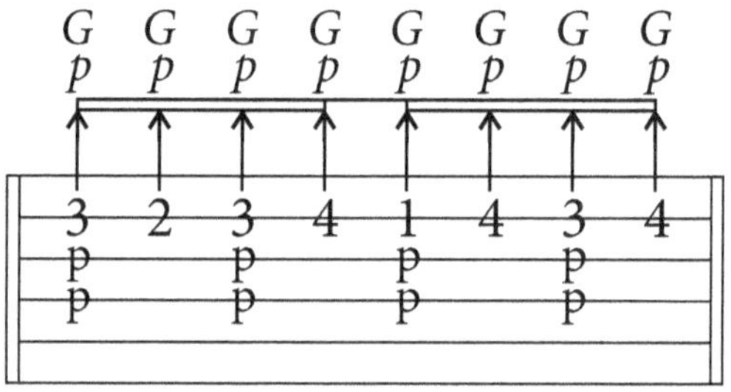

```
G   G   G   G   G   G   G   G
p   p   p   p   p   p   p   p
↑   ↑   ↑   ↑   ↑   ↑   ↑   ↑
3   2   3   4   1   4   3   4
p   p   p   p   p   p   p   p
p   p   p   p   p   p   p   p
```

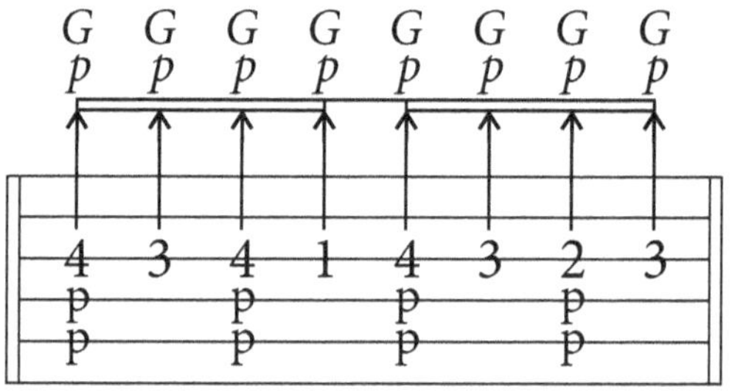

```
G   G   G   G   G   G   G   G
p   p   p   p   p   p   p   p
↑   ↑   ↑   ↑   ↑   ↑   ↑   ↑
4   3   4   1   4   3   2   3
p   p   p   p   p   p   p   p
p   p   p   p   p   p   p   p
```

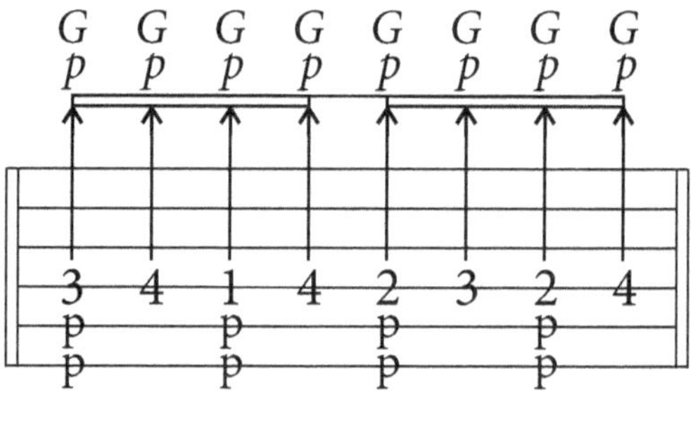

```
G   G   G   G   G   G   G   G
p   p   p   p   p   p   p   p
↑   ↑   ↑   ↑   ↑   ↑   ↑   ↑
3   4   1   4   2   3   2   4
p   p   p   p   p   p   p   p
p   p   p   p   p   p   p   p
```

§ VI

F1 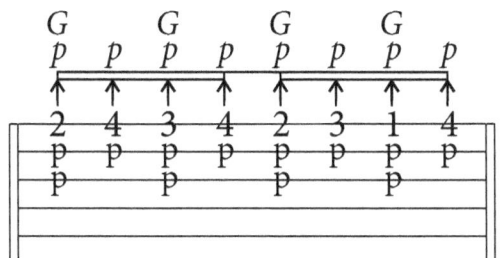 **F2**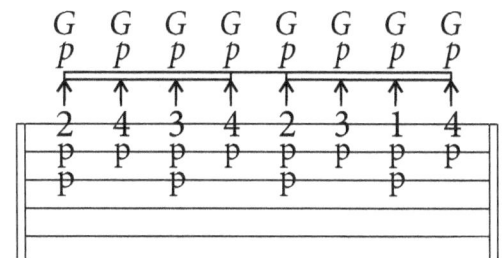

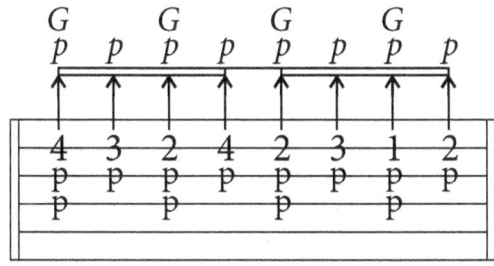 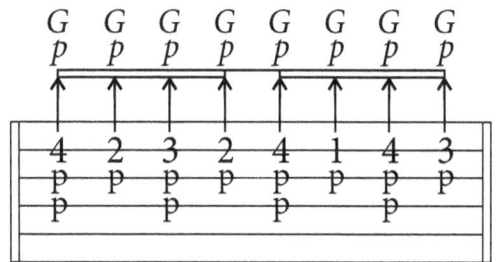

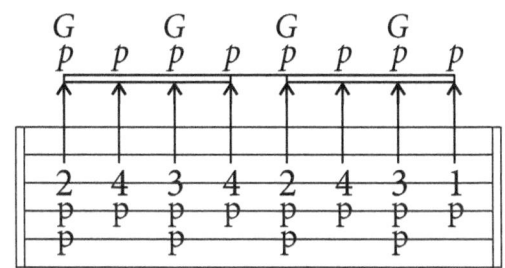 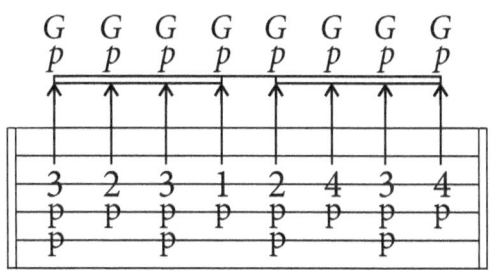

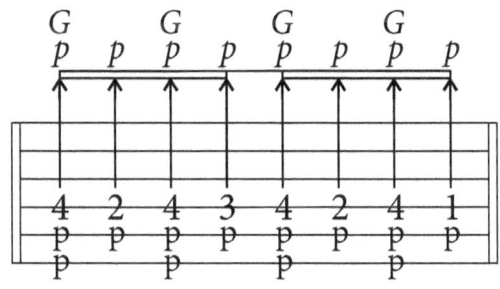 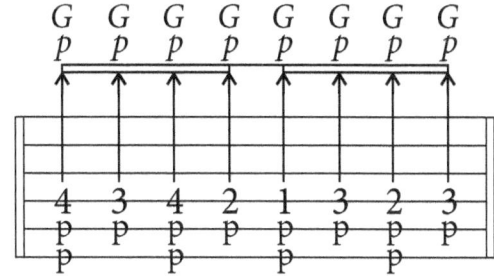

§ VII

F1   **F2**

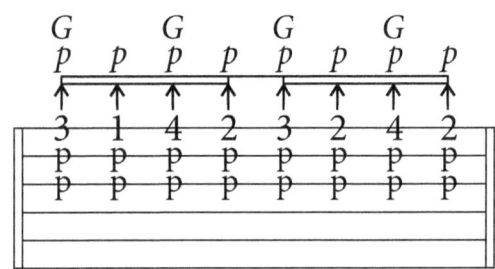 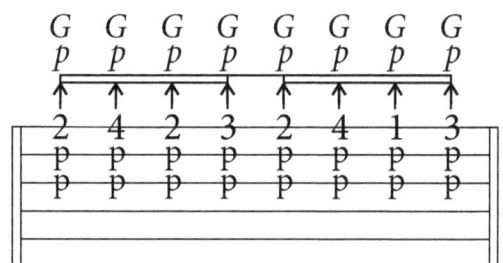

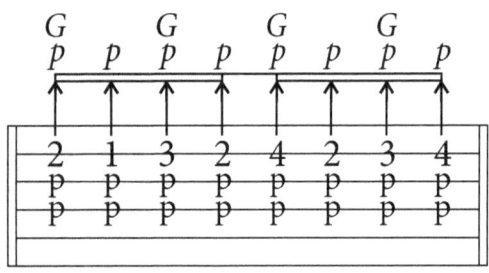 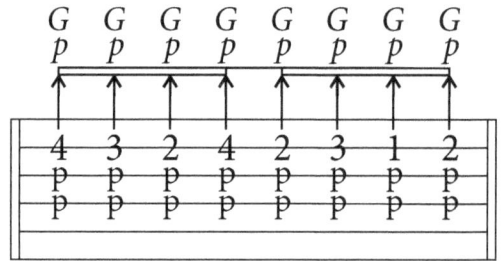

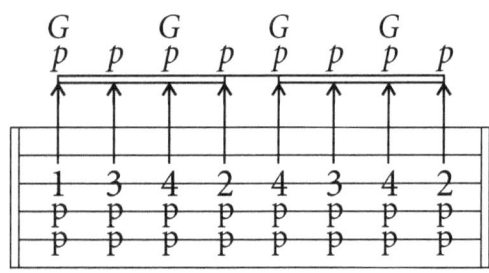 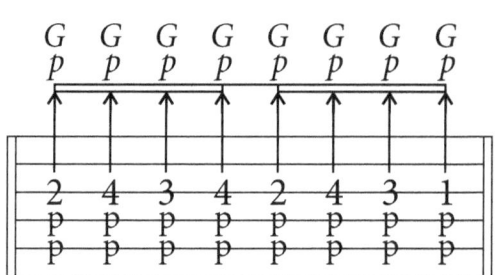

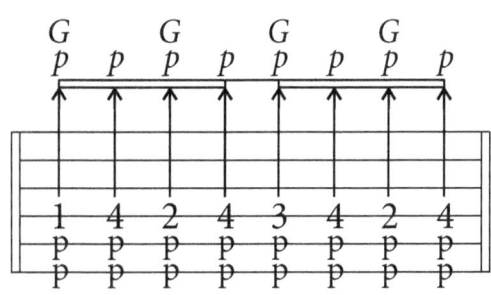 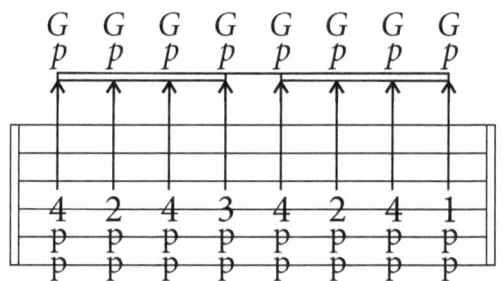

UNIT 2
Thumb stroke towards
two directions (downwards ↑ and upwards ↓).

Unit 2 contains thumb stroke of one, two or three strings simultaneously with double Golpe within the meter and thumb stroke towards two directions both downwards (↑) and upwards (↓).

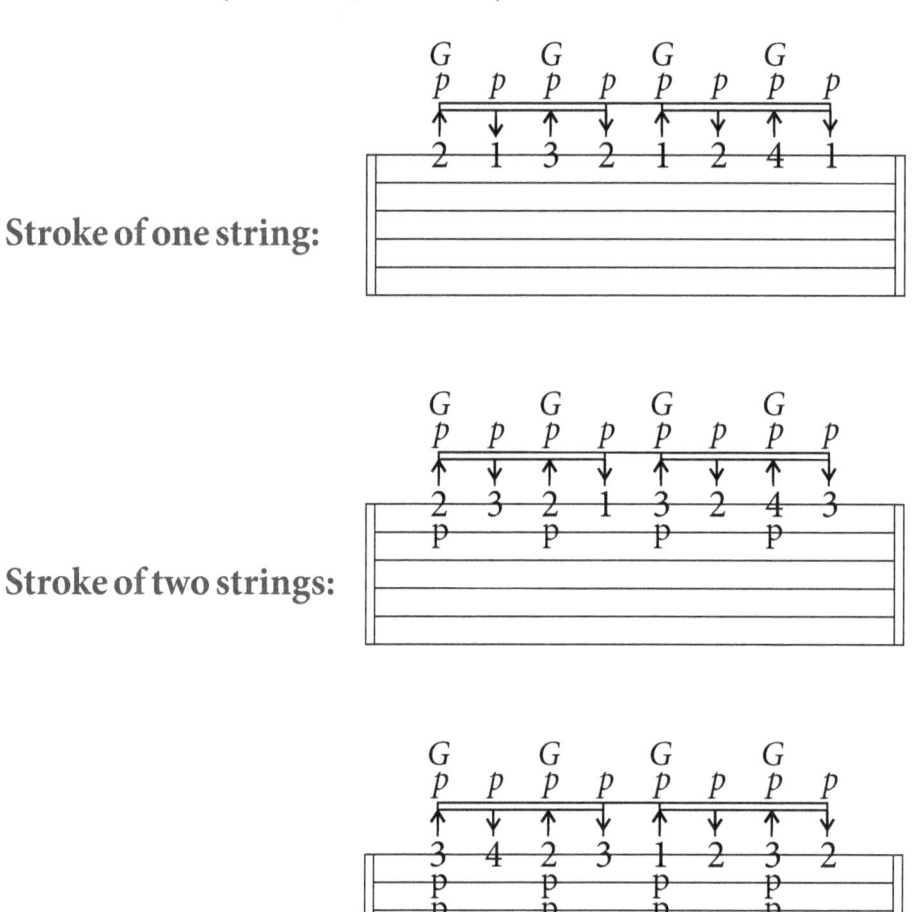

Stroke of one string:

Stroke of two strings:

Stroke of three strings:

Chromatic scale which moves every two notes from the 1st to the 4th strings and returns from the 4th to the 1st with the opposite scale.

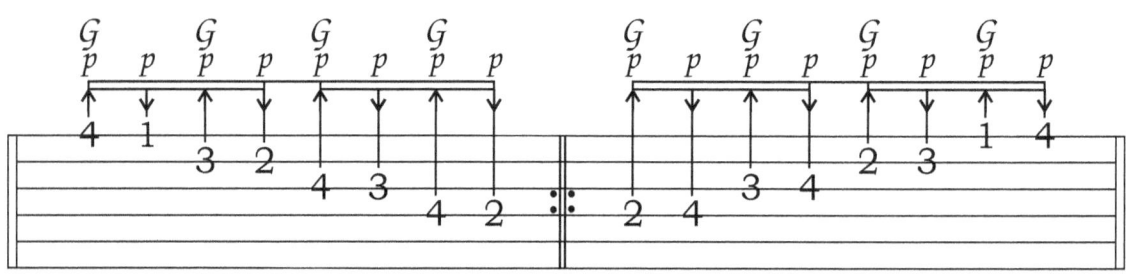

20

§ I

F1 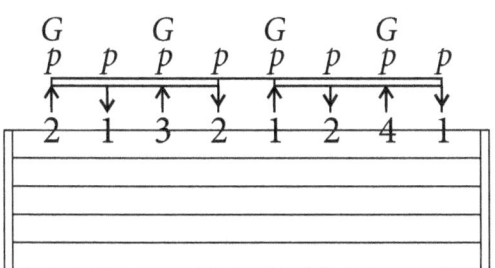 F2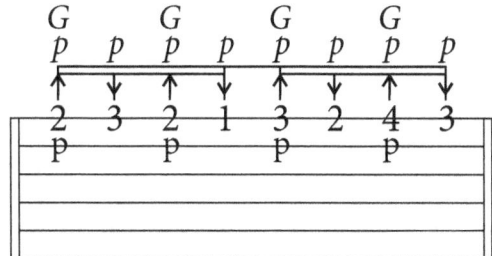

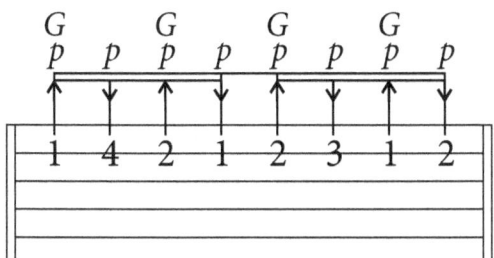 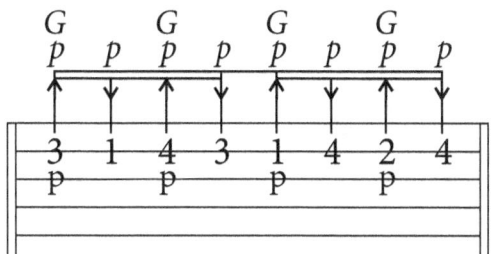

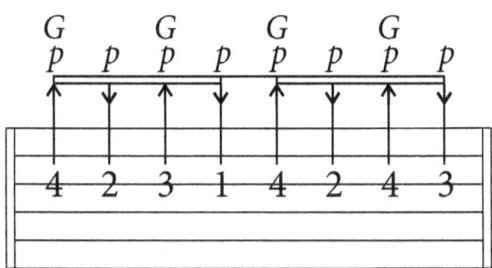 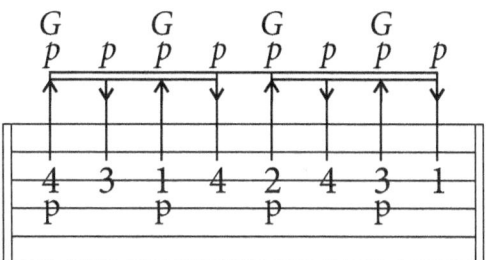

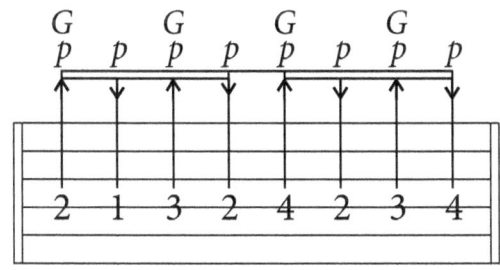 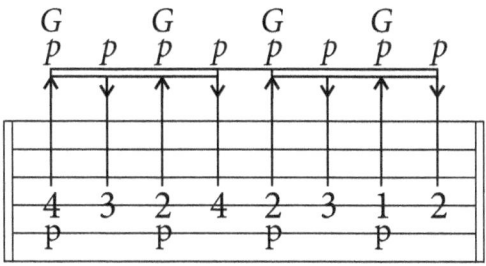

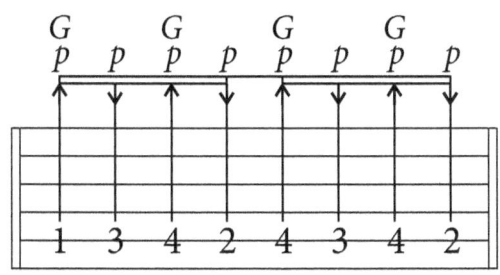 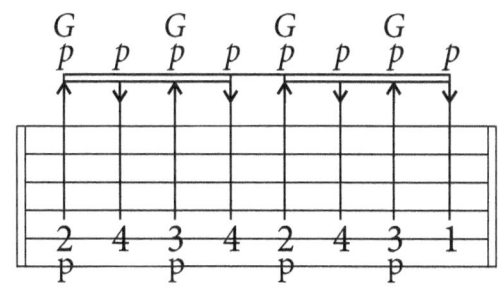

§ II

F1

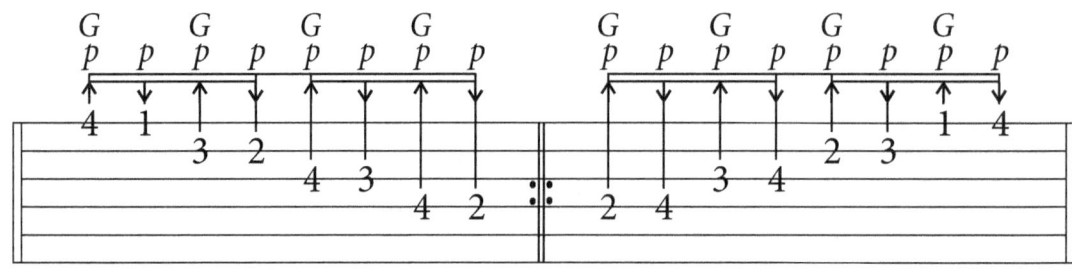

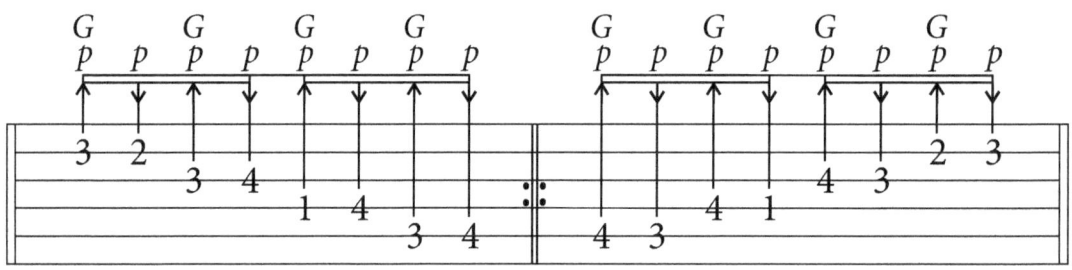

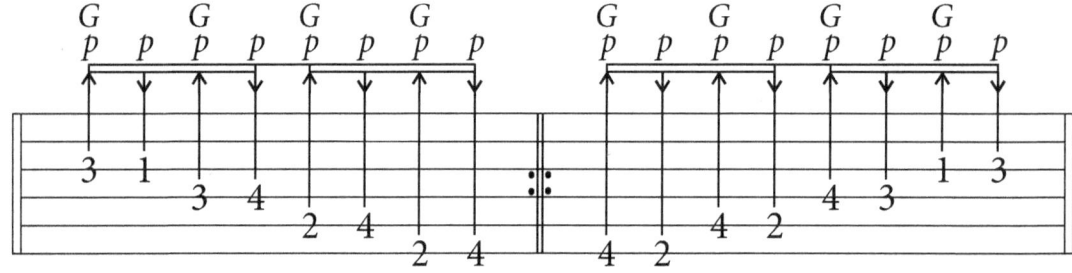

§ III

F1

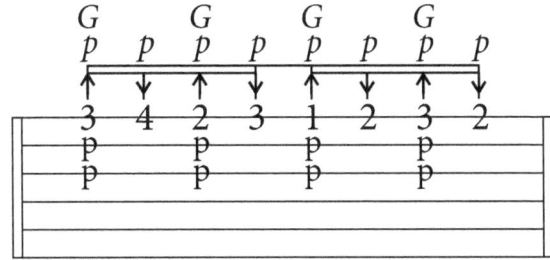
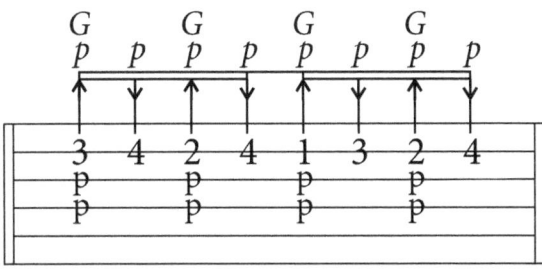
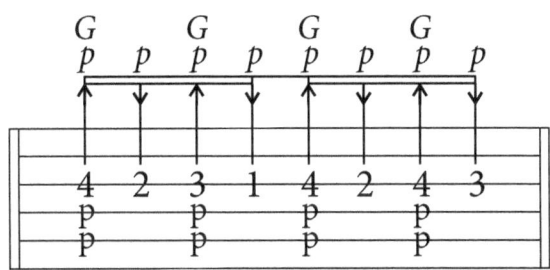
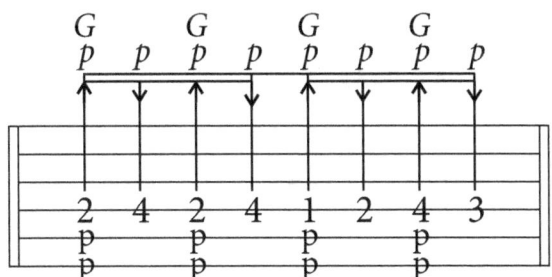

UNIT 3

Thumb stroke with Golpe towards one direction.
Two triplets in the Formula.

In Unit 3 the chromatic scales contain two triplets and two notes. Depending on the position of the triplets we have three variations.

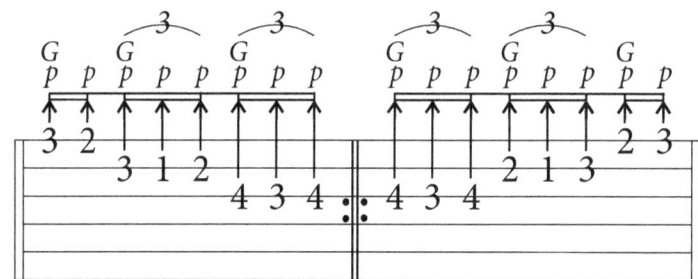

Thumb stroke with three Golpe within each Formula. The movement of the thumb is towards one direction and the chromatic scales formed are played either on one or three adjacent strings.

In the exercise of §II the chromatic scale moves in the following way from the 1st to the 3rd string and returns from the 3rd to the 1st.

In the same way we have movement from the 2nd to the 4th, from the 3rd to 5th and from the 4th to the 6th string as well as return with the opposite fingerings to the initial string.

When the chromatic scale is on the 4th string you can alternatively practice with simultaneous thumb stroke of the 5th and 6th string.

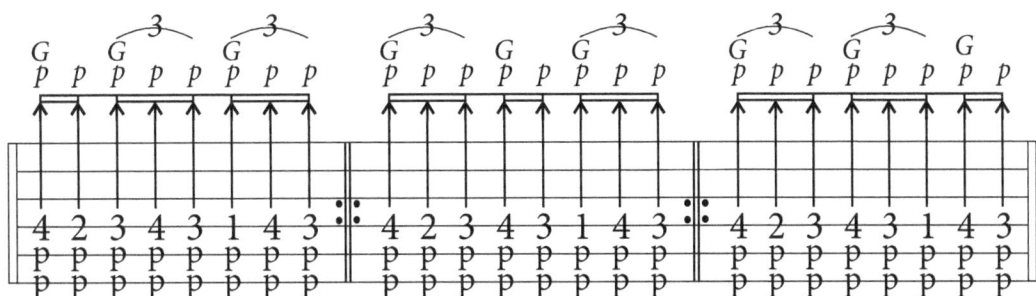

Also, when the chromatic scale is on the 5th string you can alternatively practice with simultaneous thumb stroke of the 6th string.

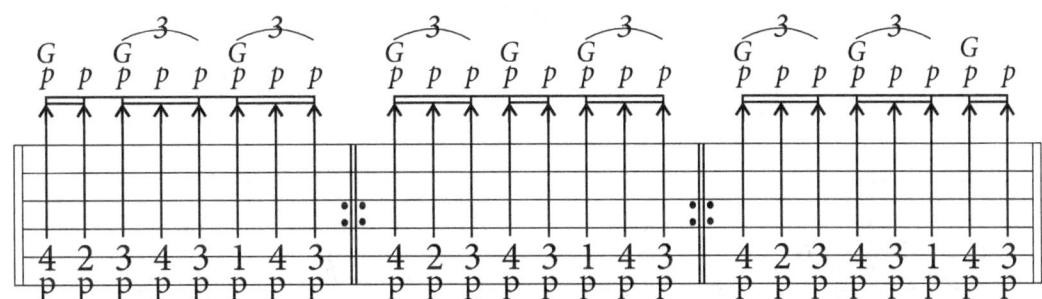

§ I

§ II

A

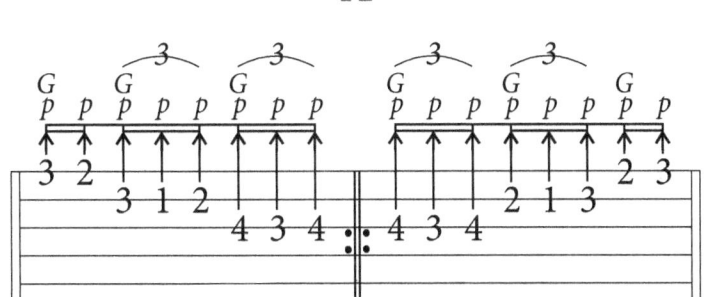

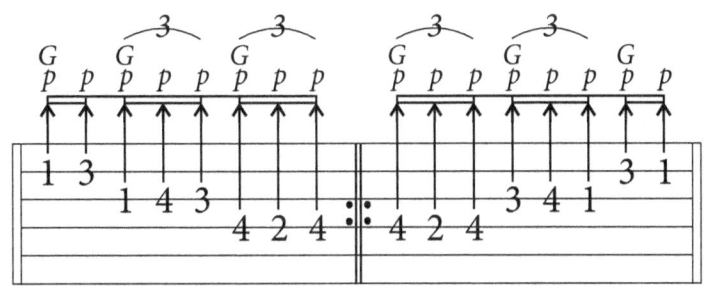

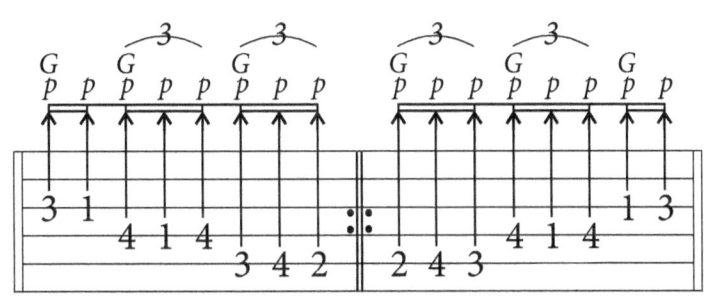

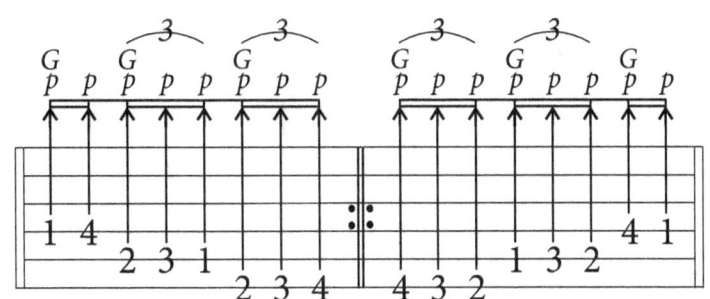

B

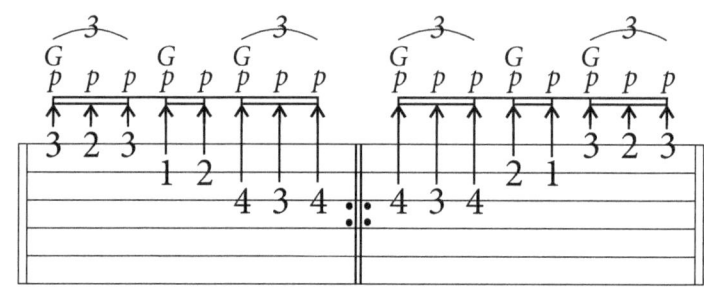
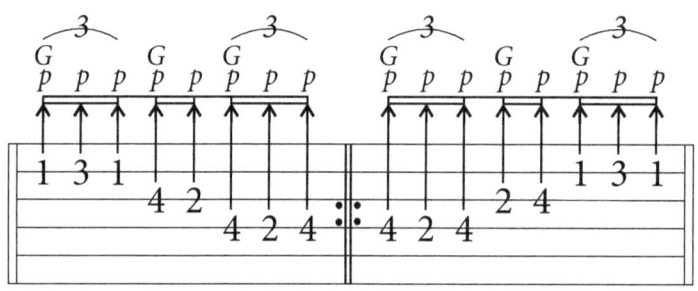
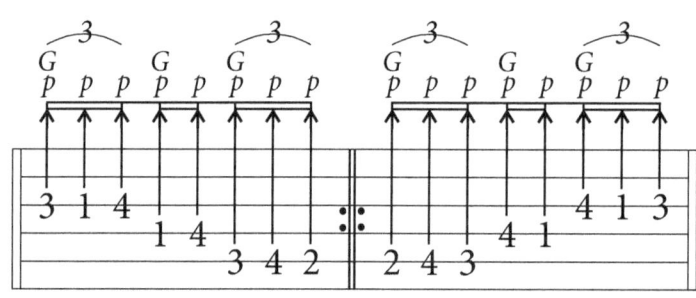
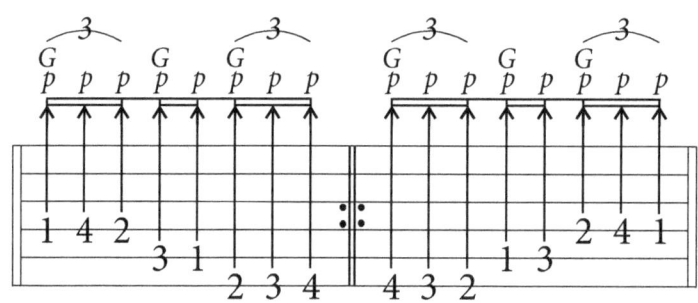

C

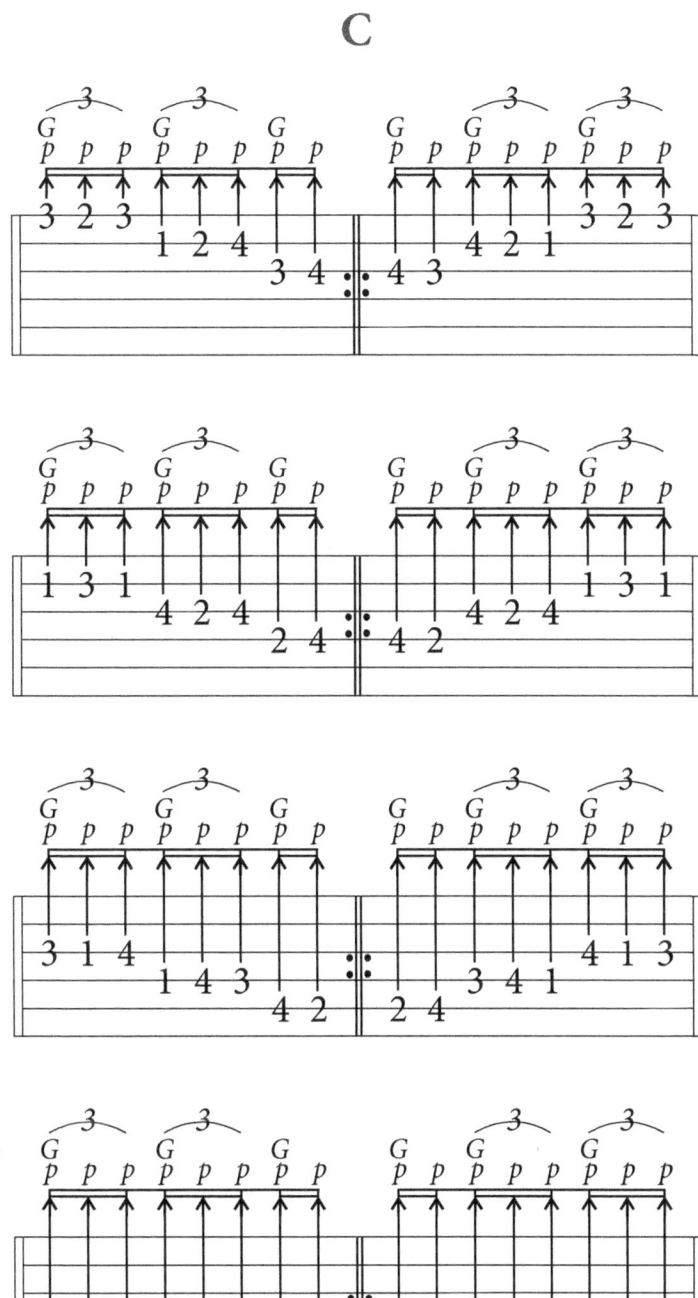

UNIT 4

Thumb stroke with Golpe towards two directions
(downwards ↑ and upwards ↓).
Two triplets within the Formula.
One Golpe within the triplet.

Unit 4 is a repetition of the previous unit with thumb stroke towards two directions both downwards (↑) and upwards (↓). The chromatic scales are played on all six strings,

VARIATION 1   **VARIATION 2**   **VARIATION 3**

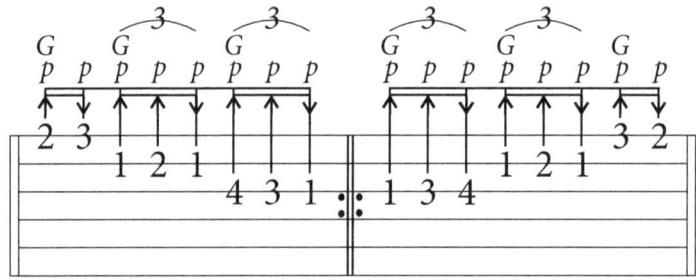

or they move from the 1st to the 3rd string, from the 3rd to the 5th string and from the 4th to the 6th string and return to the initial string with the opposite scale.

§ I

§ II

A

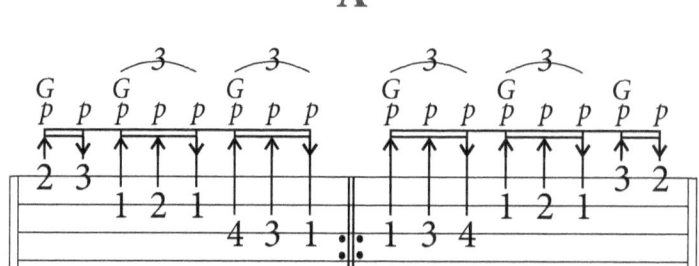

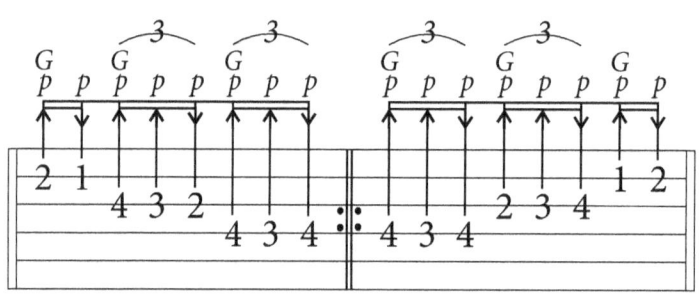

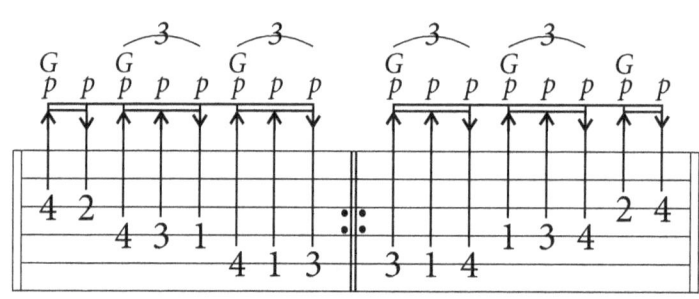

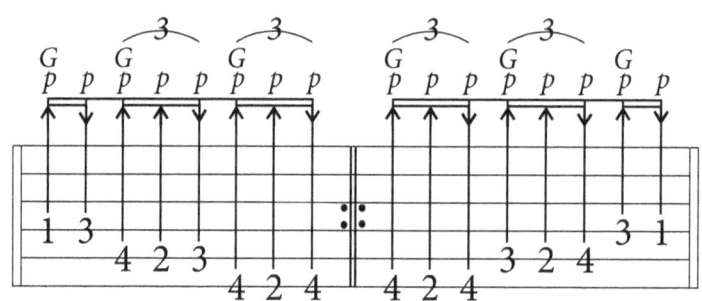

B

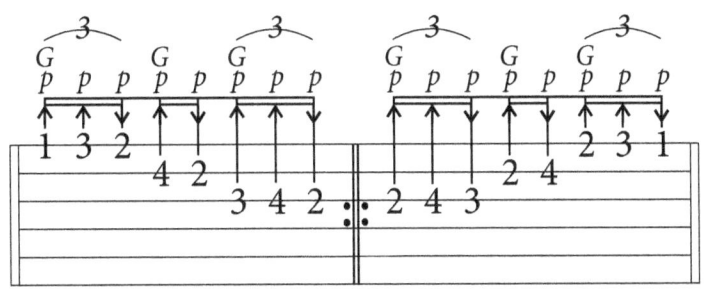
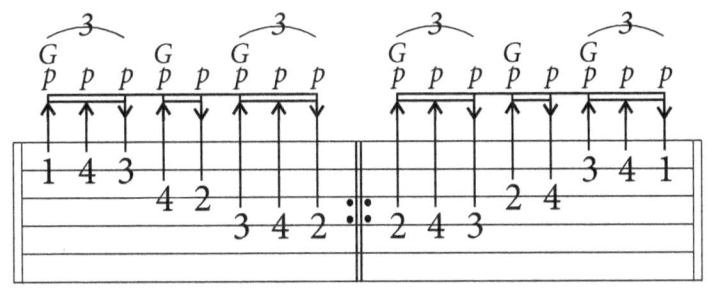
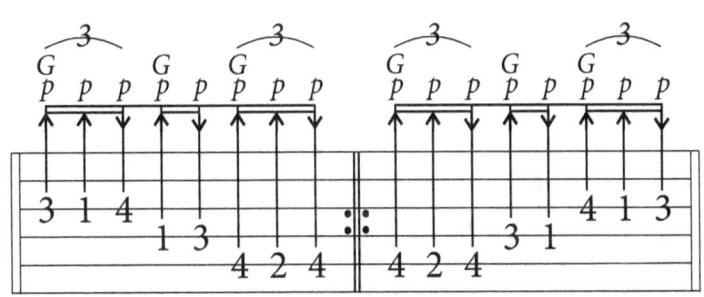
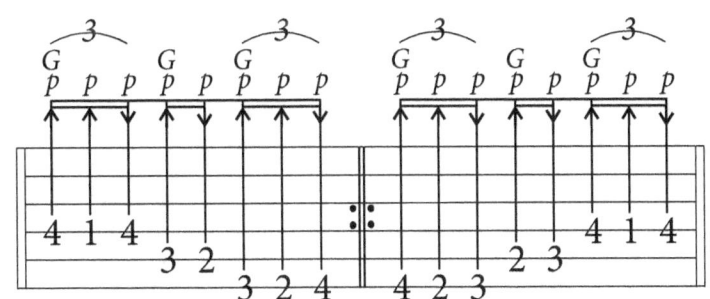

C

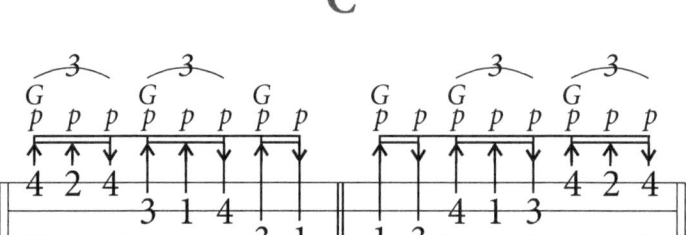

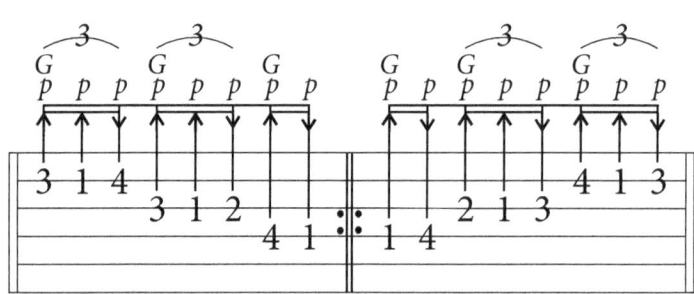

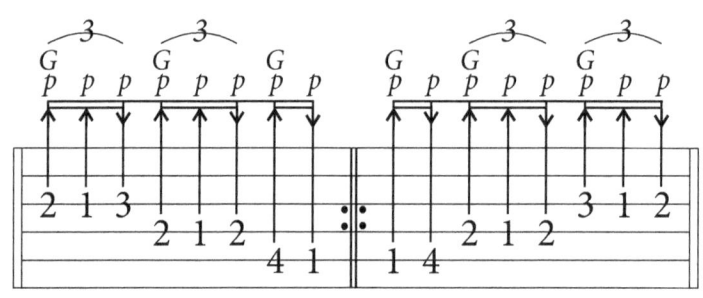

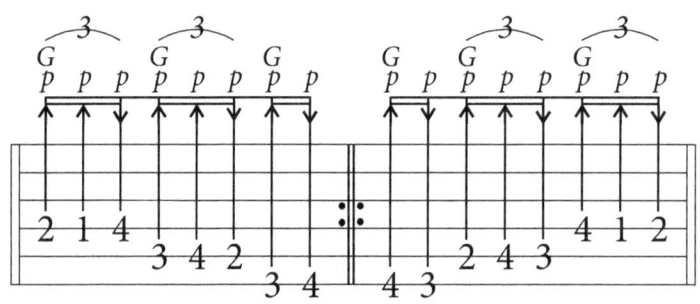

In the following paragraphs (§ III and § IV) the previous exercise is repeated with change in the thumb stroke. The triplet is played by the thumb in the following way:

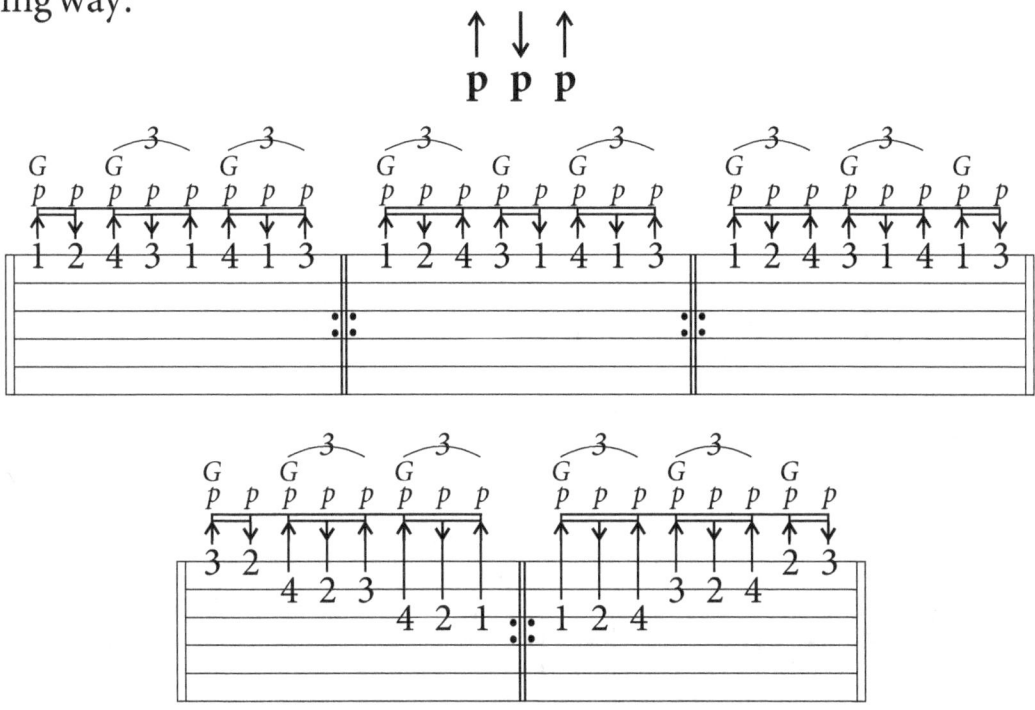

When the chromatic scale is on the 4th string, you can alternatively practice with simultaneous thumb stroke of the 5th and 6th string.

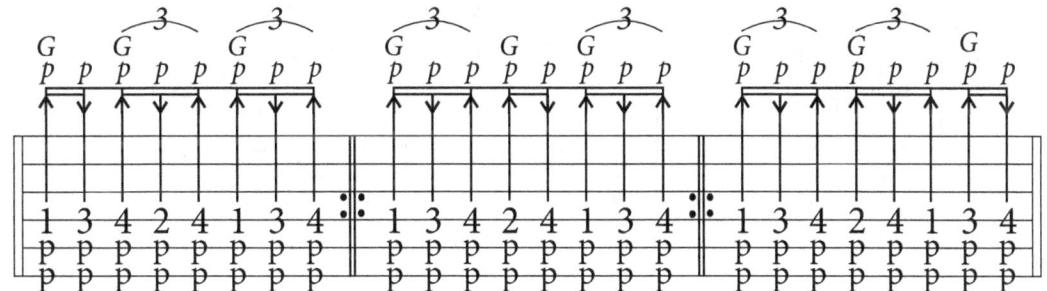

Also, when the chromatic scale is on the 5th string, you can alternatively practice with simultaneous thumb stroke of the 6th string.

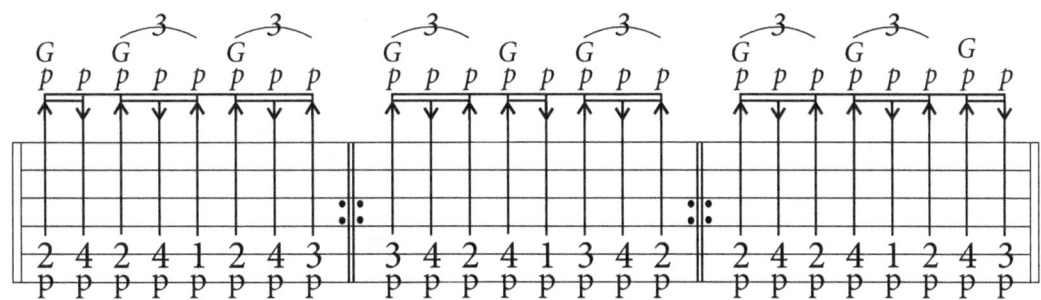

§ IV

A

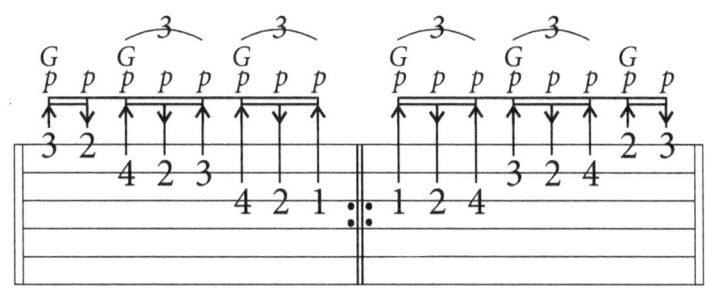

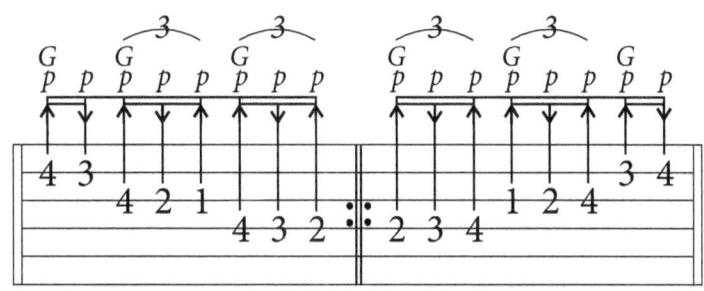

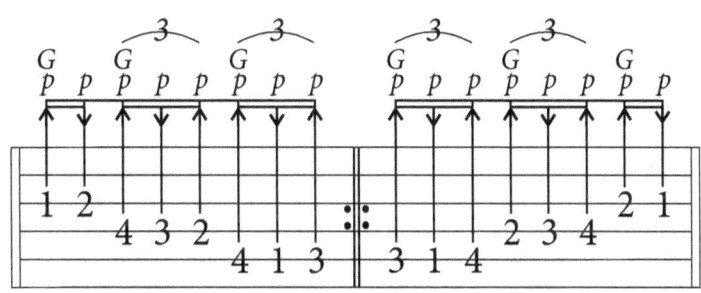

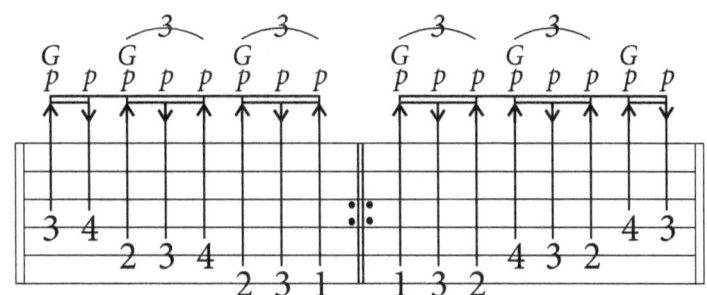

B

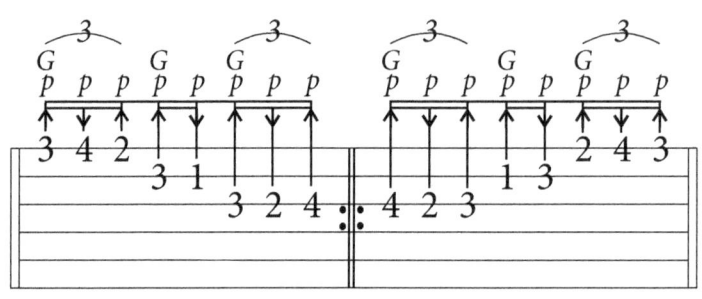

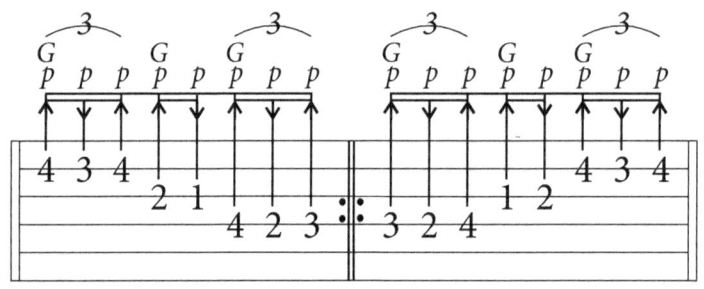

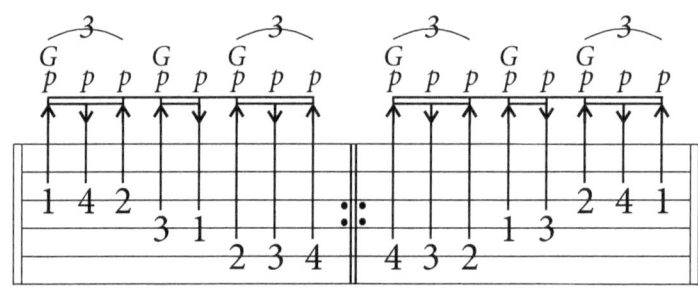

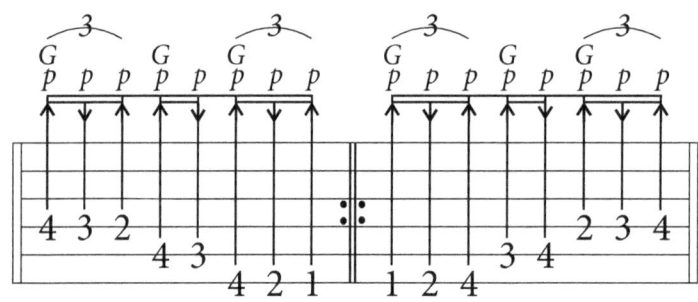

C

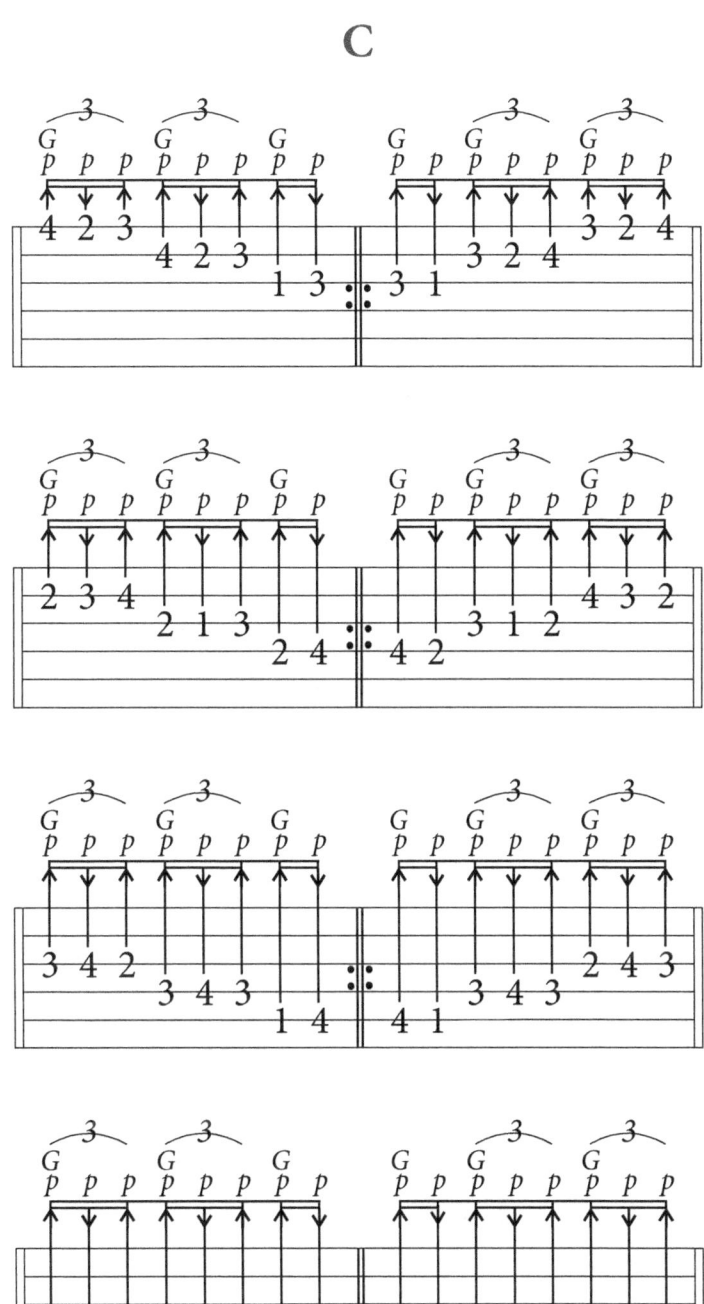

UNIT 5

Thumb stroke with Golpe towards two directions
(downwards ↑ and upwards ↓).
Two triplets within the Formula.
Two Golpe within the triplet.

The Golpe exercises which follow are variations (as far as the Golpe is concerned) on the chromatic scales of eight (8) notes (isochronous). There are three variations. The scales refer either to one string,

§ Ia

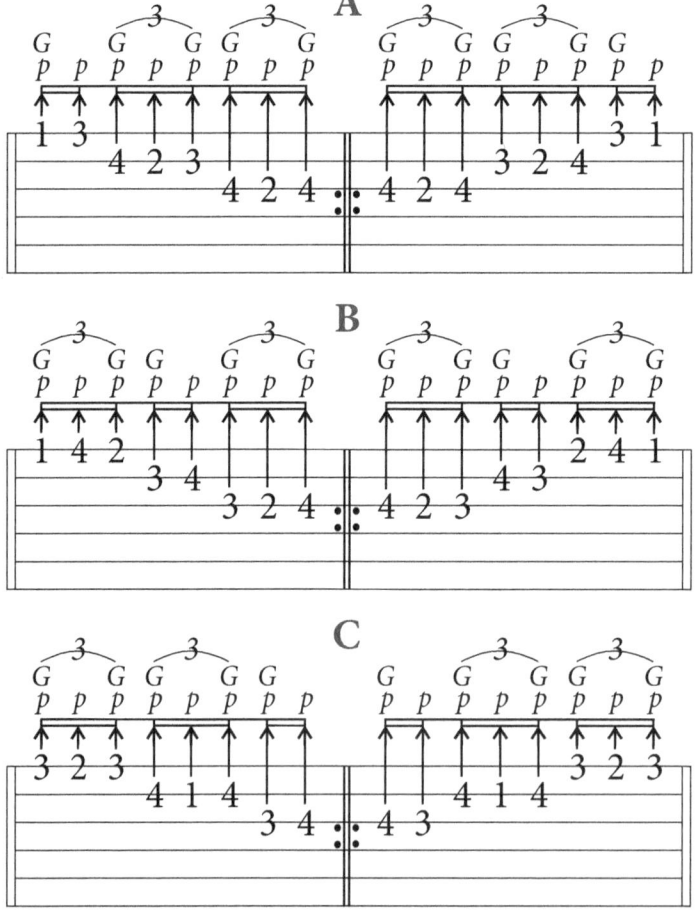

or to three adjacent strings, the 1st - 2nd - 3rd, the 2nd - 3rd - 4th, the 3rd - 4th - 5th, and the 4th - 5th - 6th.

The first (1st - 2nd - 3rd string) of each variation A, B, C is cited here:

§ Ib

In § Ia practice on the 5th line (which means that the scale is on the 5th string) by striking with the thumb the 6th string simultaneously.

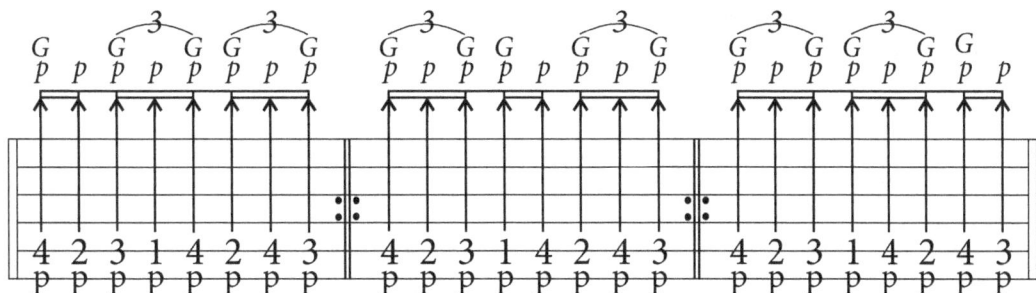

In the case where the scale is on the 4th string, the thumb can simultaneously strike the 5th and 6th string.

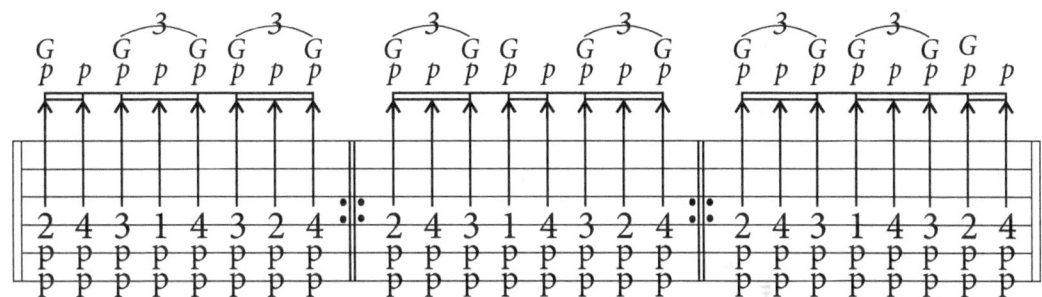

§ Ia

§ Ib

A

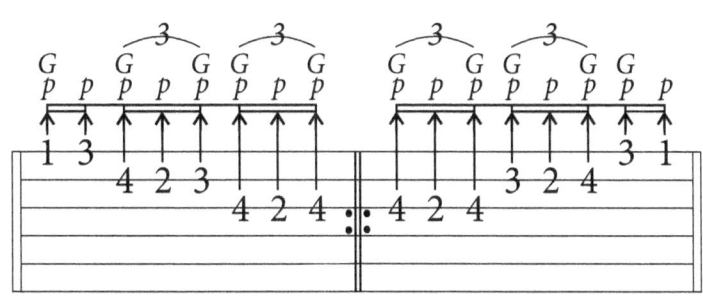

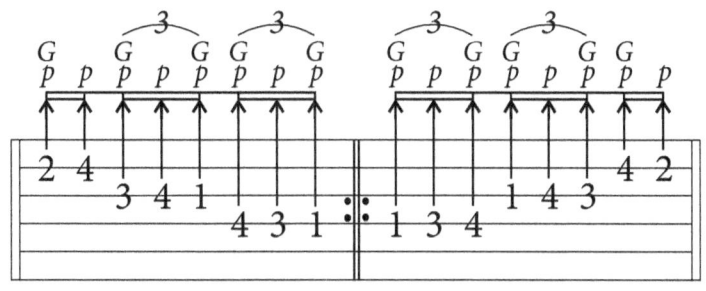

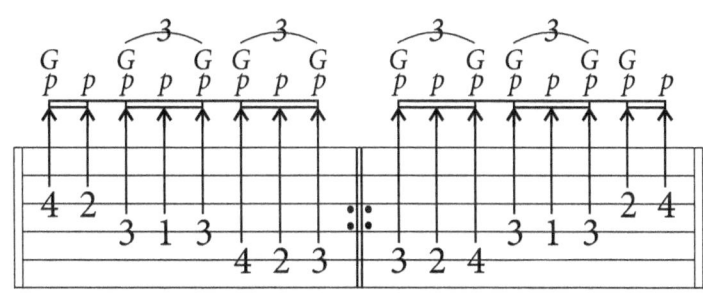

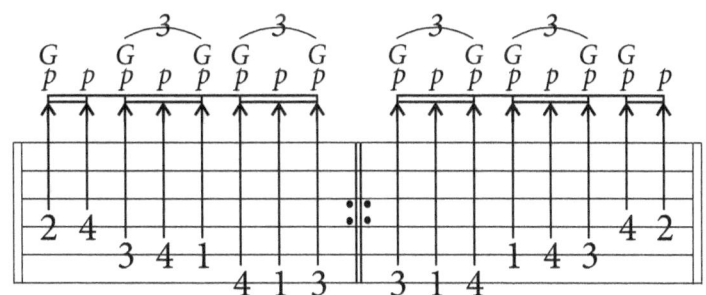

B

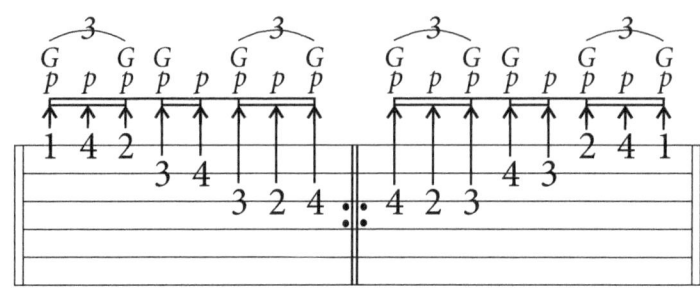

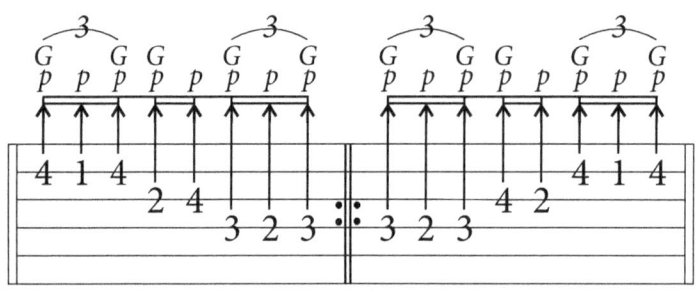

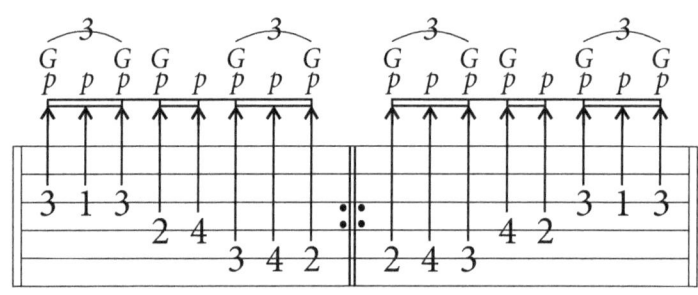

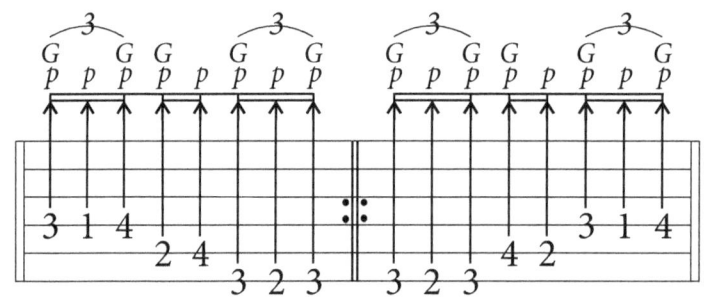

C

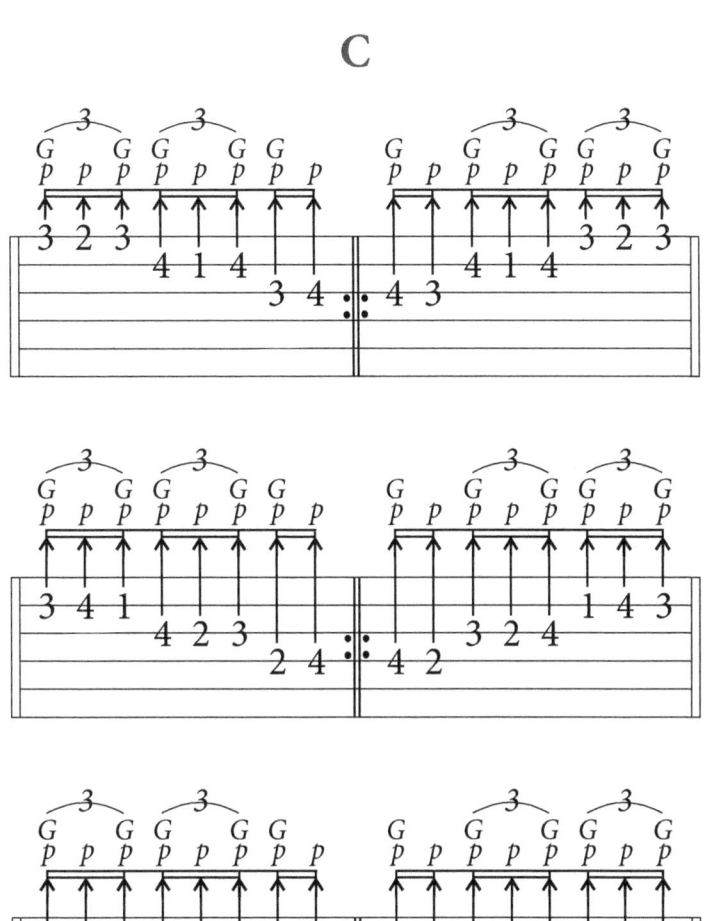

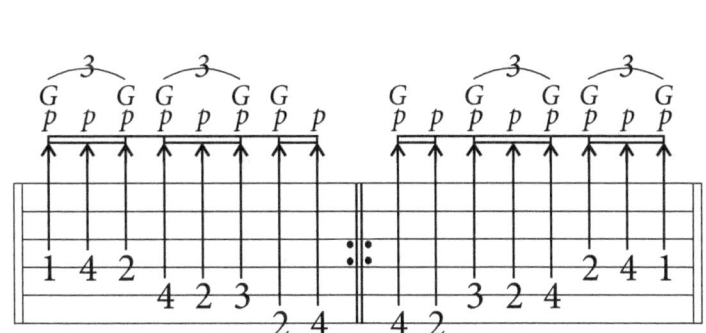

In § IIa, § IIb there is the same mechanism of exercises (as in § Ia and § Ib) but with different direction of the thumb stroke as shown below:

§ IIa

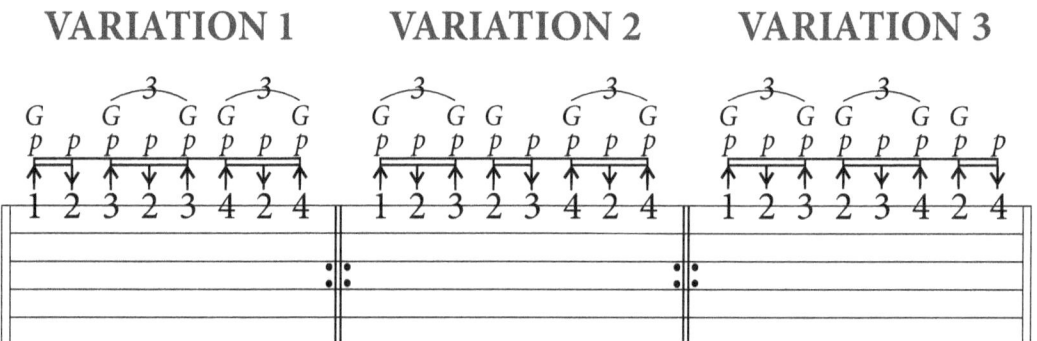

§ IIb

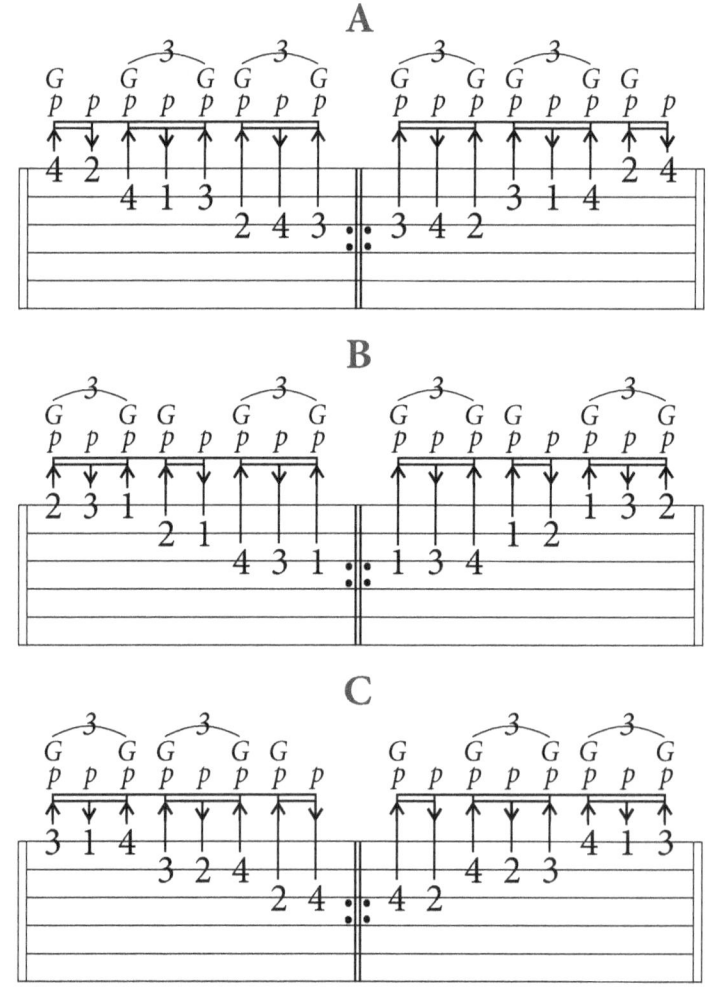

In § IIa, when the chromatic scale is on the 5th string you can practice striking the thumb and the 6th string simultaneously.

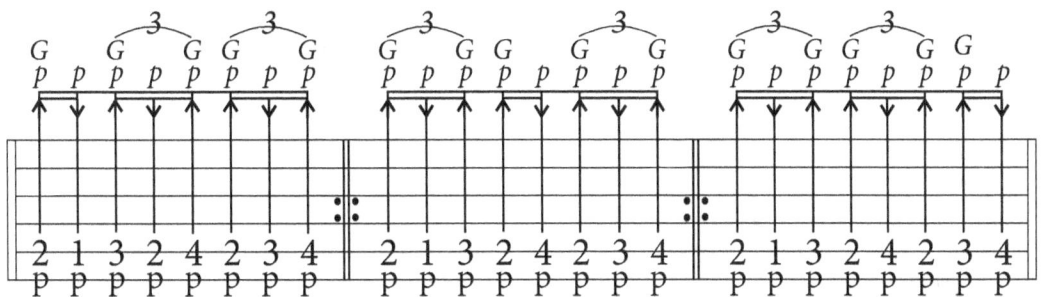

When the chromatic scale is on the 4th string you can also practice with simultaneous stroke of the 5th and 6th string.

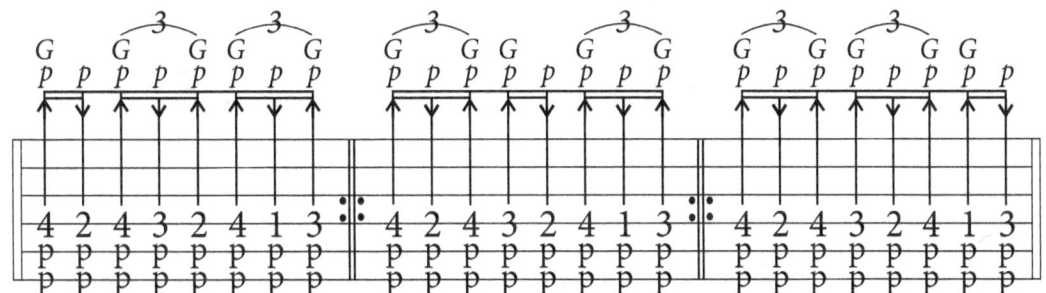

§ IIa

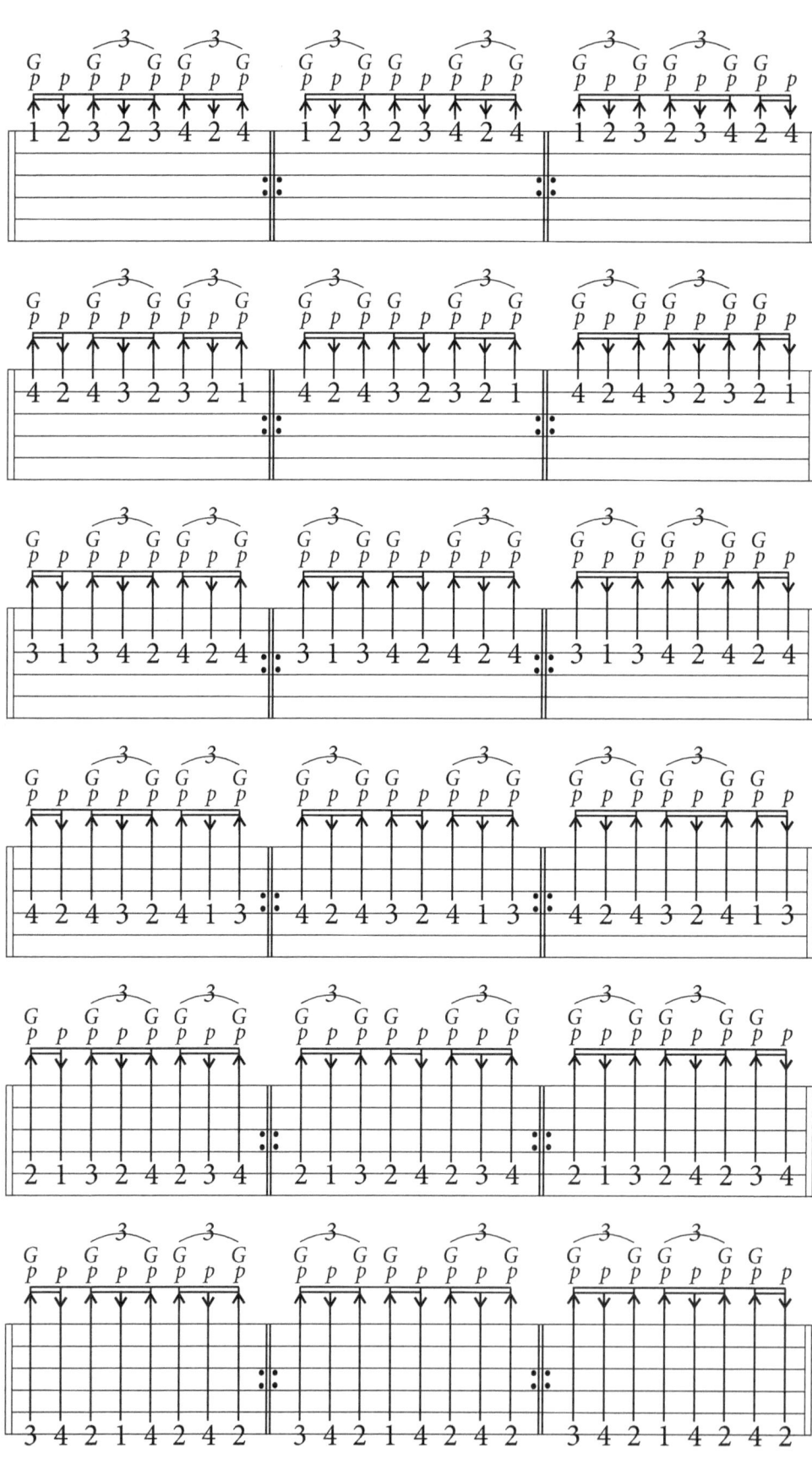

§ IIb

A

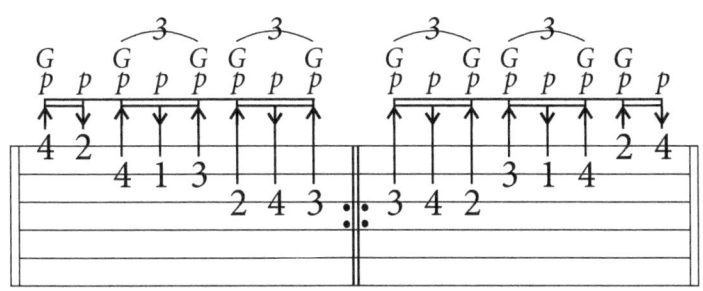

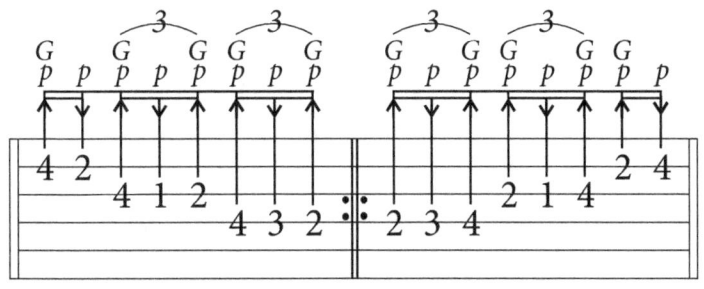

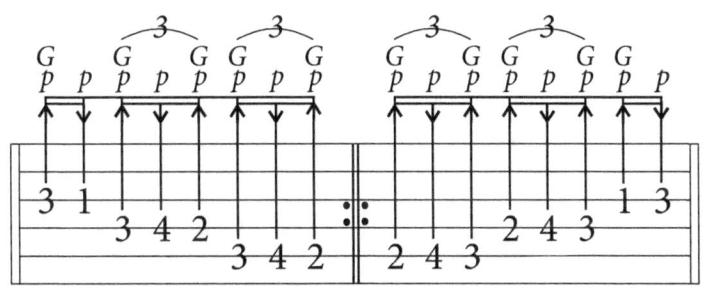

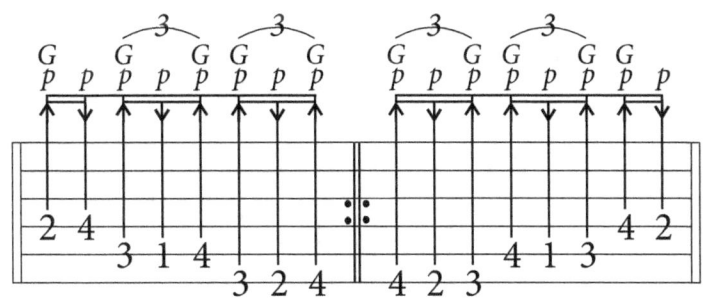

B

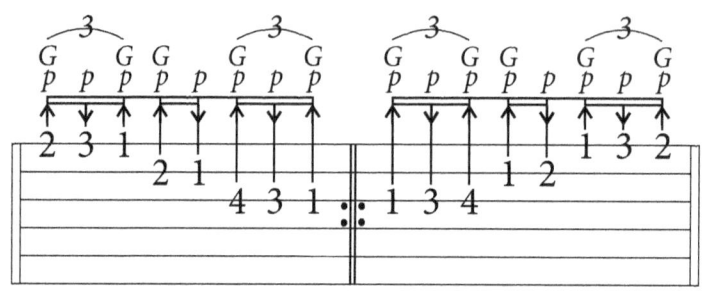
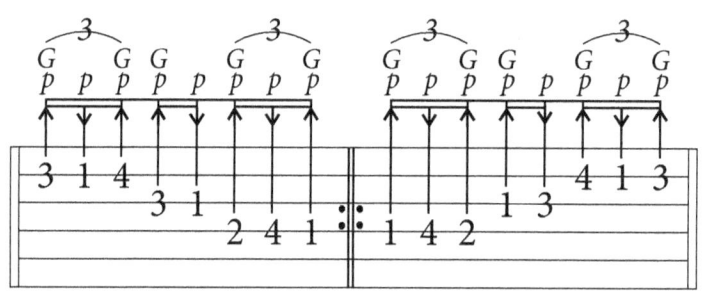
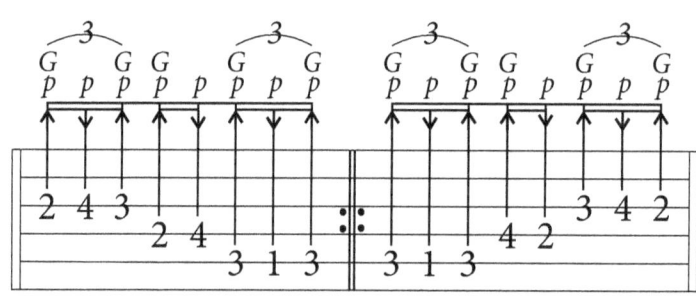
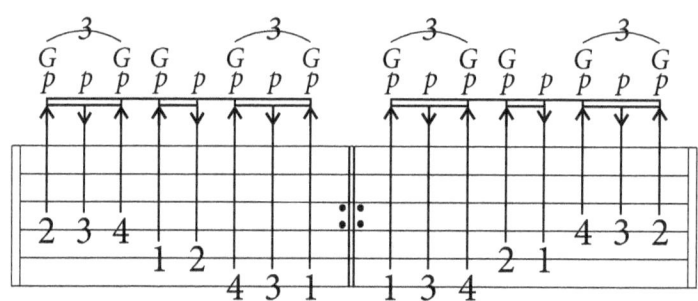

C

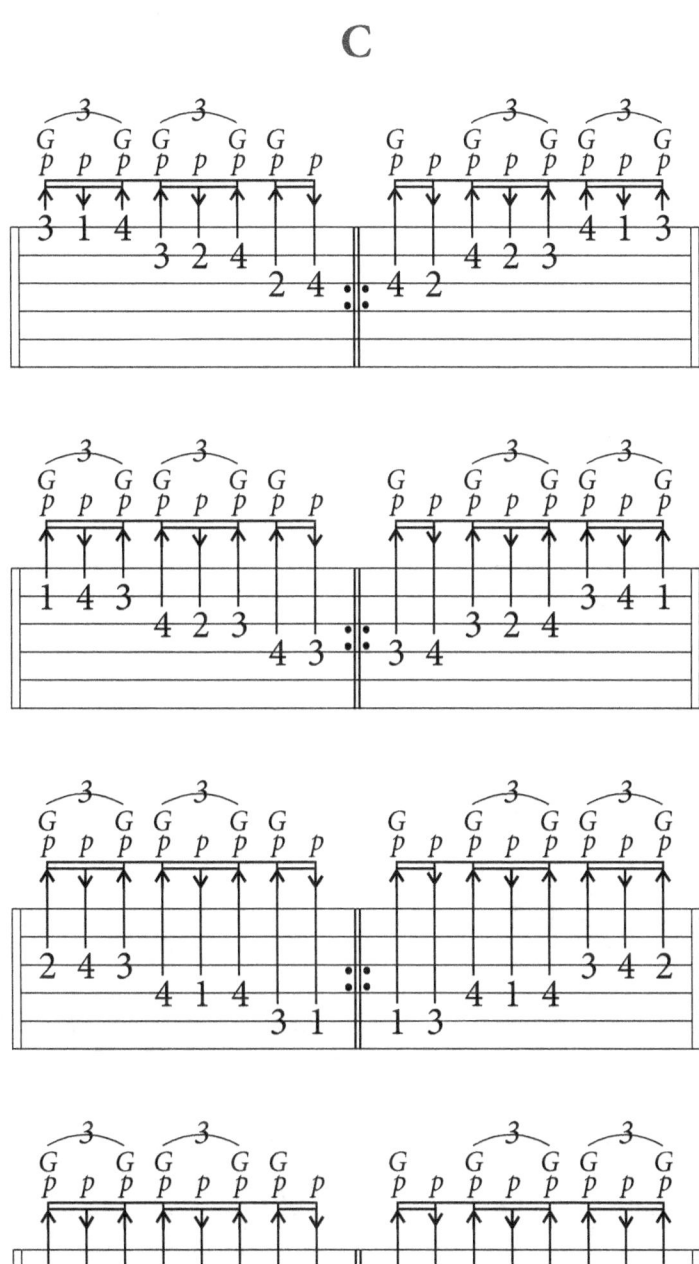

In § IIIa, § IIIb there is the same mechanism of exercises (as in § IIa and § IIb) but with different direction of the thumb stroke as shown below:

§ IIIa

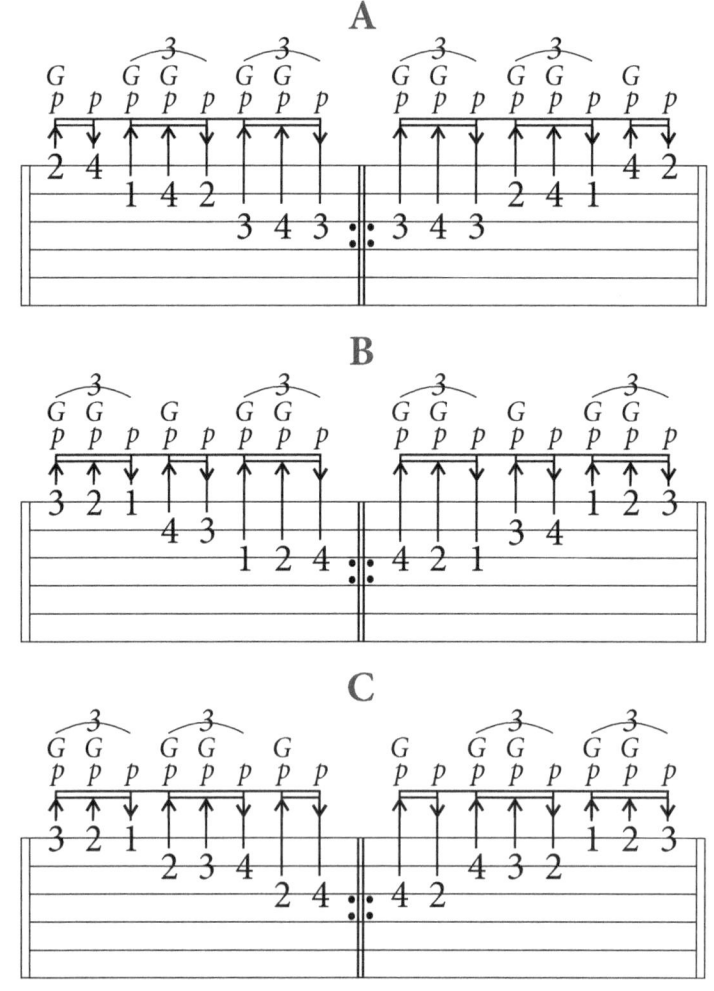

§ IIIb

In § IIIa, when the chromatic scale is on the 5th string you can practice striking the thumb and the 6th string simultaneously.

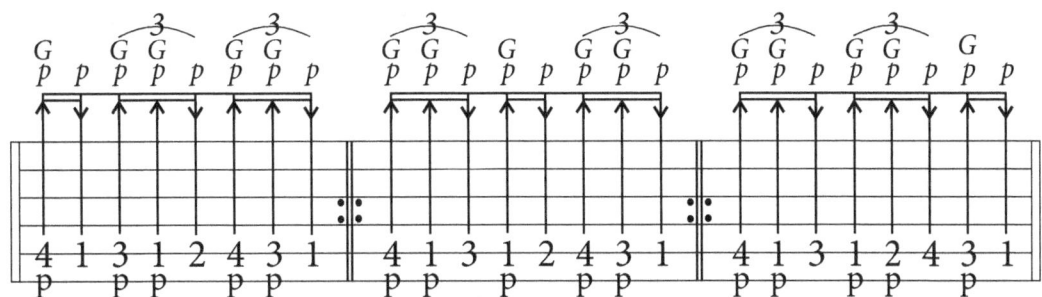

When the chromatic scale is on the 4th string you can also practice with simultaneous stroke of the 5th and 6th string.

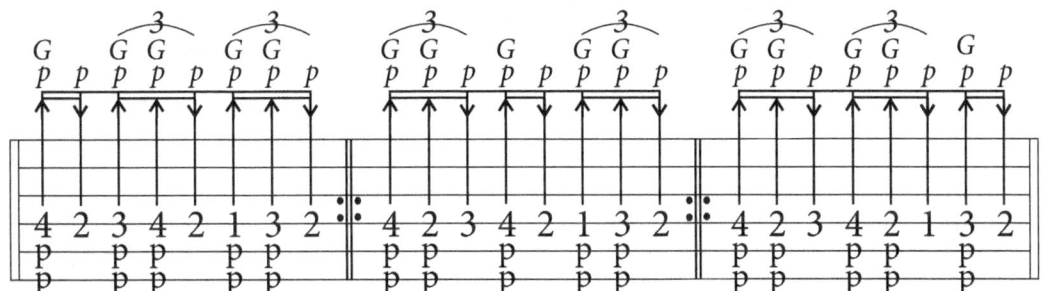

§ IIIa

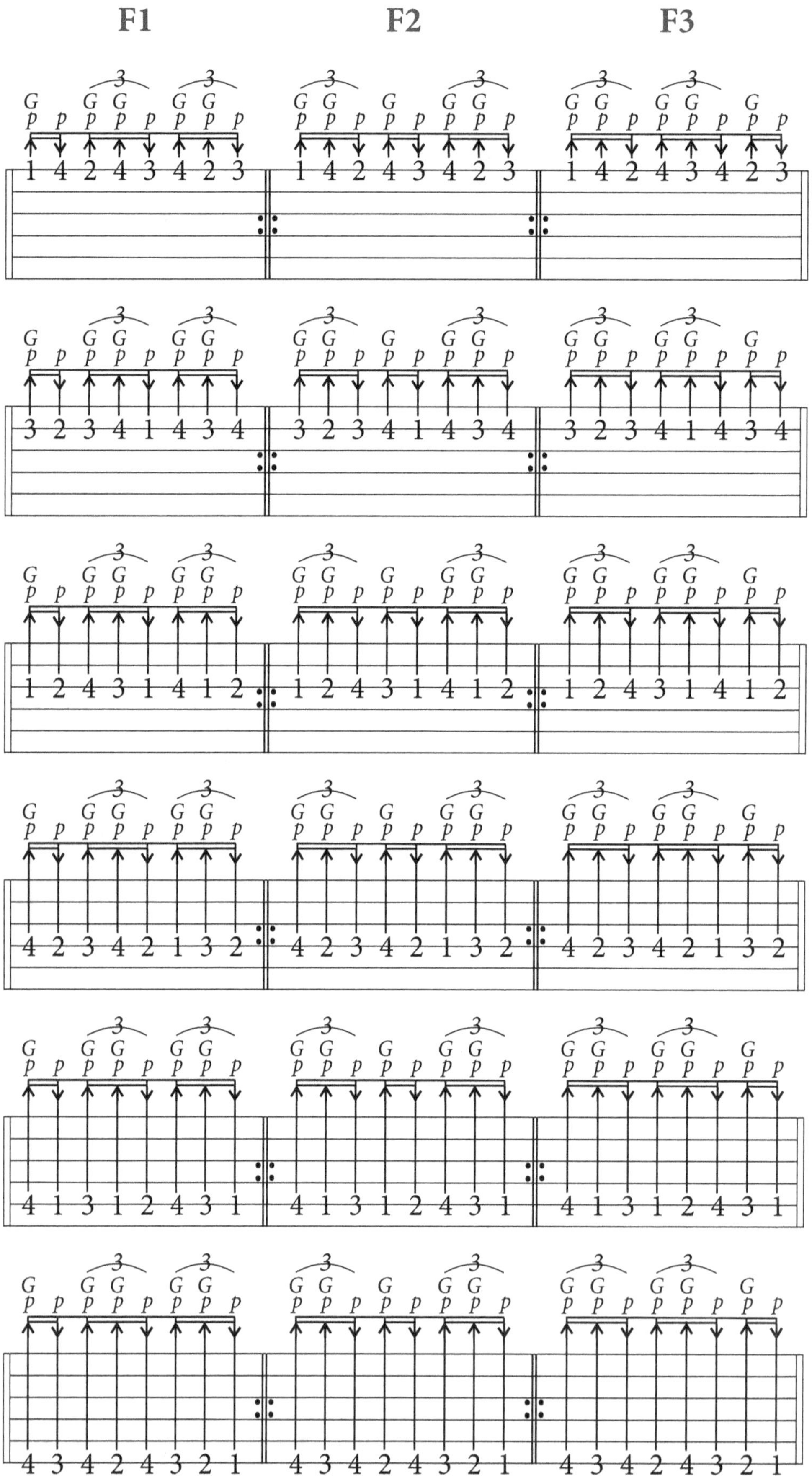

§ IIIb

A

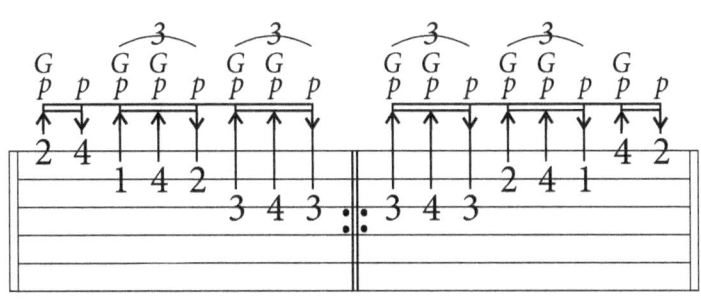

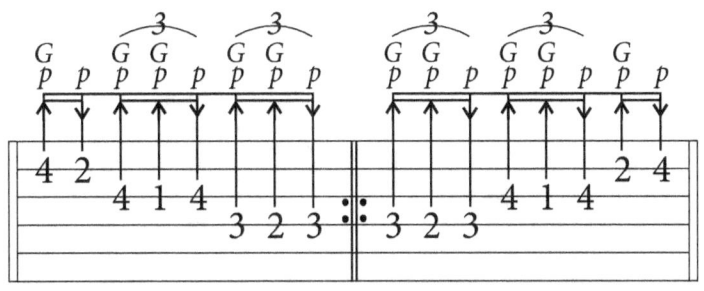

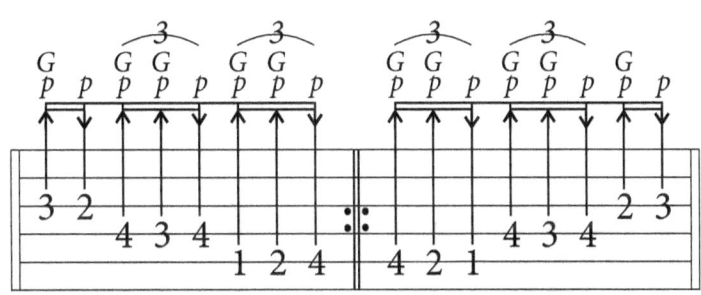

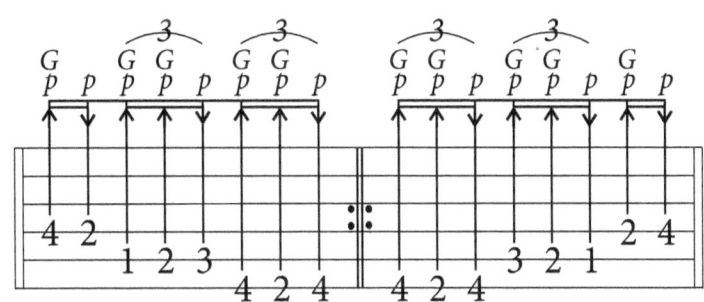

B

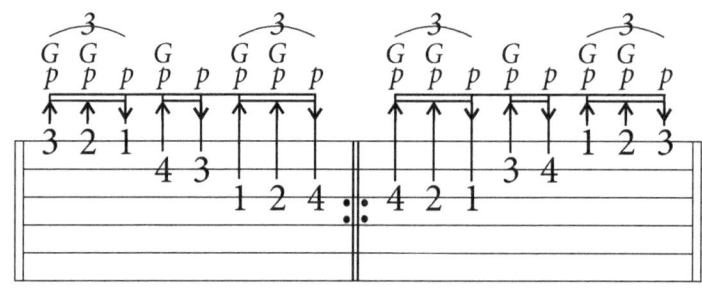

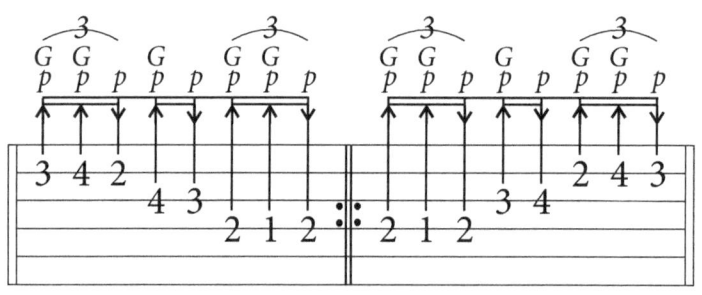

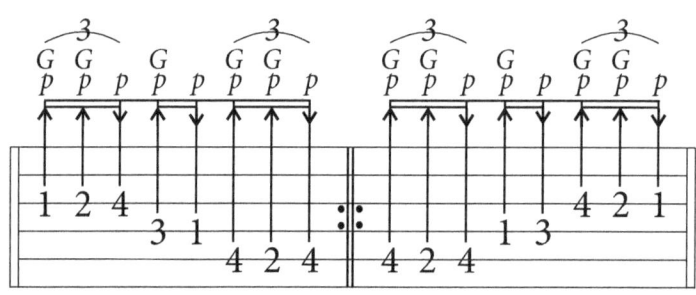

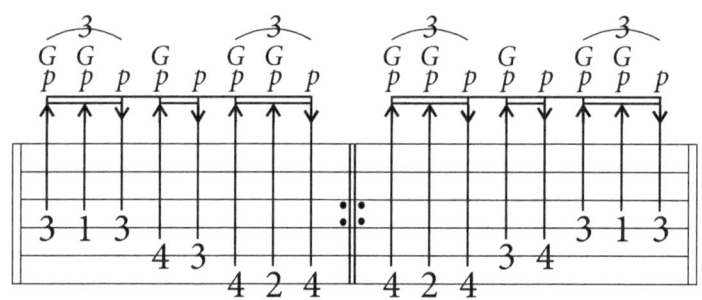

C

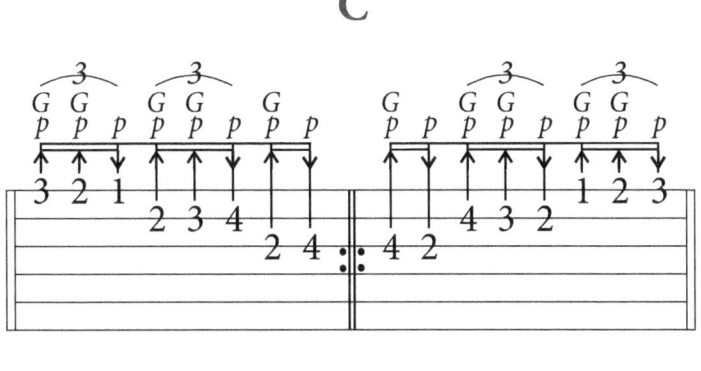
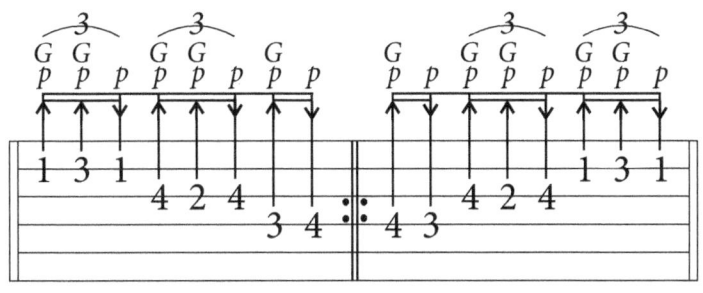
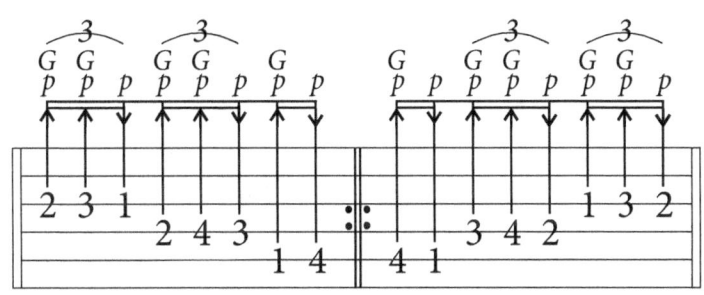
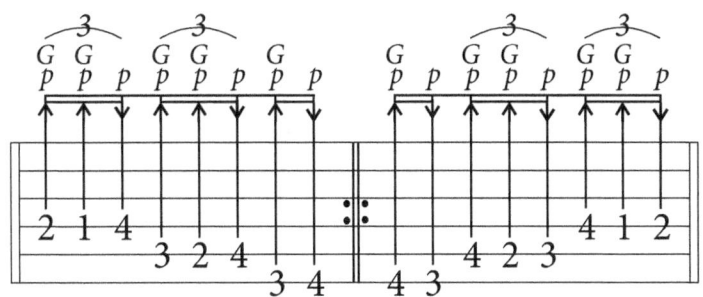

UNIT 6

Thumb stroke with Golpe and Triplets.

1/. Golpe on every thumb stroke.

2/. Thumb stroke on two or three strings simultaneously.

§ I Same mechanism of exercises as before with continuous Golpe on the varied with triplets chromatic scales.

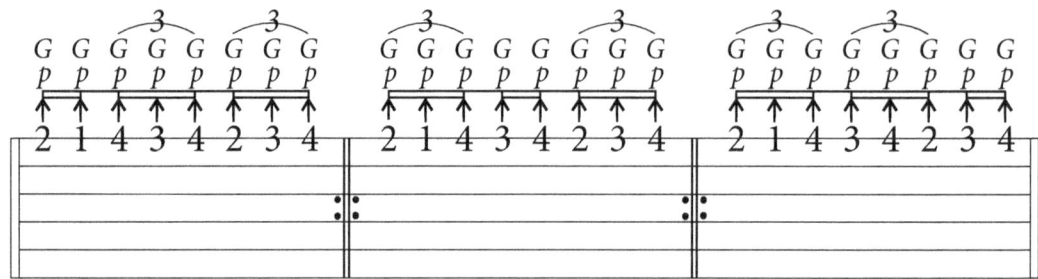

Simultaneous thumb stroke of two strings with Golpe, when the chromatic scale is on 5th string.

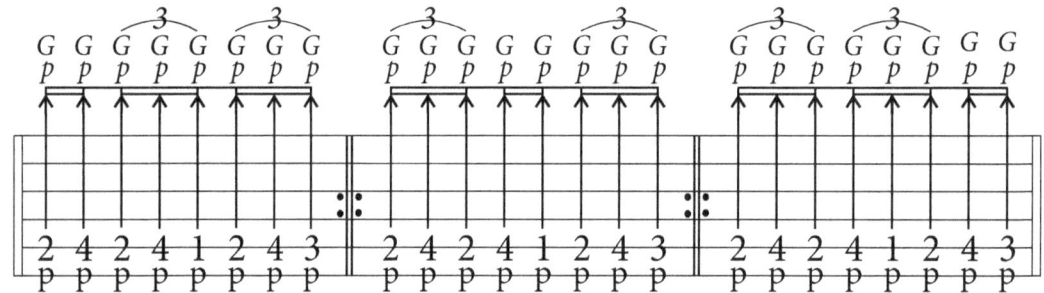

Simultaneous thumb stroke of three strings with Golpe, when the chromatic scale is on 4th string.

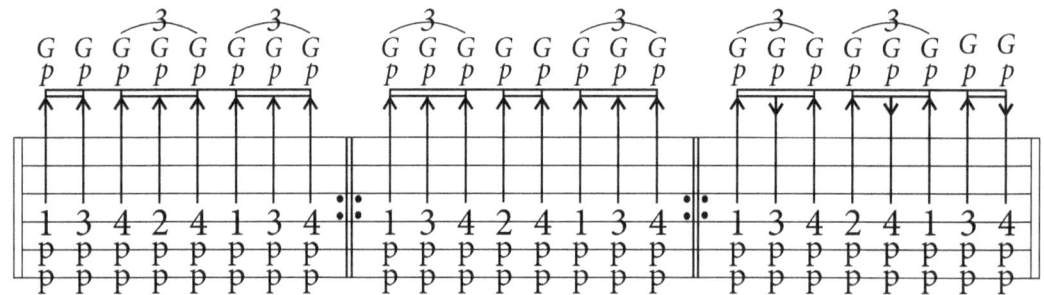

§ II Movement of the chromatic scale from the 1st to the 2nd and 3rd string and return from the 3rd to the 1st string with the opposite chromatic scale.

§ I

F1 F2 F3

§ II

A

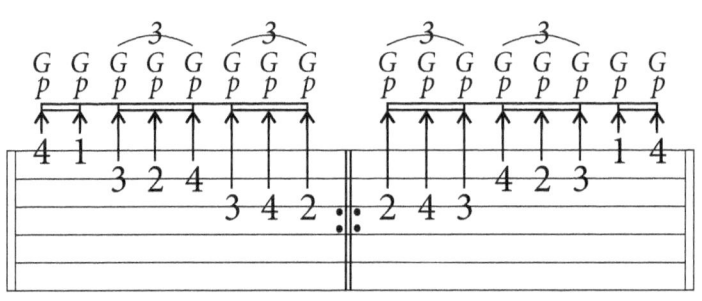

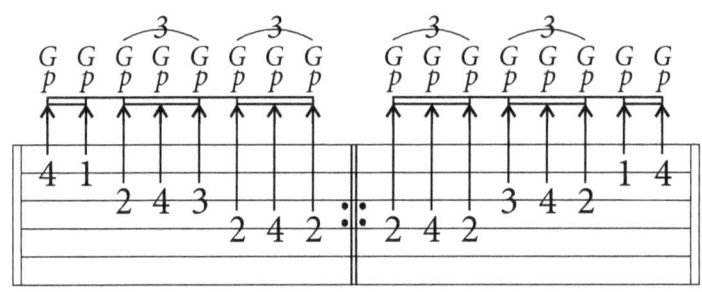

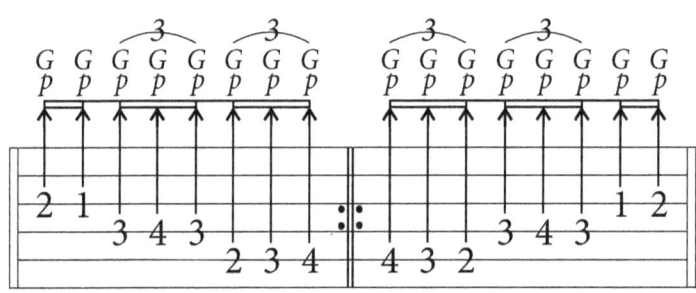

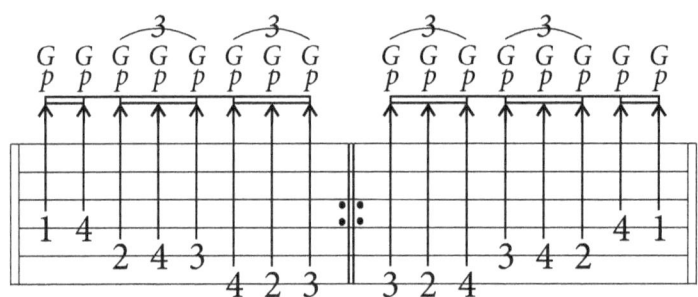

B

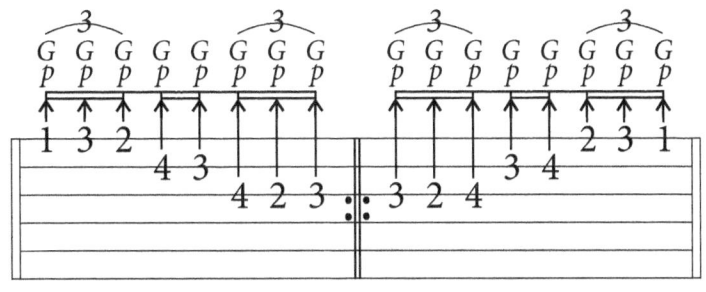
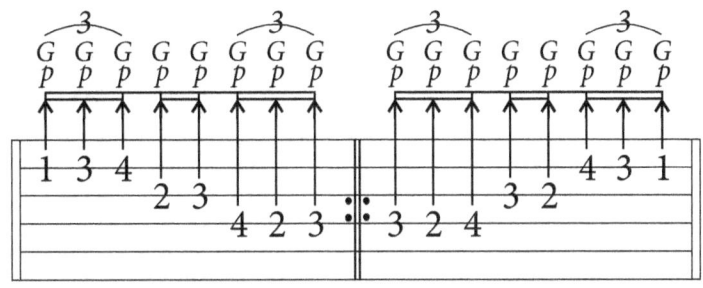
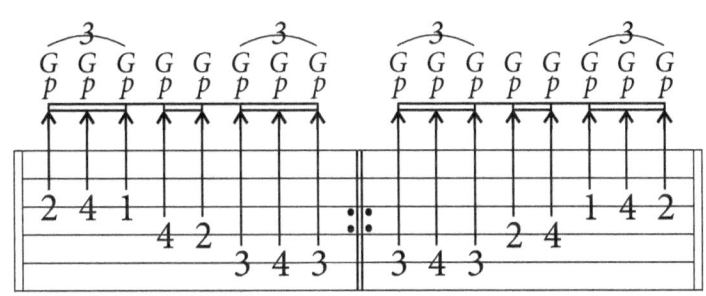
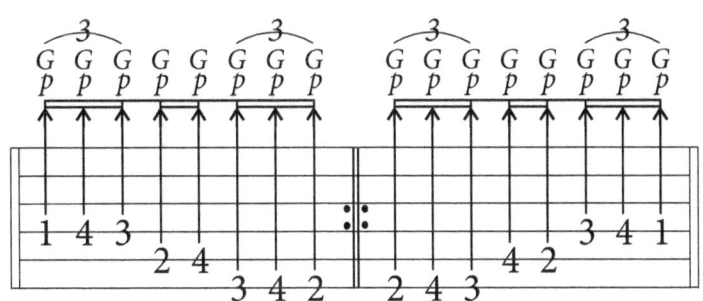

C

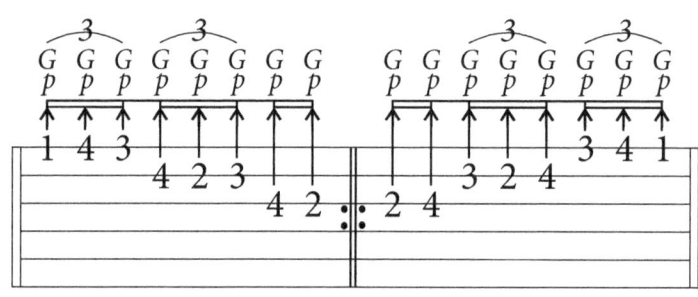
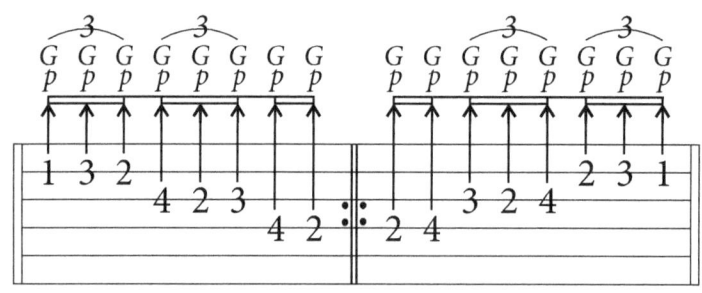
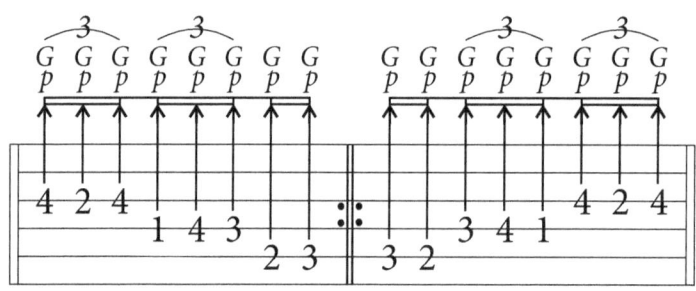
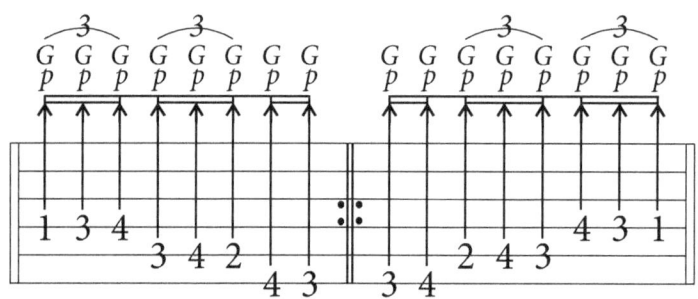

In the paragraphs that follow in this unit the first line is cited. These exercises are variations of the previous with striking of two or three strings and with differences in the direction of thumb stroke:

§ III

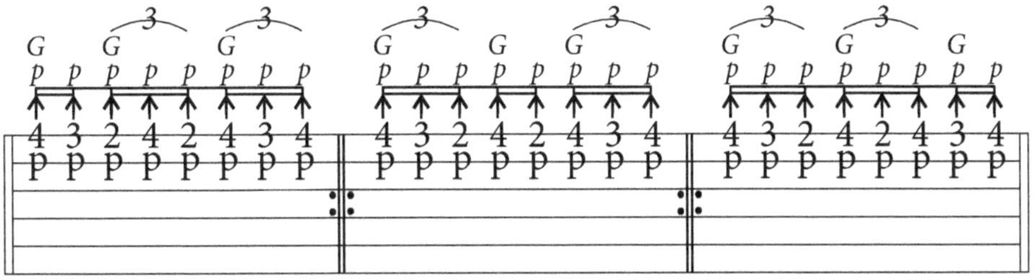

§ IV

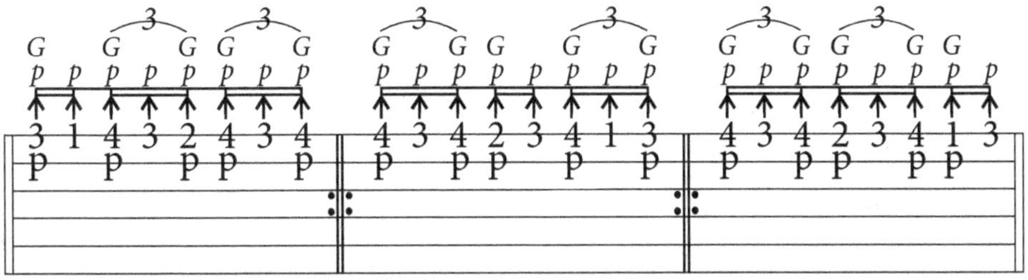

§ V

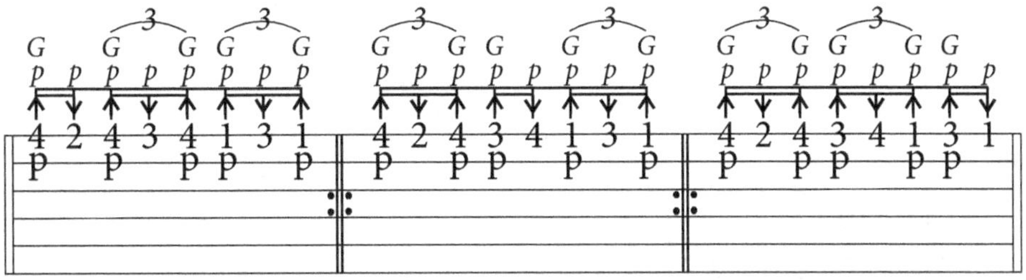

§ VI

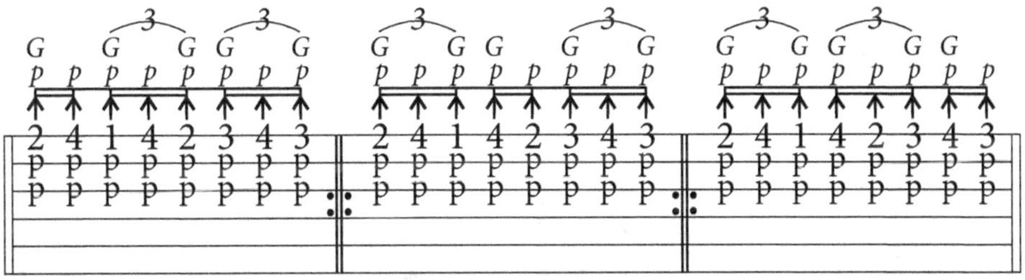

§ VII

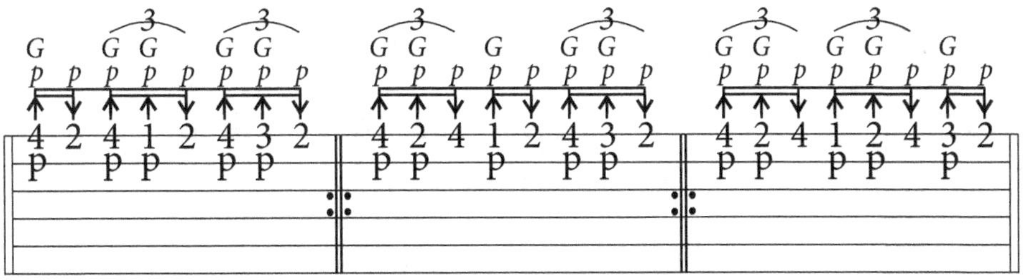

§ VIII

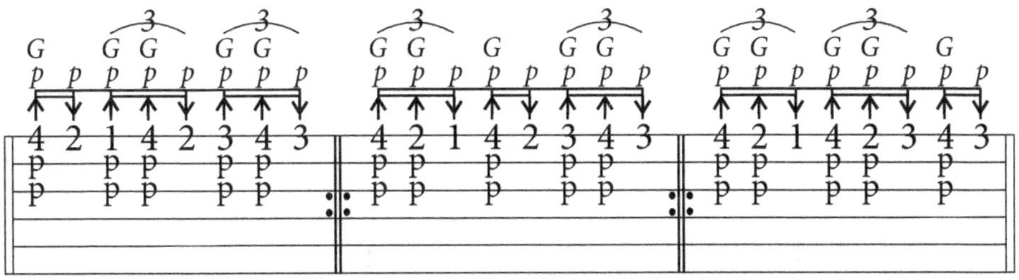

§ III

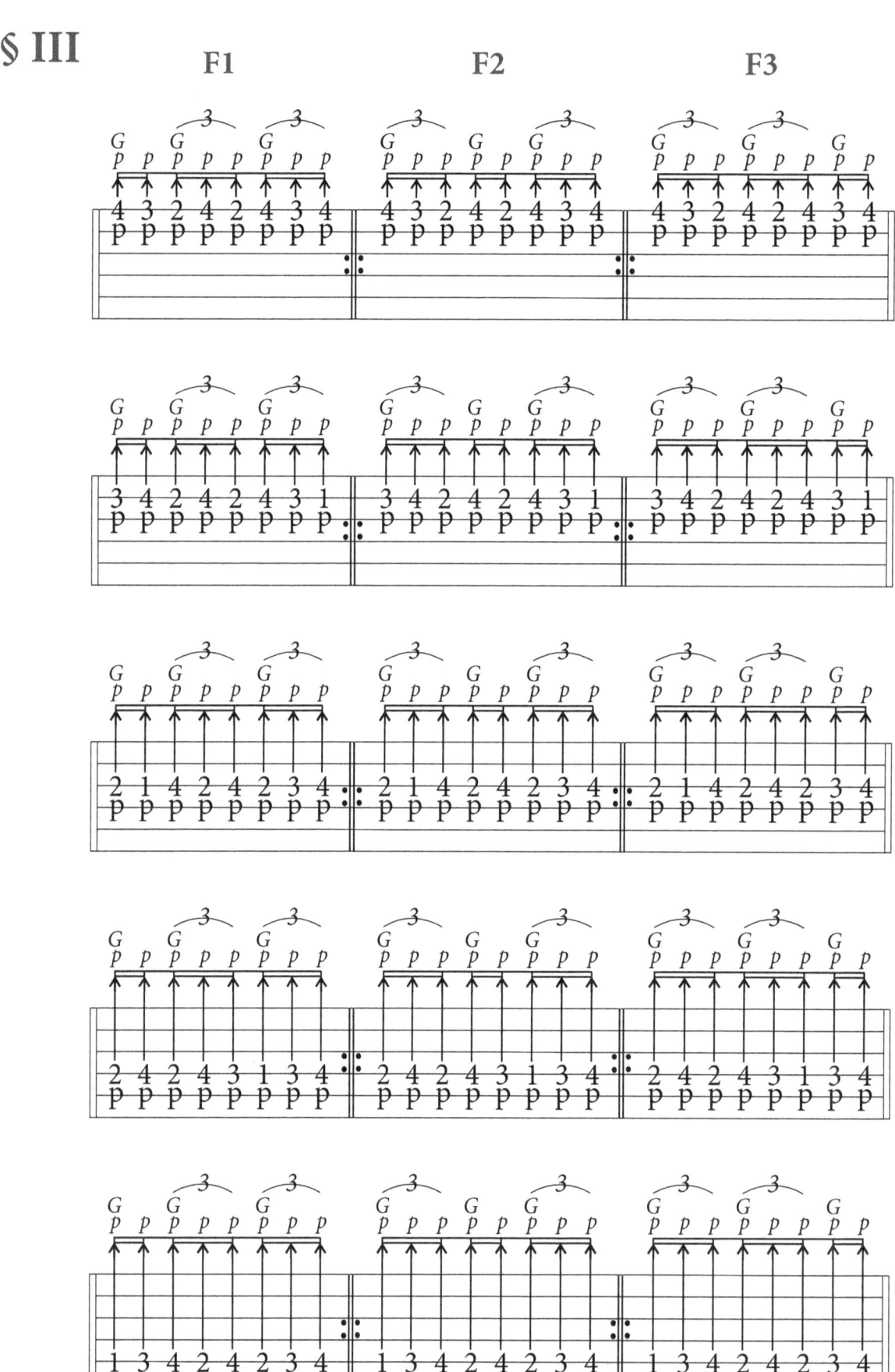

§ IV

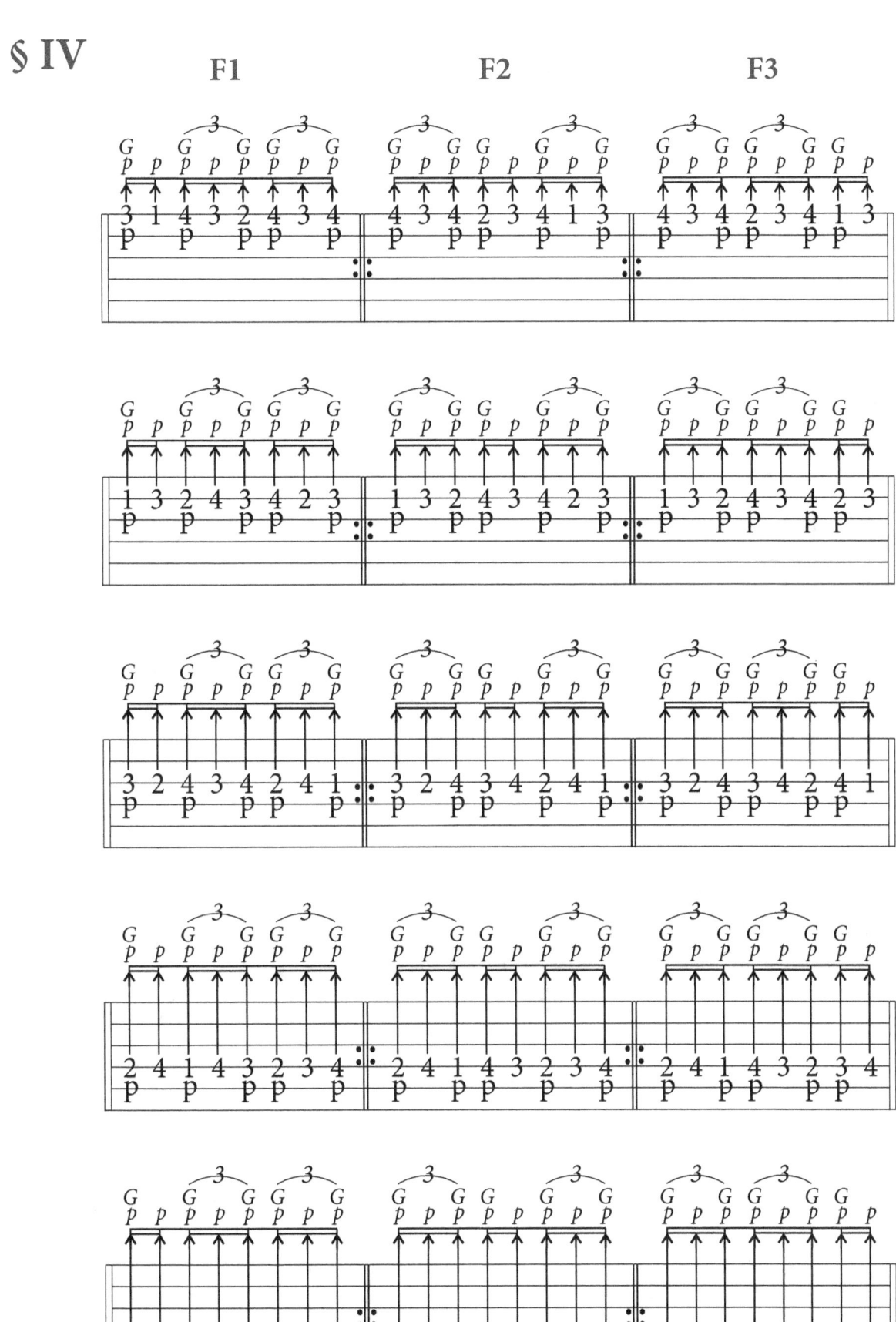

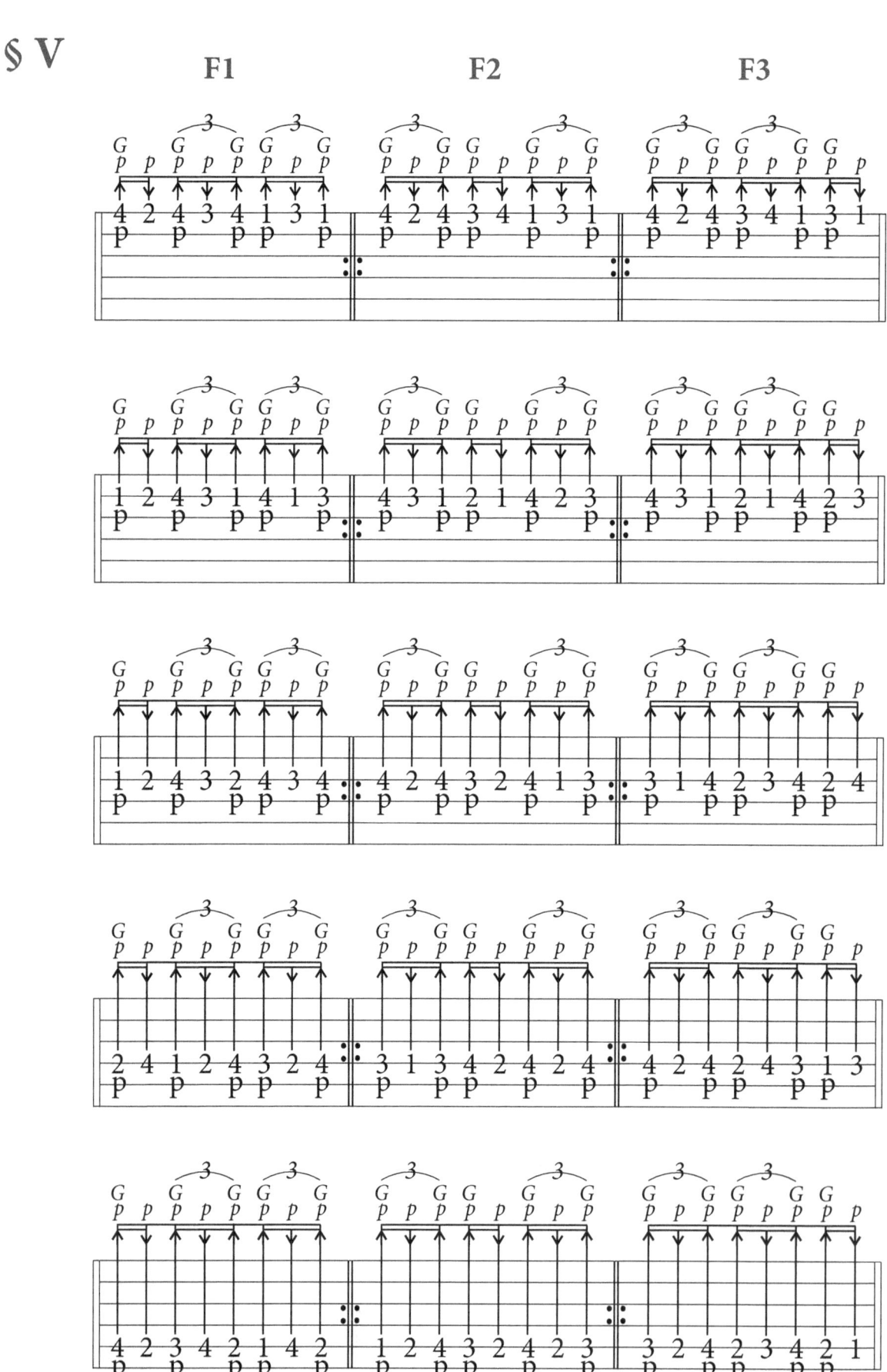

§ VI

§ VII

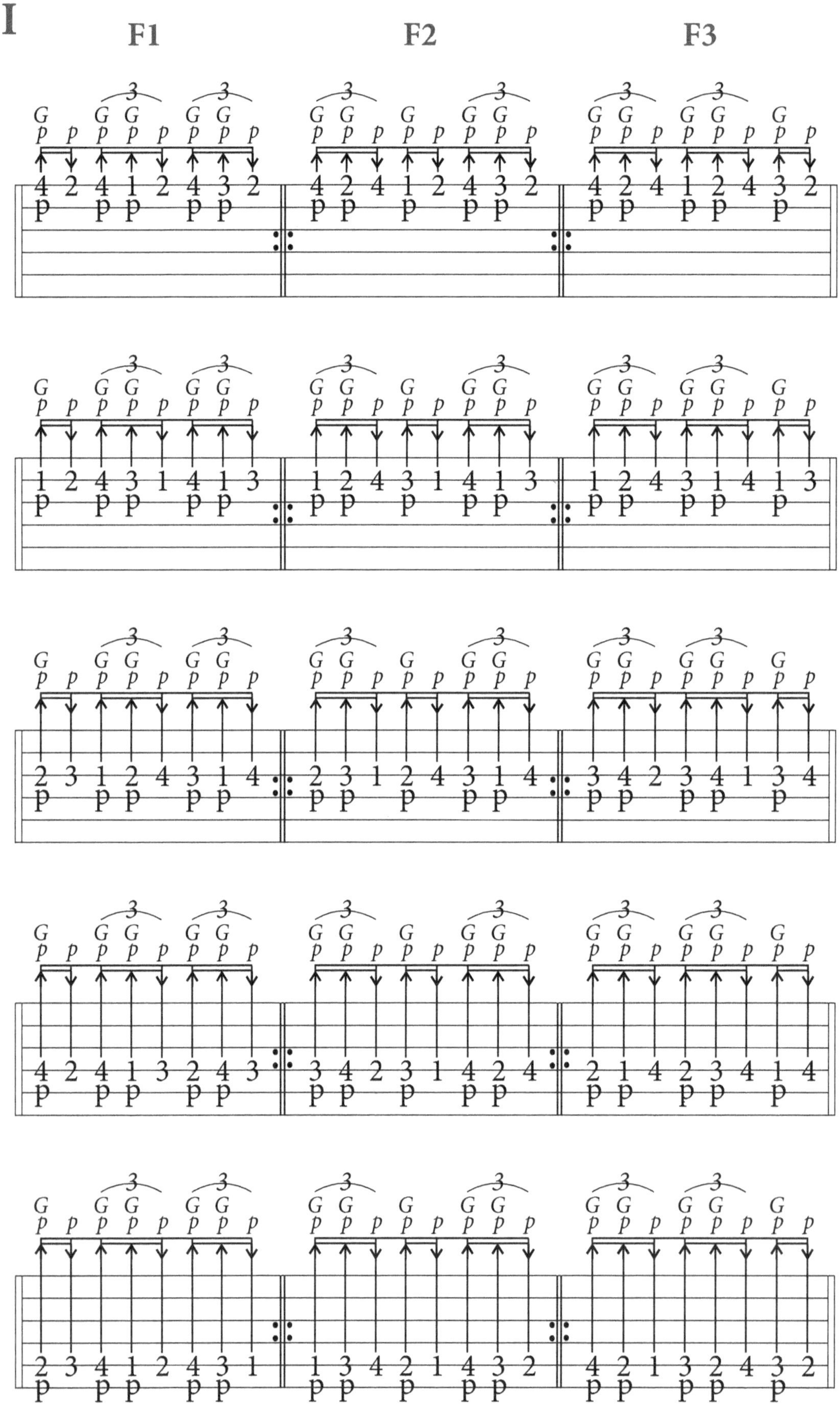

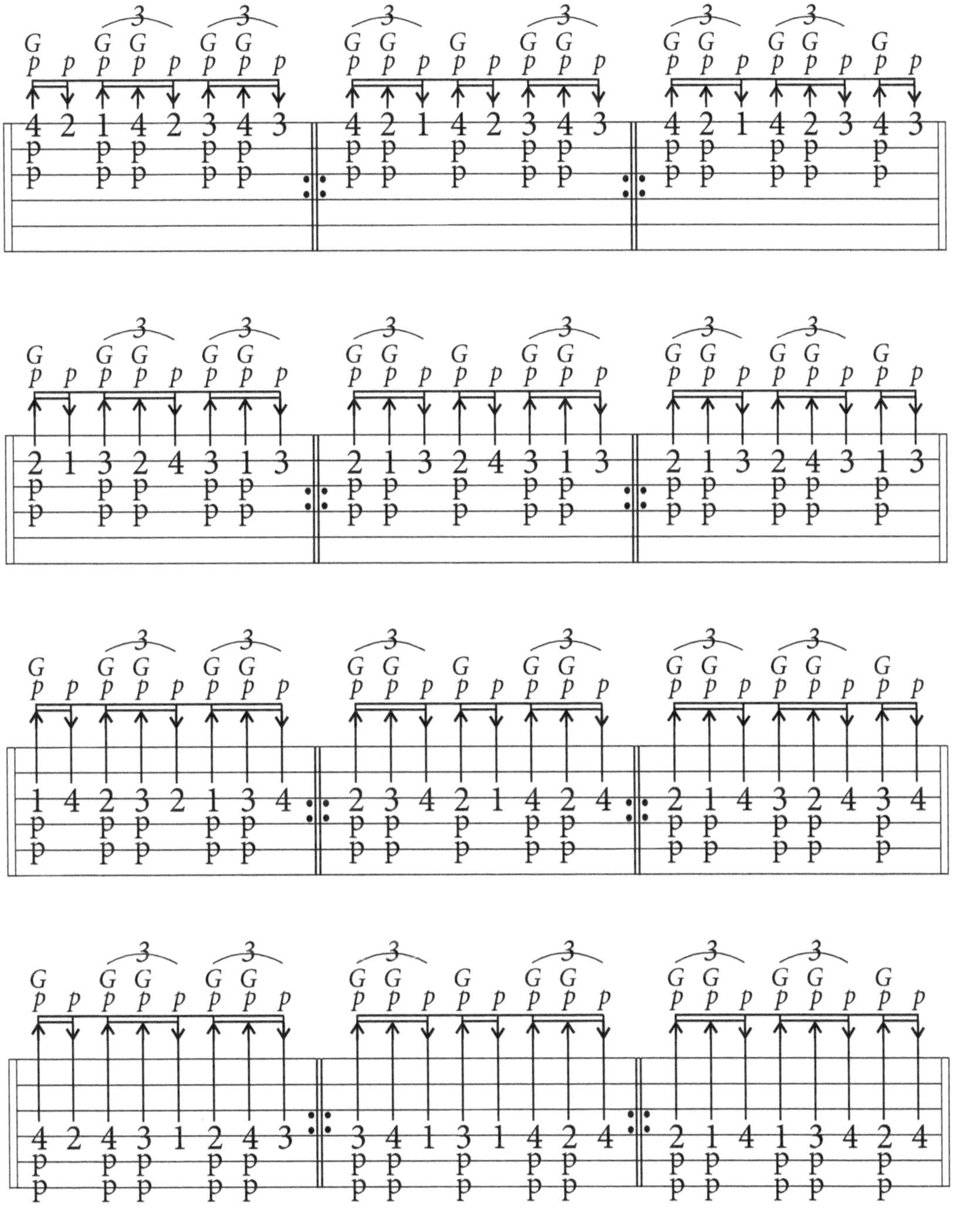

CHAPTER 2
THUMB STROKE WITH GOLPE.

UNIT 1

Thumb stroke with Golpe and Free Golpe without the participation of the thumb.

§I Chromatic scales on one string, 1st, 2nd, 3rd, 4th, 5th and 6th string.
Two Golpe within the meter. One Golpe independent from the thumb stroke (free Golpe without the participation of the thumb) and one Golpe with simultaneous stroke of the thumb within the meter.

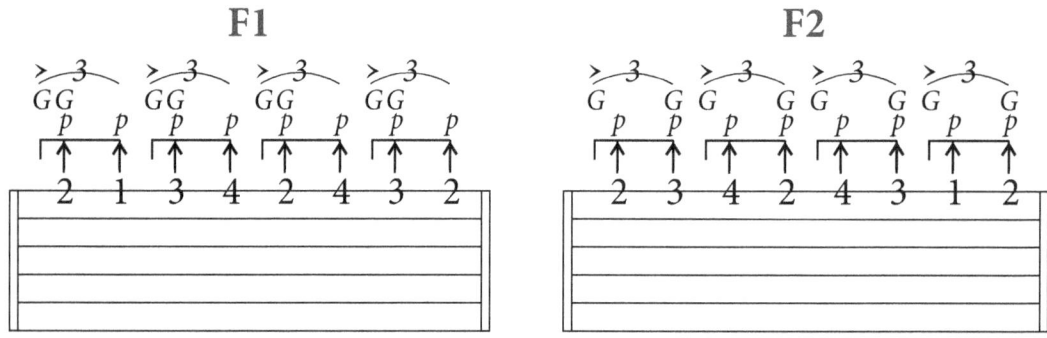

When the chromatic scale is on the 5th string, apart from the already mentioned performance way, you can also practice in another way, striking the 6th string simultaneously.

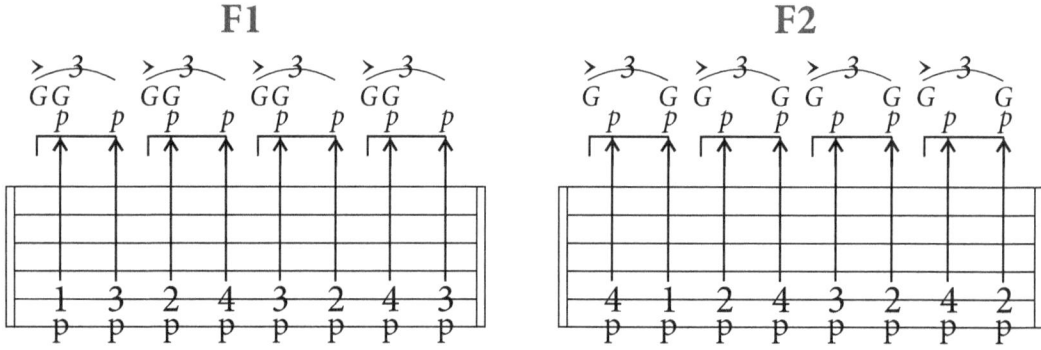

When the chromatic scale is on the 4th string you can alternatively practice striking simultaneously the 5th and 6th string as shown below.

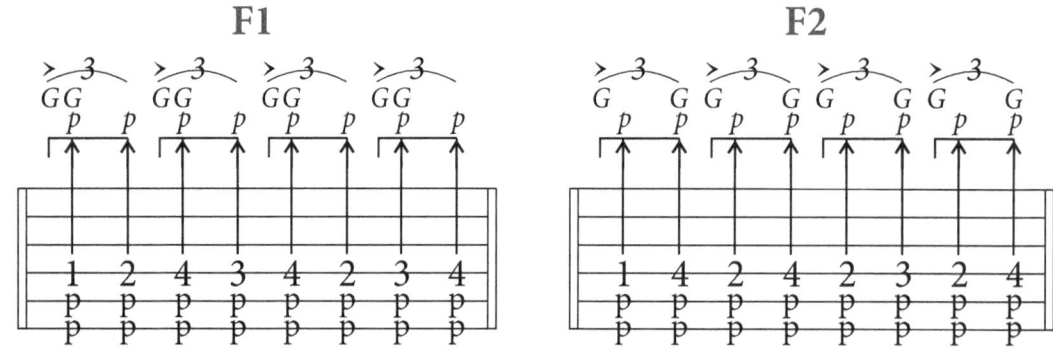

§II In this paragraph the chromatic scales move from the 1st to the 4th string (F1), from the 2nd to the 5th string (F2) and from the 3rd to the 6th string (F3) and return to the initial string with the opposite chromatic scale.

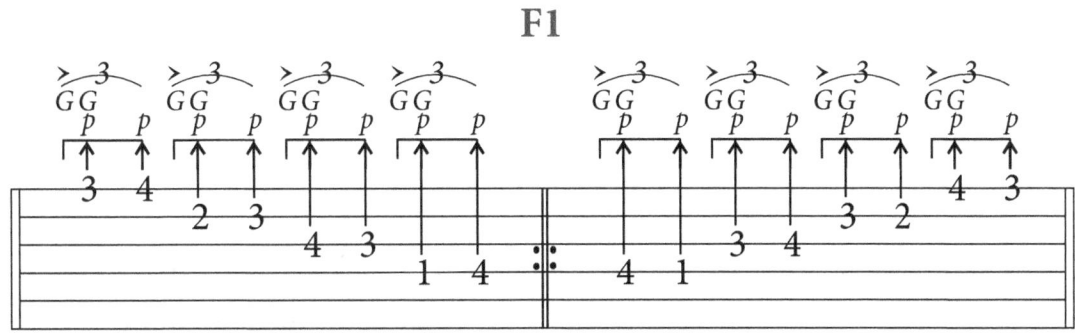

§III The exercise of §I with simultaneous thumb stroke on the above string immediately after the free Golpe (F1) and second stroke on the above string by the thumb (F2).

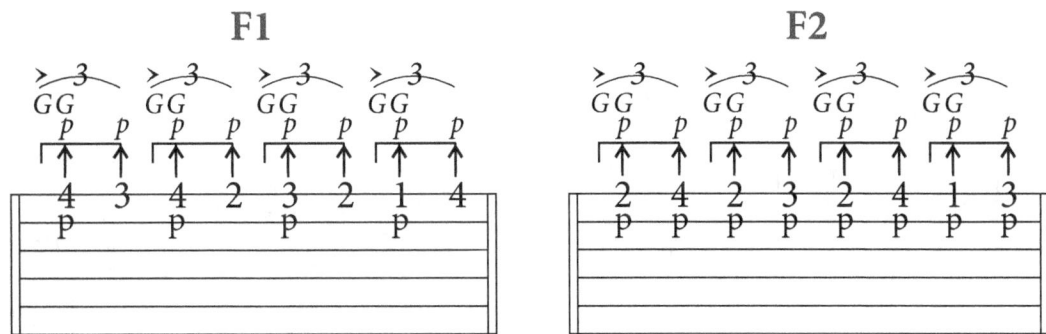

In F1 and F2 we have continuous Golpe on the first and second position of the meter (triplet).

§IV the previous exercise with Golpe on the first and third position of he meter (triplet), thumb stroke towards one direction.

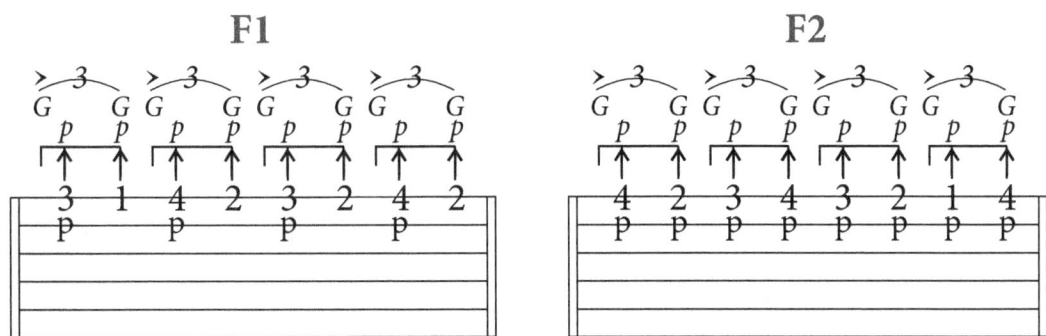

§V , §VI Repetition of the previous exercises with simultaneous stroke of three strings by the thumb, with the first Golpe free in the first position of the meter and the second Golpe:

A/ on the second position in §V and

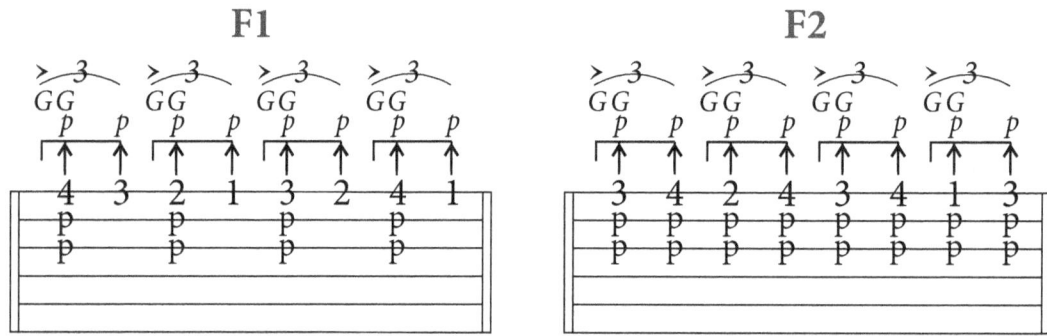

B/ on the third position in §VI.

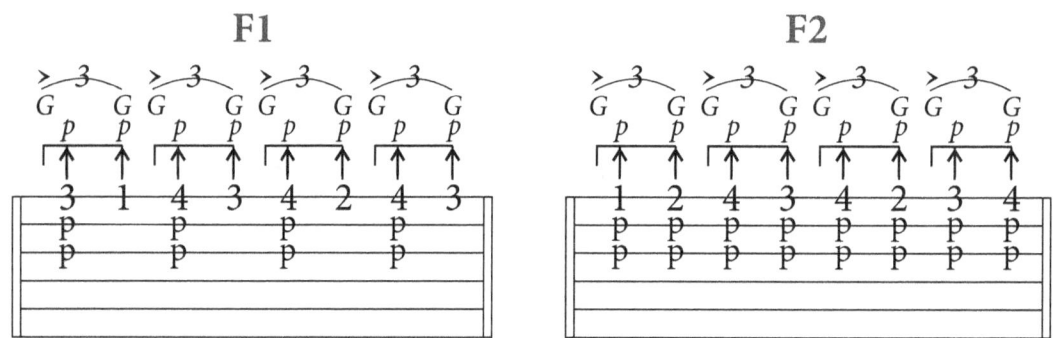

§VII Triple Golpe within the meter (the first free) with thumb stroke of one string. Chromatic scales of one string on the 1st, 2nd, 3rd, 4th. 5th and 6th string.

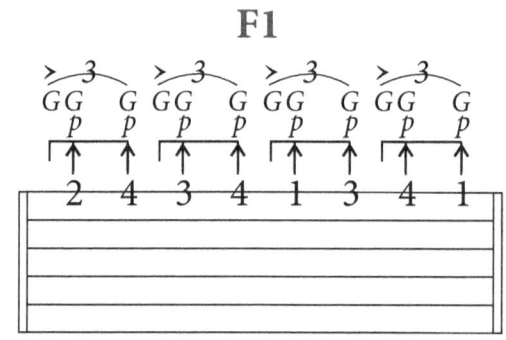

§VIII Triple Golpe within the meter (the first free) on the chromatic scales of one string which move every two notes:

A/ from the 1st to the 4th string
B/ from the 2nd to the 5th string and
C/ from the 3rd to the 6th string.

They return to the initial position. Formula A is cited below.

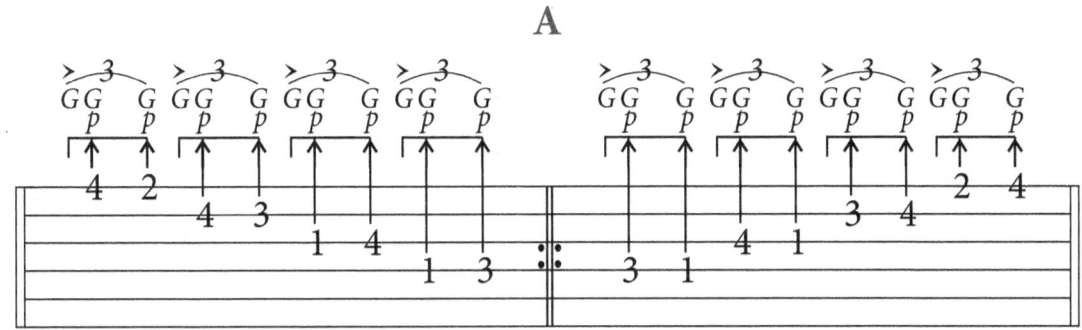

§IX, §X Same mechanism of exercises with the previous ones with triple Golpe within the meter, one free and two simultaneous with the thumb. Stroke of one, two or three strings by the thumb.

§ IX

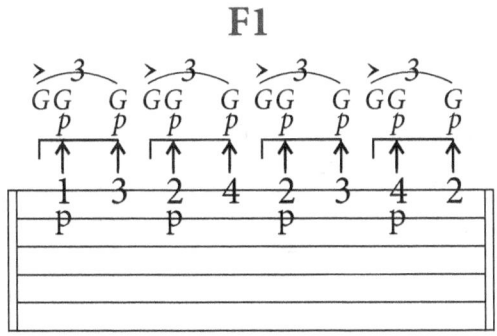
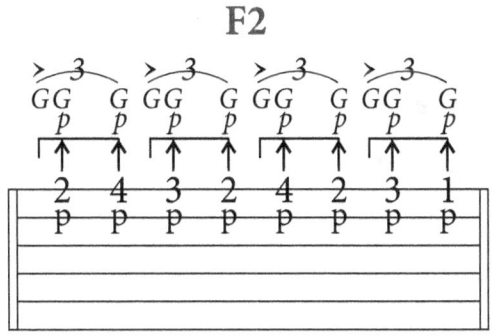

§ X

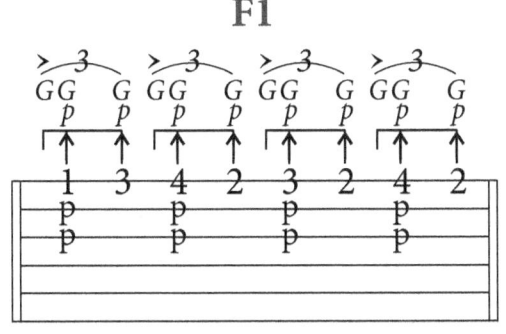
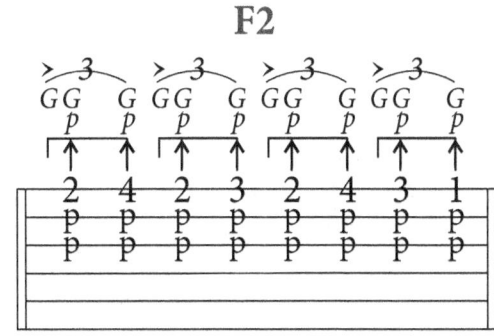

§XI, §XII, §XIII, §XIV

Variations of the previous exercises with thumb stroke towards two directions both downwards (↑) and upwards (↓) within the meter. Single free Golpe within the meter and double Golpe in the first and third position of the meter. Thumb stroke of one, two and three strings.

§ XI

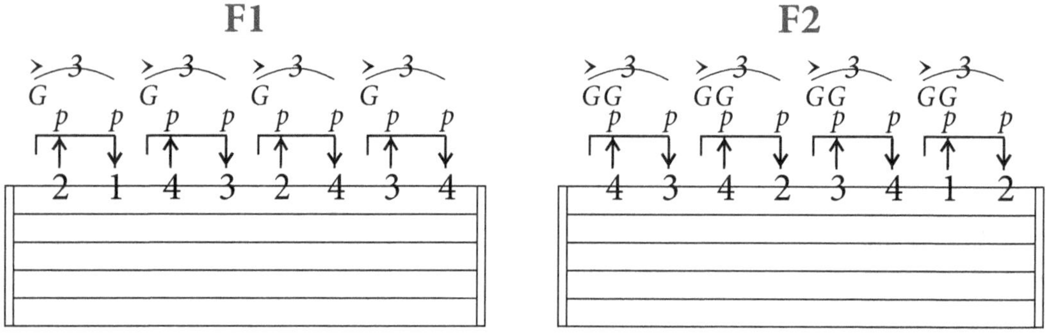

§ XII

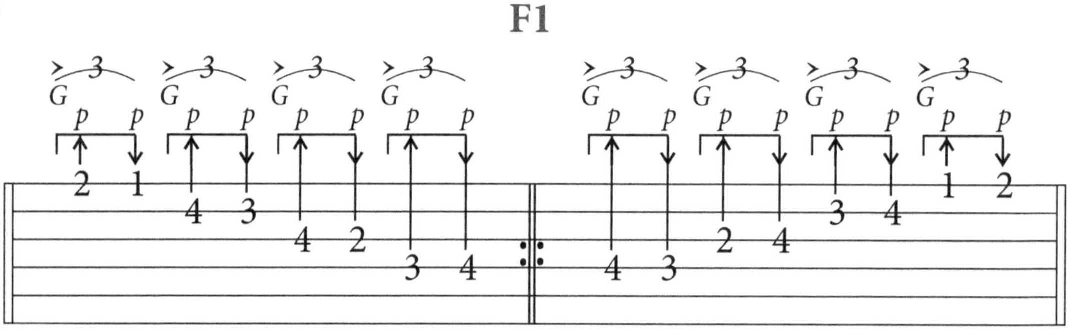

§ XIII

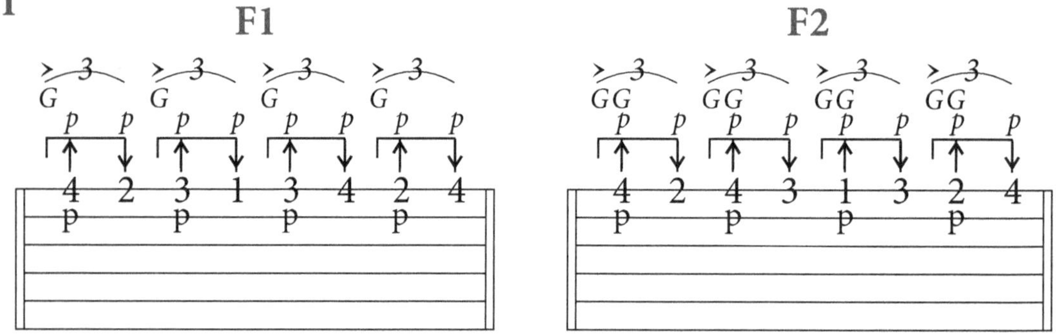

§ XIV

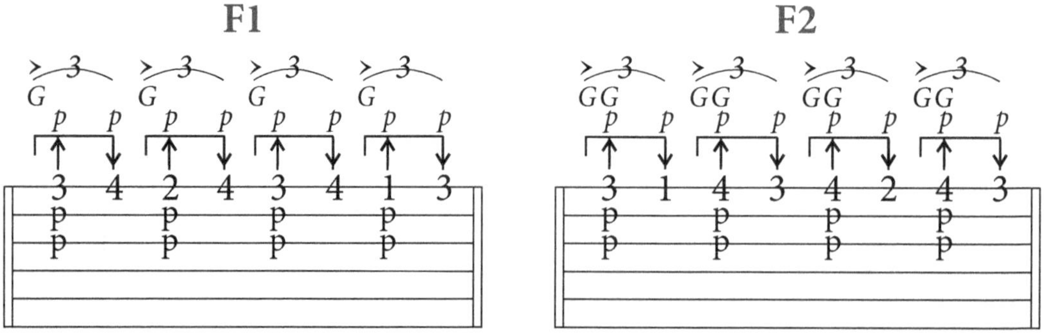

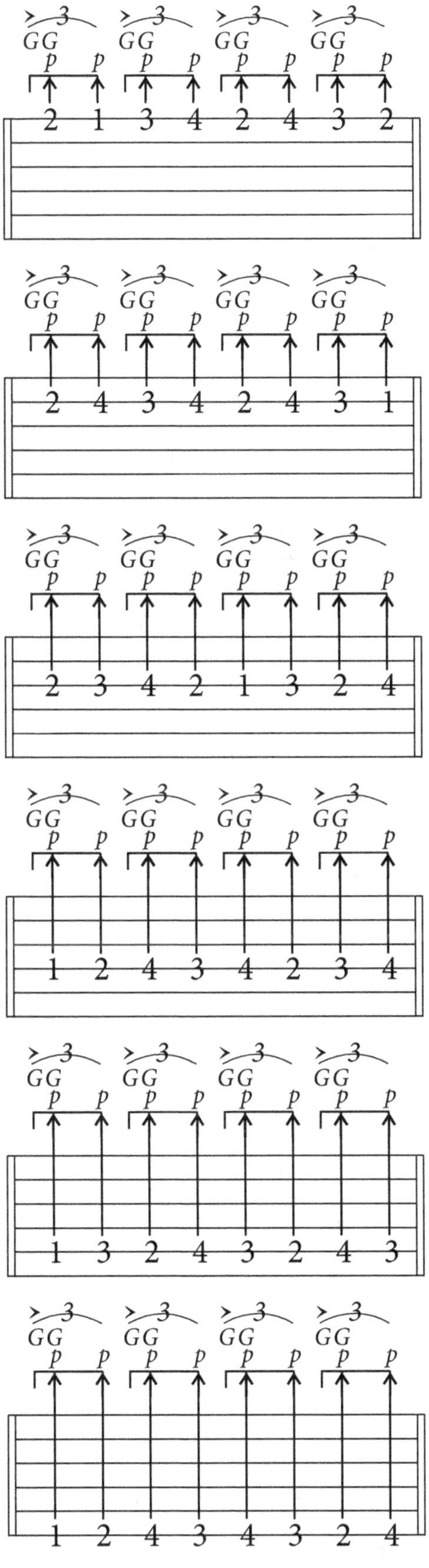

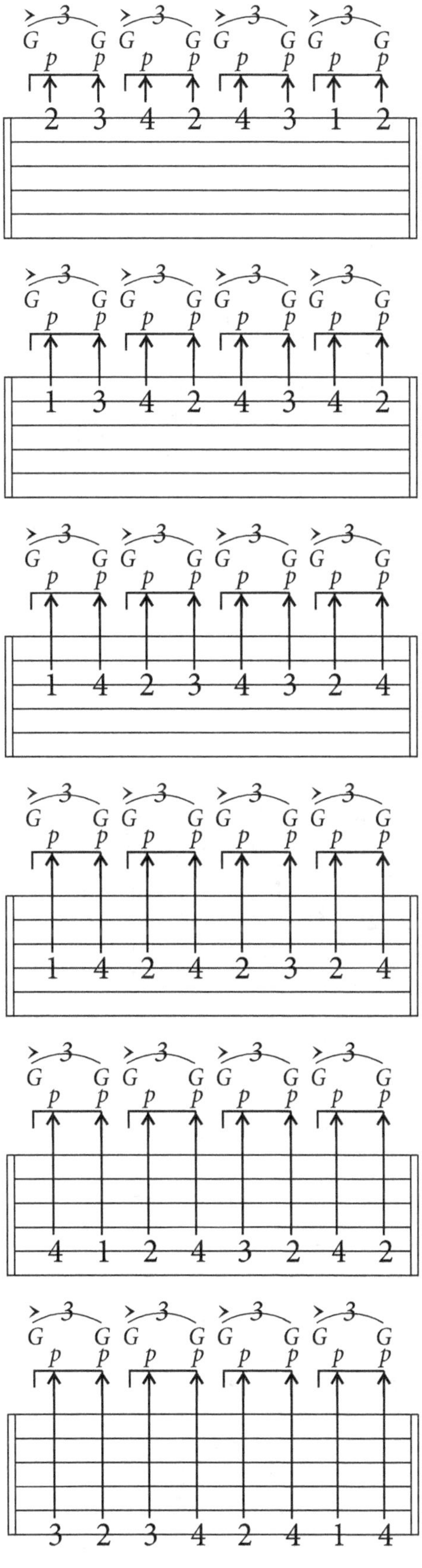

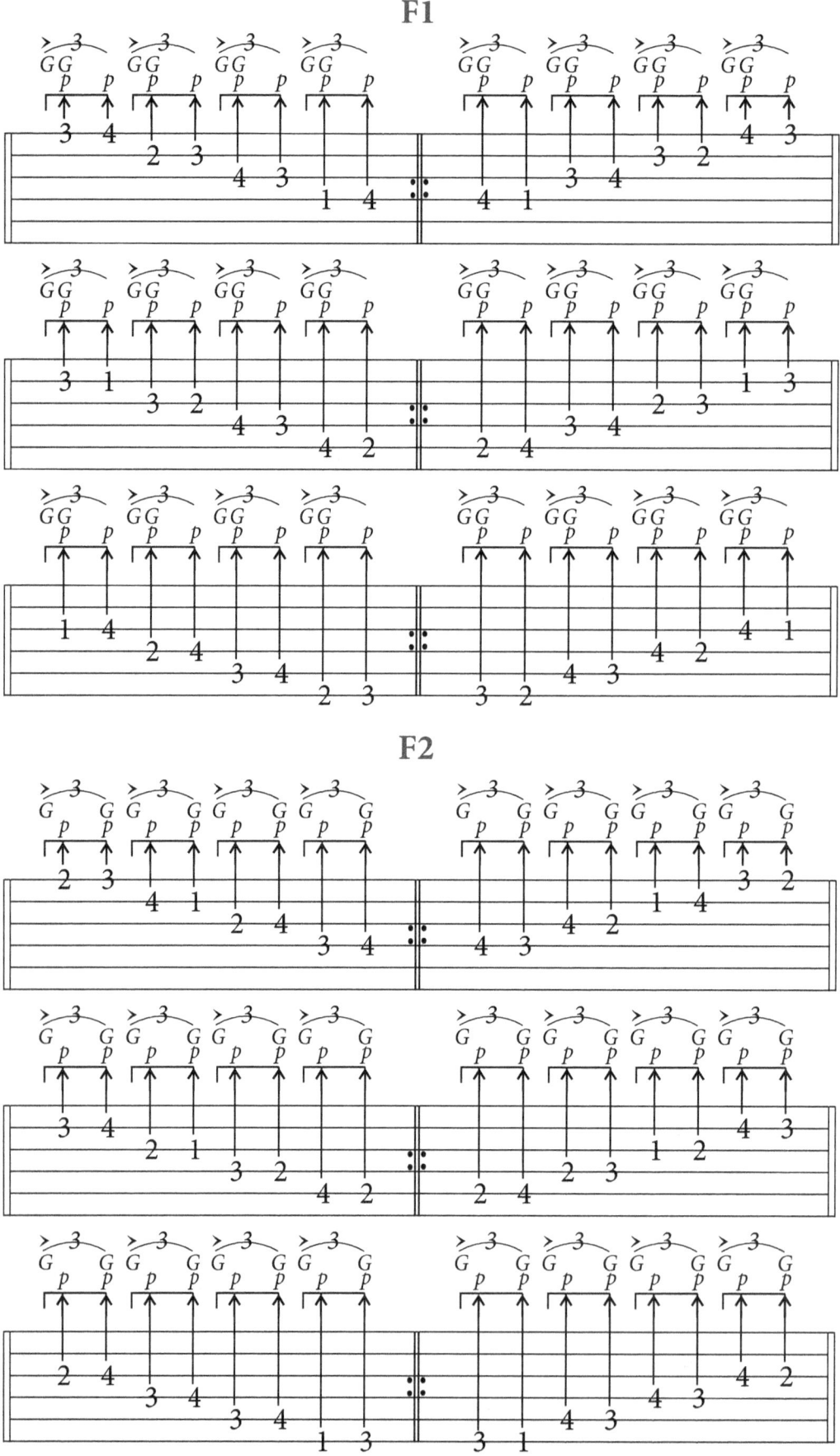

§ III

F1   F2

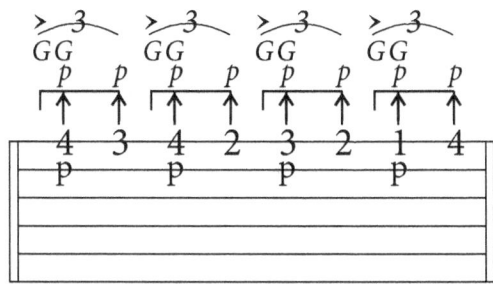 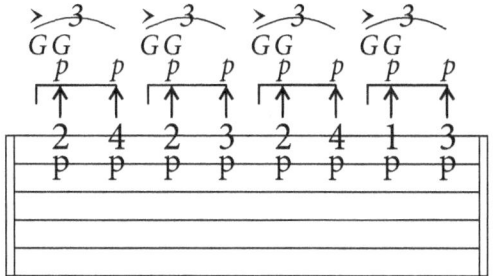
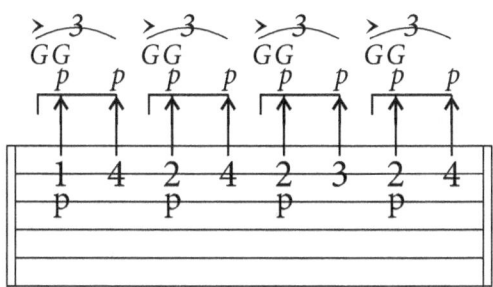 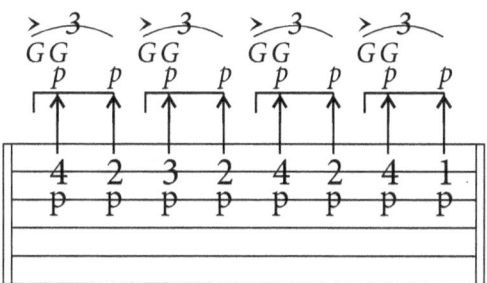
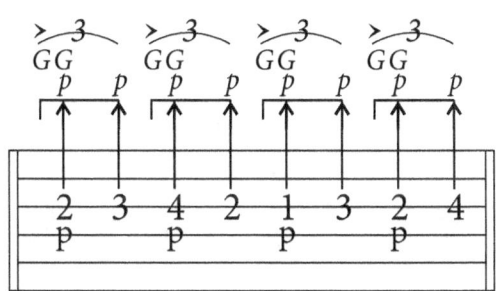 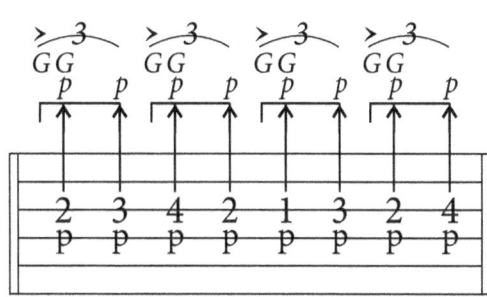
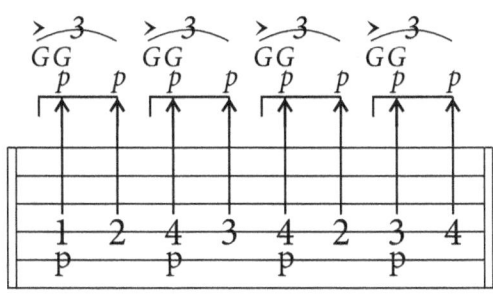 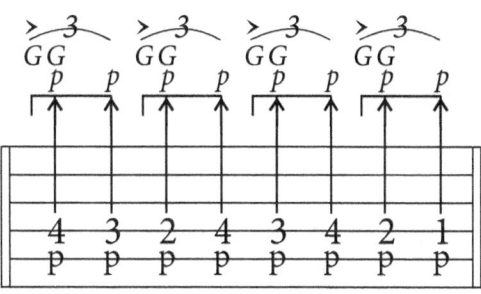
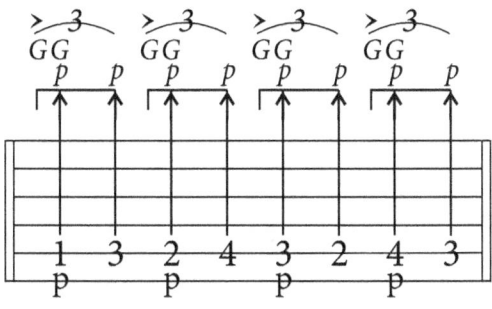 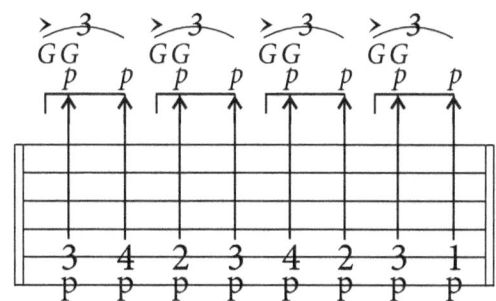

§ IV

F1 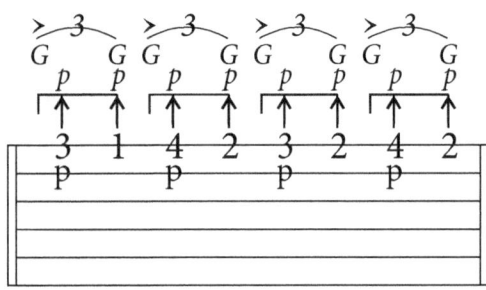 **F2**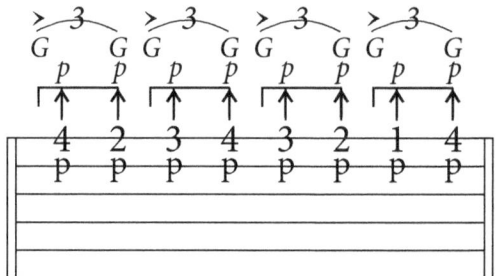

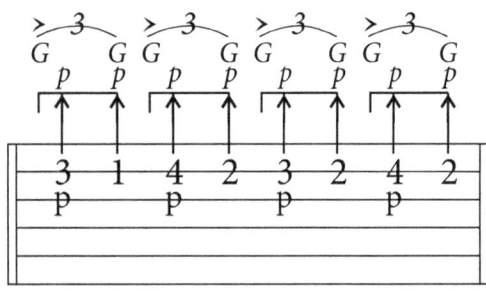 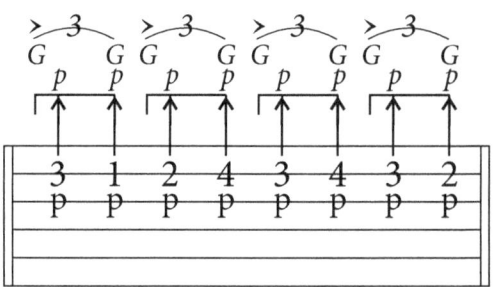

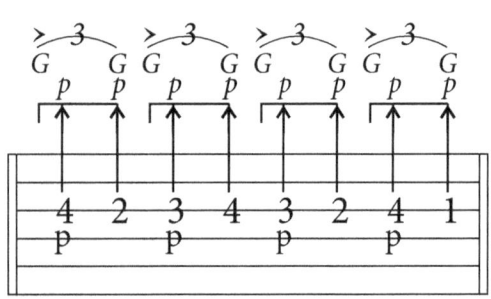 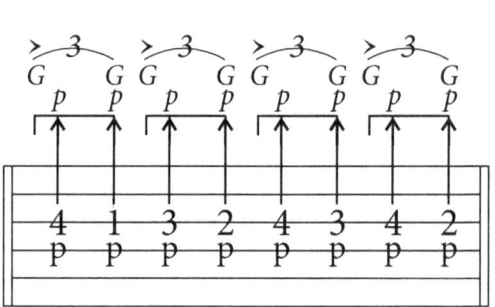

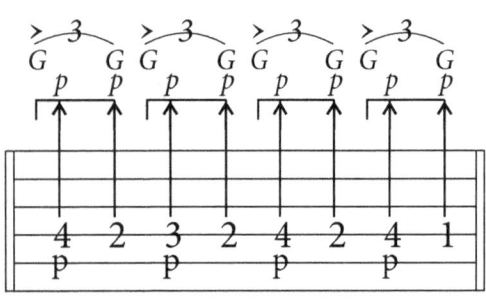 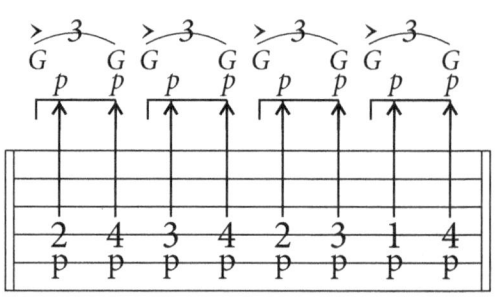

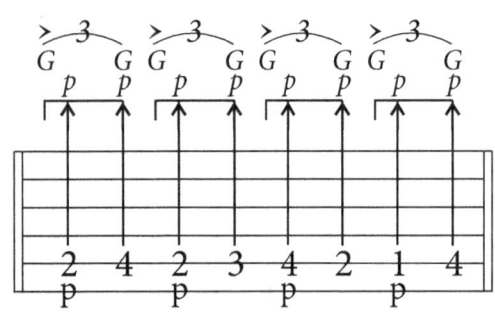 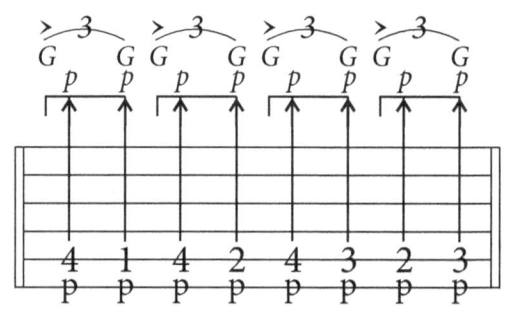

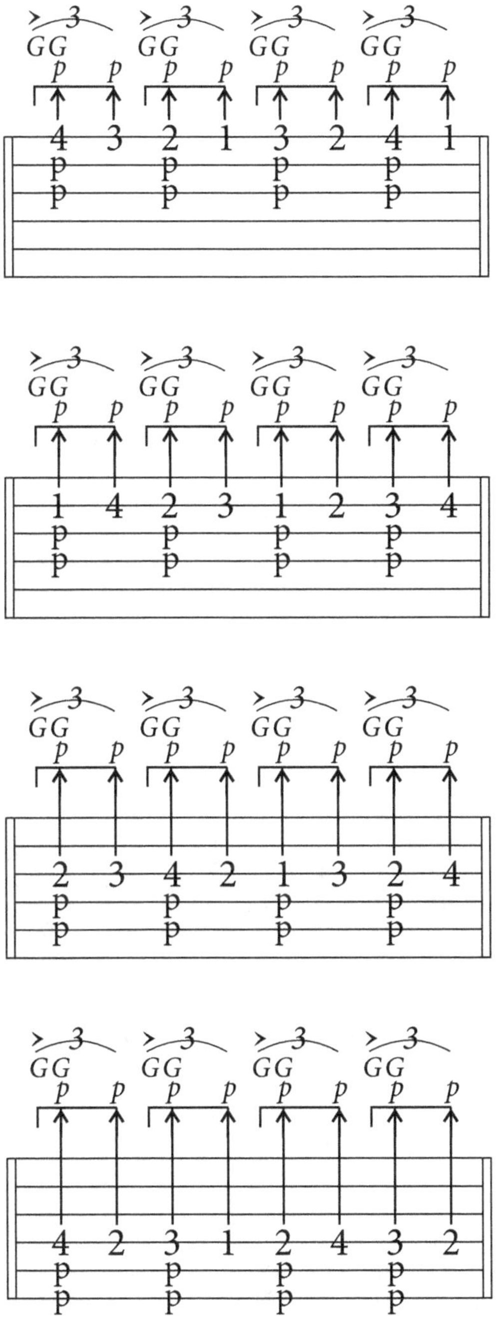

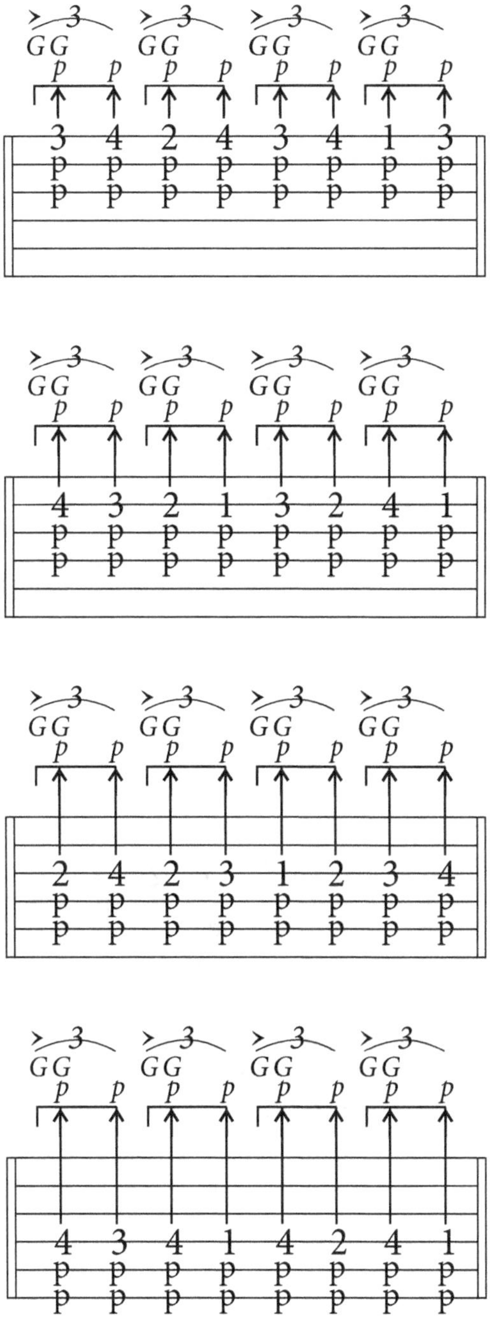

§ VI

F1   F2

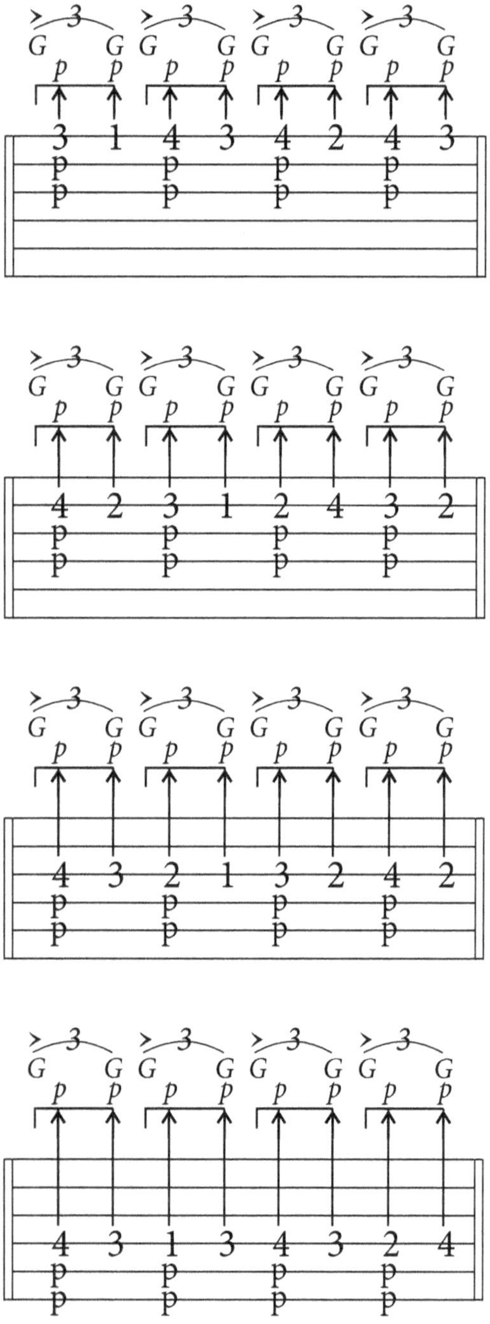

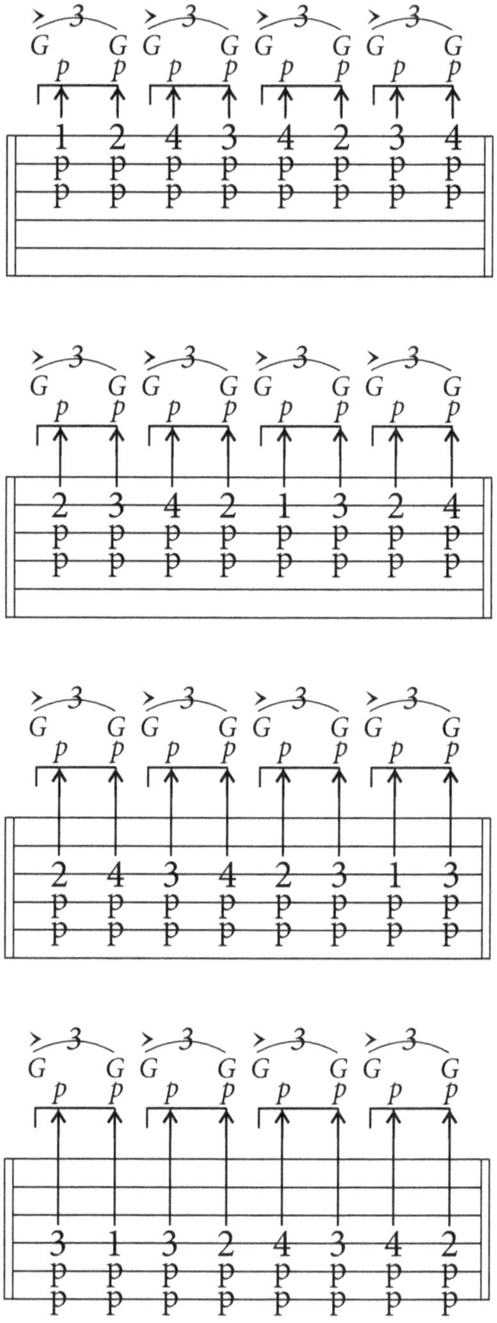

§ VII

F1

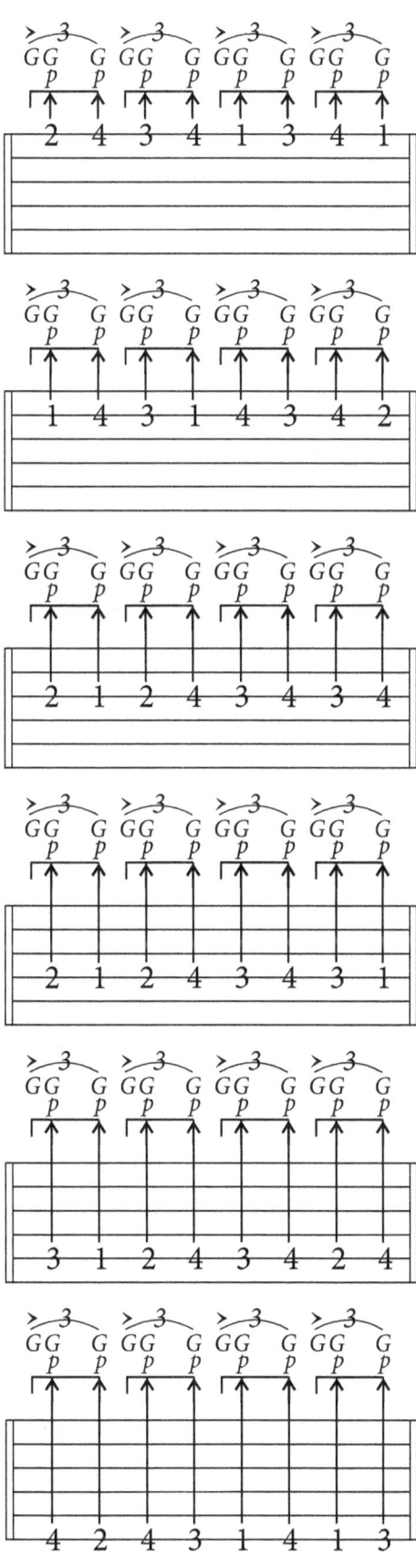

§ VIII

A

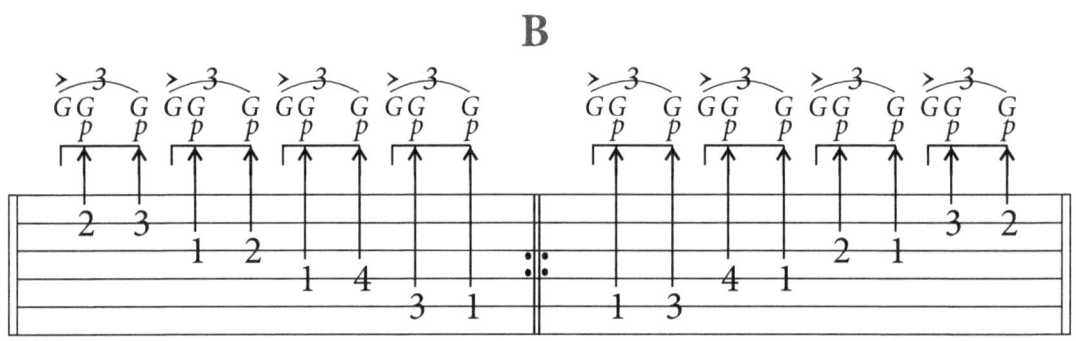

B

C

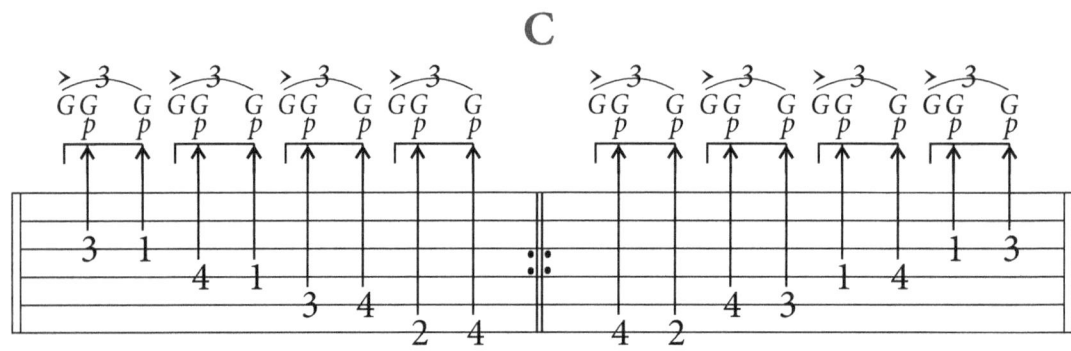

§ IX

F1   F2

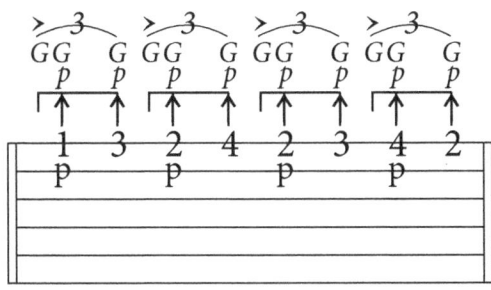
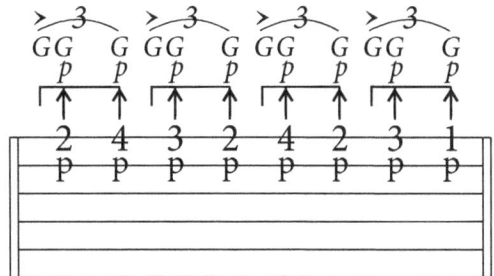
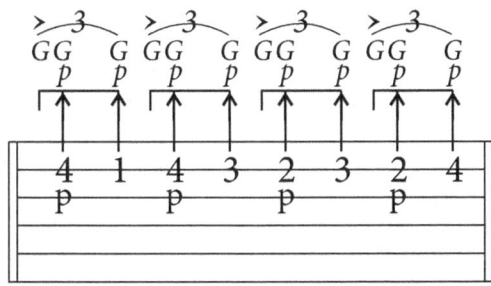
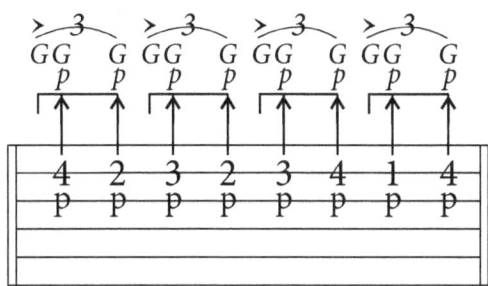
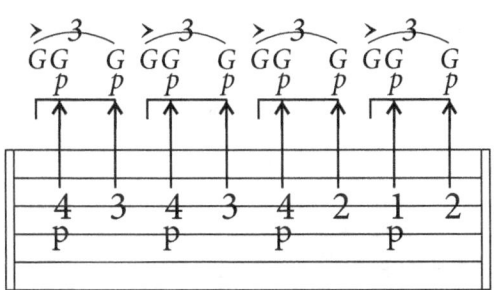
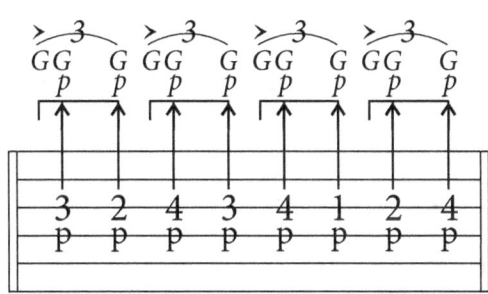
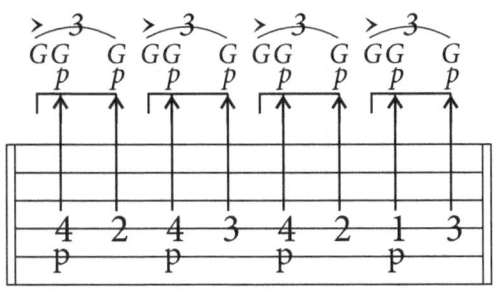
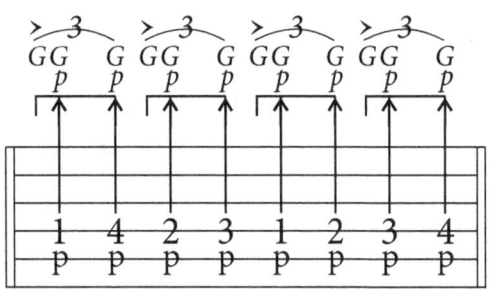
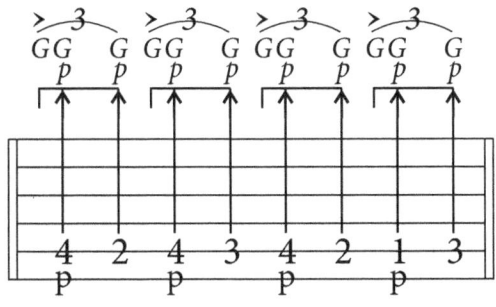
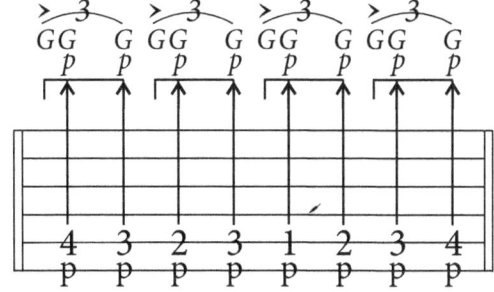

§ X

F1   **F2**

9

§ XI

F1

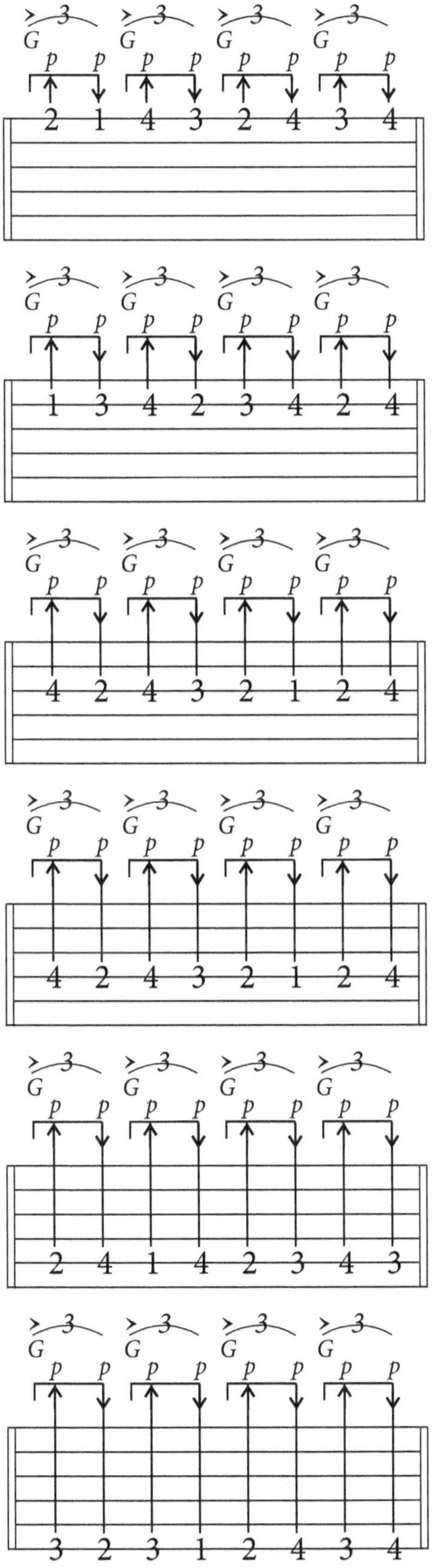
2 1 4 3 2 4 3 4
1 3 4 2 3 4 2 4
4 2 4 3 2 1 2 4
4 2 4 3 2 1 2 4
2 4 1 4 2 3 4 3
3 2 3 1 2 4 3 4

F2

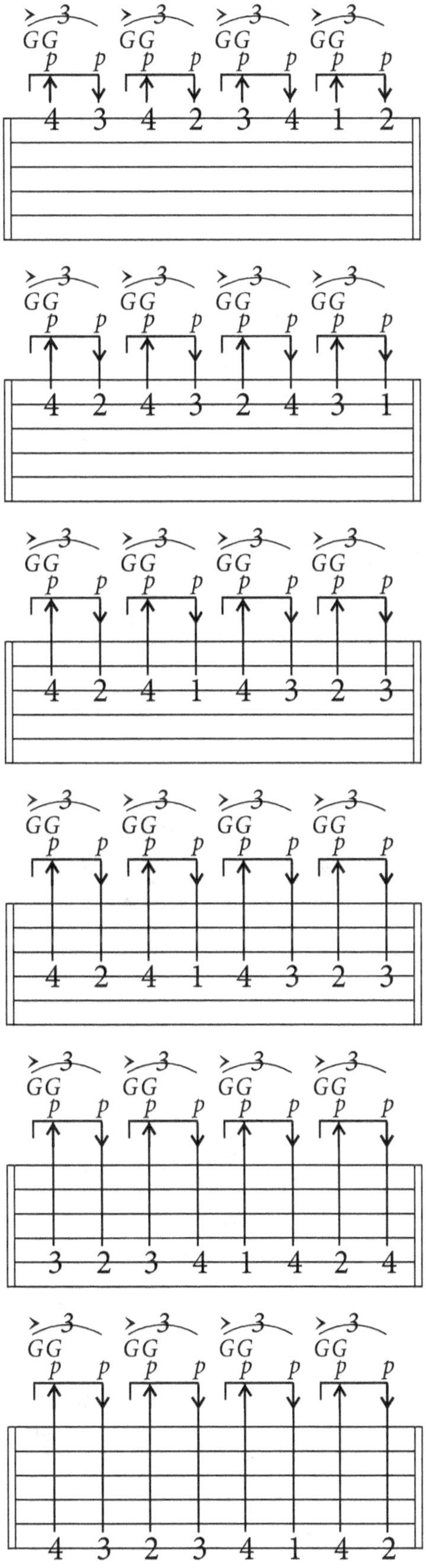
4 3 4 2 3 4 1 2
4 2 4 3 2 4 3 1
4 2 4 1 4 3 2 3
4 2 4 1 4 3 2 3
3 2 3 4 1 4 2 4
4 3 2 3 4 1 4 2

§ XII

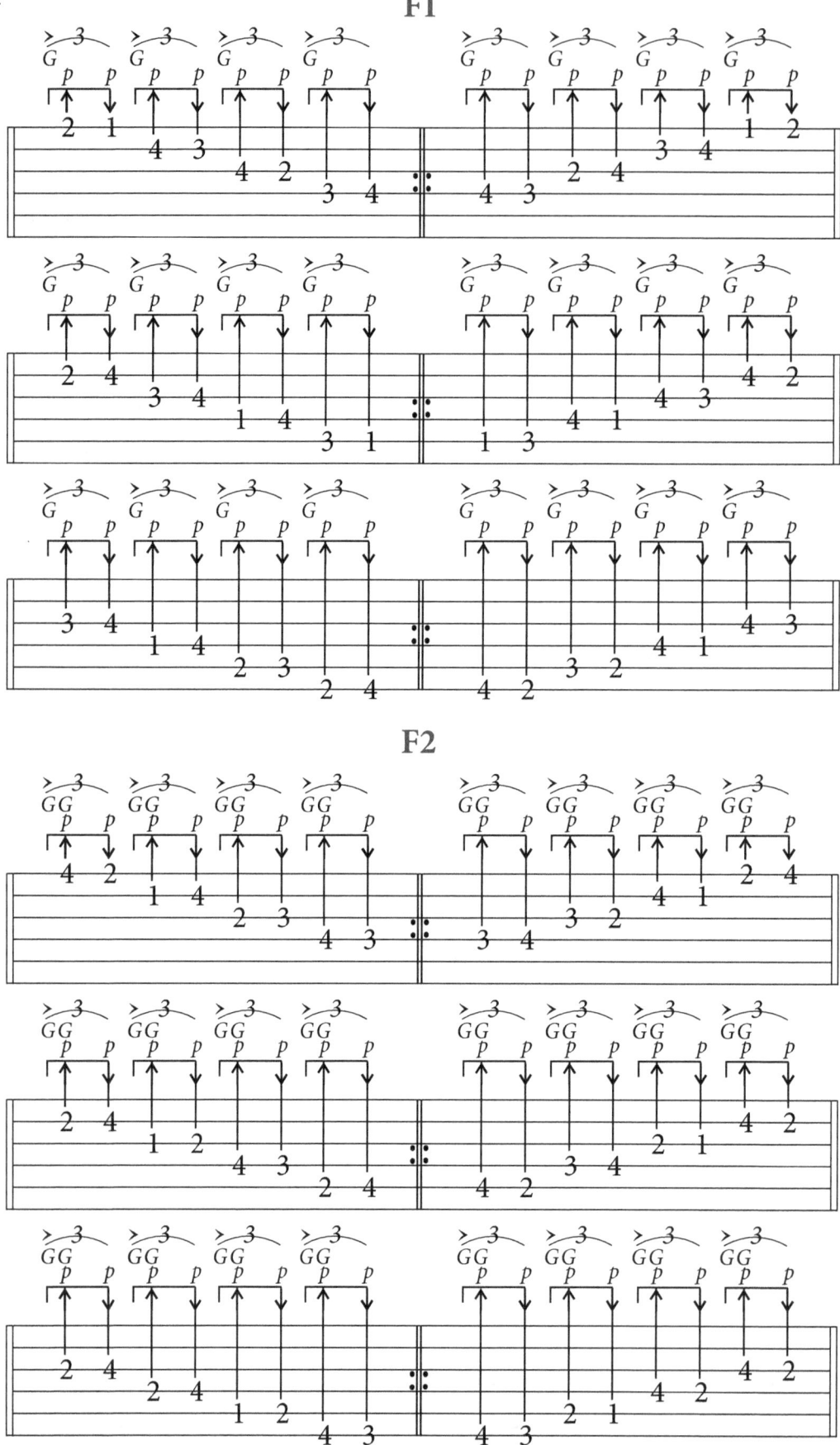

§ XIII

F1   F2

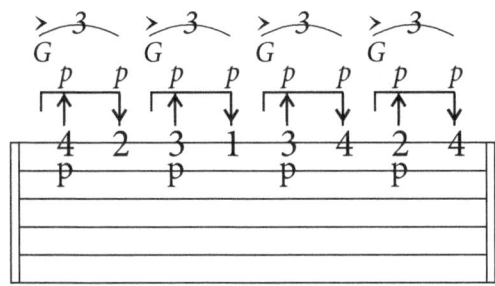 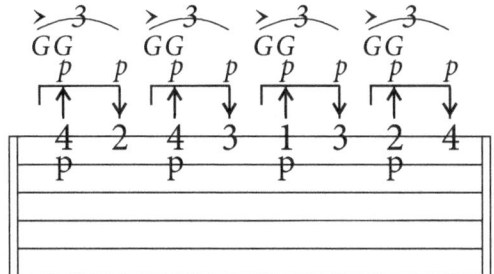

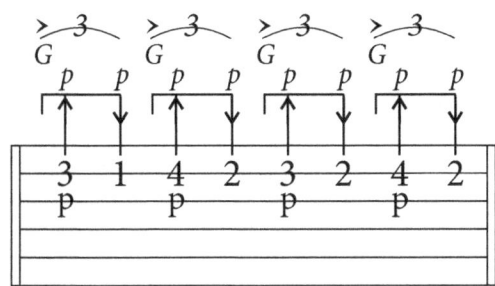 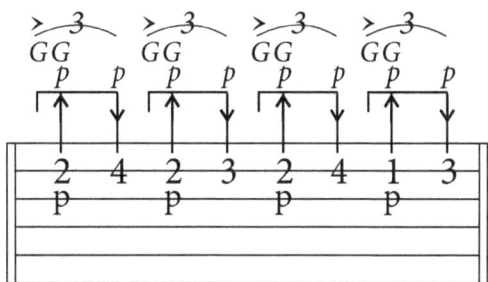

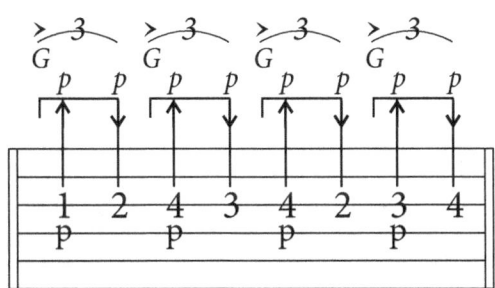 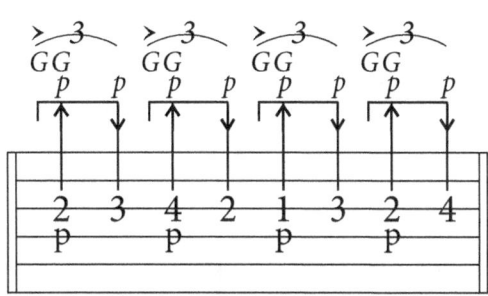

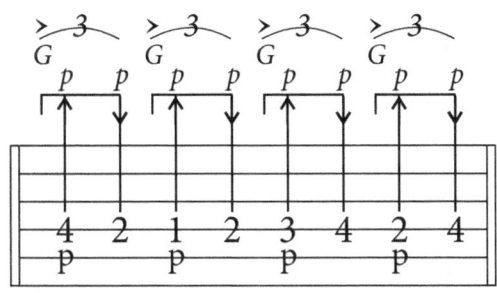 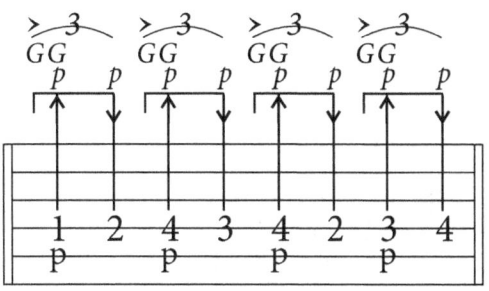

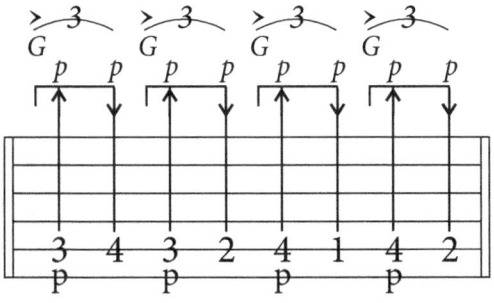 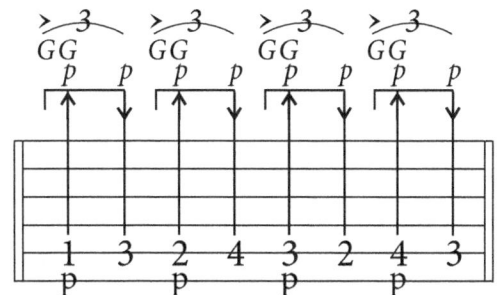

§ XIV

F1   **F2**

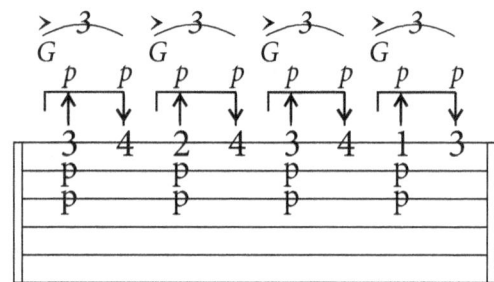 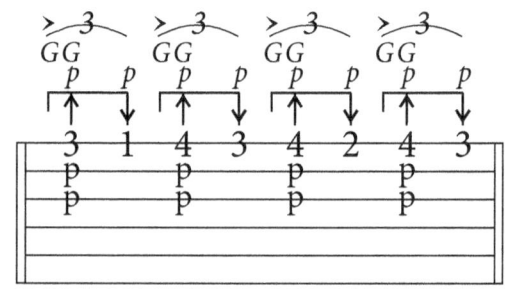

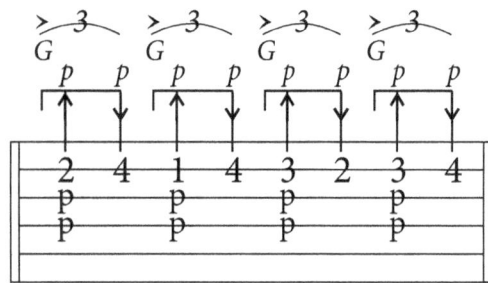 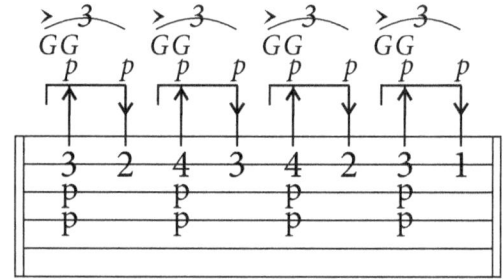

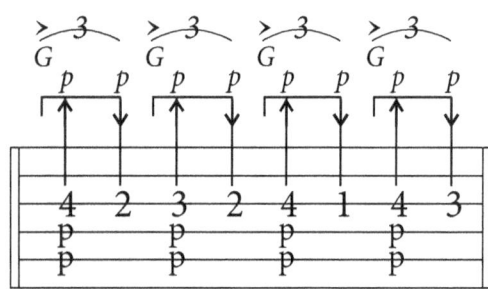 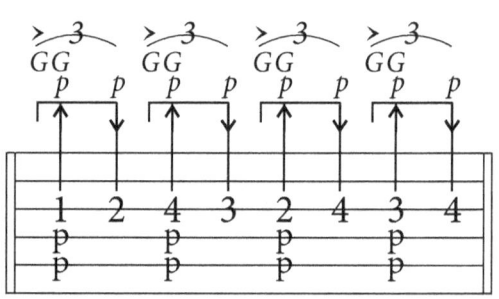

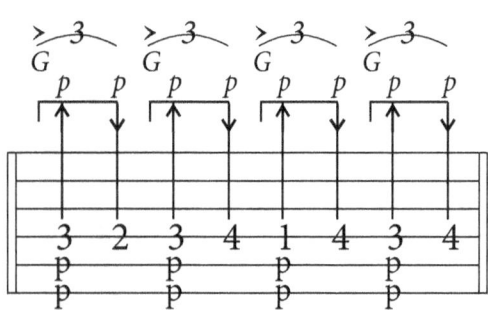 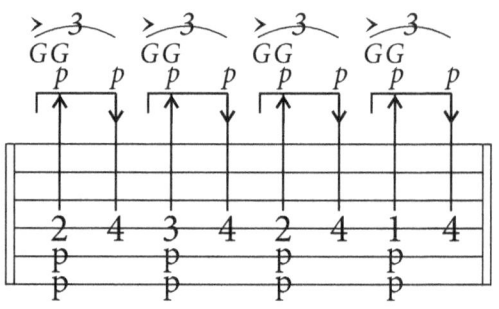

UNIT 2

Two or three Golpe within the meter (one free).
Thumb stroke on one (↑) or two (↑↓) directions.
Strike one, two or three strings simultaneously.

§I Double Golpe within the meter, one with thumb stroke and one free. The chromatic scales are formed in triplets on all strings from the 1st to the 6th. Thumb stroke towards one direction (↑).

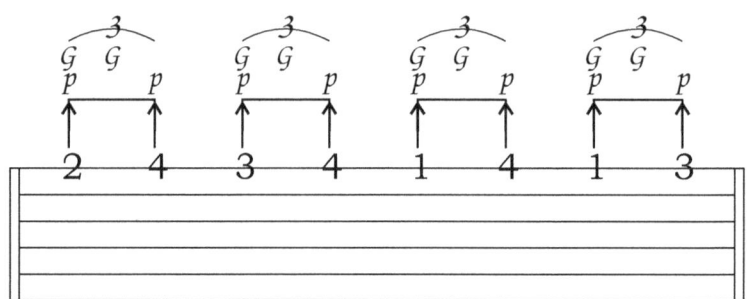

§II The chromatic scales move every two notes on four adjacent strings and return to the initial position with their opposites. Thumb stroke towards one direction (↑).

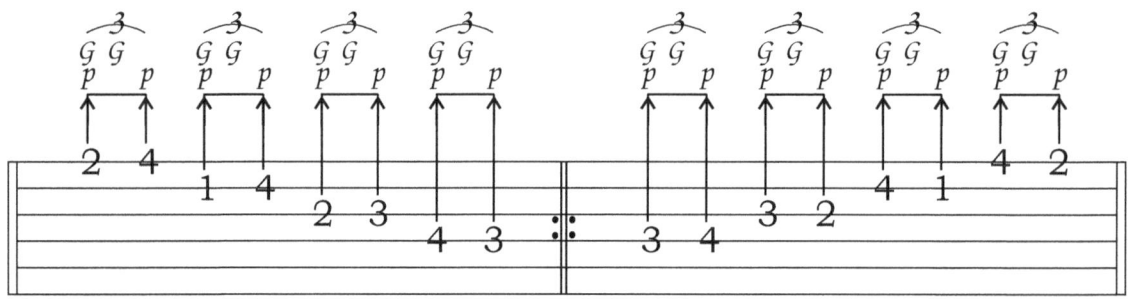

§III, §IV The previous exercises with triple Golpe within the meter, two simultaneous with the thumb and one free.

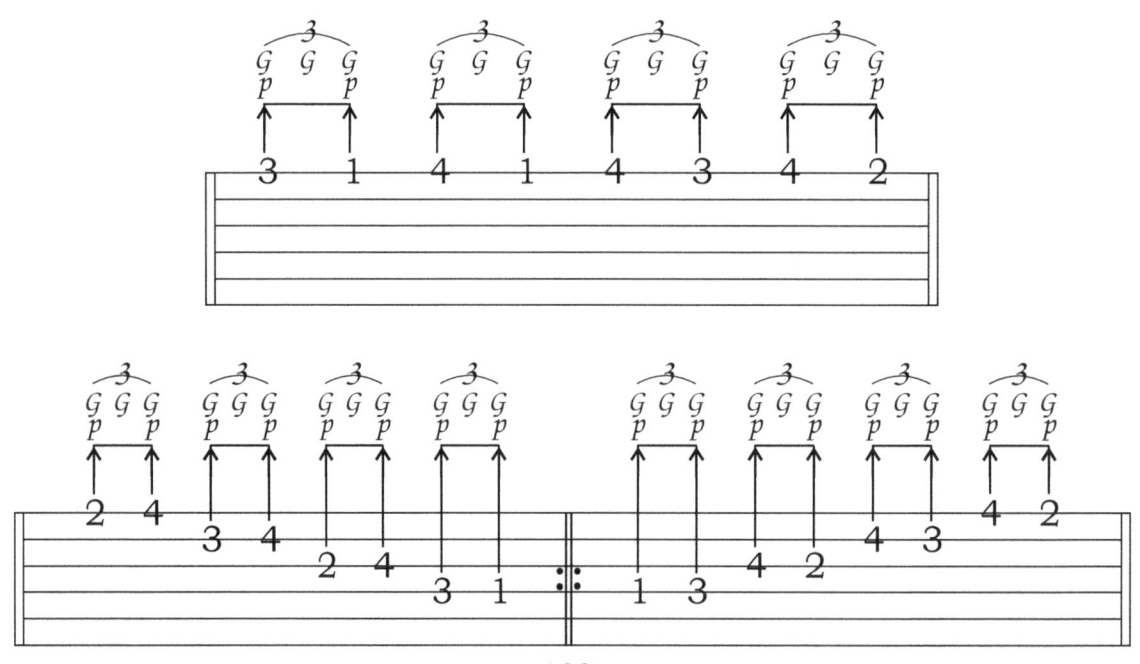

§V, §VI The exercises of §I and §II with thumb stroke downwards - upwards
(↑↓)

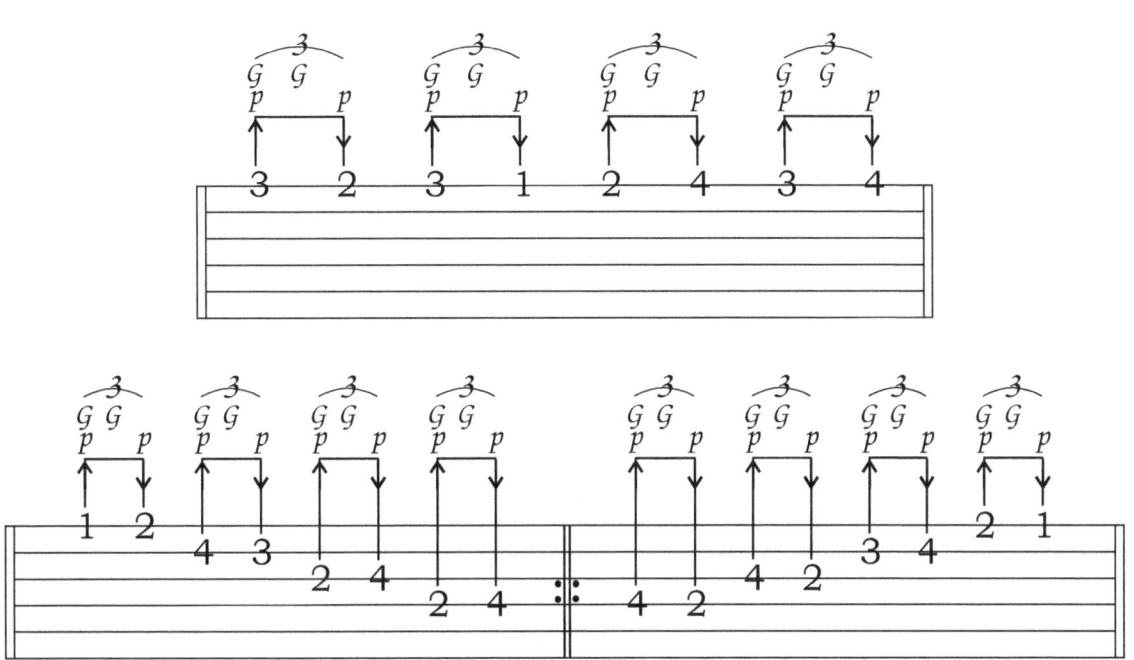

§VII, §VIII Variations of the previous exercises with three Golpe within the meter and simultaneous stroke of two and three strings by the thumb.

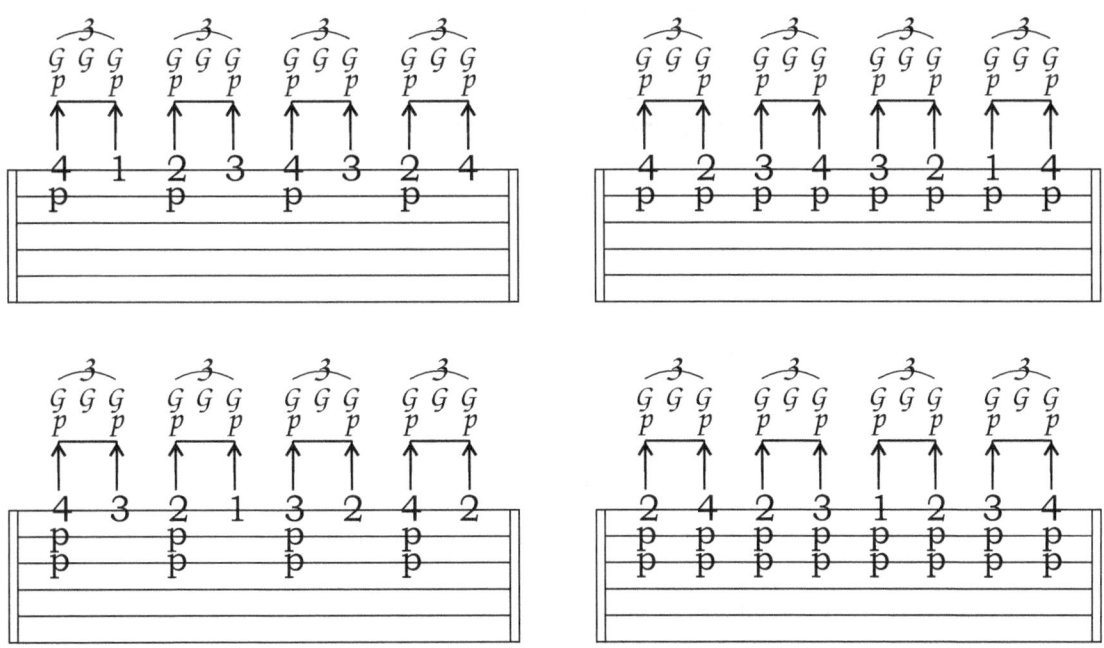

§ I

F1

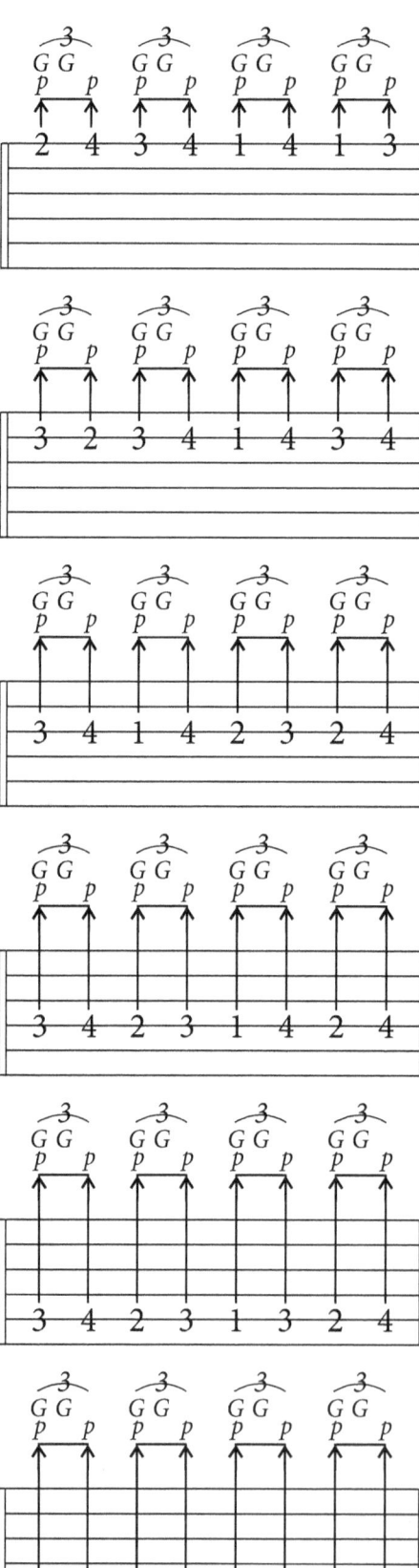

§ II

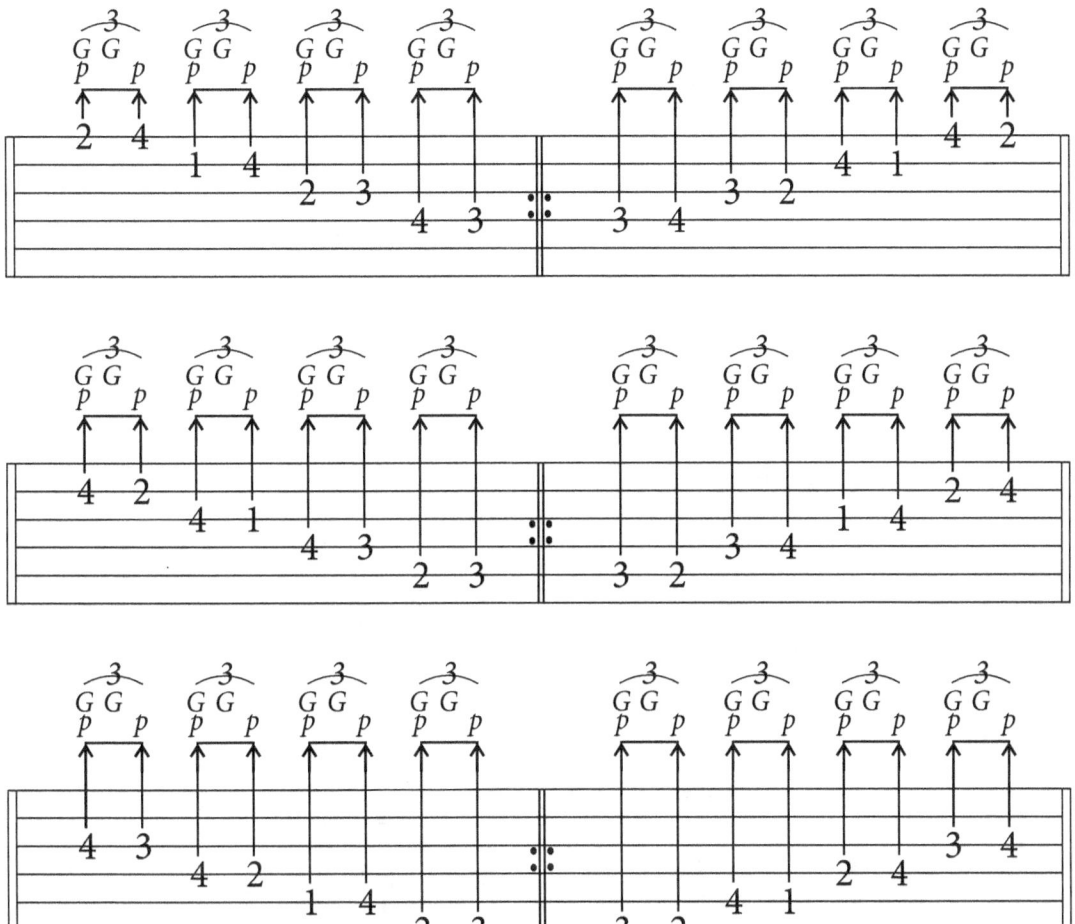

§ III

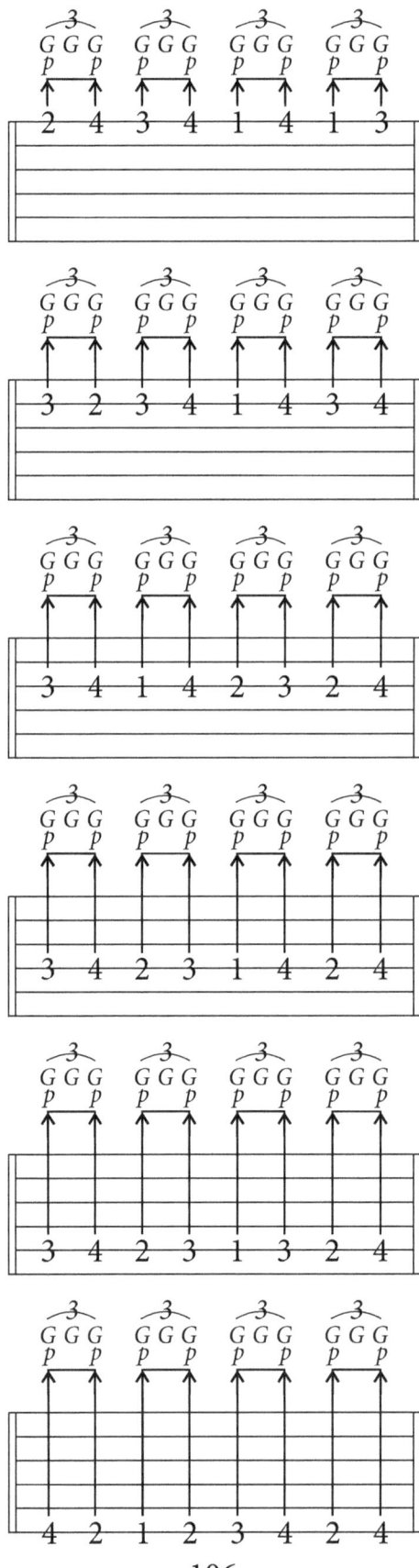

§ IV

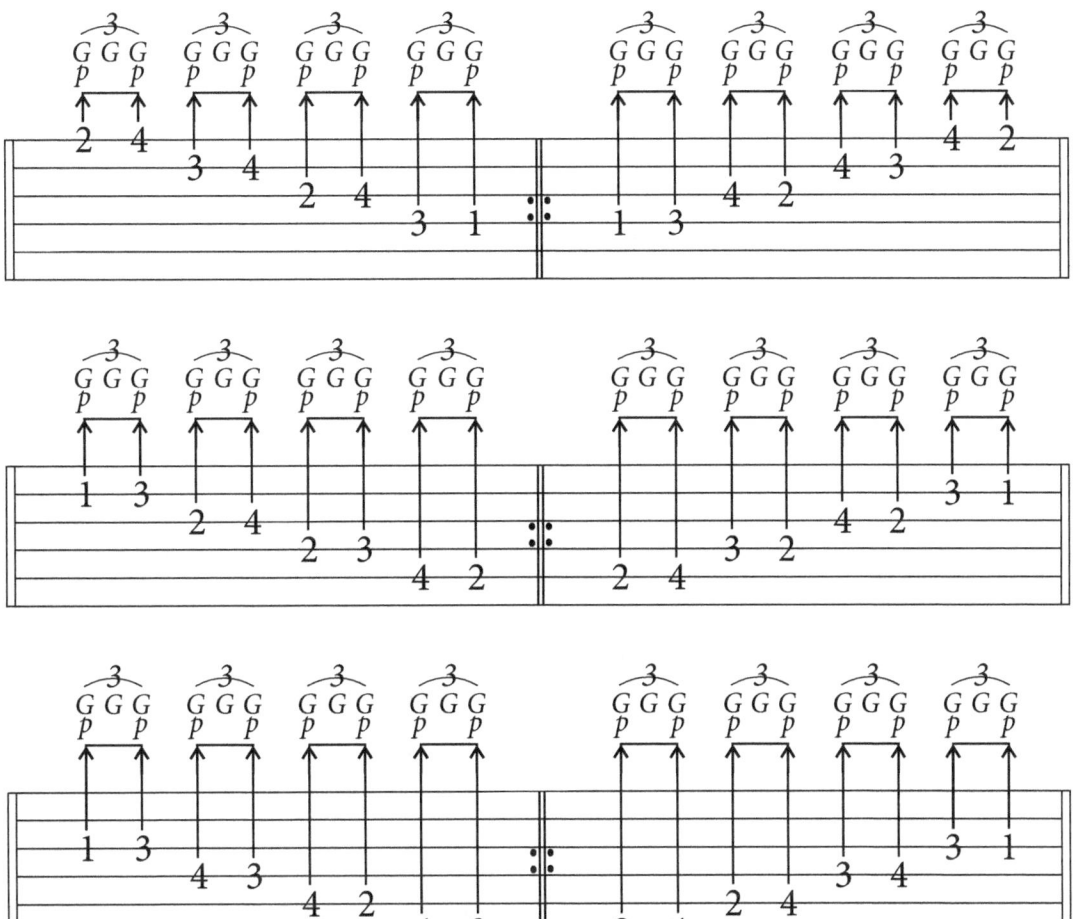

107

§ V

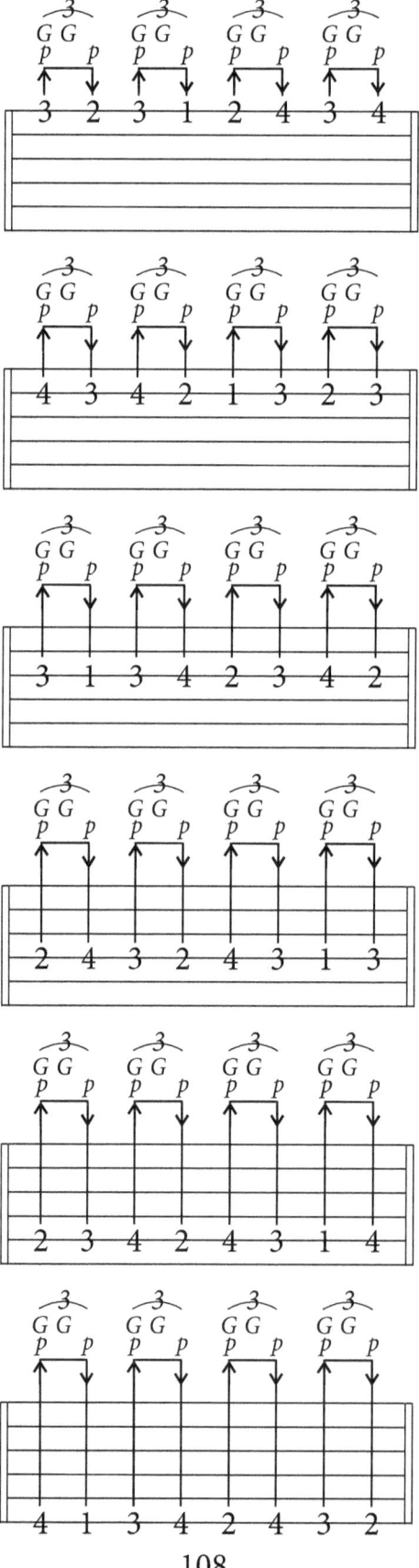

§ VI

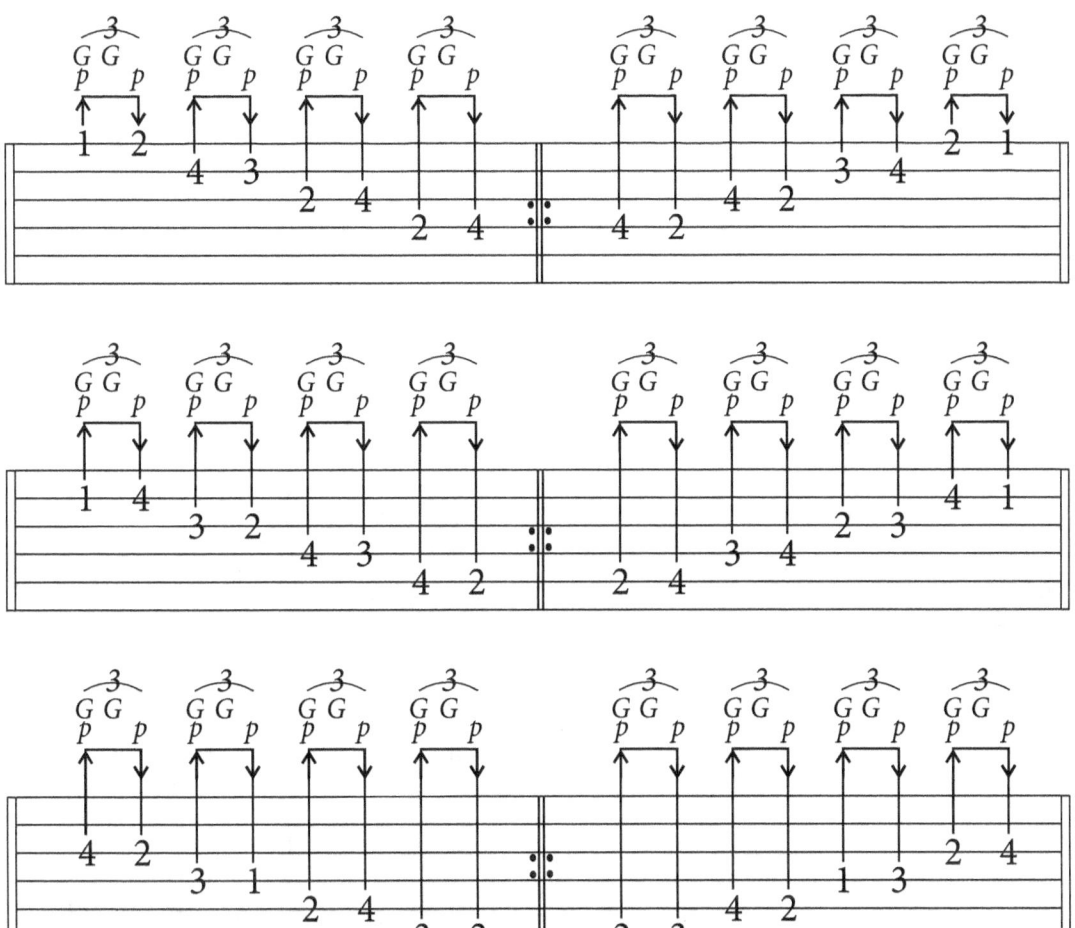

§ VII

F1 F2

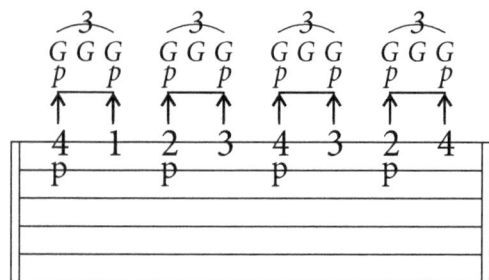 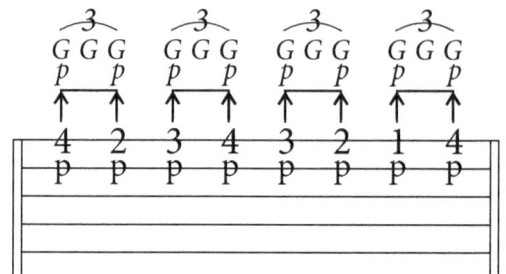

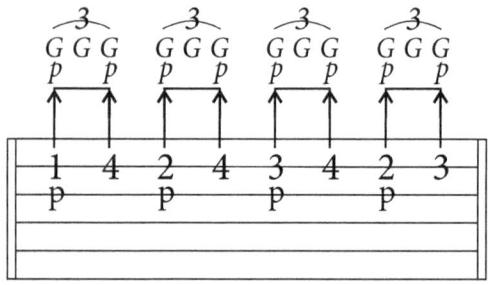 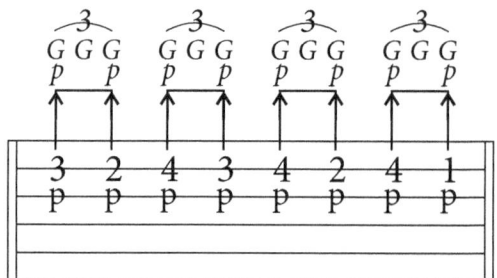

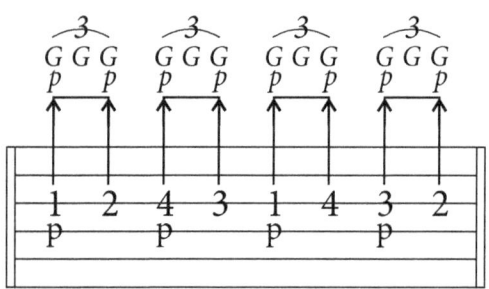 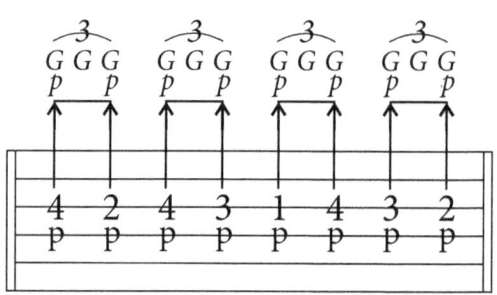

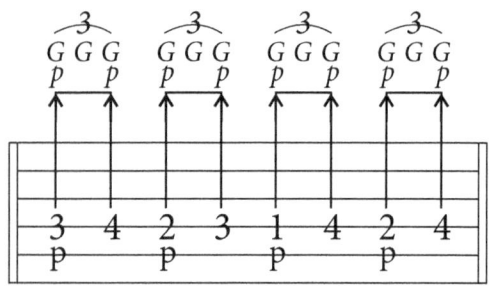 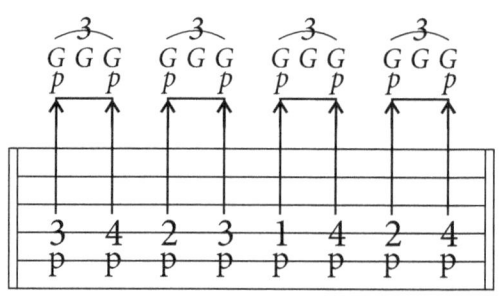

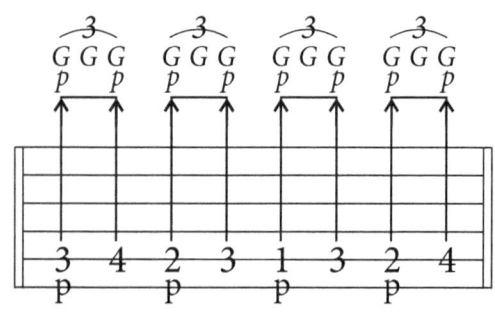 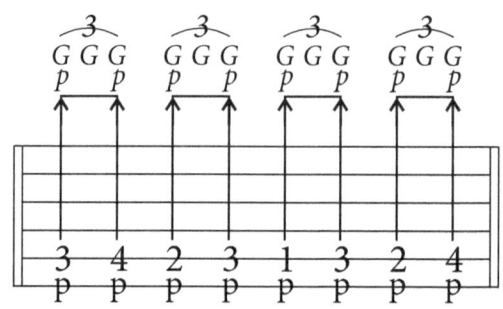

§ VIII

F1 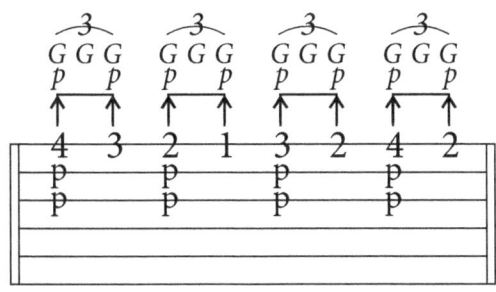 **F2**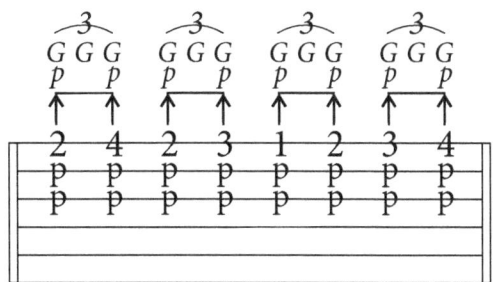

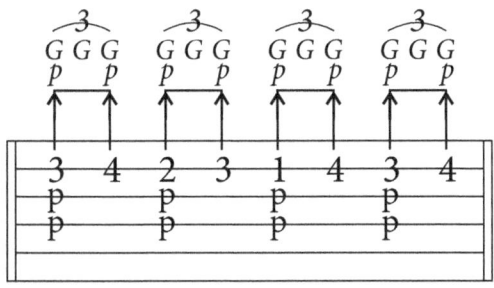 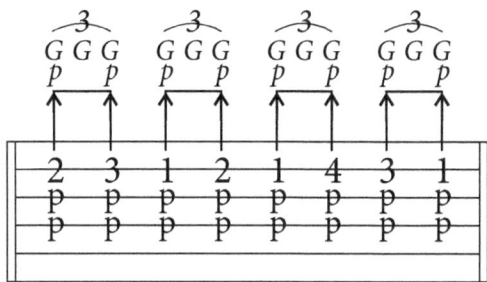

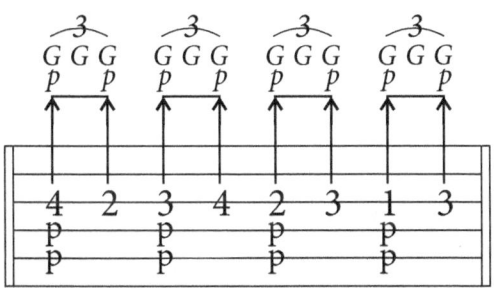 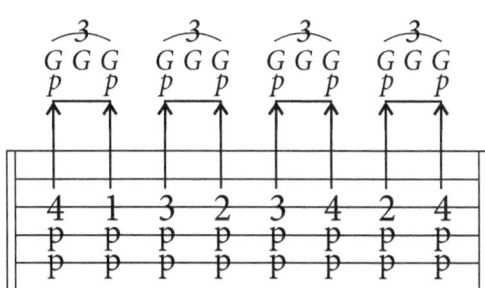

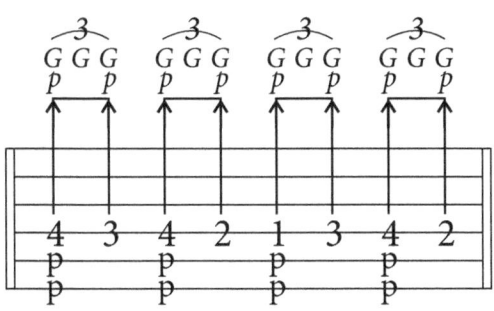 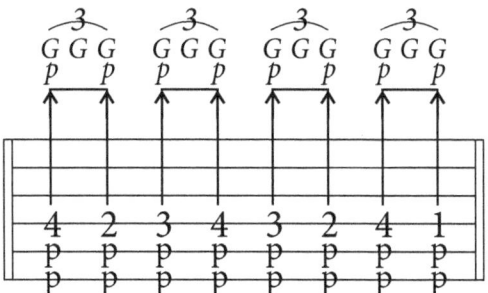

CHAPTER 3
GOLPE WITH THUMB STROKE IN COMBINATION WITH INDEX (i) AND MIDDLE FINGER (m).

Chapter 3 contains three units. In these units we find Golpe with thumb stroke on one string, on two strings or on three strings in combination with the index (i) and middle finger (m). The chromatic scales are on one string or move every two notes on four strings. The arrangement of the chromatic scales contains either isochronous notes (all of them),

eg: ‖ 1 4 2 3 4 3 2 4 ‖

or is shaped in three variations. In this case the arrangement of the chromatic scale is in two notes and two triplets as shown below:

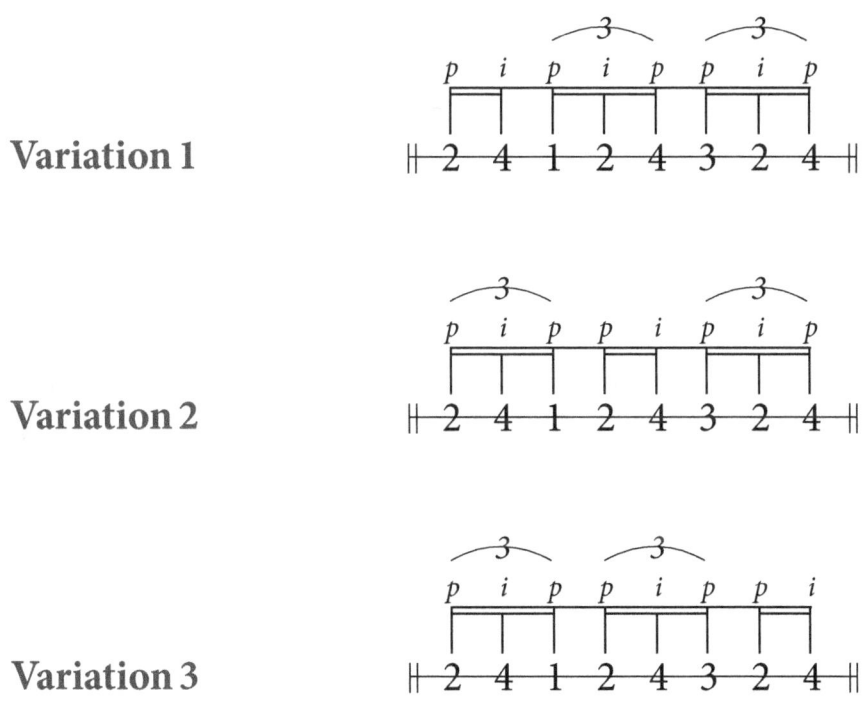

Variation 1

Variation 2

Variation 3

Double notes and triplets are isochronous. More information in the beginning of each unit.

UNIT 1

Thumb stroke with Golpe on one, two or
three strings simultaneously
and in combination with index (i) and middle finger (m).

§Ia Stroke of one string by the thumb in combination with the index (i) and middle finger (m) on the chromatic scales of one string on the 1st, 2nd, 3rd, 4th, 5th and 6th string. Double thumb stroke with Golpe within the meter in the 1st and 3rd position.

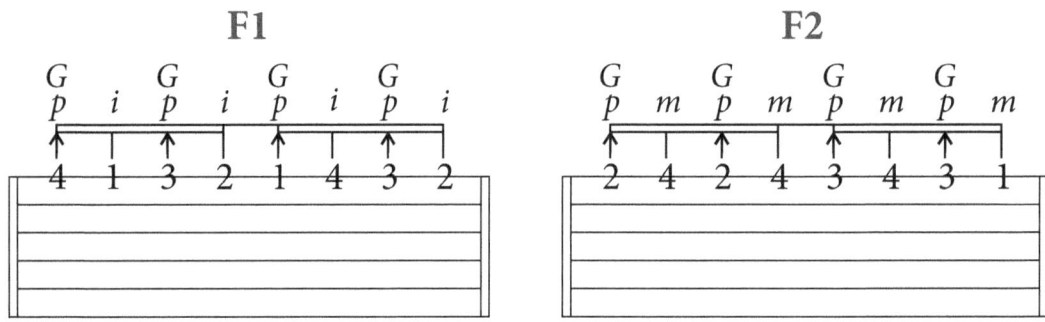

§IIa Chromatic scales on the 1st, 2nd, 3rd, 4th and 5th string. Two Golpe within the meter on the 1st and 3rd position of the meter. Simultaneous stroke of the Golpe with two strings by the thumb in combination with the index and middle finger.

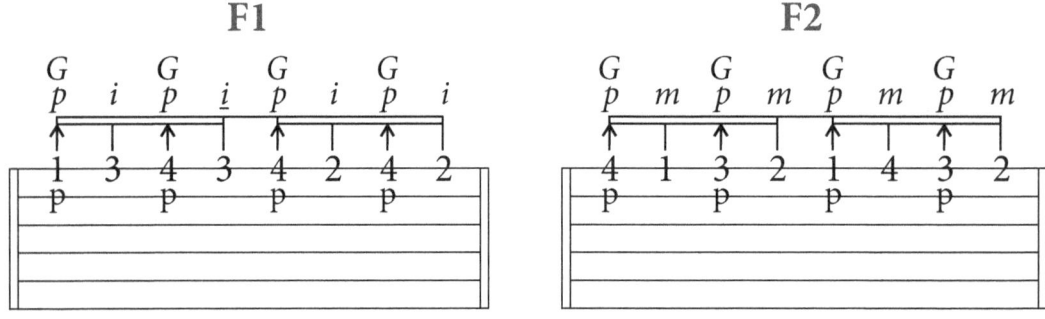

Practice with simultaneous stroke of the 6th string when the scale is on the 4th string:

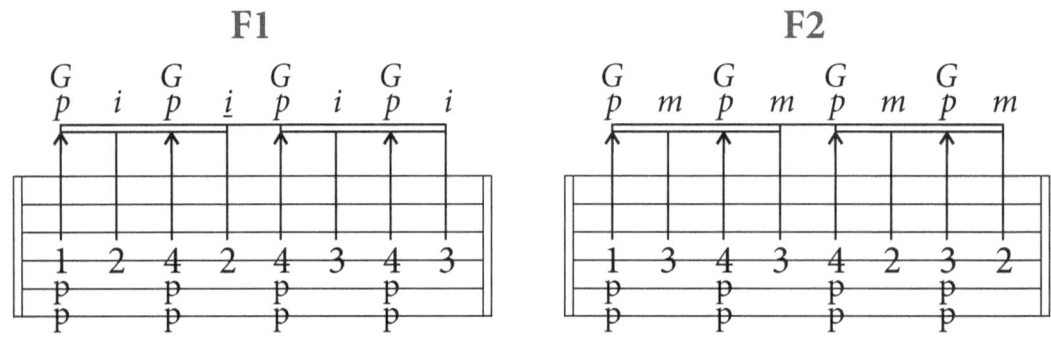

§IIIa Chromatic scales which appear every two notes on four adjacent strings and return with their opposites. Thumb stroke towards one direction (↑).

IVa Simultaneous stroke of three strings with Golpe on the chromatic scales of one string in combination with the index(i) and middle finger (m).

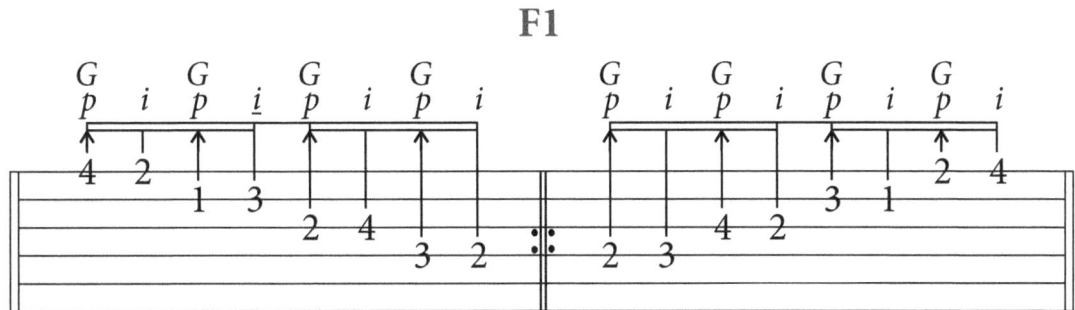

§Ib, §IIb, §IIIb The previous exercises (marked with a) with interchange of the fingers (i) and (m) within the meter. Same mechanism of the exercise. Same notes apply.

§ Ib

§ IIb

F1 F2

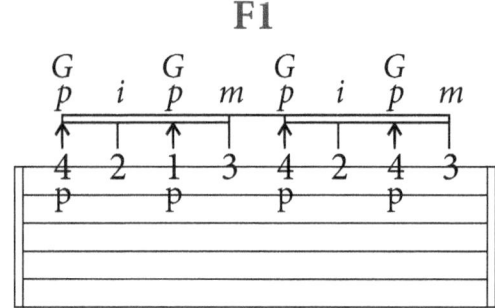
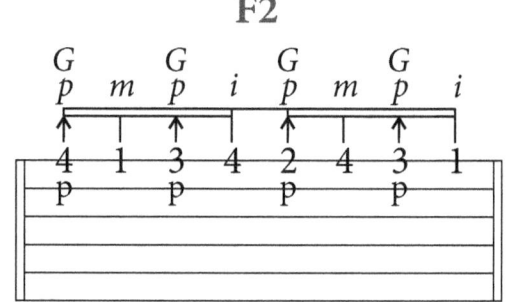

§ IIIb

A

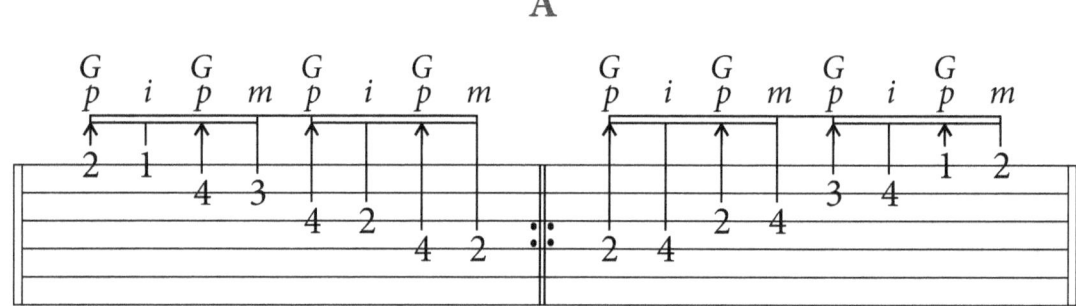

B

§ Ia

F1 **F2**

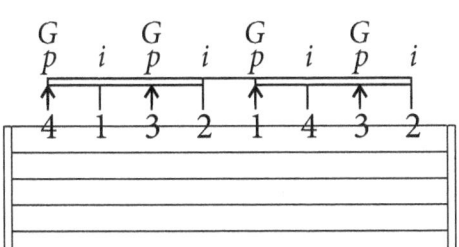 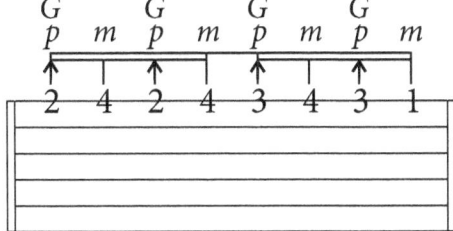

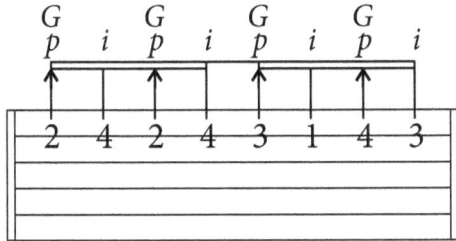 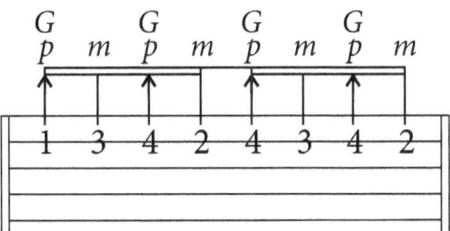

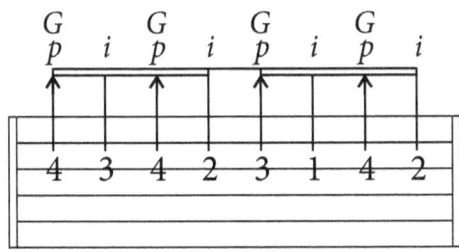 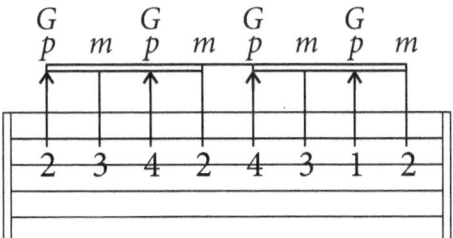

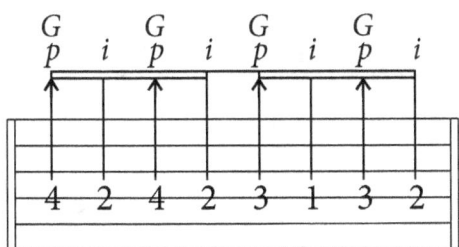 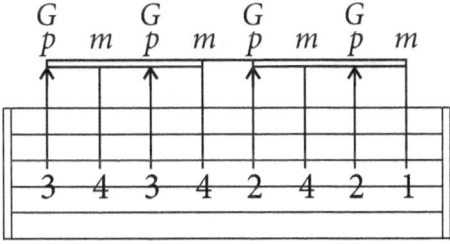

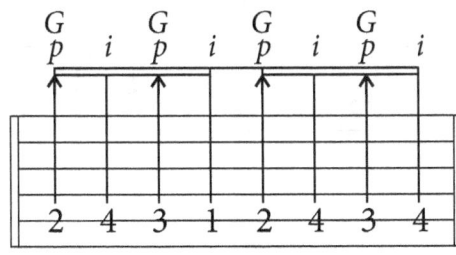 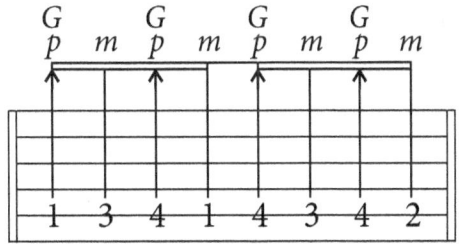

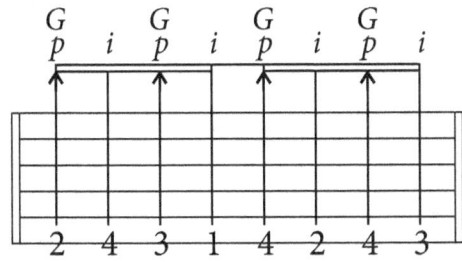 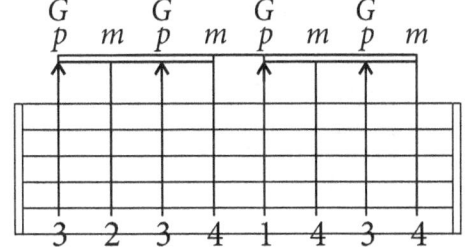

§ IIa

F1   F2

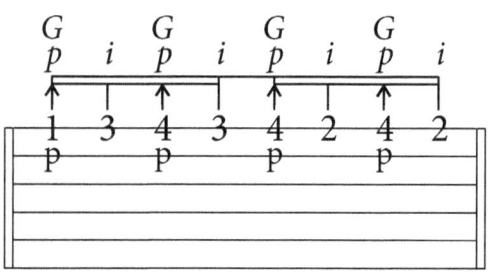 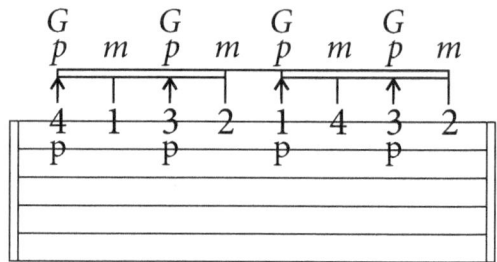
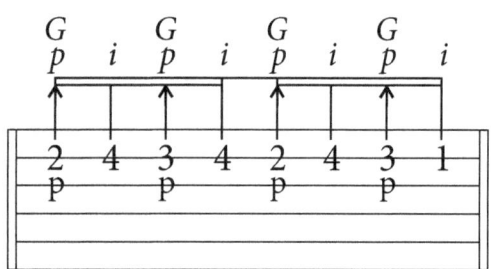 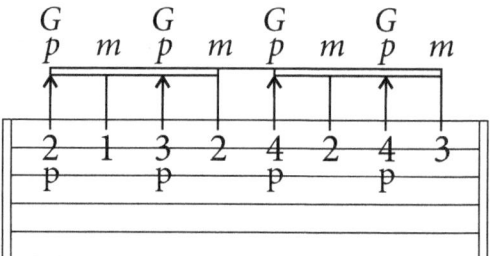
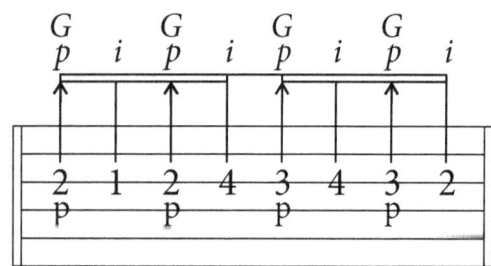 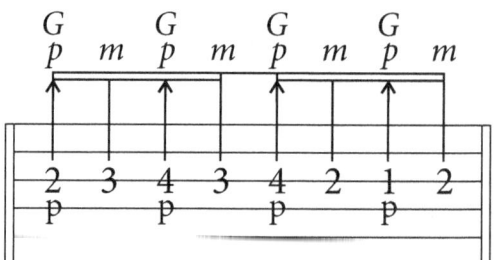
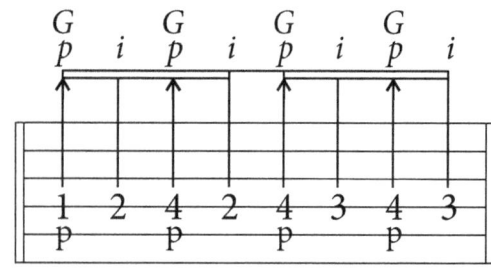 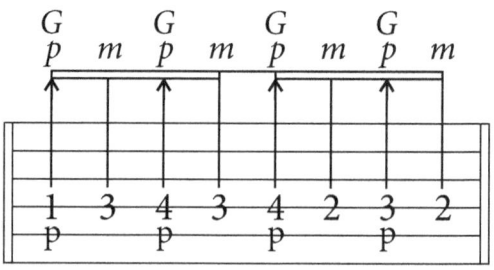
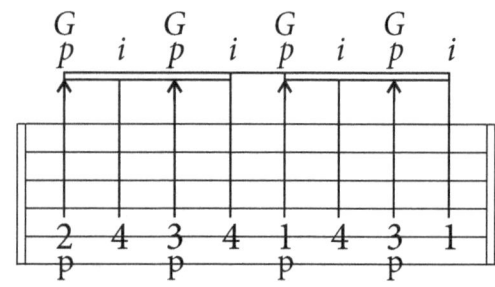 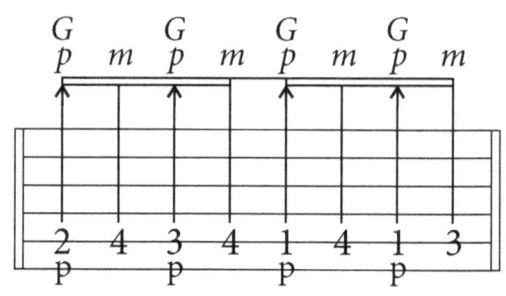

§ IIIa

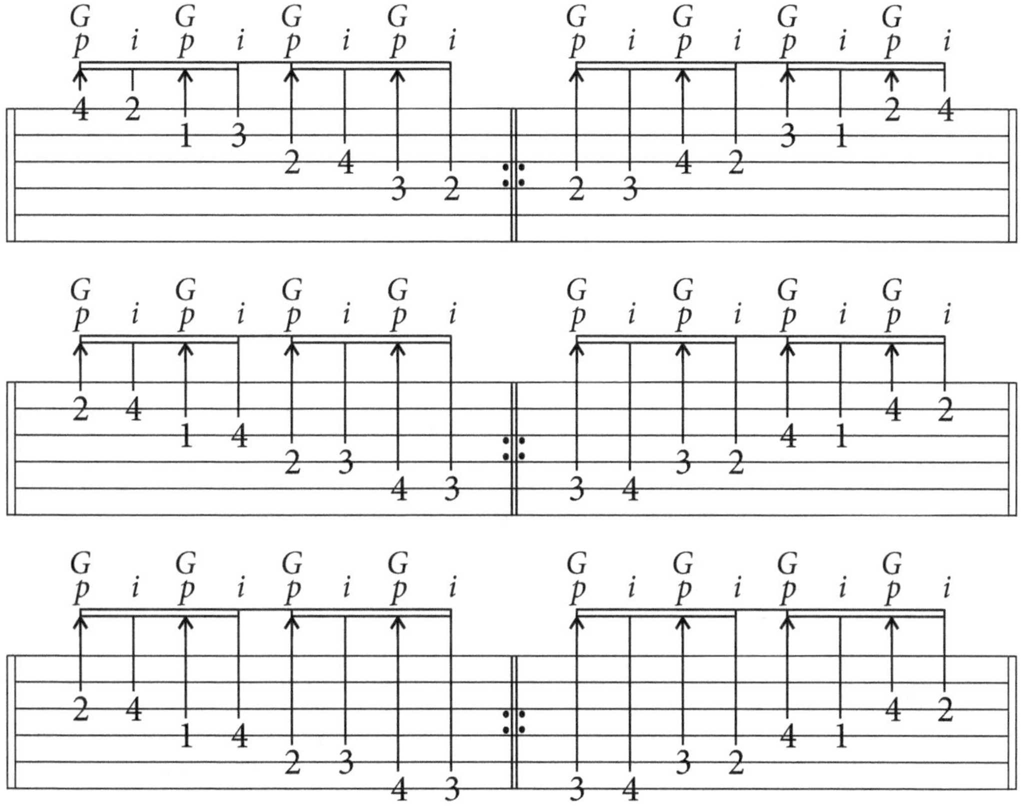

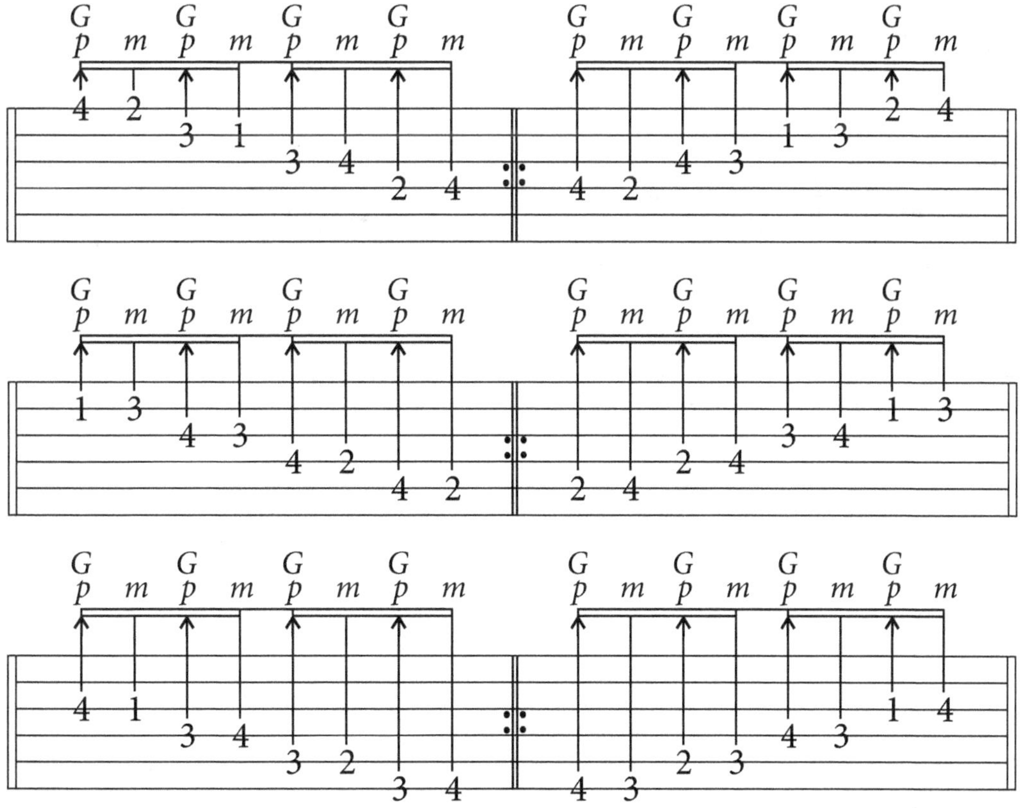

§ IVa

F1 F2

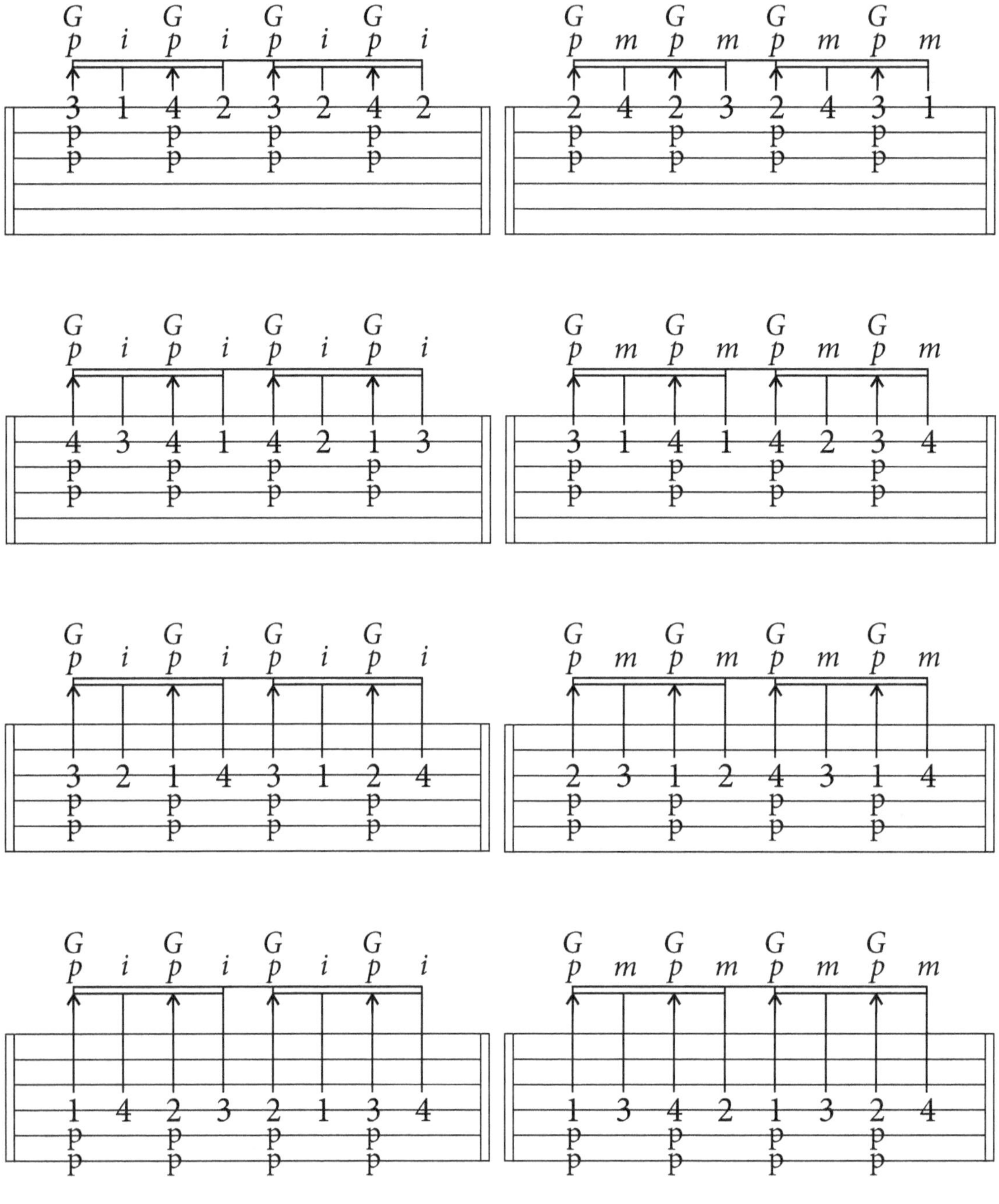

G G G G
p i p i p i p i
3 1 4 2 3 2 4 2
G G G G
p m p m p m p m
2 4 2 3 2 4 3 1
G G G G
p i p i p i p i
4 3 4 1 4 2 1 3
G G G G
p m p m p m p m
3 1 4 1 4 2 3 4
G G G G
p i p i p i p i
3 2 1 4 3 1 2 4
G G G G
p m p m p m p m
2 3 1 2 4 3 1 4
G G G G
p i p i p i p i
1 4 2 3 2 1 3 4
G G G G
p m p m p m p m
1 3 4 2 1 3 2 4

§ Ib

F1   **F2**

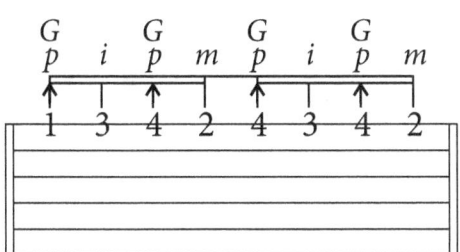 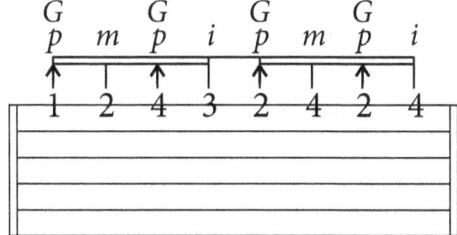

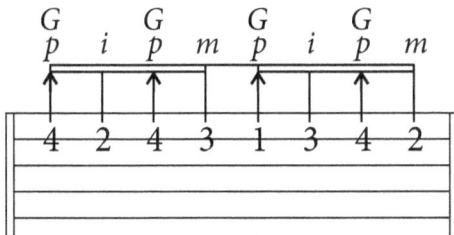 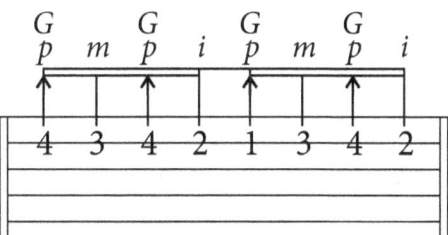

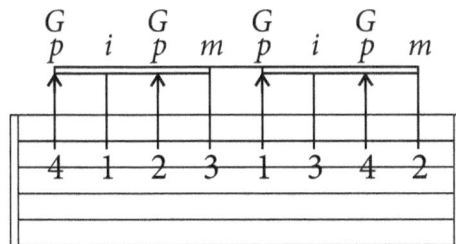 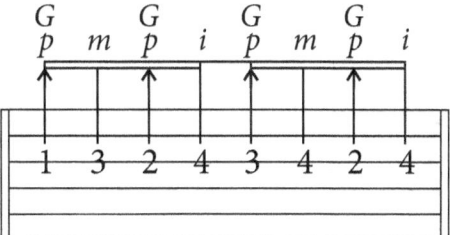

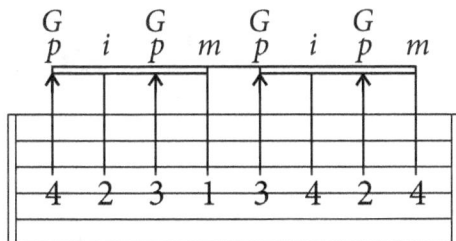 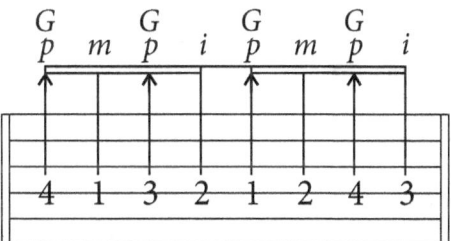

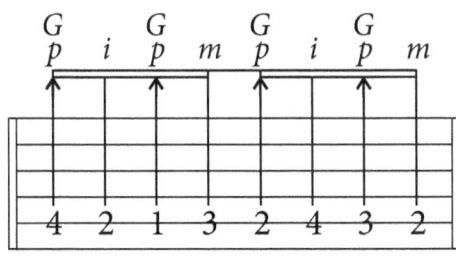 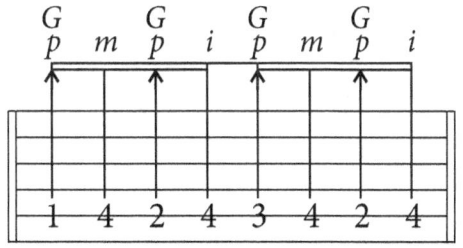

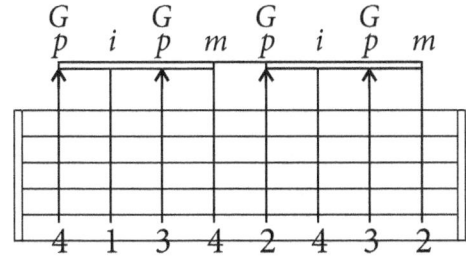 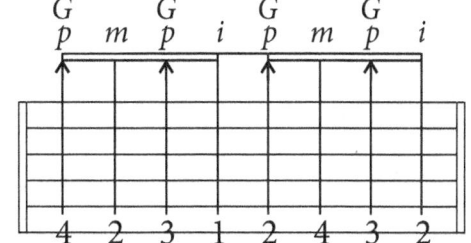

§ IIb

F1   F2

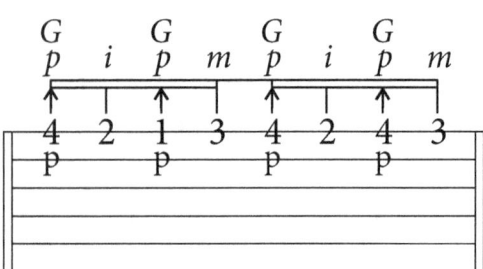 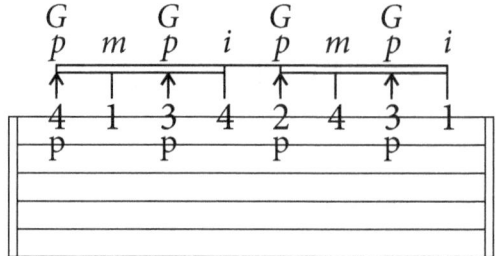

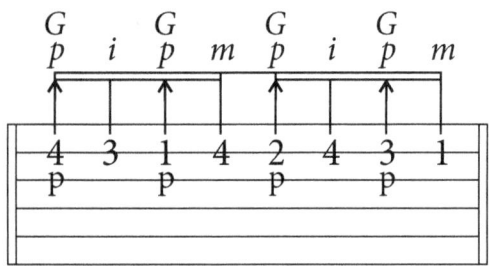 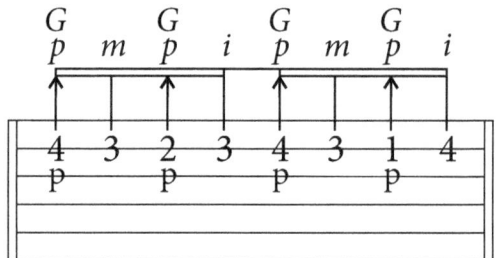

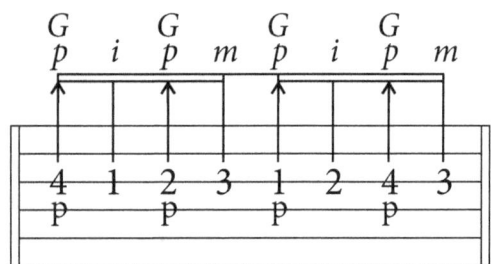 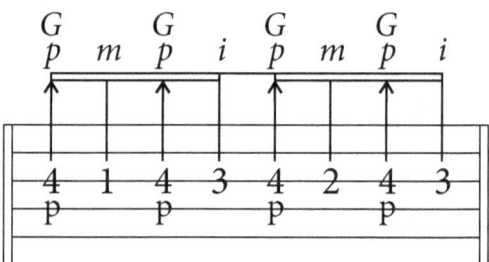

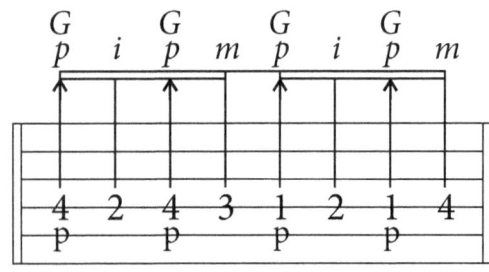 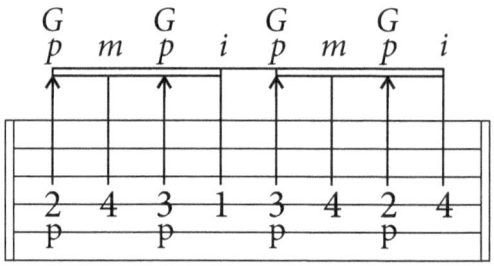

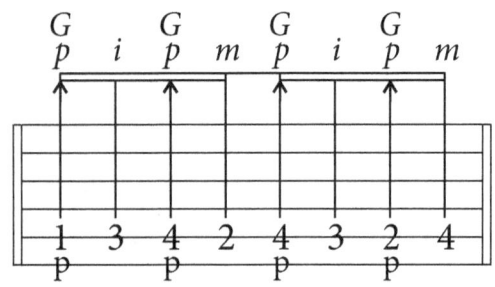 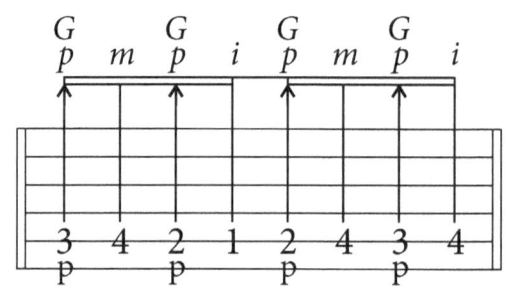

§ IIIb

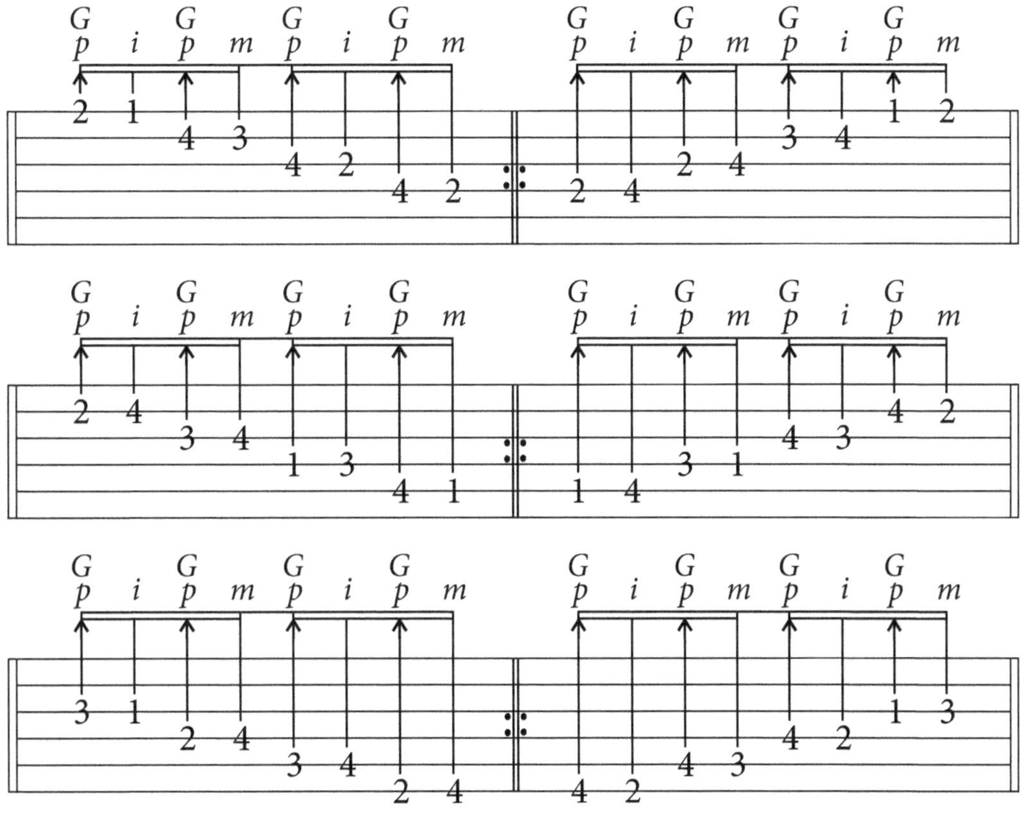

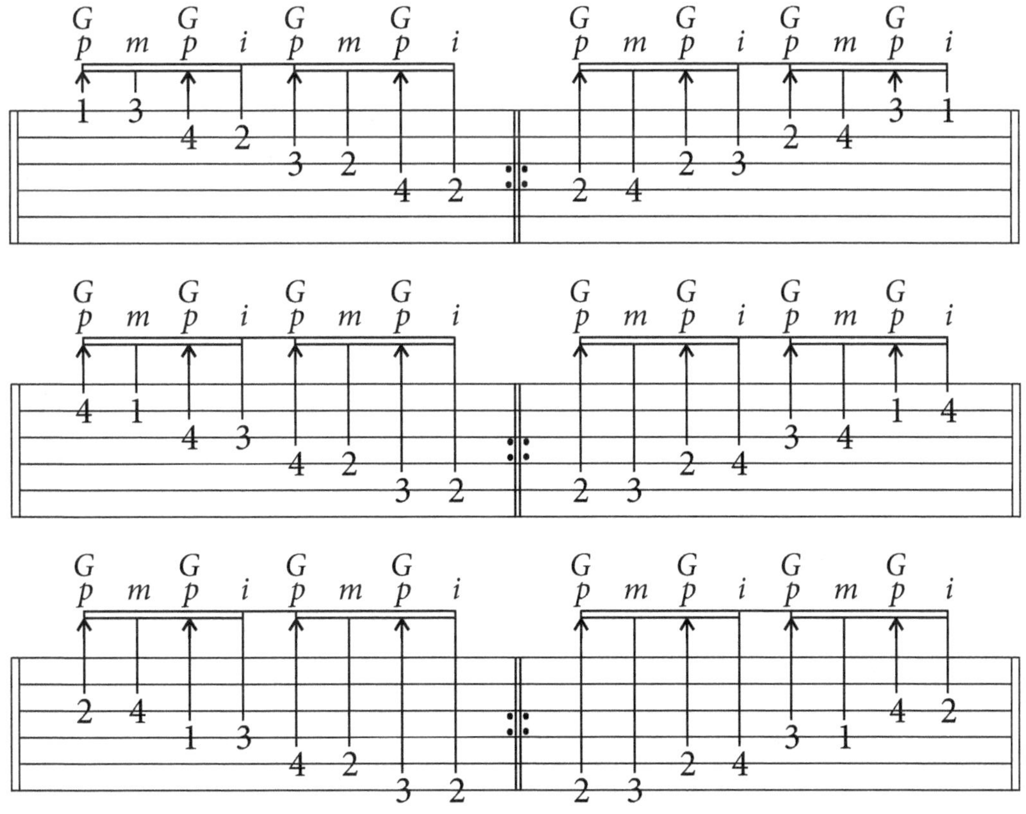

UNIT 2

Thumb stroke with Golpe on one string.
Variations with Triplets.

Unit 2 contains Golpe exercises with thumb stroke of one string in combination with the index (i) and middle finger (m) of the right hand. The exercises are based on the chromatic scales of one string and are arranged in three variations depending on the triplets:

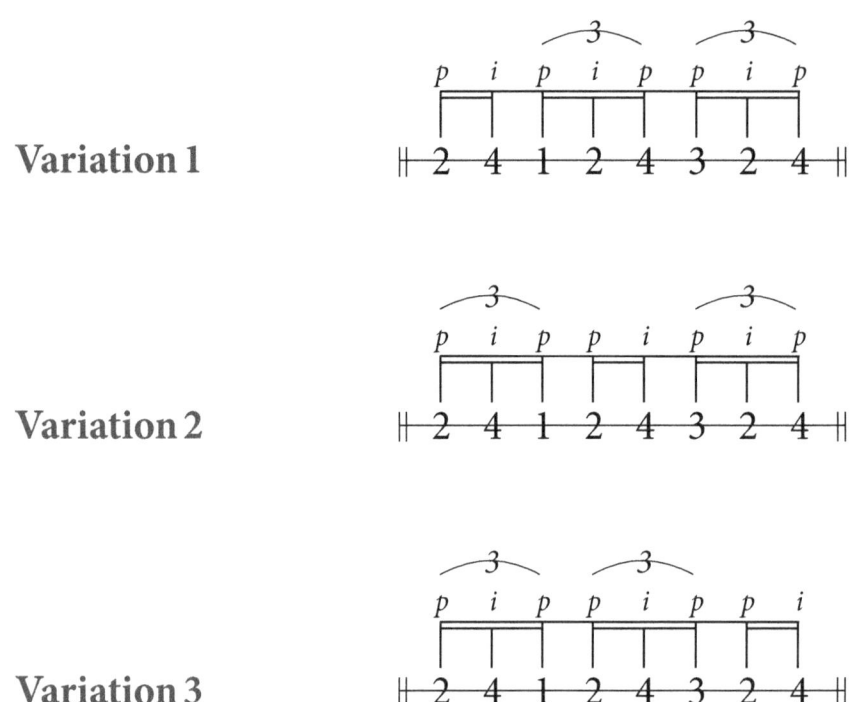

Variation 1

Variation 2

Variation 3

The exercises develop on:
A/ one string

§ Ia

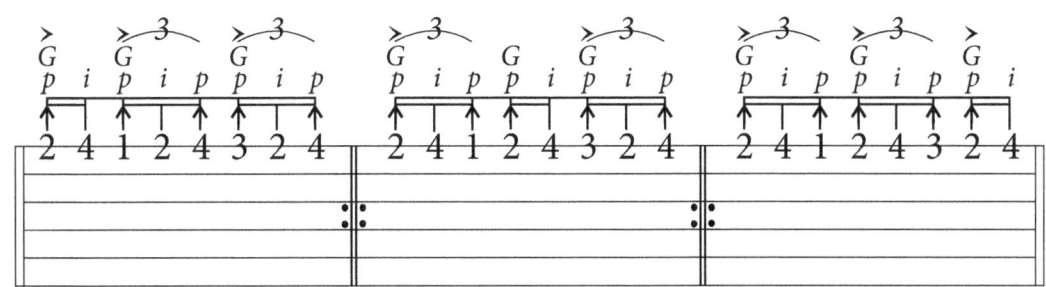

B/ three strings as follows:

        1/ 1st, 2nd and 3rd string
        2/ 2nd, 3rd and 4th string
        3/ 3rd, 4th and 5th string
        4/ 4th, 5th and 6th string

§ IIa

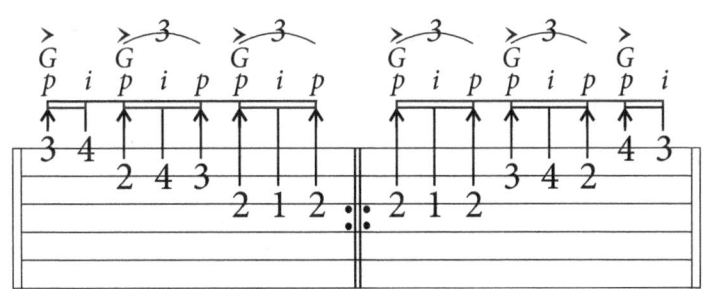

§Ic, §IIc
§Id, §IId Repetition of the previous exercises with the addition of two extra Golpe within the chromatic scales. Same mechanism of exercises.

§ Ia

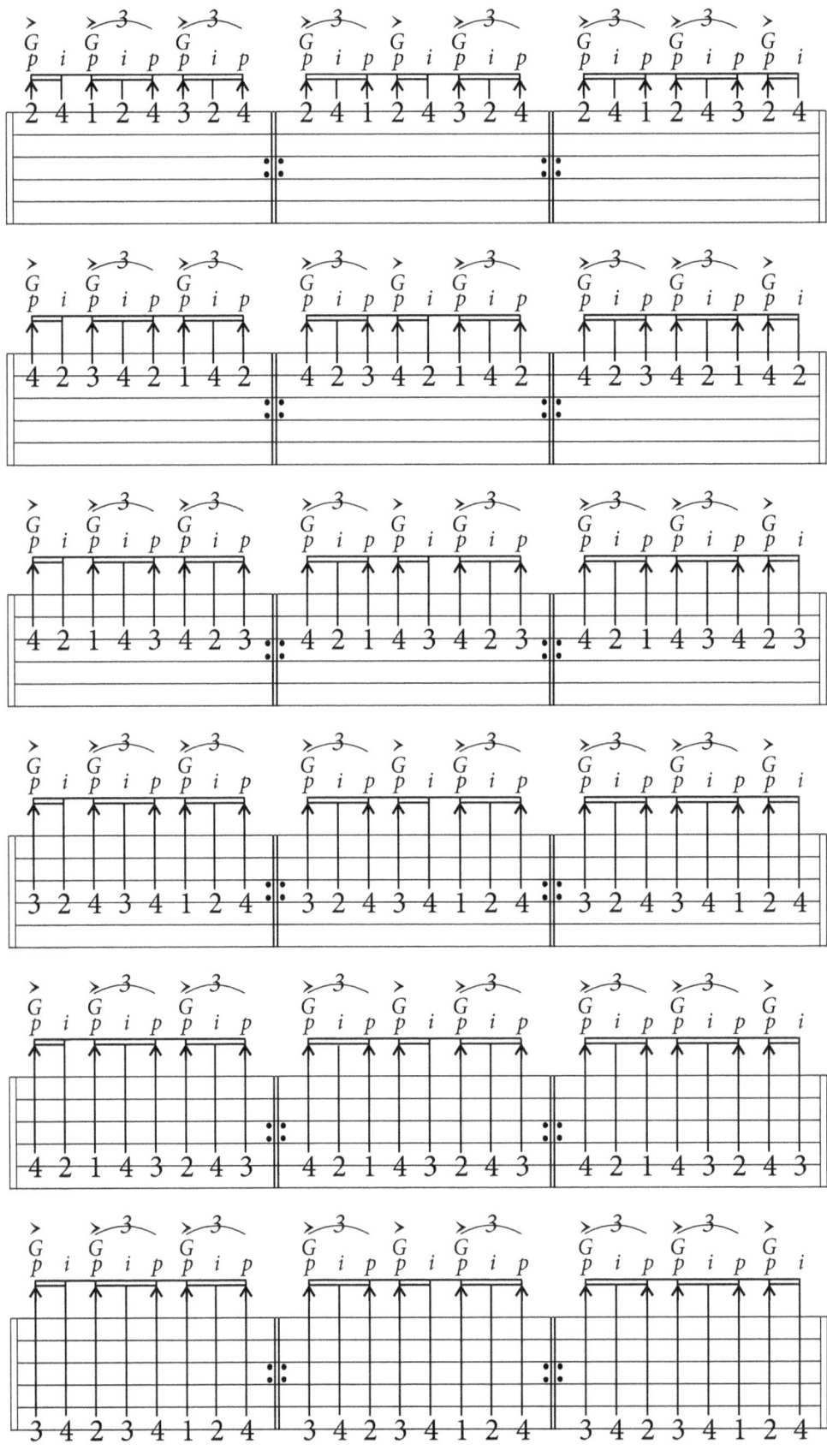

§ IIa

F1

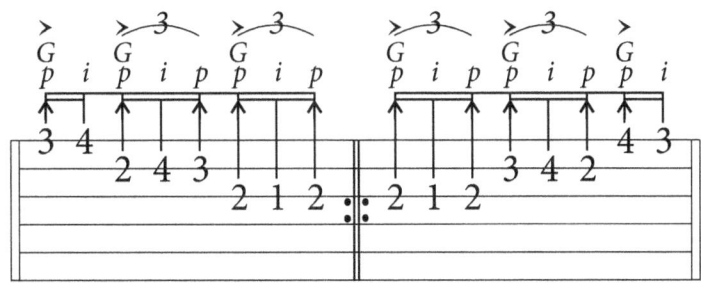
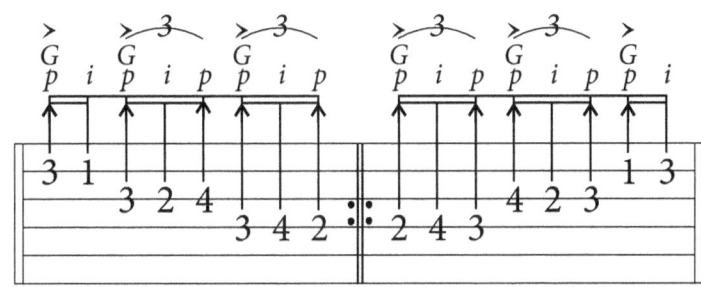
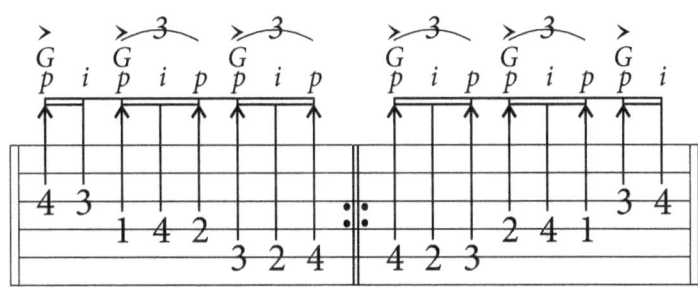
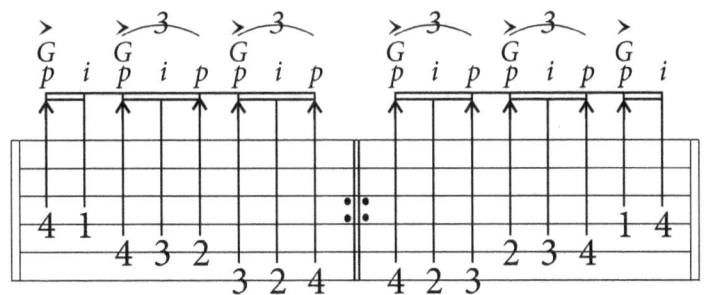

F2

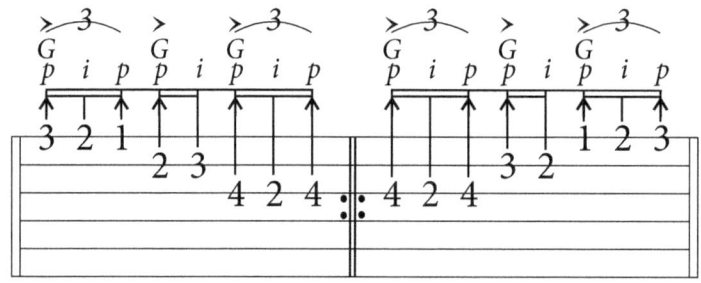
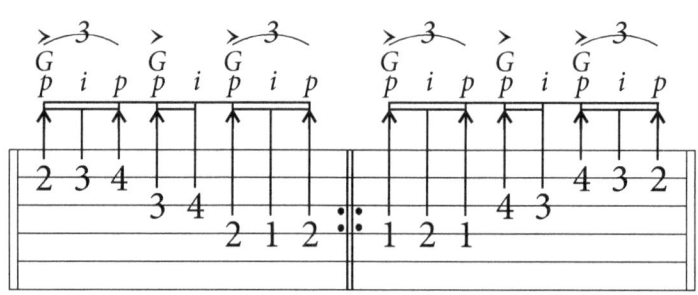
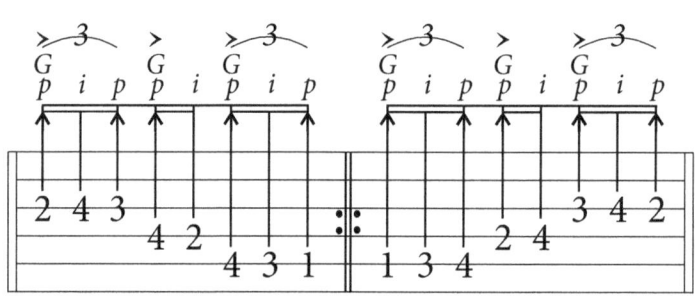
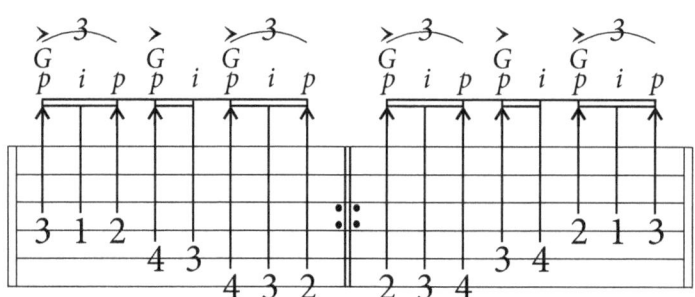

F3

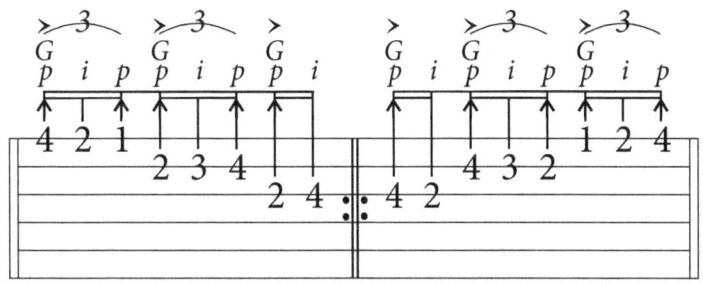
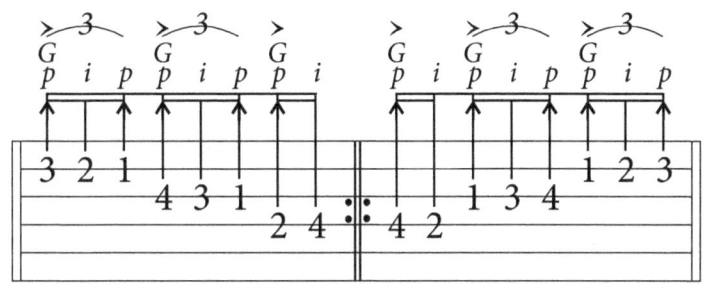
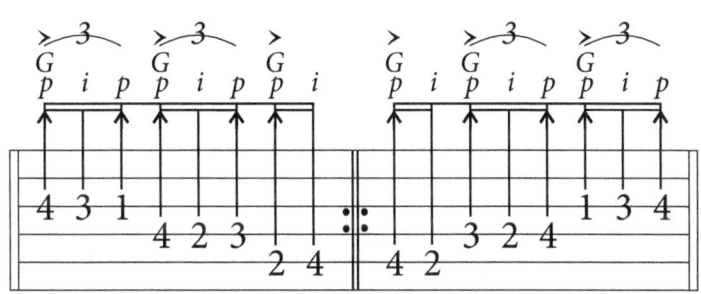
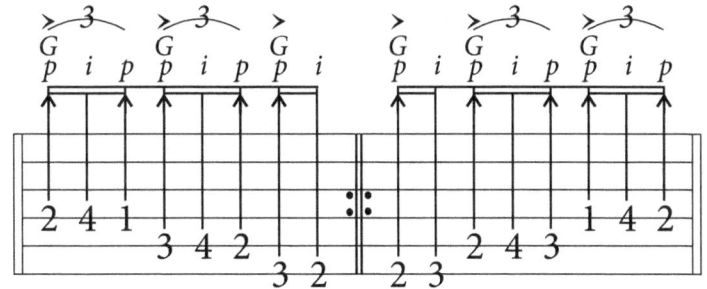

§ Ib

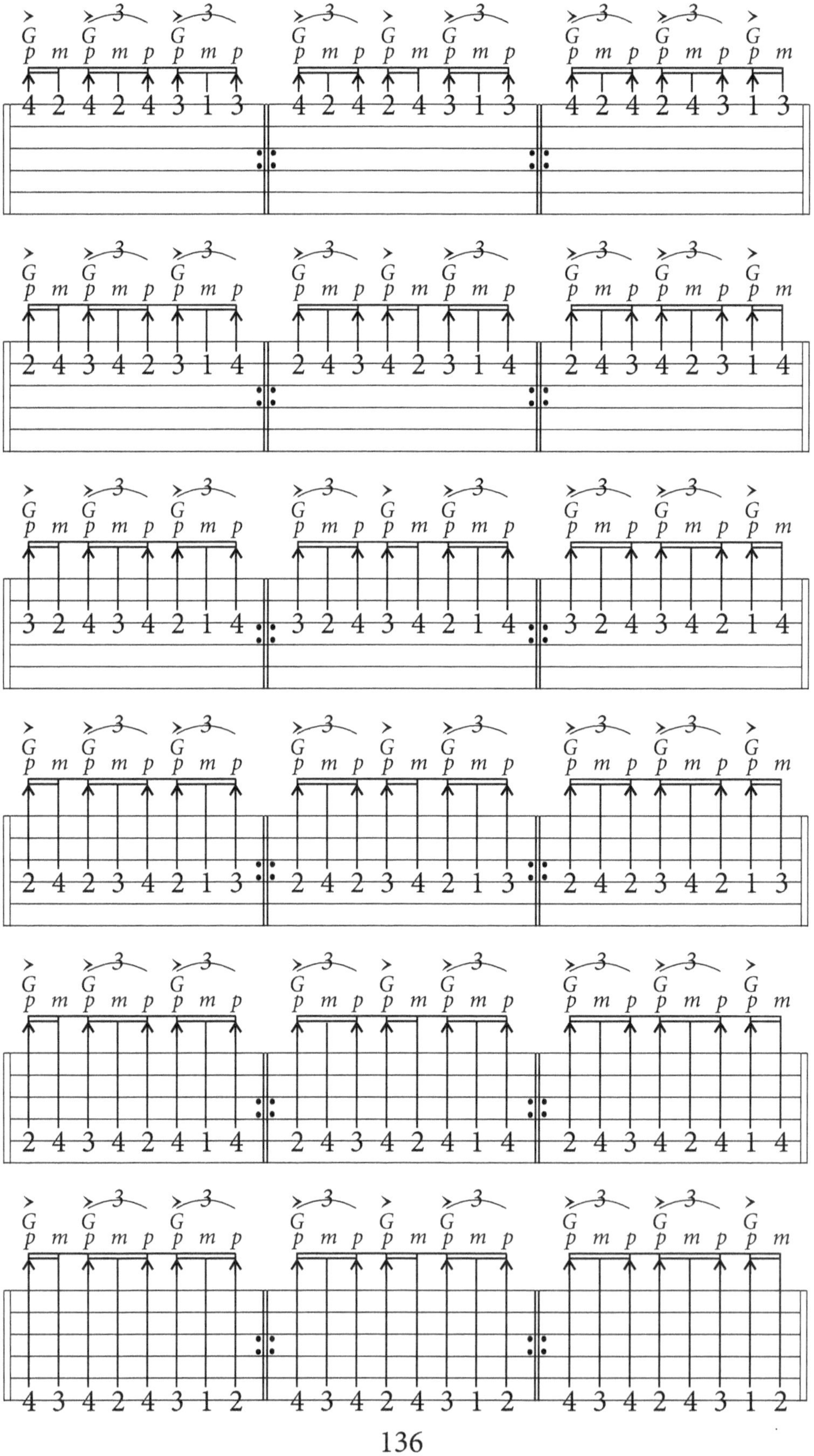

G G G G G G G G
p m p m p p m p p m p p m p m p p m p p m p p m
3 3 3 3 3 3
4 2 4 2 4 3 1 3 4 2 4 2 4 3 1 3 4 2 4 2 4 3 1 3
2 4 3 4 2 3 1 4 2 4 3 4 2 3 1 4 2 4 3 4 2 3 1 4
3 2 4 3 4 2 1 4 3 2 4 3 4 2 1 4 3 2 4 3 4 2 1 4
2 4 2 3 4 2 1 3 2 4 2 3 4 2 1 3 2 4 2 3 4 2 1 3
2 4 3 4 2 4 1 4 2 4 3 4 2 4 1 4 2 4 3 4 2 4 1 4
4 3 4 2 4 3 1 2 4 3 4 2 4 3 1 2 4 3 4 2 4 3 1 2

§ IIb

F1

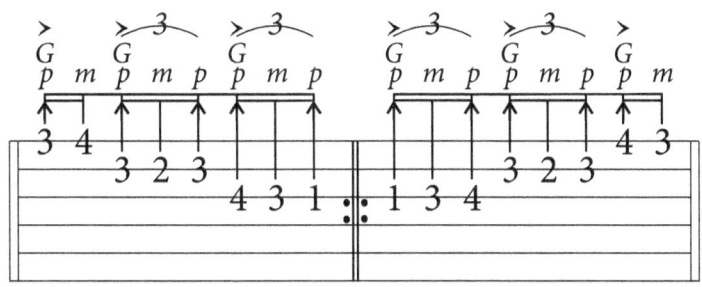
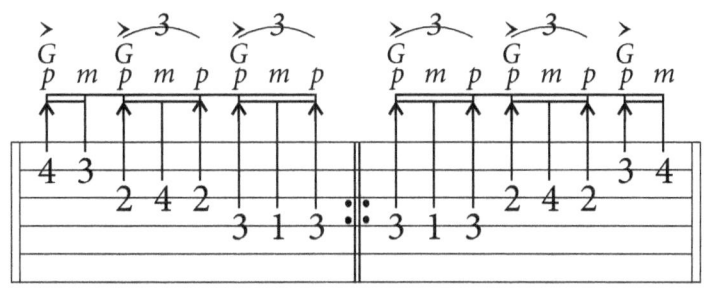
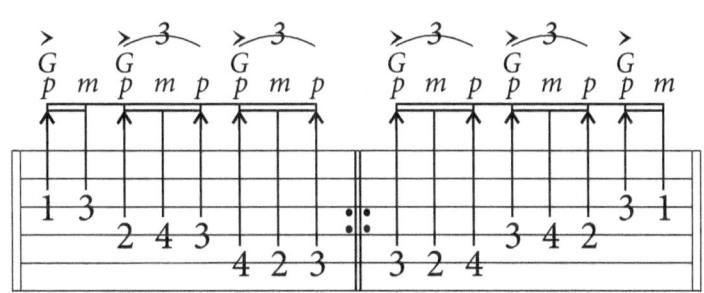
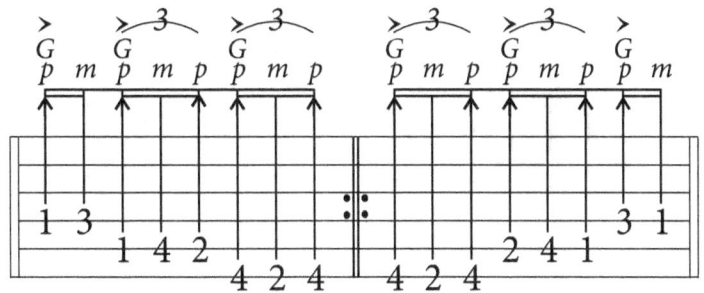

F2

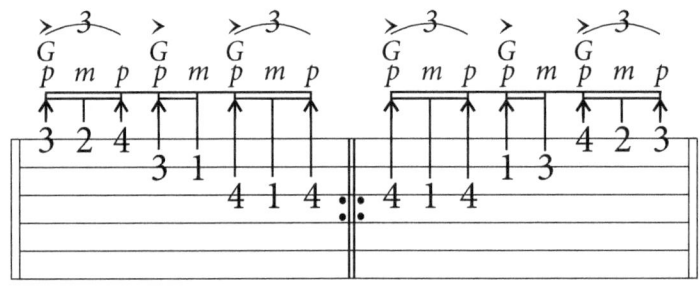
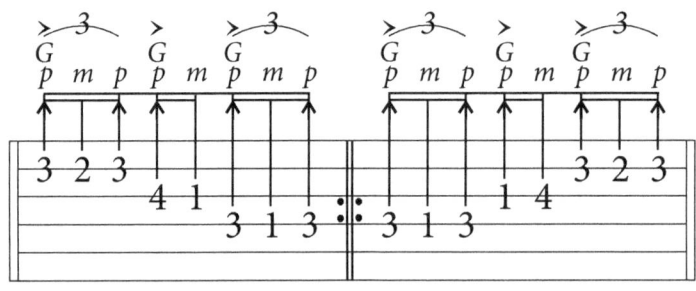
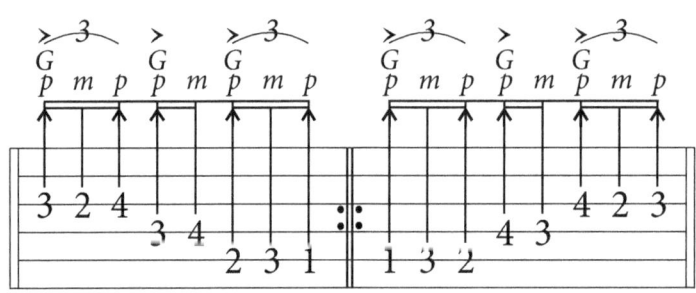
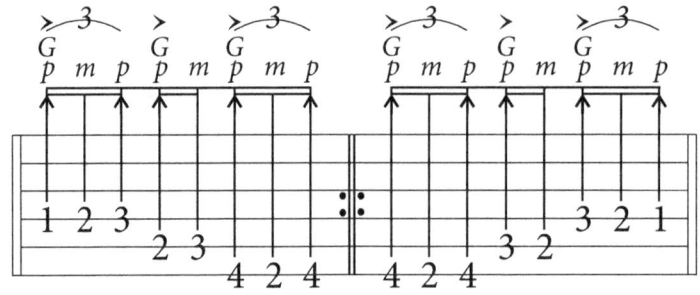

F3

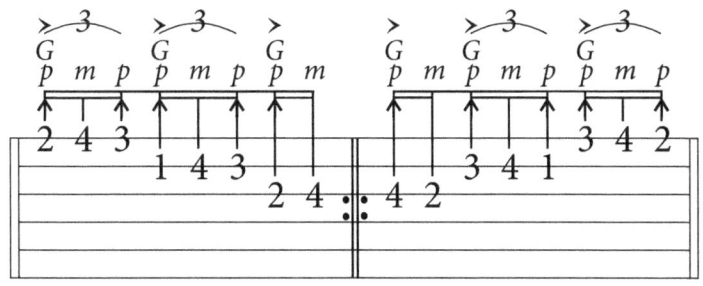
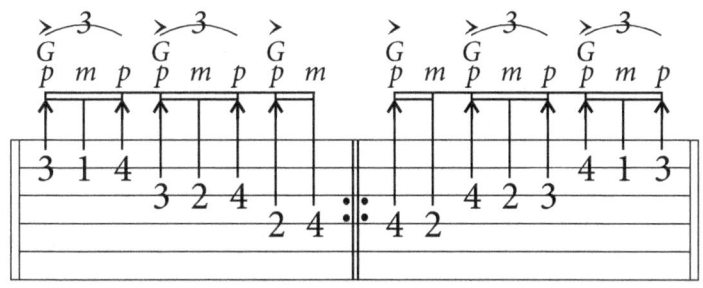
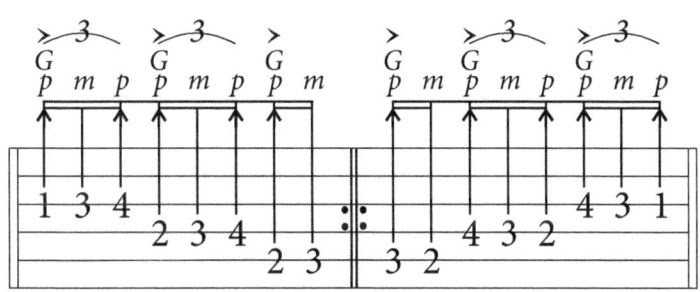
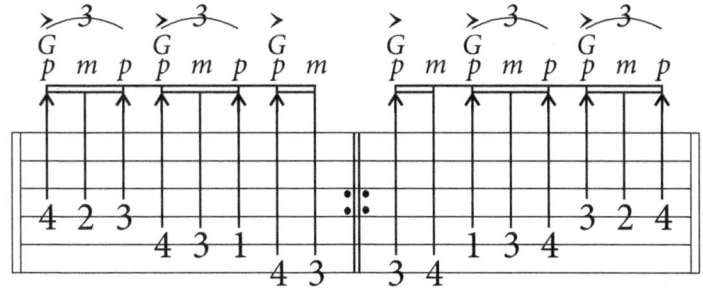

§ Ic

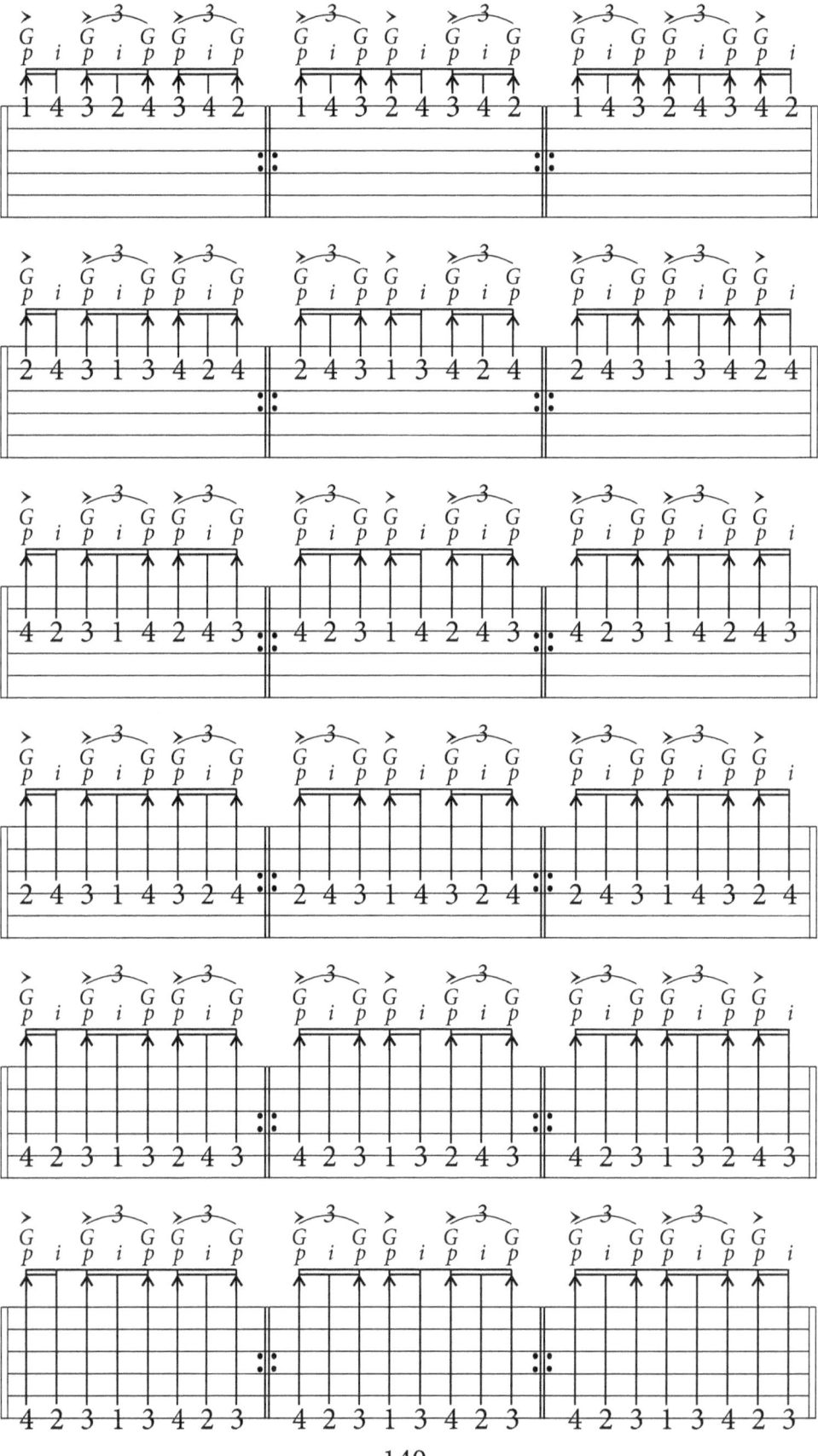

§ IIc

F1

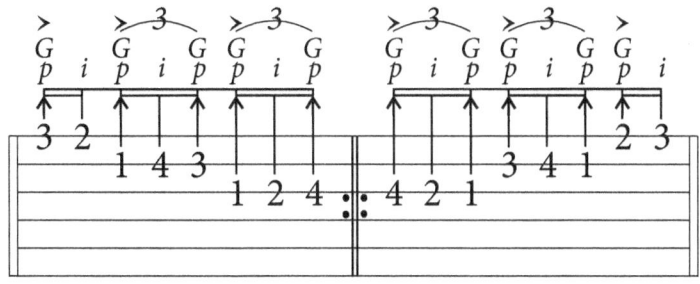
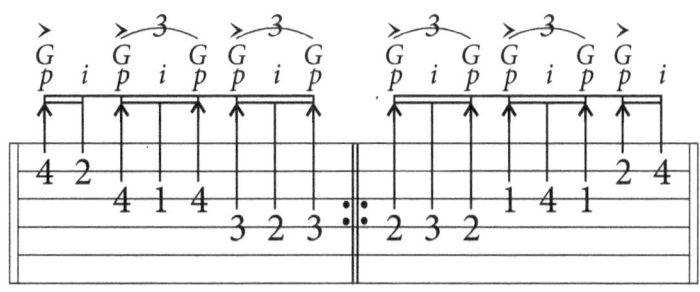
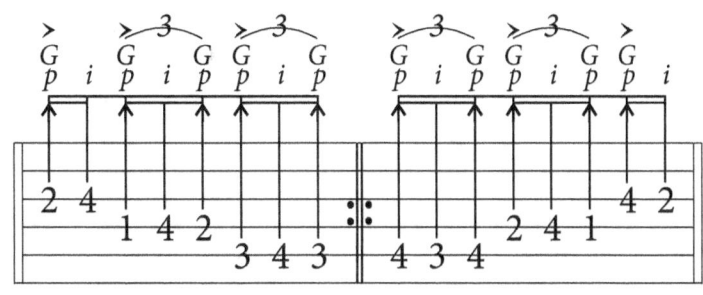
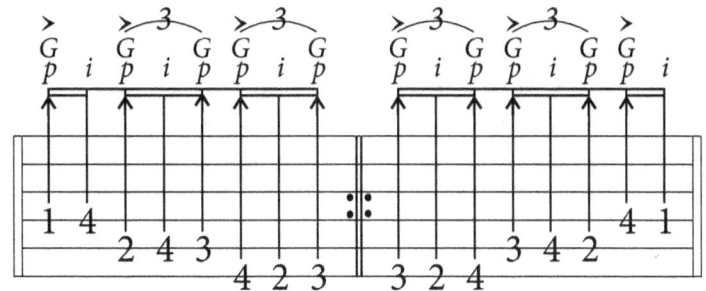

F2

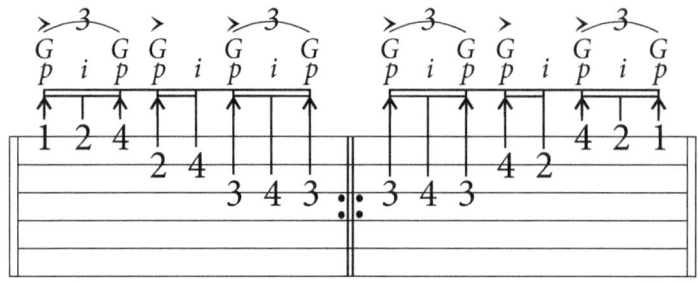
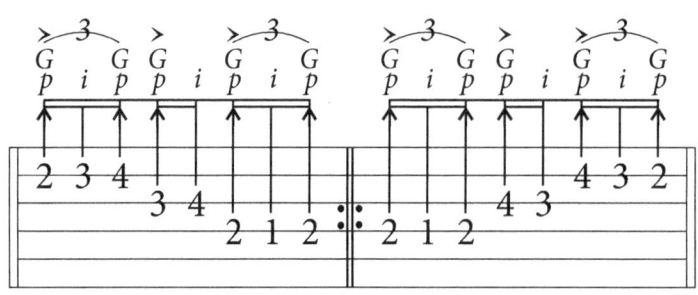
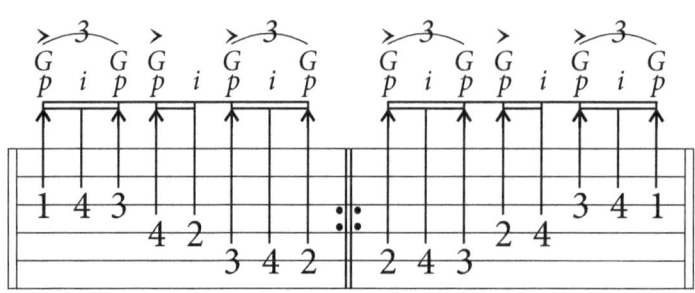
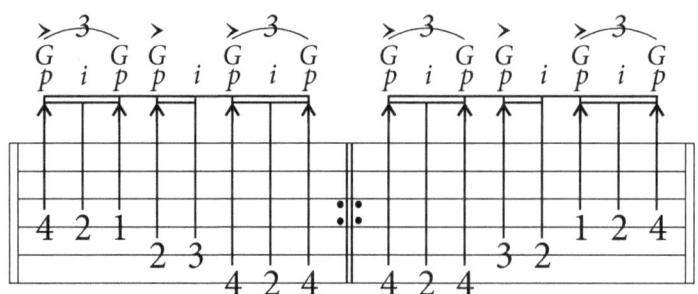

F3

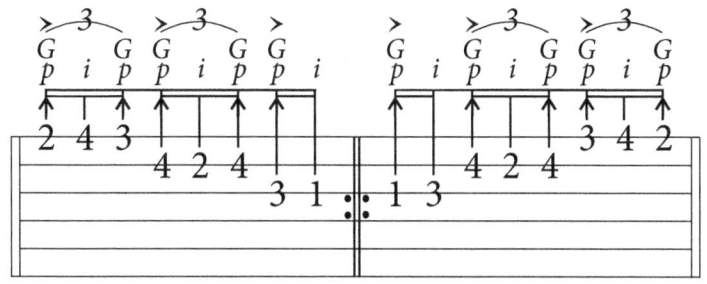
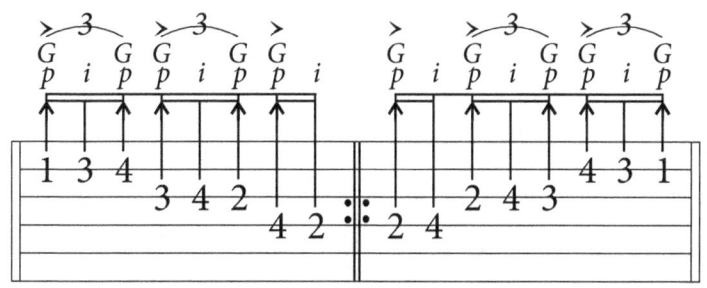
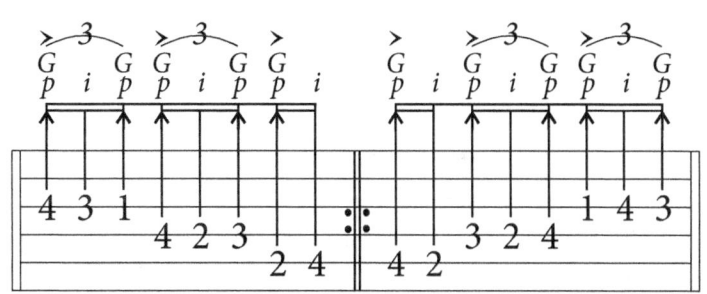
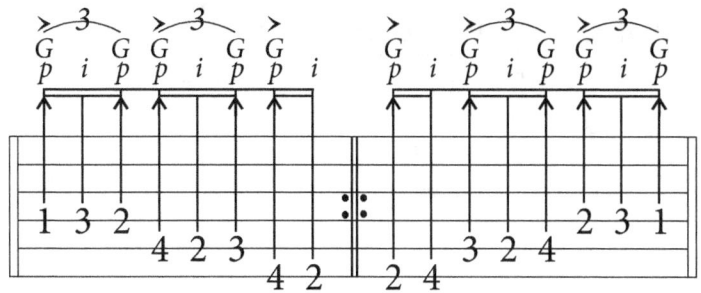

§ Id

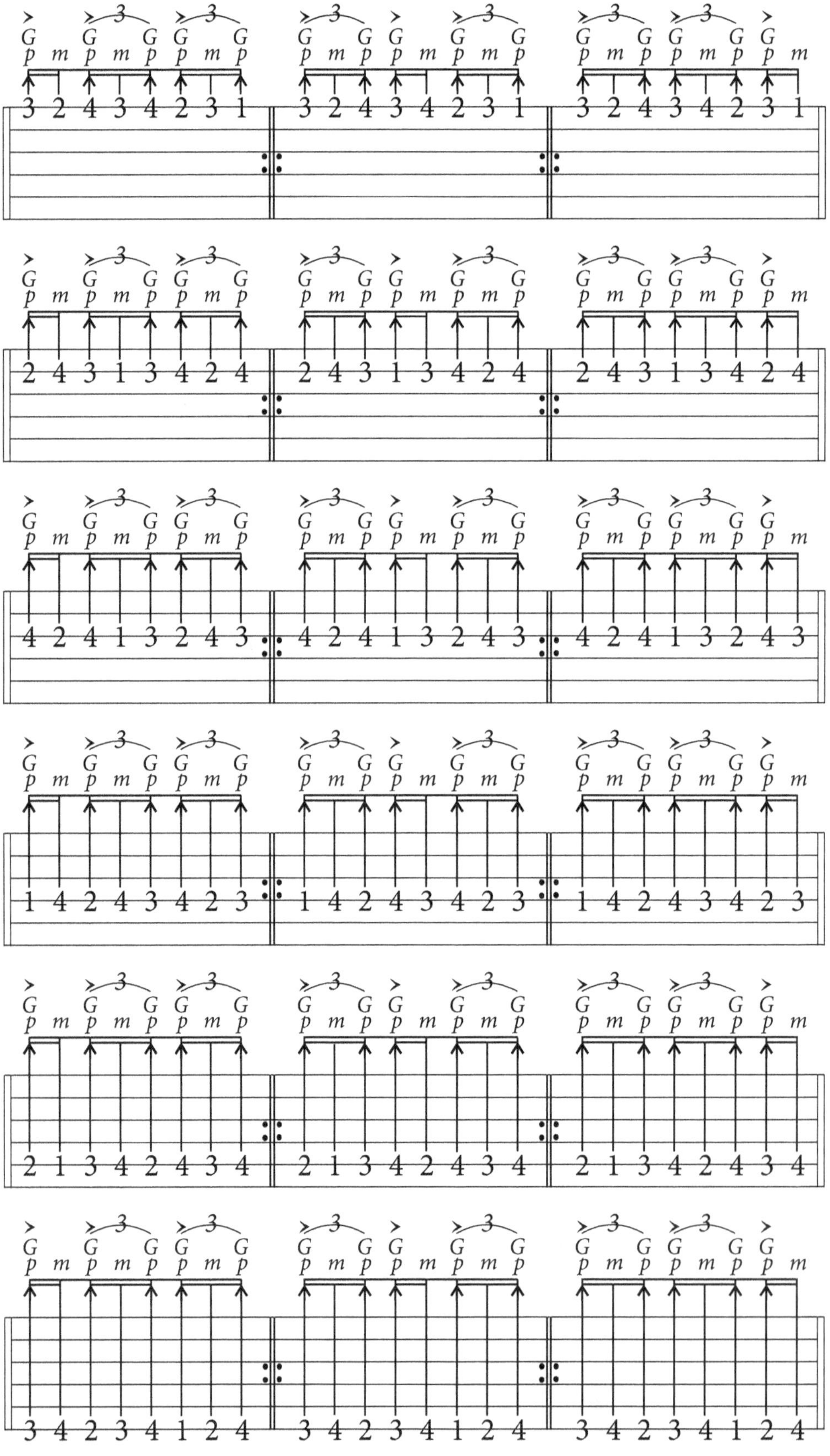
G G G G G | G G G G G | G G G G G
p m p m p p m p | p m p p m p m p | p m p p m p p m
3 2 4 3 4 2 3 1 | 3 2 4 3 4 2 3 1 | 3 2 4 3 4 2 3 1
2 4 3 1 3 4 2 4 | 2 4 3 1 3 4 2 4 | 2 4 3 1 3 4 2 4
4 2 4 1 3 2 4 3 | 4 2 4 1 3 2 4 3 | 4 2 4 1 3 2 4 3
1 4 2 4 3 4 2 3 | 1 4 2 4 3 4 2 3 | 1 4 2 4 3 4 2 3
2 1 3 4 2 4 3 4 | 2 1 3 4 2 4 3 4 | 2 1 3 4 2 4 3 4
3 4 2 3 4 1 2 4 | 3 4 2 3 4 1 2 4 | 3 4 2 3 4 1 2 4

§ IId

F1

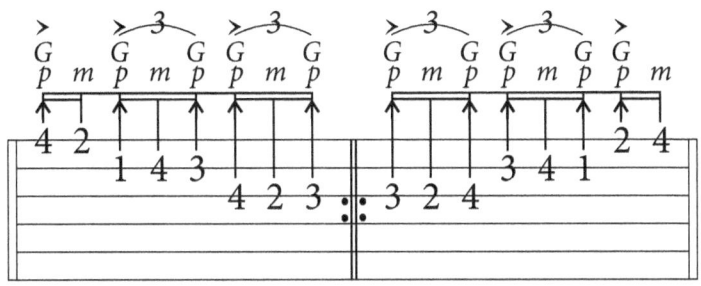

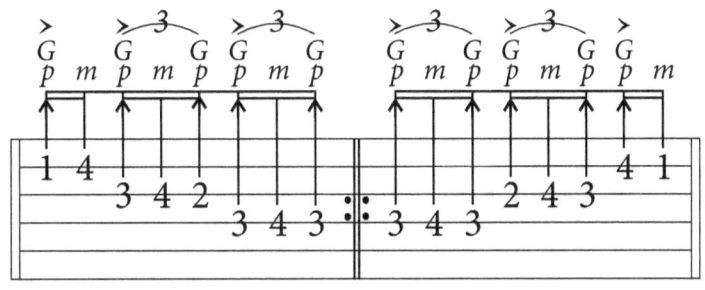

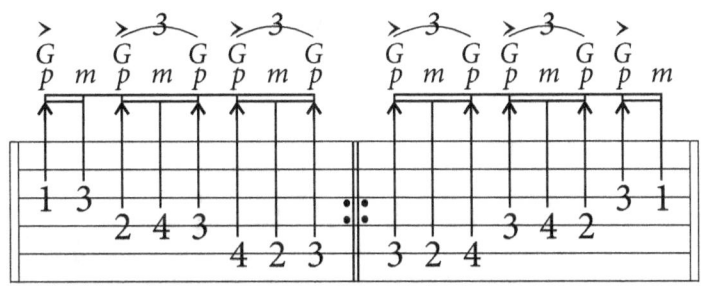

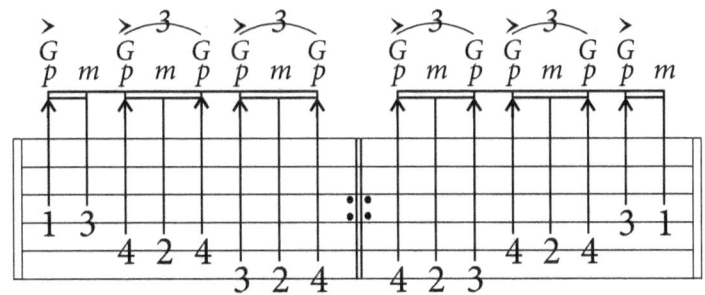

F2

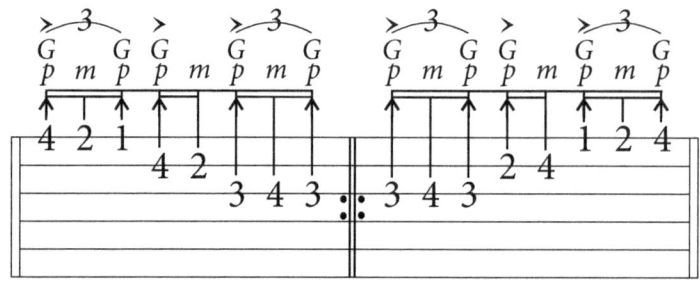

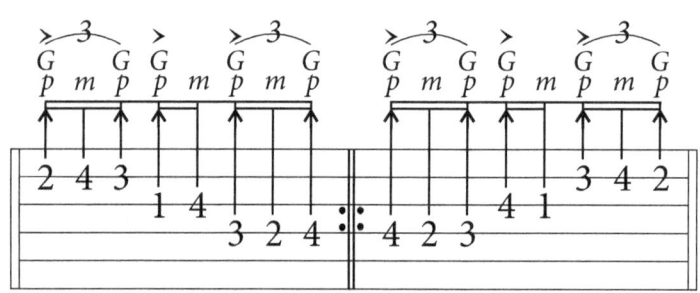

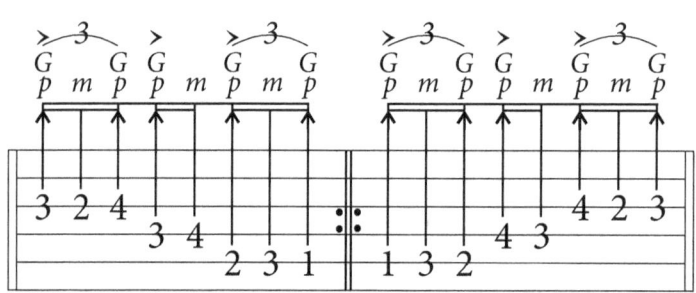

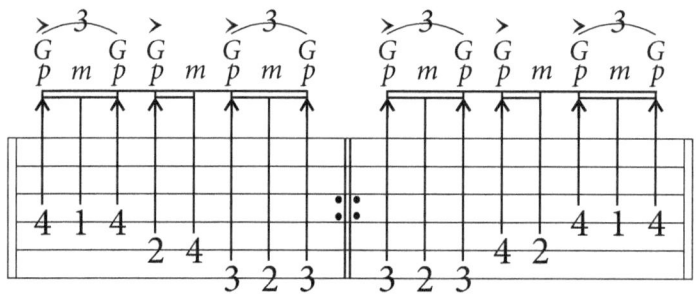

F3

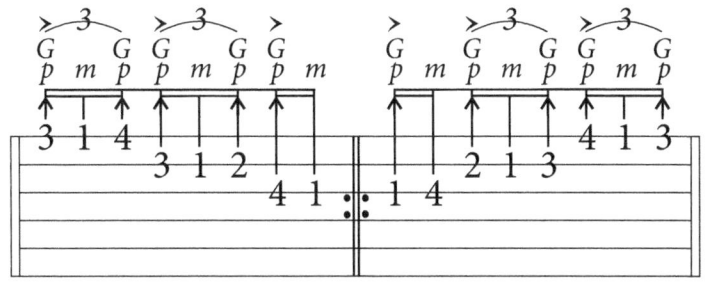
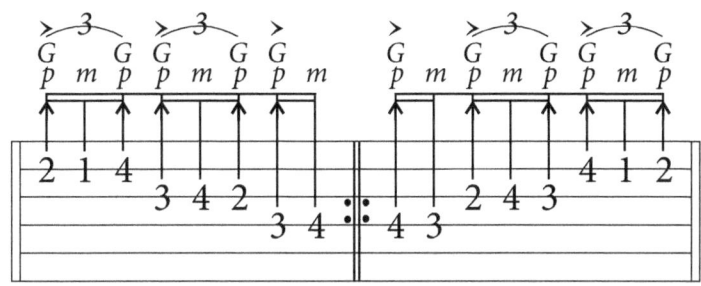
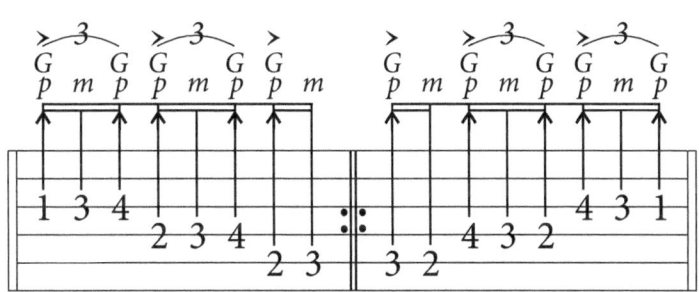
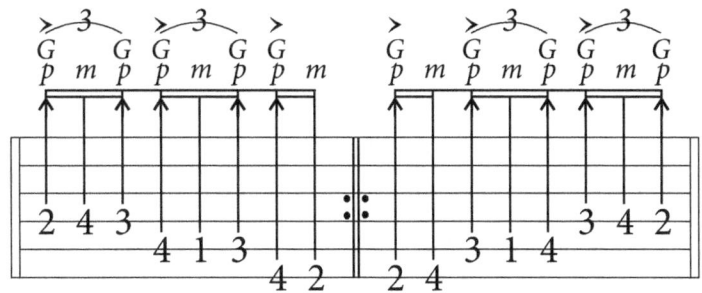

UNIT 3

Thumb stroke with Golpe on one, two
or three strings simultaneously.
Variations with Triplets.

In this unit the thumb strikes two or three strings, the string where the chromatic scale develops and the string (or strings) above it. The scales are always shaped in two triplets.

§**Ia** The chromatic scales also develop on the 1st, 2nd, 3rd, 4th and 5th string.

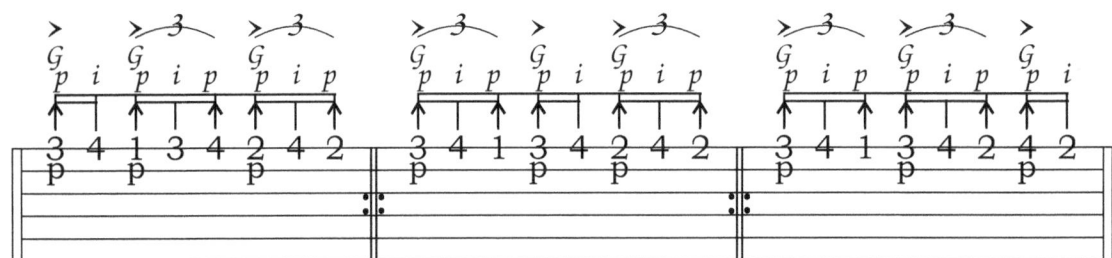

§**Ib** The chromatic scales also develop on the 1st, 2nd, 3rd and 4th string.

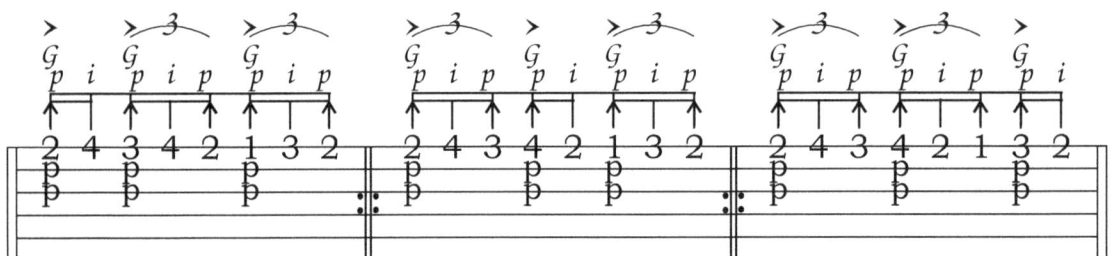

The exercises that follow refer to the simultaneous stroke of the thumb with Golpe.

§ Ia

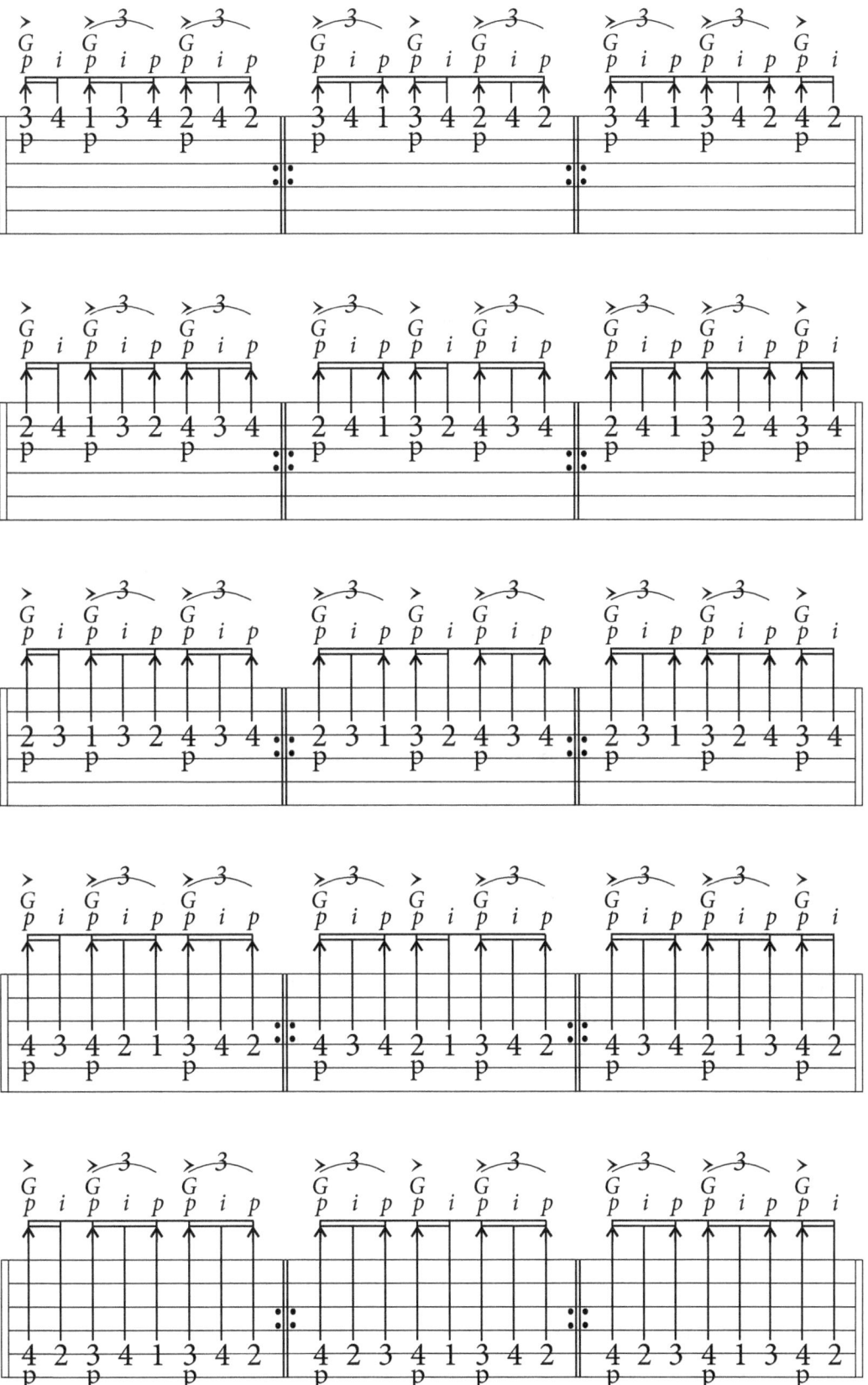

151

§ Ib

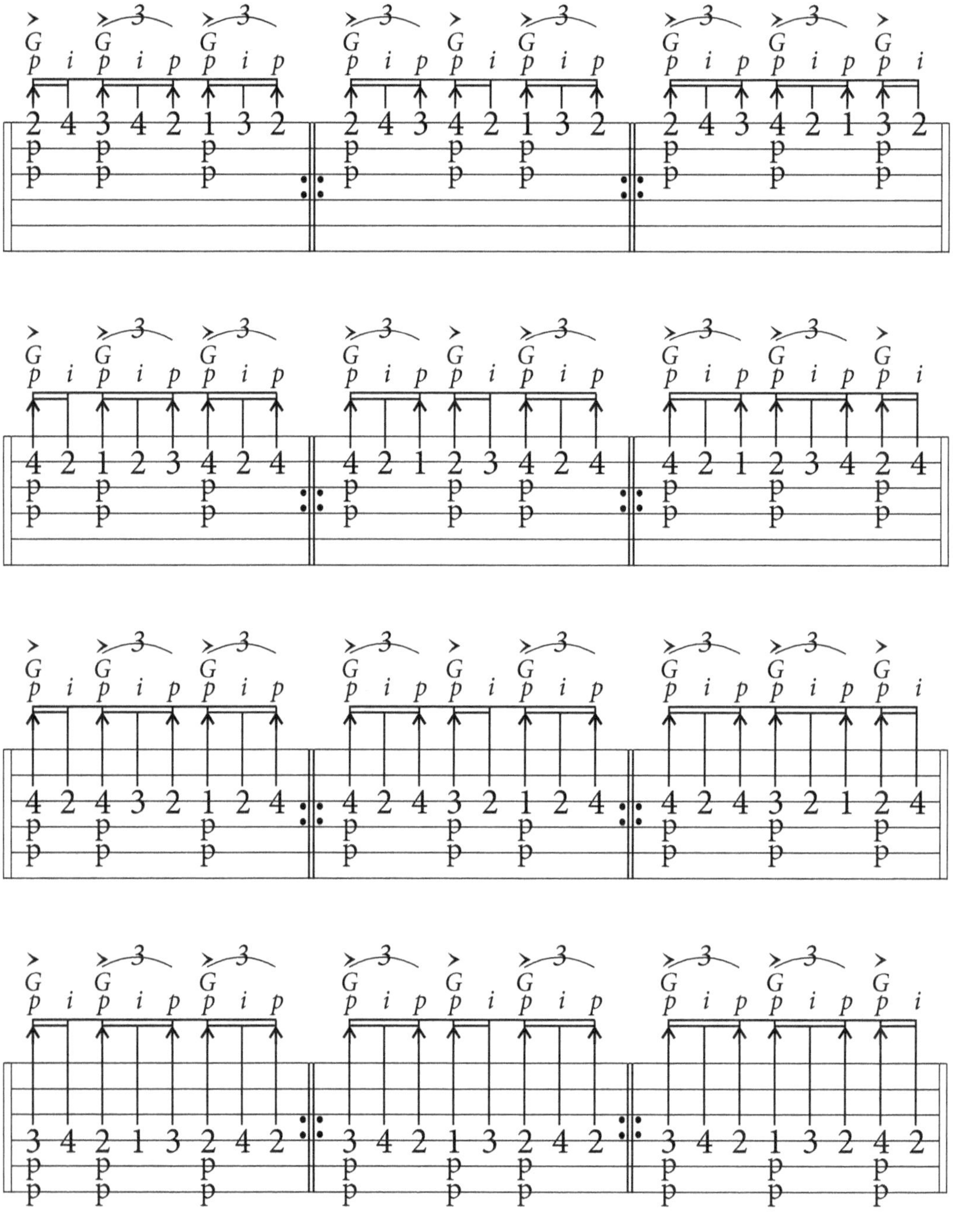

§ IIa

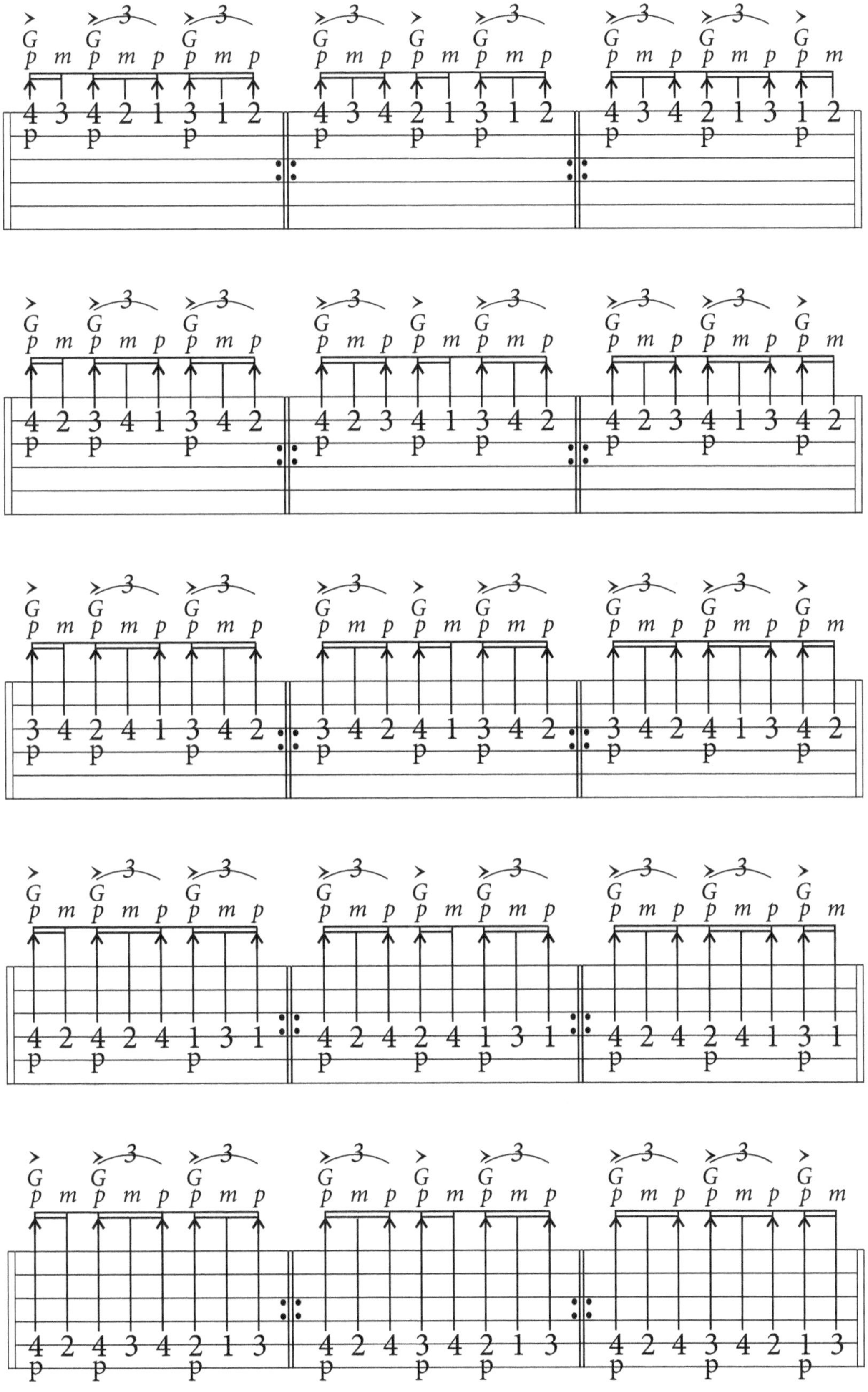

§ IIb

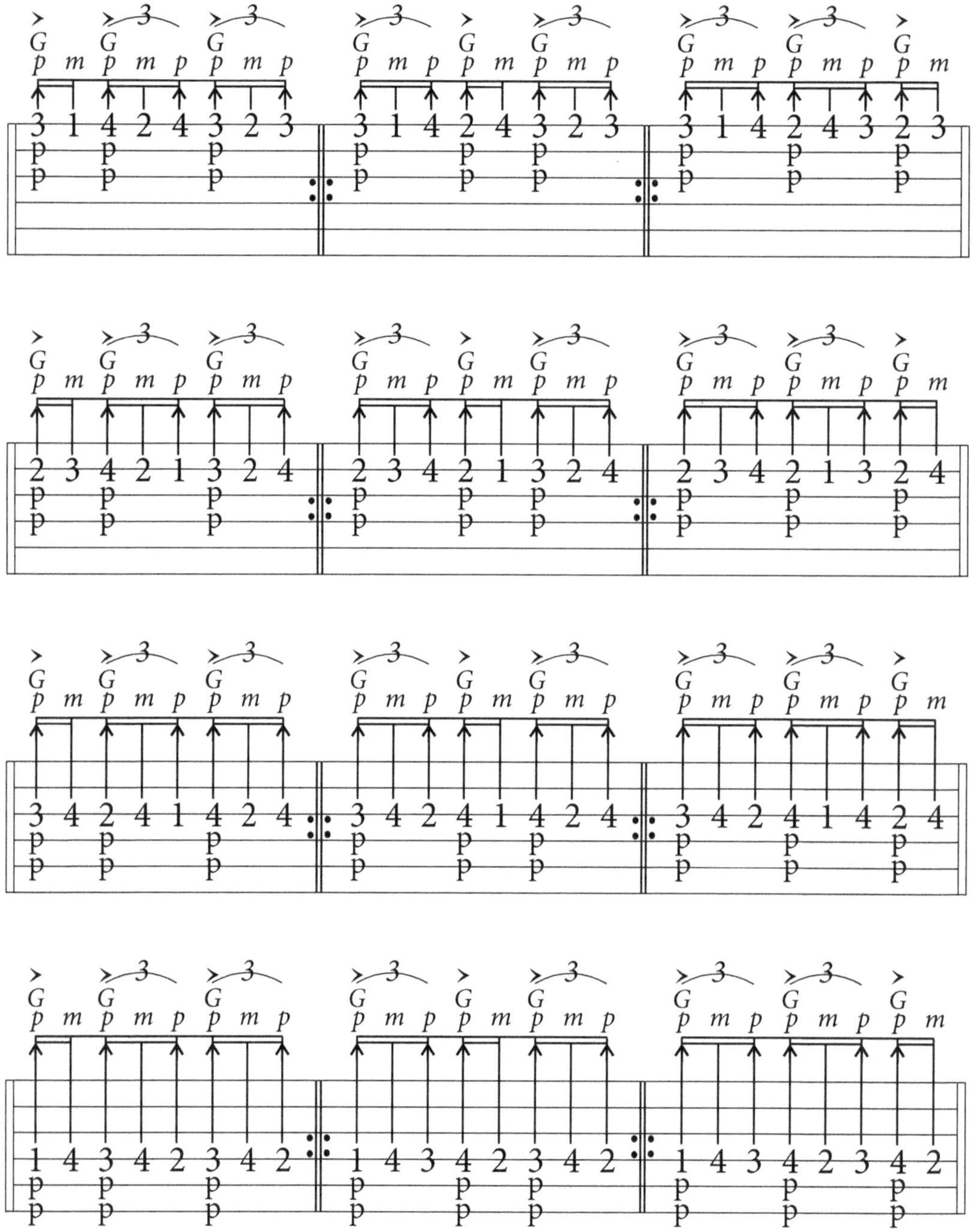

§ IIIa

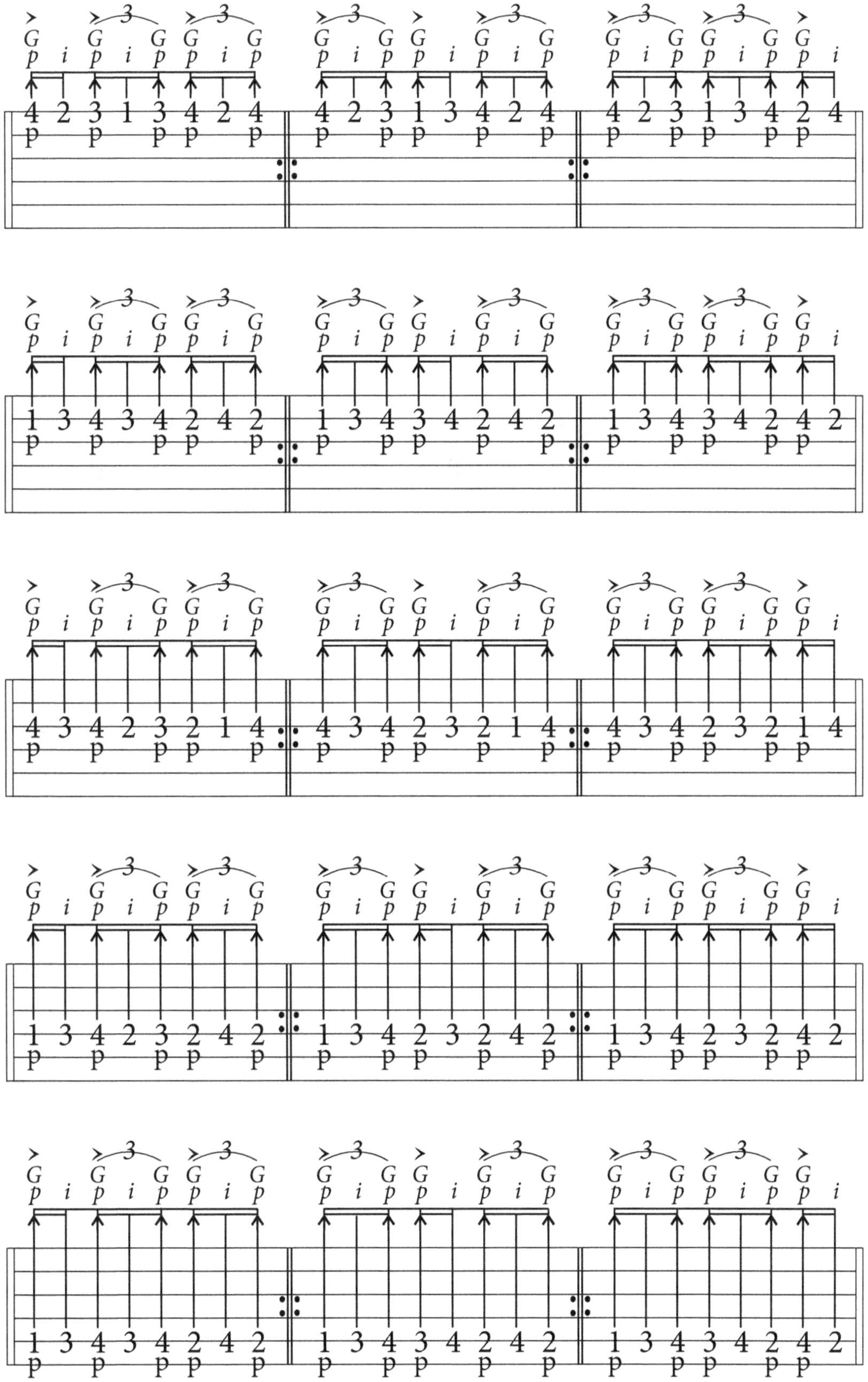

§ IIIb

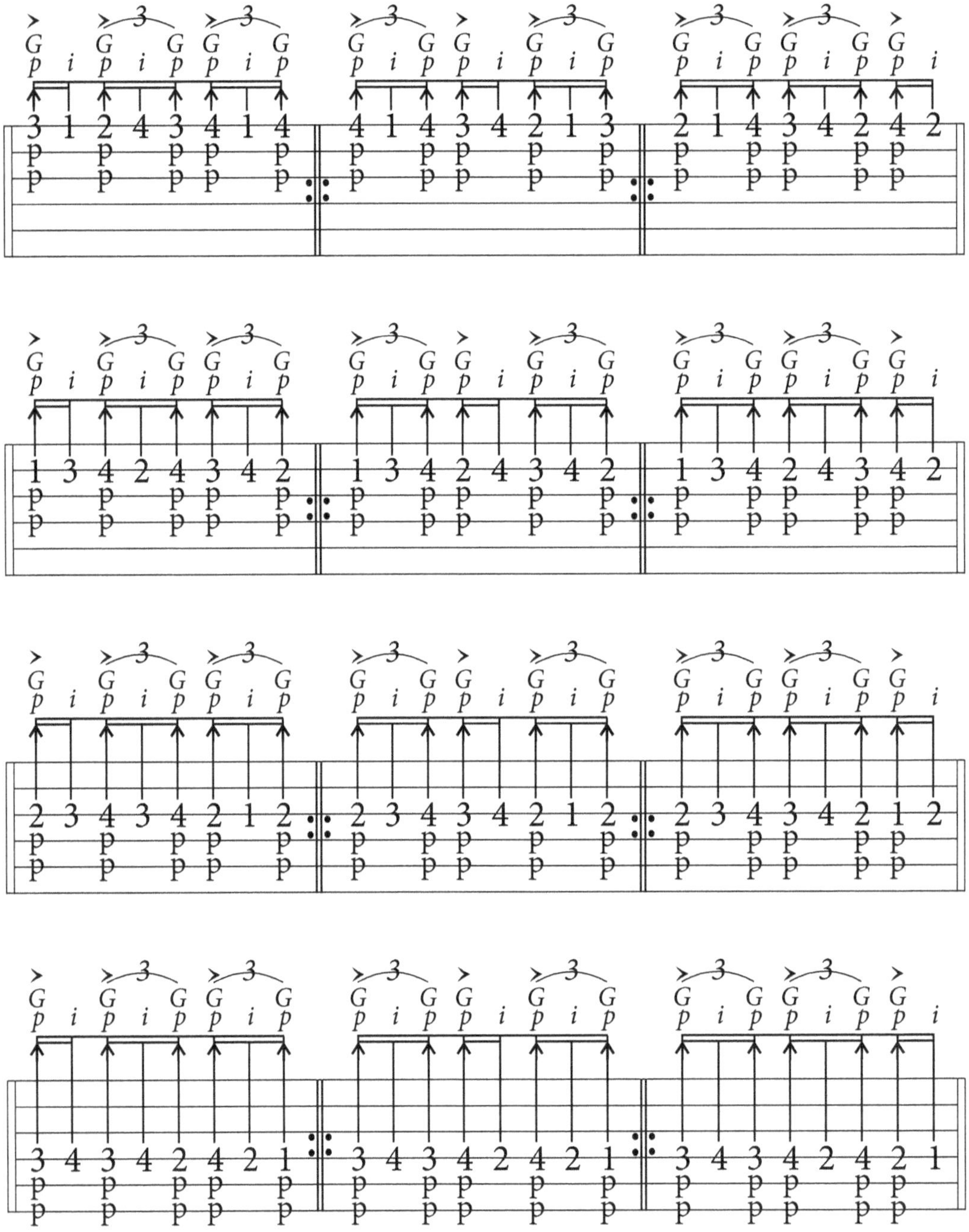

§ IVa

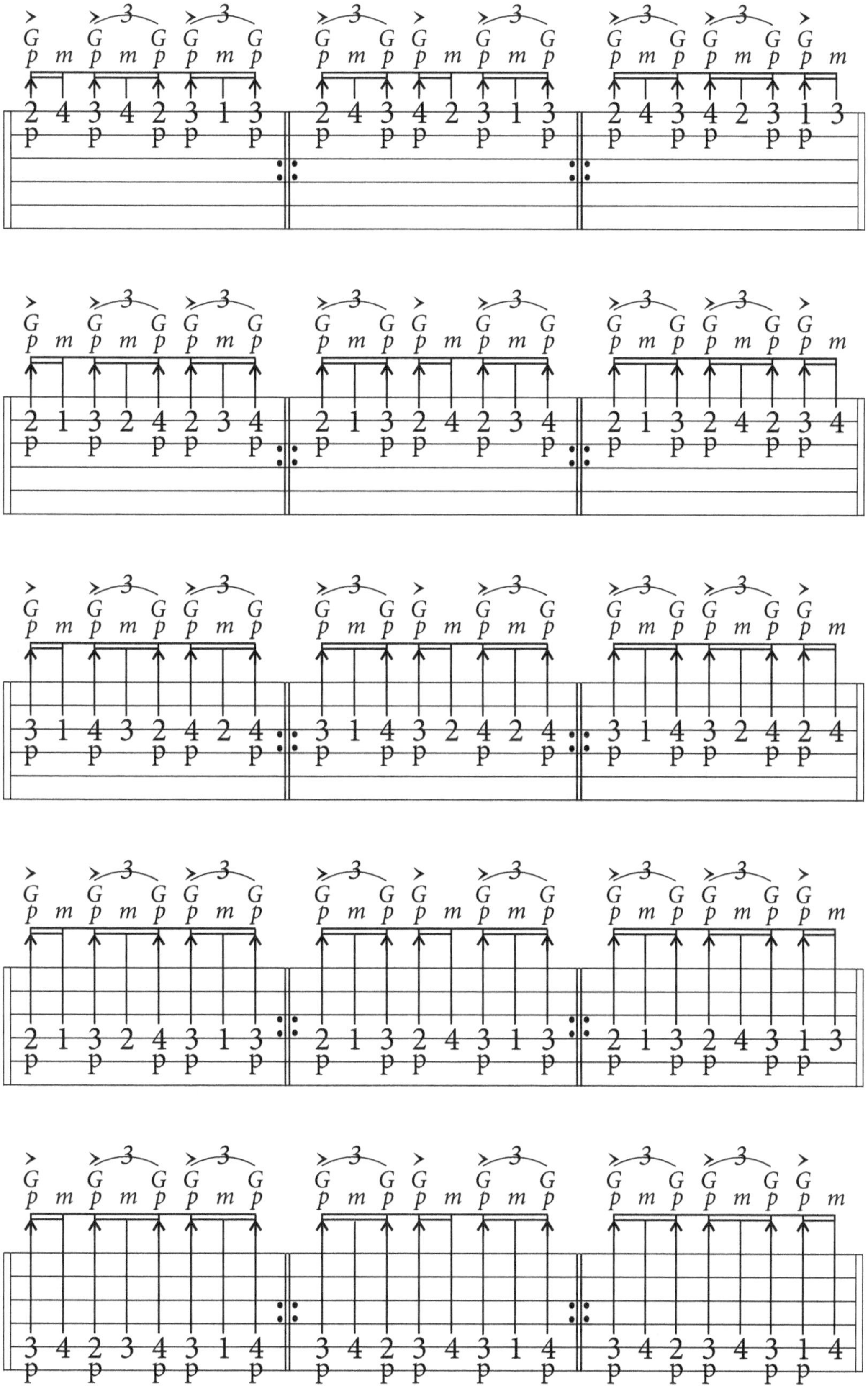

§ IVb

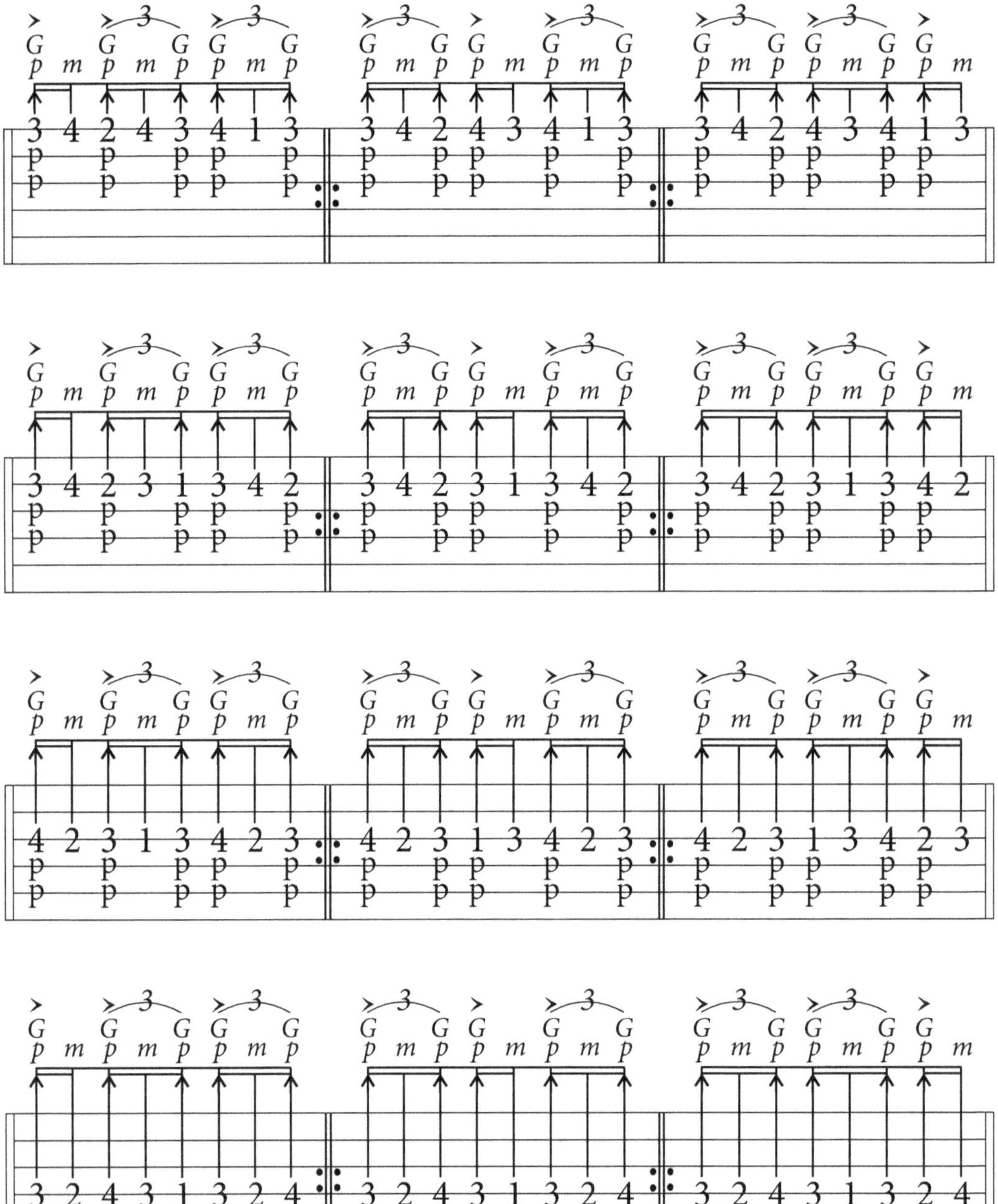

CHAPTER 4

FREE GOLPE AND THUMB STROKE ON THE
CHROMATIC SCALES OF ONE STRING (8 NOTES)
WITH THE PARTICIPATION OF INDEX (I)
AND MIDDLE FINGER (m).
ONE OR TWO GOLPE IN THE METER.
VARIATIONS IN REGARD TO FINGERS INDEX
AND RING FINGER IN REGARD TO THUMB STROKE
(DIRECTION OF STROKE).

The exercises of this chapter shaped as triplets.

UNIT 1

Free Golpe and thumb stroke
in combination with index (i) and middle finger (m).
One or two directions of thumb stroke.

§I Free Golpe without simultaneous thumb stroke on the chromatic scales of one string with the participation of index (i) and middle finger (m). The exercises of this unit are formed as triplets.

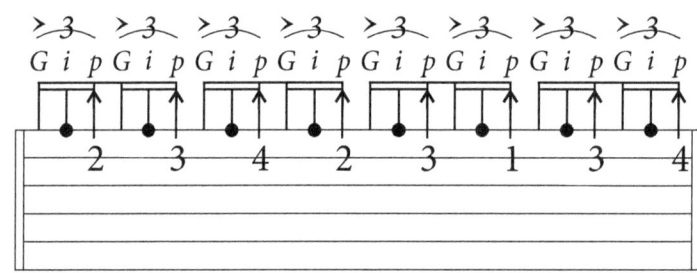

§II The above exercise with interchange of the right hand fingers, index (i) and middle finger (m).

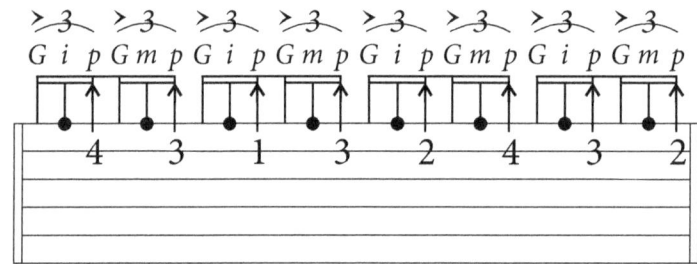

When the chromatic scale is on the 4th string, apart from the already mentioned way, you can also practice the simultaneous stroke of the 5th and 6th string.

When the chromatic scale is on the 5th string, apart from the already mentioned way, you can also practice the simultaneous stroke of the 6th string by the thumb.

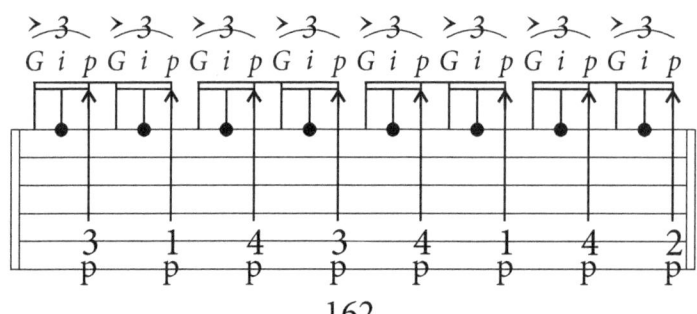

§III Chromatic scales which ascend every two notes:

1/ from the 2nd to the 5th string and return from the 5th to the 2nd string with the opposite chromatic scale.

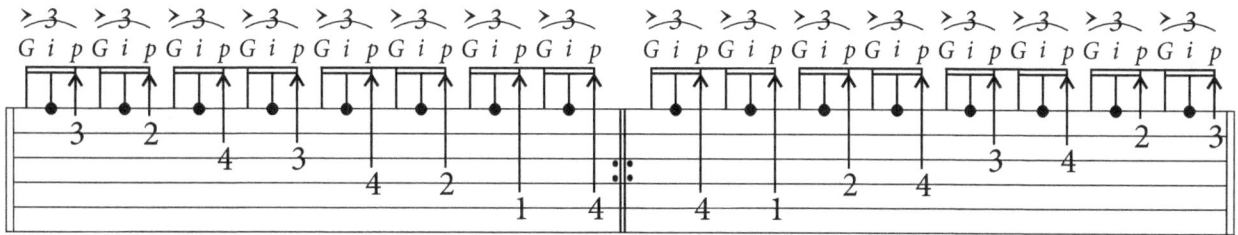

2/ from the 3rd to the 6th string and return from the 6th to the 3rd string with the opposite chromatic scale.

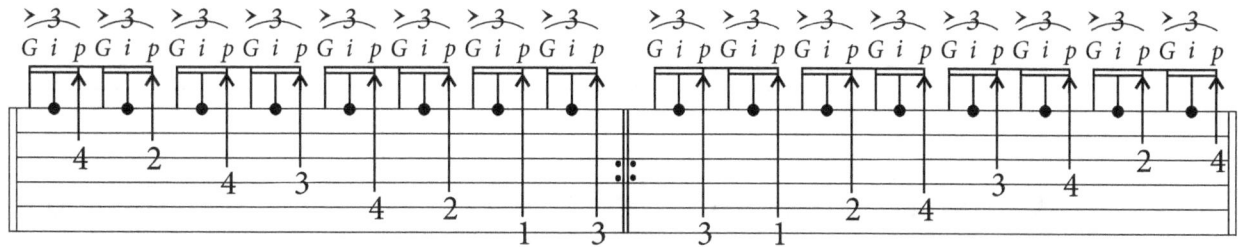

§IV The above exercise with interchange of the right hand fingers, index (i) and middle finger (m).

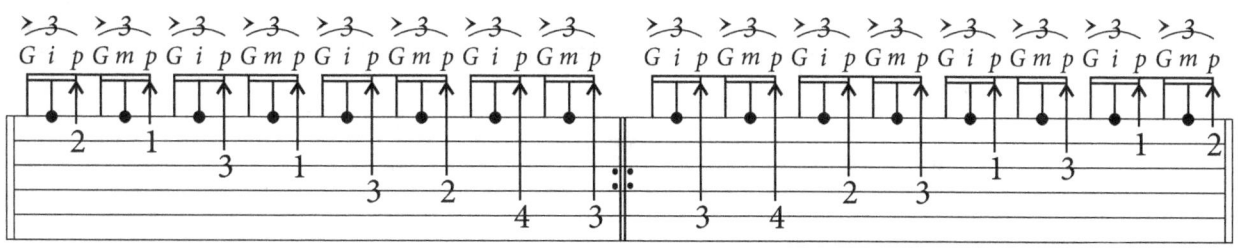

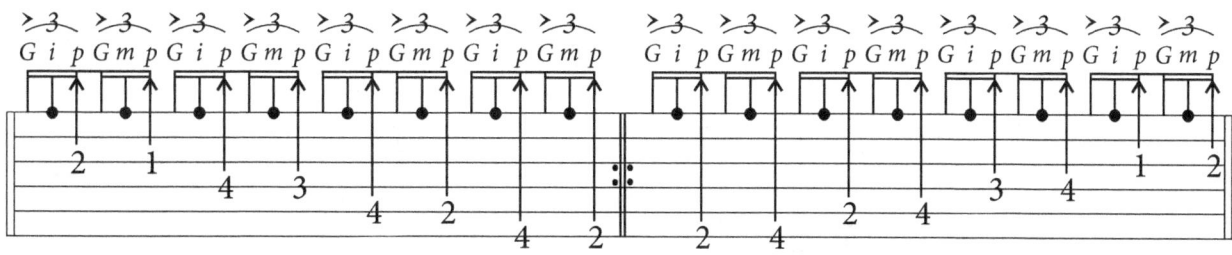

§V, §VI Variation of the previous exercises with double Golpe within the meter.

§ V

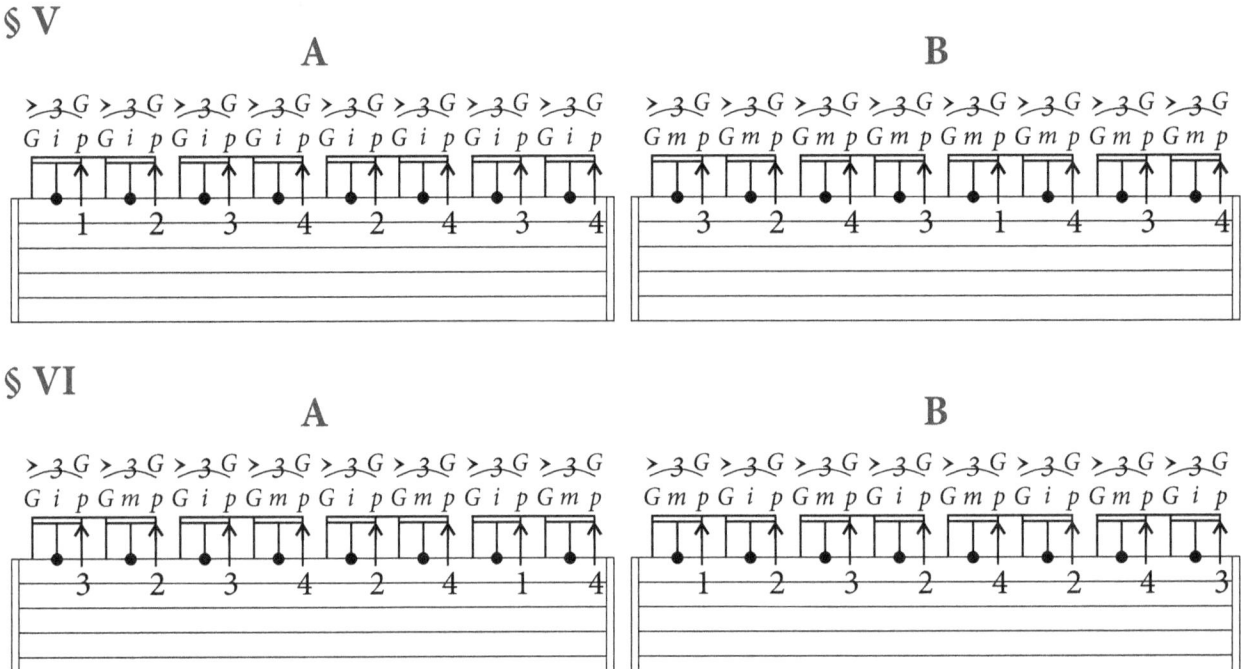

§ VI

§VII, §VIII Chromatic scales which extend every two notes, from the 2nd to the 5th string and from 3rd to 6th.

§ VII

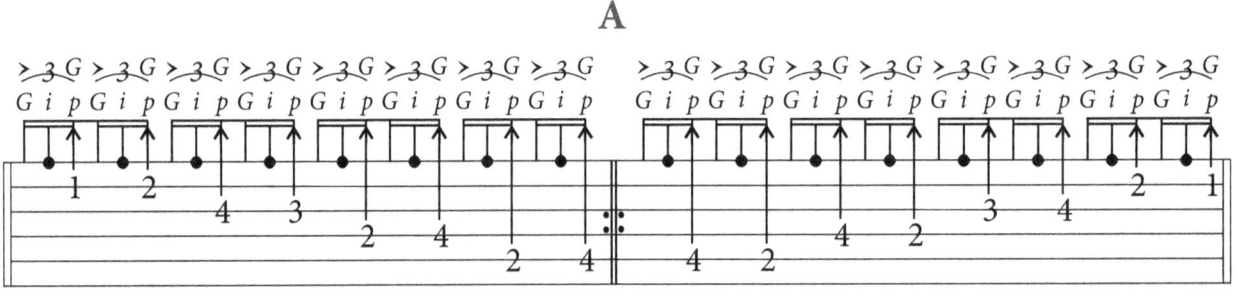

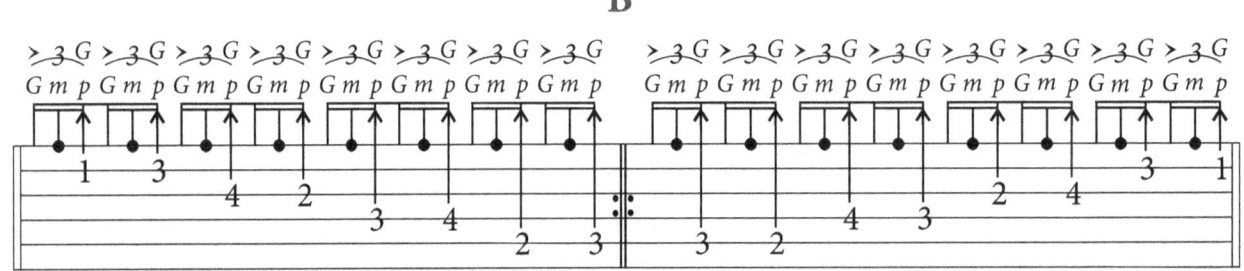

§ VIII

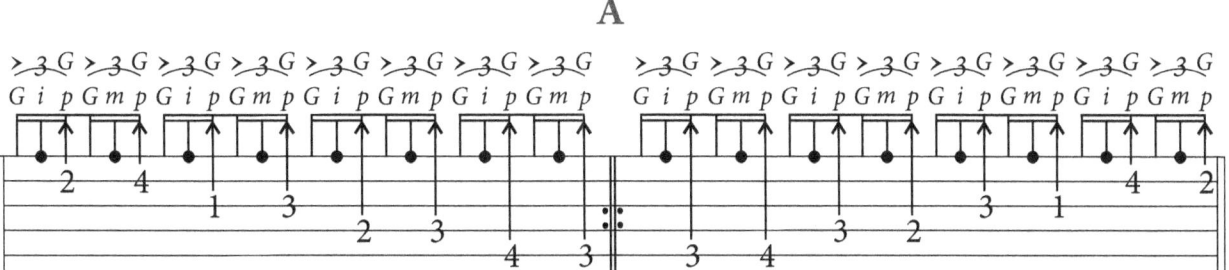

§IX , §X The previous exercises with the thumb striking towards two directions both downwards (↑) and upwards (↓).

§ IX

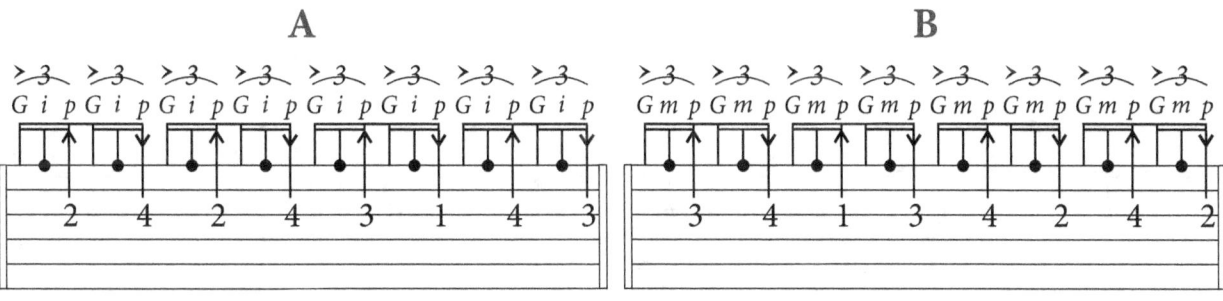

§ X

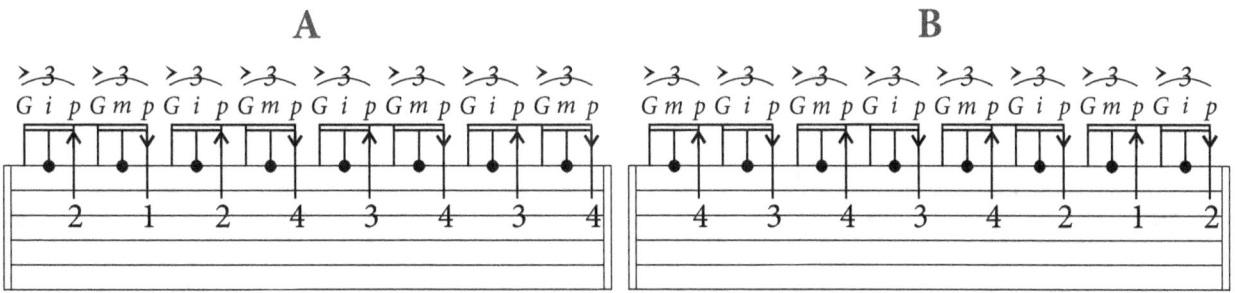

§XI Chromatic scales which extend every two nodes from the 3rd to the 6th string with one Golpe within the meter.

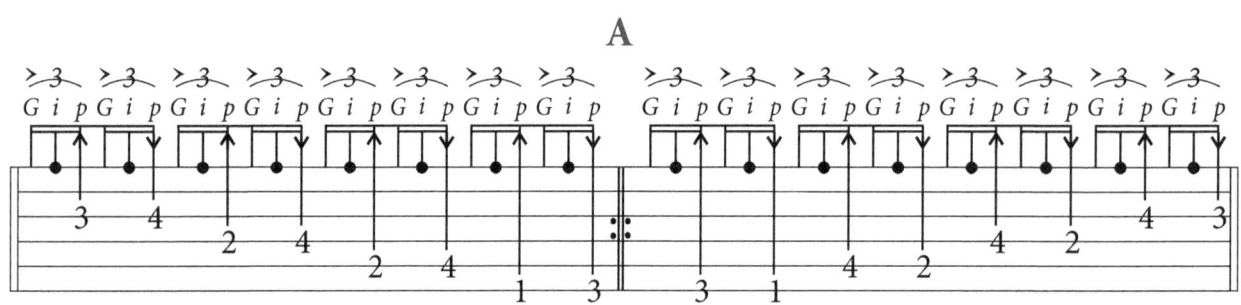

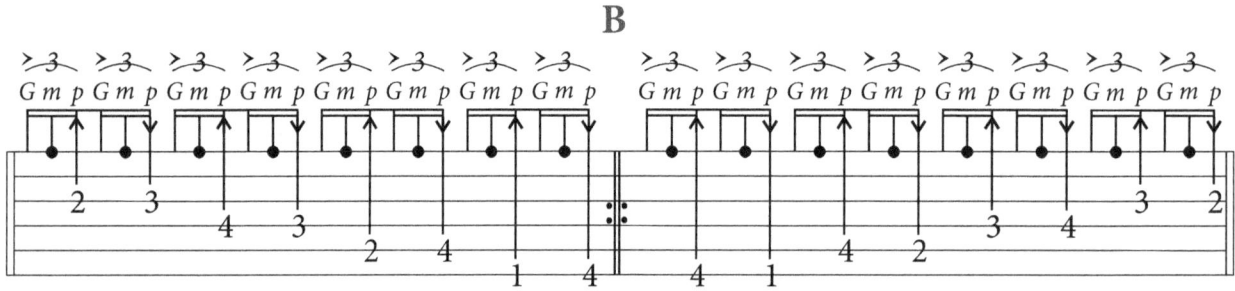

§XII, §XIII The previous exercises IX and X with the thumb striking towards two directions both downwards (↑) and upwards (↓), with Golpe addition.

§ XII

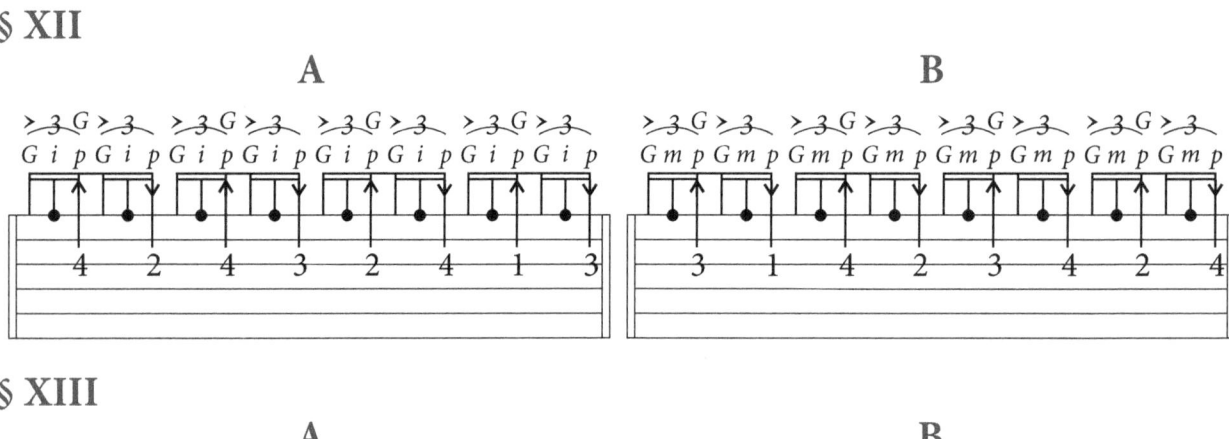

§ XIII

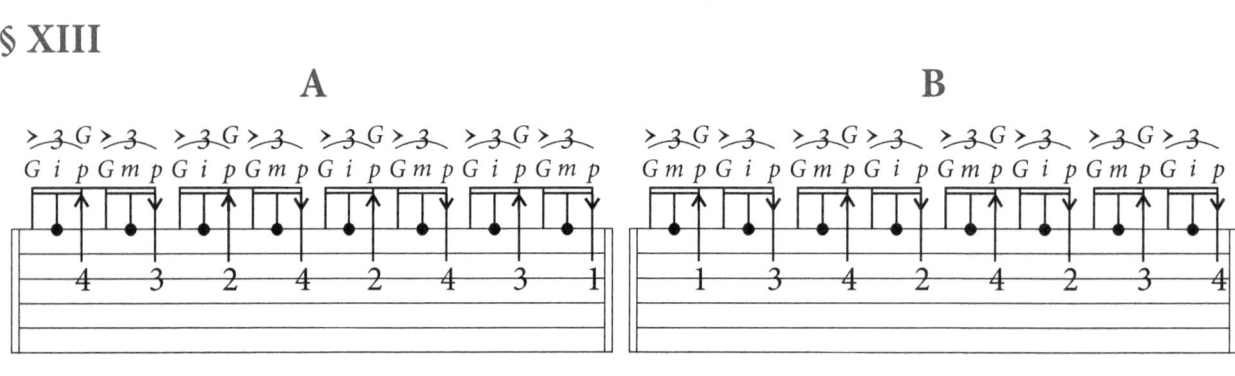

§**XIV** Chromatic scales which extend every two nodes from the 3rd to the 6th string. Thumb striking towards two directions (↑↓) with Golpe addition.

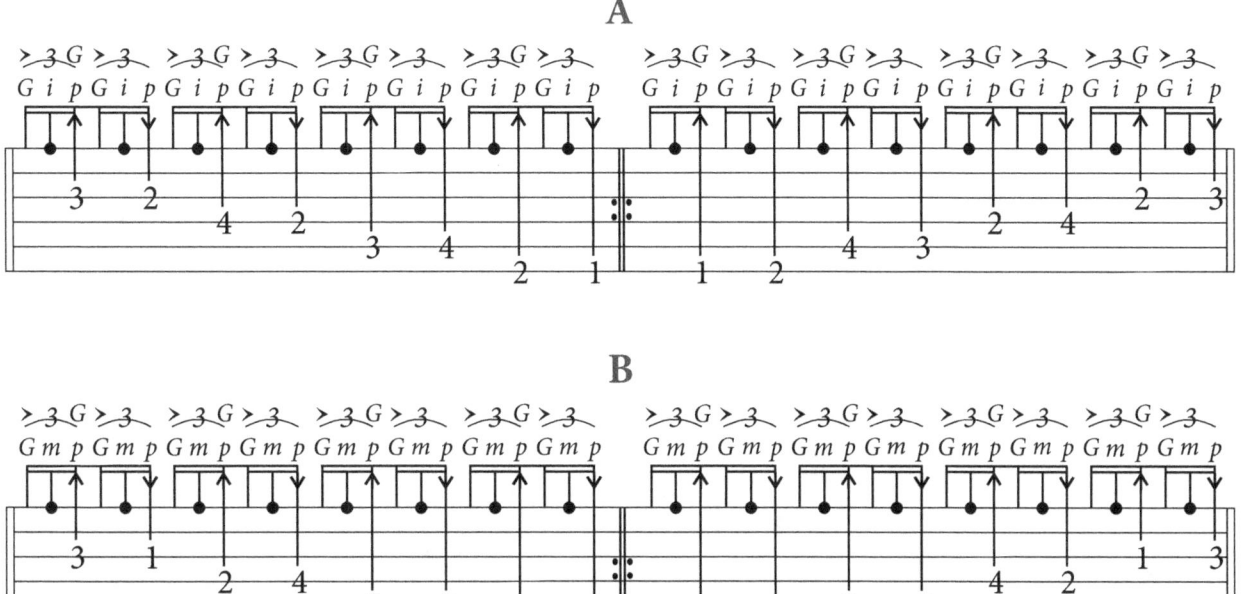

§ I

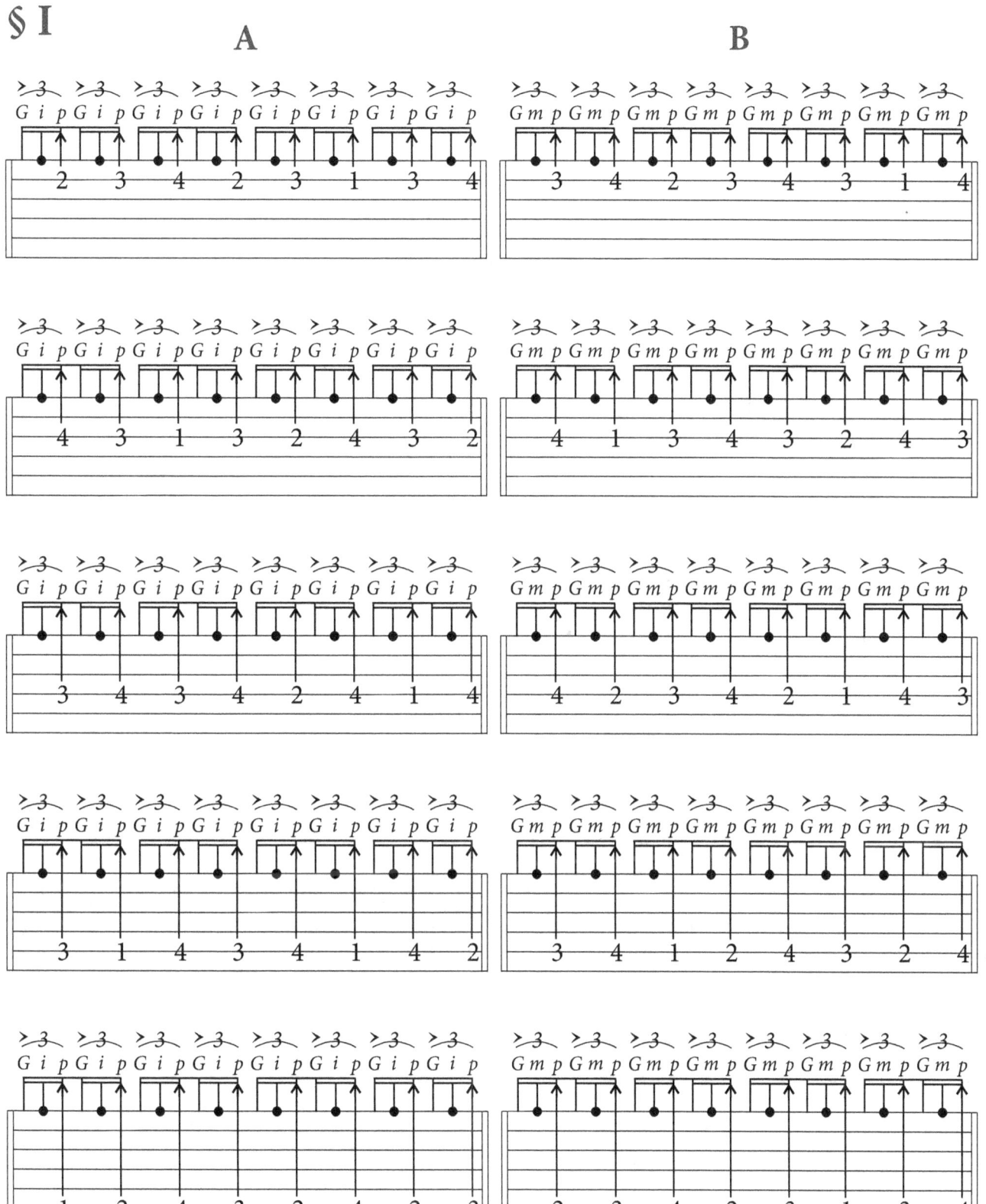

§ II

A **B**

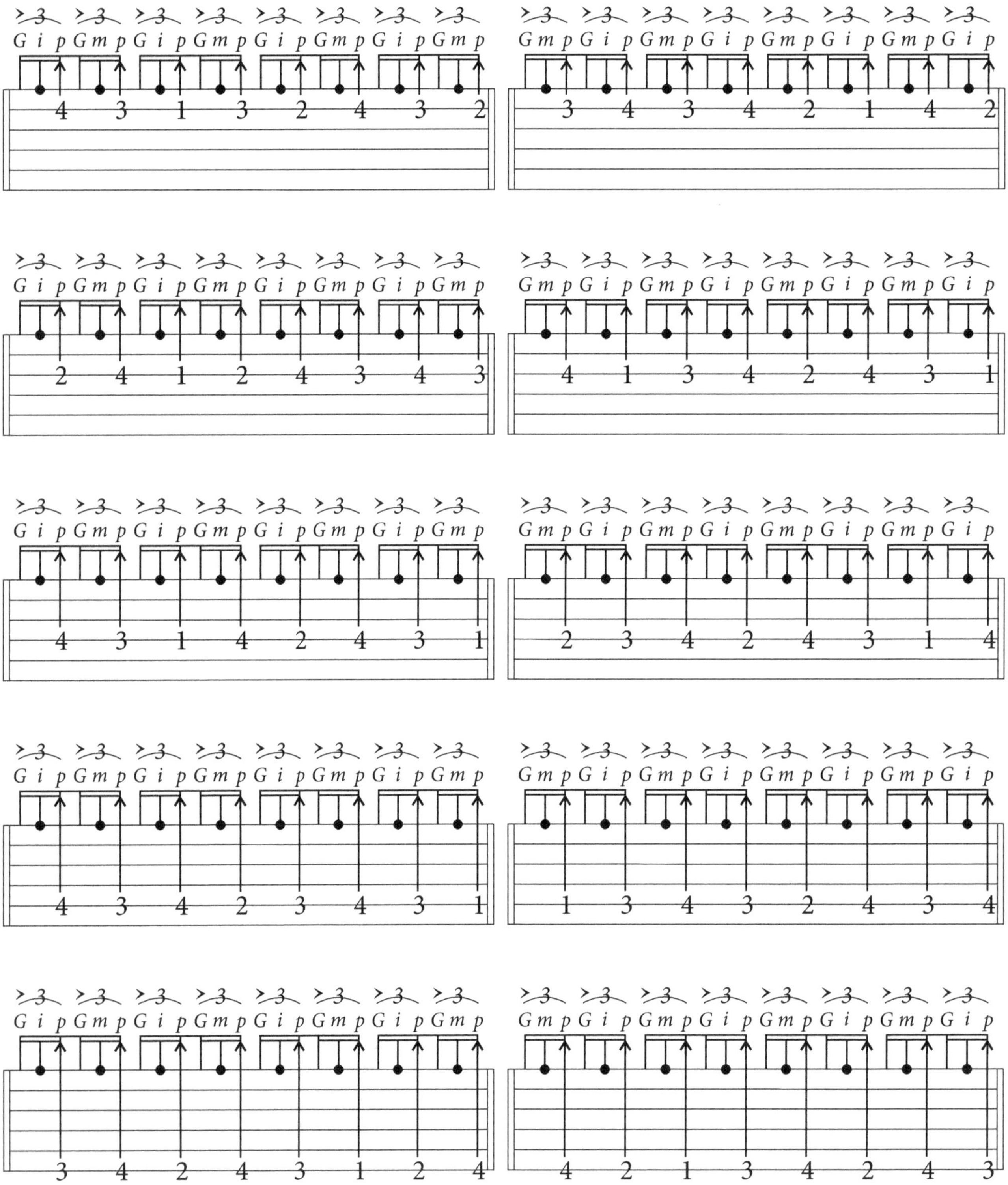
G i p G m p G i p G m p G i p G m p G i p G m p
4 3 1 3 2 4 3 2
G m p G i p G m p G i p G m p G i p G m p G i p
3 4 3 4 2 1 4 2
G i p G m p G i p G m p G i p G m p G i p G m p
2 4 1 2 4 3 4 3
G m p G i p G m p G i p G m p G i p G m p G i p
4 1 3 4 2 4 3 1
G i p G m p G i p G m p G i p G m p G i p G m p
4 3 1 4 2 4 3 1
G m p G i p G m p G i p G m p G i p G m p G i p
2 3 4 2 4 3 1 4
G i p G m p G i p G m p G i p G m p G i p G m p
4 3 4 2 3 4 3 1
G m p G i p G m p G i p G m p G i p G m p G i p
1 3 4 3 2 4 3 4
G i p G m p G i p G m p G i p G m p G i p G m p
3 4 2 4 3 1 2 4
G m p G i p G m p G i p G m p G i p G m p G i p
4 2 1 3 4 2 4 3

§ III

A

F1

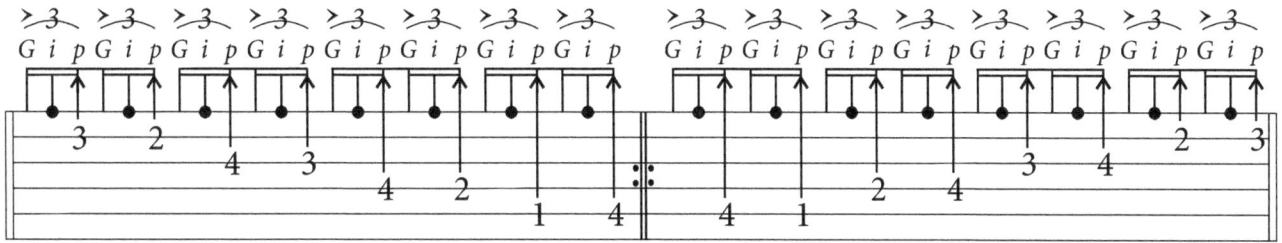

F2

B

F1

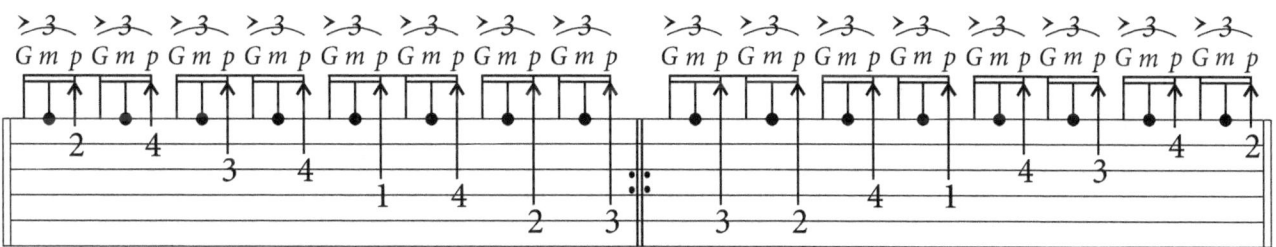

F2

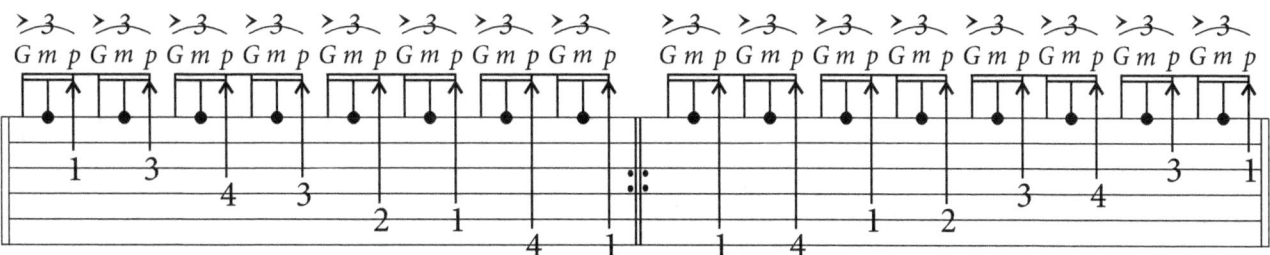

§ IV

A

F1

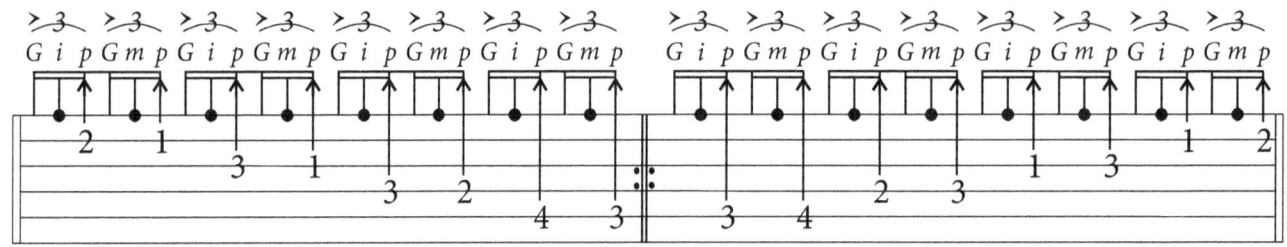

F2

B

F1

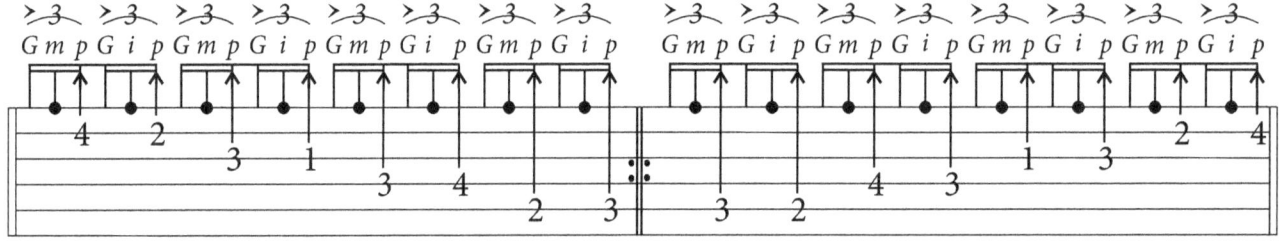

F2

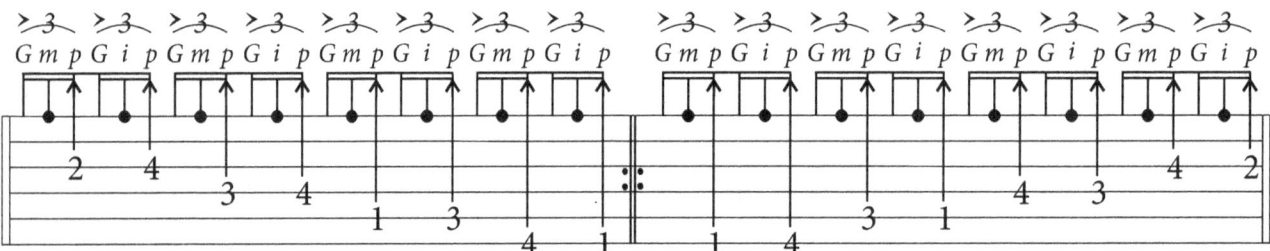

9

§ V

A **B**

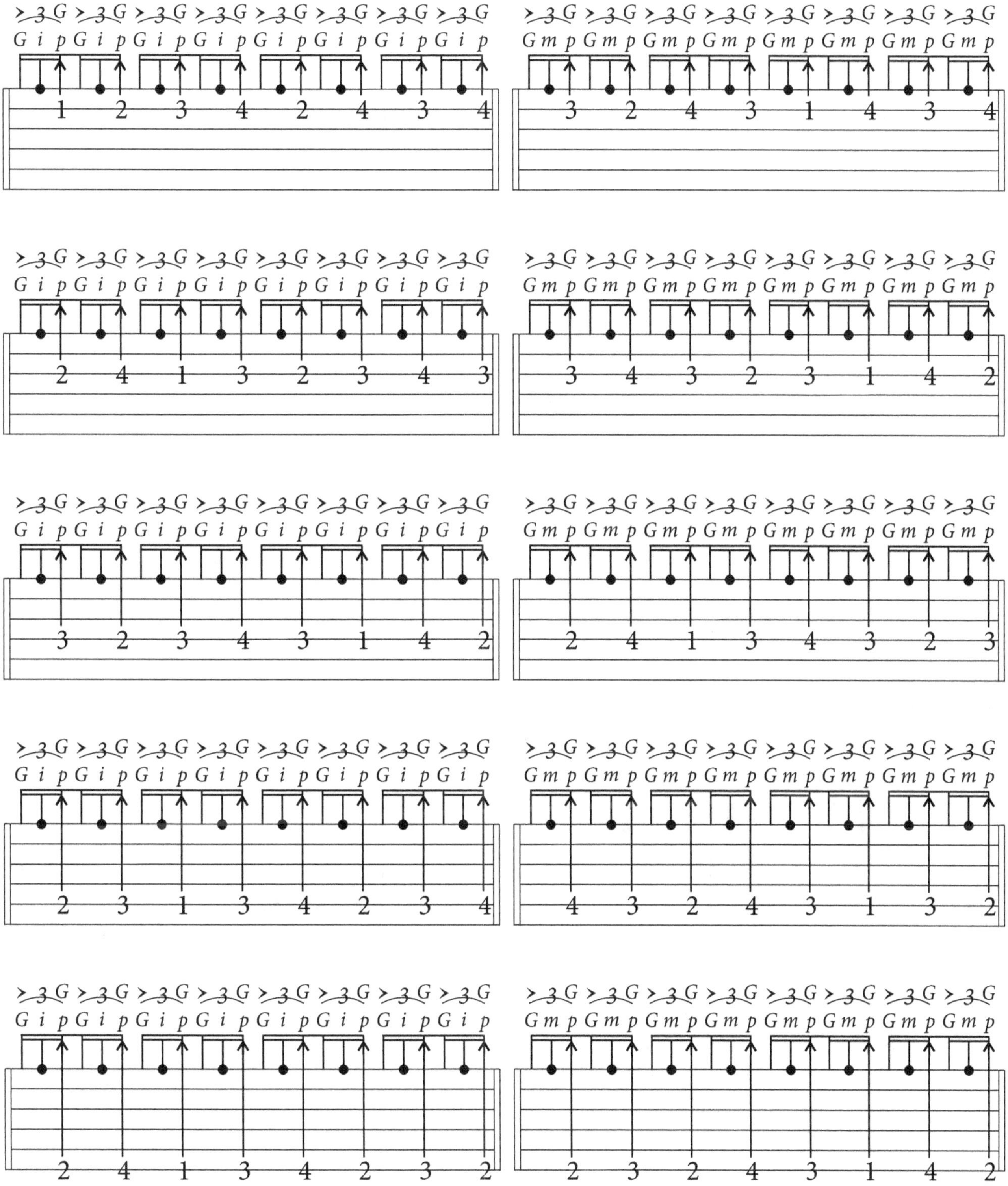
3 G 3 G 3 G 3 G 3 G 3 G 3 G 3 G
G i p G i p G i p G i p G i p G i p G i p G i p
1 2 3 4 2 4 3 4
3 G 3 G 3 G 3 G 3 G 3 G 3 G 3 G
G m p G m p G m p G m p G m p G m p G m p G m p
3 2 4 3 1 4 3 4
G i p G i p G i p G i p G i p G i p G i p G i p
2 4 1 3 2 3 4 3
G m p G m p G m p G m p G m p G m p G m p G m p
3 4 3 2 3 1 4 2
G i p G i p G i p G i p G i p G i p G i p G i p
3 2 3 4 3 1 4 2
G m p G m p G m p G m p G m p G m p G m p G m p
2 4 1 3 4 3 2 3
G i p G i p G i p G i p G i p G i p G i p G i p
2 3 1 3 4 2 3 4
G m p G m p G m p G m p G m p G m p G m p G m p
4 3 2 4 3 1 3 2
G i p G i p G i p G i p G i p G i p G i p G i p
2 4 1 3 4 2 3 2
G m p G m p G m p G m p G m p G m p G m p G m p
2 3 2 4 3 1 4 2

§ VI

A

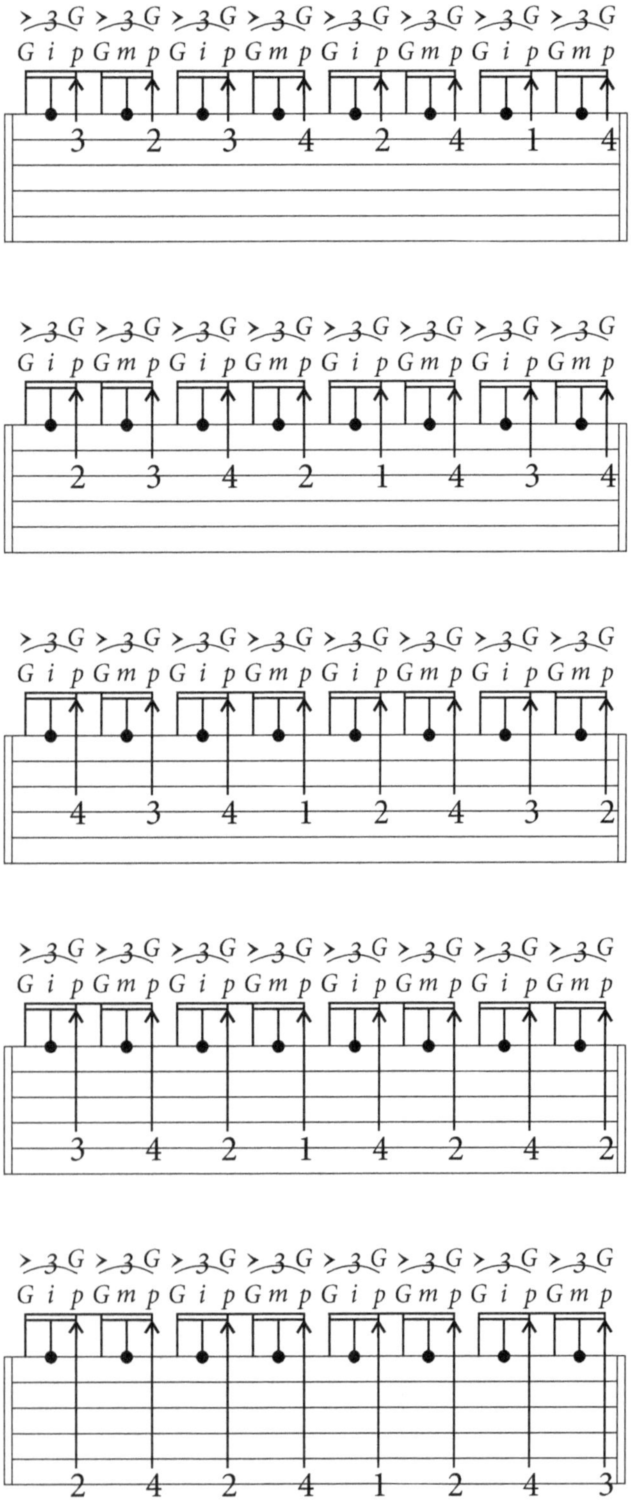
> 3 G > 3 G > 3 G > 3 G > 3 G > 3 G > 3 G > 3 G
G i p G m p G i p G m p G i p G m p G i p G m p
3 2 3 4 2 4 1 4
2 3 4 2 1 4 3 4
4 3 4 1 2 4 3 2
3 4 2 1 4 2 4 2
2 4 2 4 1 2 4 3

B

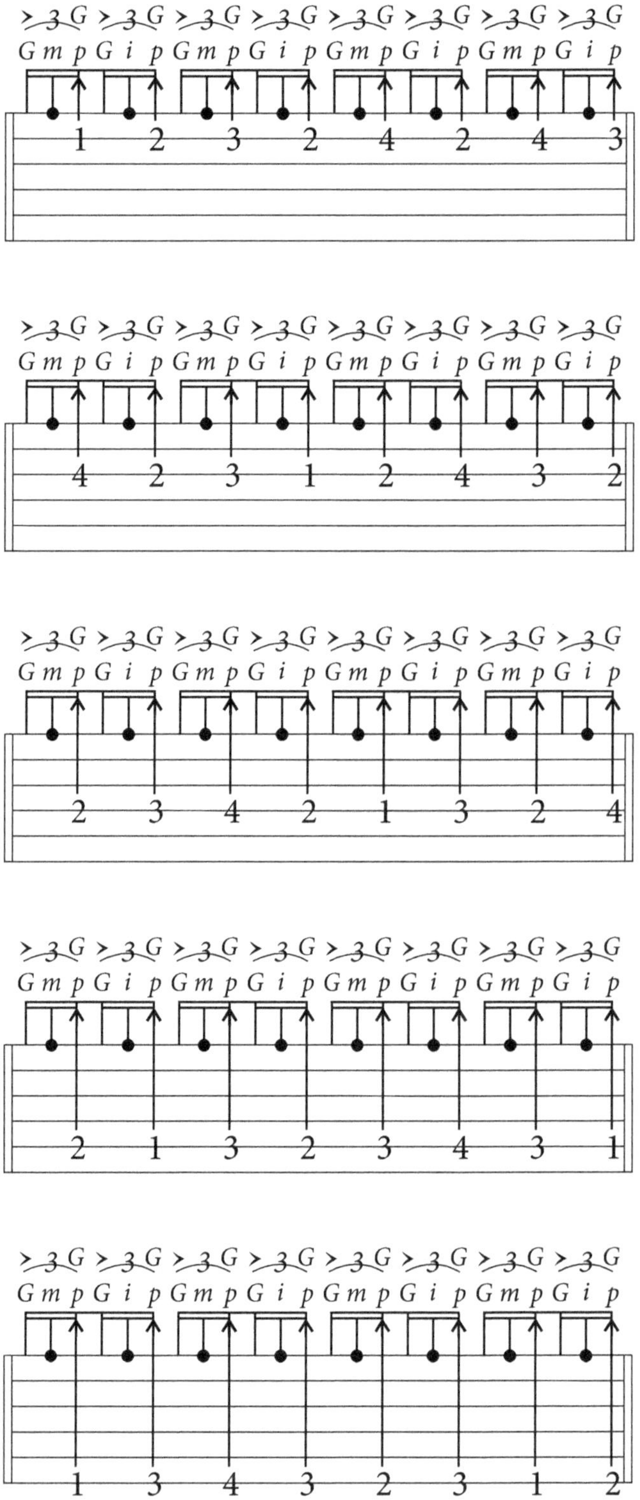
> 3 G > 3 G > 3 G > 3 G > 3 G > 3 G > 3 G > 3 G
G m p G i p G m p G i p G m p G i p G m p G i p
1 2 3 2 4 2 4 3
4 2 3 1 2 4 3 2
2 3 4 2 1 3 2 4
2 1 3 2 3 4 3 1
1 3 4 3 2 3 1 2

§ VII

A

F1

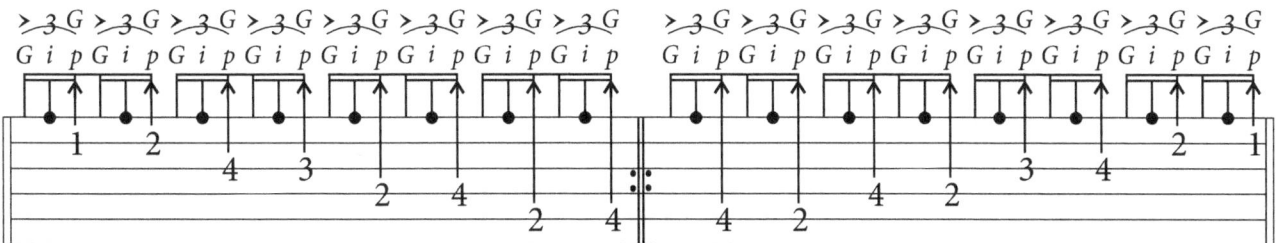

F2

B

F1

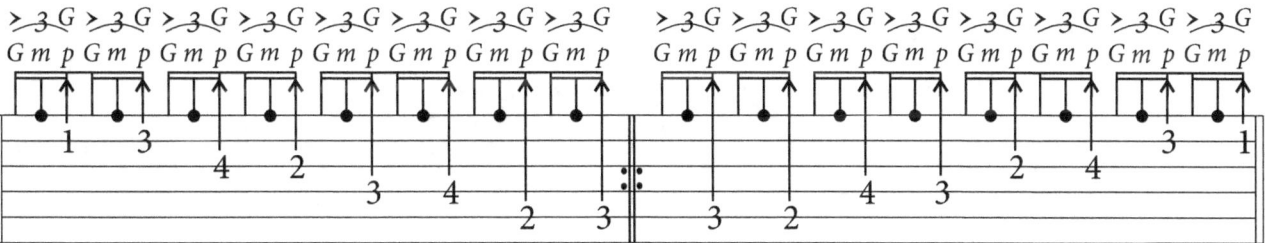

F2

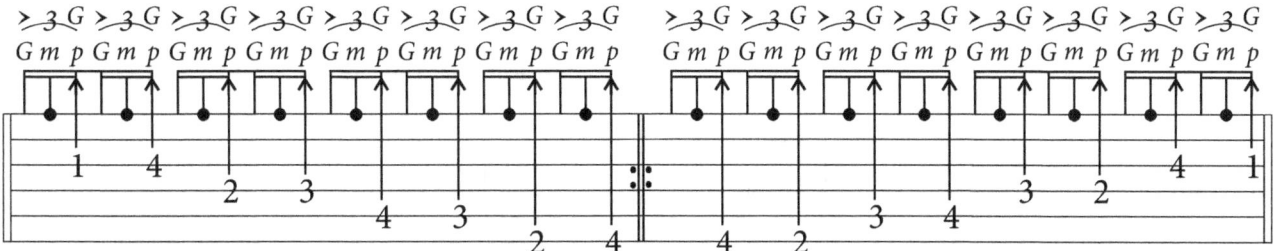

§ VIII

A

F1
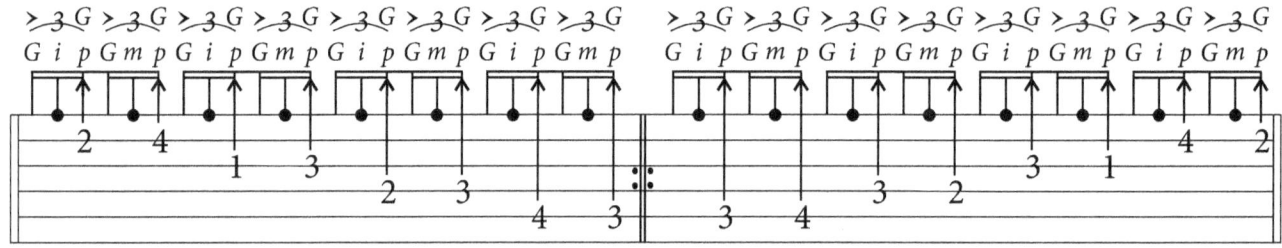

F2
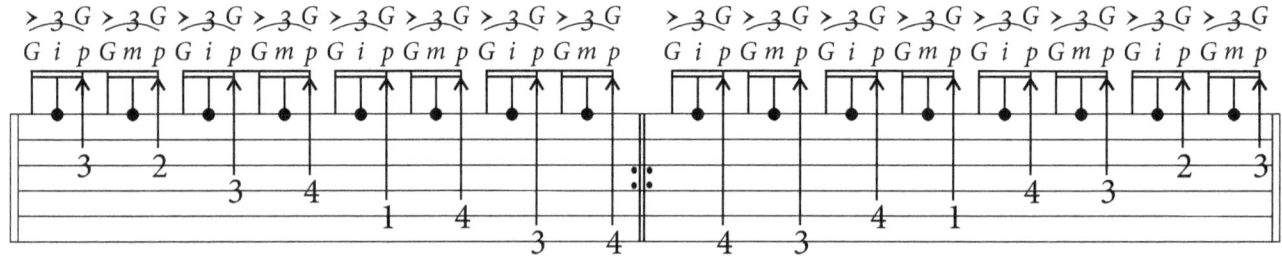

B

F1
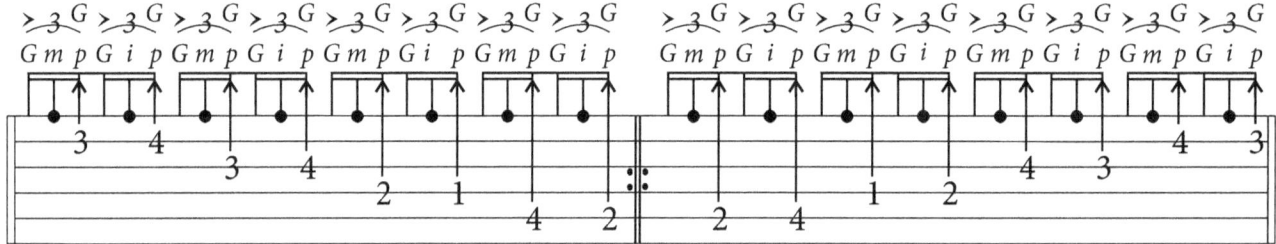

F2
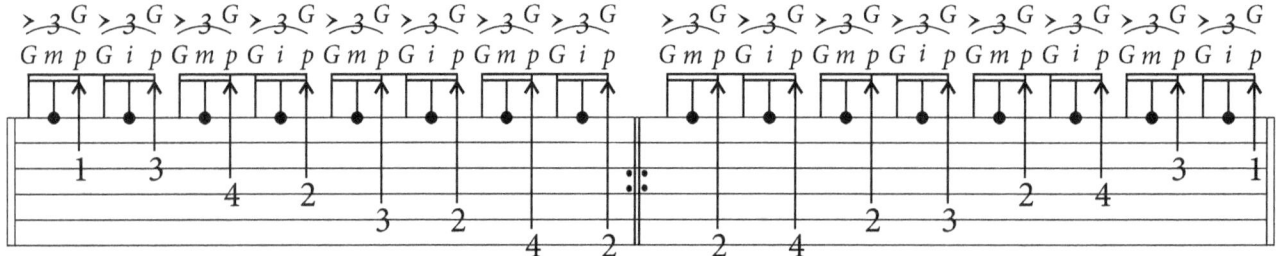

§ IX

A

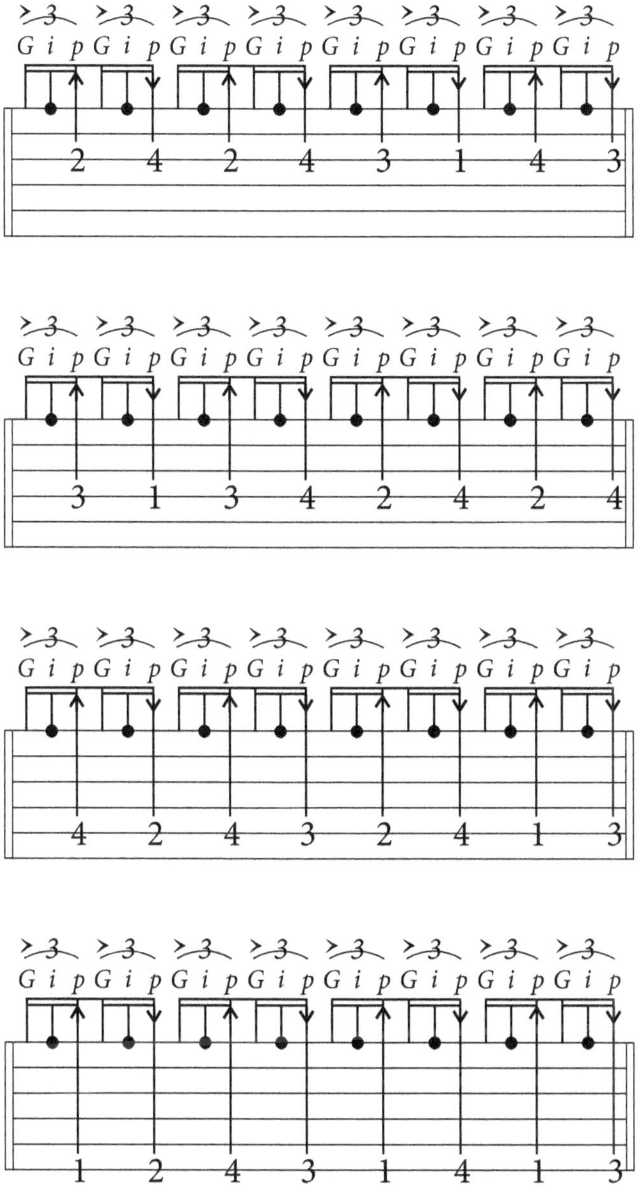

3 3 3 3 3 3 3 3
G i p G i p G i p G i p G i p G i p G i p G i p
2 4 2 4 3 1 4 3
3 1 3 4 2 4 2 4
4 2 4 3 2 4 1 3
1 2 4 3 1 4 1 3

B

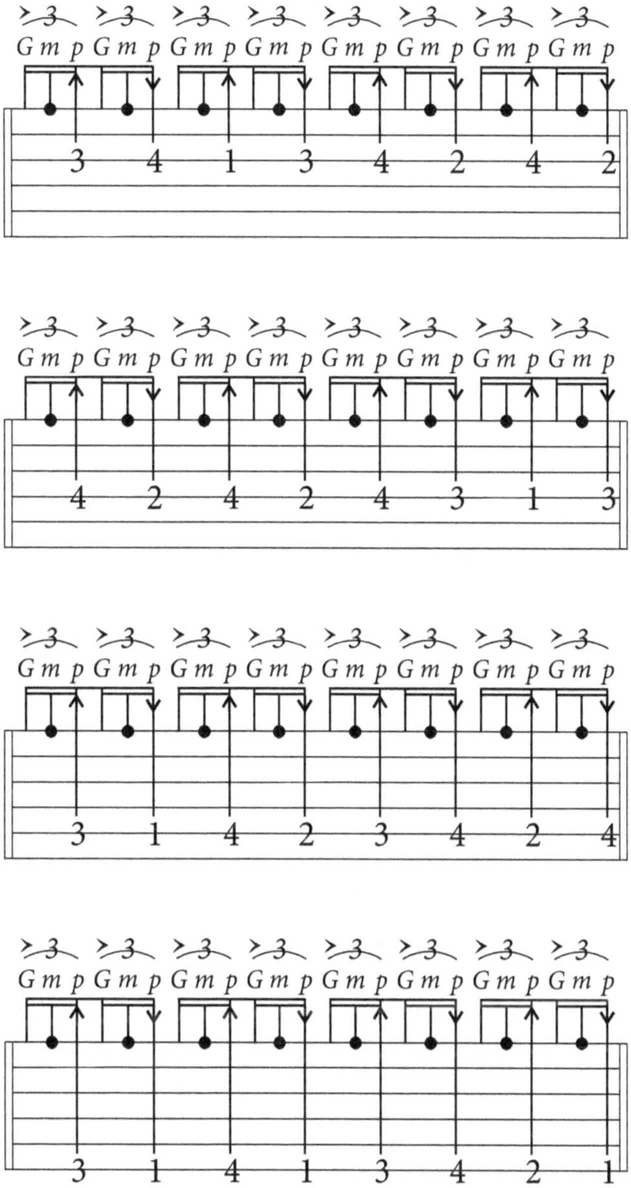

3 3 3 3 3 3 3 3
G m p G m p G m p G m p G m p G m p G m p G m p
3 4 1 3 4 2 4 2
4 2 4 2 4 3 1 3
3 1 4 2 3 4 2 4
3 1 4 1 3 4 2 1

§ X

A B

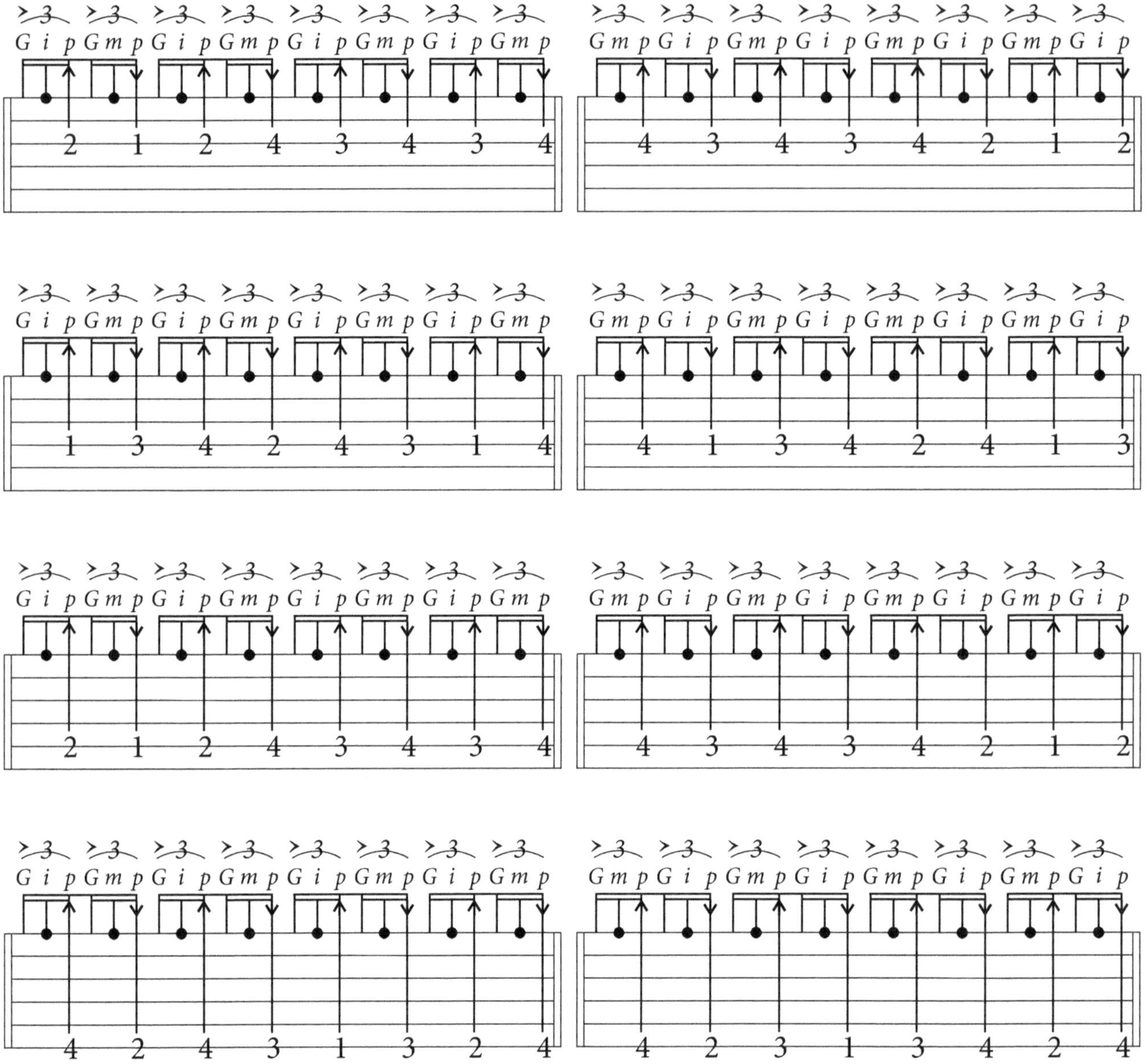
G i p G m p G i p G m p G i p G m p G i p G m p
2 1 2 4 3 4 3 4
G m p G i p G m p G i p G m p G i p G m p G i p
4 3 4 3 4 2 1 2
G i p G m p G i p G m p G i p G m p G i p G m p
1 3 4 2 4 3 1 4
G m p G i p G m p G i p G m p G i p G m p G i p
4 1 3 4 2 4 1 3
G i p G m p G i p G m p G i p G m p G i p G m p
2 1 2 4 3 4 3 4
G m p G i p G m p G i p G m p G i p G m p G i p
4 3 4 3 4 2 1 2
G i p G m p G i p G m p G i p G m p G i p G m p
4 2 4 3 1 3 2 4
G m p G i p G m p G i p G m p G i p G m p G i p
4 2 3 1 3 4 2 4

§ XI

A

F1

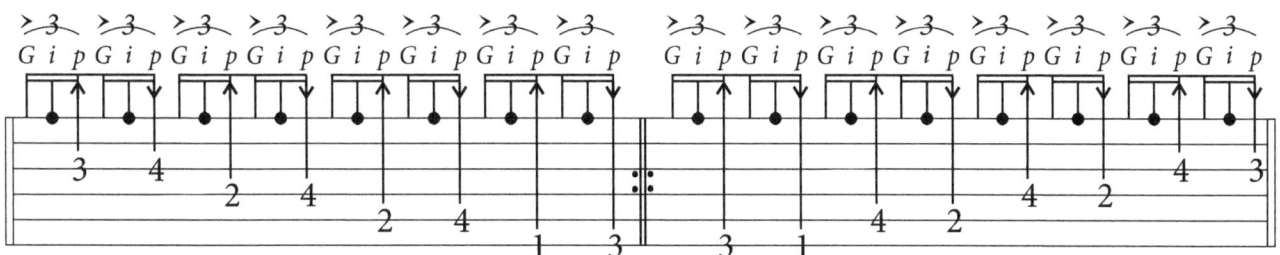

B

F2

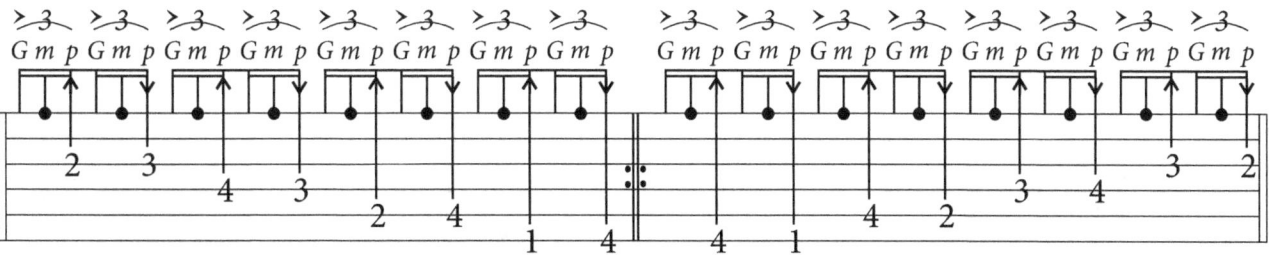

C

F3

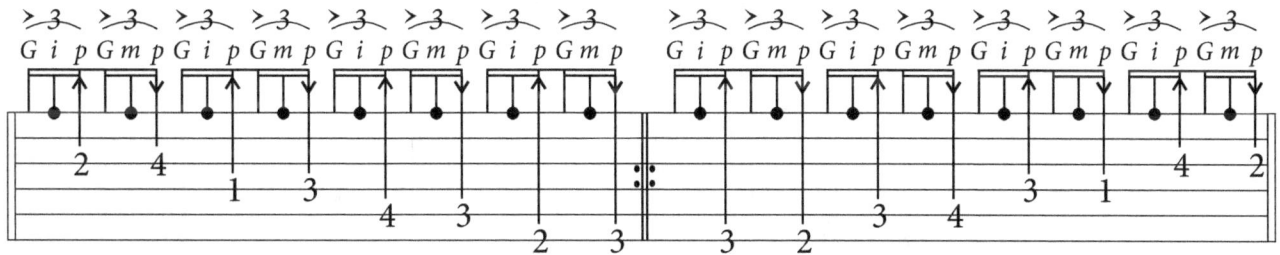

D

F4

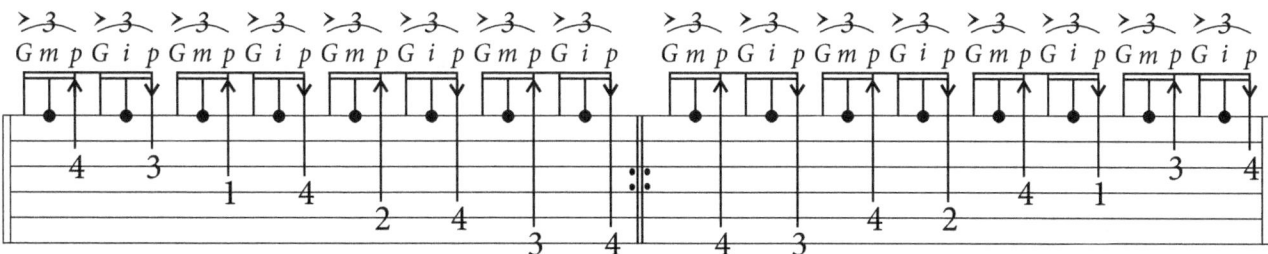

§ XII

A B

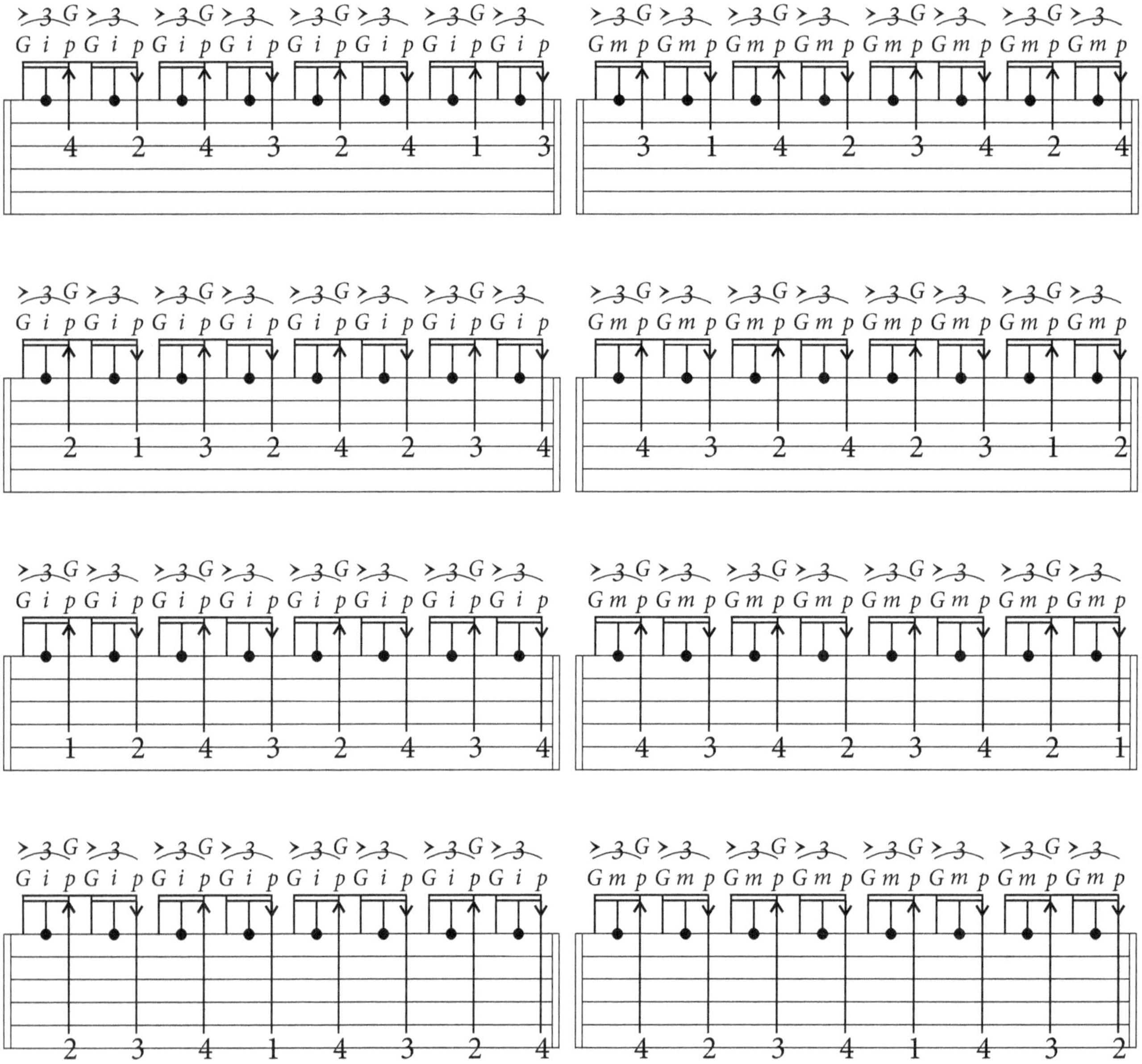

3 G 3 3 G 3 3 G 3 3 G 3
G i p G i p G i p G i p G i p G i p G i p G i p
4 2 4 3 2 4 1 3
3 G 3 3 G 3 3 G 3 3 G 3
G m p G m p G m p G m p G m p G m p G m p G m p
3 1 4 2 3 4 2 4
G i p G i p G i p G i p G i p G i p G i p G i p
2 1 3 2 4 2 3 4
G m p G m p G m p G m p G m p G m p G m p G m p
4 3 2 4 2 3 1 2
G i p G i p G i p G i p G i p G i p G i p G i p
1 2 4 3 2 4 3 4
G m p G m p G m p G m p G m p G m p G m p G m p
4 3 4 2 3 4 2 1
G i p G i p G i p G i p G i p G i p G i p G i p
2 3 4 1 4 3 2 4
G m p G m p G m p G m p G m p G m p G m p G m p
4 2 3 4 1 4 3 2

§ XIII

A

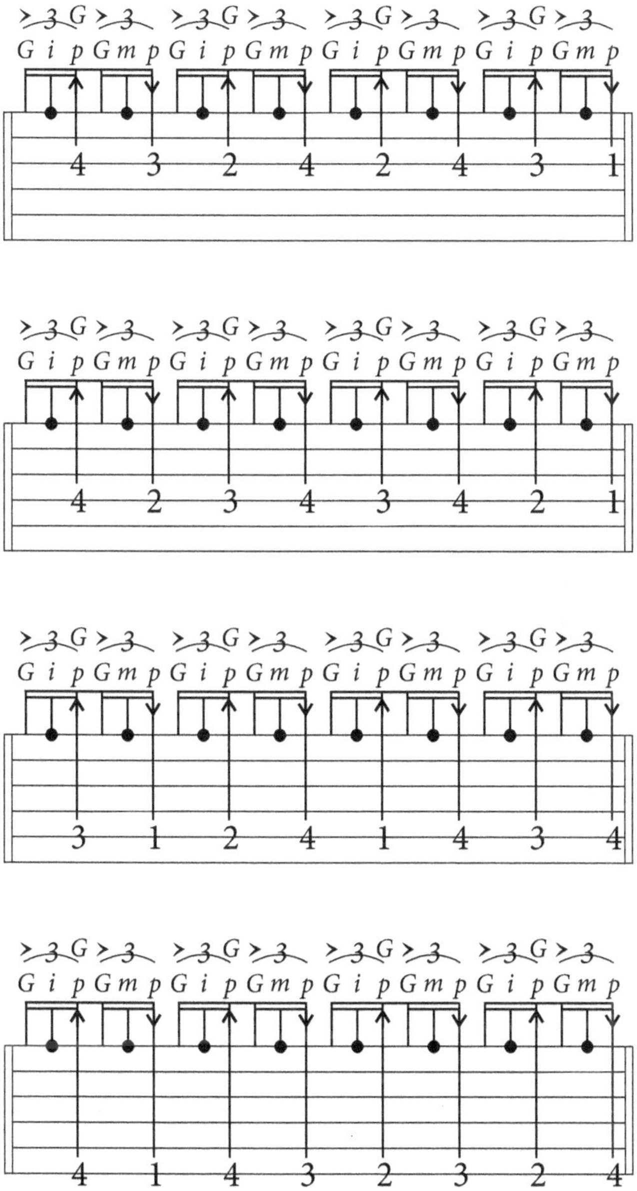
G i p G m p G i p G m p G i p G m p G i p G m p
4 3 2 4 2 4 3 1
G i p G m p G i p G m p G i p G m p G i p G m p
4 2 3 4 3 4 2 1
G i p G m p G i p G m p G i p G m p G i p G m p
3 1 2 4 1 4 3 4
G i p G m p G i p G m p G i p G m p G i p G m p
4 1 4 3 2 3 2 4

B

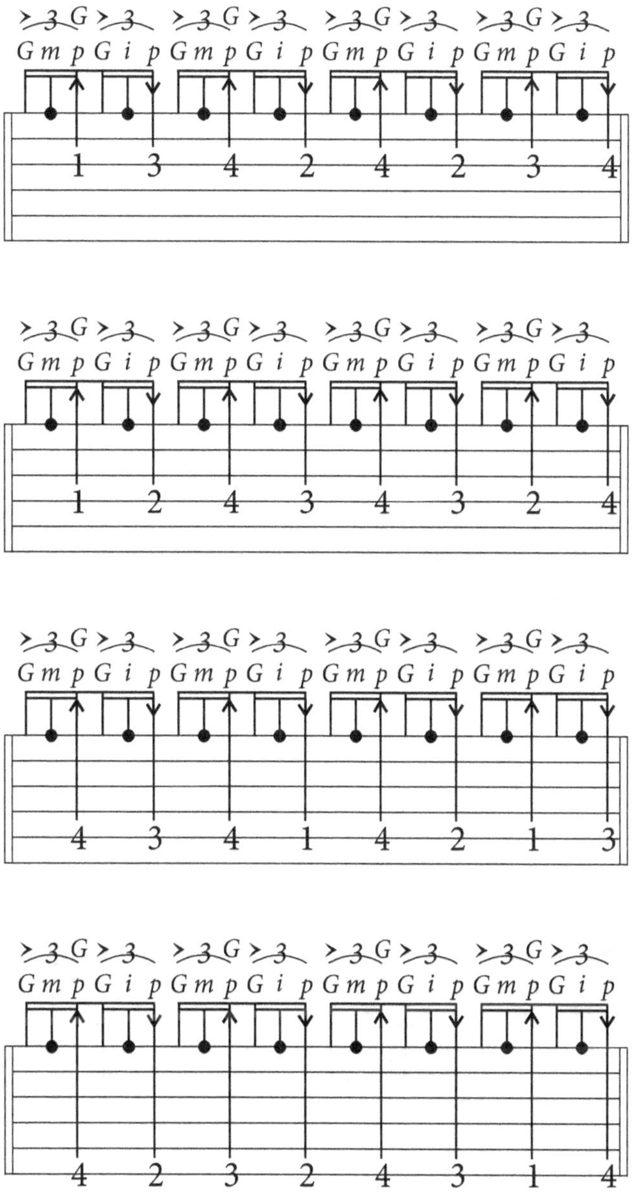
G m p G i p G m p G i p G m p G i p G m p G i p
1 3 4 2 4 2 3 4
G m p G i p G m p G i p G m p G i p G m p G i p
1 2 4 3 4 3 2 4
G m p G i p G m p G i p G m p G i p G m p G i p
4 3 4 1 4 2 1 3
G m p G i p G m p G i p G m p G i p G m p G i p
4 2 3 2 4 3 1 4

§ XIV

A
F1

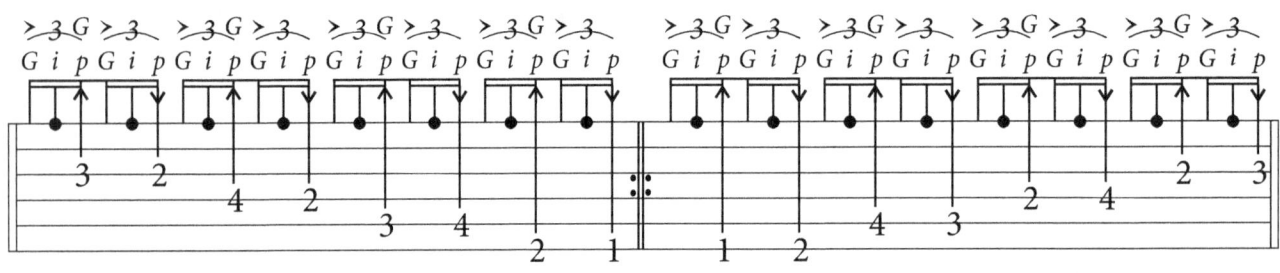

B
F2

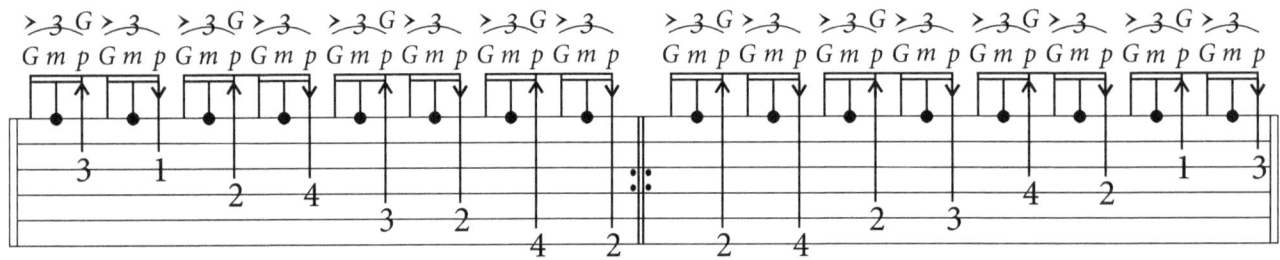

C
F3

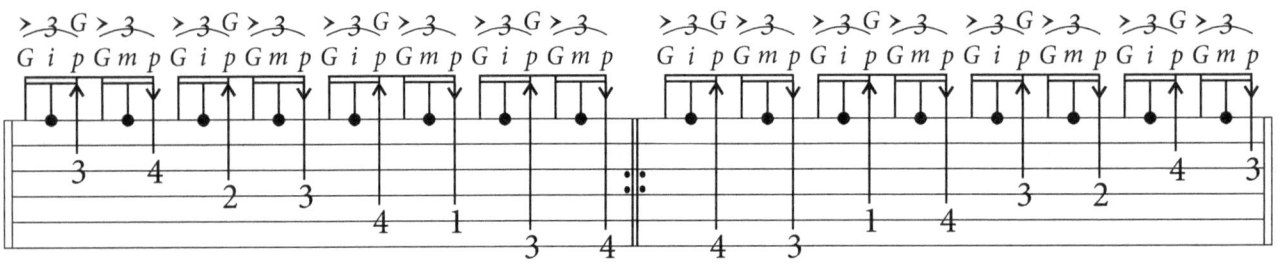

D
F4

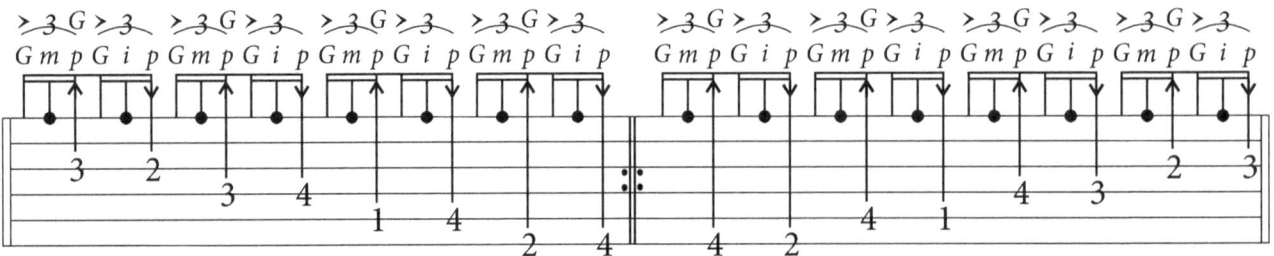

UNIT 2

Thumb stroke with Golpe on two or three strings simultaneously.
Free Golpe within the Formulas.

The exercises of this unit are formed into triplets. They are the exercises of the previous unit varied as far as the thumb is concerned. More specifically, we find thumb stroke of two or three strings simultaneously with free Golpe in the first position of the triplet or with simultaneous thumb stroke in the third position of the triplet. We also find exercises that refer to the thumb stroke. Irrespective of the index (i) and middle finger (m) as well as exercises with interchange among the above fingers (i) and (m). Finally, there are exercises with thumb stroke towards one direction, only downwards (↑) as shown below:

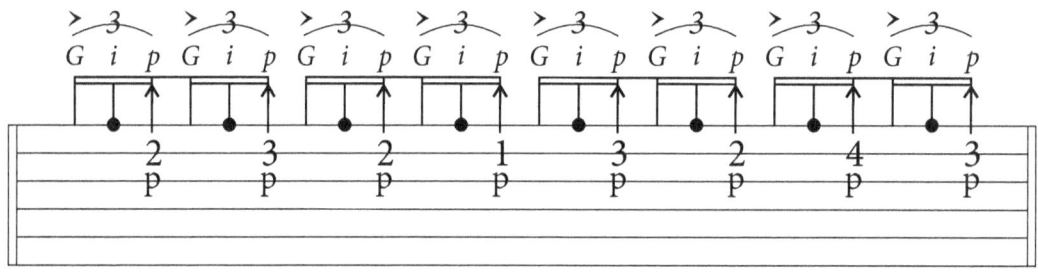

and towards two directions both downwards (↑) and upwards (↓):

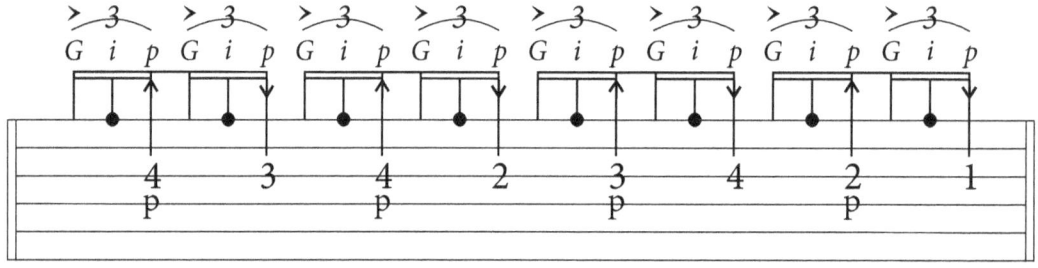

Also there are exercises where there is a thump stroke of two chords (as the above) or thump stroke of three chords.

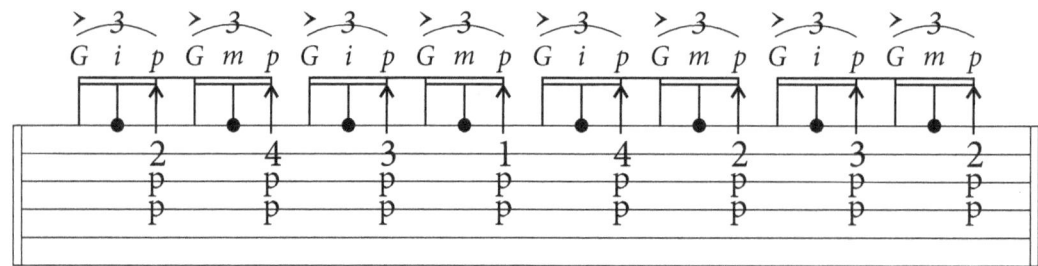

§ I

A

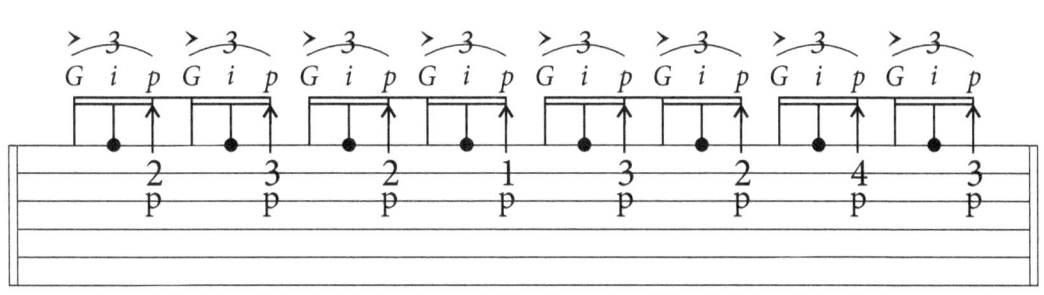

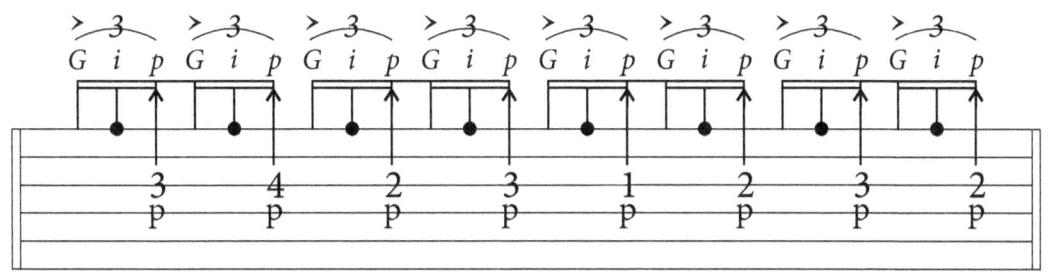

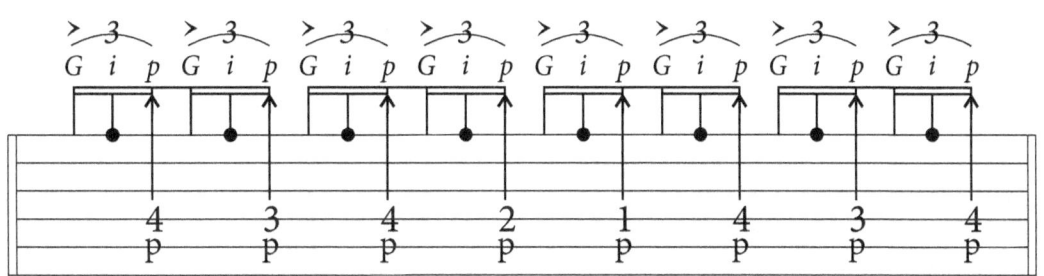

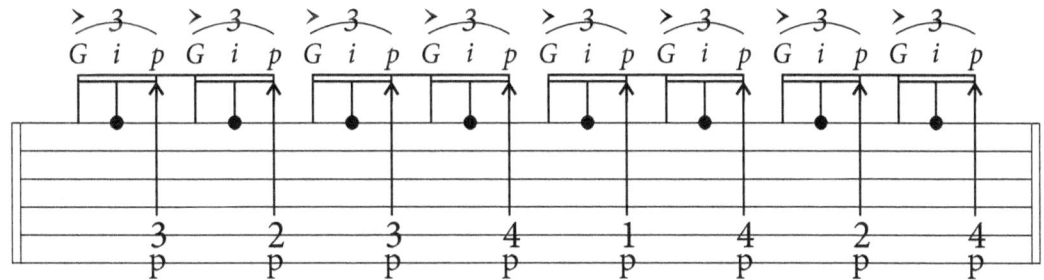

B

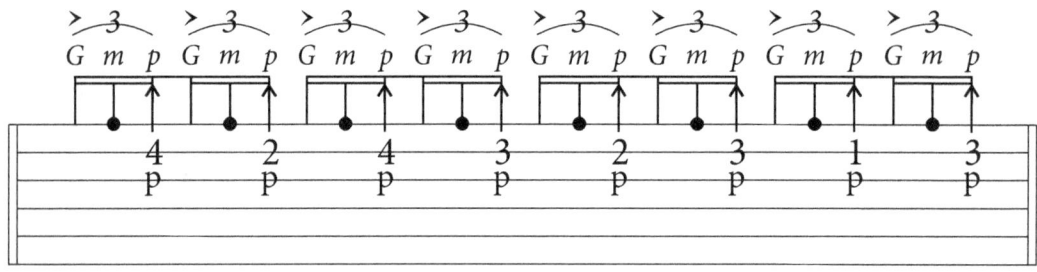
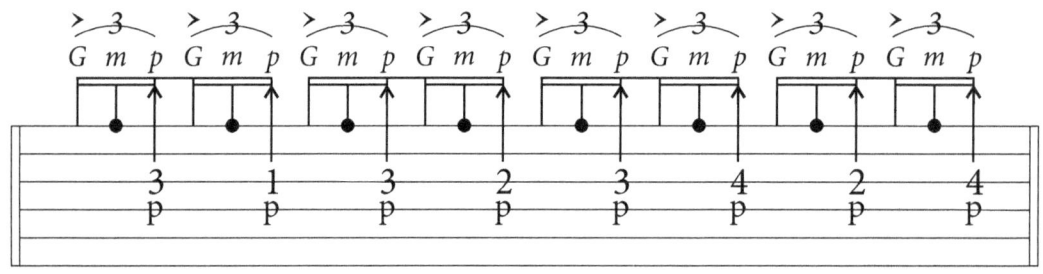
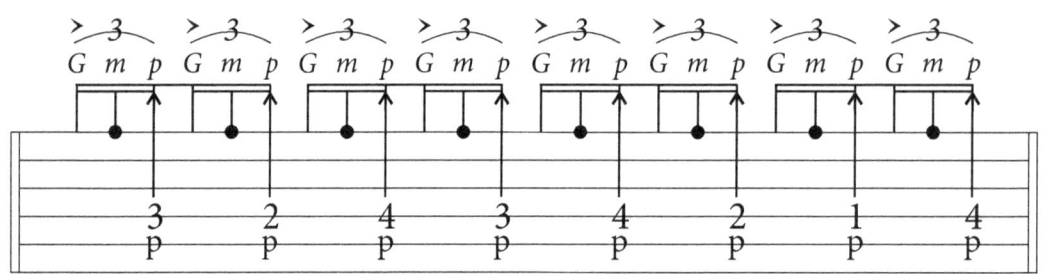
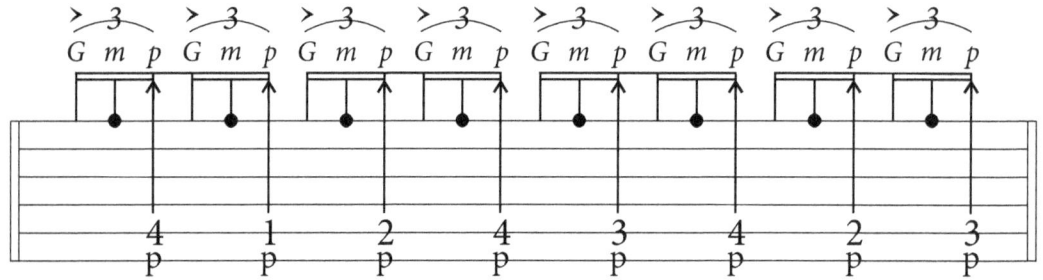

§ II

A

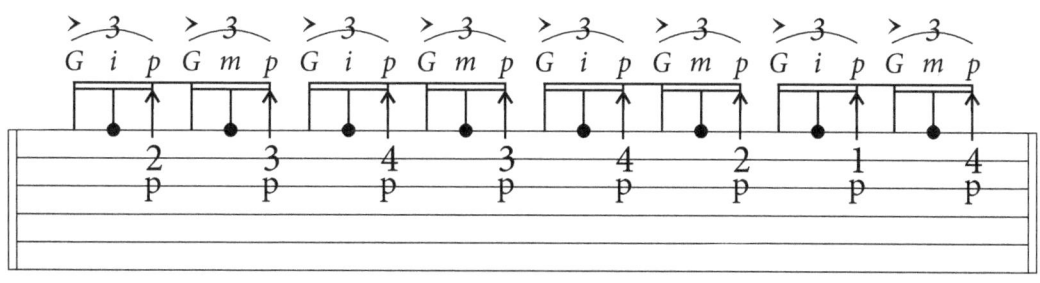

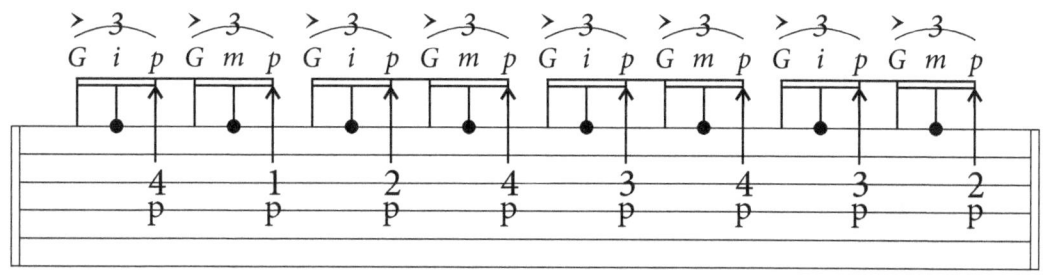

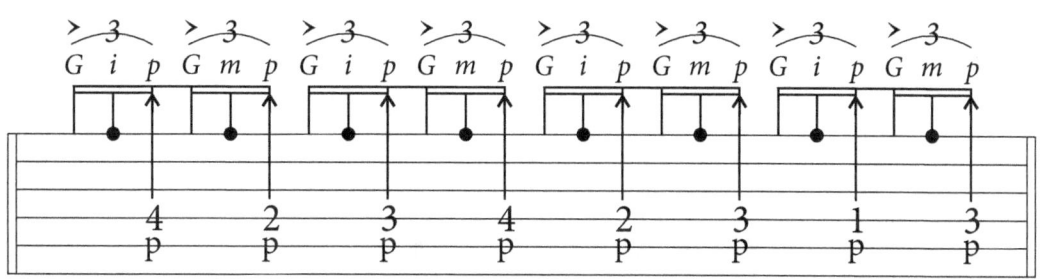

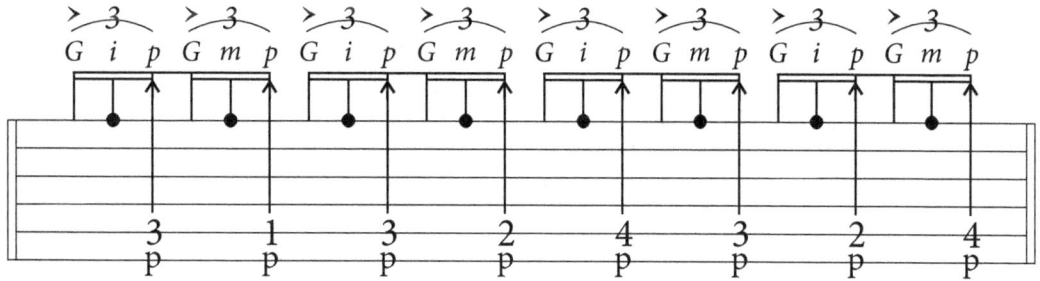

B

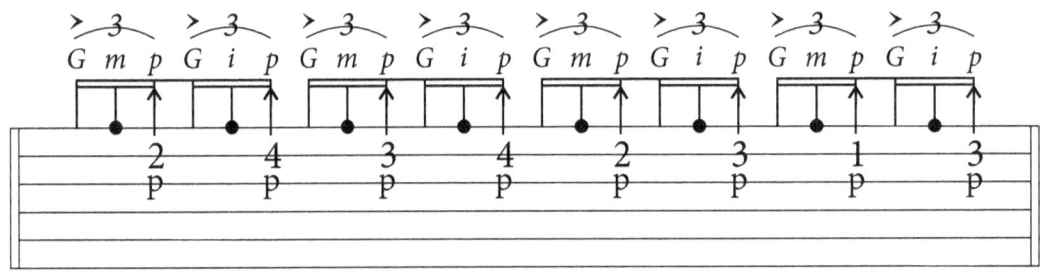
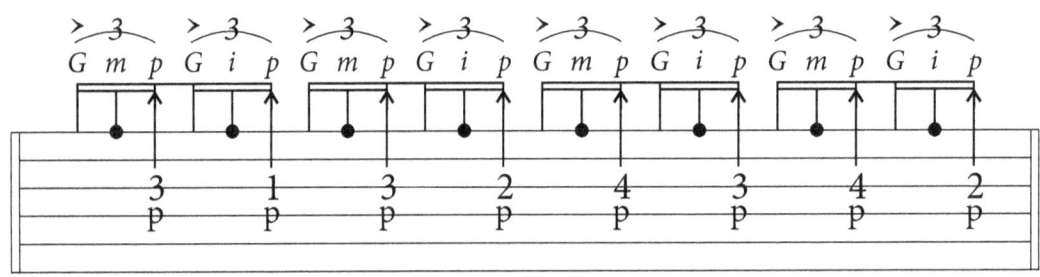
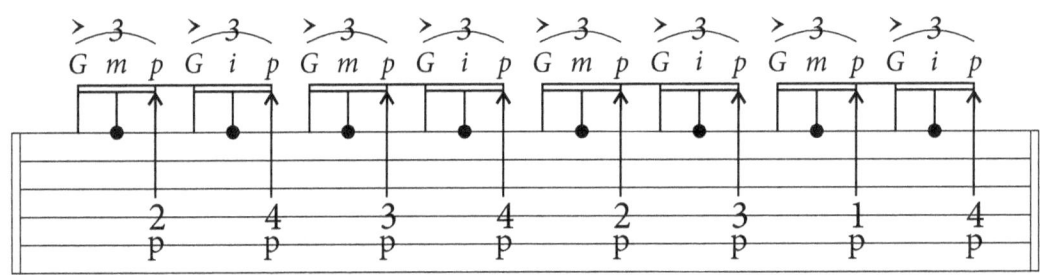
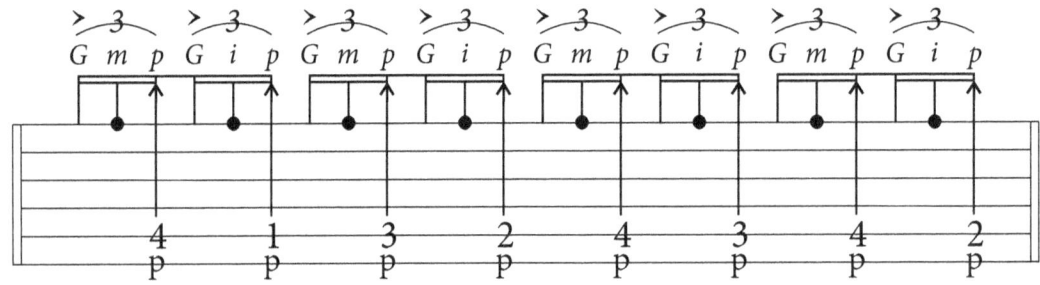

§ III

A

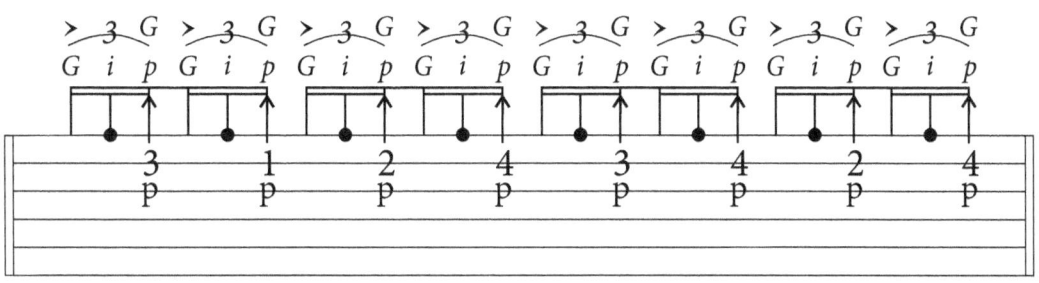

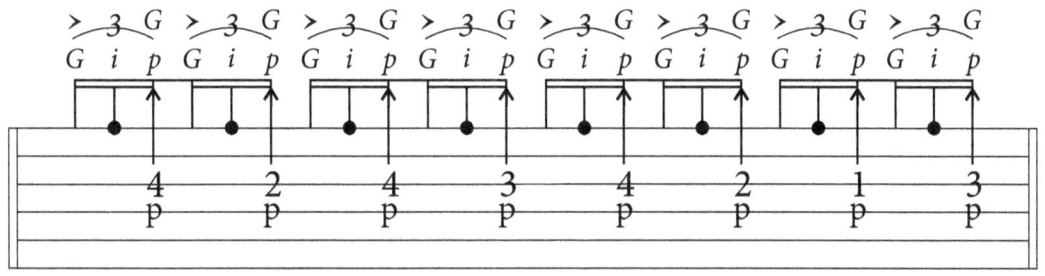

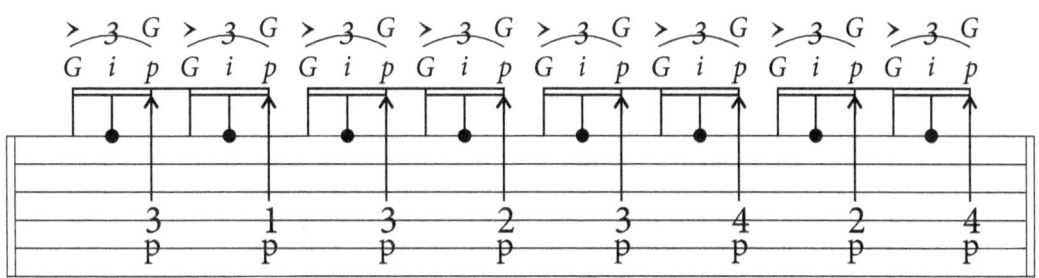

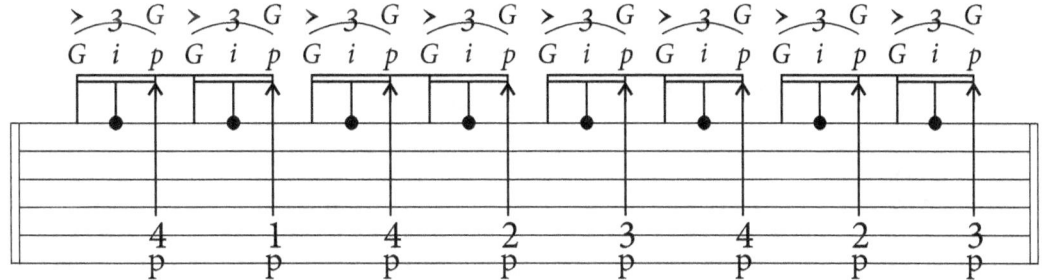

B

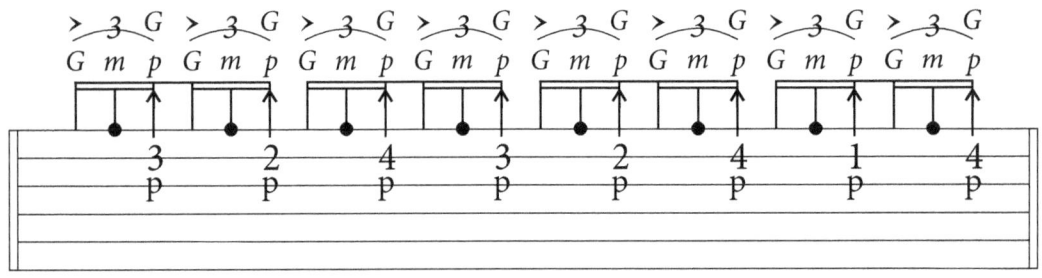
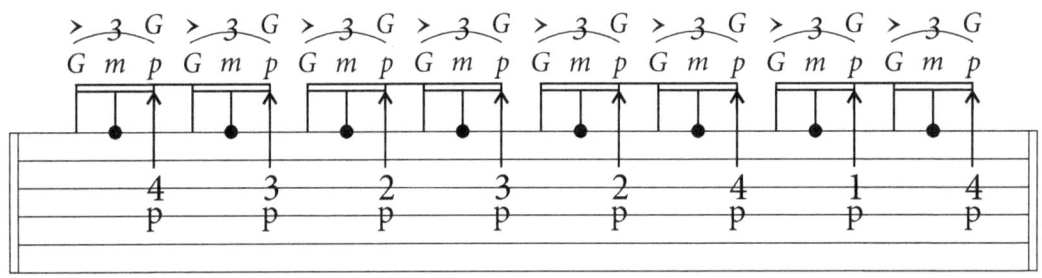
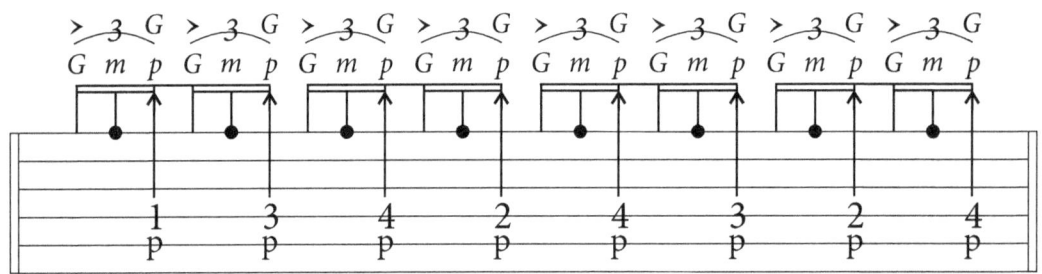
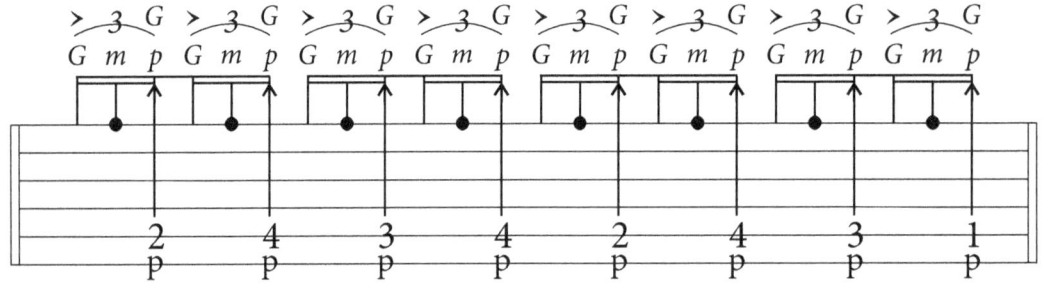

§ IV

A

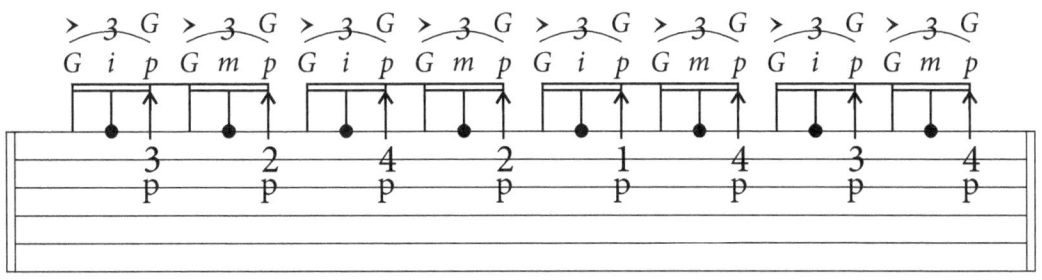

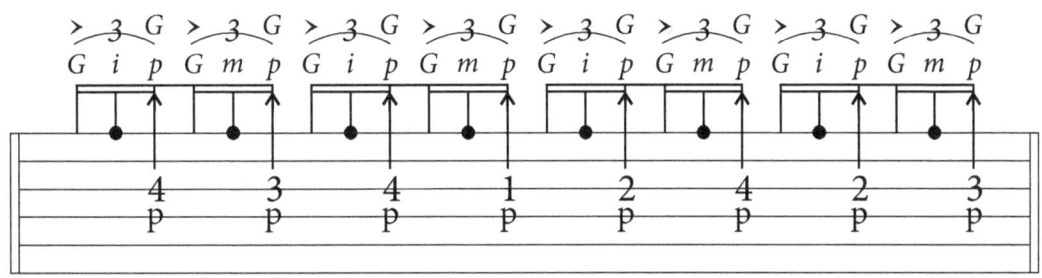

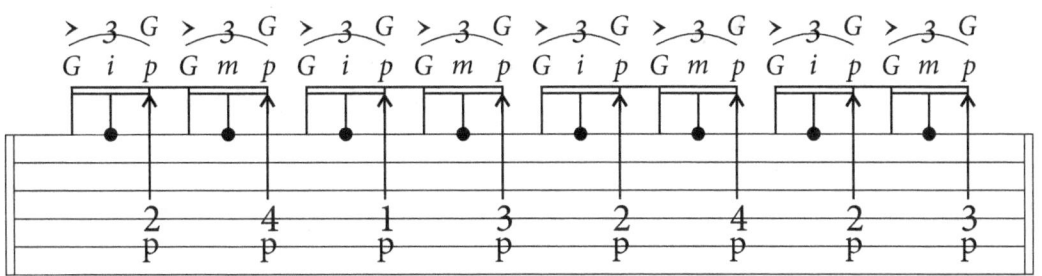

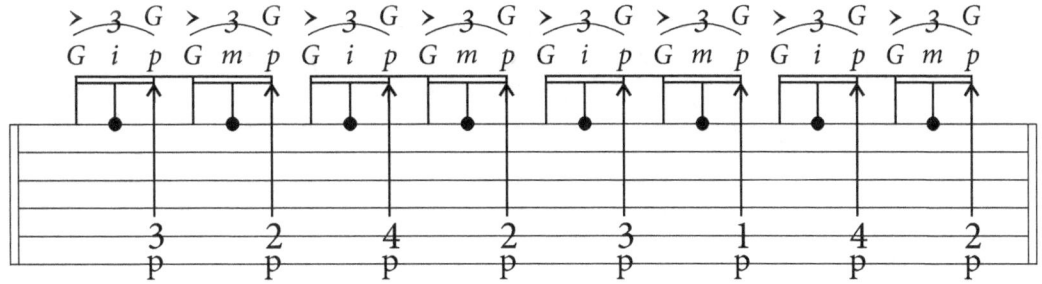

B

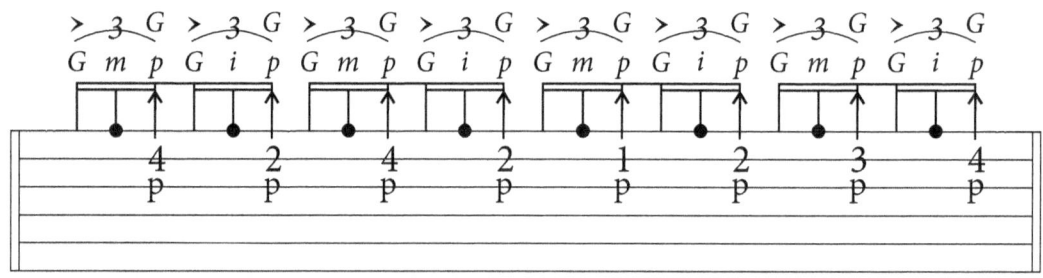
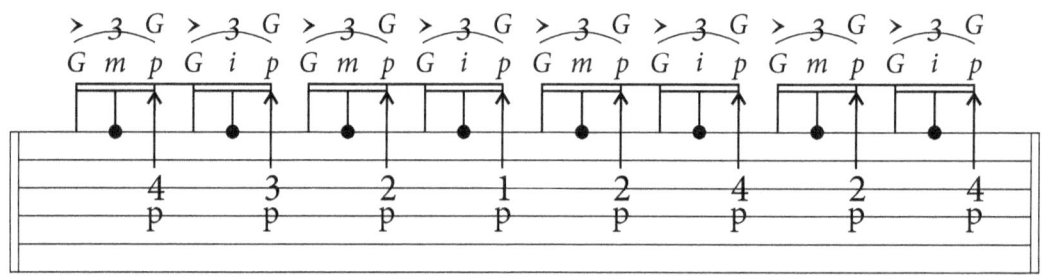
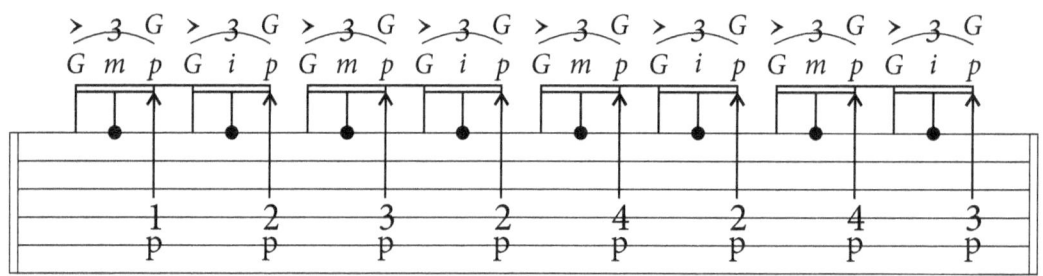
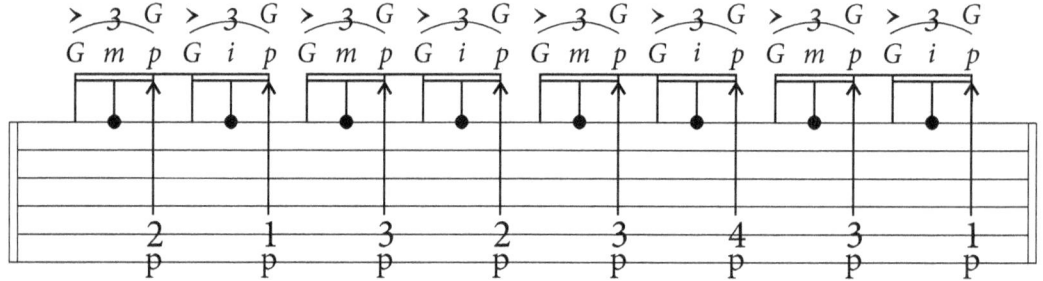

§ V

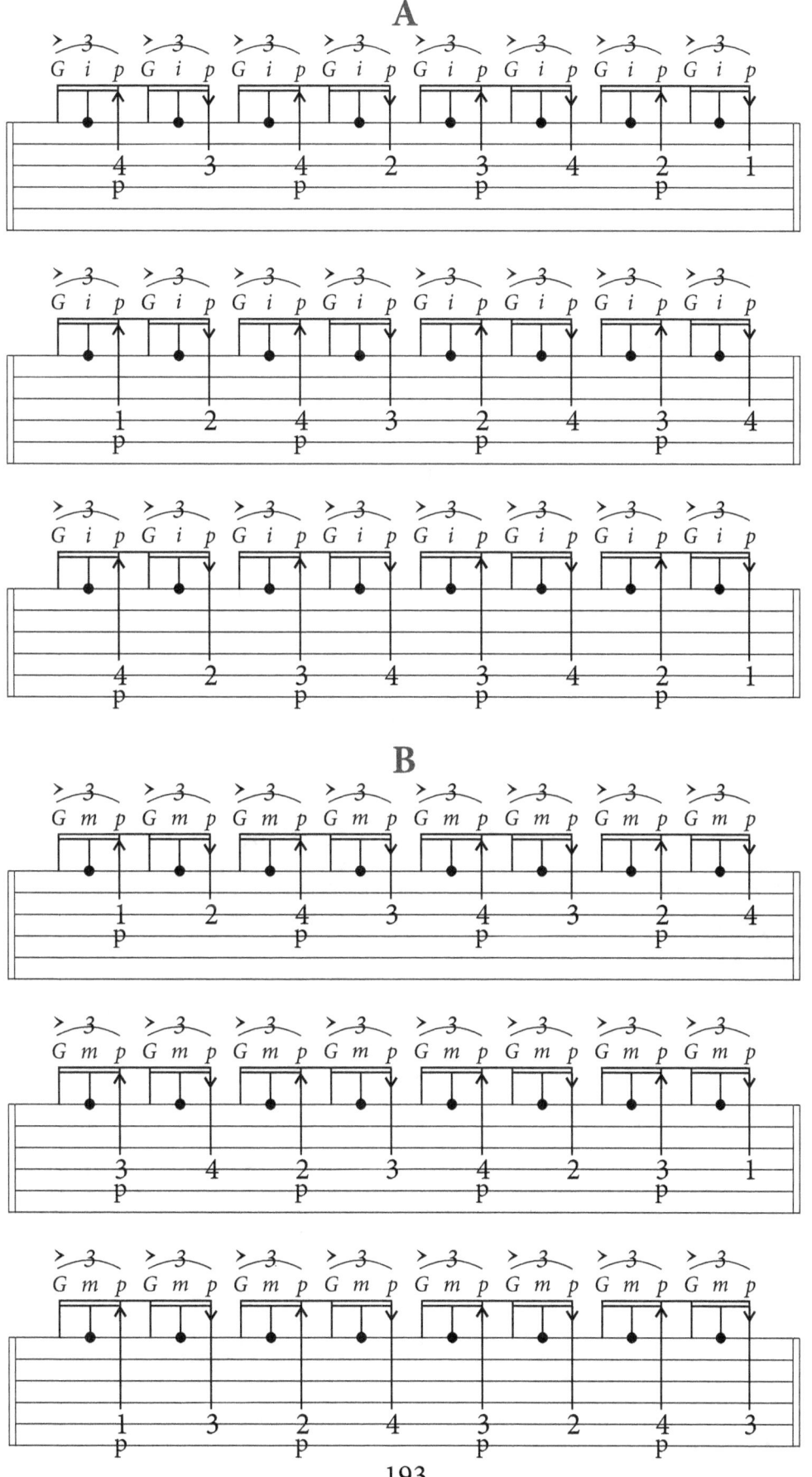

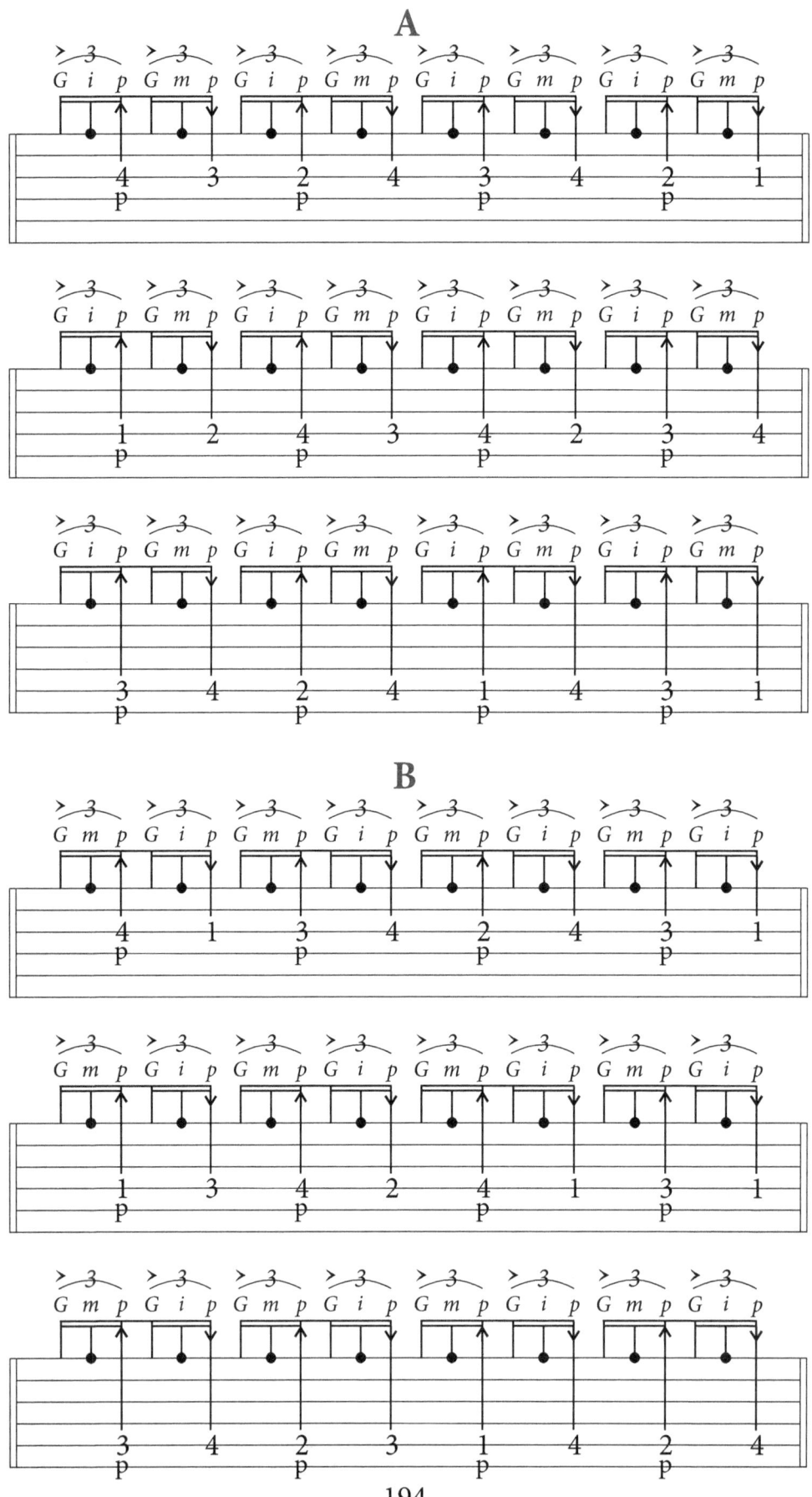

§ VII

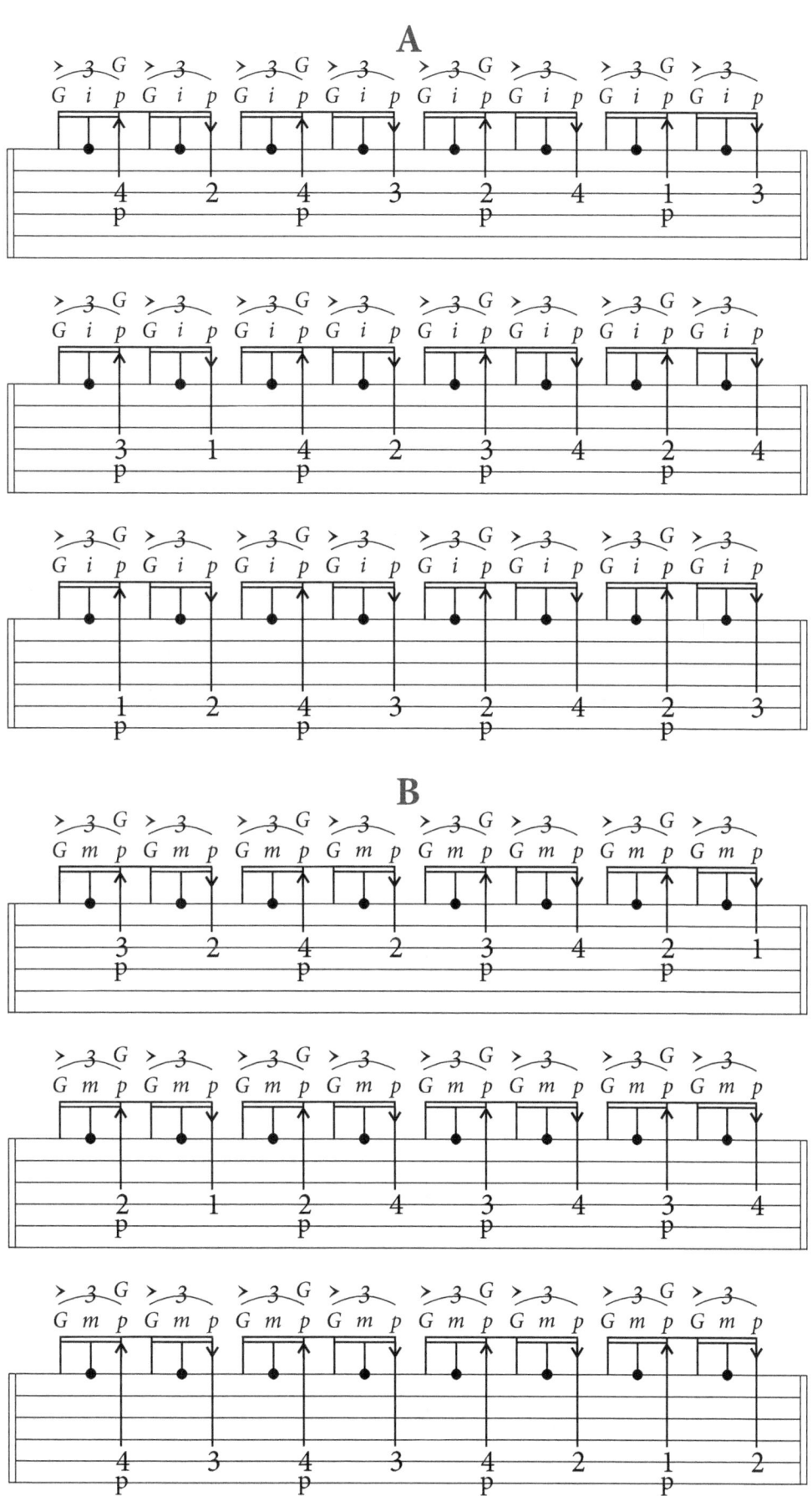

§ VIII

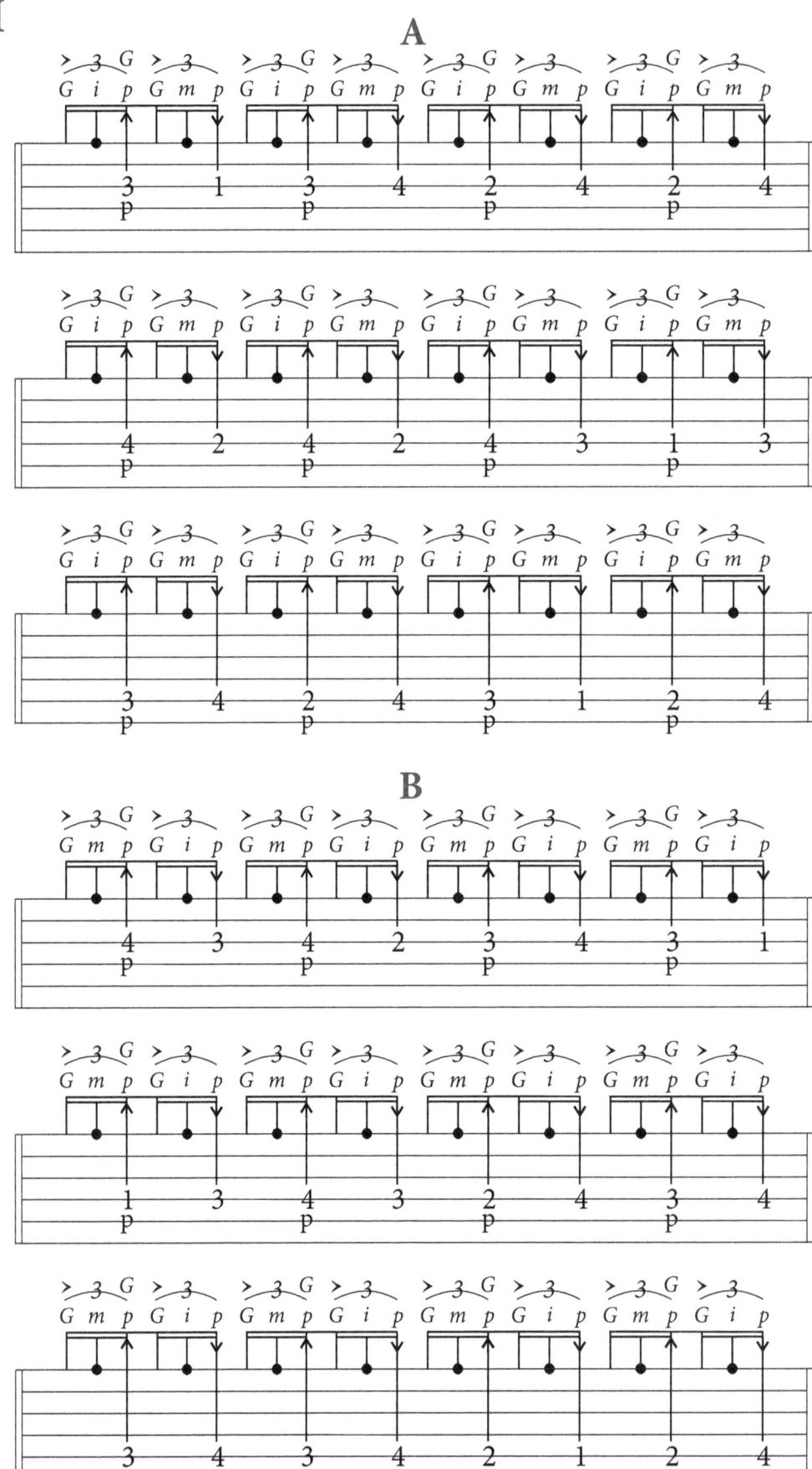

§ IX

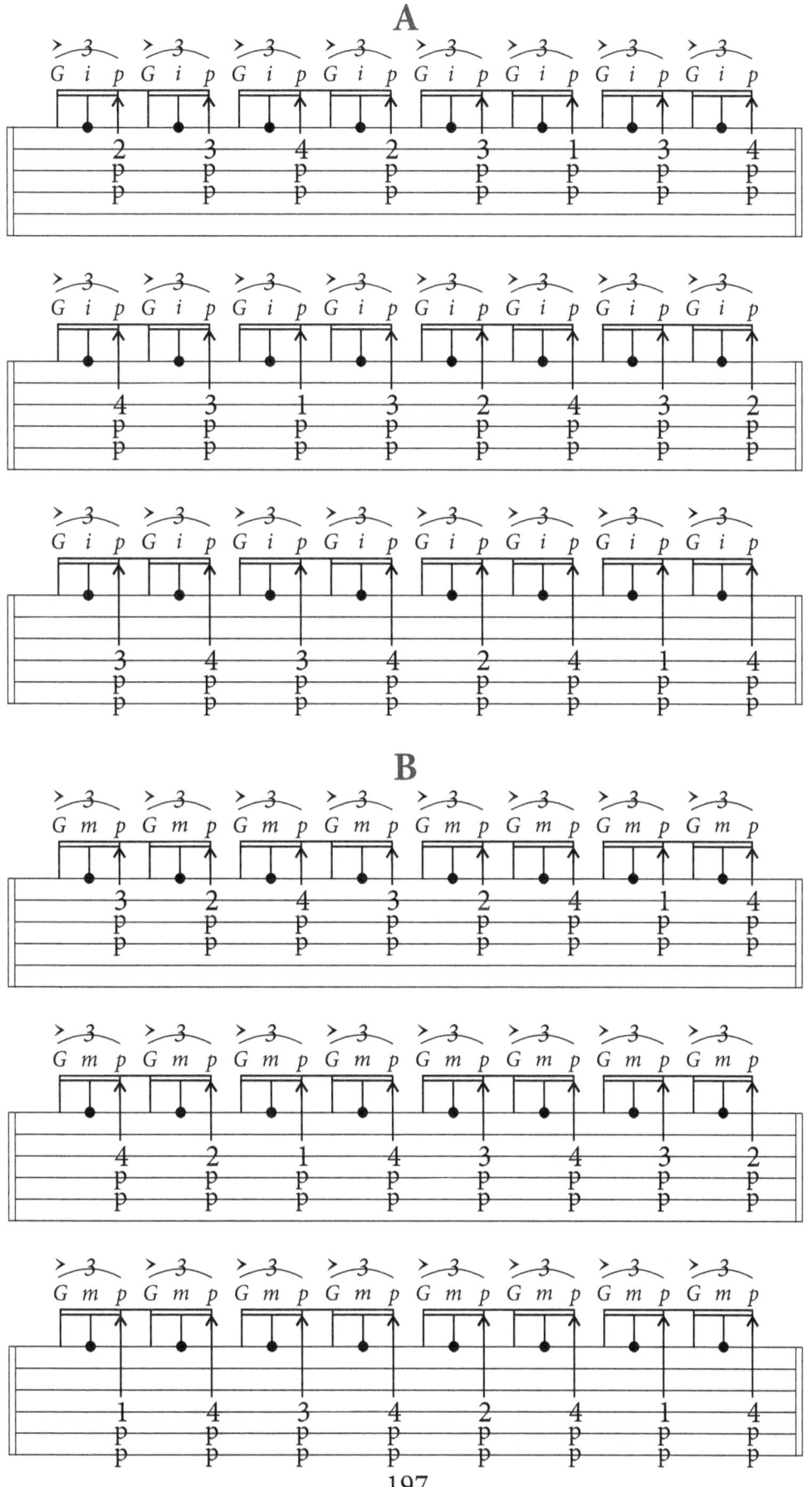

§ X

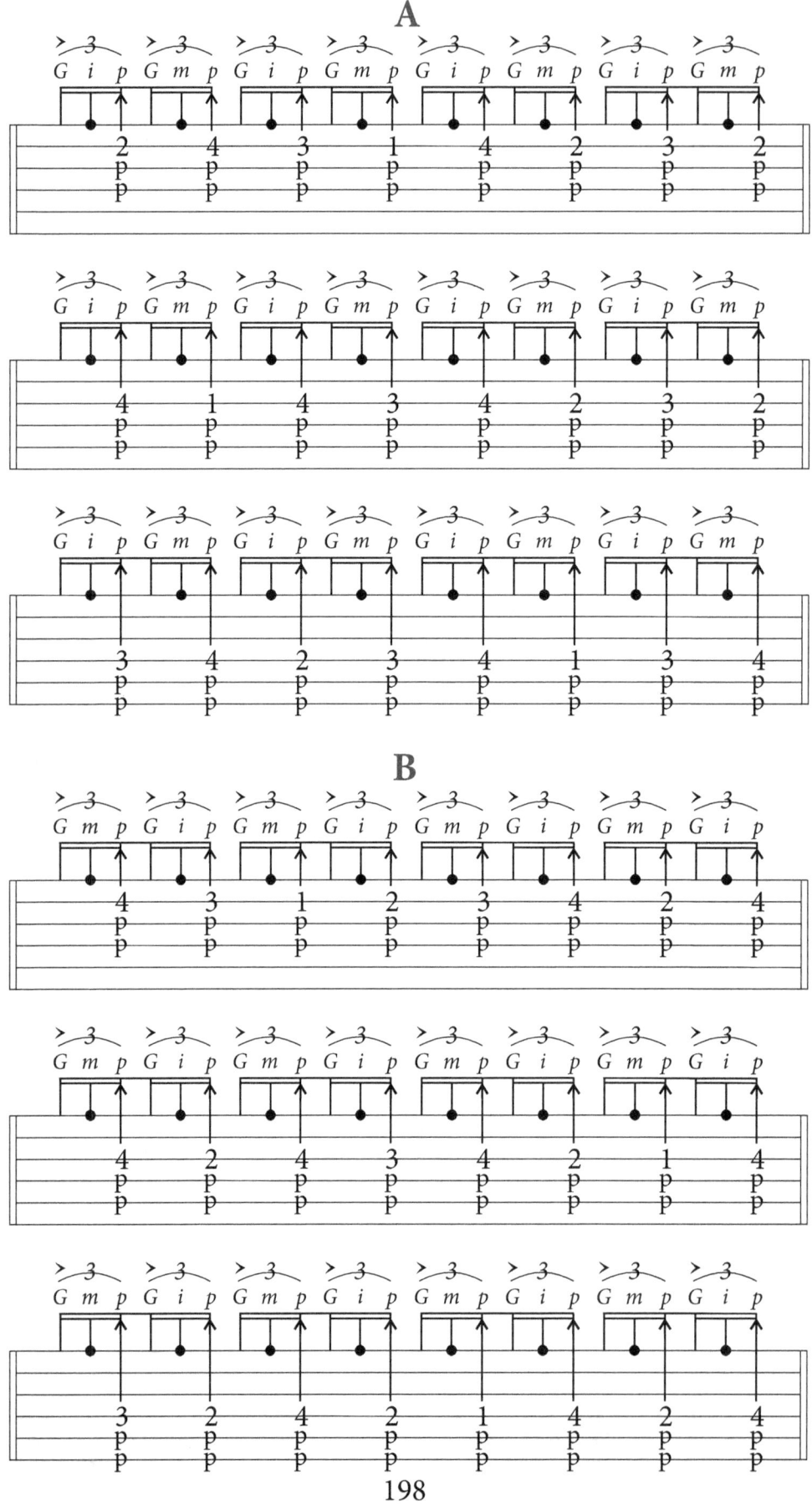

§ XI

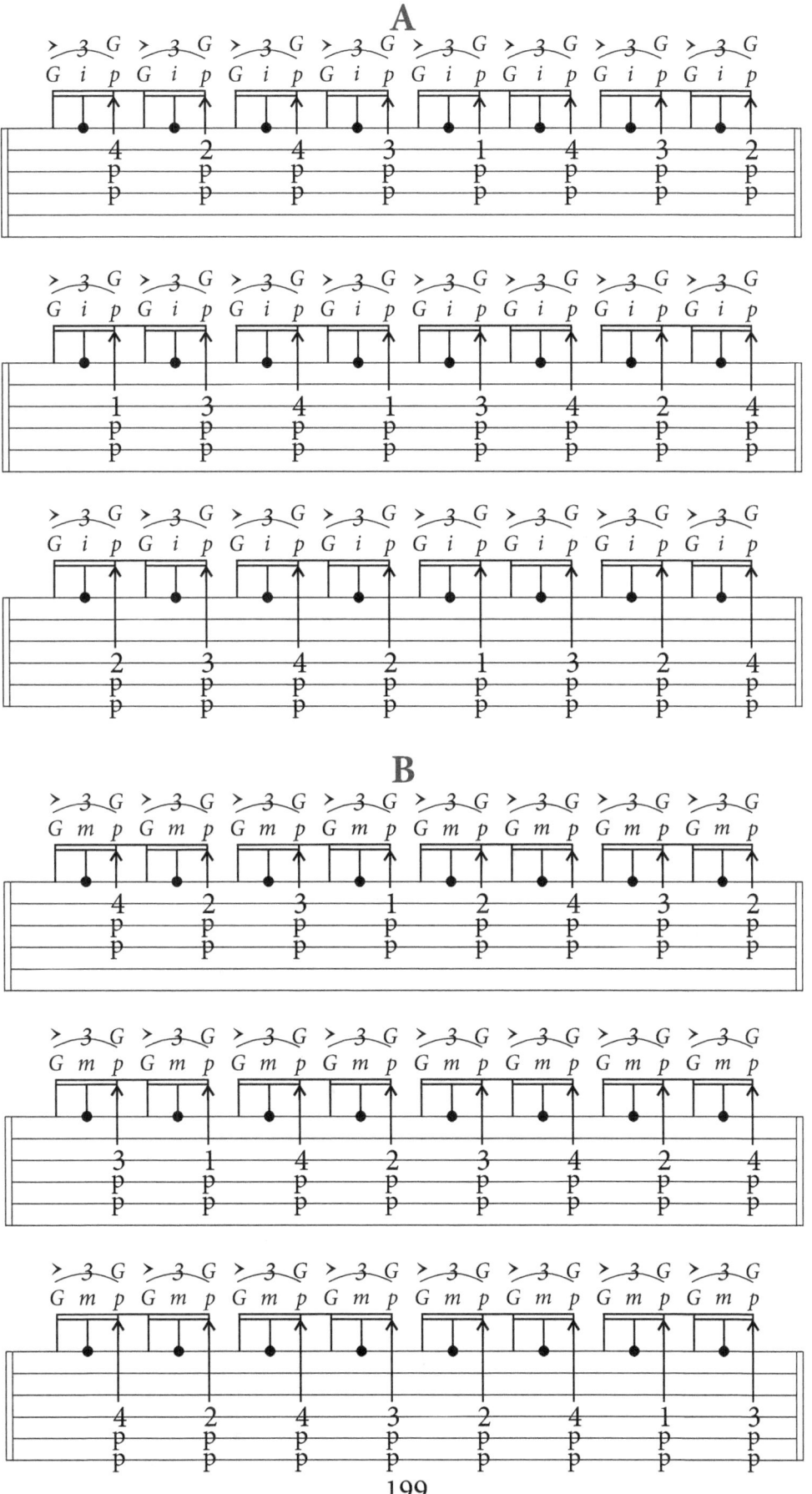

§ XII

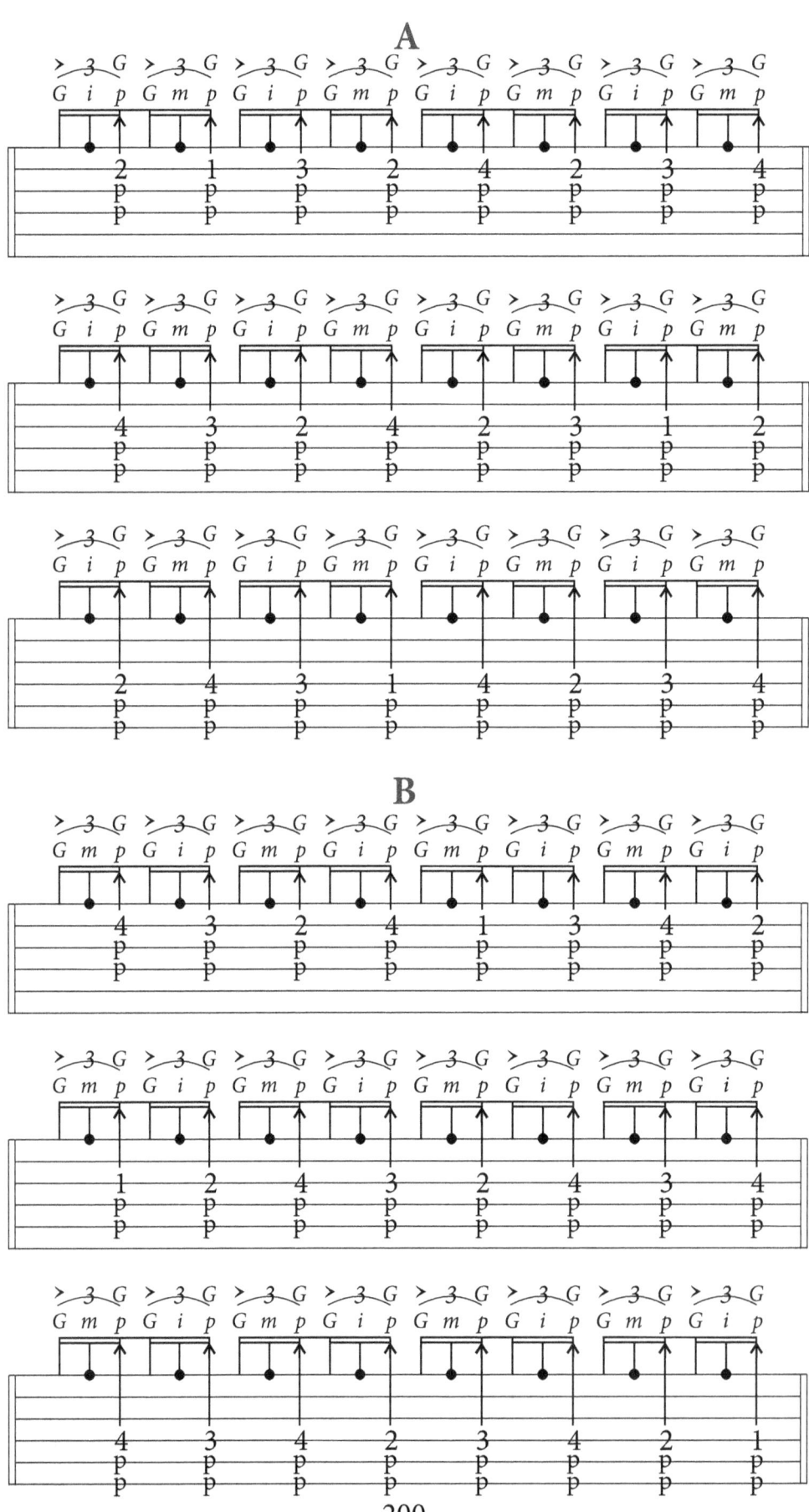

UNIT 3

Golpe exercises in combination with arpegios and ligados.

§I Golpe exercises in combination with arpeggios on the chromatic scales of one string from the 1st to the 6th and also formed as triplets. Right hand fingerings im and mi.

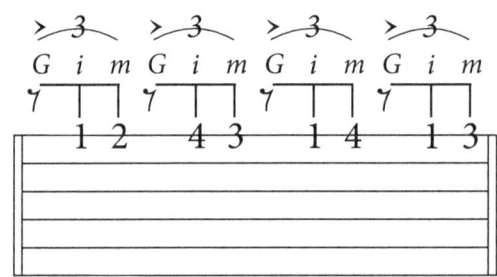

§II Golpe on the chromatic scales of one string which move every two notes:
1/ from the 1st to the 4th string

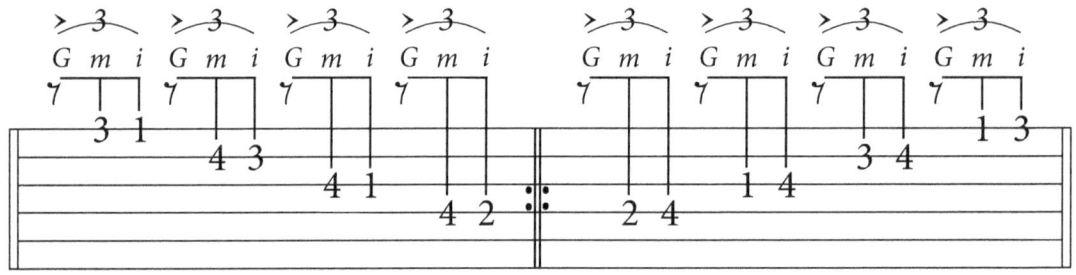

2/ from the 2nd to the 5th string
3/ from the 3rd to the 6th string, returning to the initial strings with the opposite chromatic scales.

§III, §IV, §V, §VI
Variations on the previous exercises with the insertion of ligados within the chromatic scales.

§ I

F1   **F2**

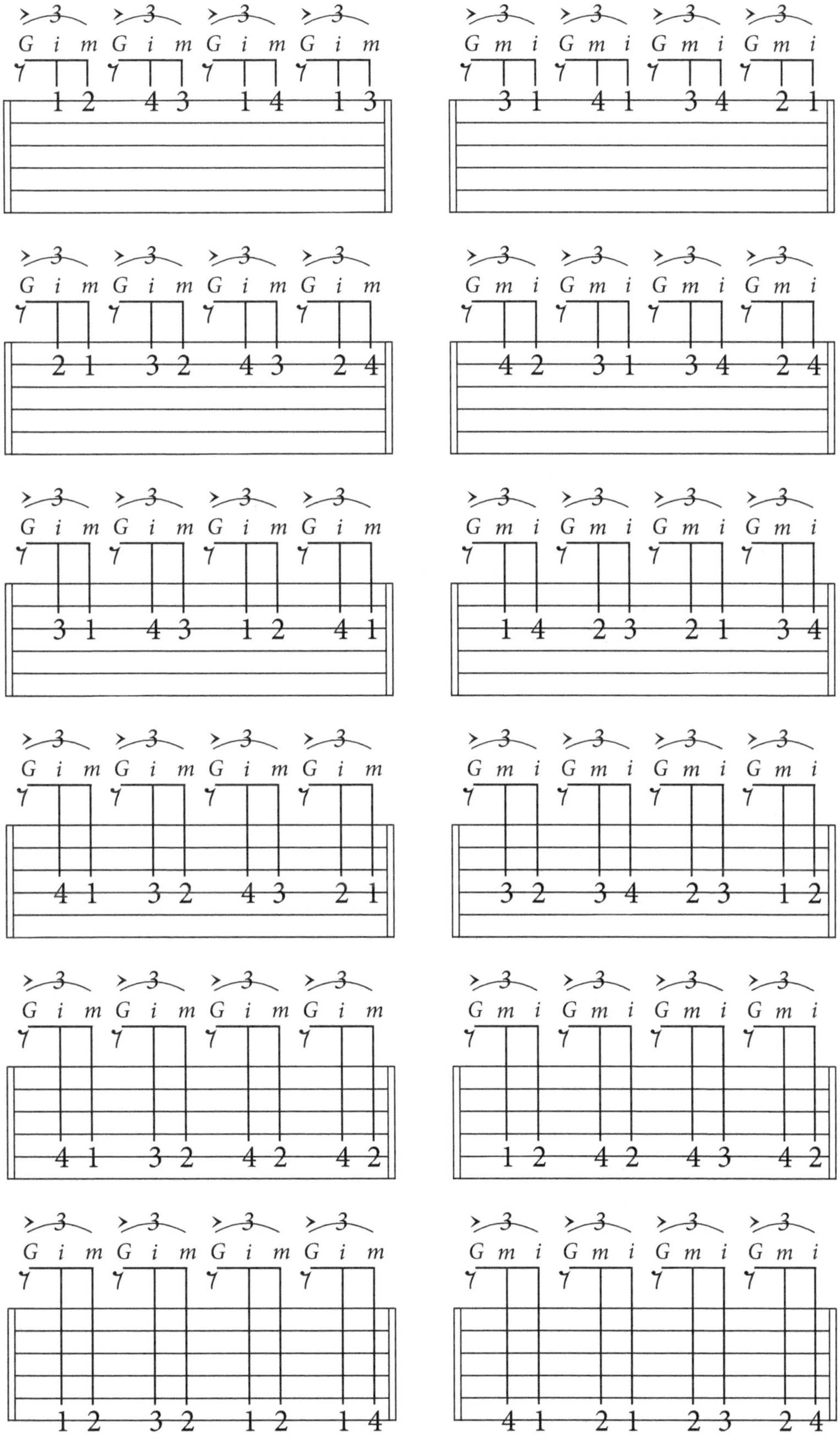

§ II

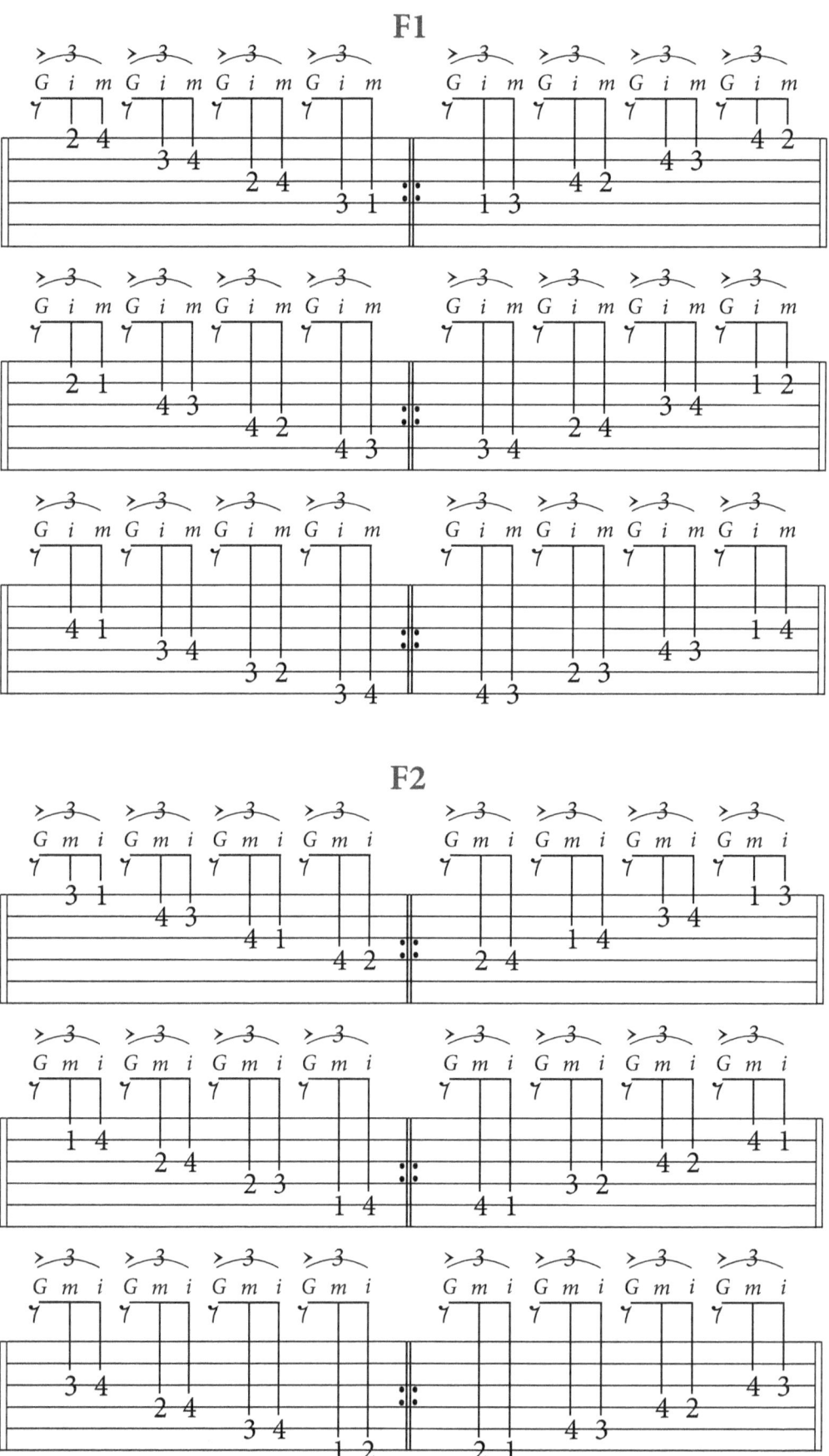

§ III

F1

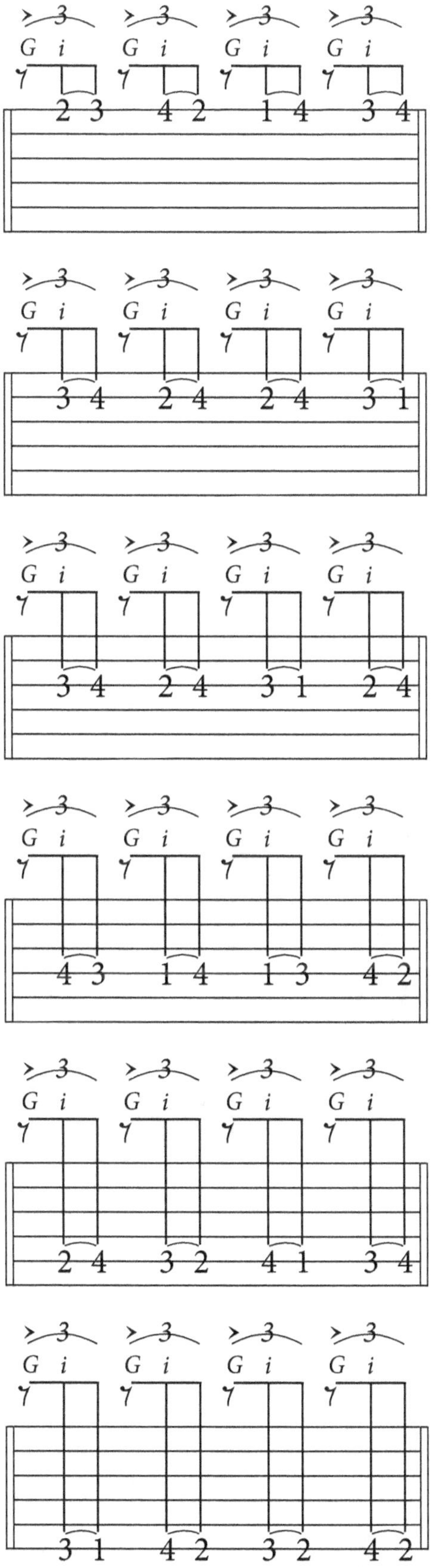
G i G i G i G i
2 3 4 2 1 4 3 4
3 4 2 4 2 4 3 1
3 4 2 4 3 1 2 4
4 3 1 4 1 3 4 2
2 4 3 2 4 1 3 4
3 1 4 2 3 2 4 2

F2

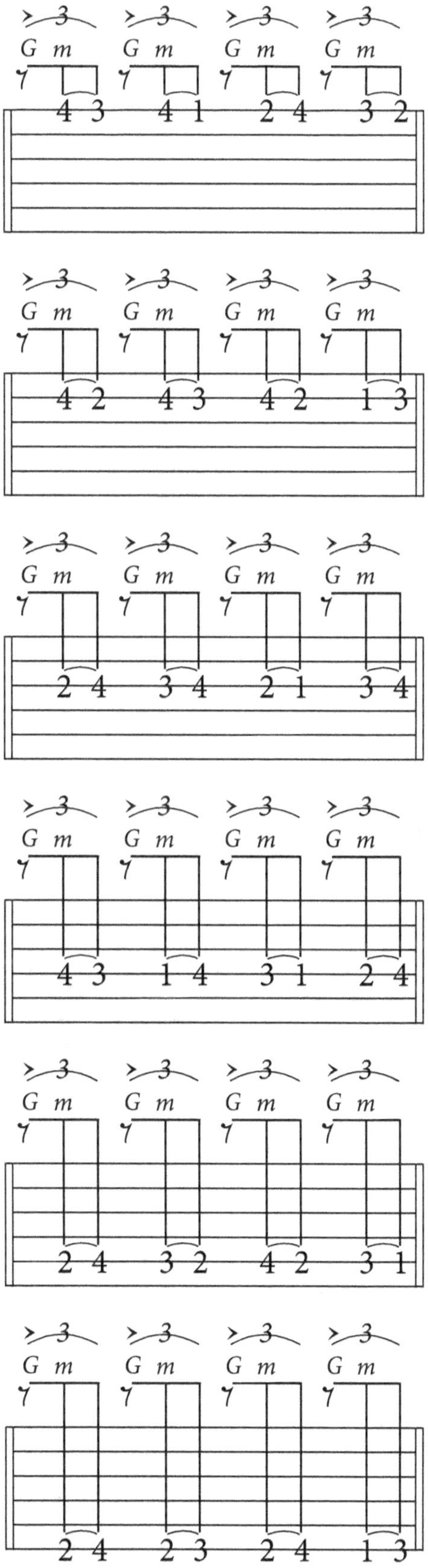
G m G m G m G m
4 3 4 1 2 4 3 2
4 2 4 3 4 2 1 3
2 4 3 4 2 1 3 4
4 3 1 4 3 1 2 4
2 4 3 2 4 2 3 1
2 4 2 3 2 4 1 3

§ IV

F1

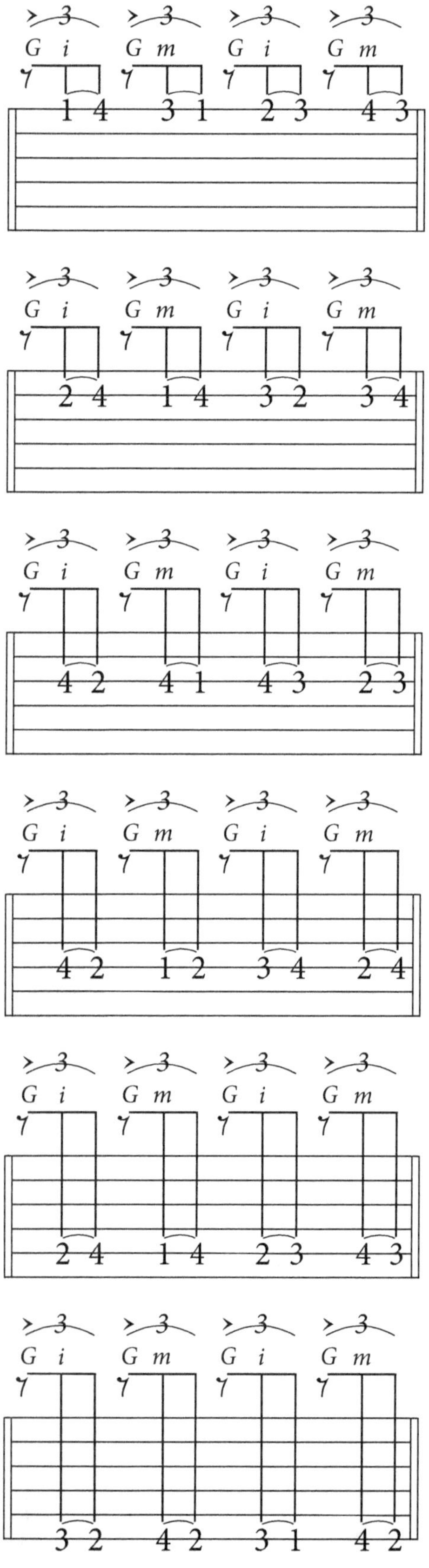
3 3 3 3
G i G m G i G m
1 4 3 1 2 3 4 3
2 4 1 4 3 2 3 4
4 2 4 1 4 3 2 3
4 2 1 2 3 4 2 4
2 4 1 4 2 3 4 3
3 2 4 2 3 1 4 2

F2

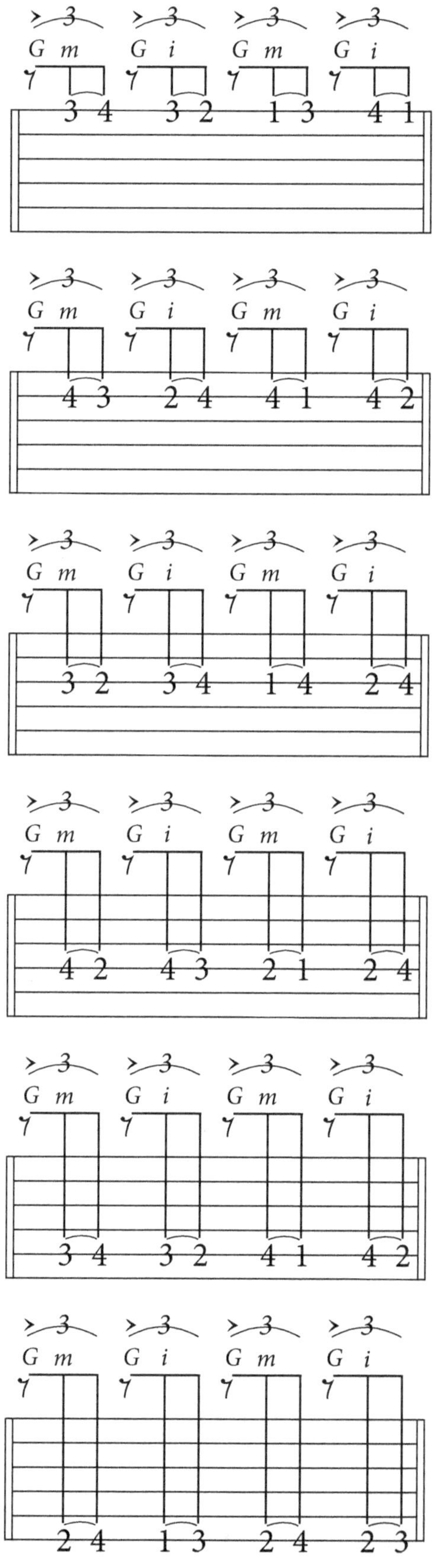
3 3 3 3
G m G i G m G i
3 4 3 2 1 3 4 1
4 3 2 4 4 1 4 2
3 2 3 4 1 4 2 4
4 2 4 3 2 1 2 4
3 4 3 2 4 1 4 2
2 4 1 3 2 4 2 3

§ V

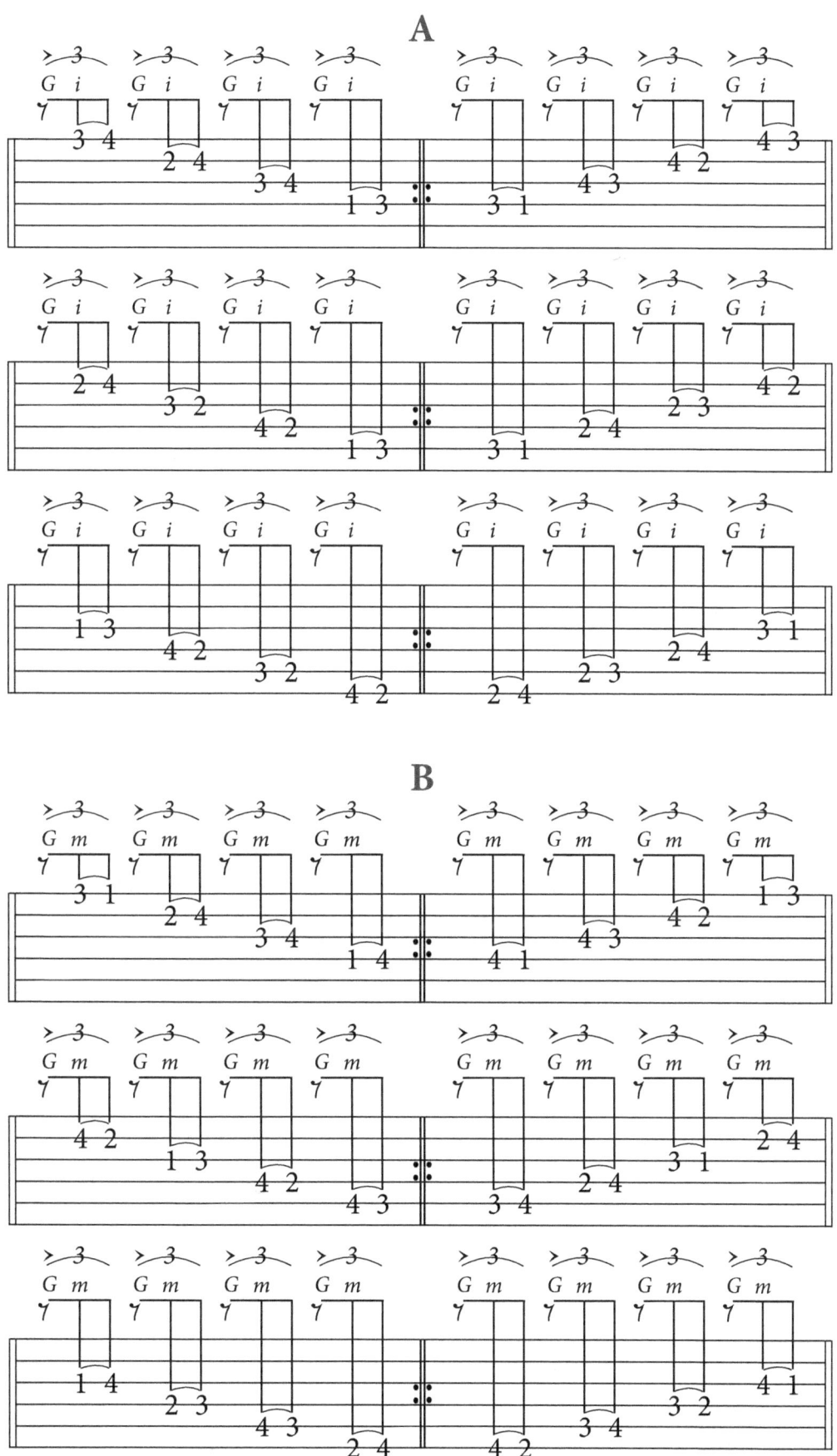

§ VI

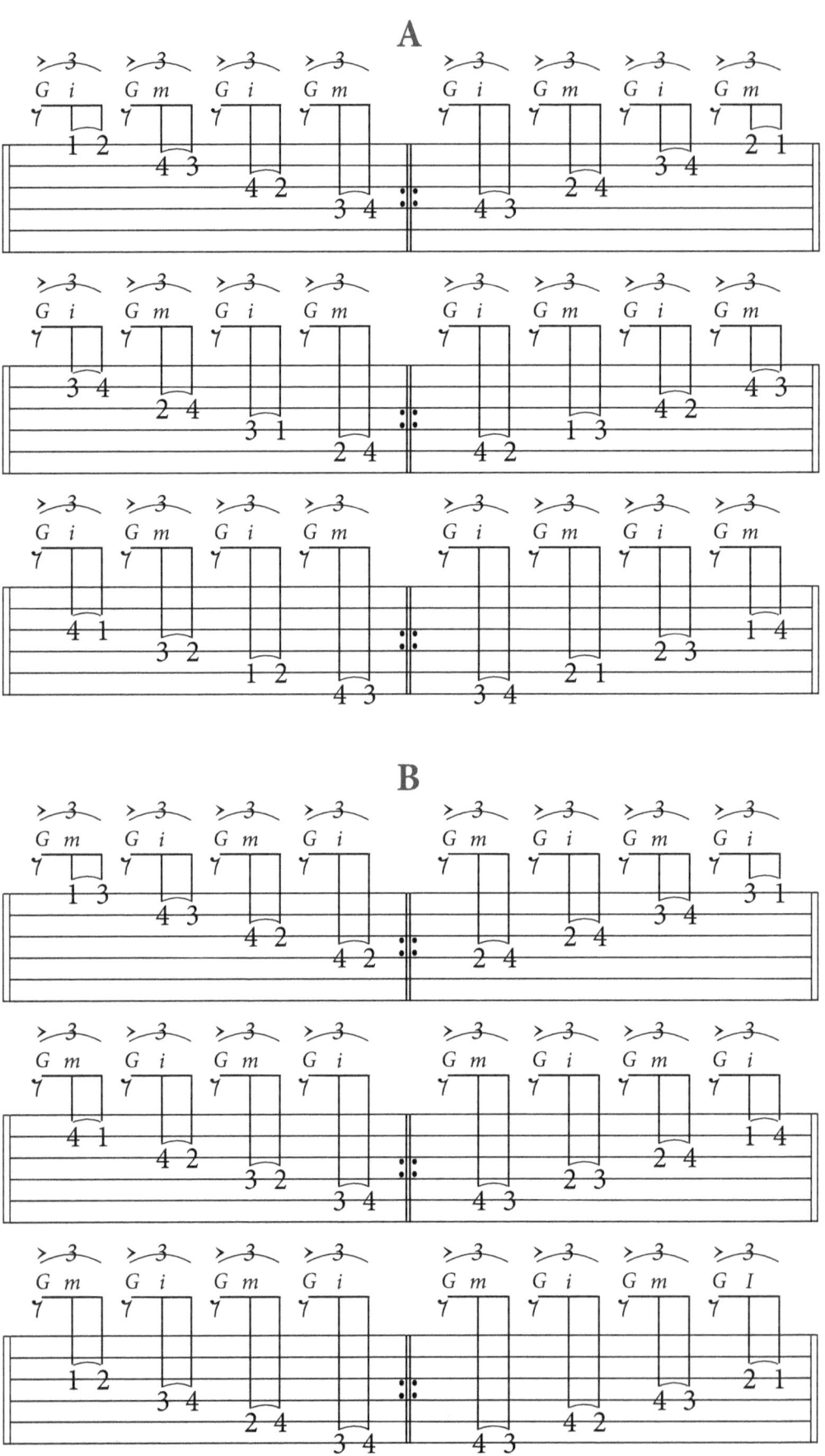

CHAPTER 5
SIMULTANEOUS STROKE OF THUMB
WITH INDEX (i) OR MIDDLE (m) FINGER AND GOLPE.

UNIT 1

Thumb stroke simultaneously
with index (i) or middle finger (m).
Two Golpe within meter.

§I Simultaneous stroke of the thumb and the index (i) or middle finger (m) of the right hand. Chromatic scales of one string on the 1st, 2nd, 3rd, 4th and 5th string. Two Golpe within each meter.

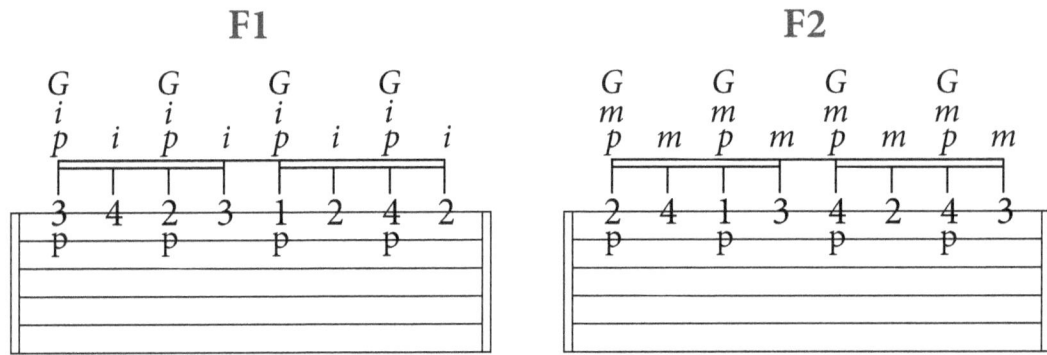

§II The thumb strikes steadily the 6th string and the chromatic scale moves every two notes:

1/ from the 1st to the 4th string and returns from the 4th to the 1st string with the opposite scale.

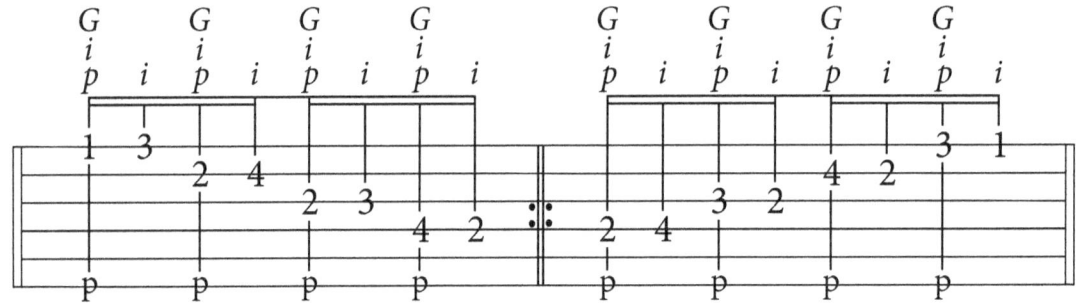

2/ from the 2nd to the 5th string and returns from the 5th to the 2nd string with the opposite scale.

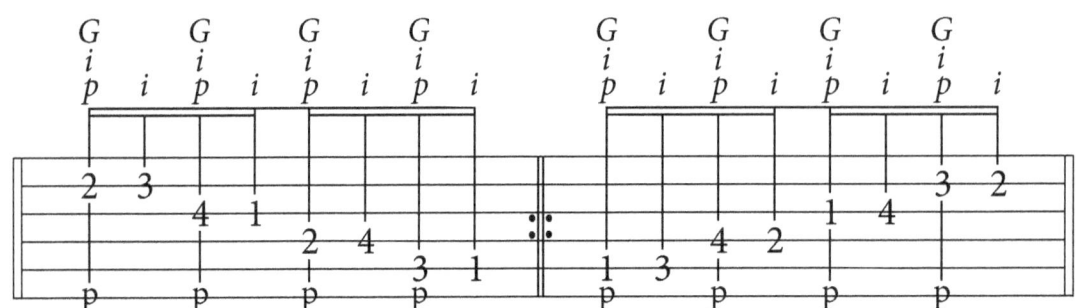

§III, §IV, §V Variations on the previous exercises.

§ III

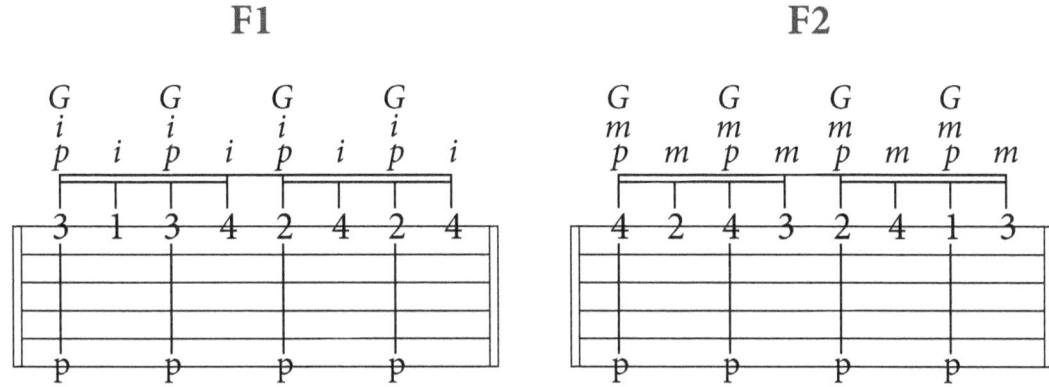

§ IV

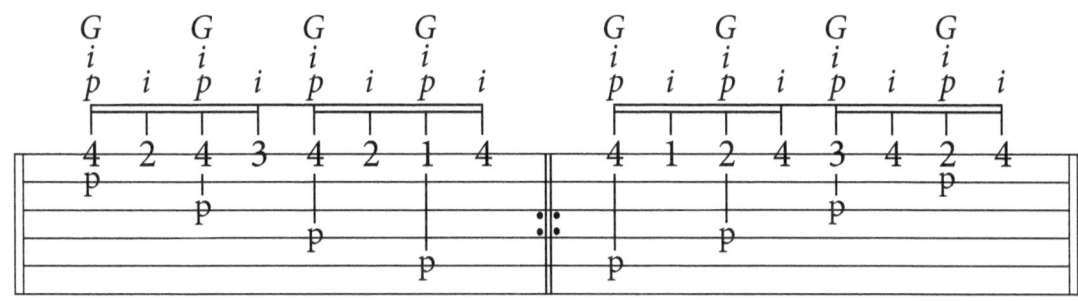

§ V

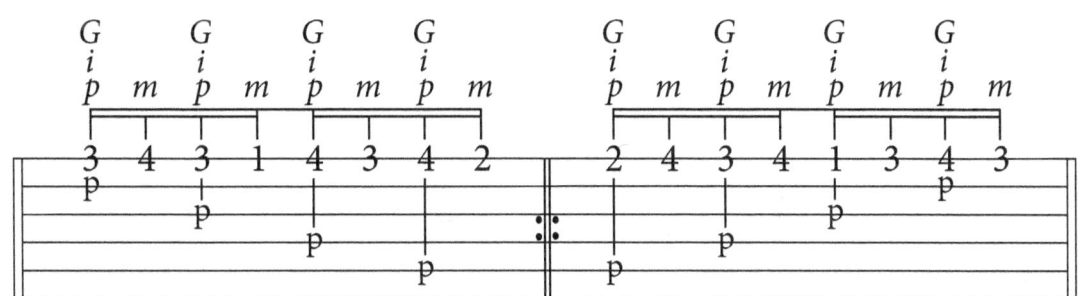

§VI, §VII Variations with interchange of index and middle finger.

§ VI

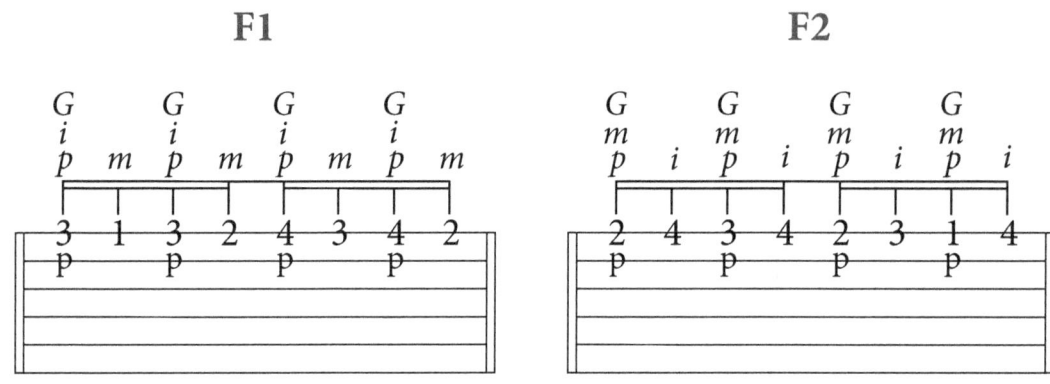

§ VII

A

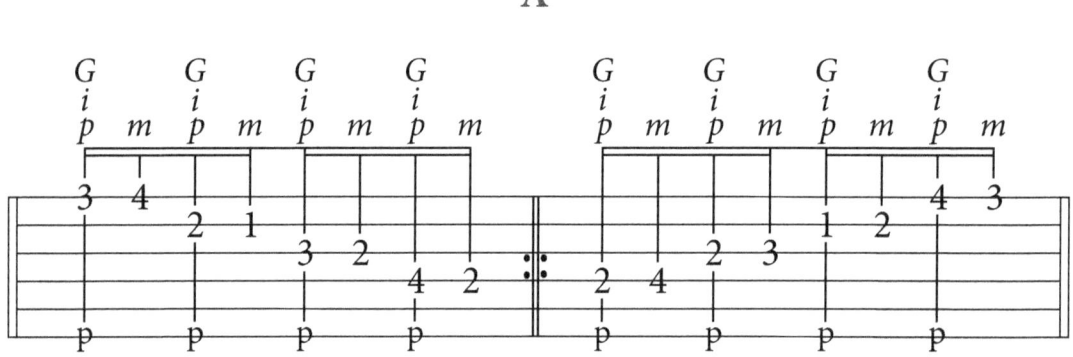

B

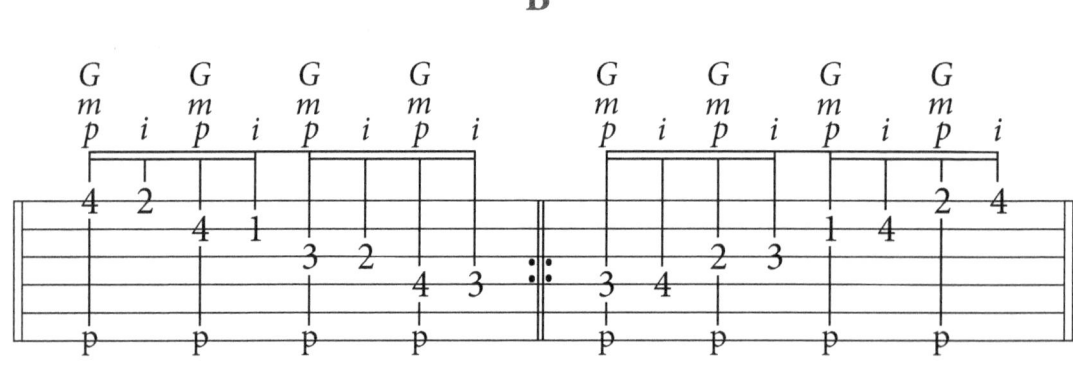

§ I

F1 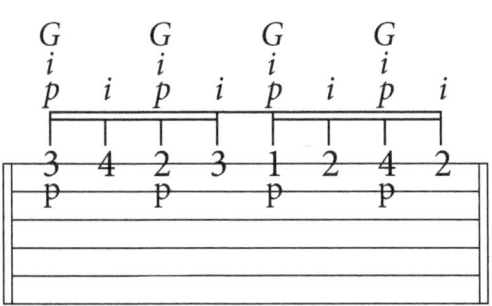 **F2**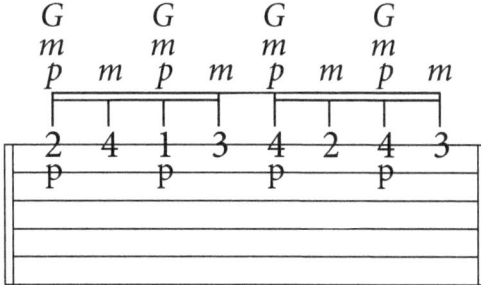

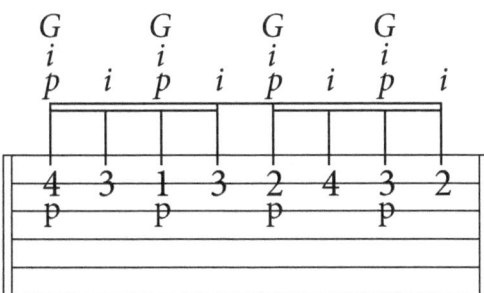 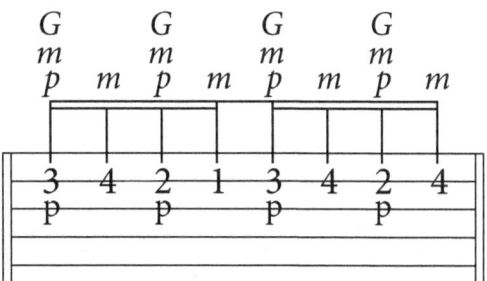

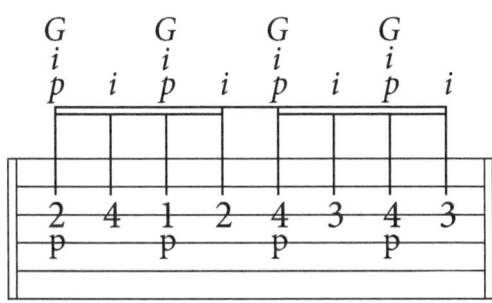 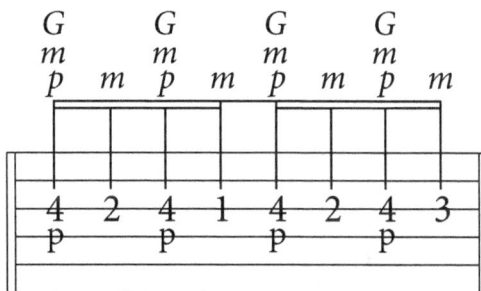

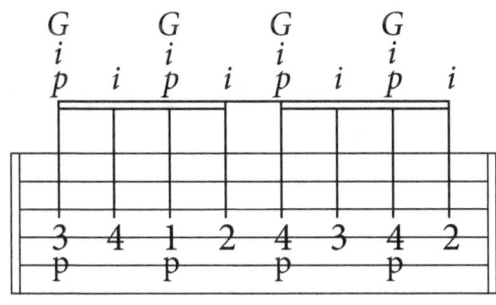 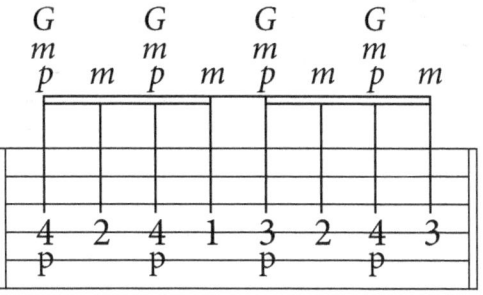

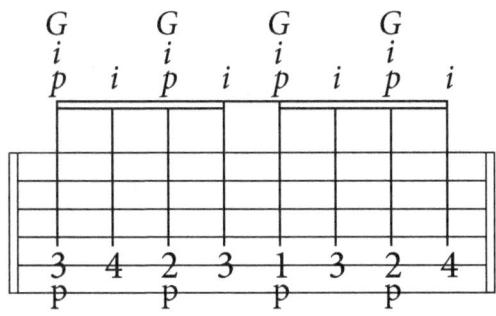 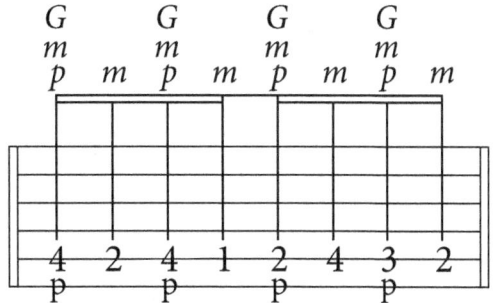

§ II

A

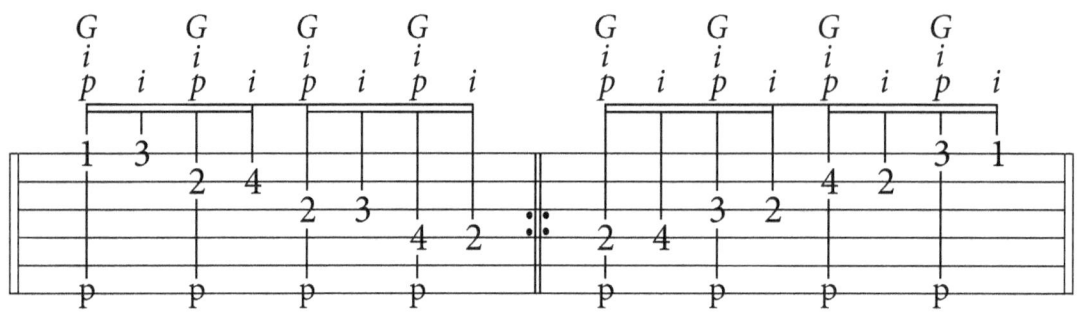

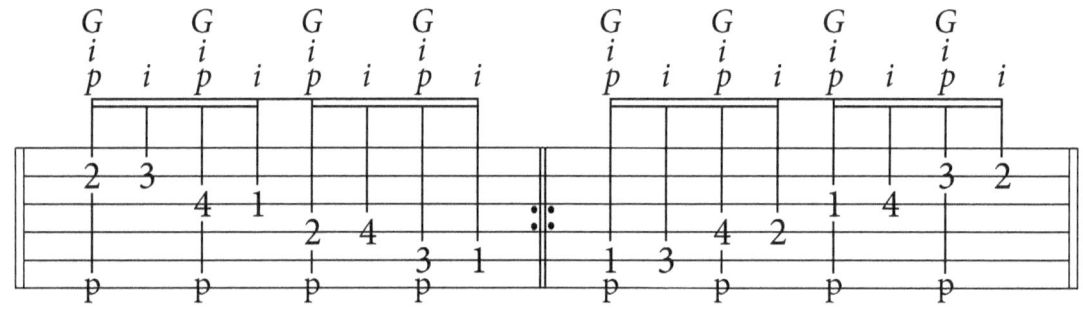

B

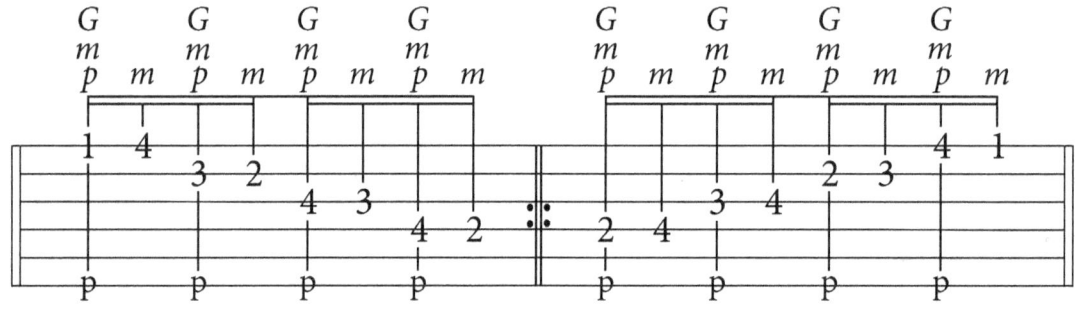

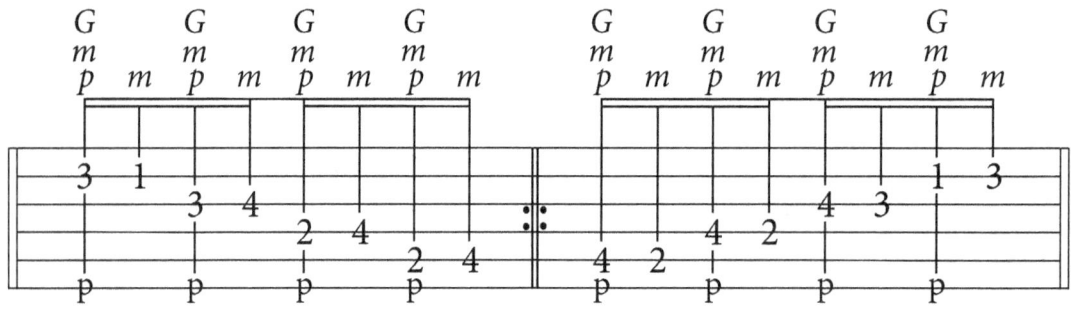

§ III

F1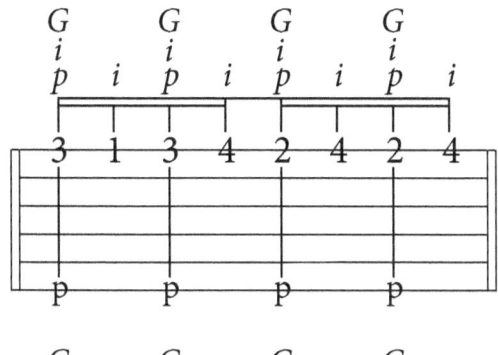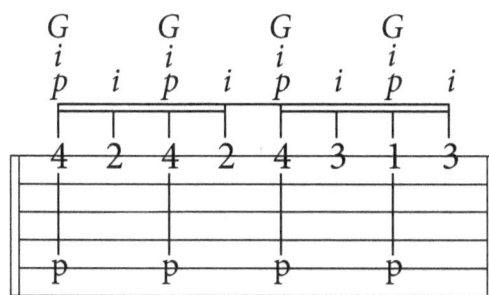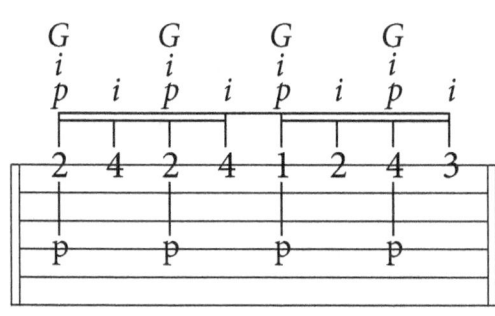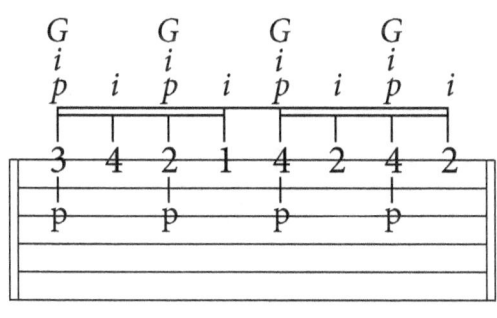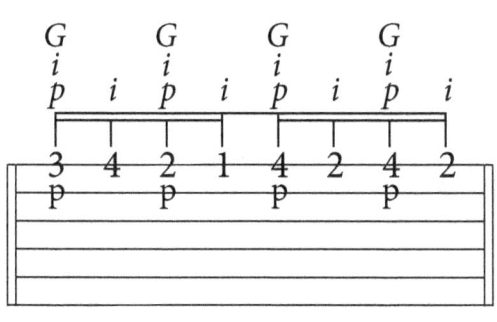

F2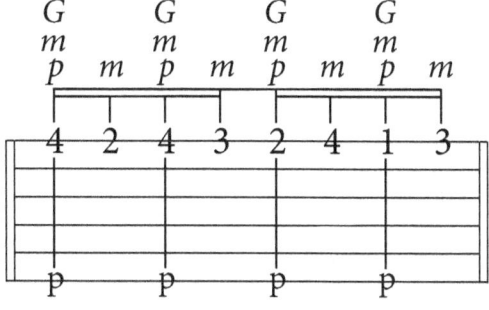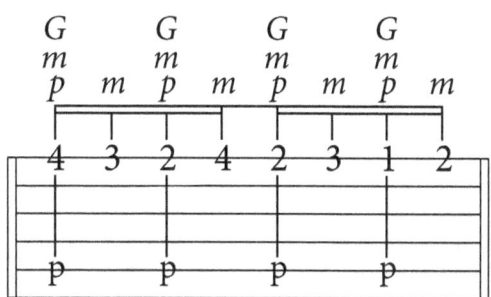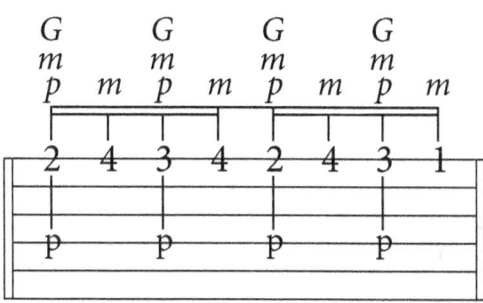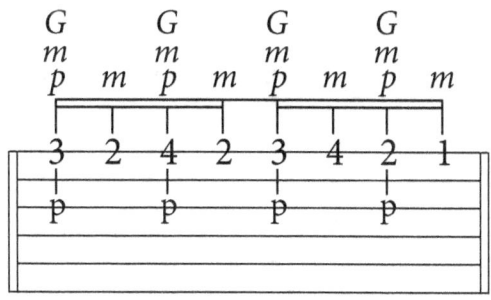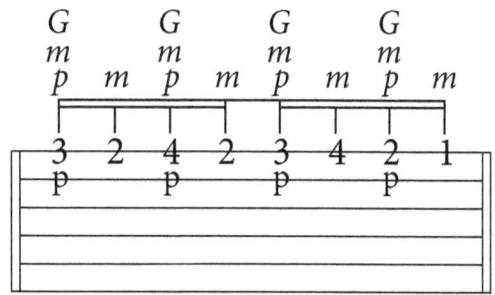

F3

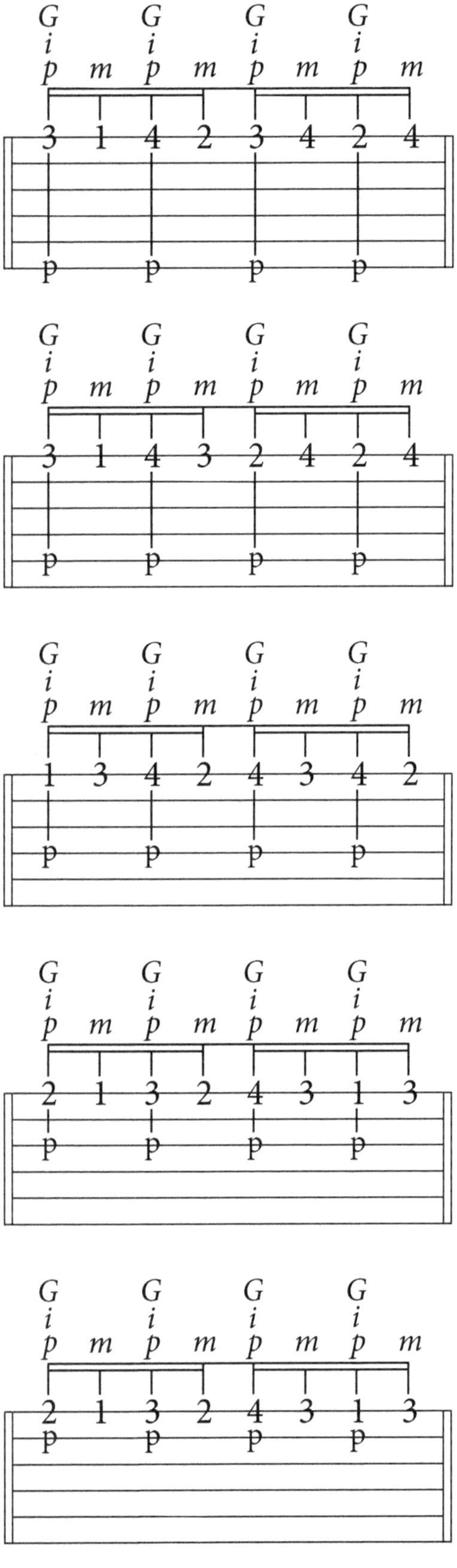
G G G G
i i i i
p m p m p m p m
3 1 4 2 3 4 2 4
p p p p
G G G G
i i i i
p m p m p m p m
3 1 4 3 2 4 2 4
p p p p
G G G G
i i i i
p m p m p m p m
1 3 4 2 4 3 4 2
p p p p
G G G G
i i i i
p m p m p m p m
2 1 3 2 4 3 1 3
p p p p
G G G G
i i i i
p m p m p m p m
2 1 3 2 4 3 1 3
p p p p

F4

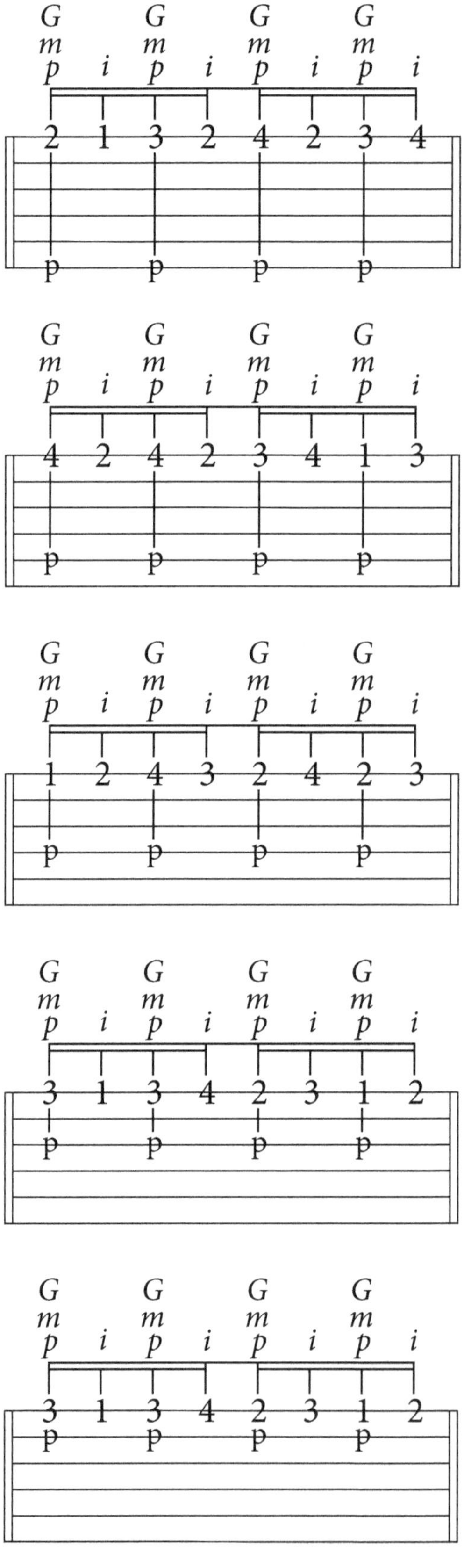
G G G G
m m m m
p i p i p i p i
2 1 3 2 4 2 3 4
p p p p
G G G G
m m m m
p i p i p i p i
4 2 4 2 3 4 1 3
p p p p
G G G G
m m m m
p i p i p i p i
1 2 4 3 2 4 2 3
p p p p
G G G G
m m m m
p i p i p i p i
3 1 3 4 2 3 1 2
p p p p
G G G G
m m m m
p i p i p i p i
3 1 3 4 2 3 1 2
p p p p

§ IV

A

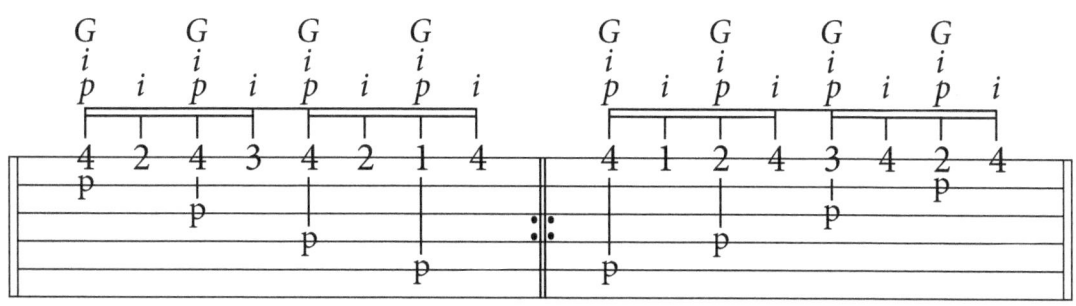

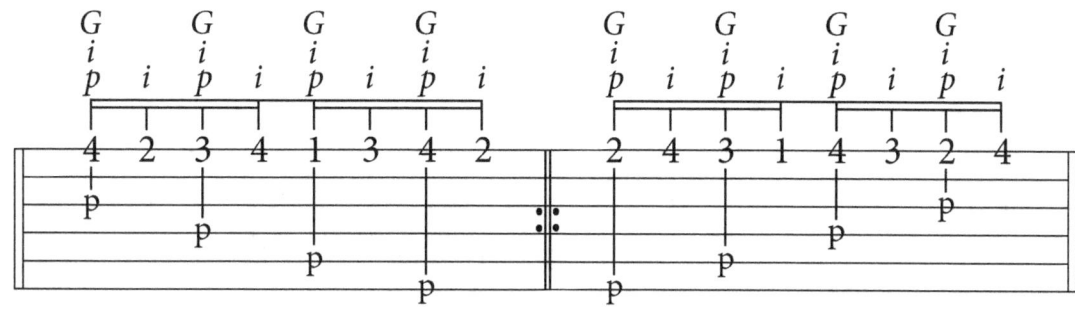

B

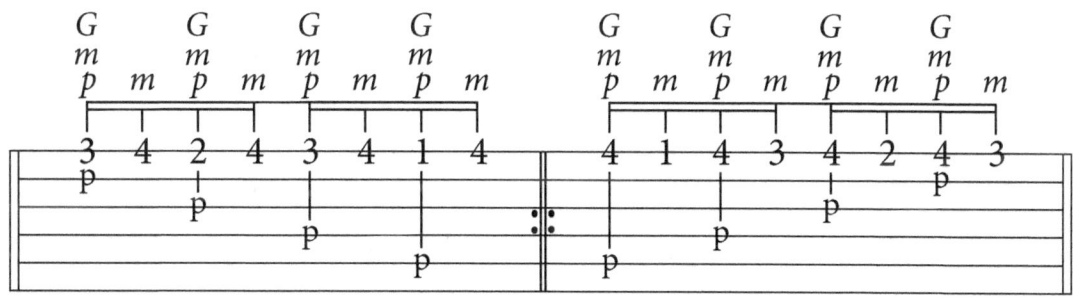

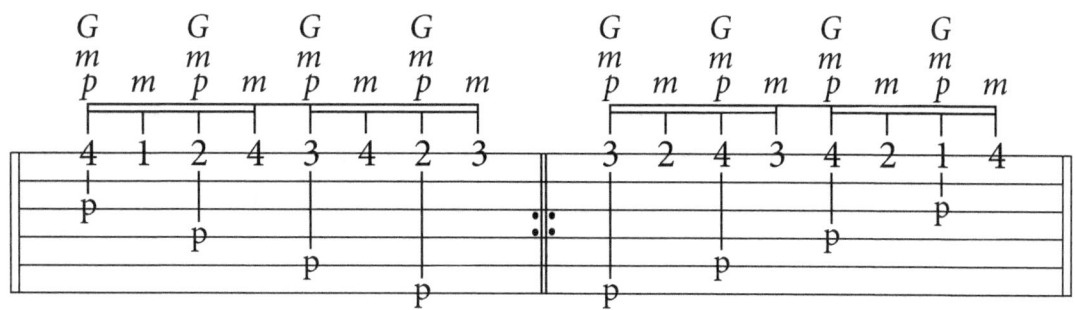

§ V

A

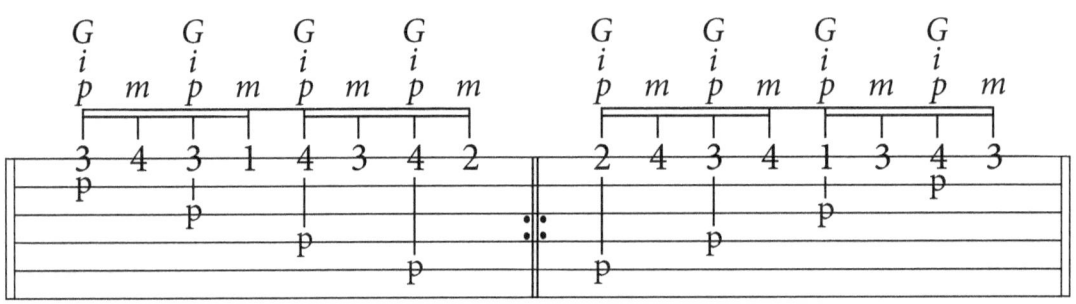

B

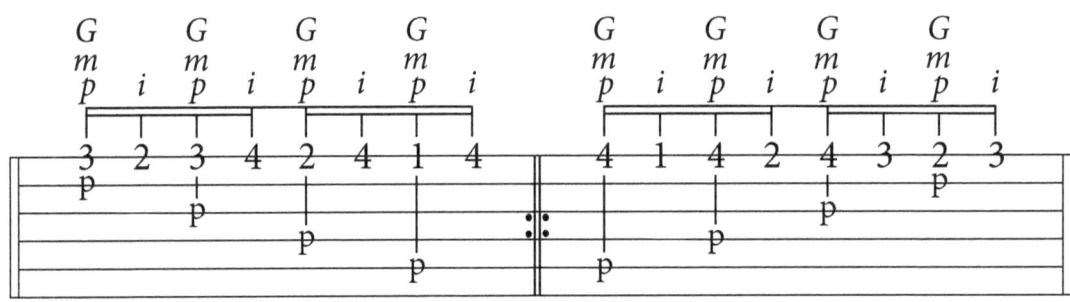

§ VI

           F1   **F2**

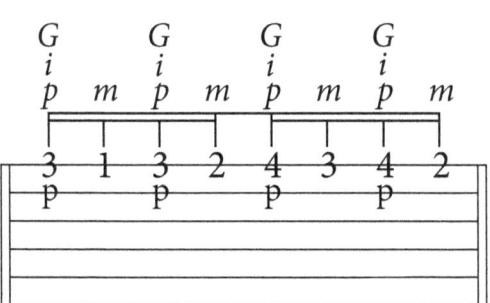 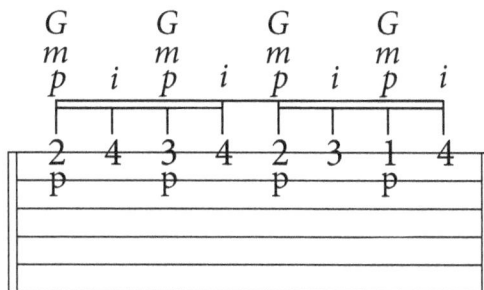

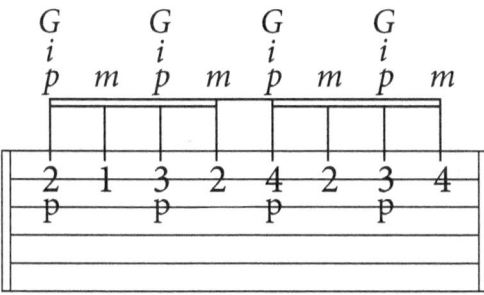 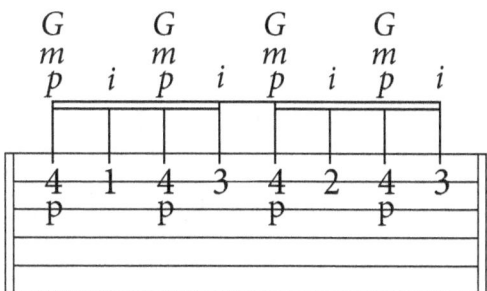

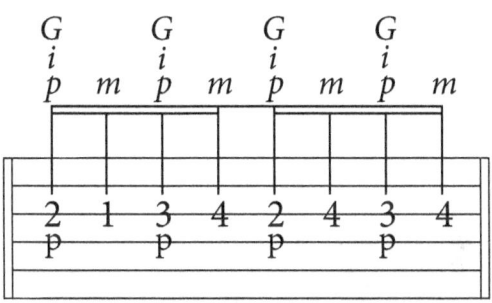 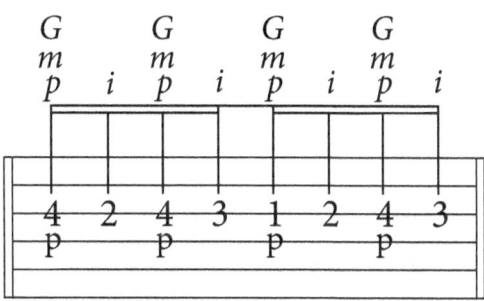

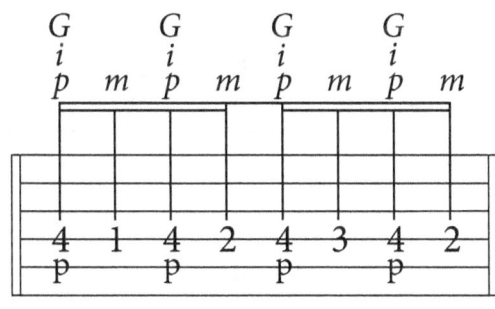 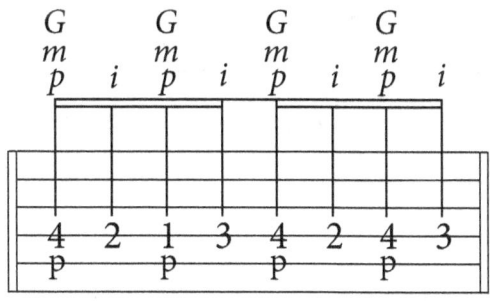

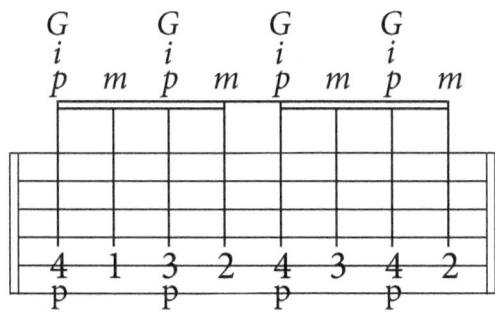 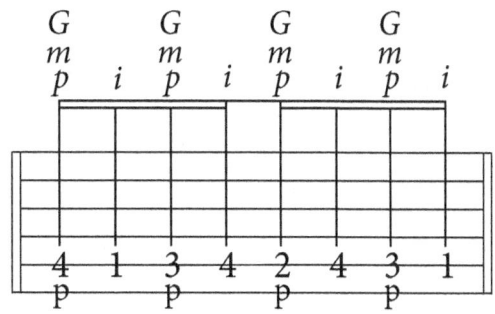

§ VII

A

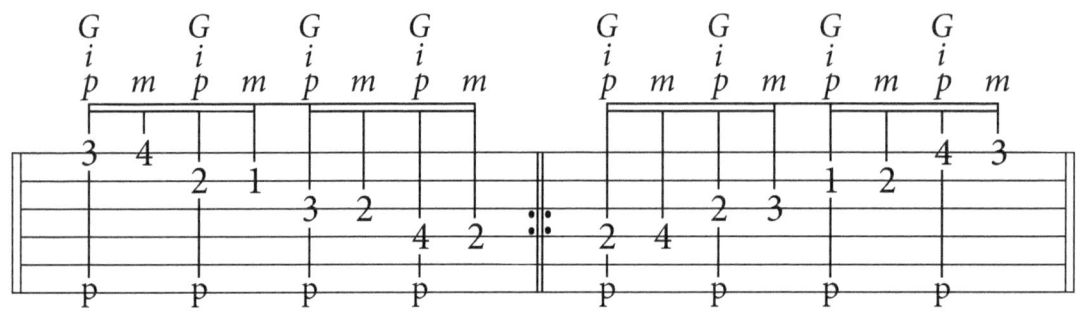

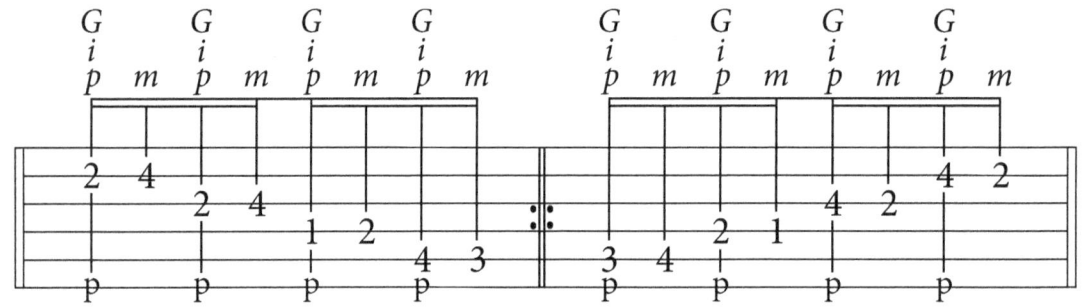

B

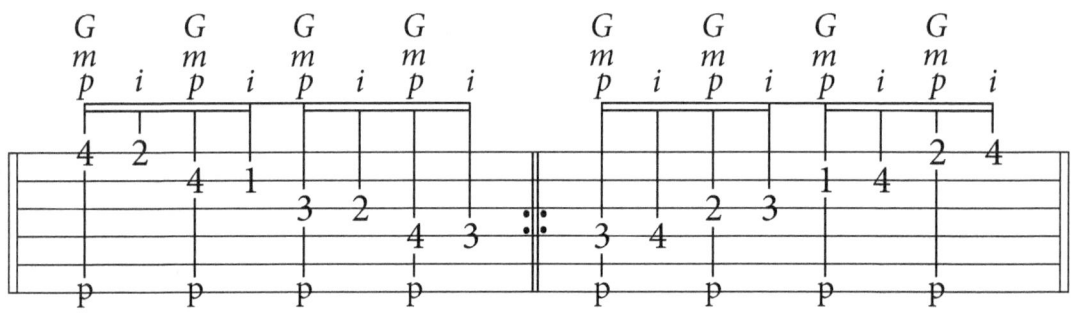

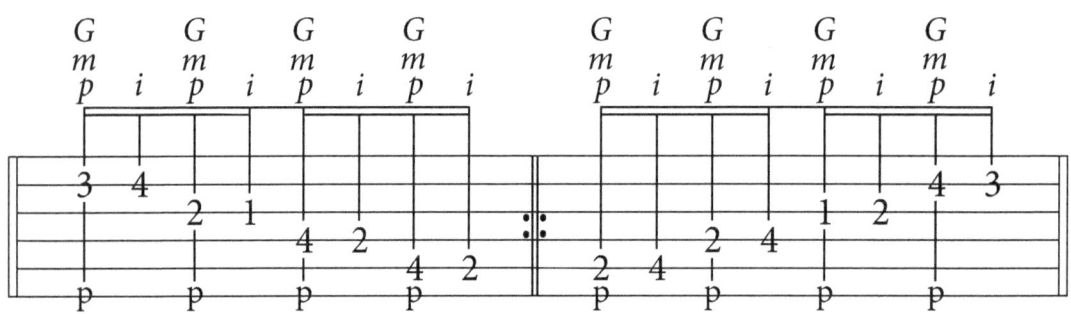

UNIT 2

Thumb stroke simultaneously
with index (i) or middle finger (m).
Two Triplets within the Formula variations.

§I Chromatic scales of one string which develop on the 1st, 2nd, 3rd, 4th and 5th string and are arranged in three variations with one double and two triple strokes. The double and triple strokes are isochronous.

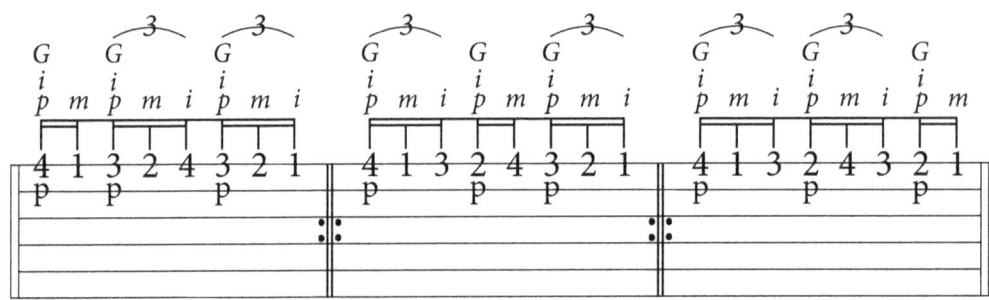

§II Chromatic scales expressed in three variations:

1/ on the 1st, 2nd and 3rd string and return from the 3rd to the 1st string with the opposite scale.

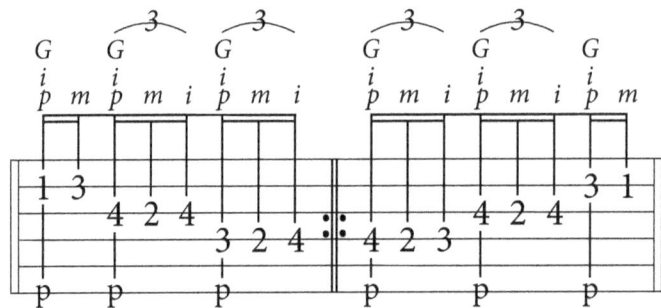

2/ on the 2nd, 3rd and 4th string and return from the 4th to the 2nd string withthe opposite scale.

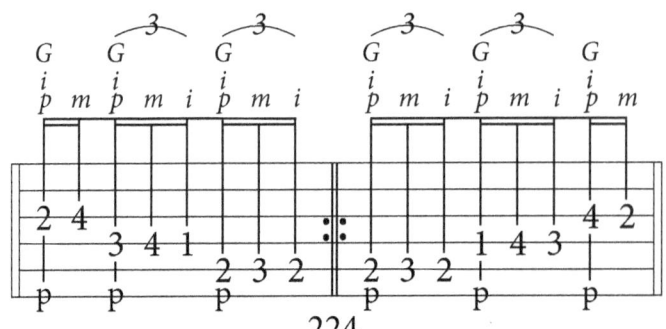

3/ on the 3rd, 4th and 5th string and return from the 5th to the 3rd string with the opposite scale.

§III Same exercise as in §I with difference only in the fingerings of he right hand.

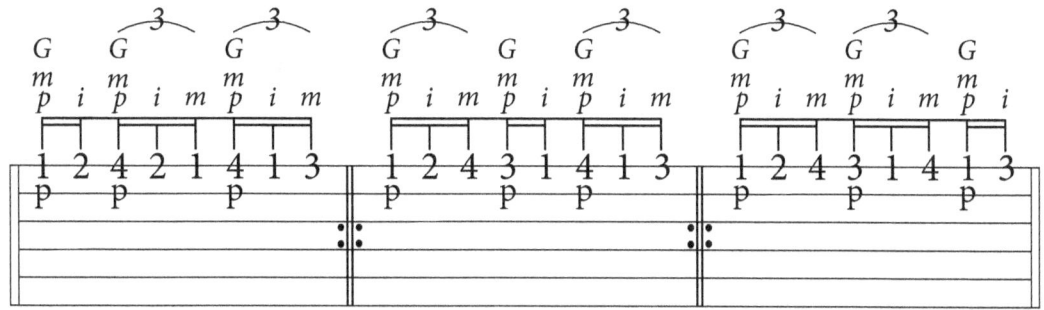

§IV Same exercise as in §II with difference only in the fingerings of he right hand.

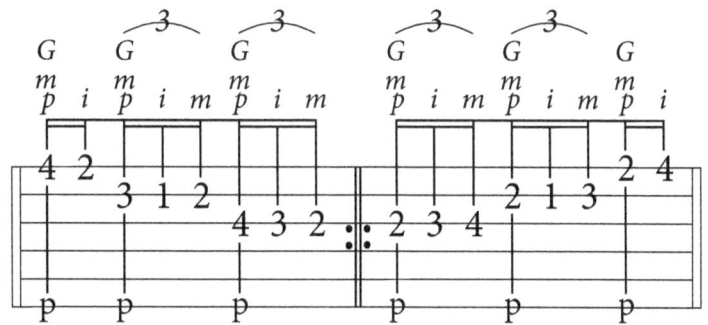

§V, §VI, §VII, §VIII

The exercises of these paragraphs are in a way variations of the previous ones, always in relation to the fingerings of the right hand.

§ I

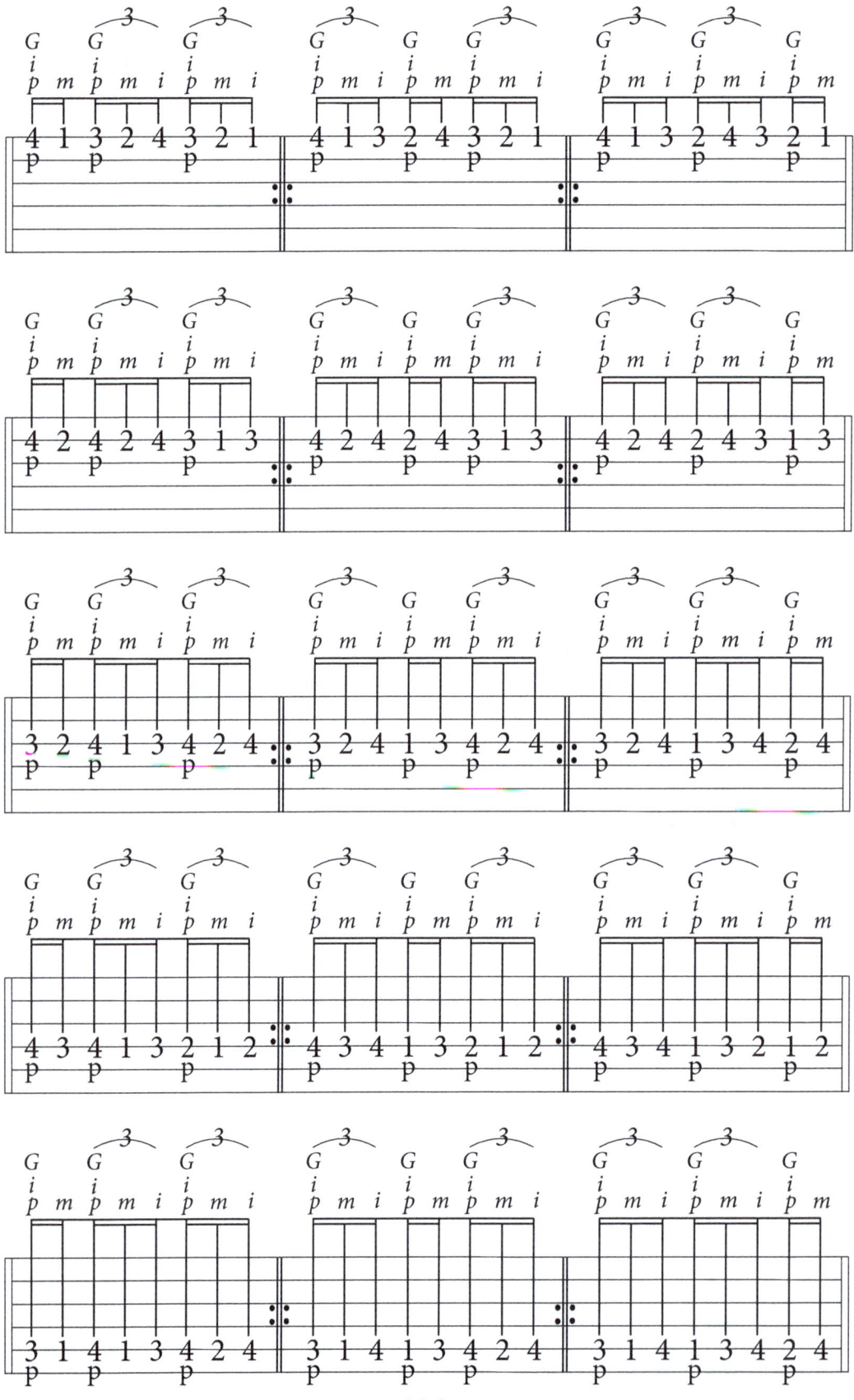

§ II

A

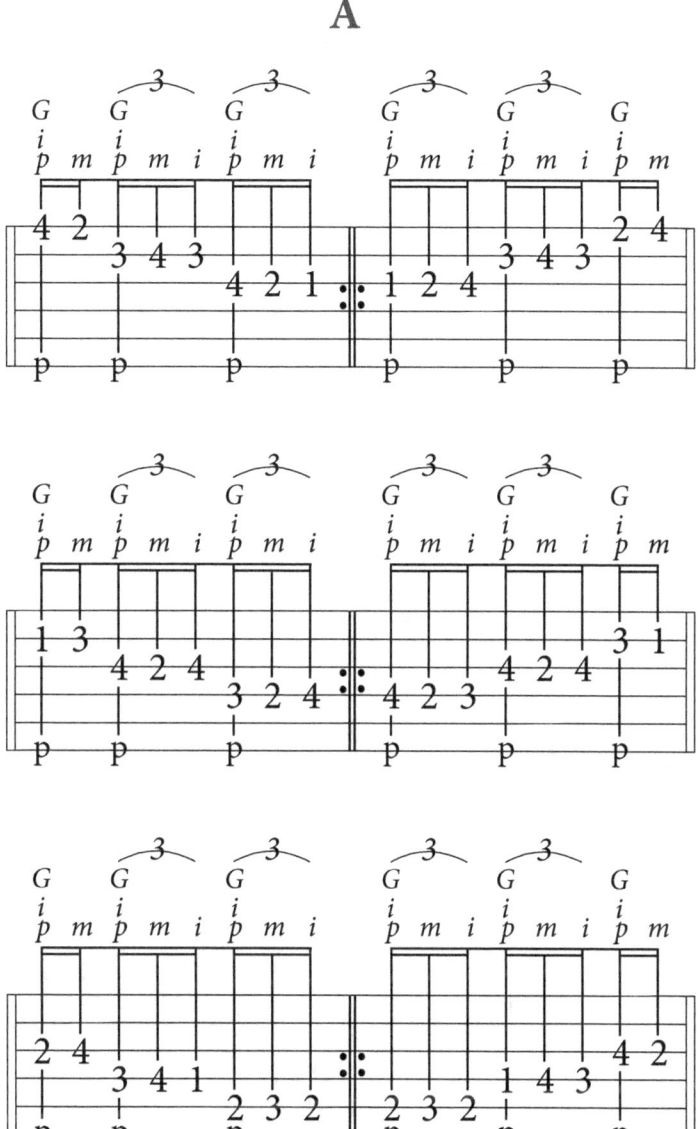

B

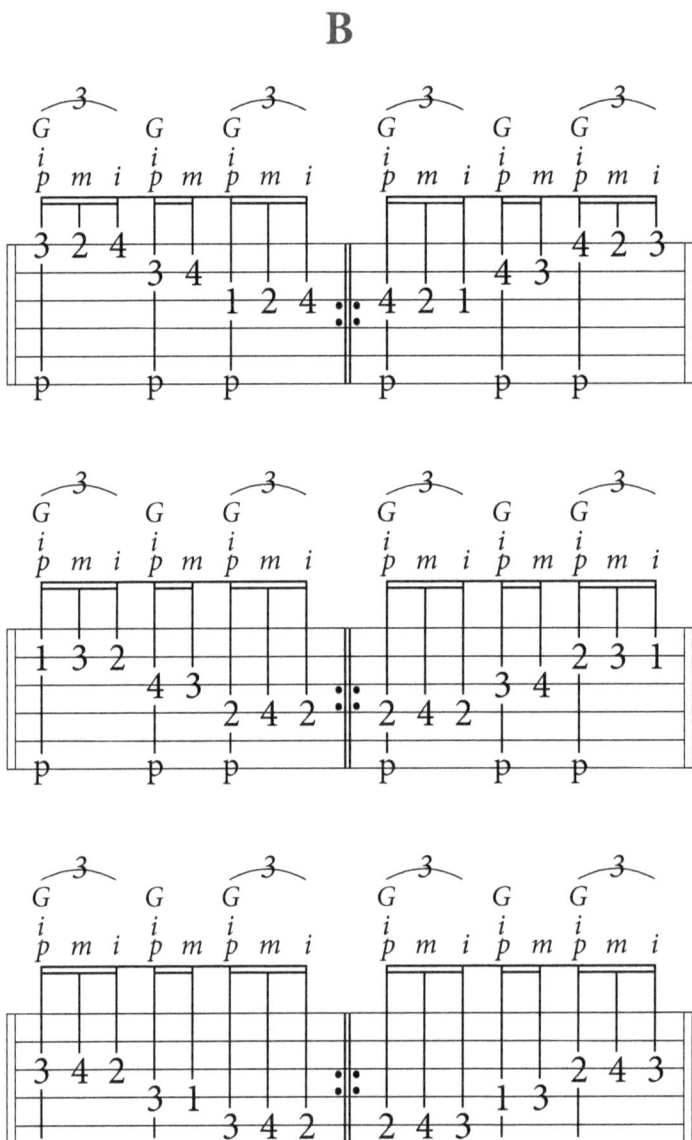

C

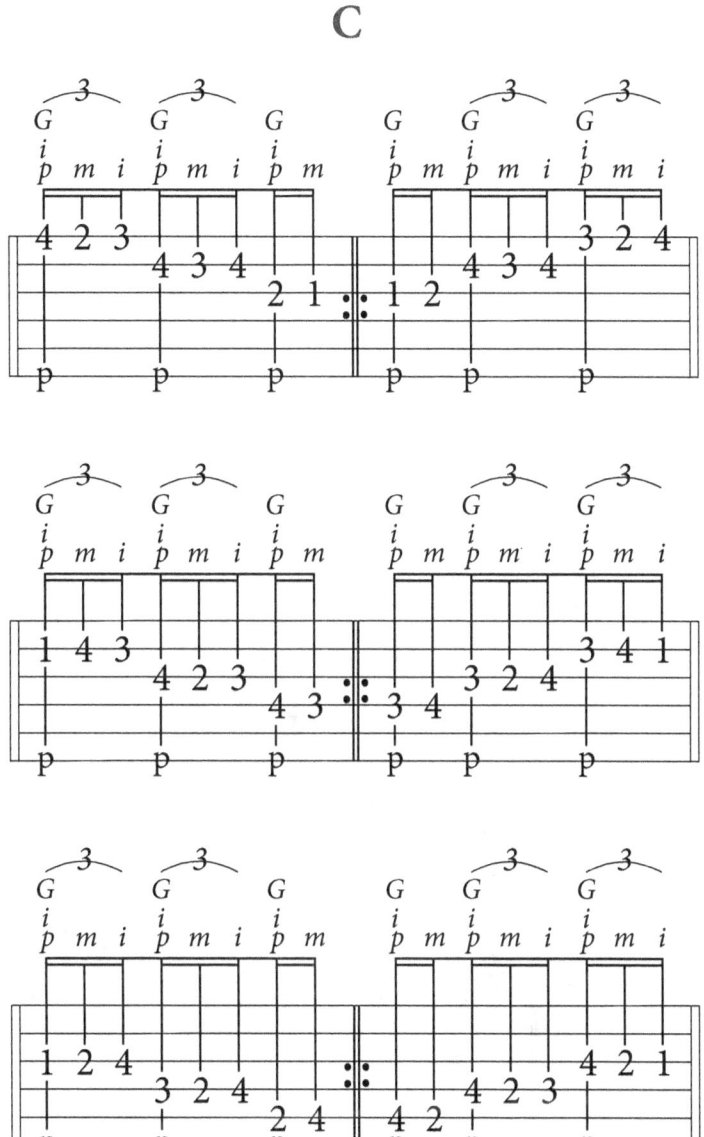

§ III

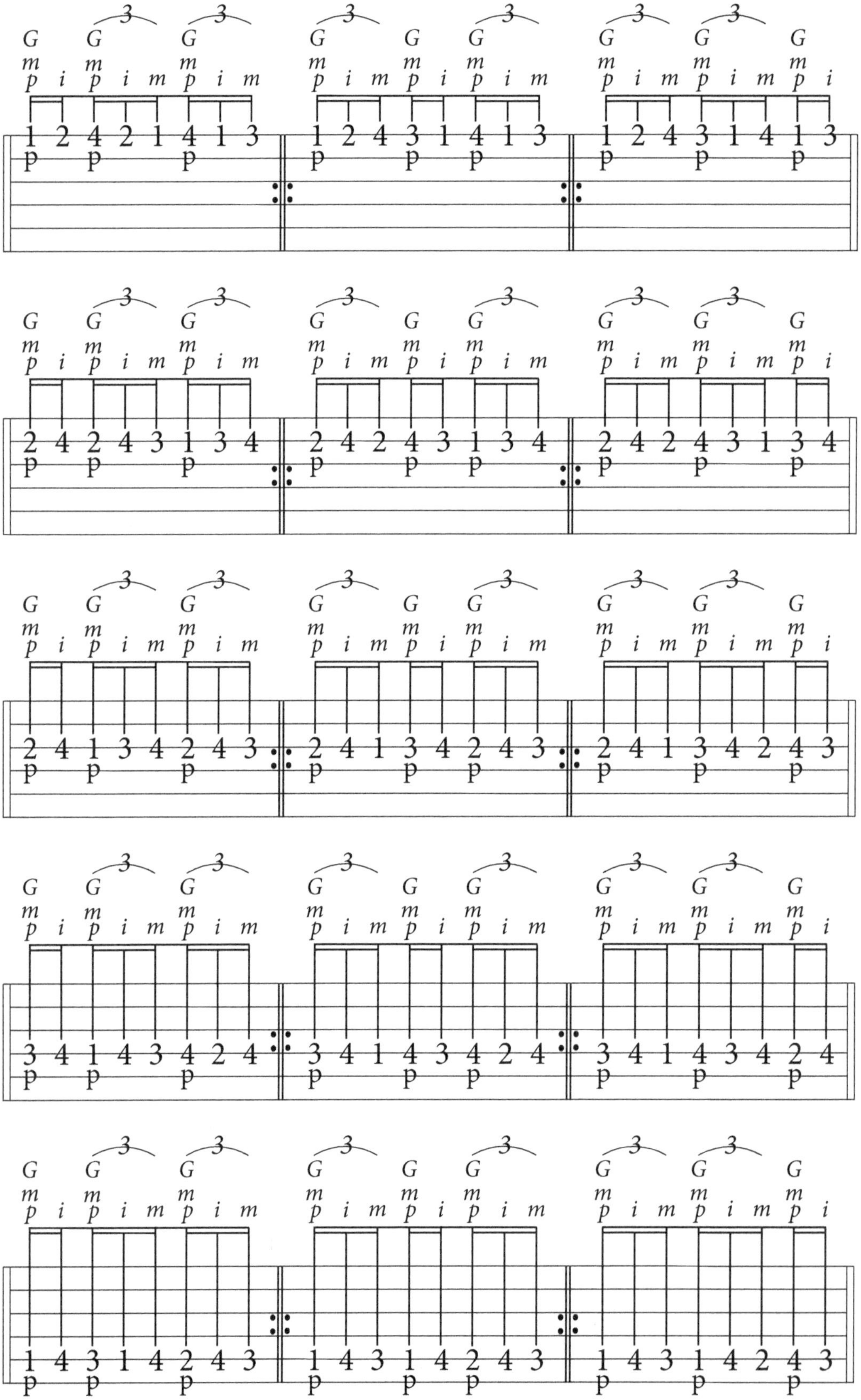

p i p i m p i m | p i m p i p i m | p i m p i m p i
1 2 4 2 1 4 1 3 | 1 2 4 3 1 4 1 3 | 1 2 4 3 1 4 1 3
2 4 2 4 3 1 3 4 | 2 4 2 4 3 1 3 4 | 2 4 2 4 3 1 3 4
2 4 1 3 4 2 4 3 | 2 4 1 3 4 2 4 3 | 2 4 1 3 4 2 4 3
3 4 1 4 3 4 2 4 | 3 4 1 4 3 4 2 4 | 3 4 1 4 3 4 2 4
1 4 3 1 4 2 4 3 | 1 4 3 1 4 2 4 3 | 1 4 3 1 4 2 4 3

§ IV

A

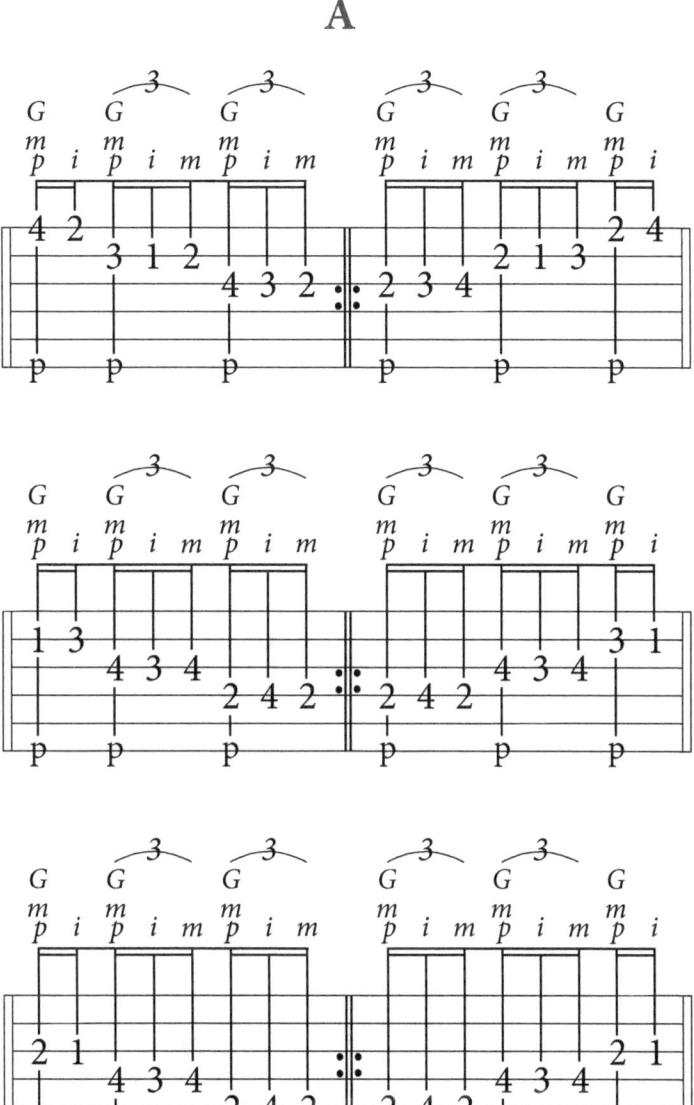

B

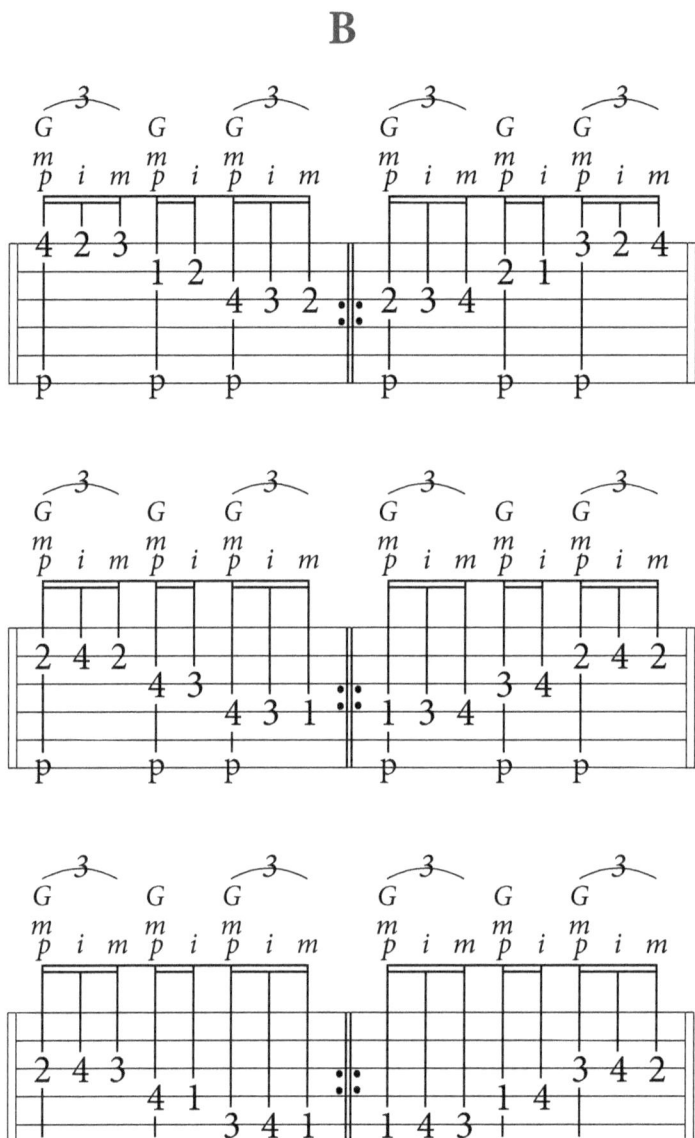

C

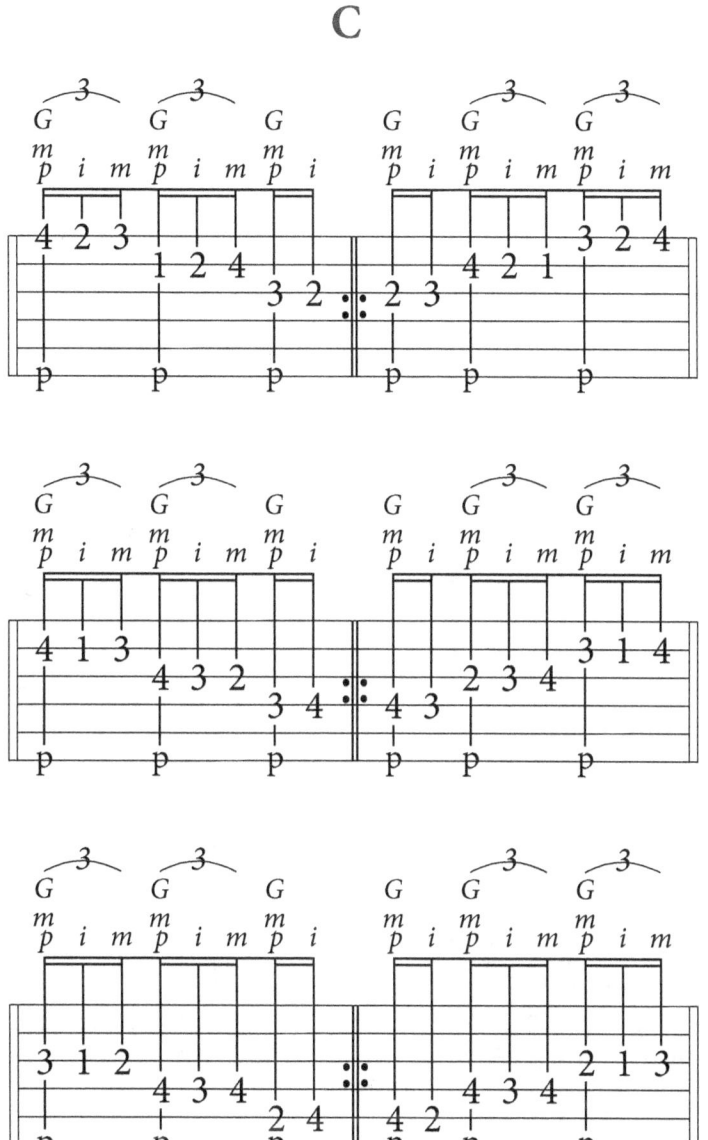

§ V

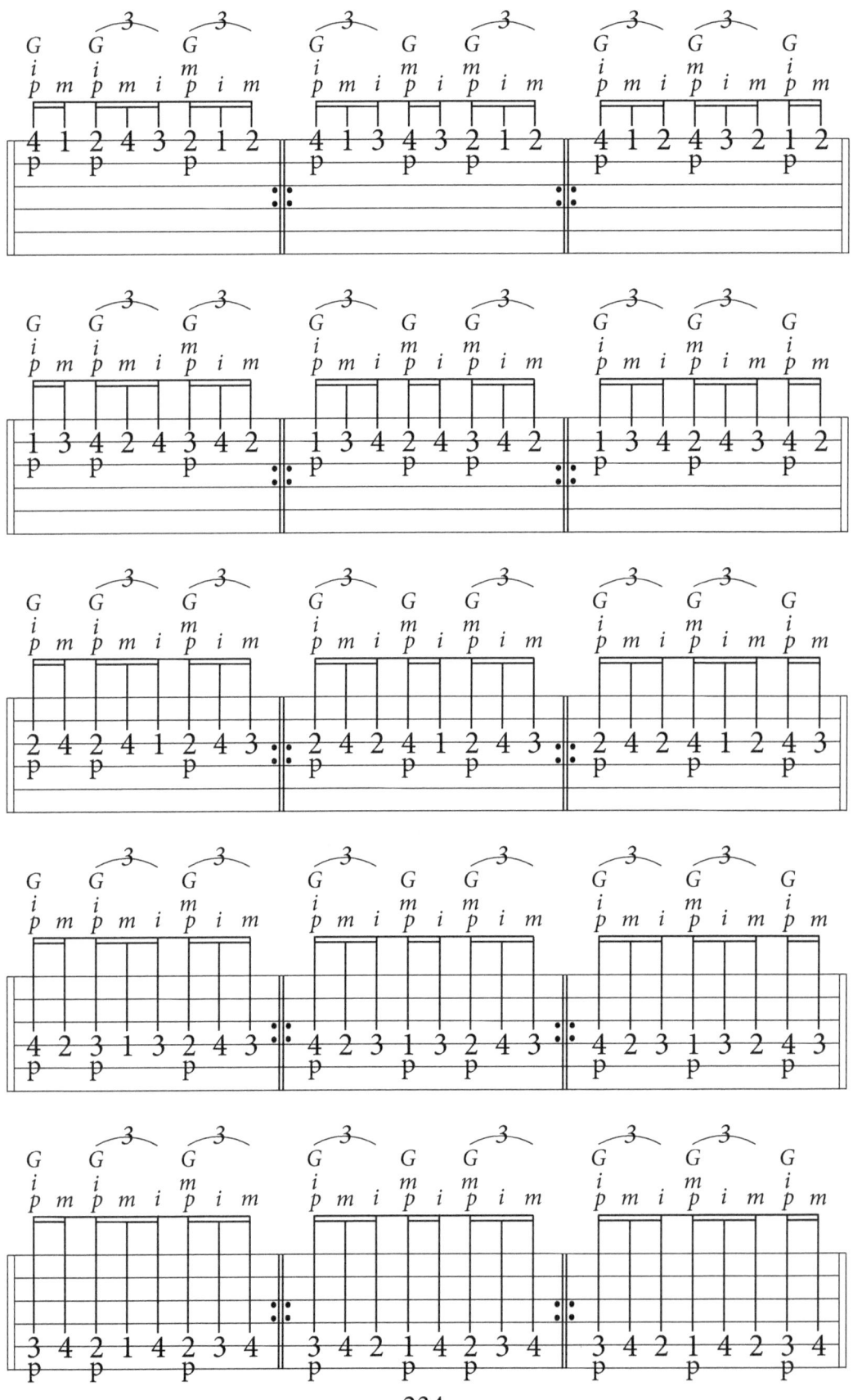

§ VI

A

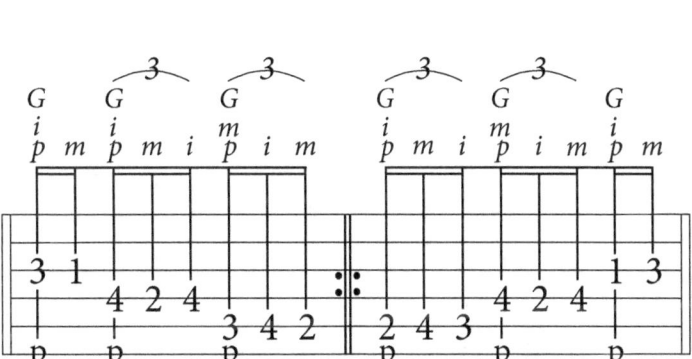

B

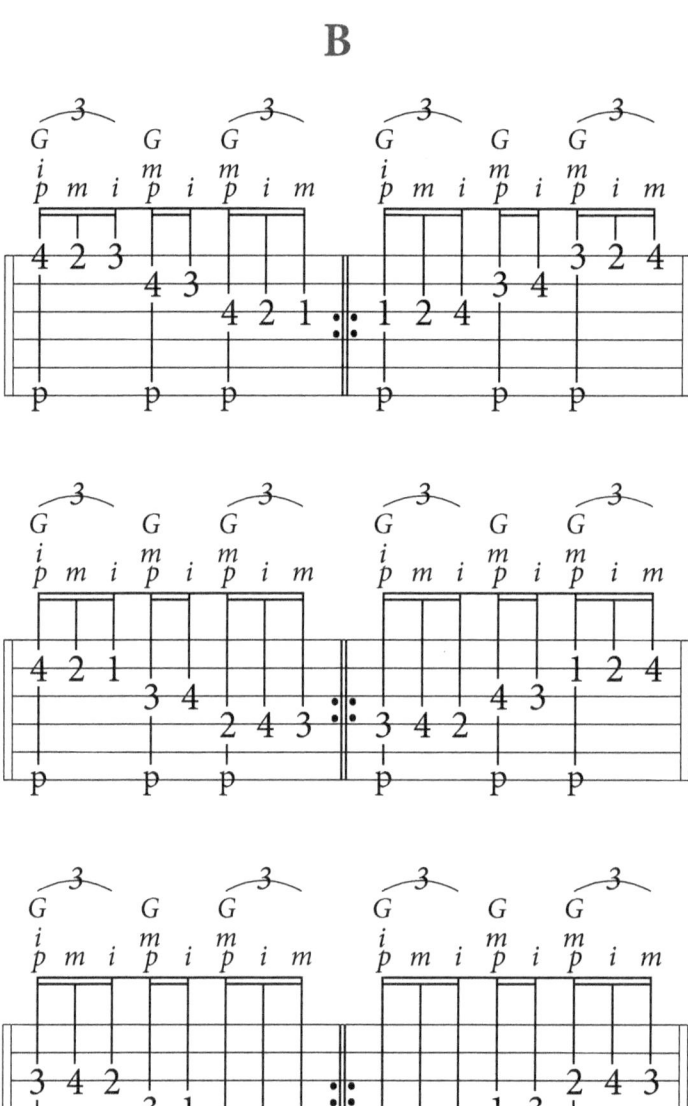

C

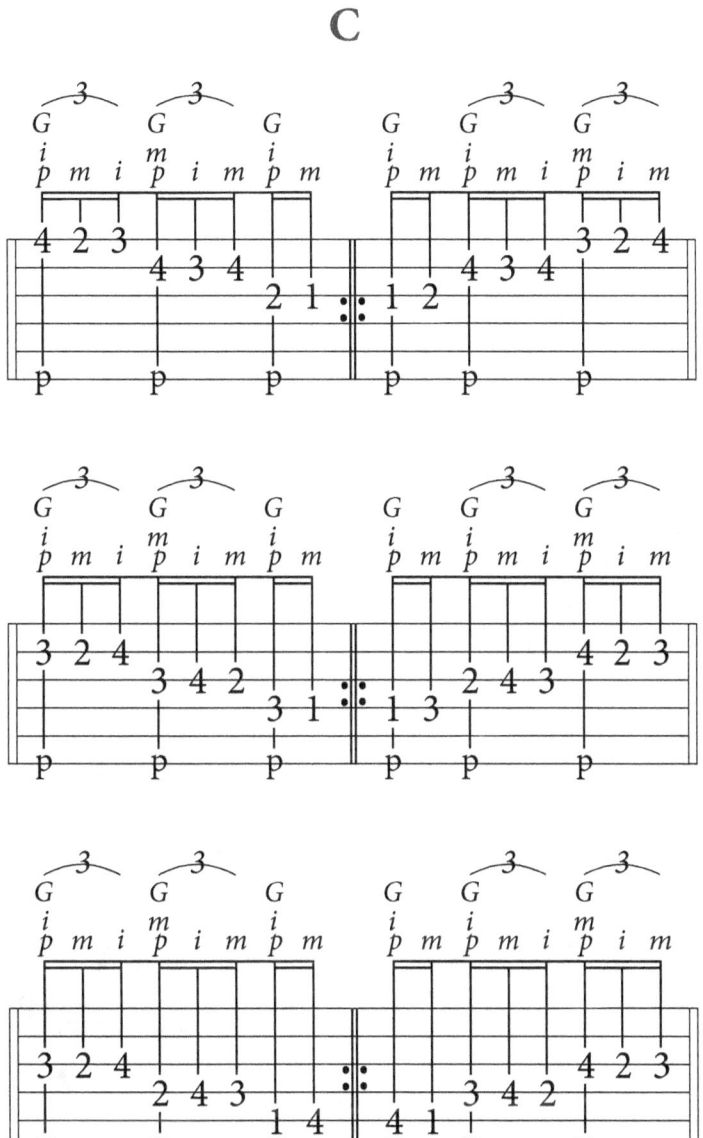

§ VII

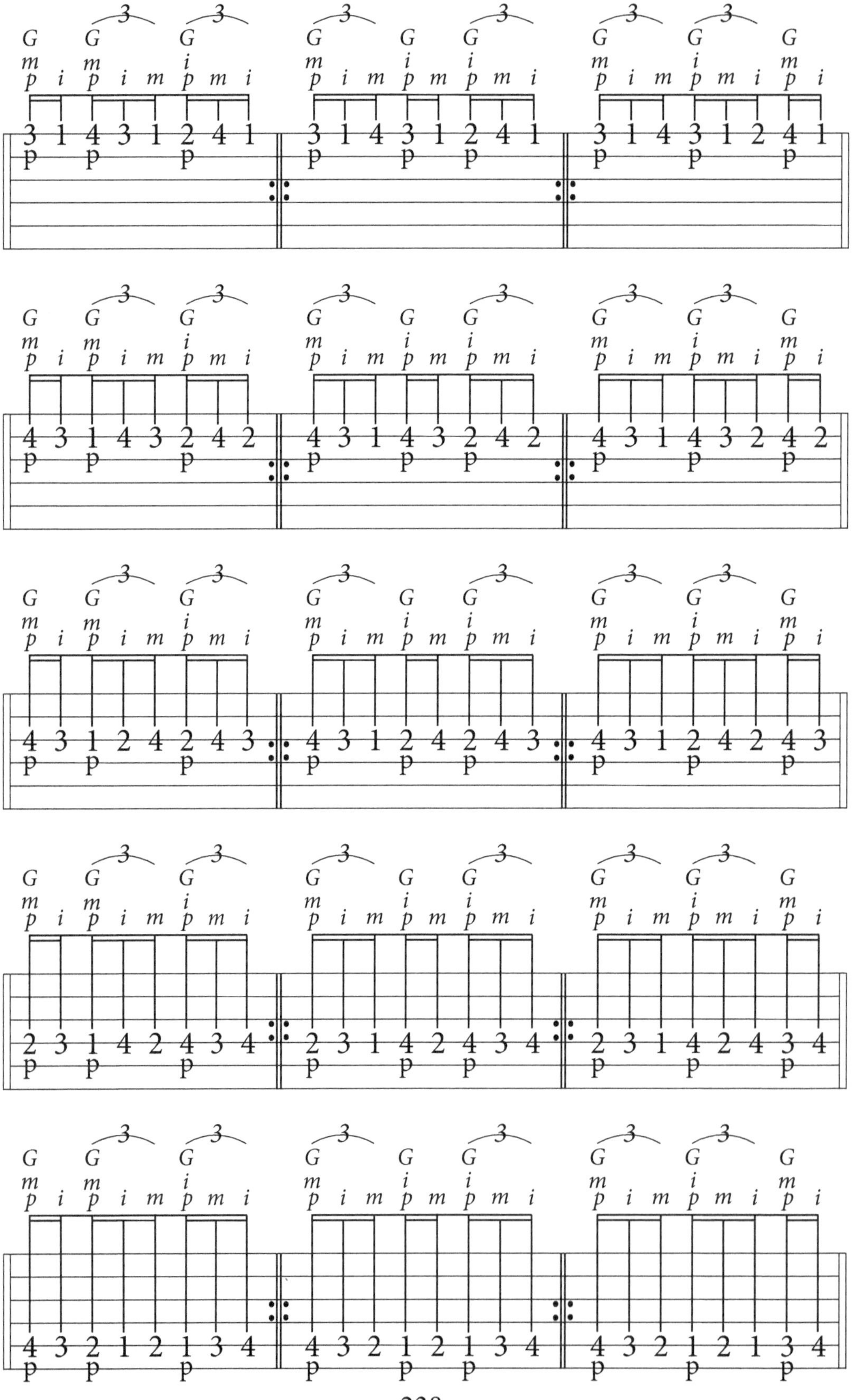

§ VIII

A

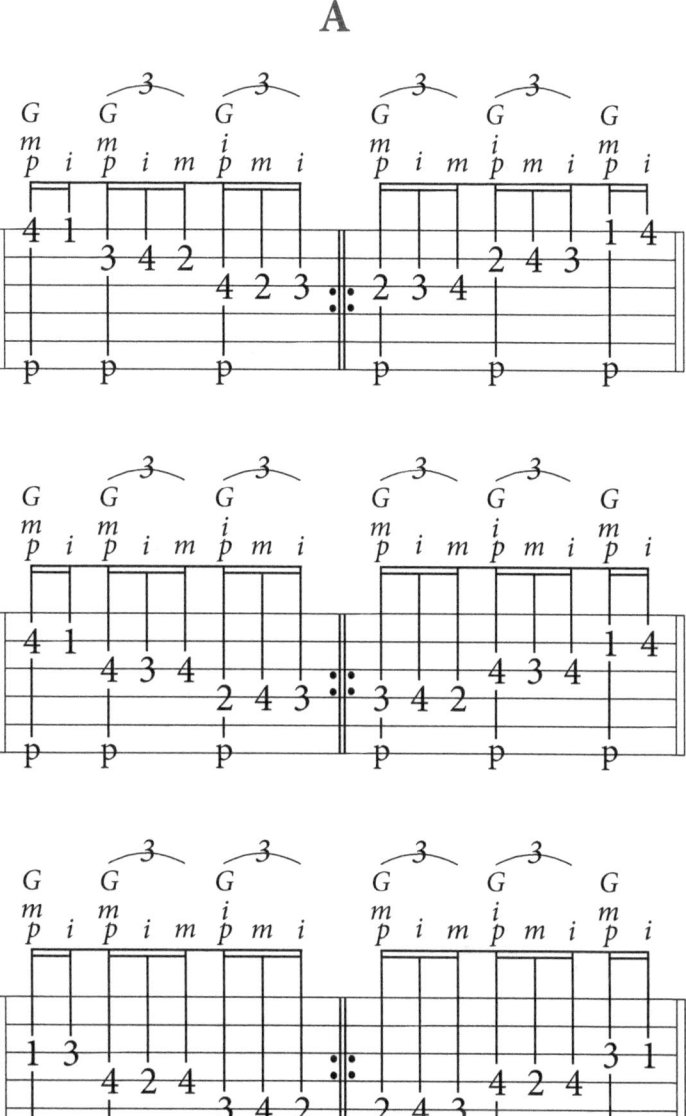

B

C

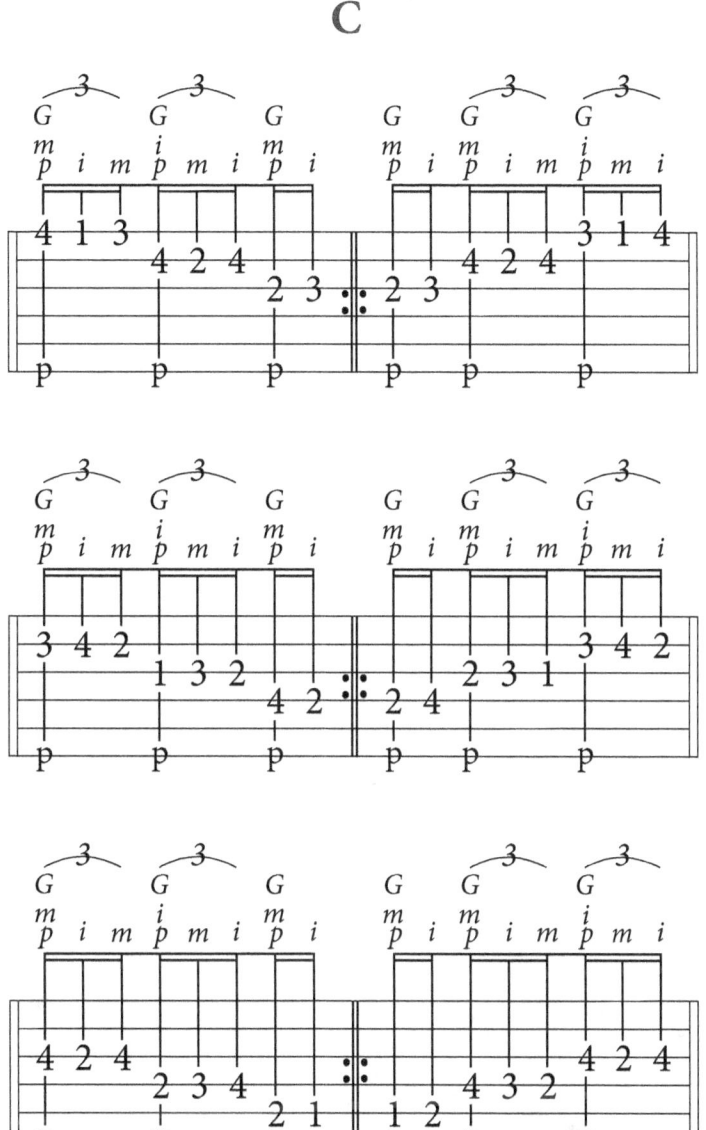

CHAPTER 6

COMBINATION OF GOLPE
AND SIMULTANEOUS STROKE OF THUMB
WITH INDEX AND MIDDLE FINGER.
TWO TRIPLETS WITHIN THE FORMULA.

UNIT 1

Combination of Golpe
and simultaneous stroke of thumb
and right hand fingers
index (i) and middle finger (m).

Combination of Golpe with simultaneous stroke of the thumb with the right hand fingers, index and middle finger.

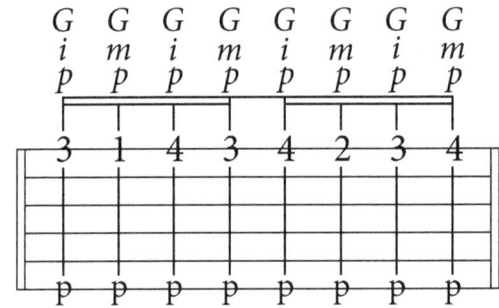

The paragraphs marked with 1 refer to the simultaneous stroke of the thumb with the index and middle finger that play on the chromatic scales of one string. The thumb plays on the 6th, 5th, 4th and 3rd string.

Arrangement of the chromatic scales of one string in three variations:

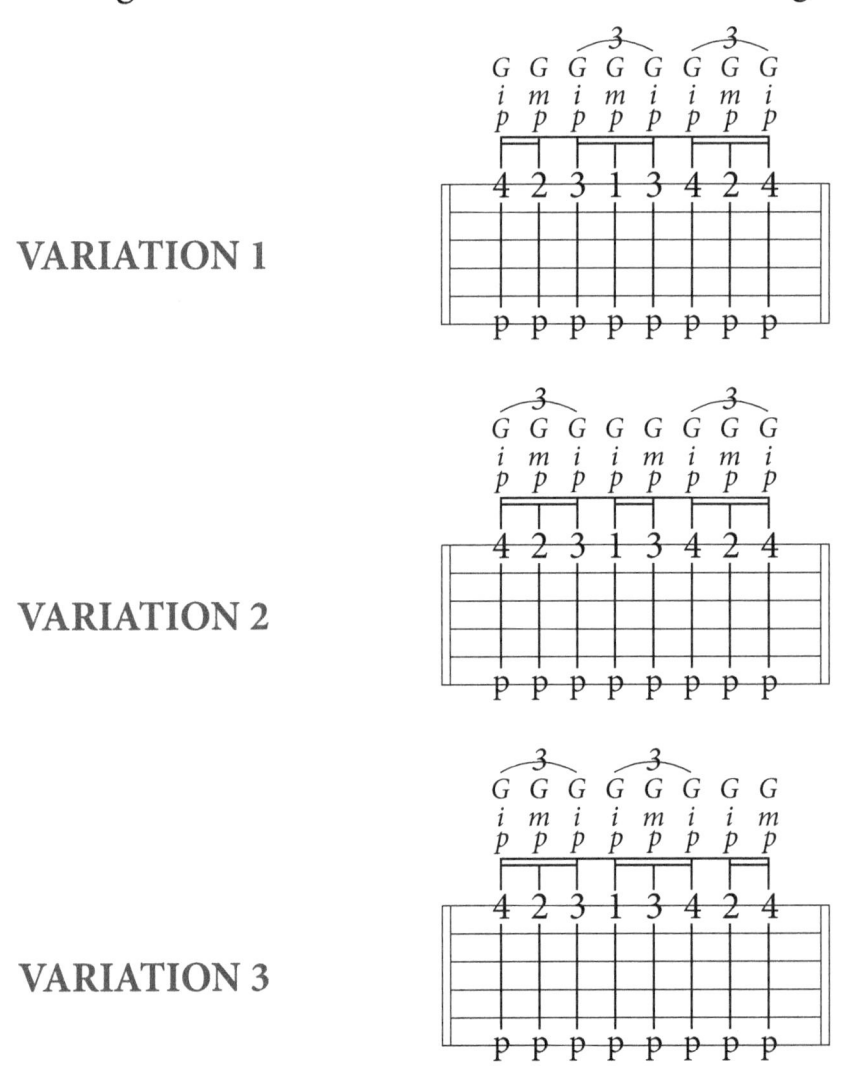

VARIATION 1

VARIATION 2

VARIATION 3

The paragraphs marked with 2 exhibit greater degrees of difficulty as the chromatic scale moves.

1/ from the 1st to the 3rd string and returns from the 3rd to the 1st string with the opposite scale.

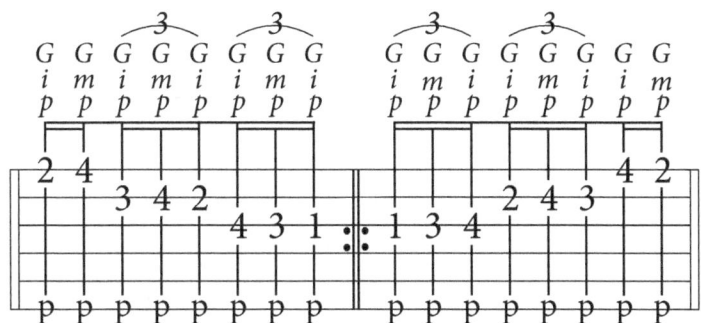

2/ from the 2nd to the 4th string and returns from the 4th to the 2nd string with the opposite scale.

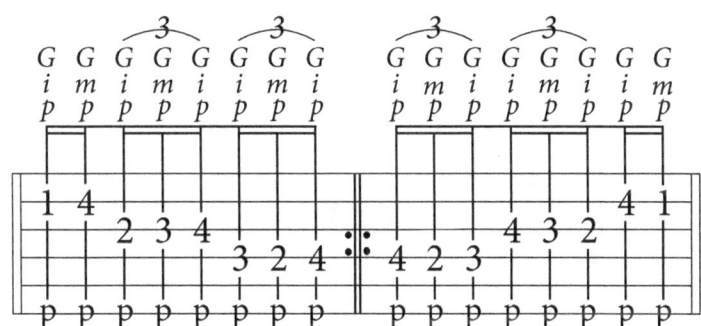

3/ from the 3rd to the 5th string and returns from the 5th to the 3rd string with the opposite scale.

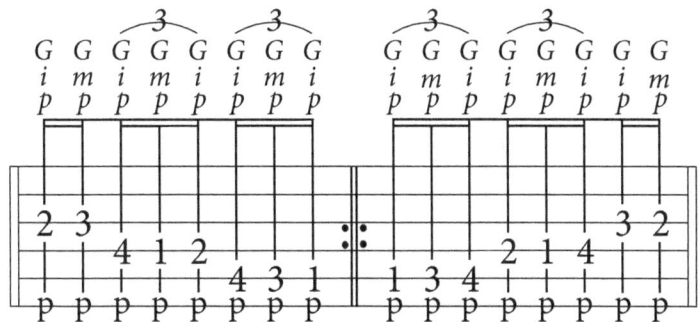

§ I

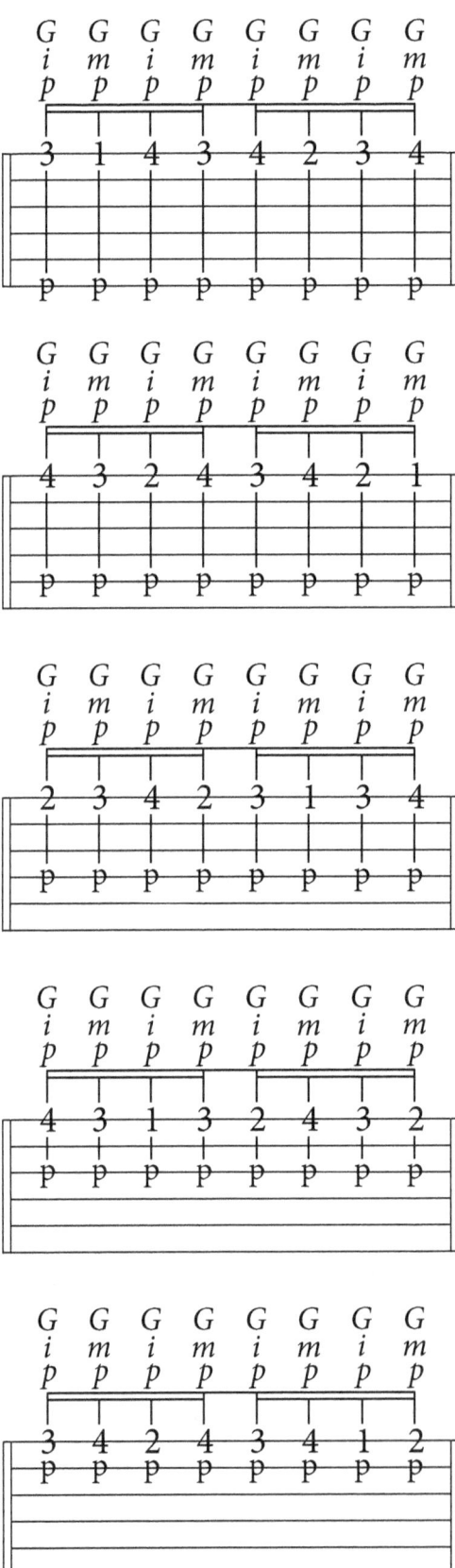

§ II/1

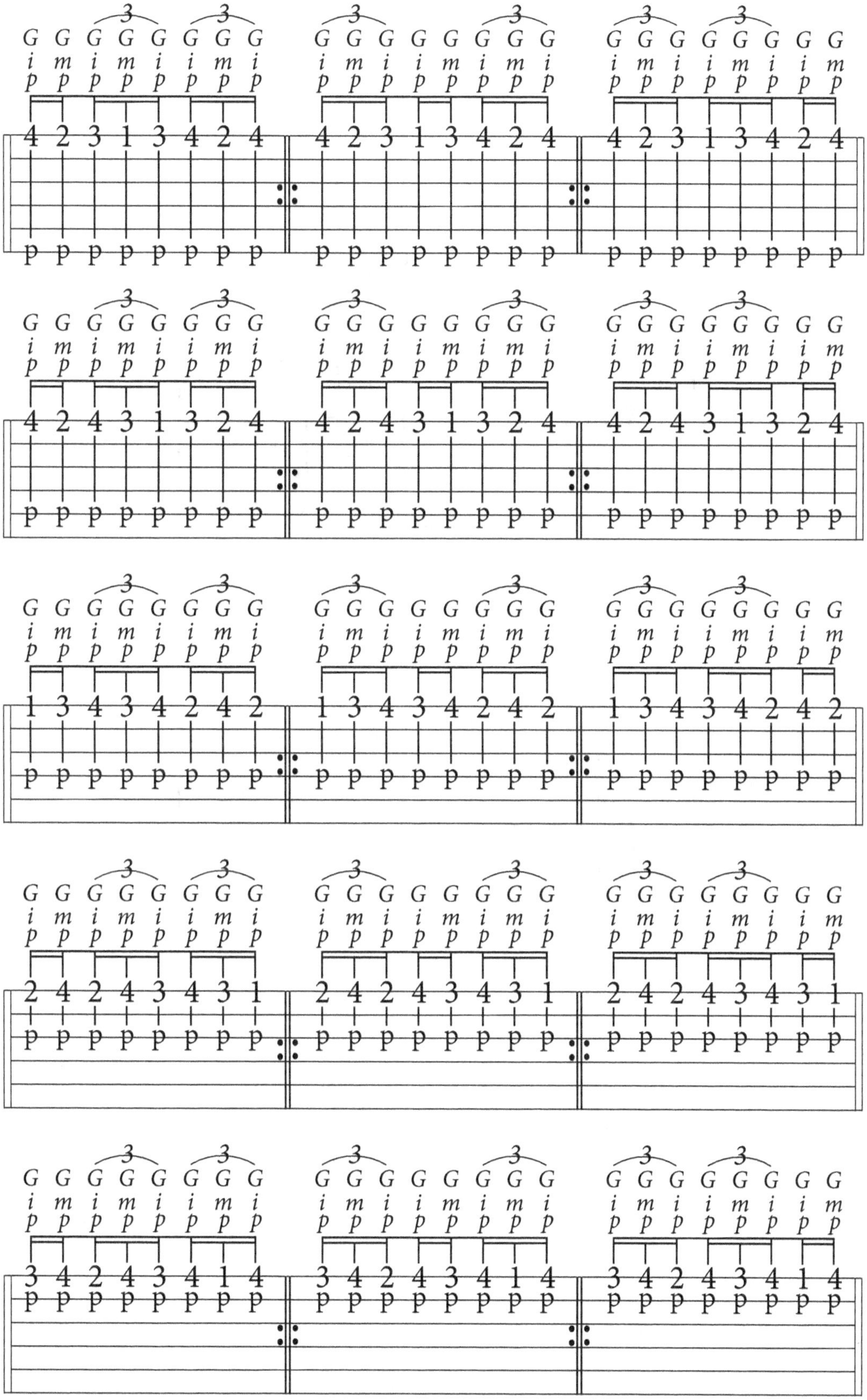

§ II/2

A

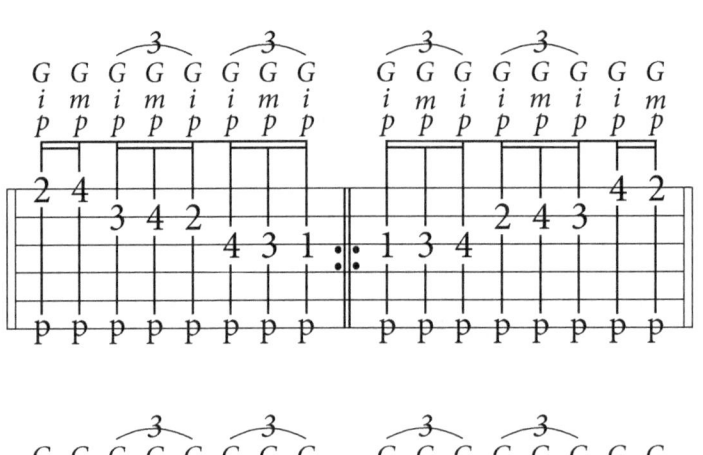
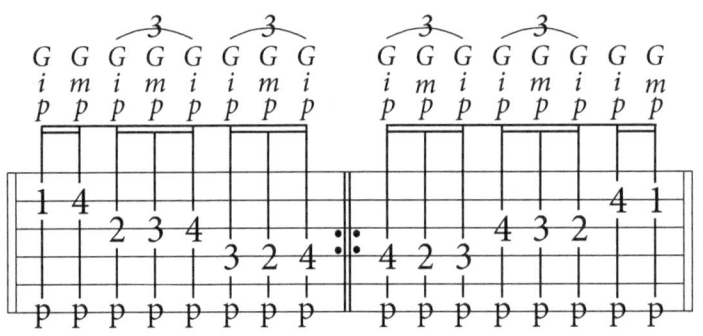
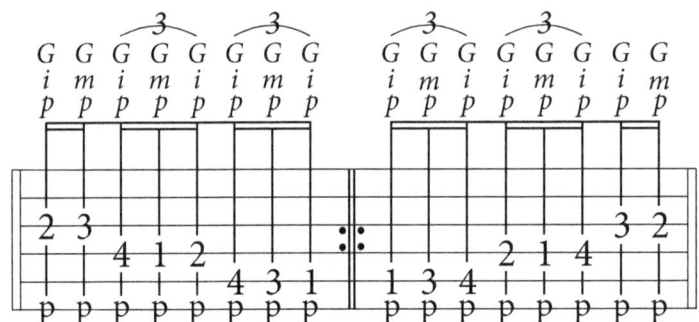

B

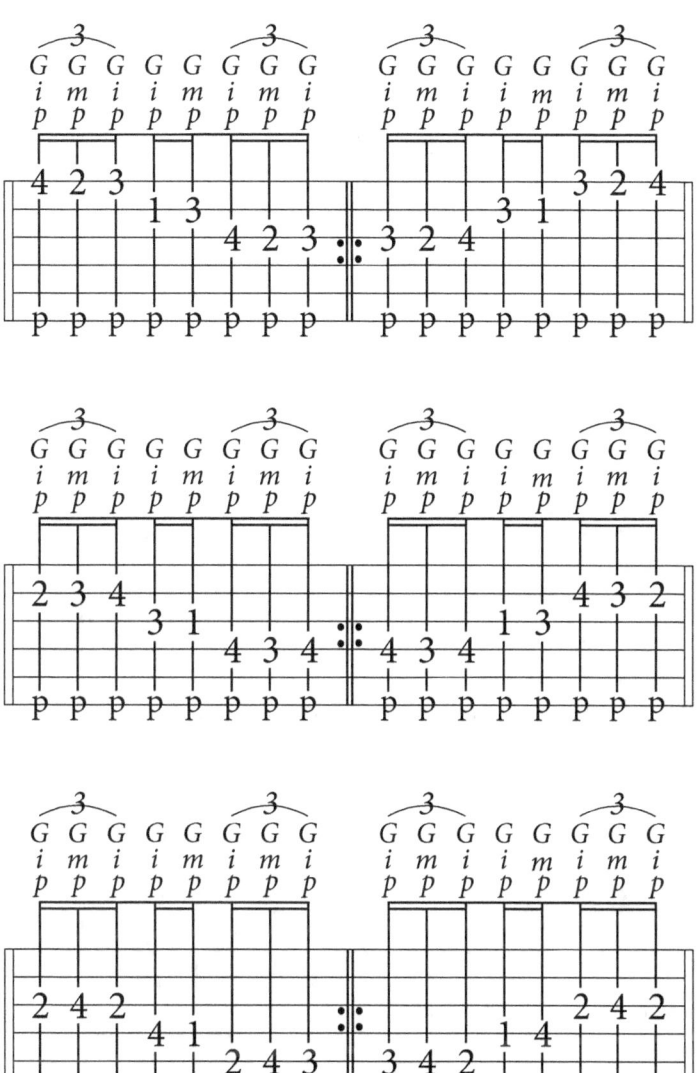

C

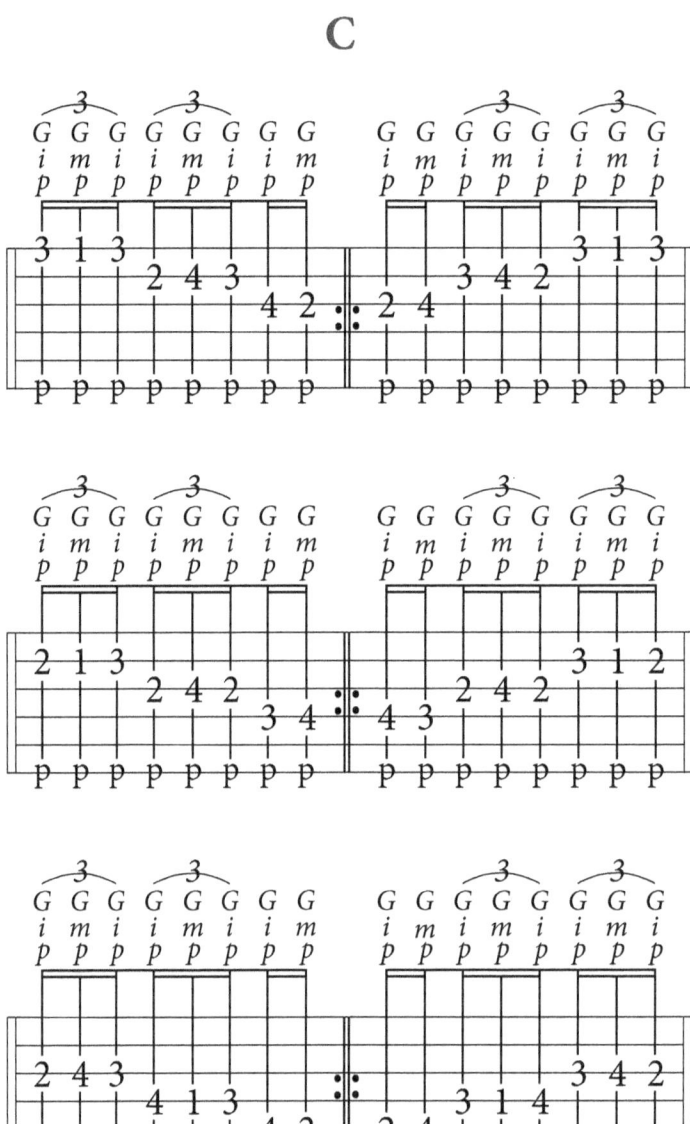

§ III/1

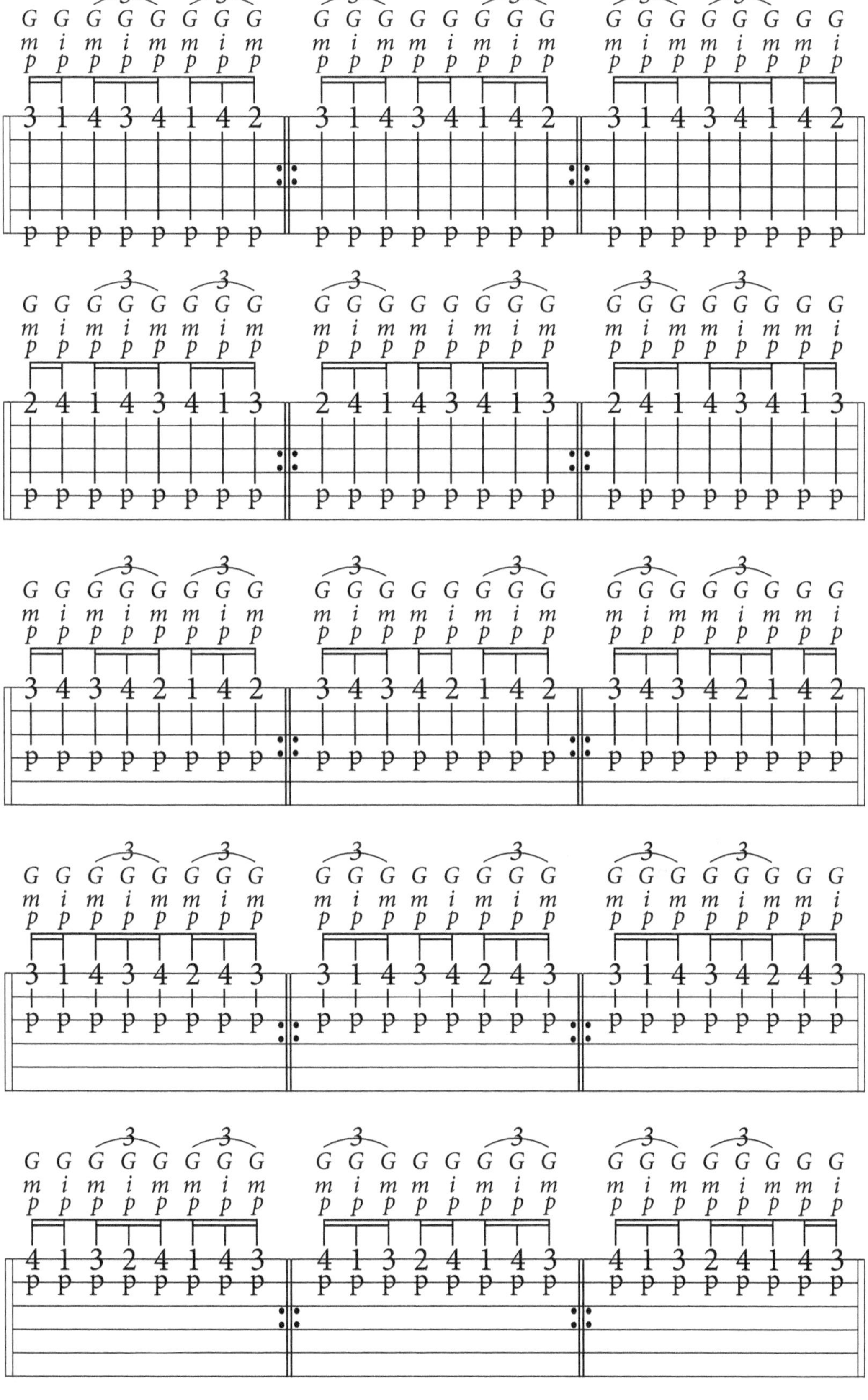
3 1 4 3 4 1 4 2 | 3 1 4 3 4 1 4 2 | 3 1 4 3 4 1 4 2
2 4 1 4 3 4 1 3 | 2 4 1 4 3 4 1 3 | 2 4 1 4 3 4 1 3
3 4 3 4 2 1 4 2 | 3 4 3 4 2 1 4 2 | 3 4 3 4 2 1 4 2
3 1 4 3 4 2 4 3 | 3 1 4 3 4 2 4 3 | 3 1 4 3 4 2 4 3
4 1 3 2 4 1 4 3 | 4 1 3 2 4 1 4 3 | 4 1 3 2 4 1 4 3

§ III/2

A

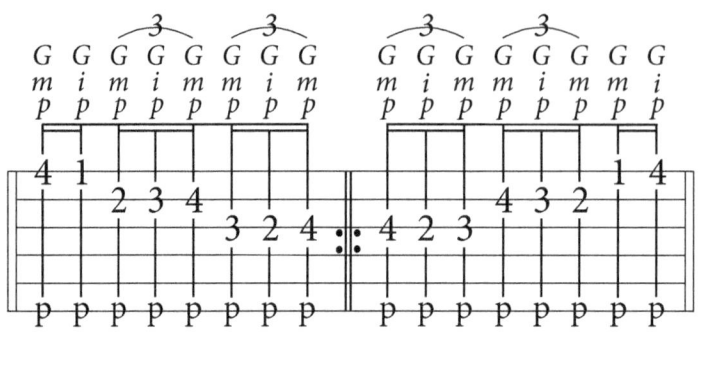
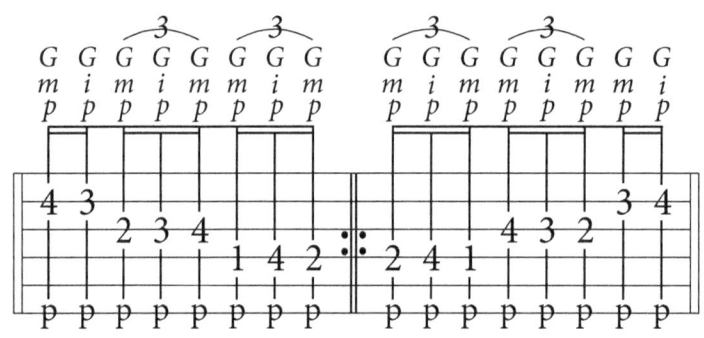
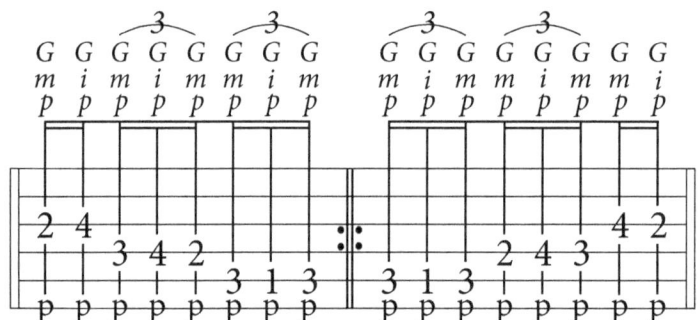

B

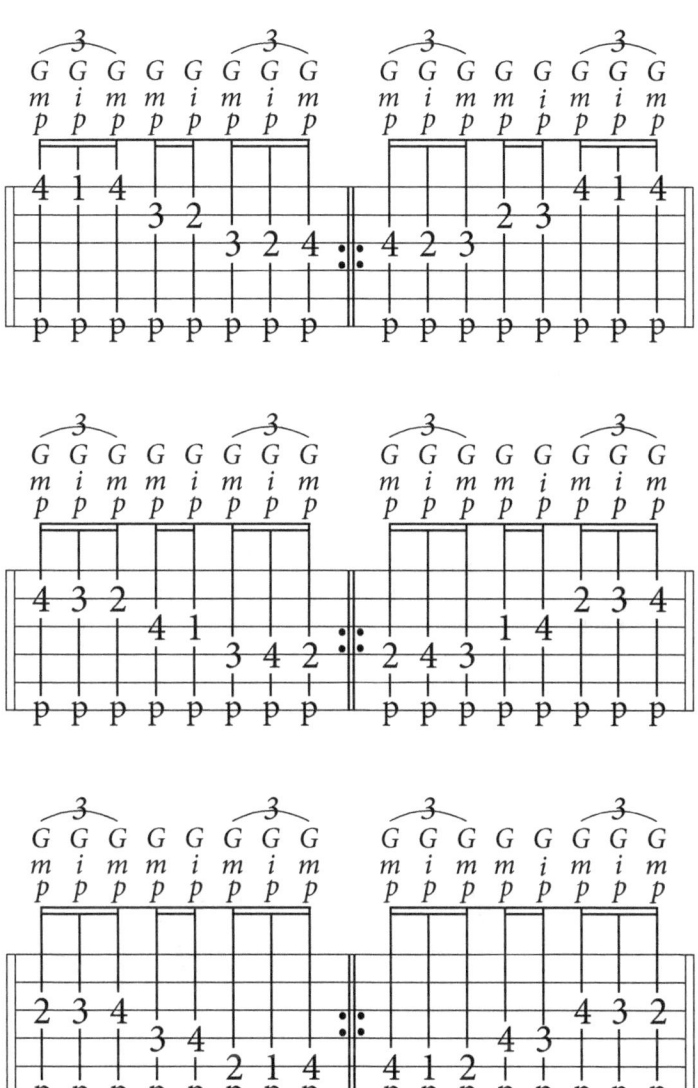

C

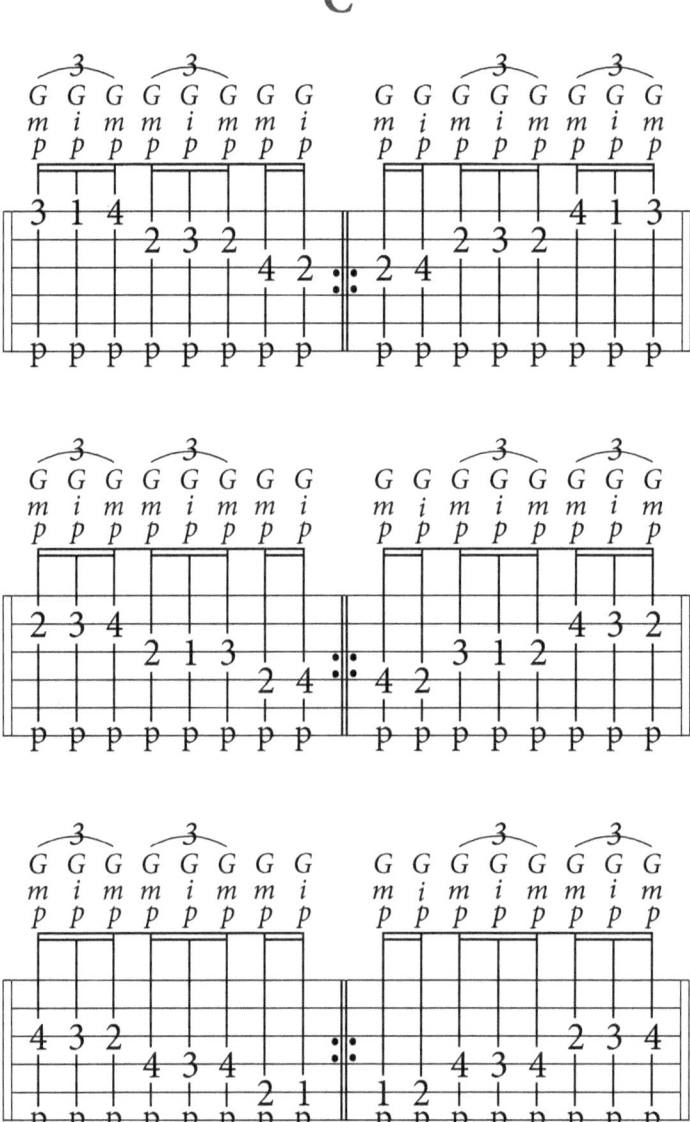

§ IV/1

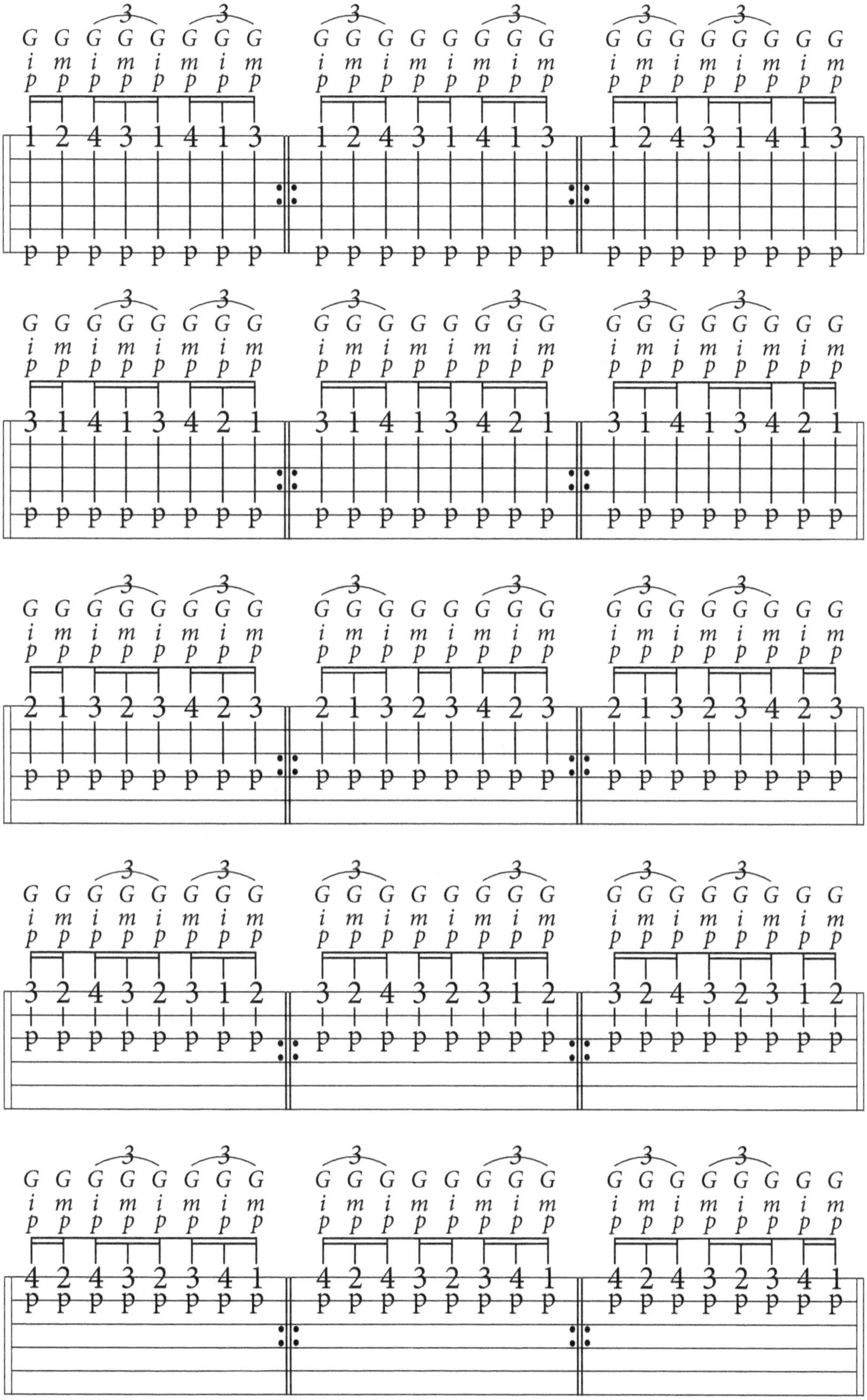
3 3 3 3 3 3
G G G G G G G G G G G G G G G G G G G G G G G G
i m i m i m i m i m i m i m i m i m i m i m i m
p p p p p p p p p p p p p p p p p p p p p p p p
1 2 4 3 1 4 1 3 1 2 4 3 1 4 1 3 1 2 4 3 1 4 1 3
p p p p p p p p p p p p p p p p p p p p p p p p
3 3 3 3 3 3
G G G G G G G G G G G G G G G G G G G G G G G G
i m i m i m i m i m i m i m i m i m i m i m i m
p p p p p p p p p p p p p p p p p p p p p p p p
3 1 4 1 3 4 2 1 3 1 4 1 3 4 2 1 3 1 4 1 3 4 2 1
p p p p p p p p p p p p p p p p p p p p p p p p
3 3 3 3 3 3
G G G G G G G G G G G G G G G G G G G G G G G G
i m i m i m i m i m i m i m i m i m i m i m i m
p p p p p p p p p p p p p p p p p p p p p p p p
2 1 3 2 3 4 2 3 2 1 3 2 3 4 2 3 2 1 3 2 3 4 2 3
p p p p p p p p p p p p p p p p p p p p p p p p
3 3 3 3 3 3
G G G G G G G G G G G G G G G G G G G G G G G G
i m i m i m i m i m i m i m i m i m i m i m i m
p p p p p p p p p p p p p p p p p p p p p p p p
3 2 4 3 2 3 1 2 3 2 4 3 2 3 1 2 3 2 4 3 2 3 1 2
p p p p p p p p p p p p p p p p p p p p p p p p
3 3 3 3 3 3
G G G G G G G G G G G G G G G G G G G G G G G G
i m i m i m i m i m i m i m i m i m i m i m i m
p p p p p p p p p p p p p p p p p p p p p p p p
4 2 4 3 2 3 4 1 4 2 4 3 2 3 4 1 4 2 4 3 2 3 4 1
p p p p p p p p p p p p p p p p p p p p p p p p

§ IV/2

A

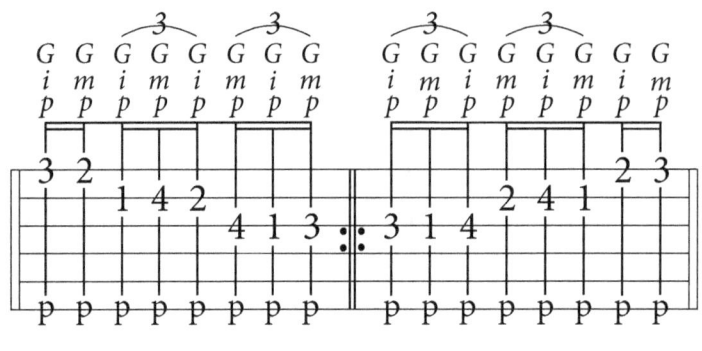
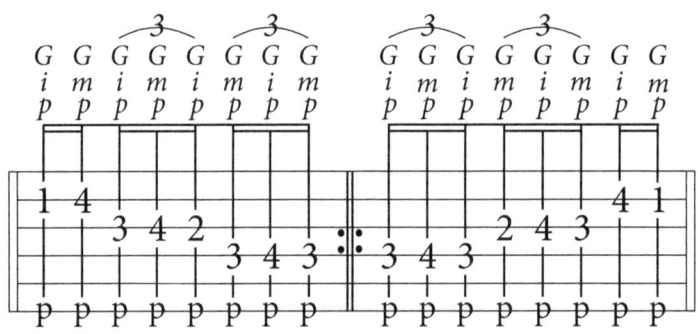
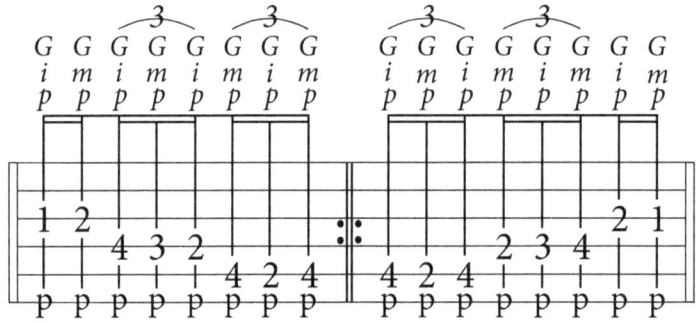

B

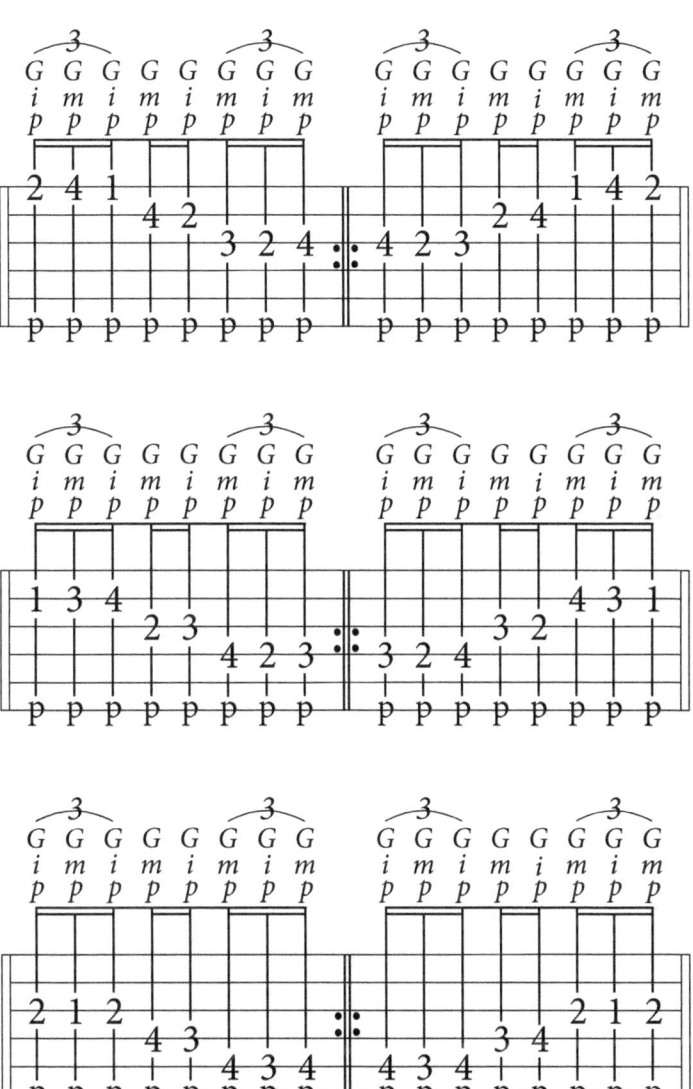

C

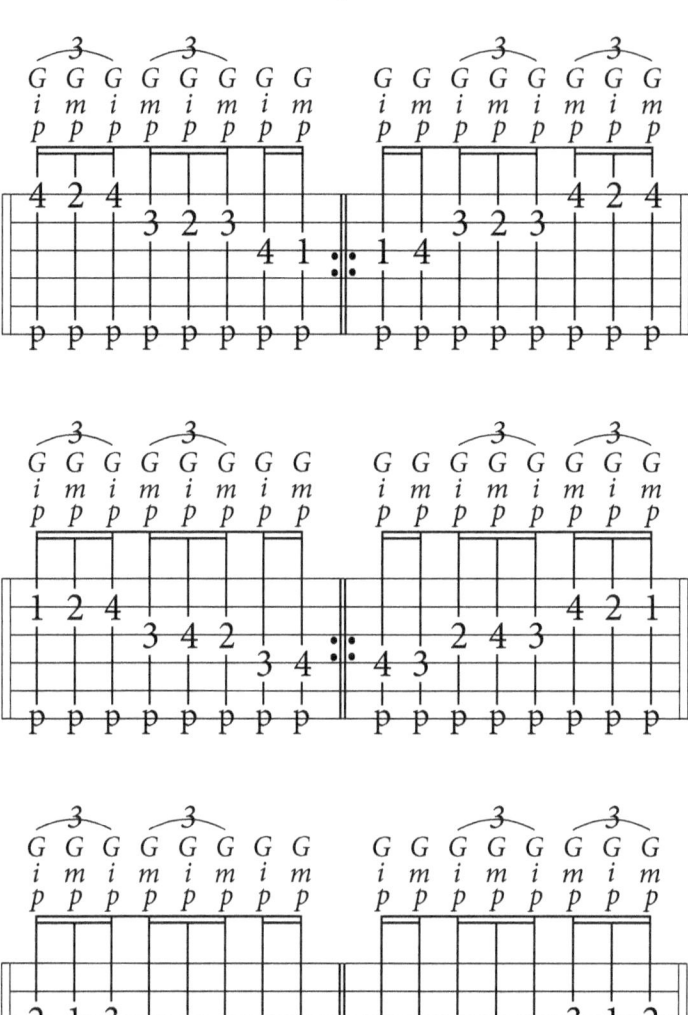

§ V/1

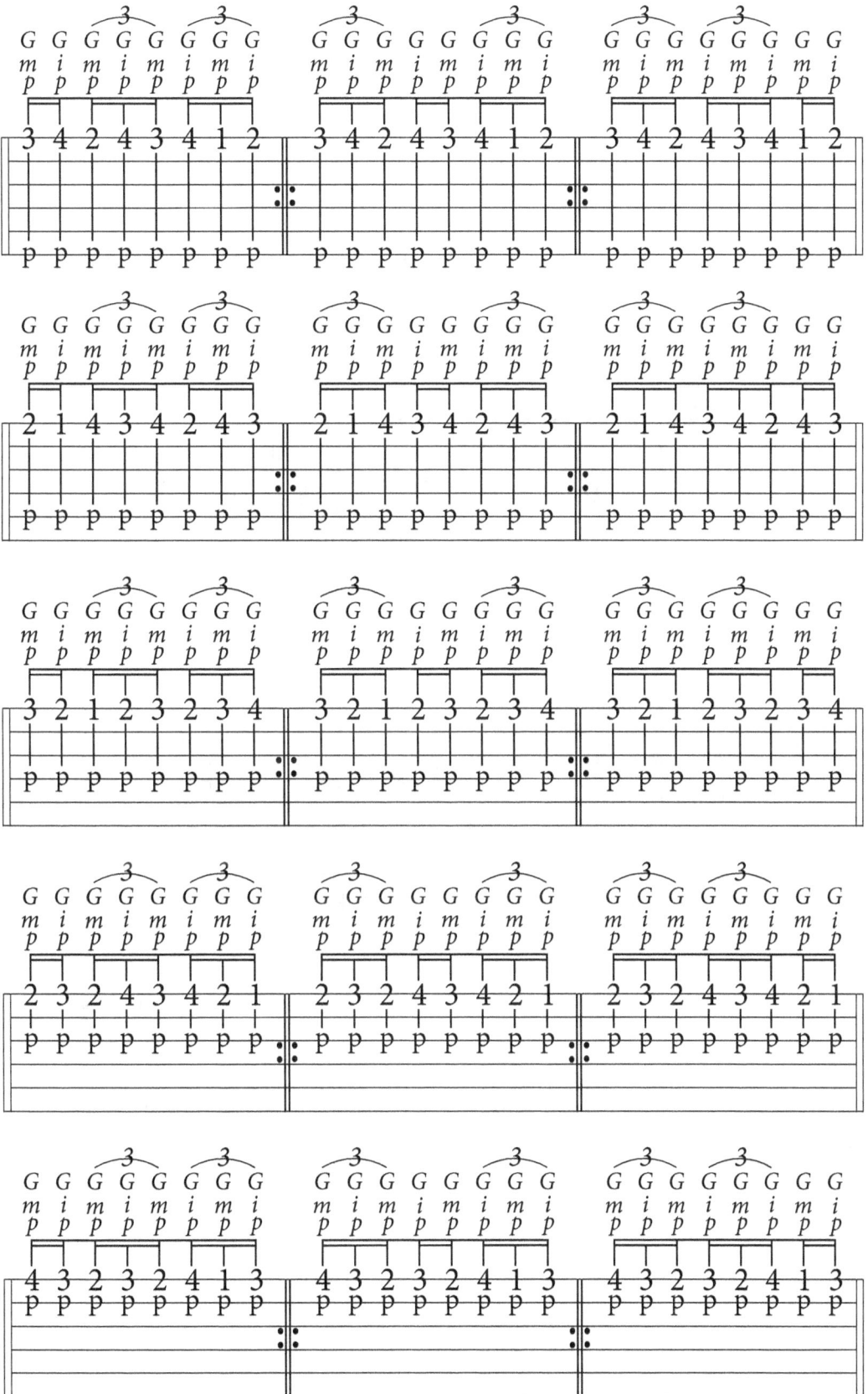

§ V/2

A

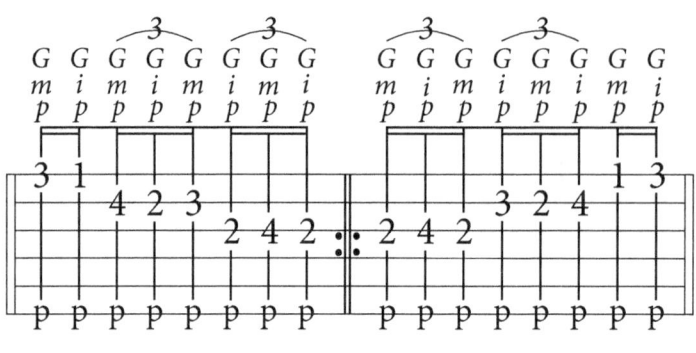

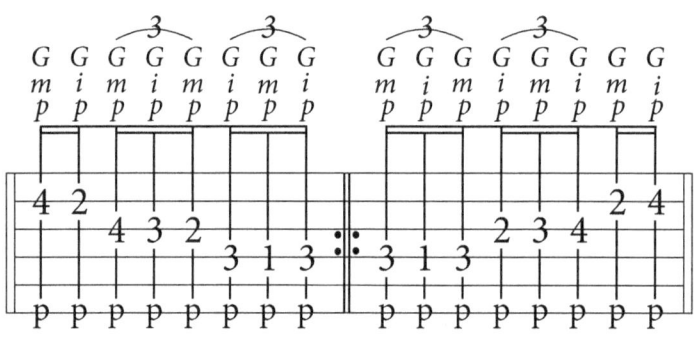

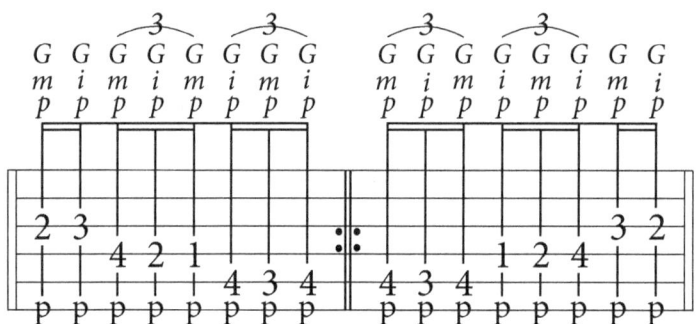

B

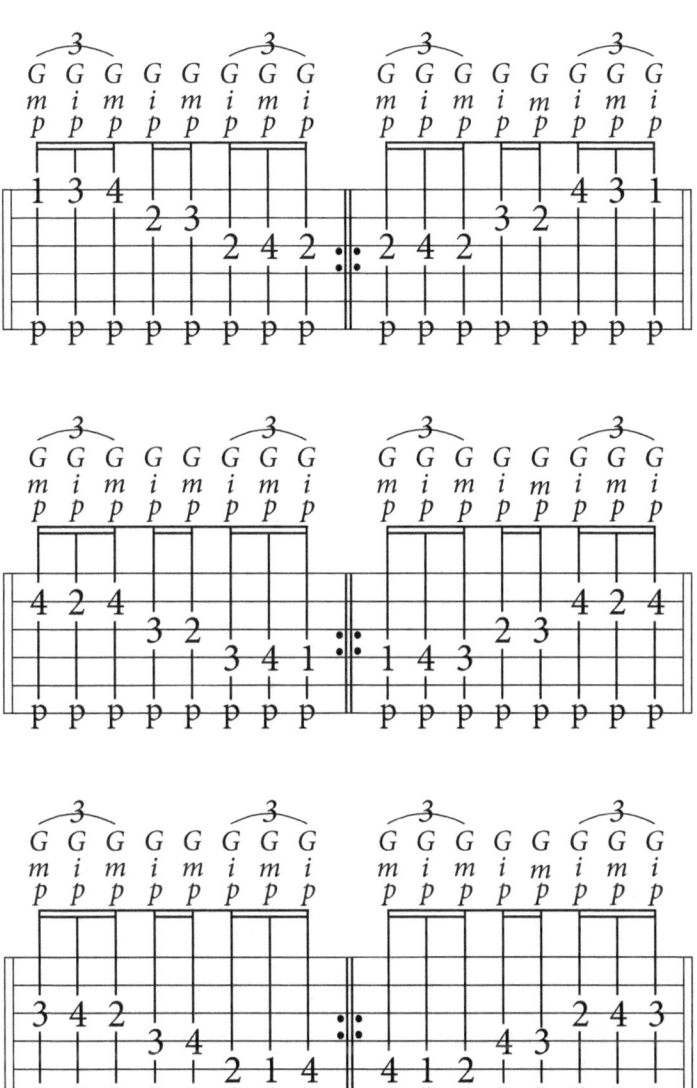

C

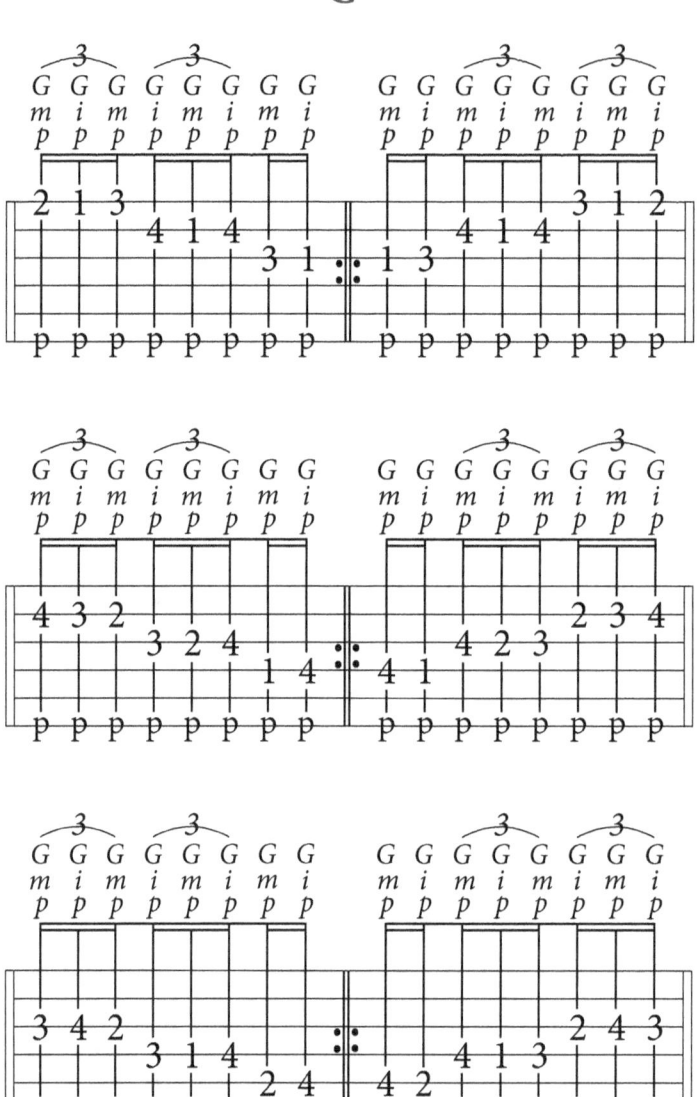

UNIT 2

Simultaneous stroke of thumb
with index (i), middle finger (m) and Golpe.
Continuous Golpe in every stroke.

Simultaneous stroke of the thumb with the index and middle finger with continuous Golpe. The chromatic scale is on the 1st, 2nd, 3rd, 4th and 5th string. The thumb always strikes the adjacent strings which are above the ones where the chromatic scales develop. There are variations in relation to the sequencing of the fingers (i) and (m).

§ Ia

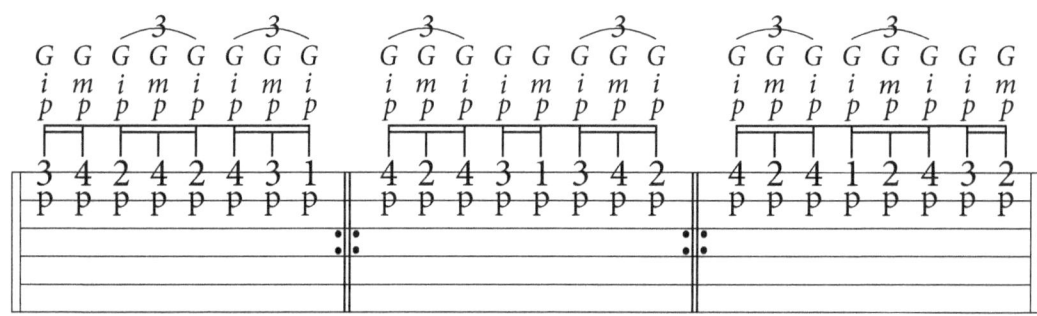

§ Ib

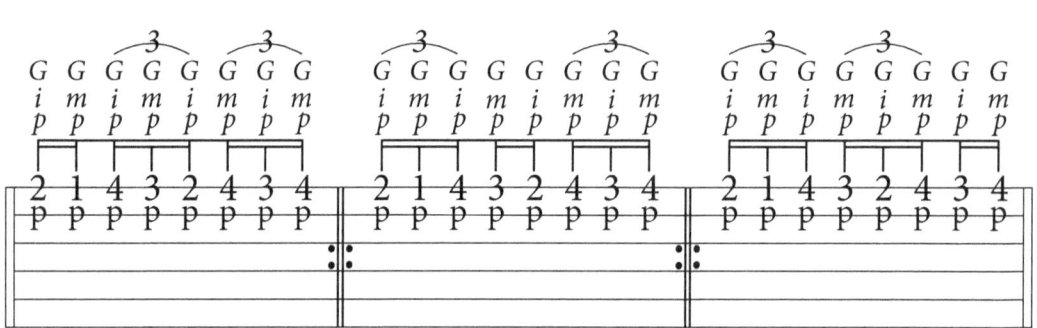

§ IIa

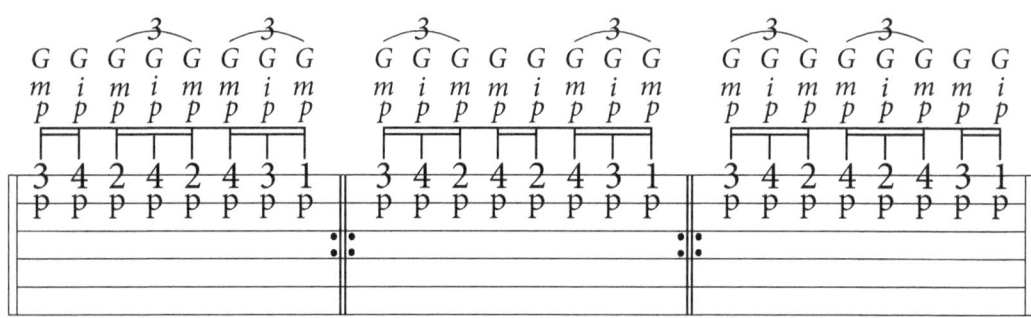

§ IIb

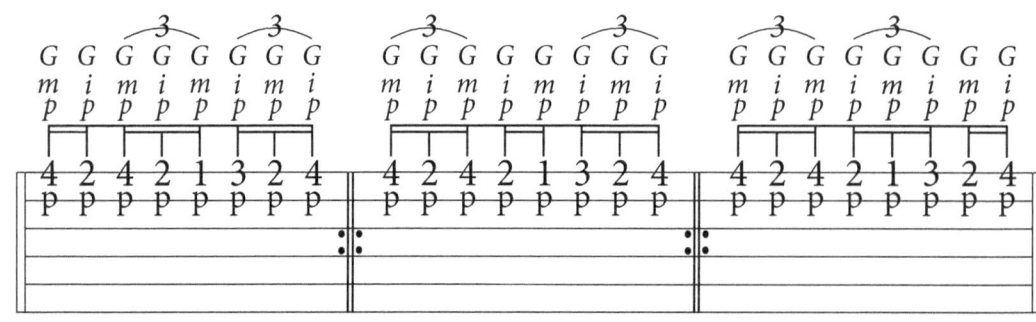

§ Ia

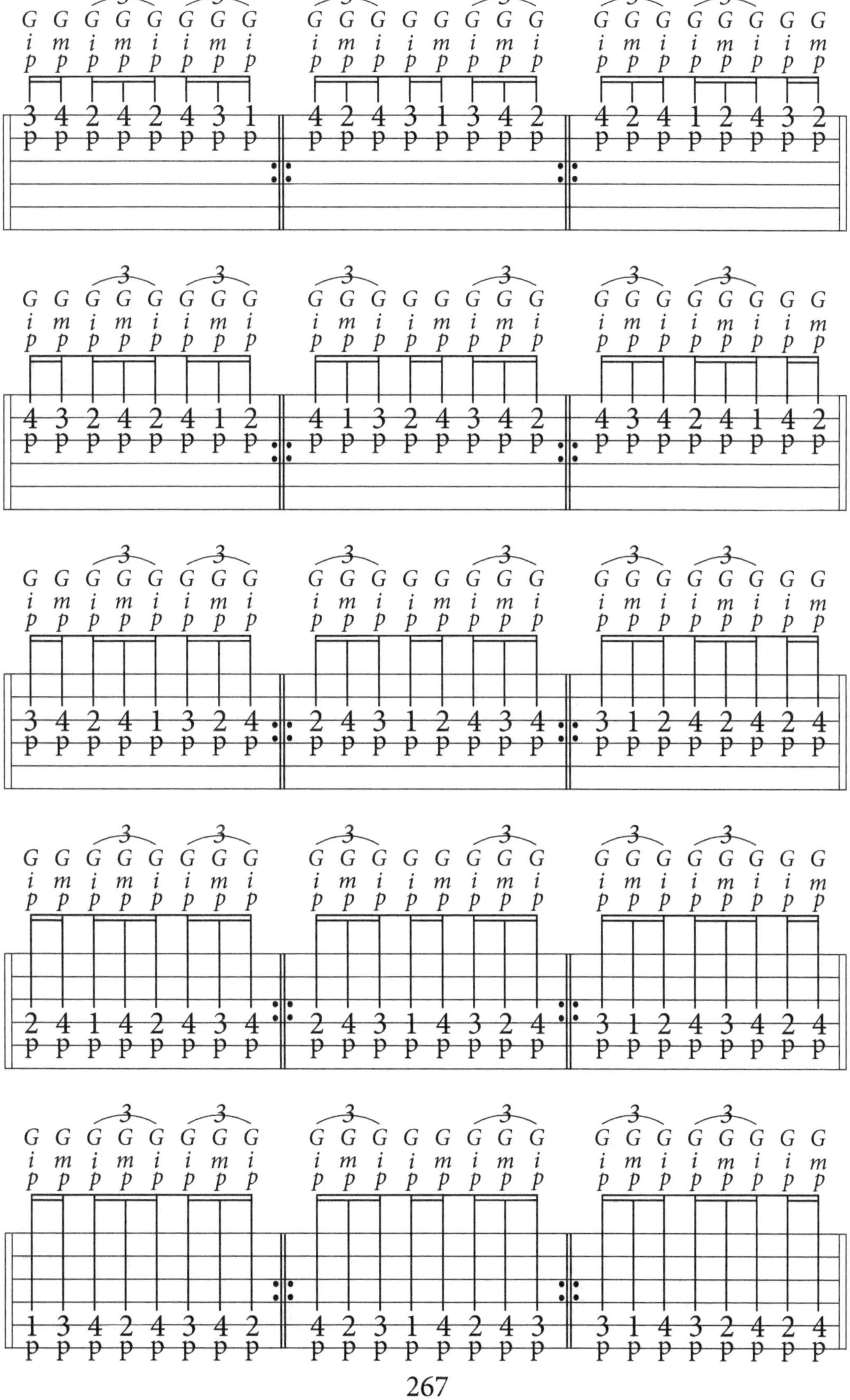

§ Ib

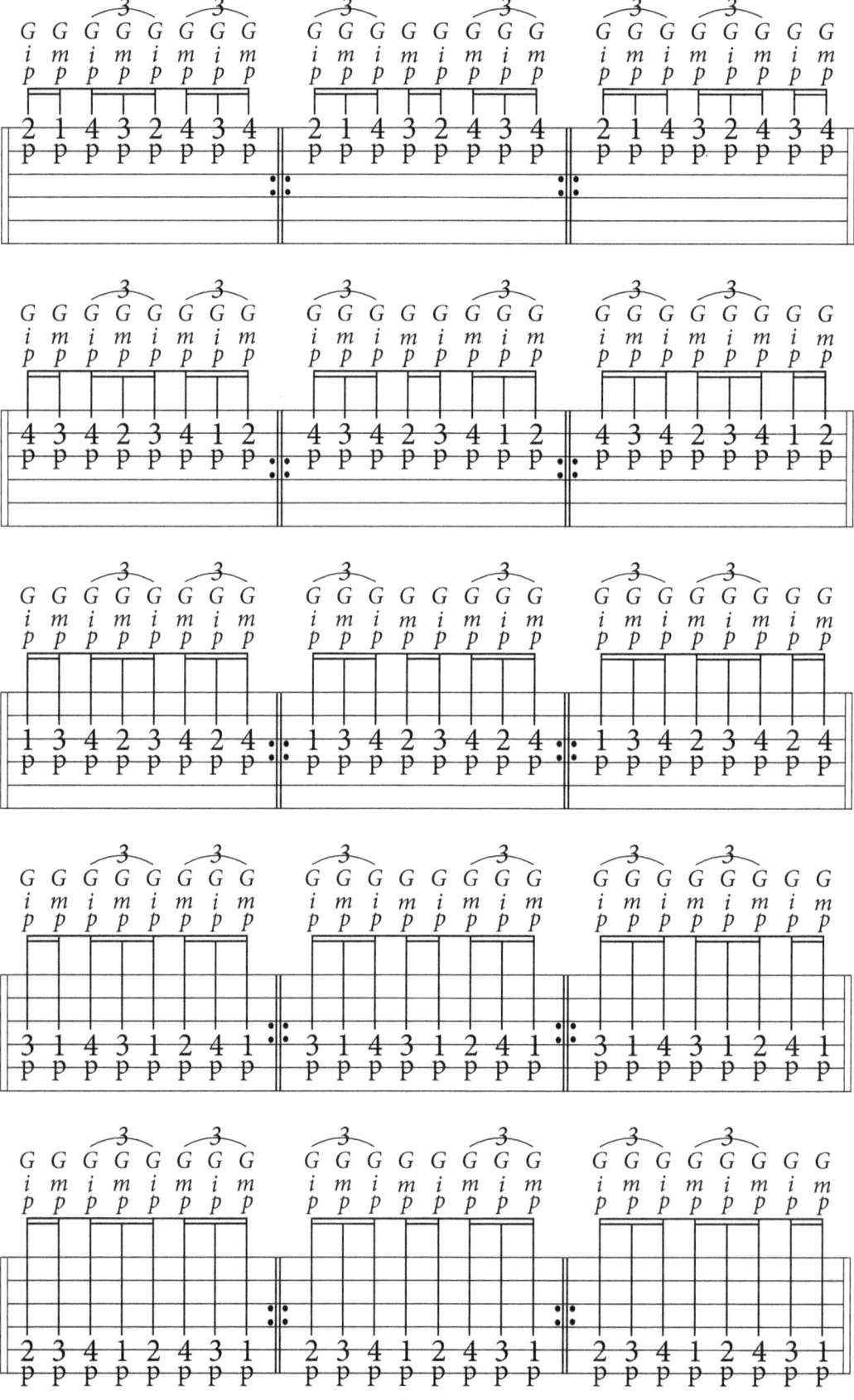

§ IIa

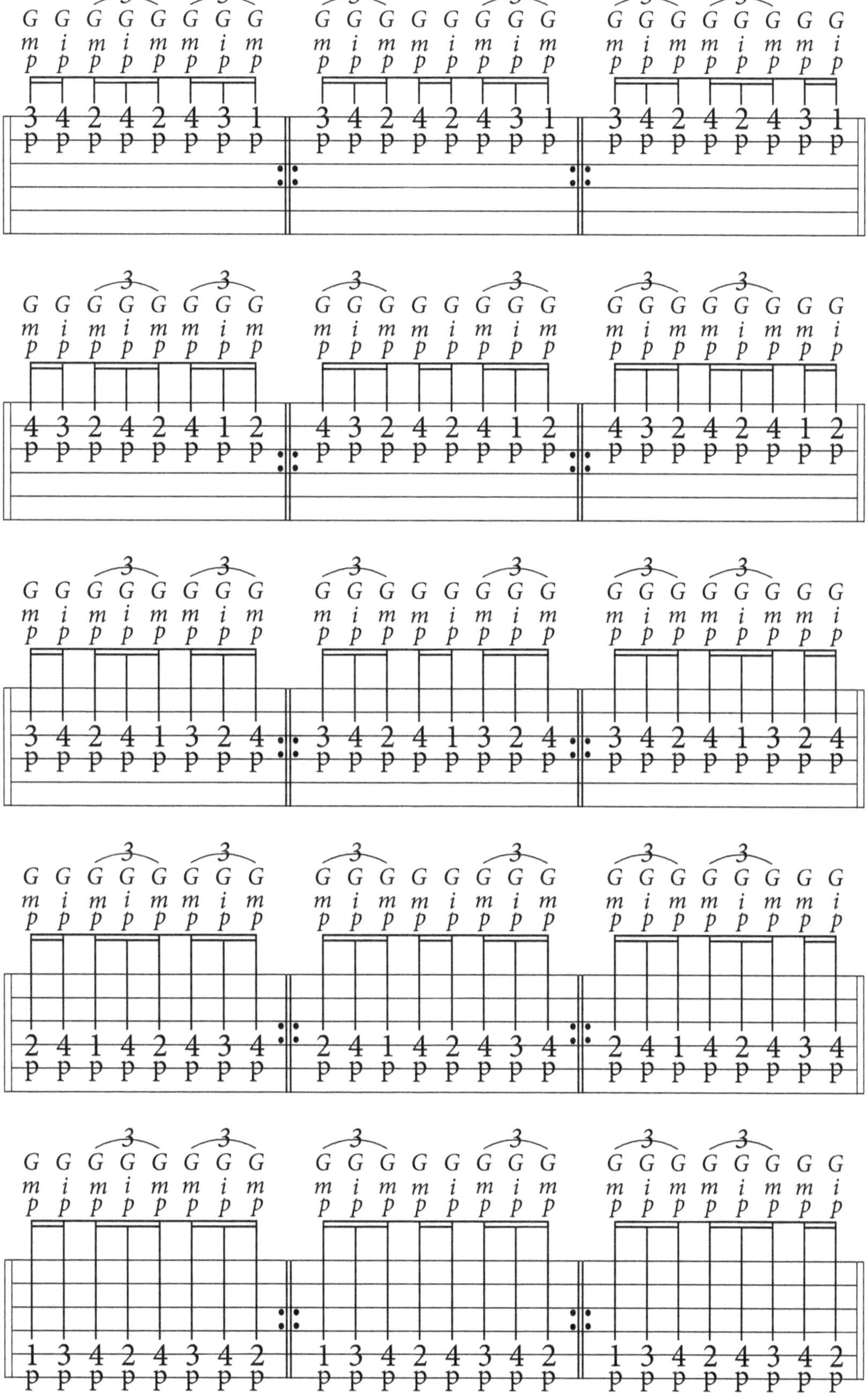

§ IIb

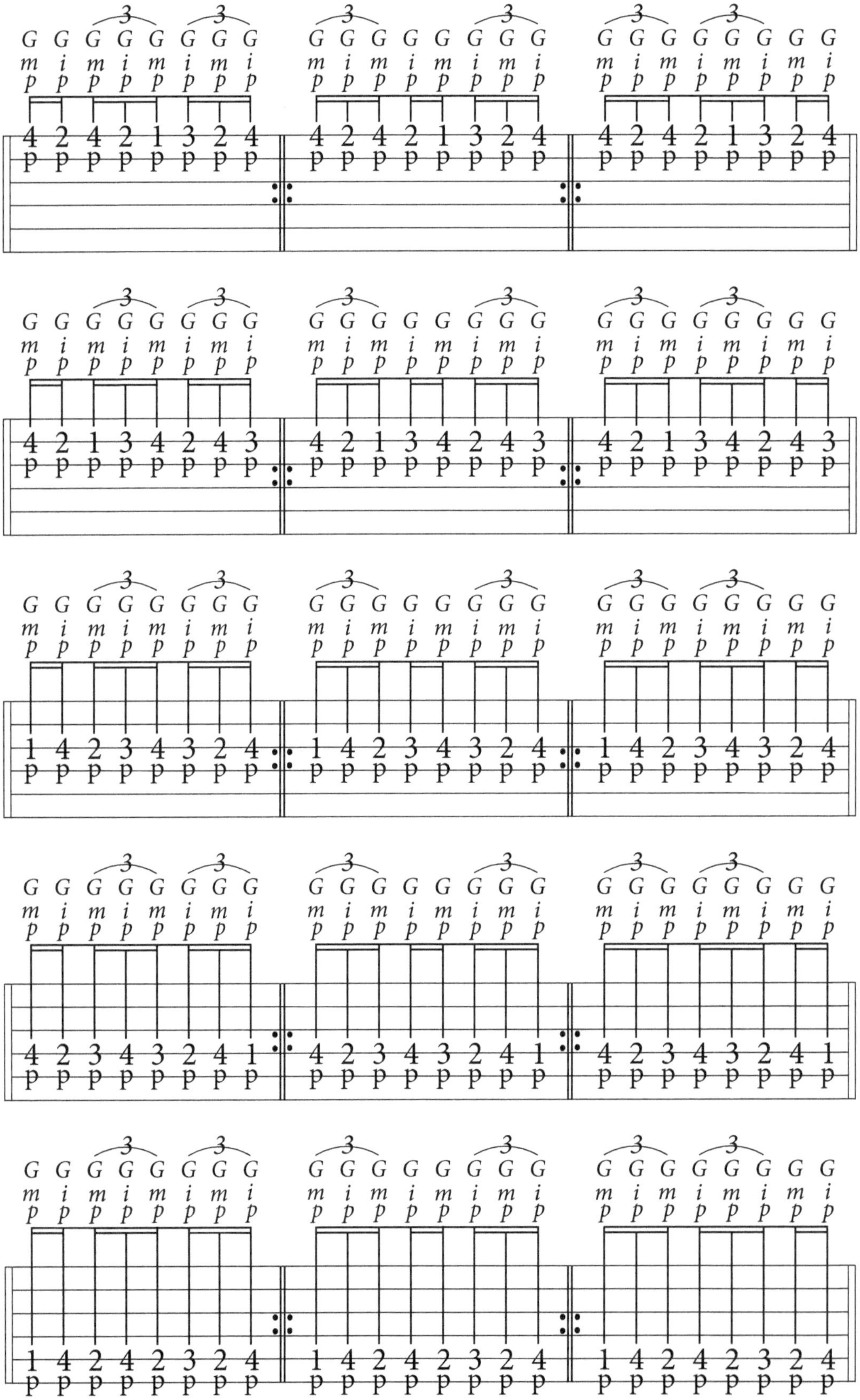

BOOK ON GOLPE

SECOND PART

The second part of the book contains exercises based on:

1/. SCALES OF TWO ADJACENT STRINGS.
2/. SCALES OF ONE STRING.
3/. ASCENDING SCALES.
4/. DESCENDING SCALES.

The second part of the book contains Golpe exercises based on the scales of two adjacent strings which apart from their original arrangement,

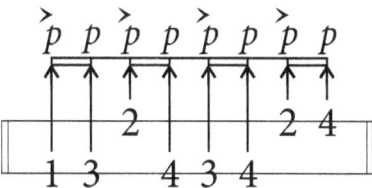

can be also arranged with two triplets in three variations:

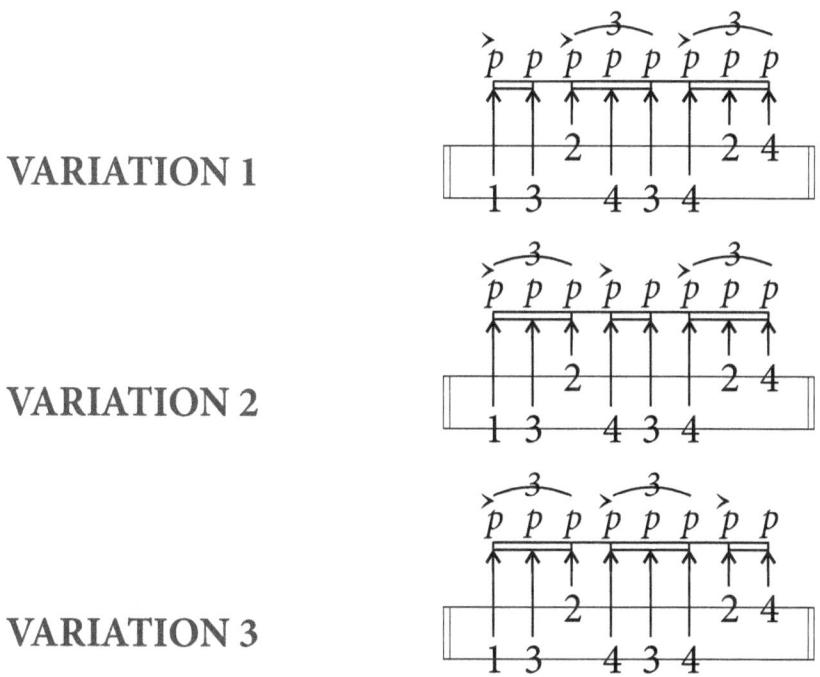

VARIATION 1

VARIATION 2

VARIATION 3

The above scales which function on two adjacent strings can be also applied in some exercises on remote strings with insertion of:

one string

two strings

or three strings

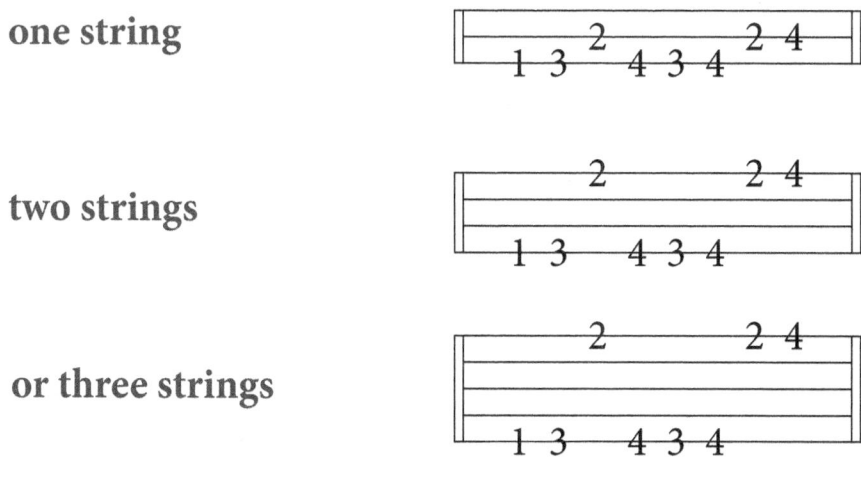

CHAPTER 1
THUMB STROKE AND GOLPE ON SCALES OF TWO ADJACENT STRINGS.

UNIT 1

Various exercises of Golpe:
1/. Only thumb Golpe.
2/. Thumb Golpe in combination.
with index (i) or middle finger (m).
3/. Exercises with free Golpe.

§ I Practice on the Formula without Golpe, only with the thumb in the normal form and in the three variations with the triplets. The two notes and the triplet have the same duration (they are isochronous).
Also practice in the following Formulas (scales of two adjacent strings) with Golpe as it is noted.

§ II Variation of the previous exercise with insertion, within the scales, of the right hand fingers, index (i) and middle finger (m), either each one seperately within the exercise or in combination (i-m) and (m-i).

§ III Golpe exercises on the Formulas with normal finger sequencing. Ascending and descending rolling Formulas which I call Formulas ROTATION. Here we find Golpe with simultaneous thumb stroke and free Golpe.

§ IV Golpe exercises on the chromatic scales of two adjacent strings with simultaneous Golpe with the thumb and free within the meter.

The exercises of §III and §IV are in triplets.

The exercises of unit 1 are written in order to be performed on two adjacent strings (any pair of adjacent strings). Different pairs of strings exhibit different degrees of difficulty. Start practicing with the pair of strings that exhibits the less difficulties in your hand and then practice with all pairs. These exercises can be also performed with inserted strings, one, two, three or even four. Insist in this way of practice, too.

§ I

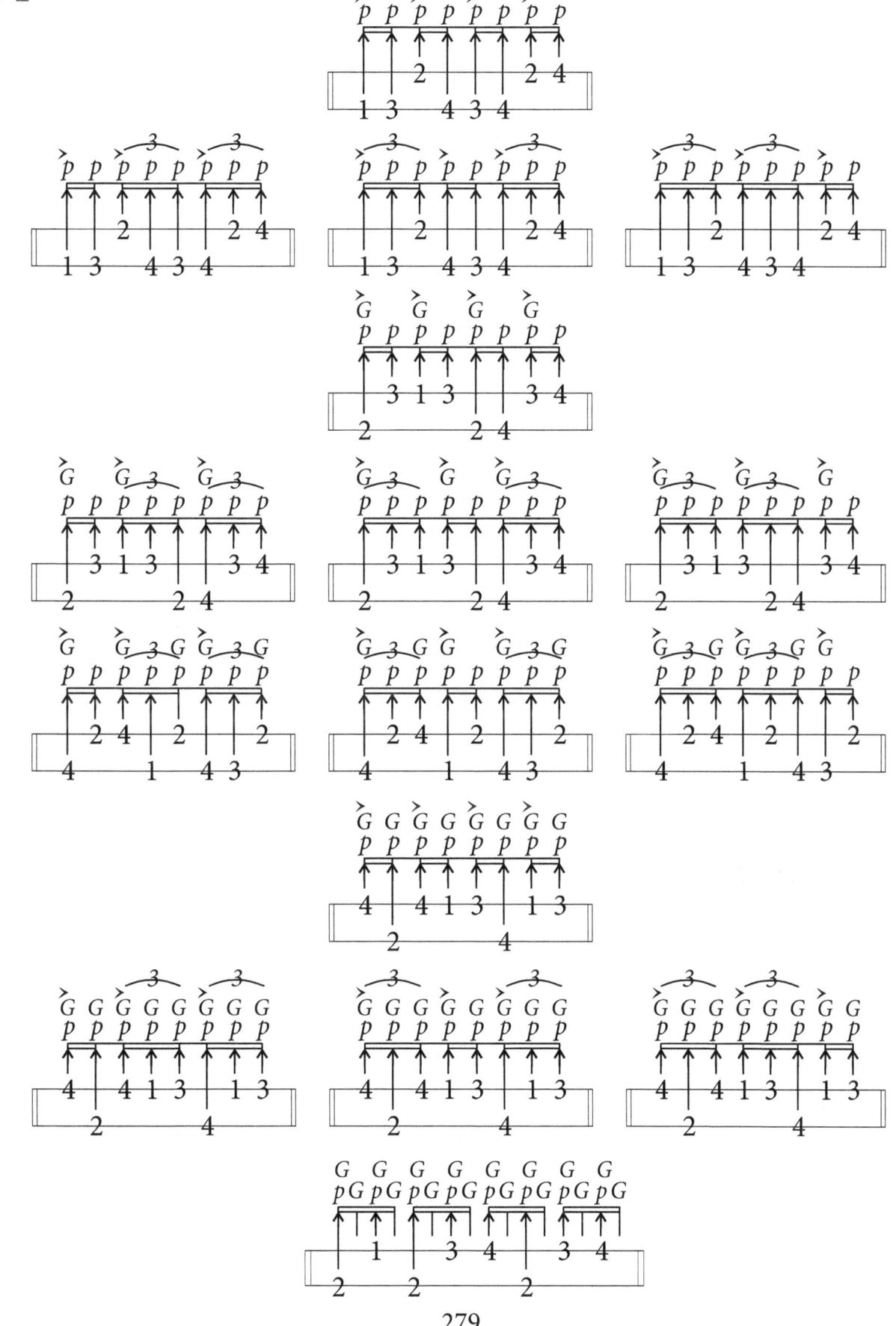

§ II

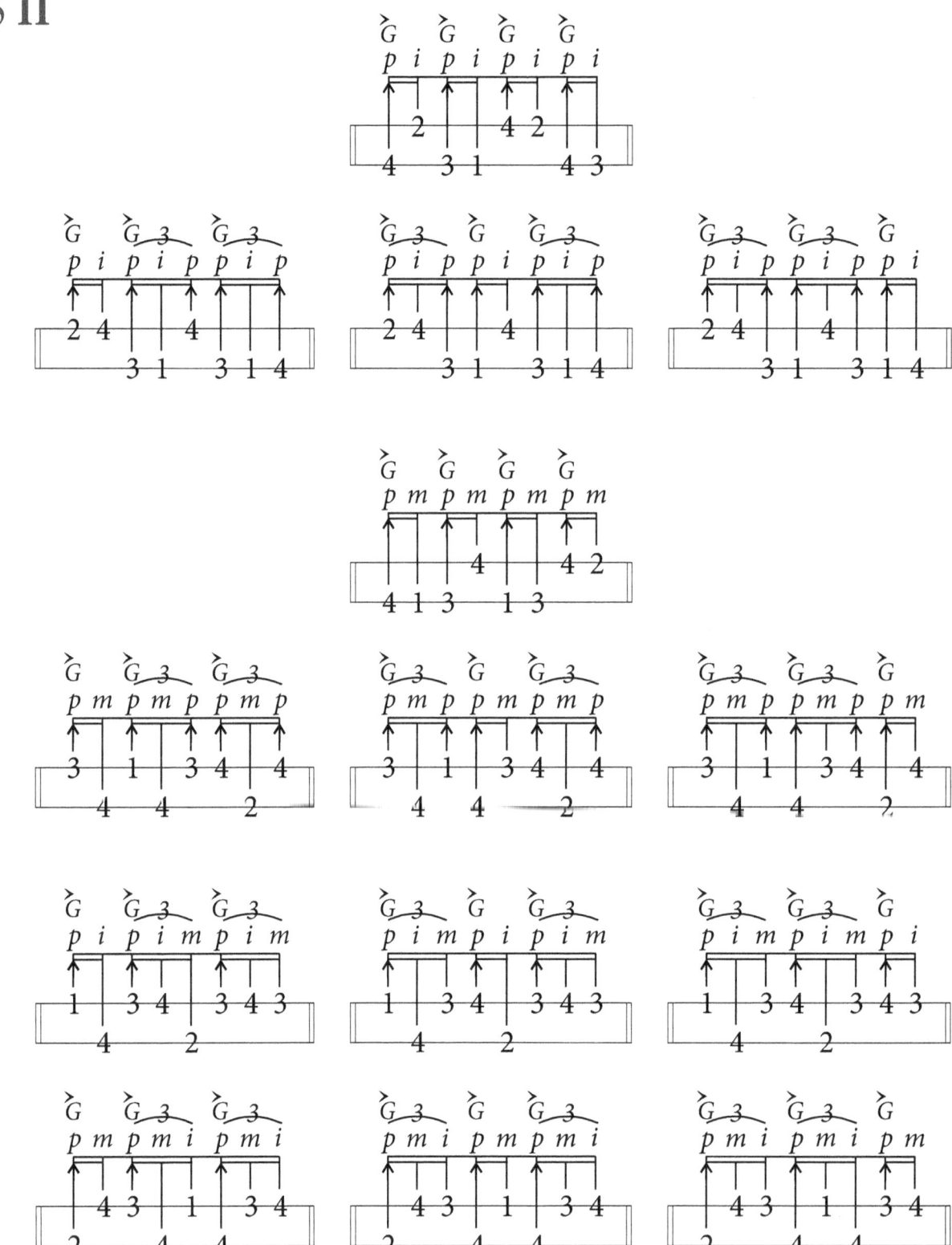

§ III

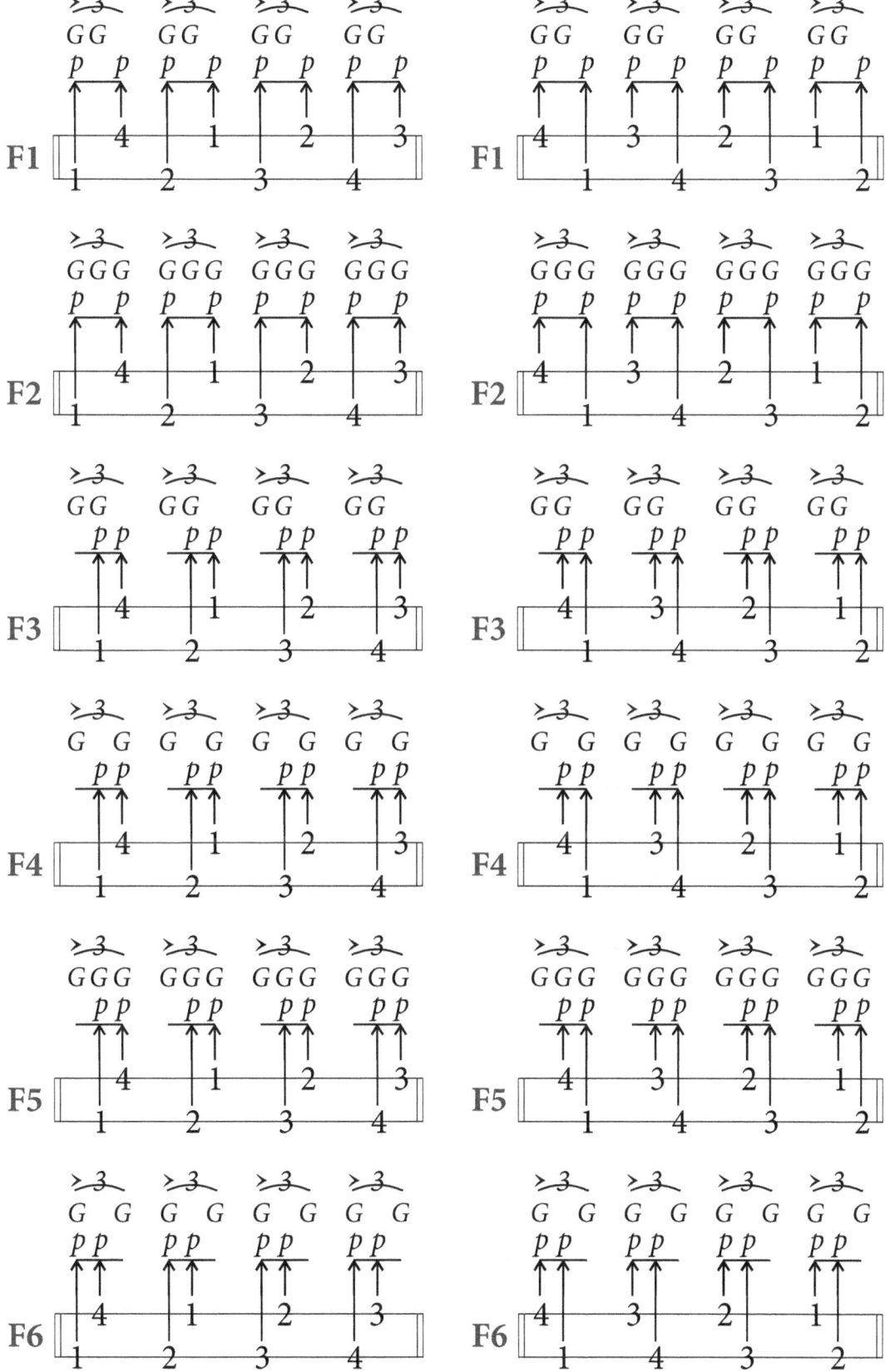

§ IV

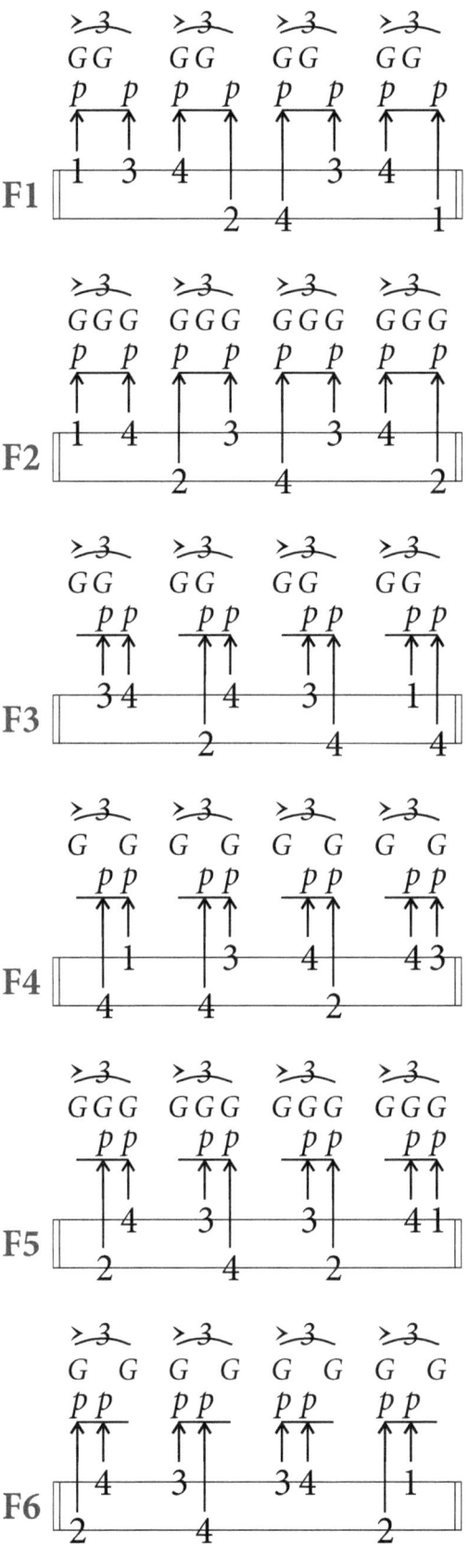

282

UNIT 2

Golpe exercises without the participation of the thumb.
Exercises based on the ascending and descending rolling scales.

9

This unit contains Golpe exercises without the participation of the thumb. These exercises are based on the ascending and descending rolling scales which are played either on two adjacent strings in § I and § II or on remote strings in § III.

§ I

A

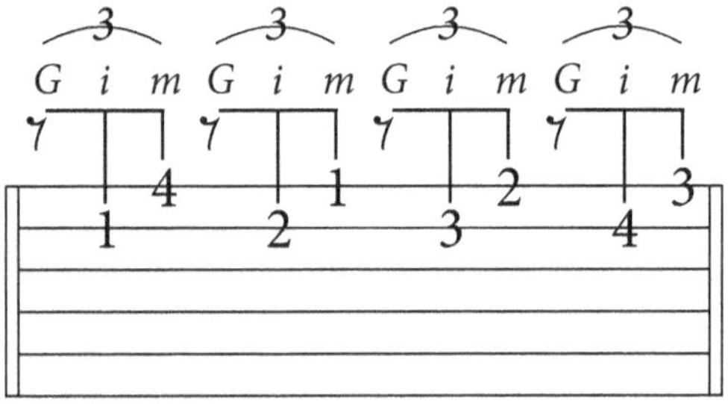

B

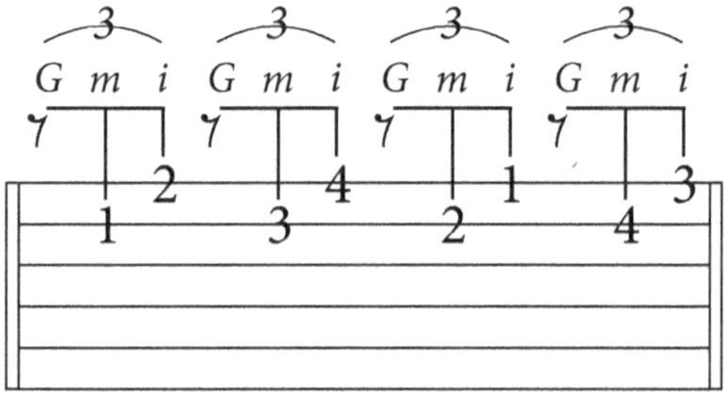

§ II

A

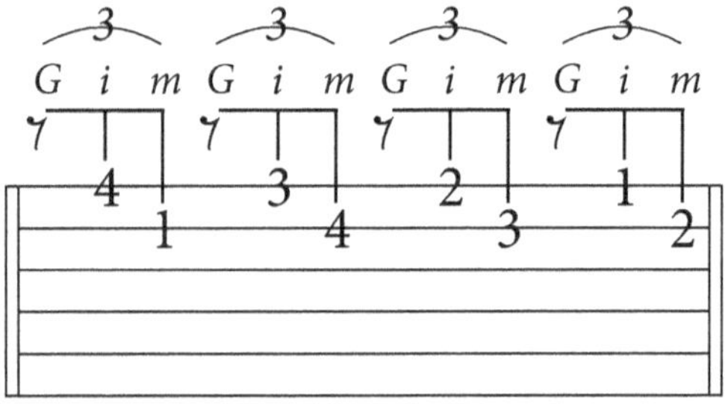

B

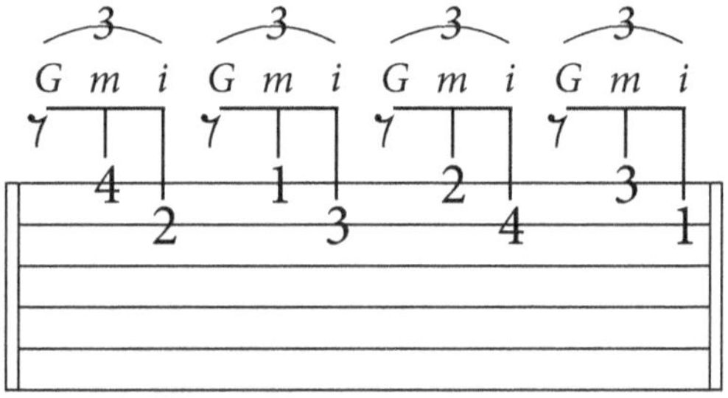

§ III

A

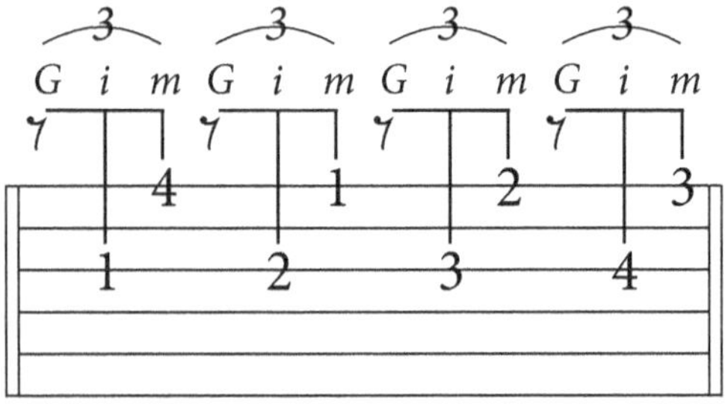

B

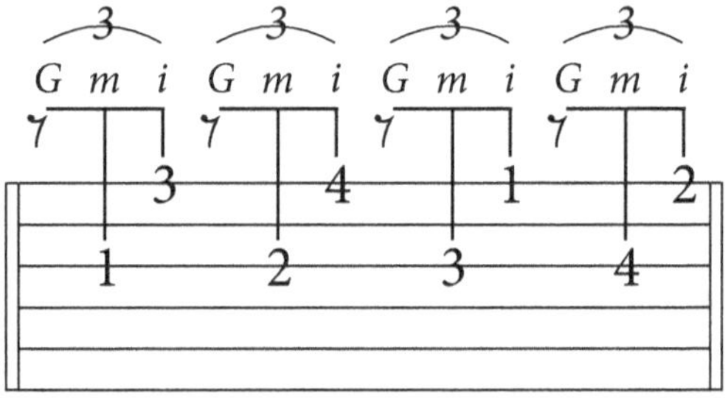

§ IV

A

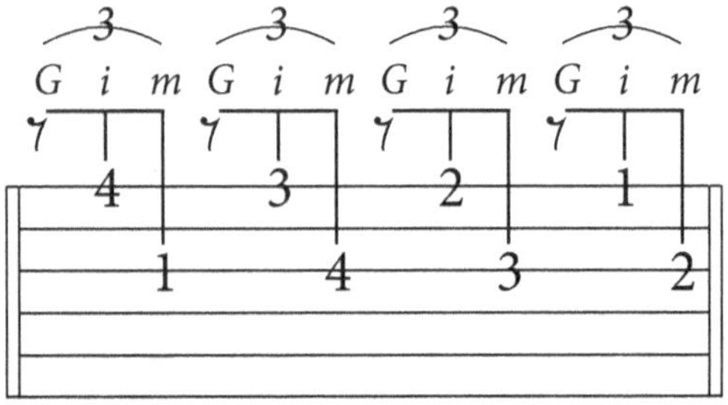

B

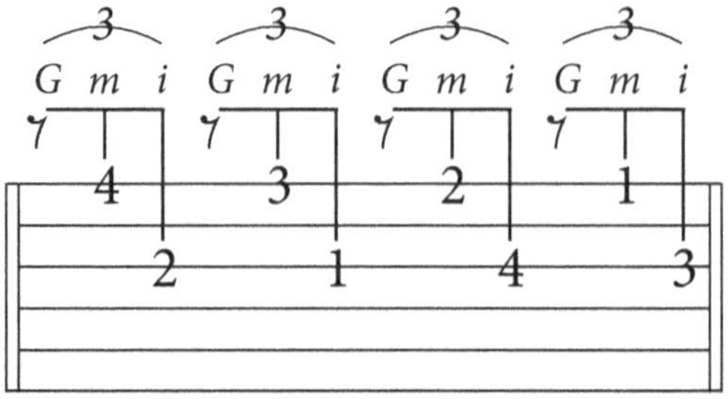

In the exercises of unit 2 use exclusively the index and middle finger apart from the already mentioned way (with of the fingers im and mi). For example the exercise of § I:

§ I

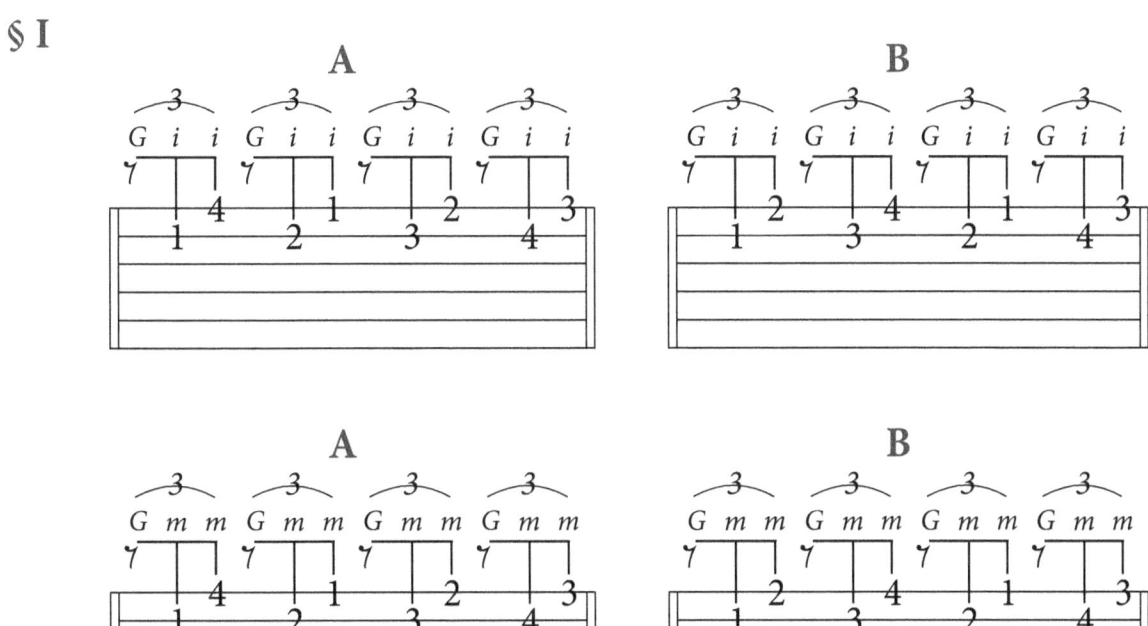

§ I

F1 F2

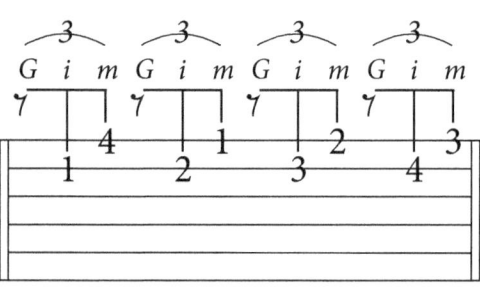 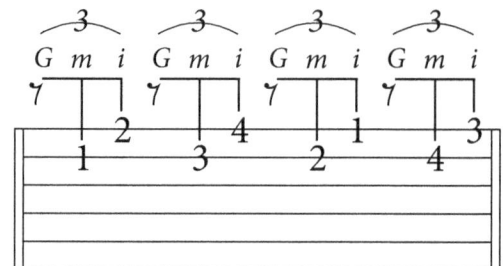
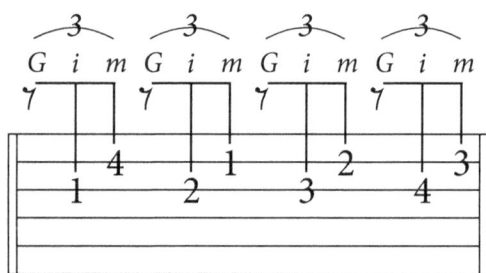 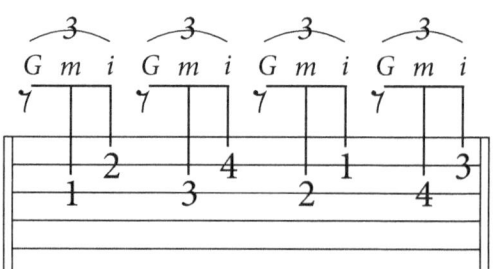
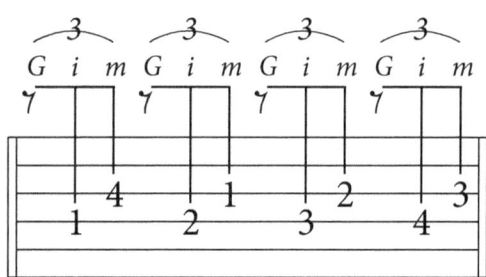 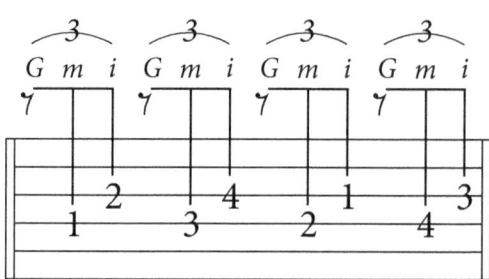
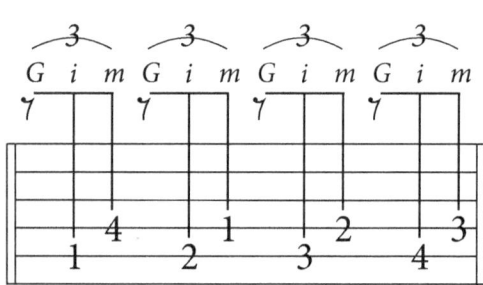 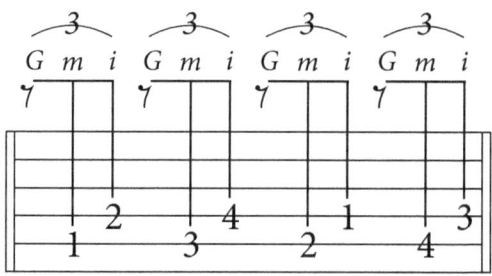
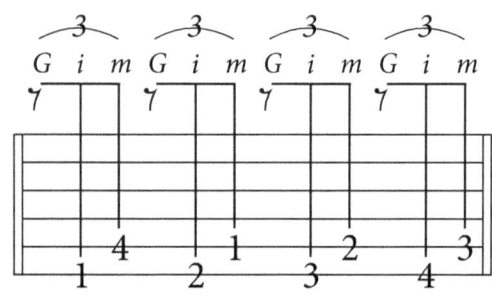 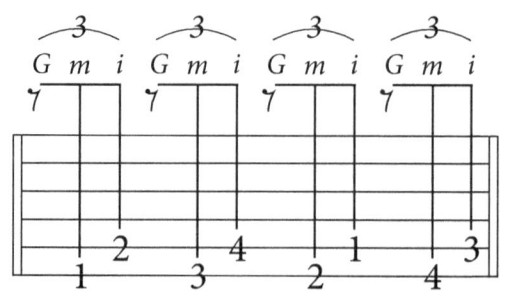

§ II

F1 **F2**

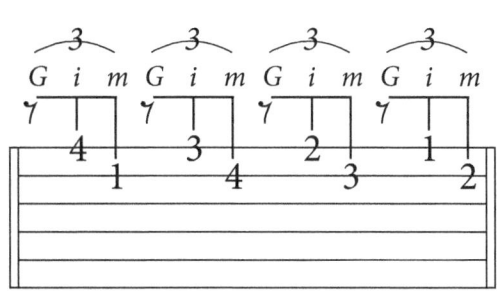 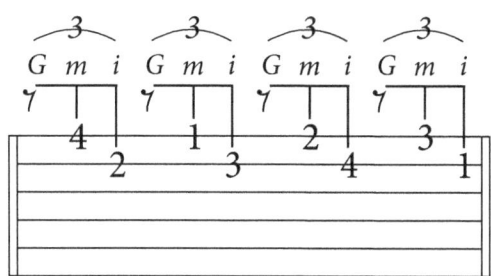

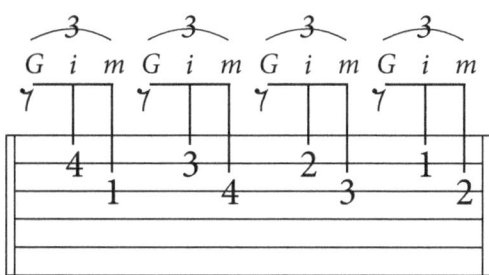 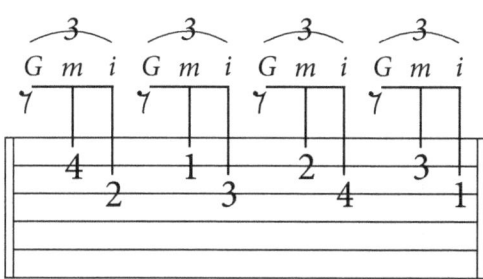

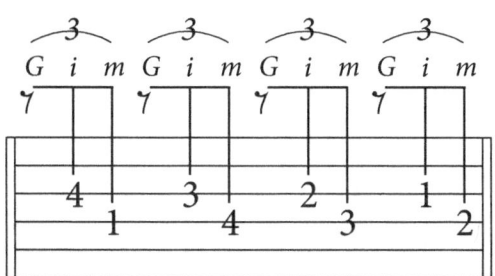 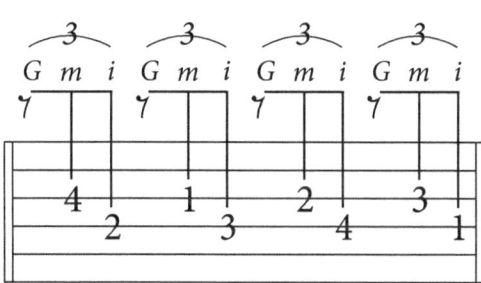

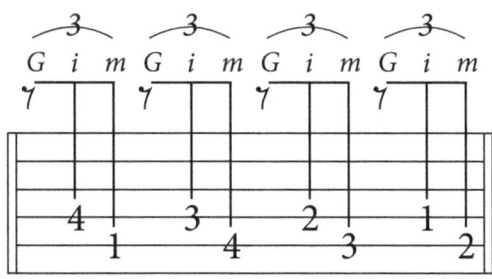 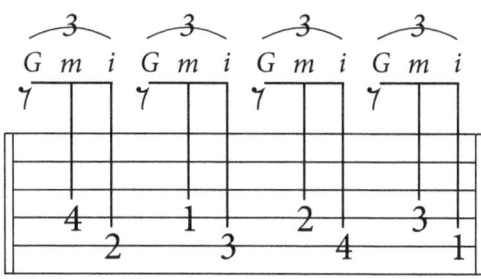

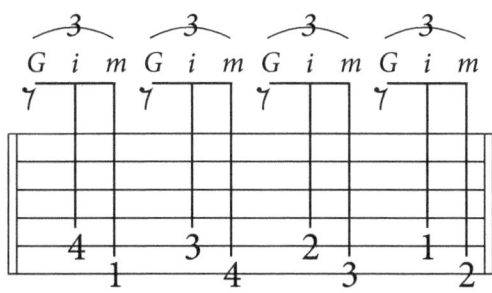 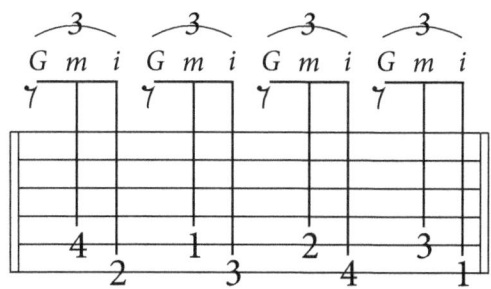

§ III

F1   F2

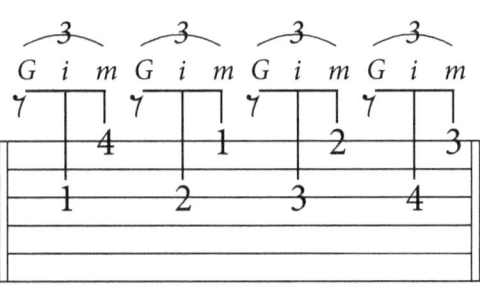 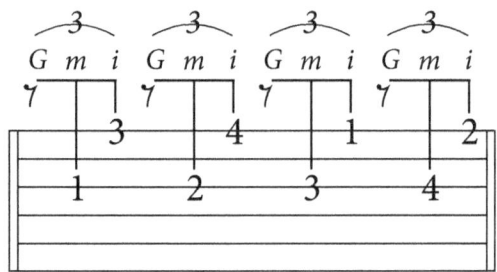

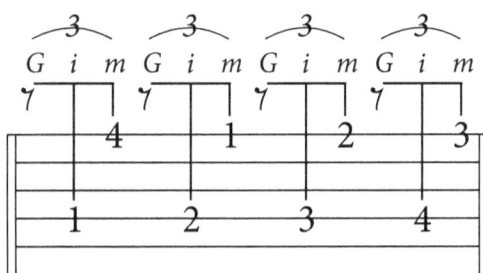 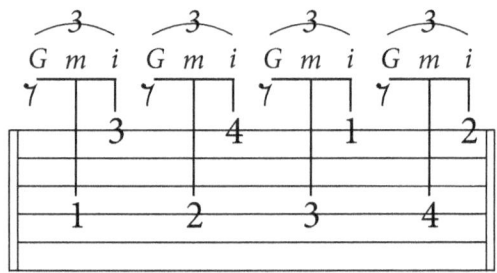

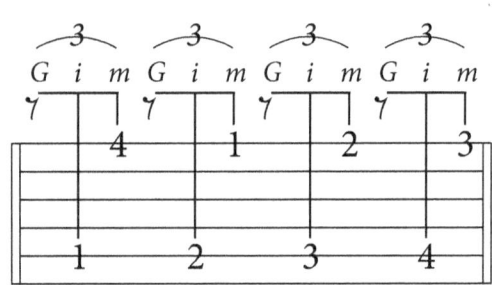 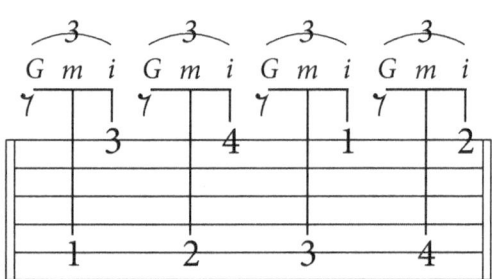

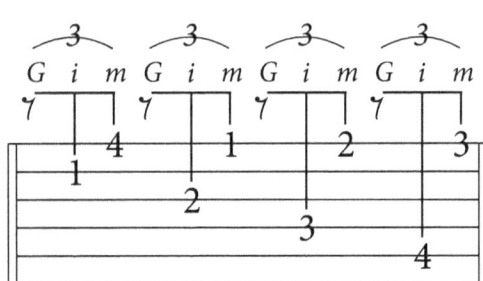 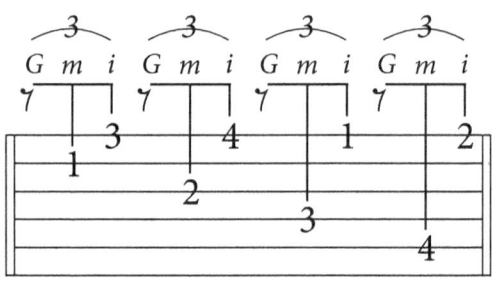

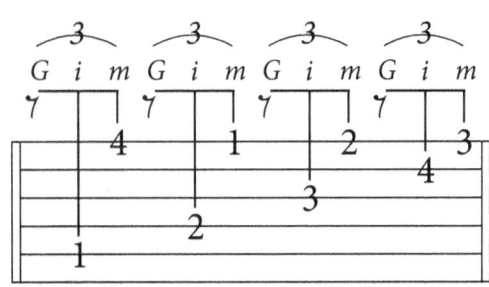 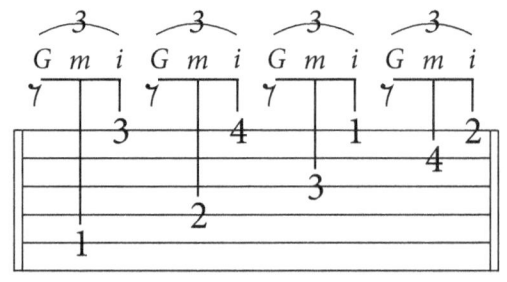

§ IV

F1   **F2**

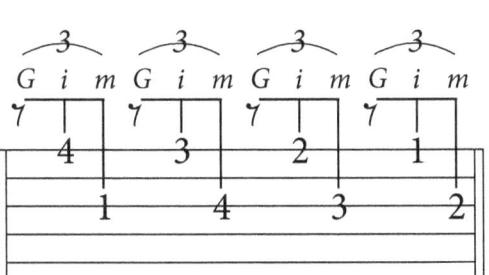 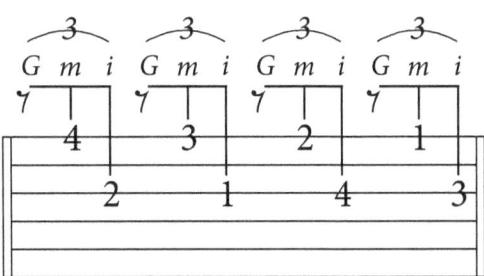

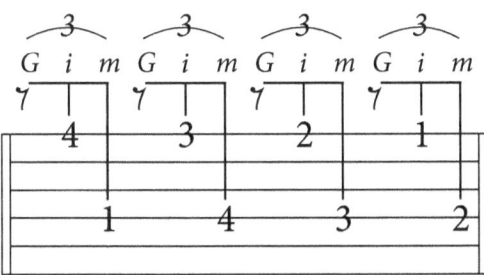 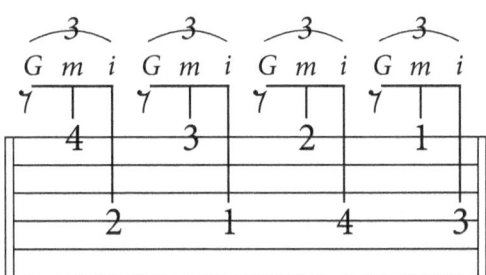

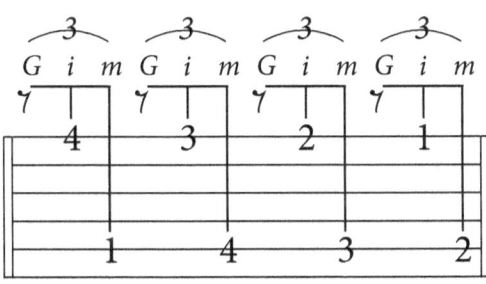 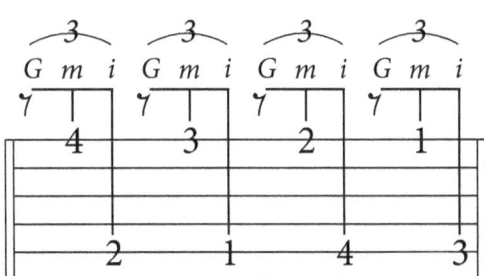

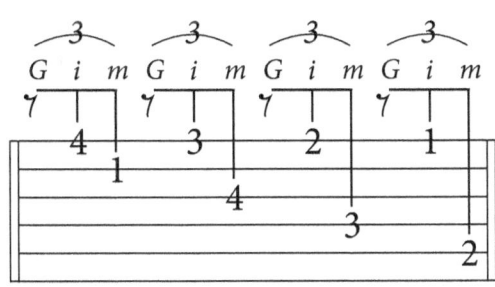 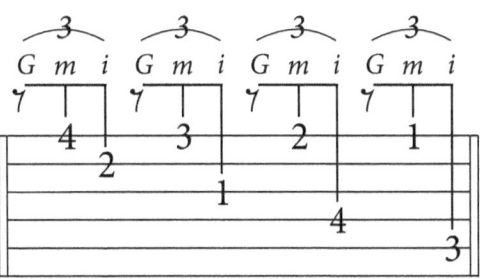

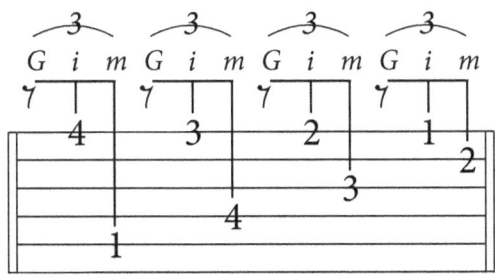 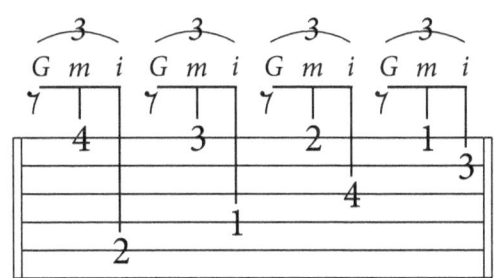

UNIT 3

Golpe exercises without the participation of the thumb.
Golpe exercises with Ligados.

This unit contains Golpe exercises without thumb participation. These exercises are based on the scales of two adjacent strings which are played either on two adjacent strings as in § I or on remote strings as in § II.

§ I

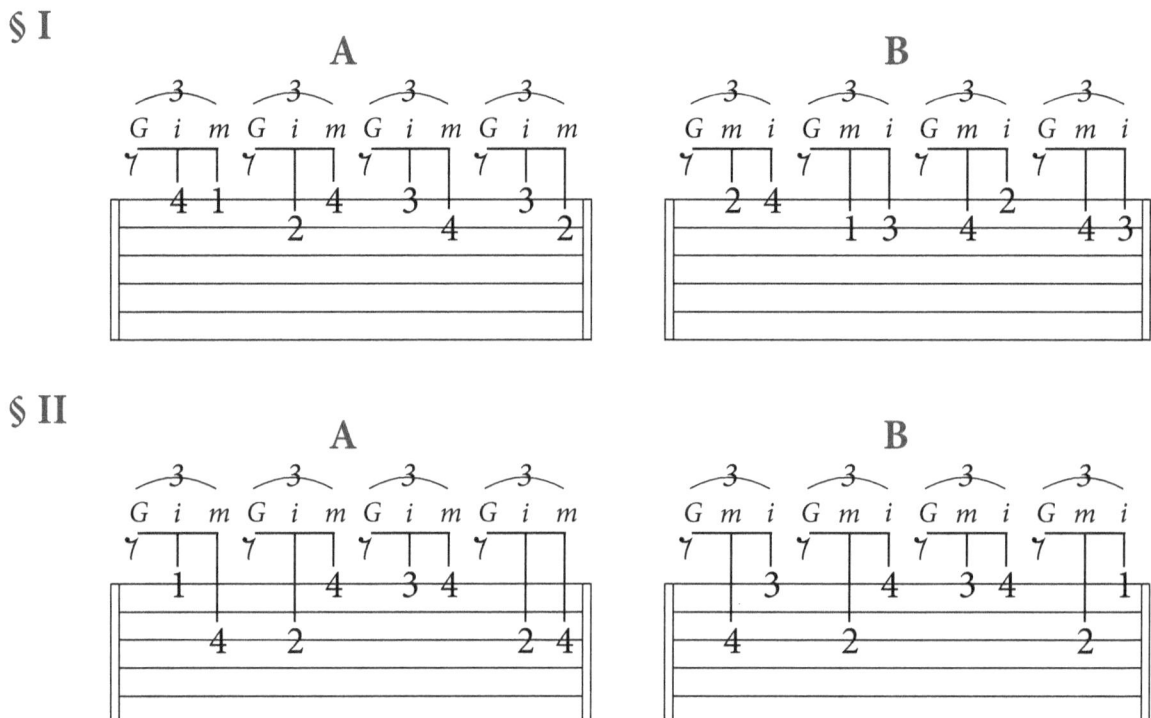

§ II

In § III we find Golpe in combination with legatos. You can also practice with insertion of strings in the Formulas of this paragraph.

§ III

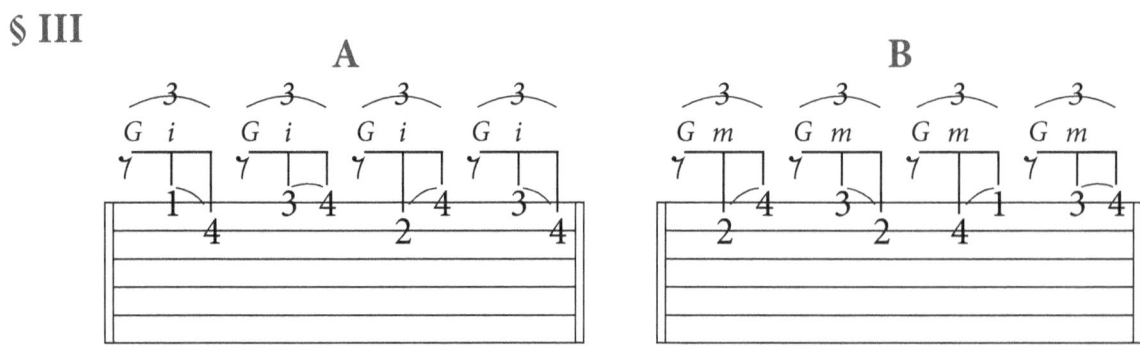

Practice exclusively with the index and middle finger in the exercises of § I, § II of this unit apart from the already mentioned way of finger sequencing (im and mi).

The first line of §I is cited below which uses exclusively the index:

§ I

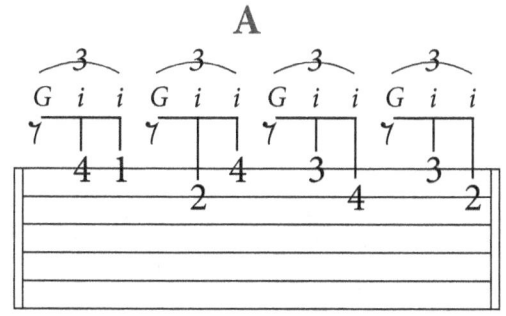

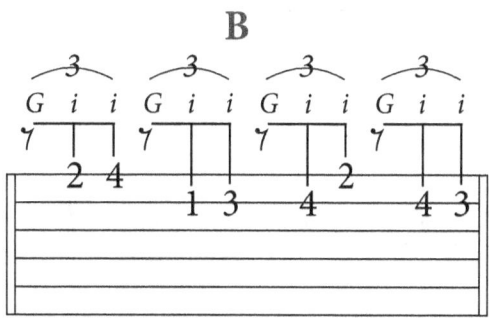

or exclusively the middle finger:

§ I

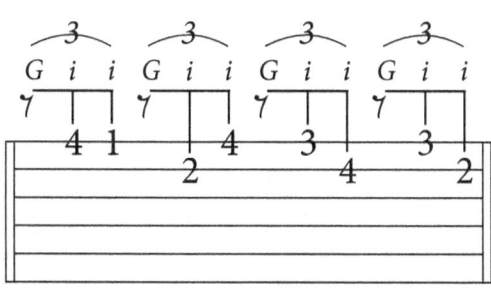

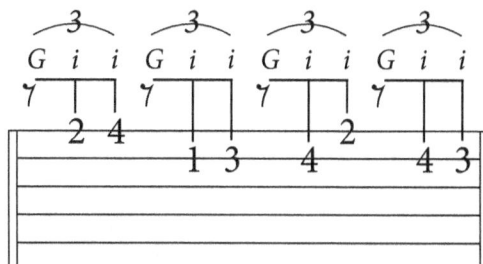

§ I

F1   F2

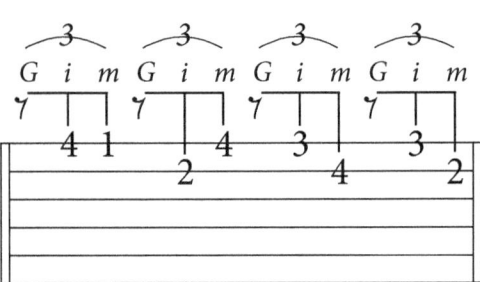 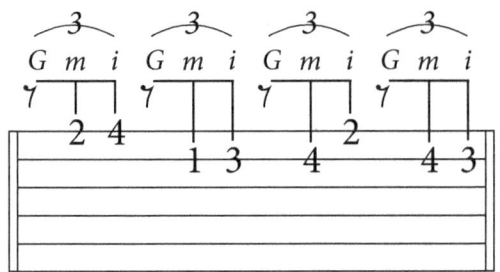

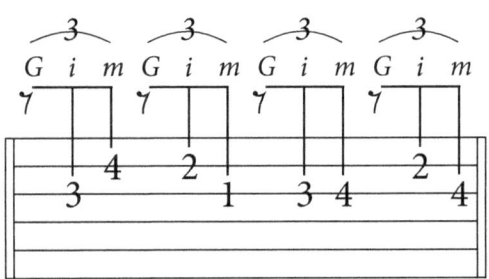 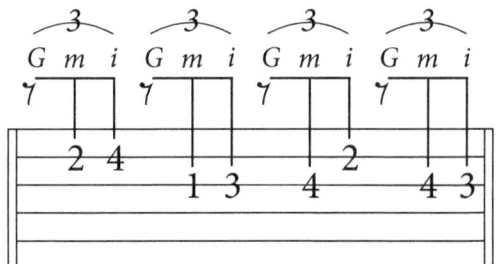

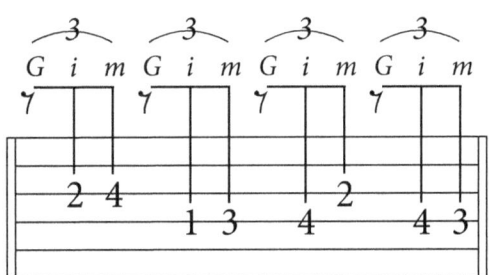 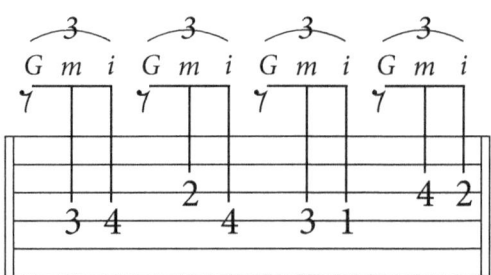

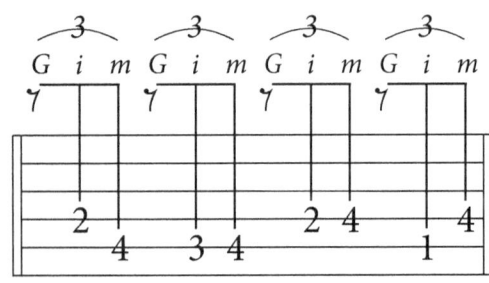 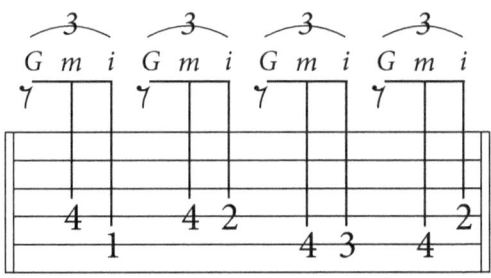

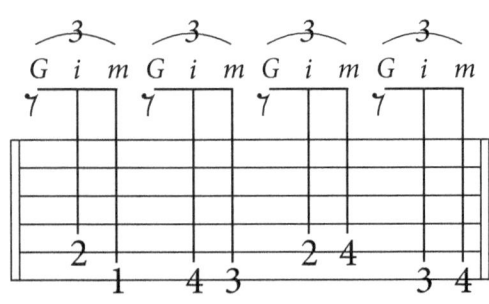 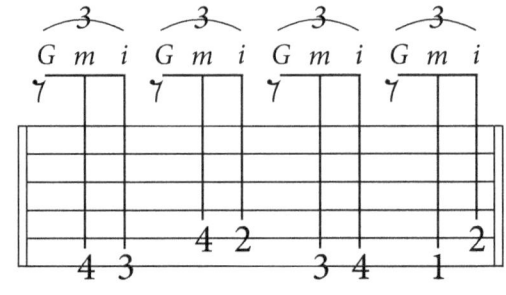

§ II

F1   **F2**

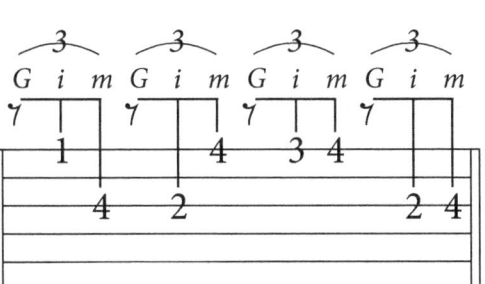 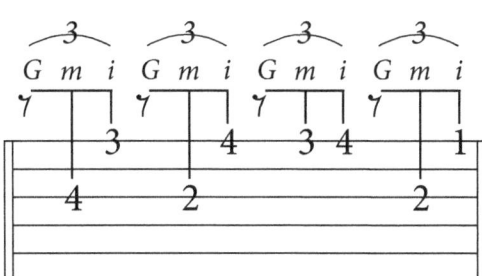

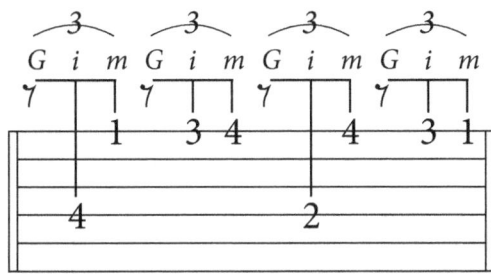 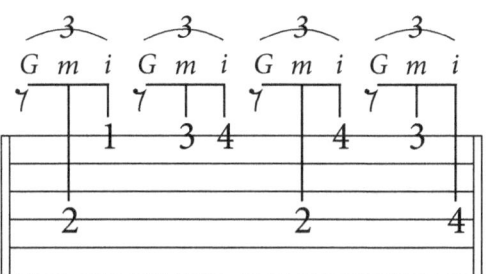

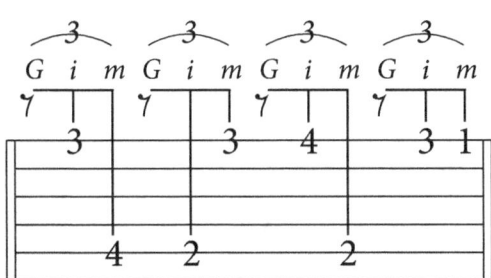 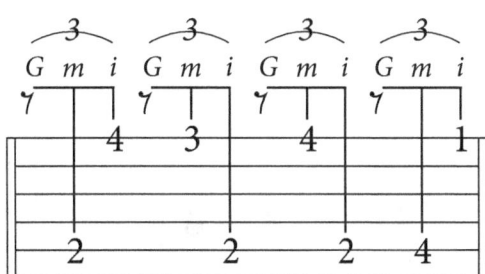

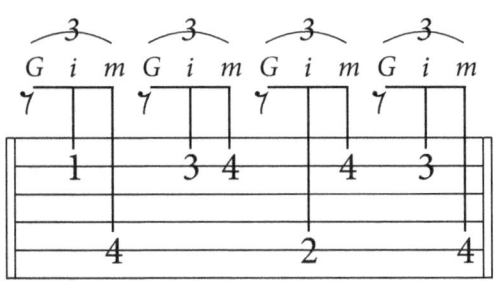 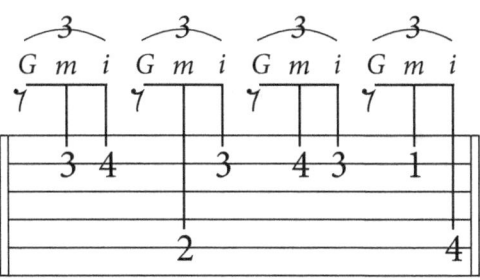

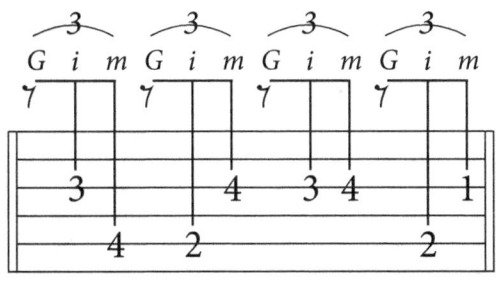 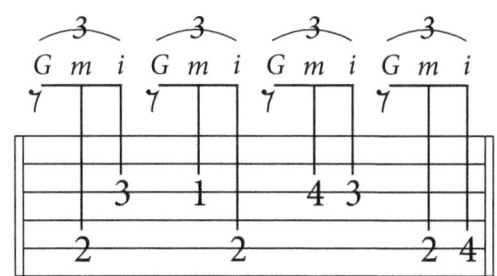

§ III

A							B

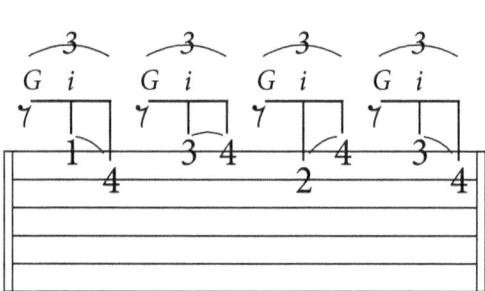 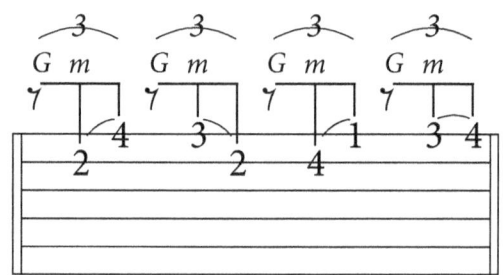
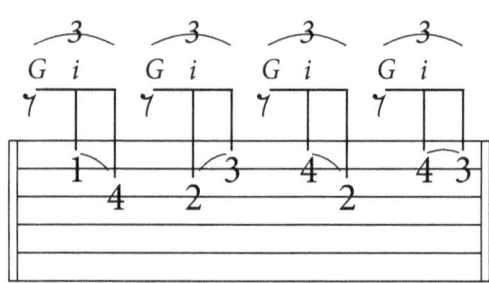 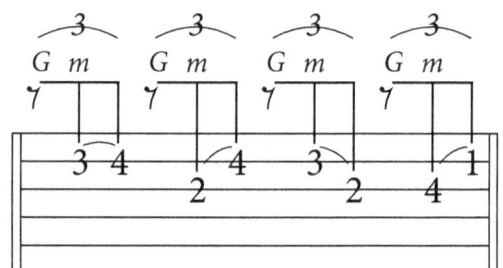
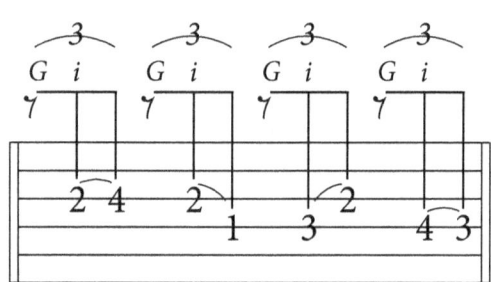 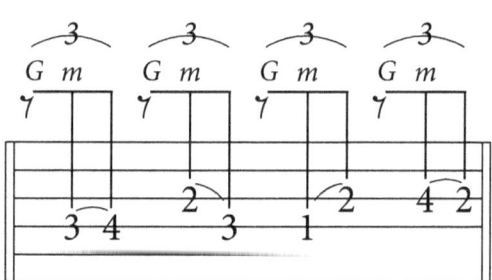
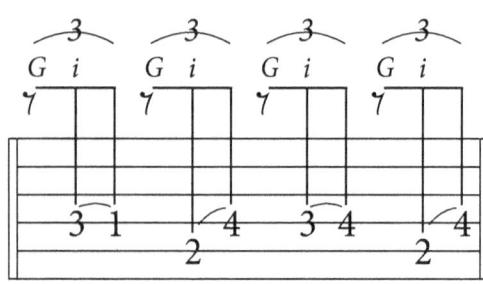 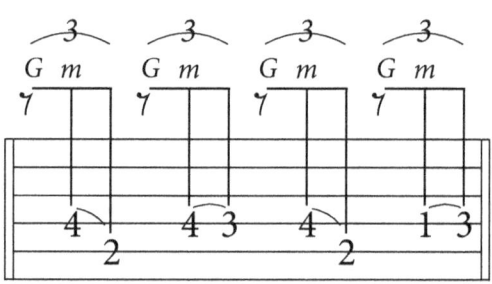
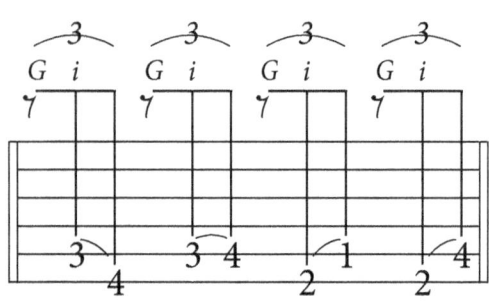 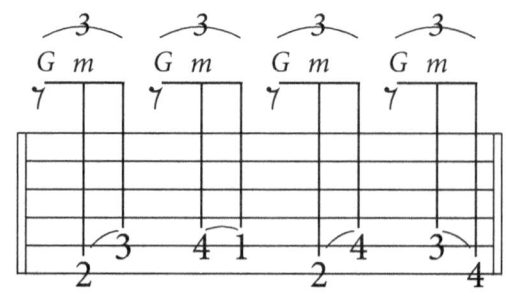

CHAPTER 2
FREE GOLPE OR GOLPE SIMULTANEOUS WITH THUMB STROKE.

UNIT 1

Free Golpe or Golpe simultaneous
with thumb stroke.

Unit 1 of chapter 2 contains Golpe exercises based on the scales of two adjacent strings as in the following example:

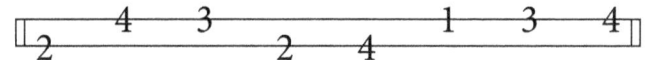

Within the meter we may have free Golpe:

§ I1

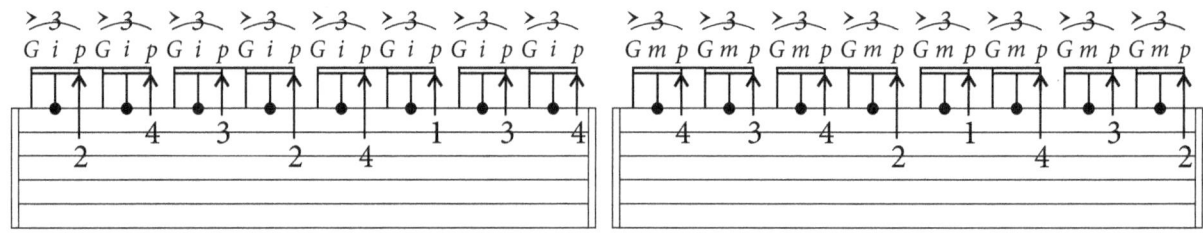

Or Golpe with simultaneous thumb stroke:

§ I2

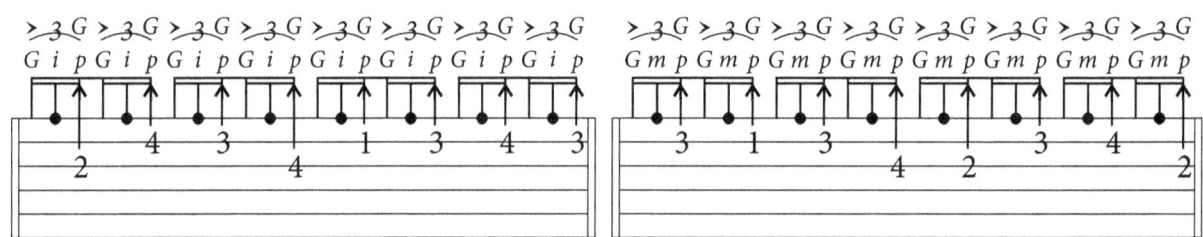

Participation within the Formula only of the index or middle finger as in § I1 and § I2 or participation of both index and middle finger with interchange of these within the Formulas as follows:

§ II1

§ II2

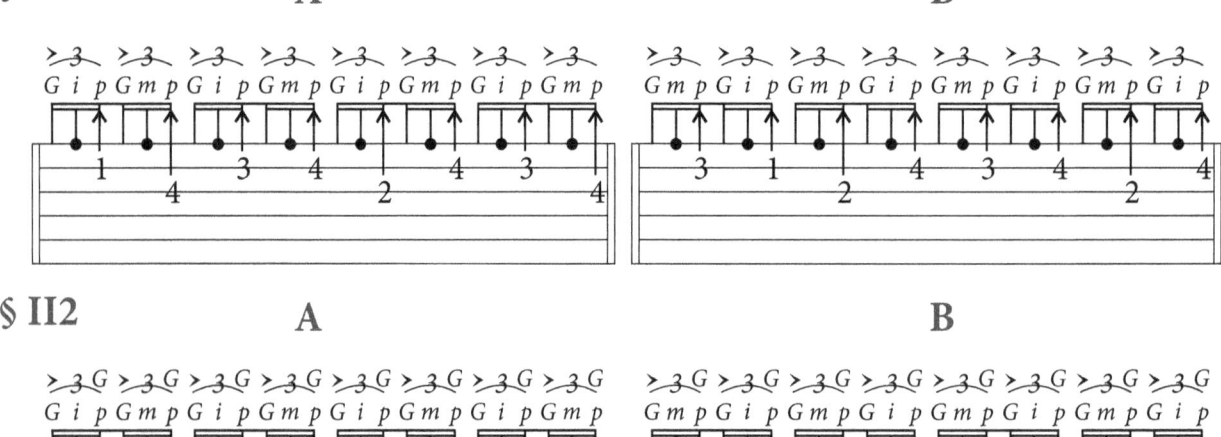

The scales of two adjacent strings are played either on two adjacent strings as shown in (§ I1, § I2) and in (§ II1, § II2) or on remote strings with the insertion of one string (§ III1),

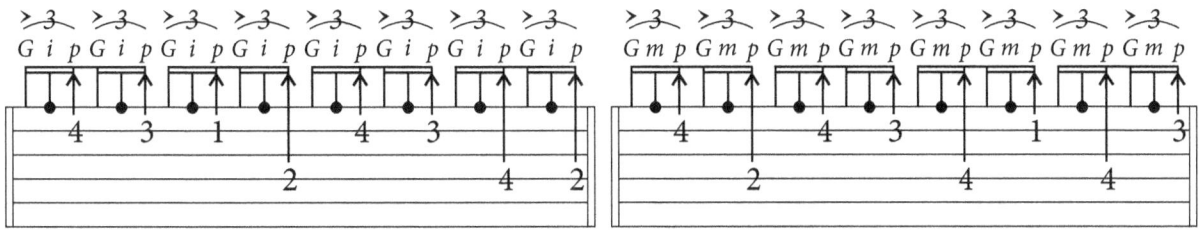

two strings,

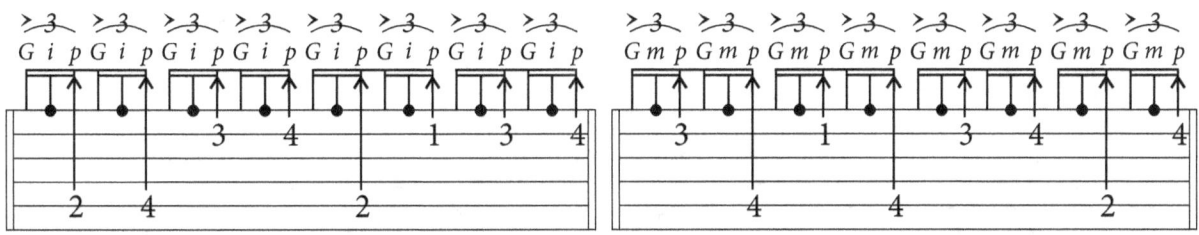

or three strings.

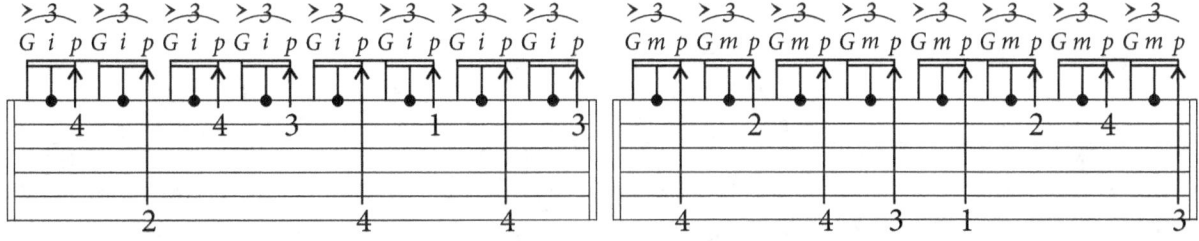

§ I1

A **B**

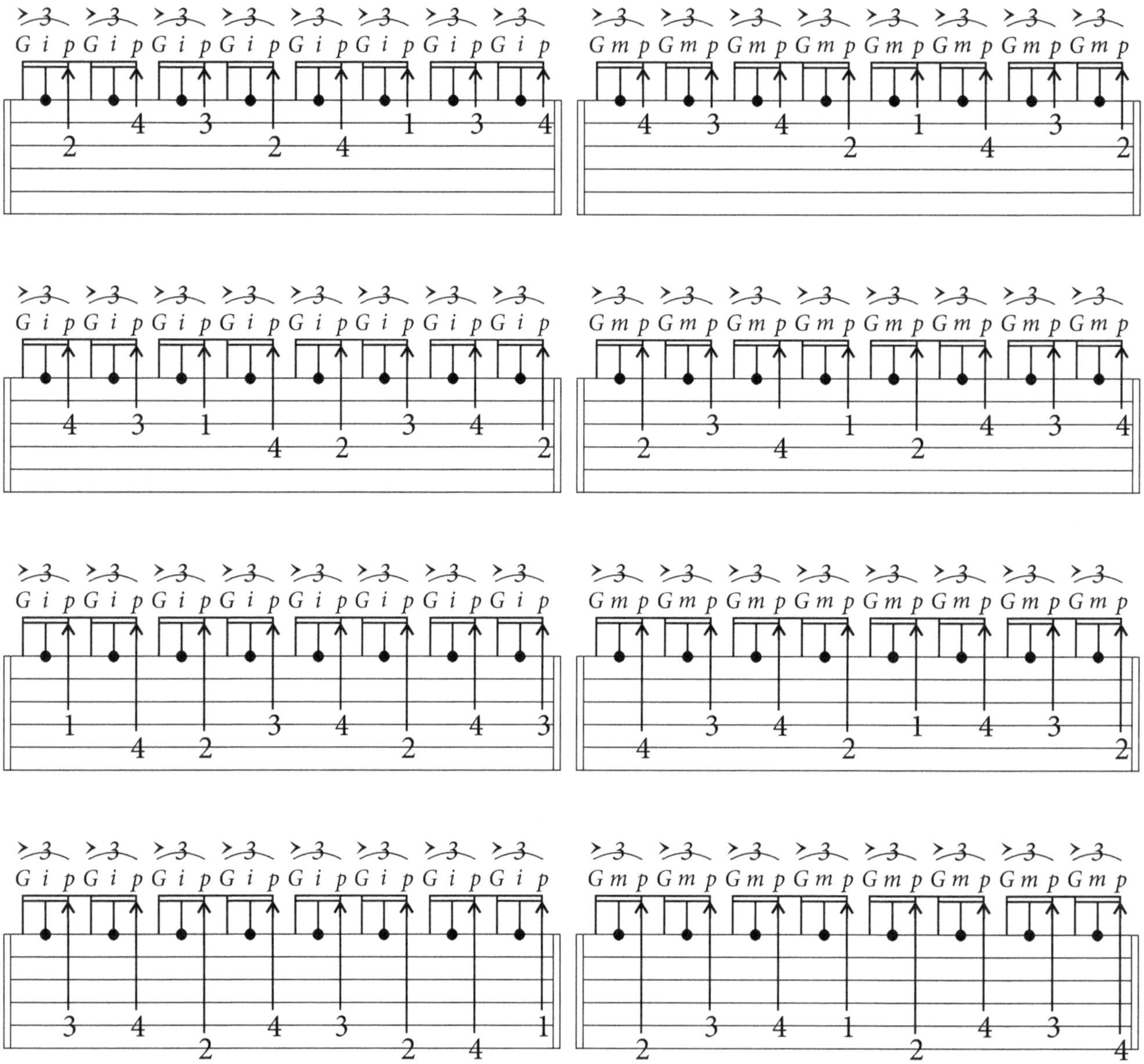
G i p G i p G i p G i p G i p G i p G i p G i p
G m p G m p G m p G m p G m p G m p G m p G m p
G i p G i p G i p G i p G i p G i p G i p G i p
G m p G m p G m p G m p G m p G m p G m p G m p
G i p G i p G i p G i p G i p G i p G i p G i p
G m p G m p G m p G m p G m p G m p G m p G m p
G i p G i p G i p G i p G i p G i p G i p G i p
G m p G m p G m p G m p G m p G m p G m p G m p

§ I2

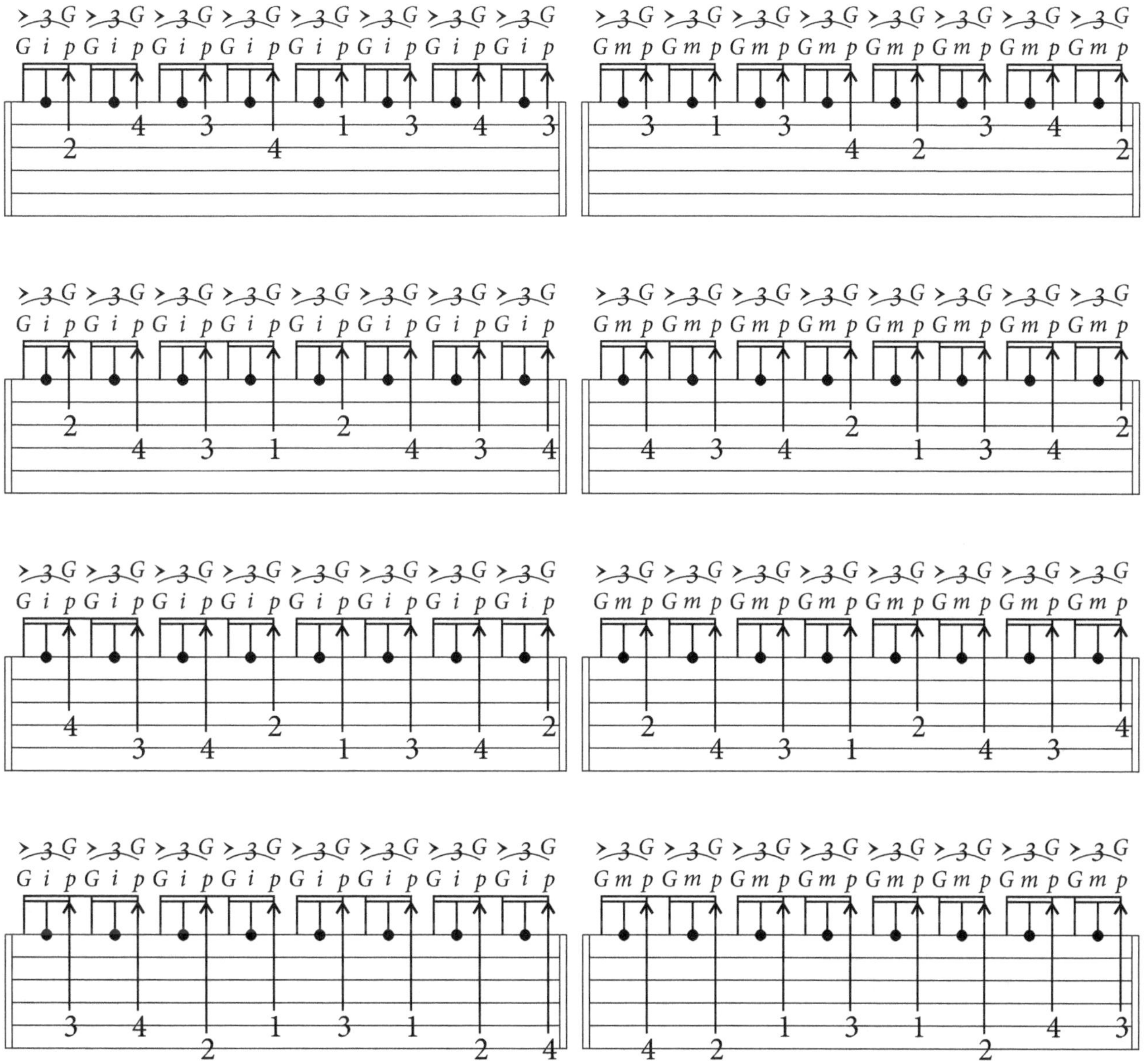

§ II1

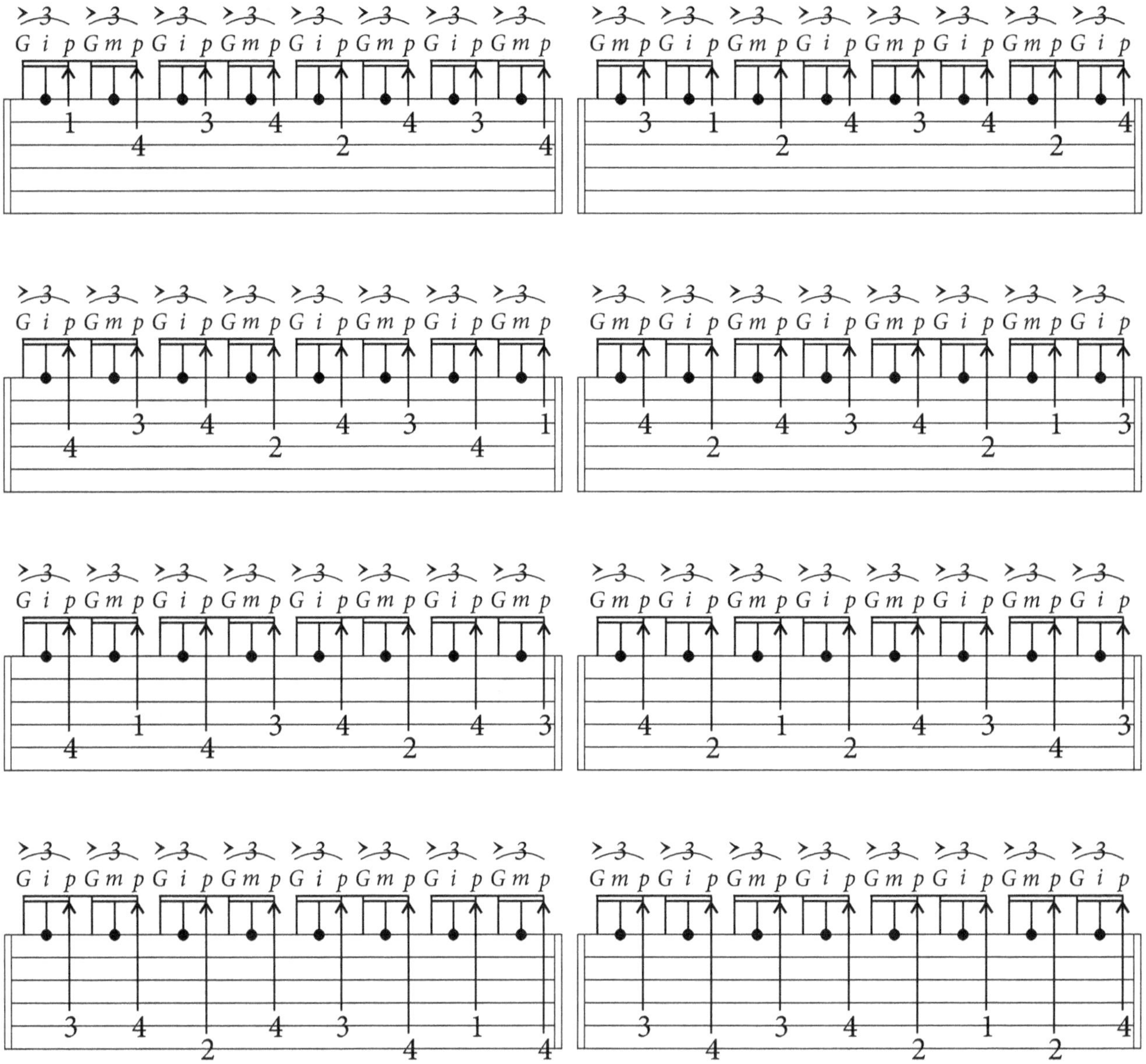

§ II2

A **B**

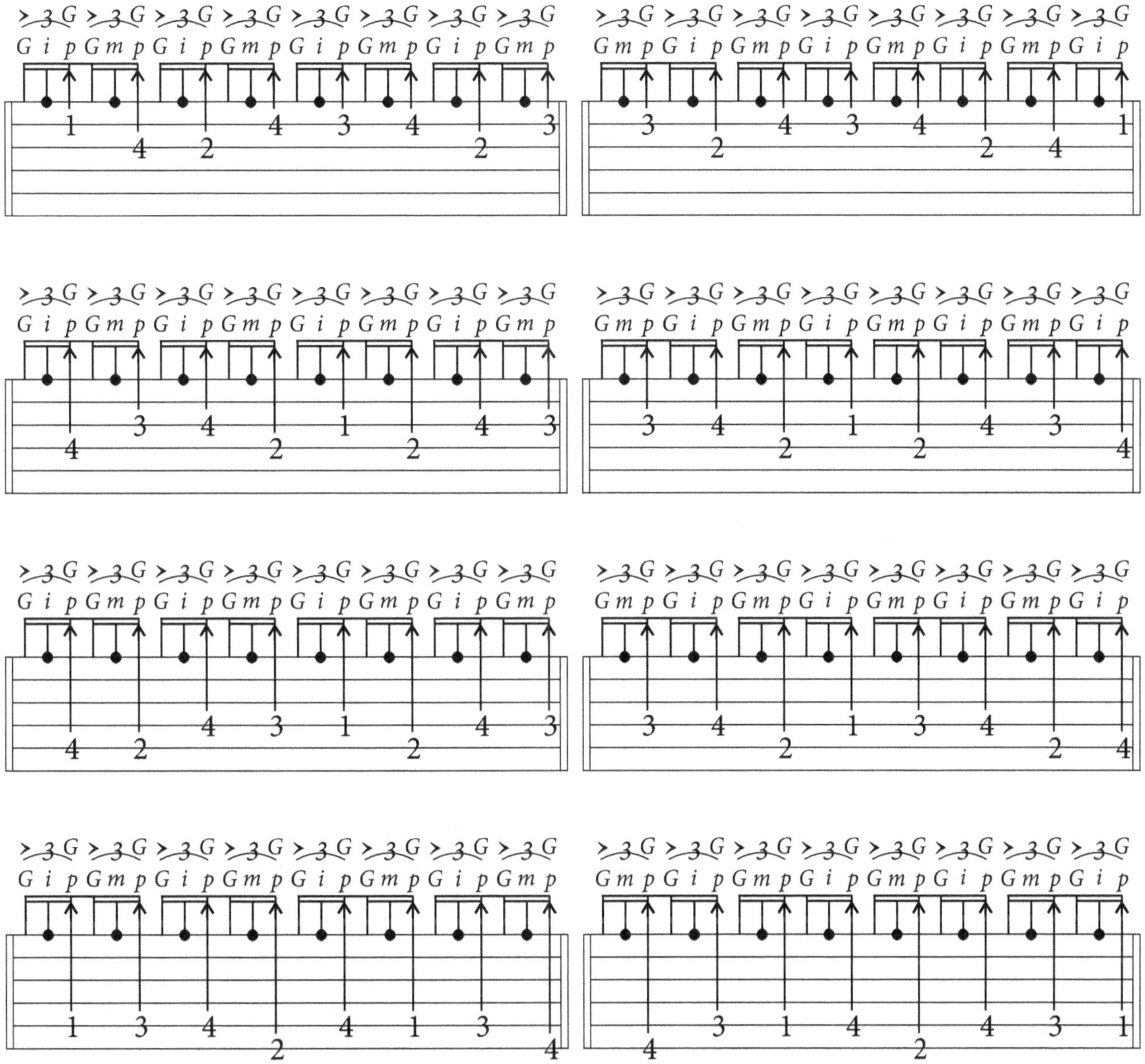
3 G 3 G 3 G 3 G 3 G 3 G 3 G 3 G
G i p G m p G i p G m p G i p G m p G i p G m p
3 G 3 G 3 G 3 G 3 G 3 G 3 G 3 G
G m p G i p G m p G i p G m p G i p G m p G i p
3 G 3 G 3 G 3 G 3 G 3 G 3 G 3 G
G i p G m p G i p G m p G i p G m p G i p G m p
3 G 3 G 3 G 3 G 3 G 3 G 3 G 3 G
G m p G i p G m p G i p G m p G i p G m p G i p
3 G 3 G 3 G 3 G 3 G 3 G 3 G 3 G
G i p G m p G i p G m p G i p G m p G i p G m p
3 G 3 G 3 G 3 G 3 G 3 G 3 G 3 G
G m p G i p G m p G i p G m p G i p G m p G i p
3 G 3 G 3 G 3 G 3 G 3 G 3 G 3 G
G i p G m p G i p G m p G i p G m p G i p G m p
3 G 3 G 3 G 3 G 3 G 3 G 3 G 3 G
G m p G i p G m p G i p G m p G i p G m p G i p

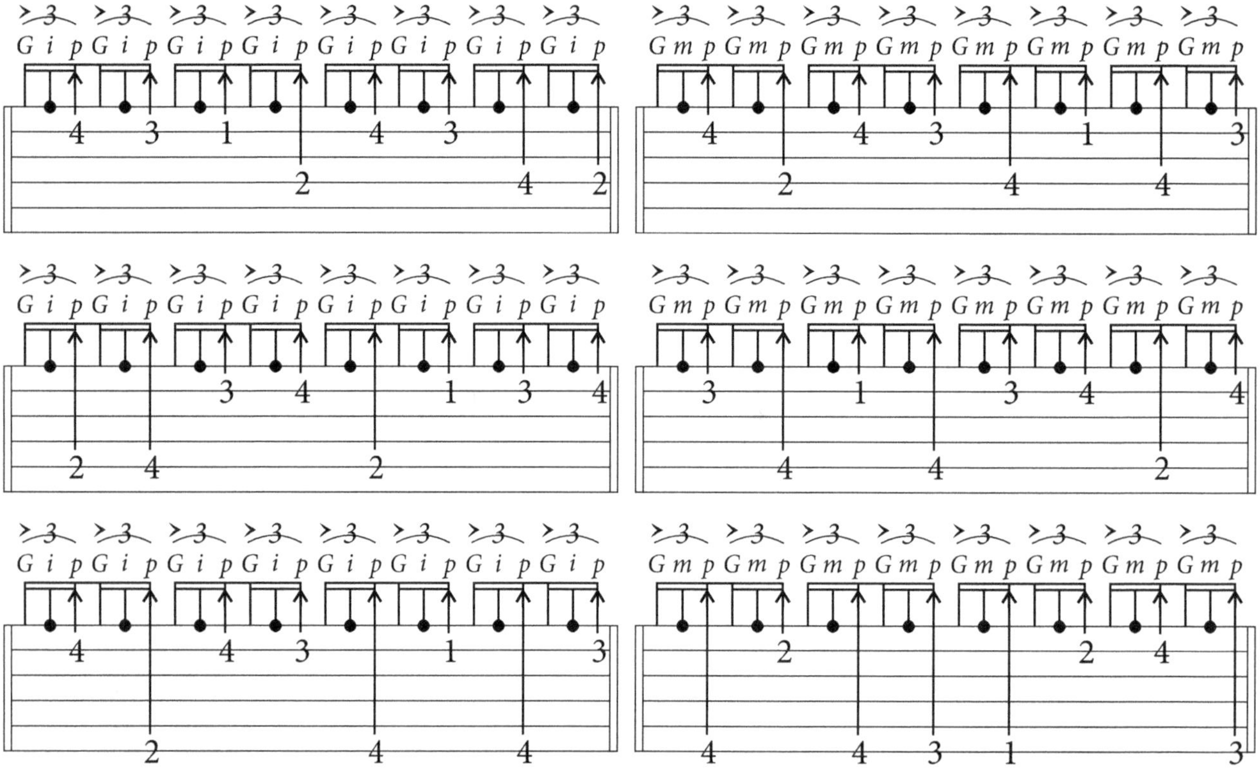

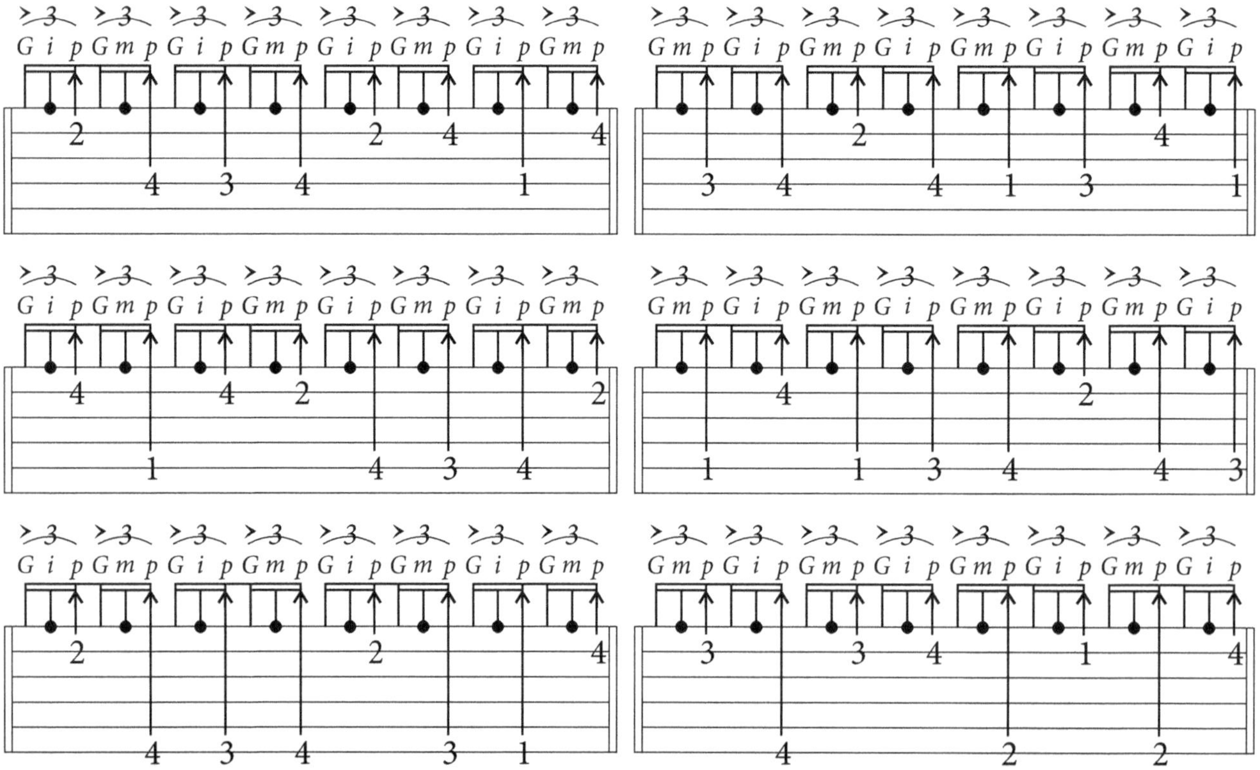

§ III2

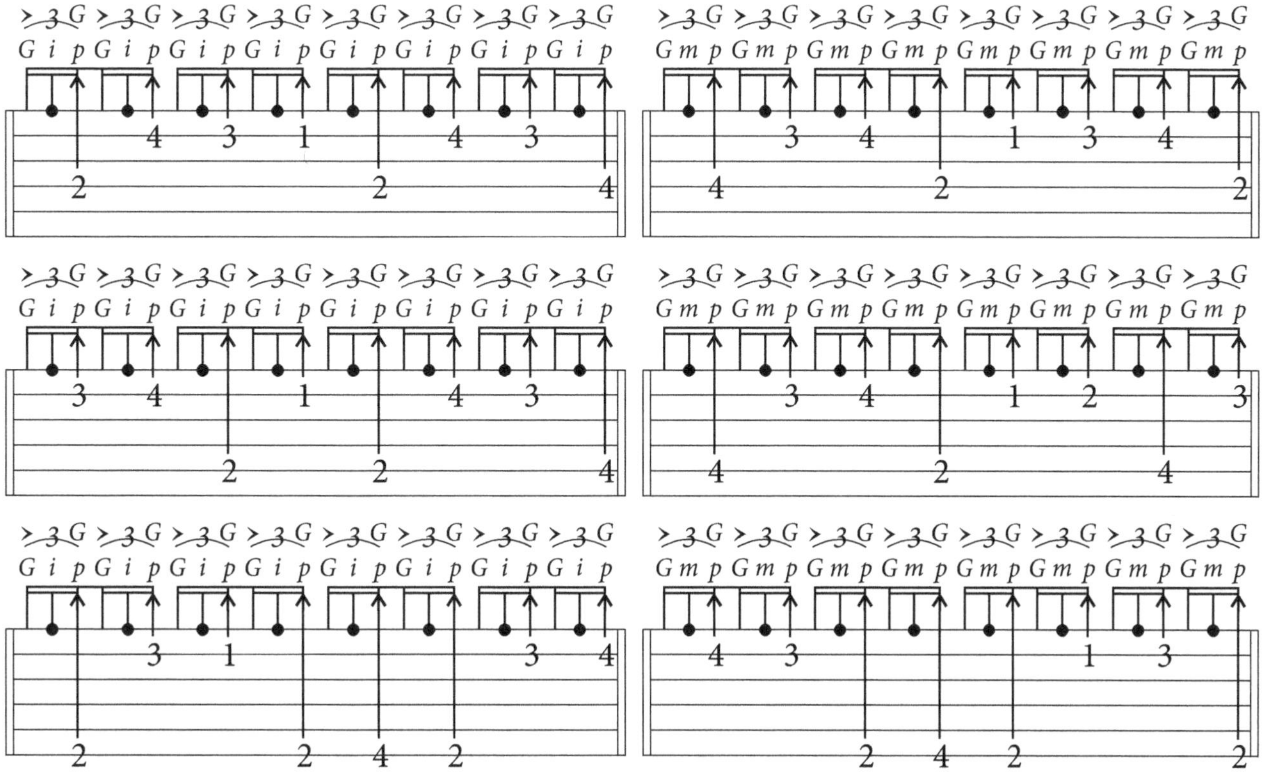

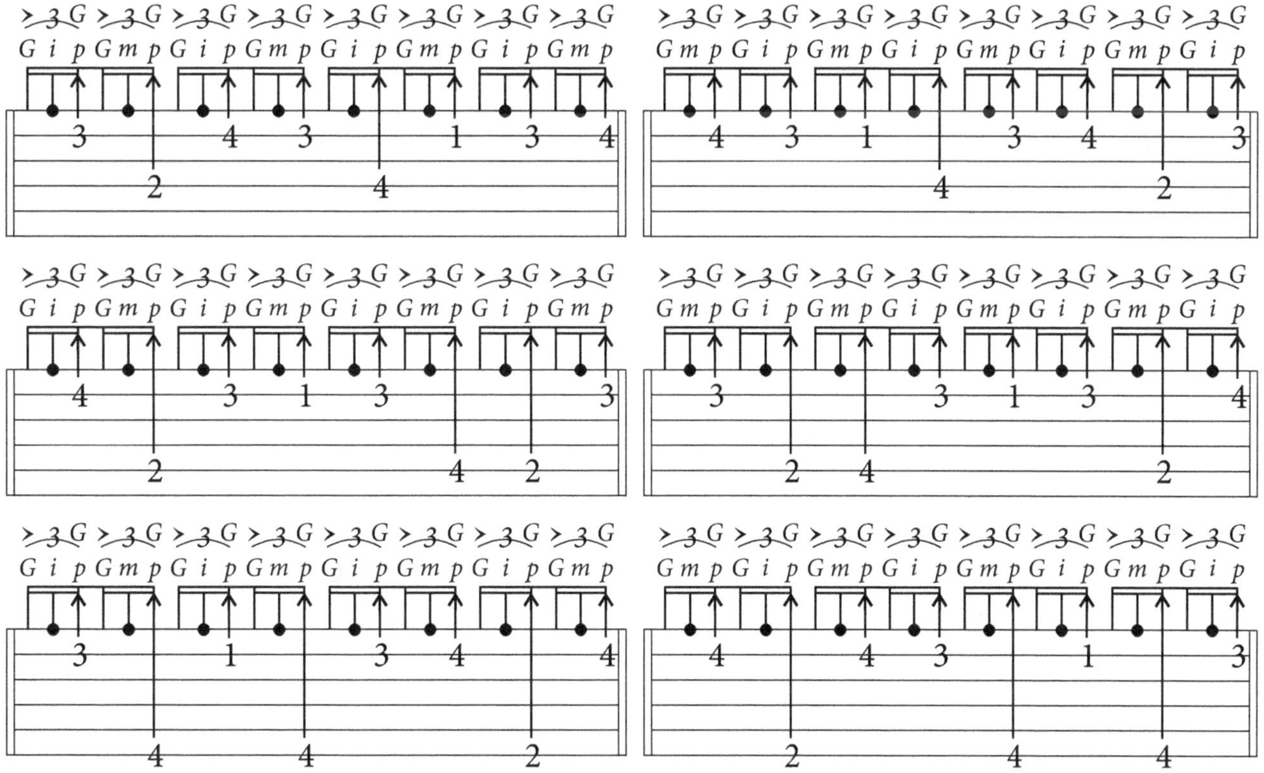

UNIT 2

A/. Gople exercises shaped in Triplets.
One or two Golpe within the meter.
B/. Golpe exercises with Ligado in the Triplet.

§I Golpe exercises on the scales of two adjacent strings shaped in triplets with one Golpe,

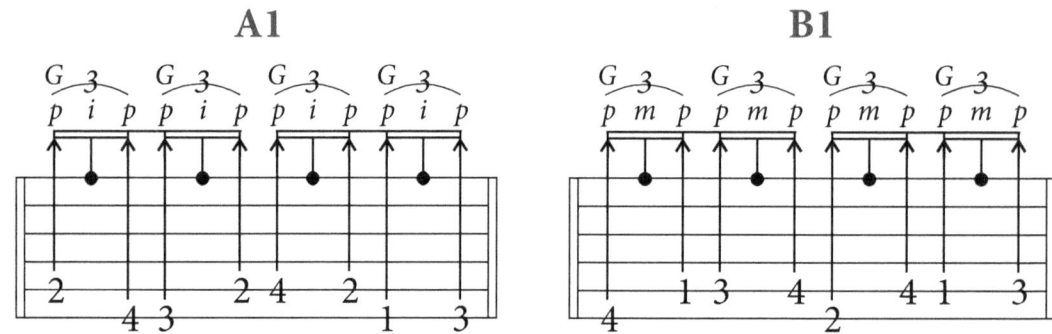

or with two Golpe within the meter and in combination with the index and middle finger of the right hand.

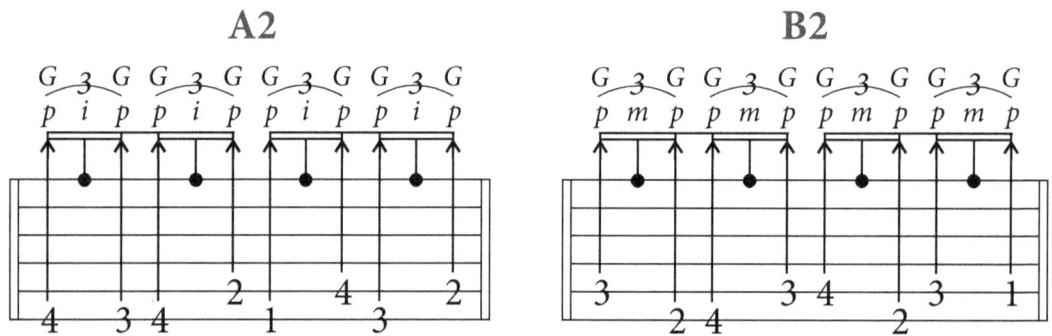

§II The same exercises with legato within the triplet.

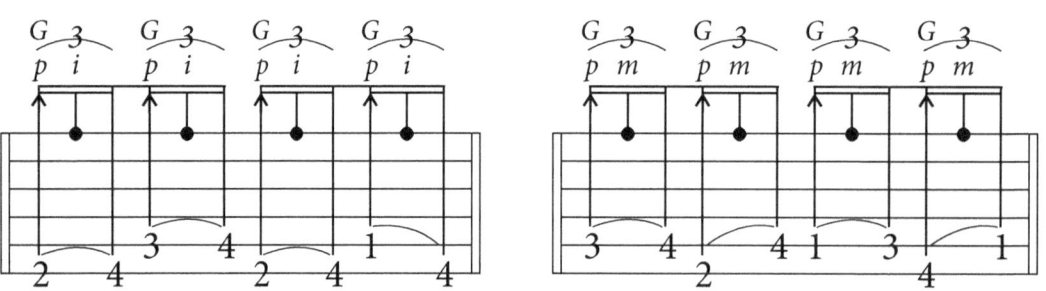

§ I

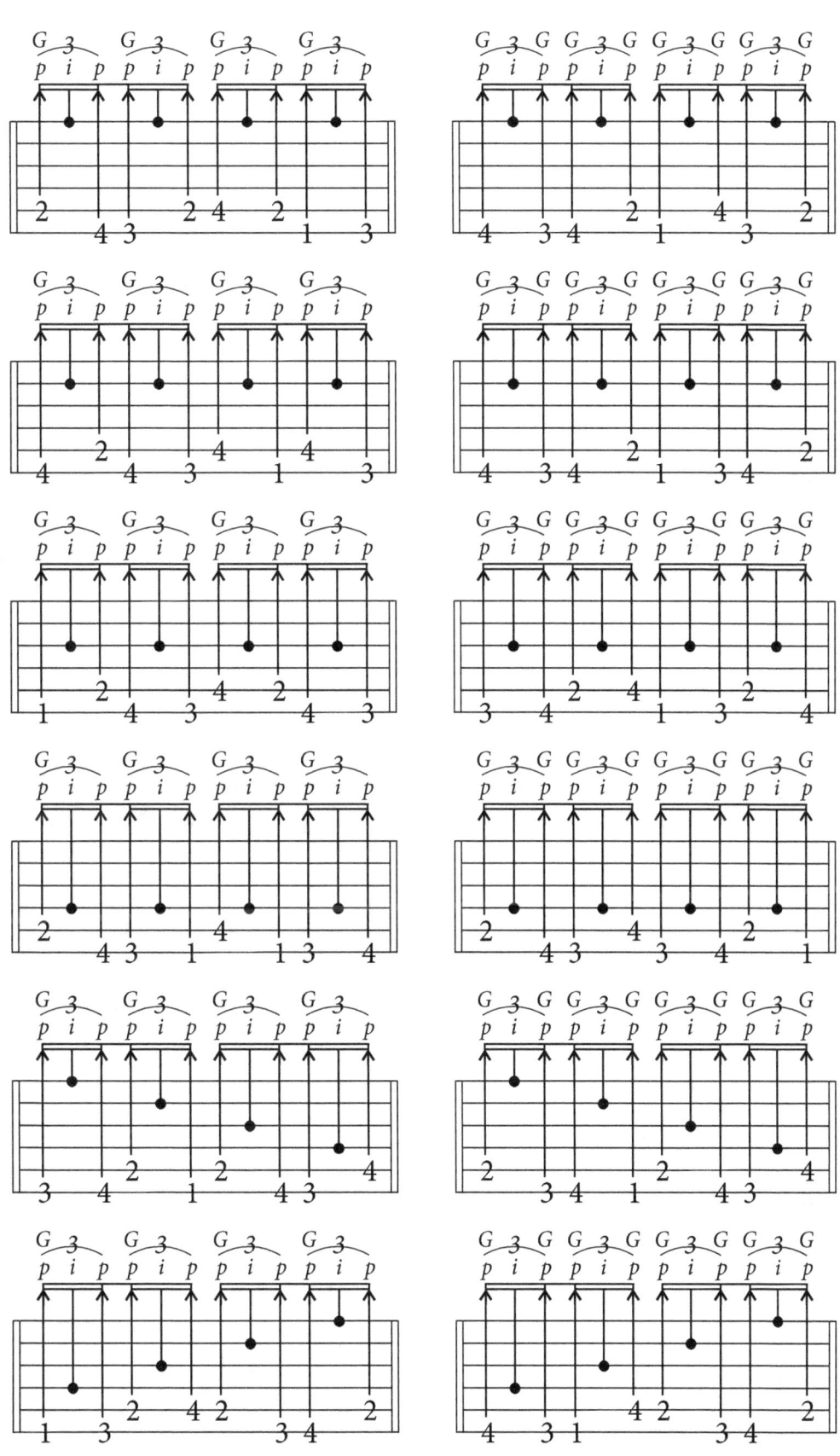

311

B1 **B2**

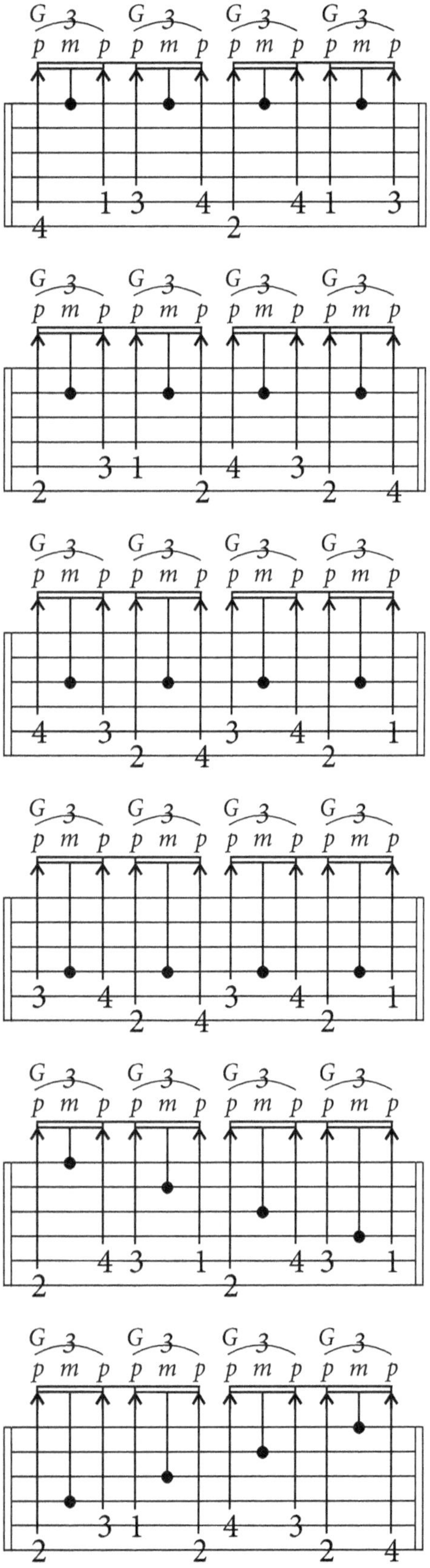

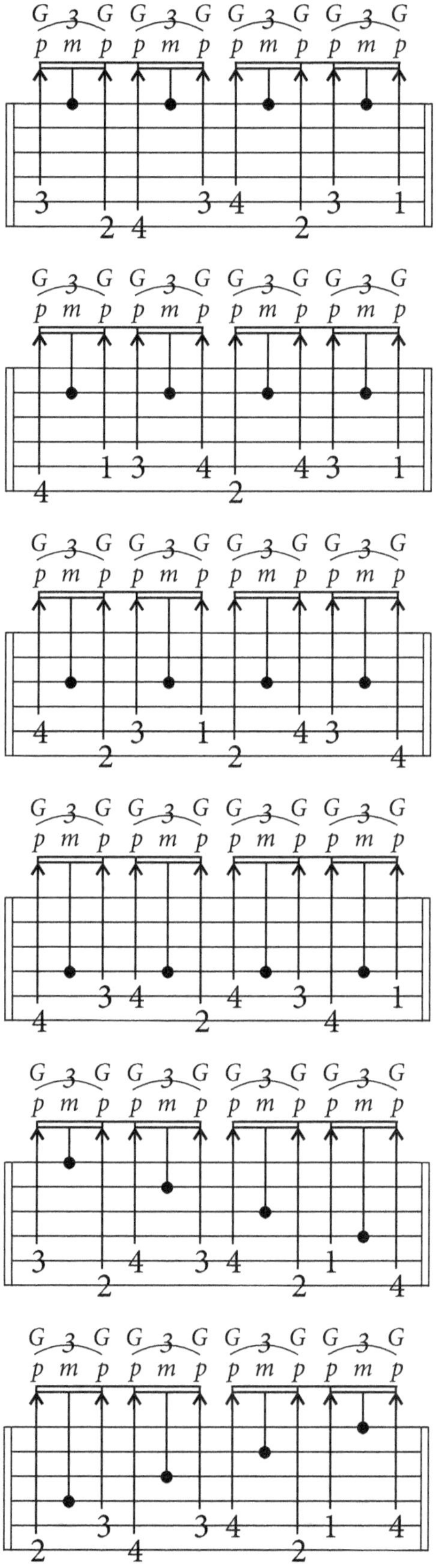

§ II

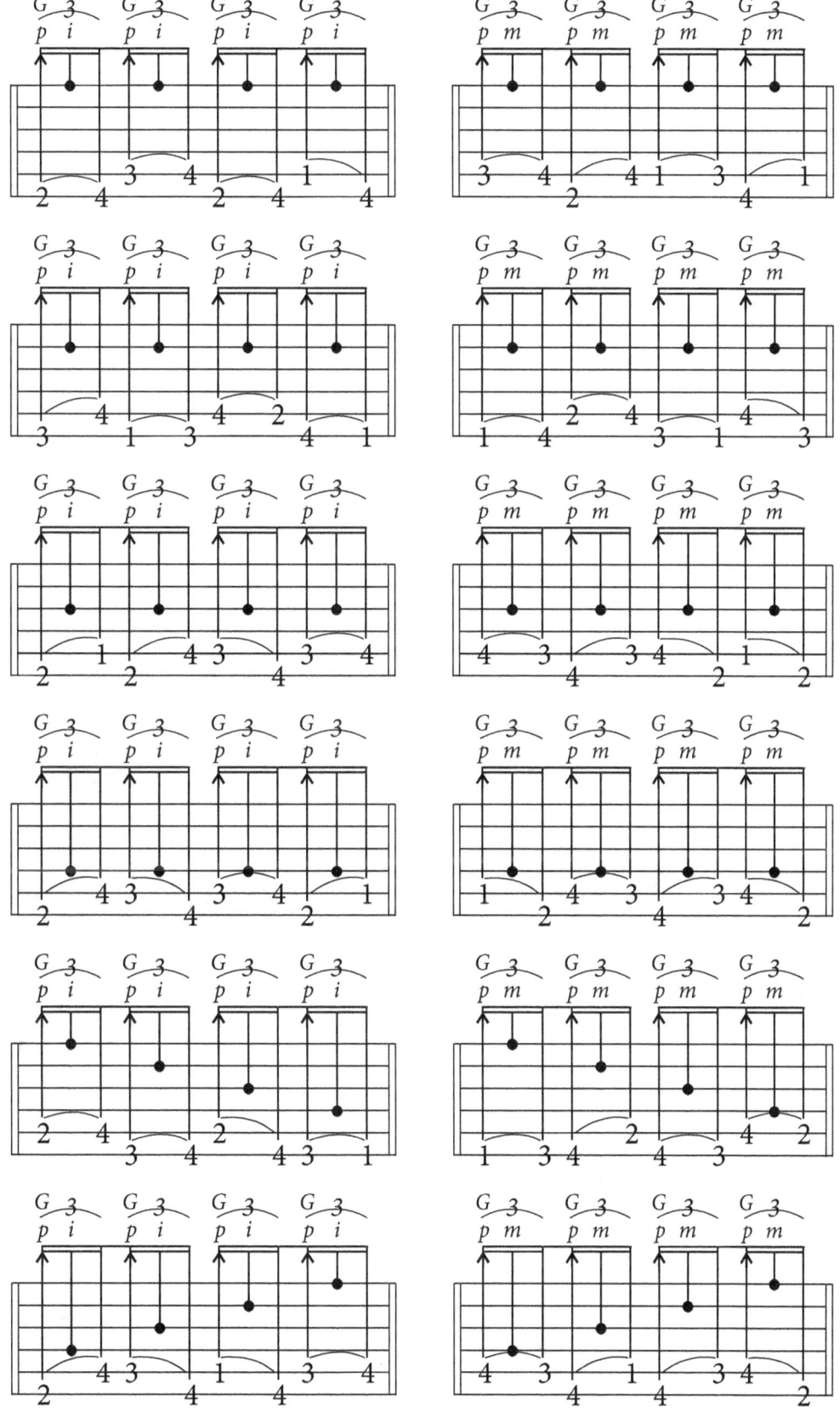

313

TWO VARIATIONS OF THE EXERCISE IN § II
VARIATION 1

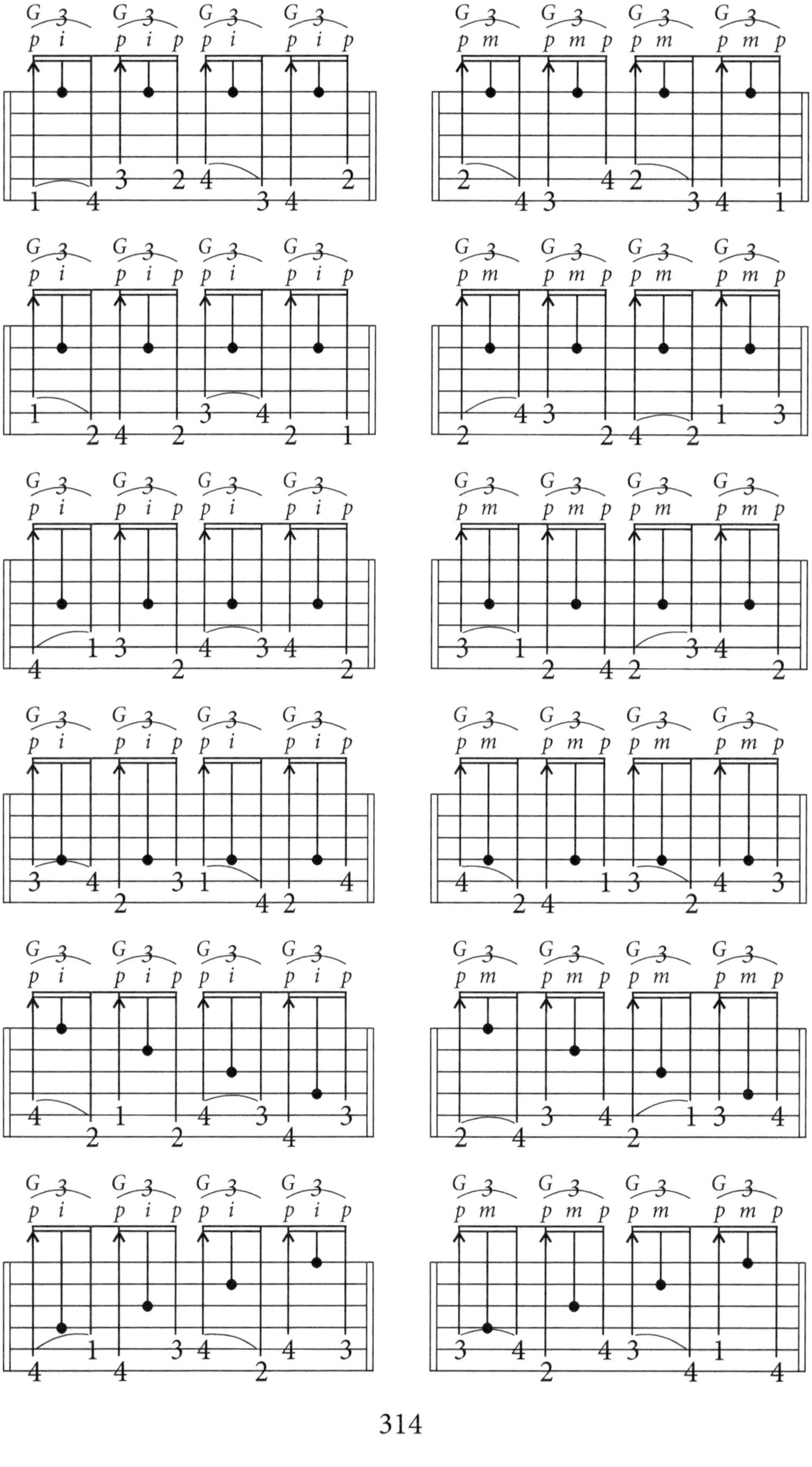

VARIATION 2

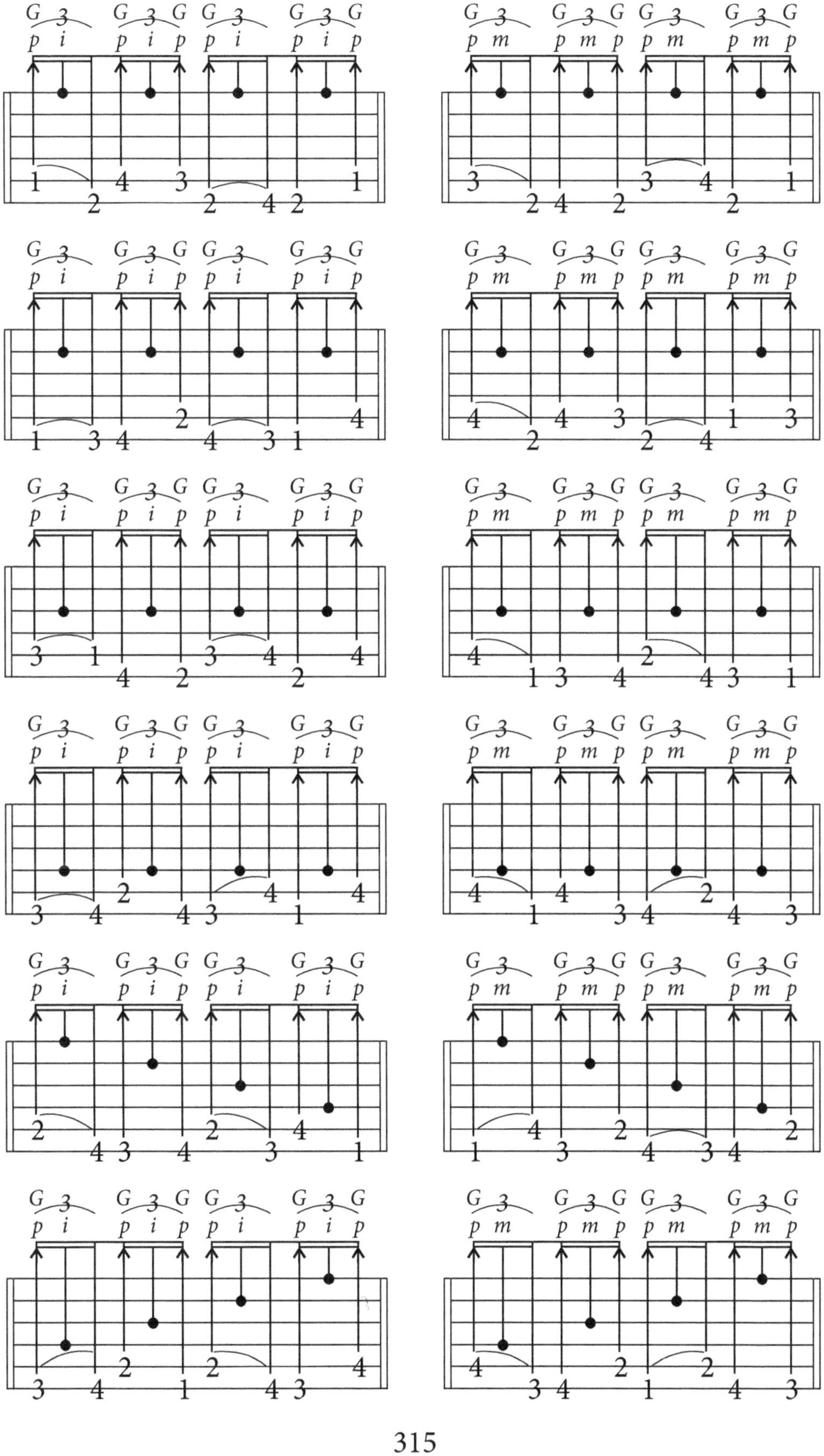

UNIT 3
Combination of Golpe with Arpegios.

§ I Combination of Golpe with arpeggios of three notes. These exercises are based on the scales of two adjacent strings. The arpeggios refer to:

a/ one string,

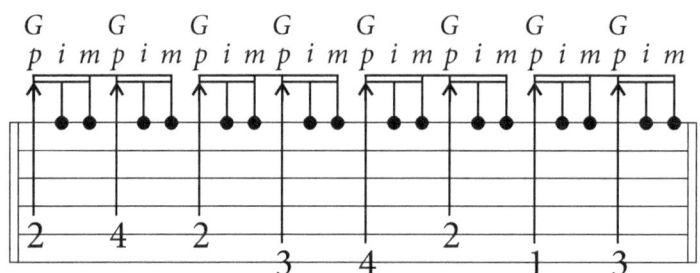

b/ two adjacent strings,

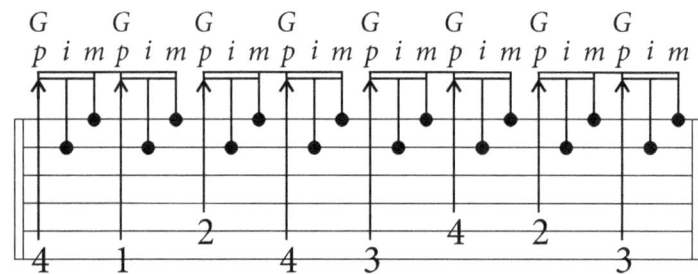

c/ remote strings with insertion of one or two strings.

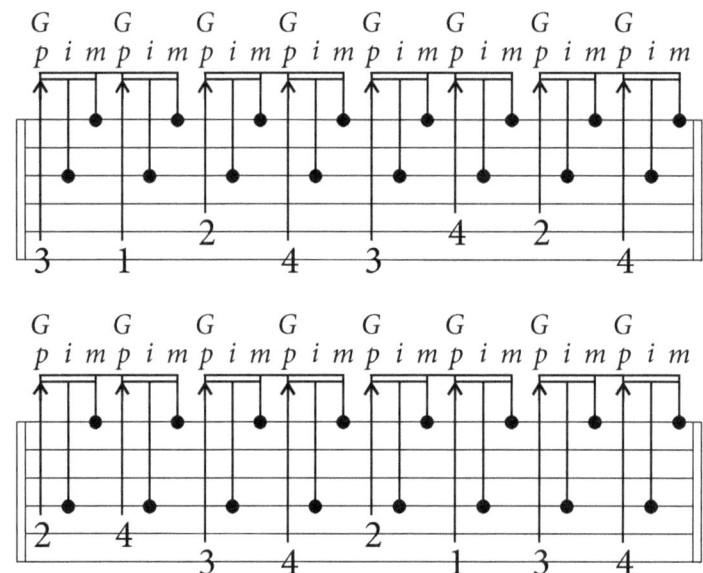

The fingerings of the right hand are simple (pim, pmi, pma, pia) or more complicated (pmipma, pmapmi).

§ II Variations on the arpeggios strings of the previous exercise.

§ I

1 **2**

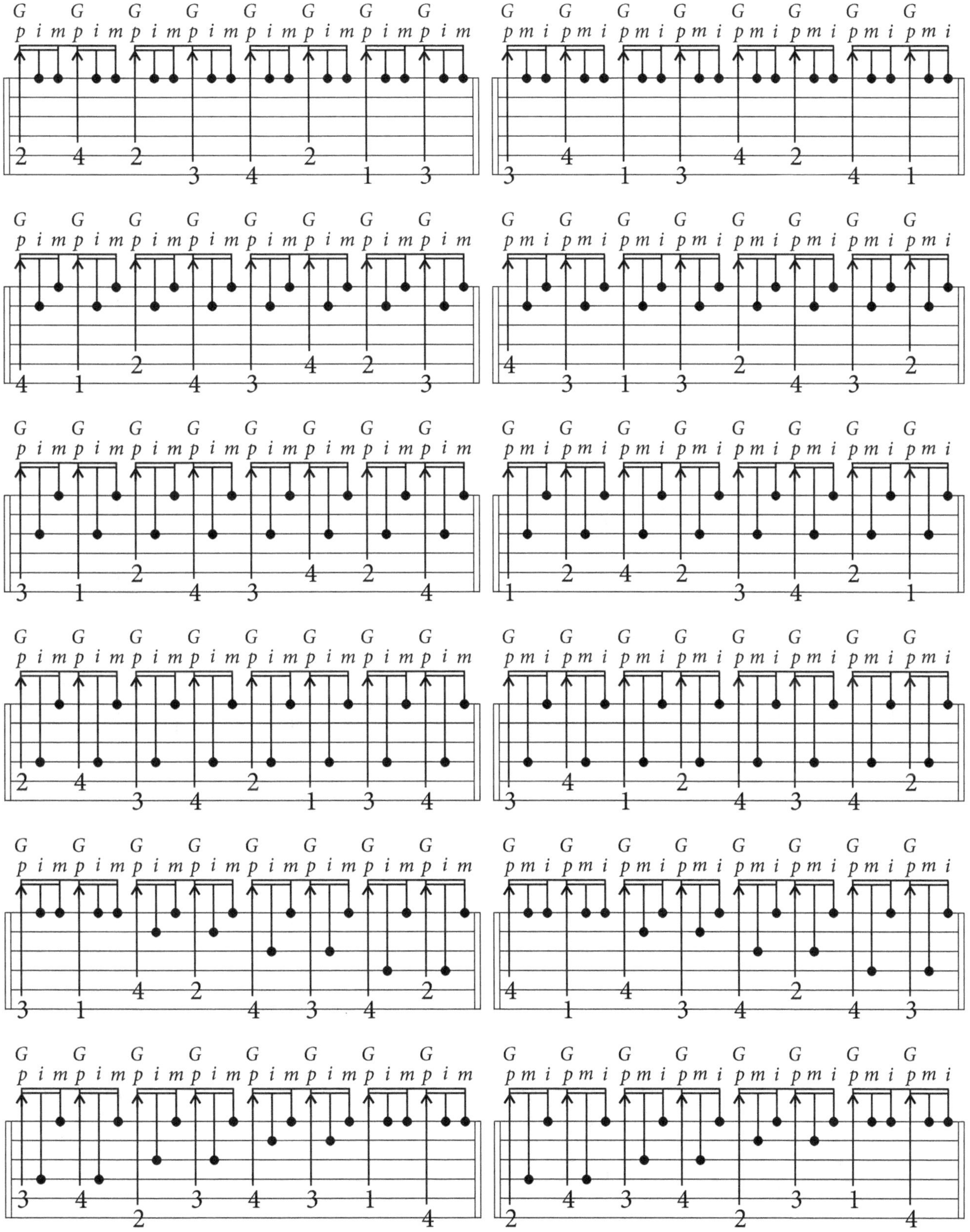

G G G G G G G G
p i m p i m p i m p i m p i m p i m p i m p i m
G G G G G G G G
p m i p m i p m i p m i p m i p m i p m i p m i
G G G G G G G G
p i m p i m p i m p i m p i m p i m p i m p i m
G G G G G G G G
p m i p m i p m i p m i p m i p m i p m i p m i
G G G G G G G G
p i m p i m p i m p i m p i m p i m p i m p i m
G G G G G G G G
p m i p m i p m i p m i p m i p m i p m i p m i
G G G G G G G G
p i m p i m p i m p i m p i m p i m p i m p i m
G G G G G G G G
p m i p m i p m i p m i p m i p m i p m i p m i
G G G G G G G G
p i m p i m p i m p i m p i m p i m p i m p i m
G G G G G G G G
p m i p m i p m i p m i p m i p m i p m i p m i
G G G G G G G G
p i m p i m p i m p i m p i m p i m p i m p i m
G G G G G G G G
p m i p m i p m i p m i p m i p m i p m i p m i

3

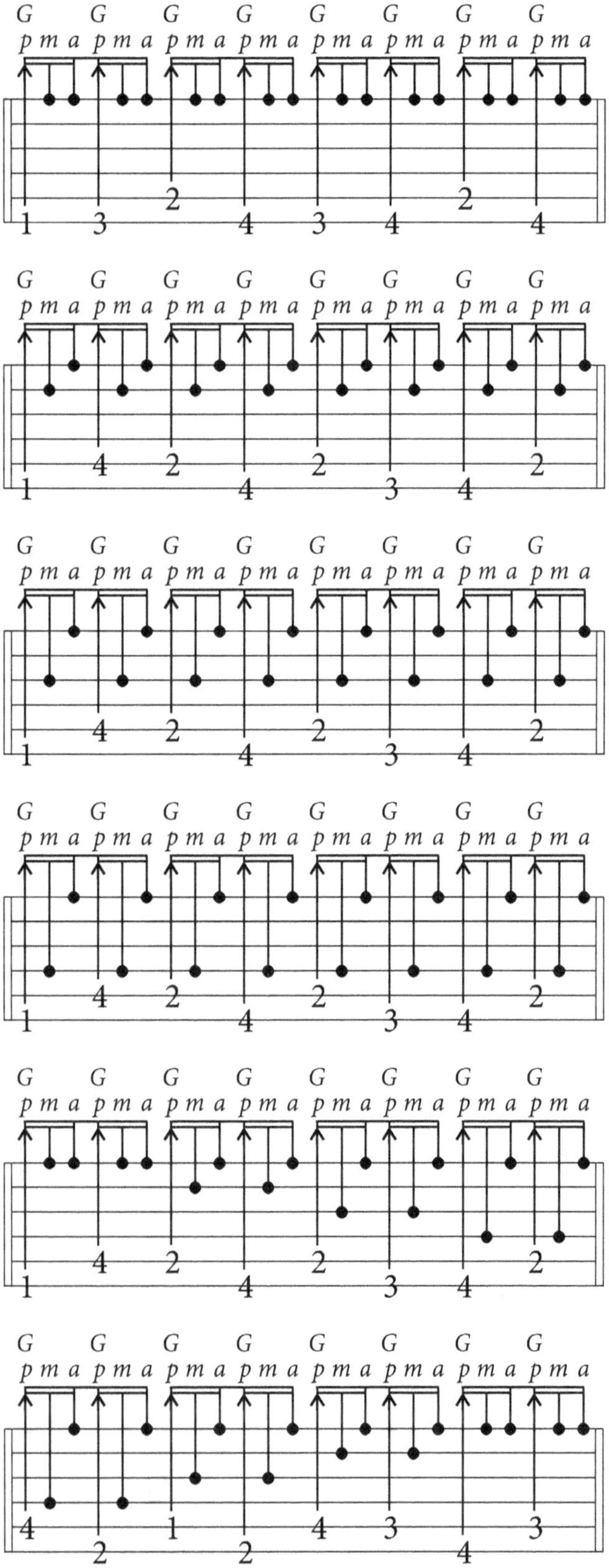
G G G G G G G G
p m a p m a p m a p m a p m a p m a p m a p m a
G G G G G G G G
p m a p m a p m a p m a p m a p m a p m a p m a
G G G G G G G G
p m a p m a p m a p m a p m a p m a p m a p m a
G G G G G G G G
p m a p m a p m a p m a p m a p m a p m a p m a
G G G G G G G G
p m a p m a p m a p m a p m a p m a p m a p m a
G G G G G G G G
p m a p m a p m a p m a p m a p m a p m a p m a

4

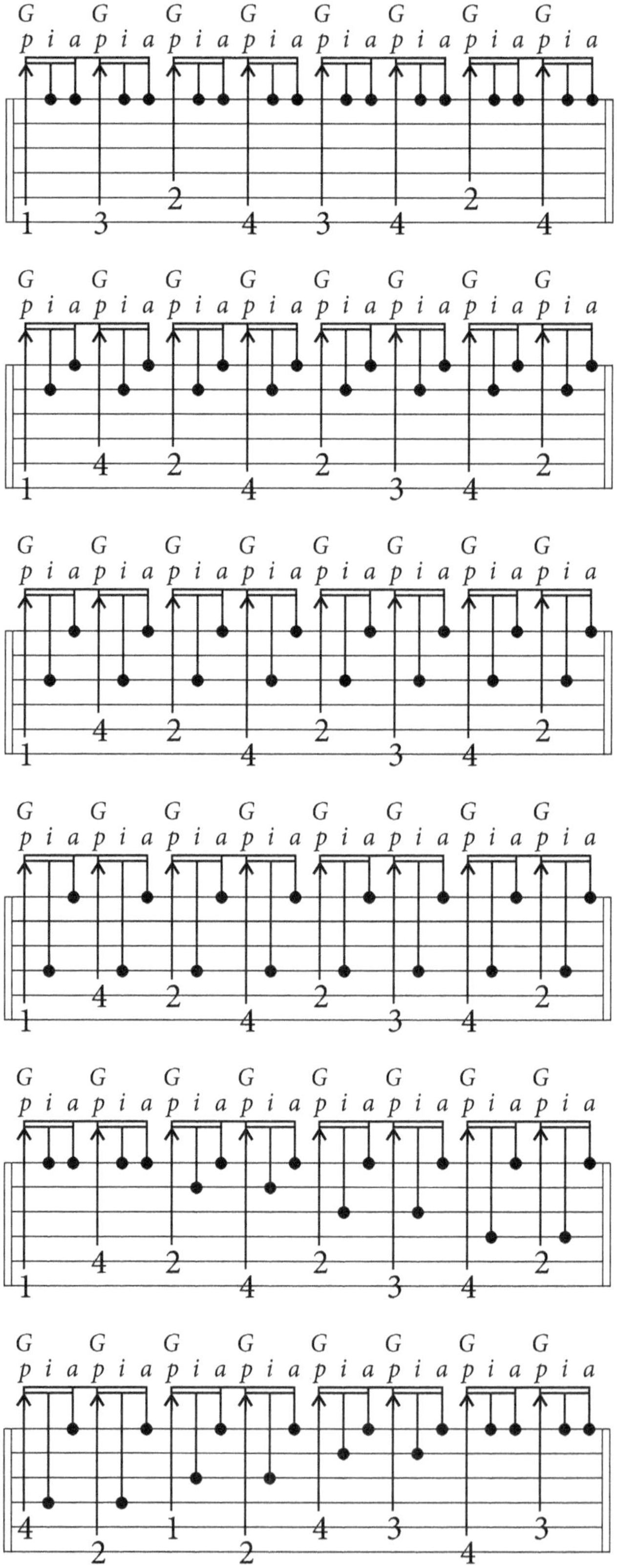
G G G G G G G G
p i a p i a p i a p i a p i a p i a p i a p i a
G G G G G G G G
p i a p i a p i a p i a p i a p i a p i a p i a
G G G G G G G G
p i a p i a p i a p i a p i a p i a p i a p i a
G G G G G G G G
p i a p i a p i a p i a p i a p i a p i a p i a
G G G G G G G G
p i a p i a p i a p i a p i a p i a p i a p i a
G G G G G G G G
p i a p i a p i a p i a p i a p i a p i a p i a

5

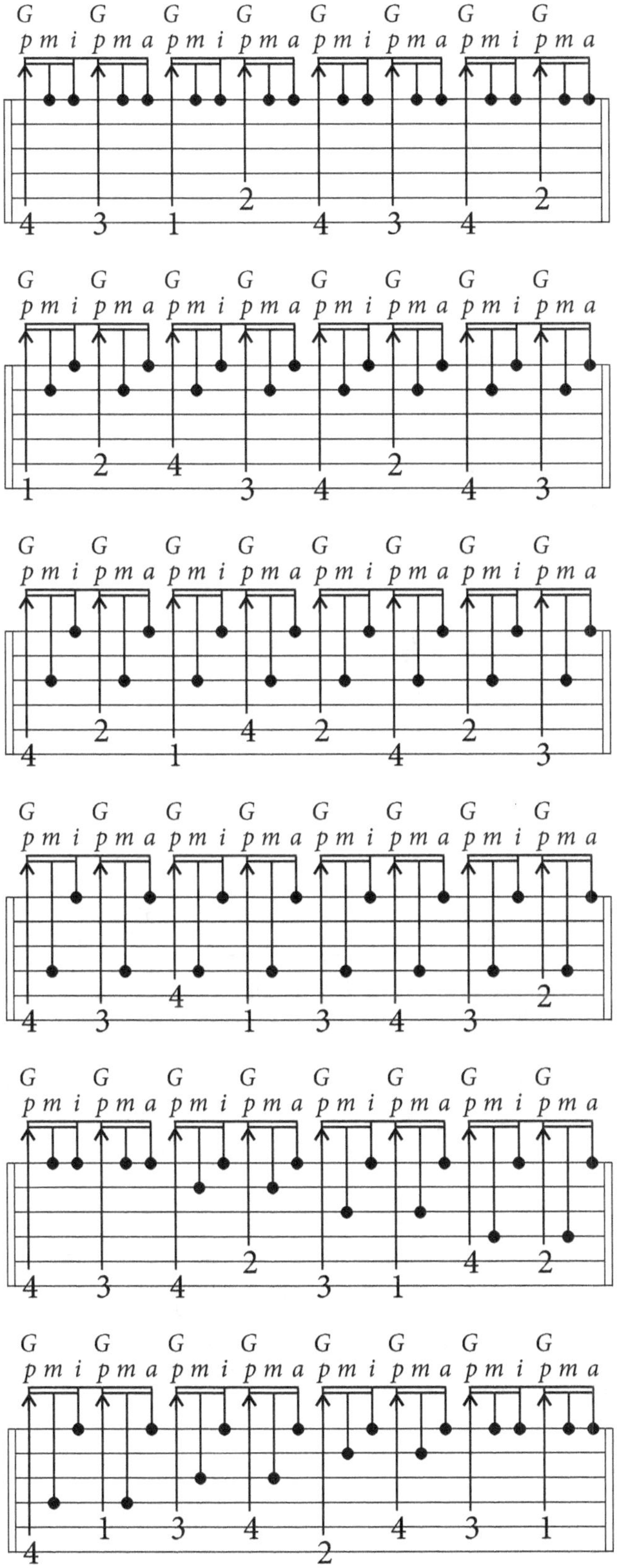
G G G G G G G G
p m i p m a p m i p m a p m i p m a p m i p m a
G G G G G G G G
p m i p m a p m i p m a p m i p m a p m i p m a
G G G G G G G G
p m i p m a p m i p m a p m i p m a p m i p m a
G G G G G G G G
p m i p m a p m i p m a p m i p m a p m i p m a
G G G G G G G G
p m i p m a p m i p m a p m i p m a p m i p m a
G G G G G G G G
p m i p m a p m i p m a p m i p m a p m i p m a

6

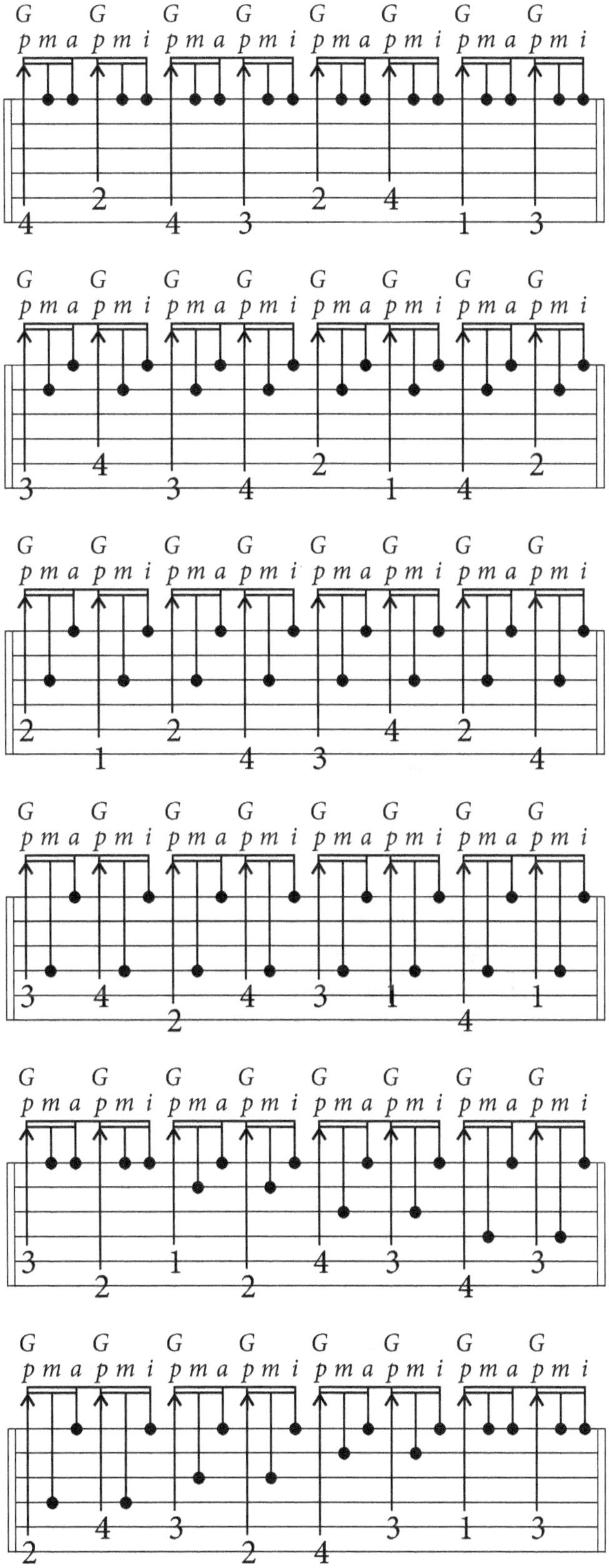
G G G G G G G G
p m a p m i p m a p m i p m a p m i p m a p m i
G G G G G G G G
p m a p m i p m a p m i p m a p m i p m a p m i
G G G G G G G G
p m a p m i p m a p m i p m a p m i p m a p m i
G G G G G G G G
p m a p m i p m a p m i p m a p m i p m a p m i
G G G G G G G G
p m a p m i p m a p m i p m a p m i p m a p m i
G G G G G G G G
p m a p m i p m a p m i p m a p m i p m a p m i

§ II

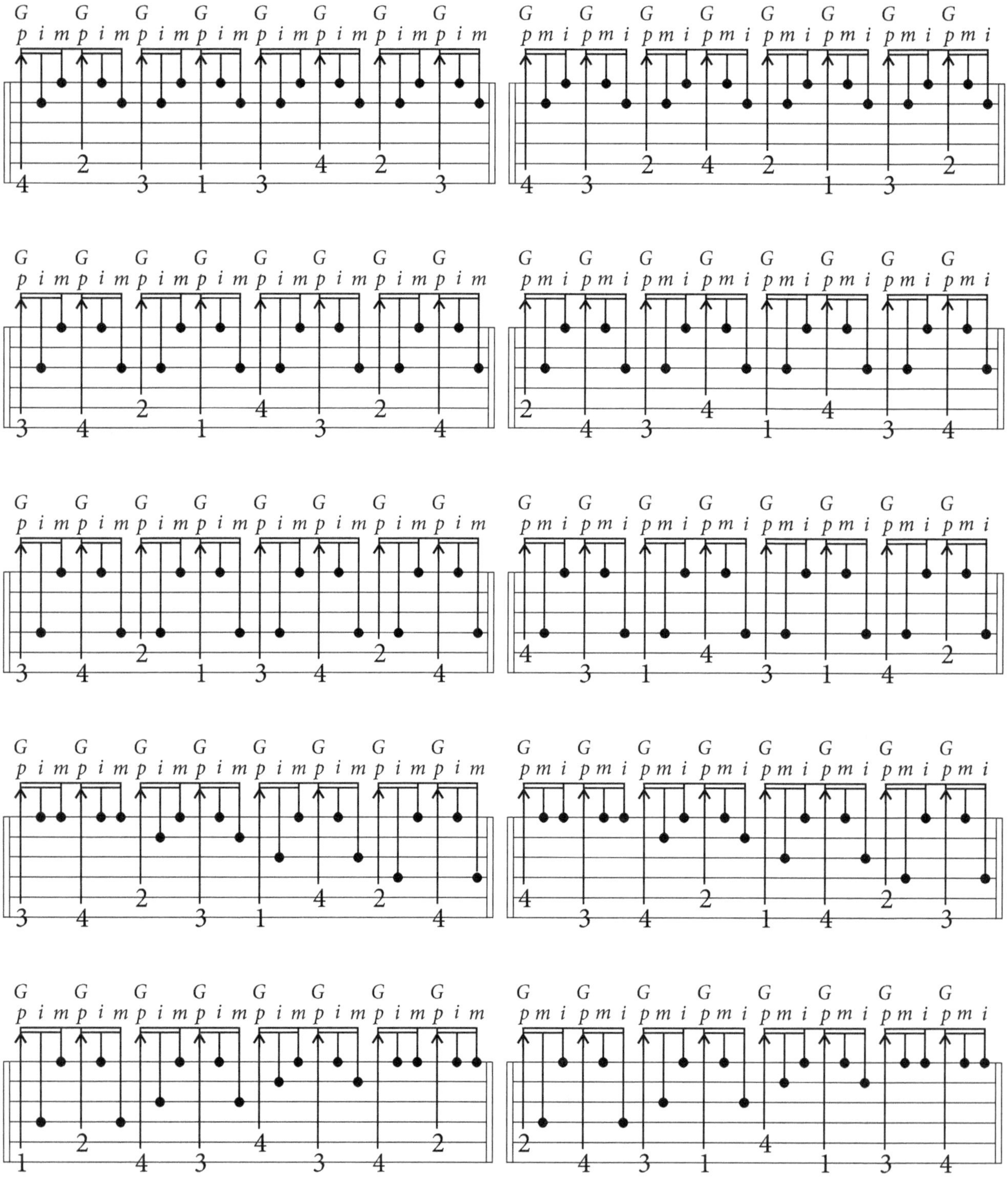

3

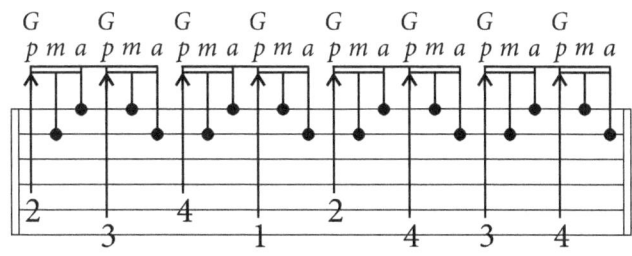
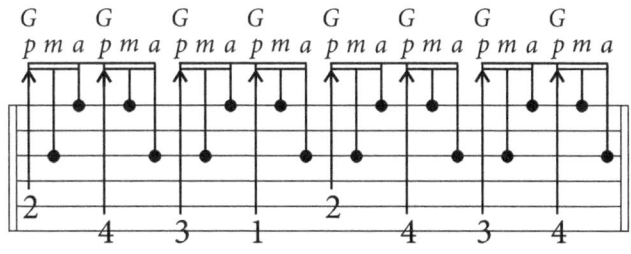
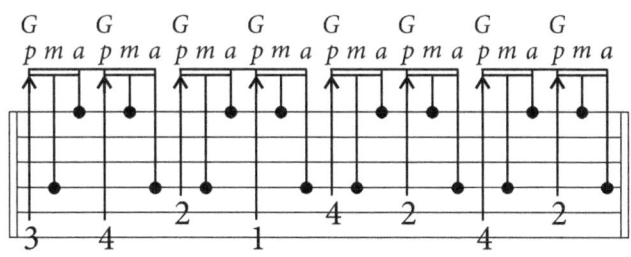
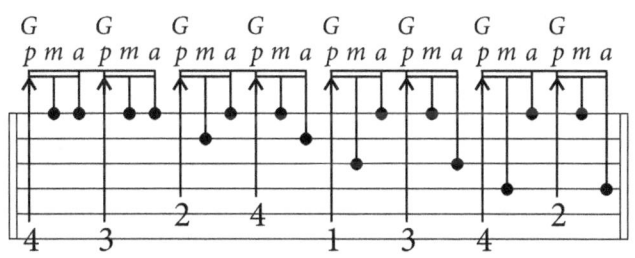
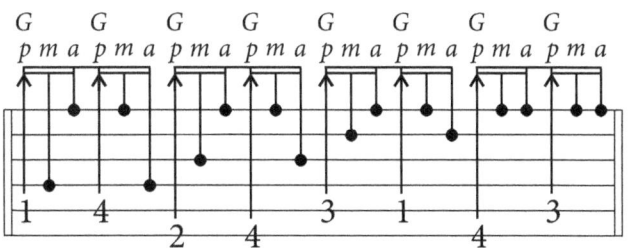

UNIT 4

Golpe exercises on the ascending and descending rolling Formulas.

In Unit 4 we find Golpe exercises on the ascending,

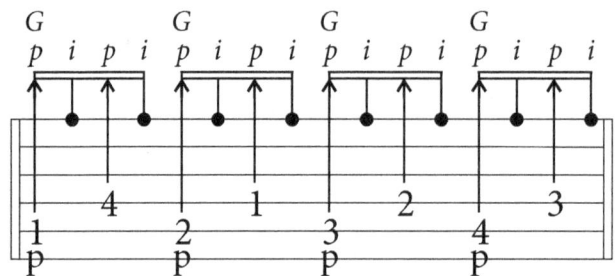

And descending rolling Formulas of the left hand.

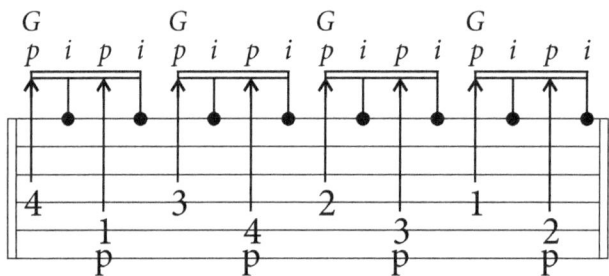

§ I Thumb stroke with Golpe in combination with the right hand fingers, index and middle finger. The scales in § I refer to adjacent strings. Practice on the exercises of § I and § II adding a second Golpe within the meter as follows:

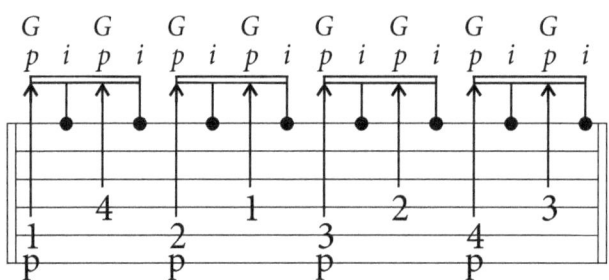

§ **III** Insertion of string or strings in the rolling Formulas. Double Golpe within the meter. Practice apart from the already mentioned way with interchange between the index and middle finger. So the following exercise,

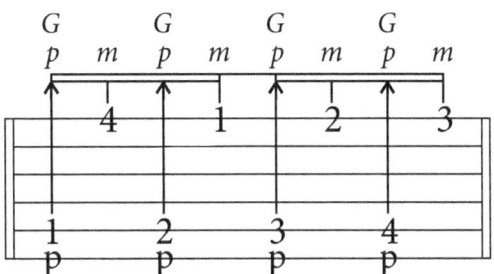

can be performed as follows:

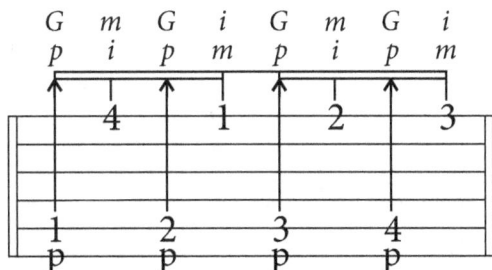

§ **Iva**, § **IVb** Exercise with greater difficulty in performance. Simultaneous strike of thumb with index or middle finger with Golpe. Practice interchanging the index and middle finger.

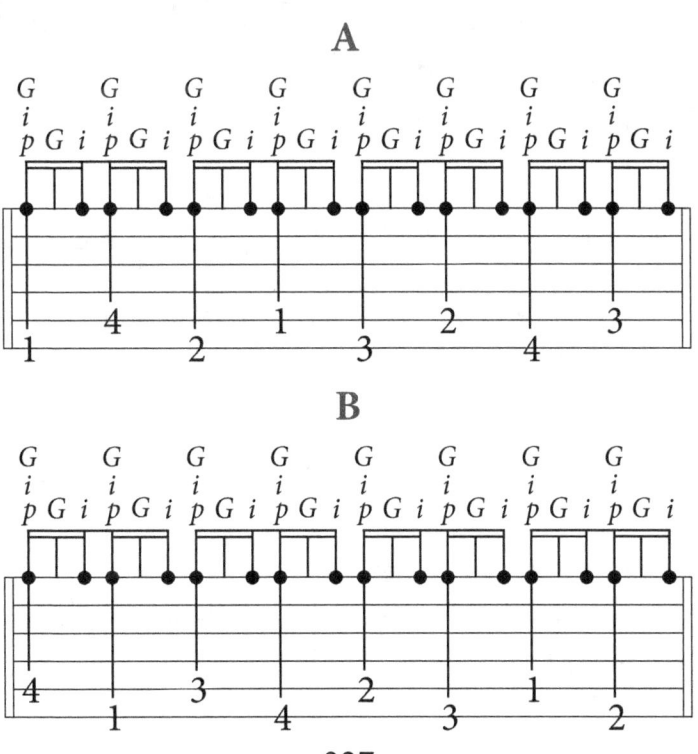

§ I

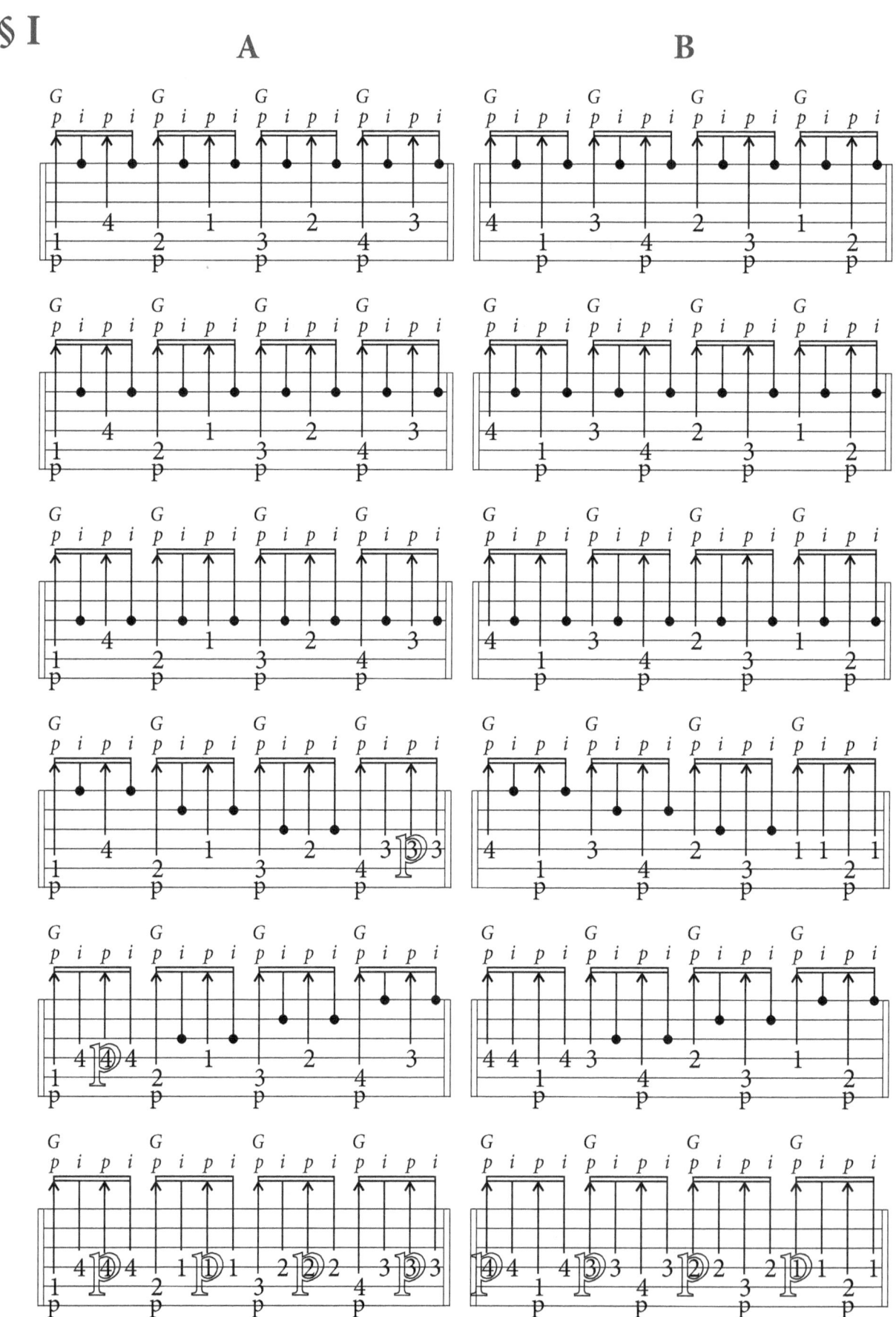

328

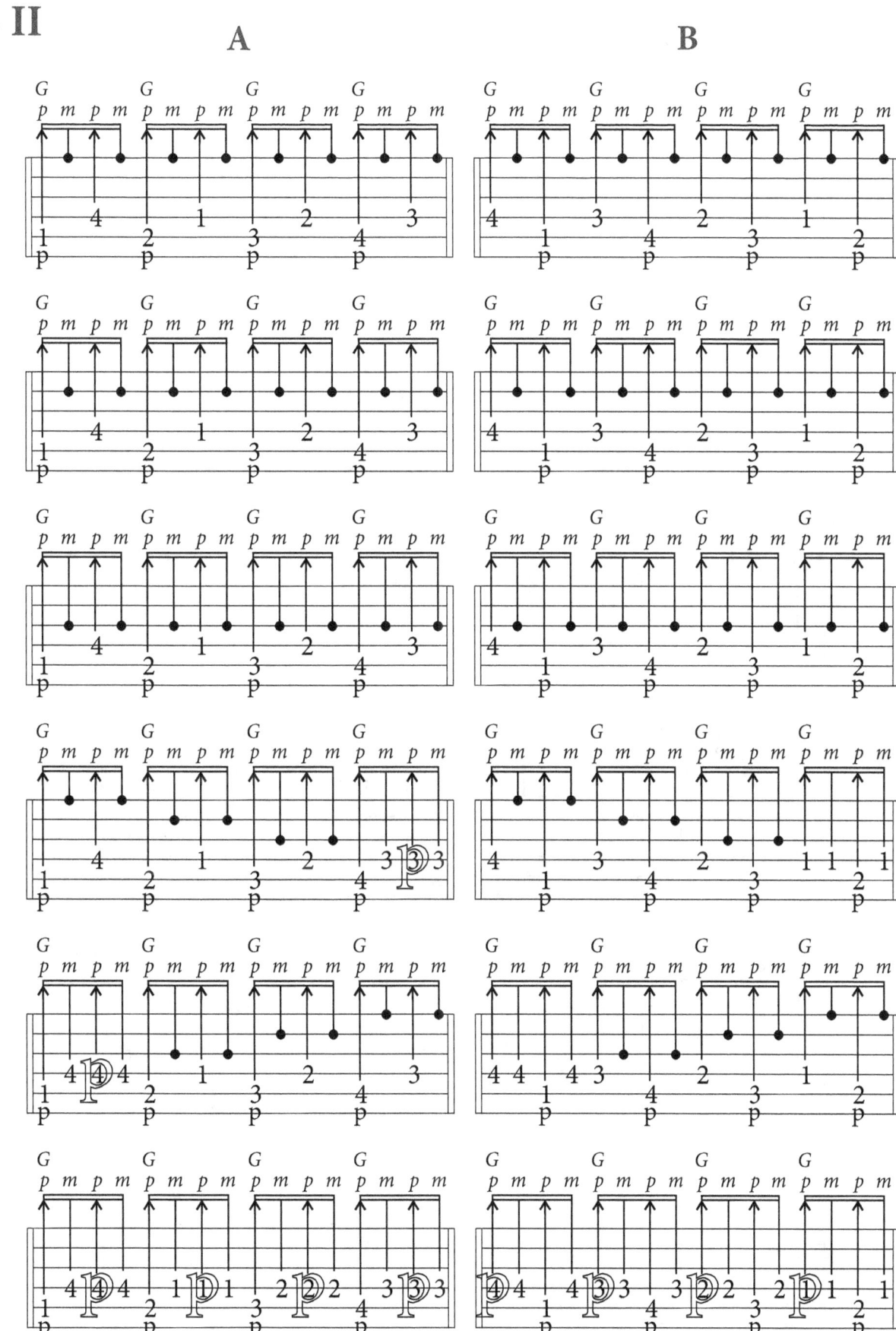

§ III

A   B

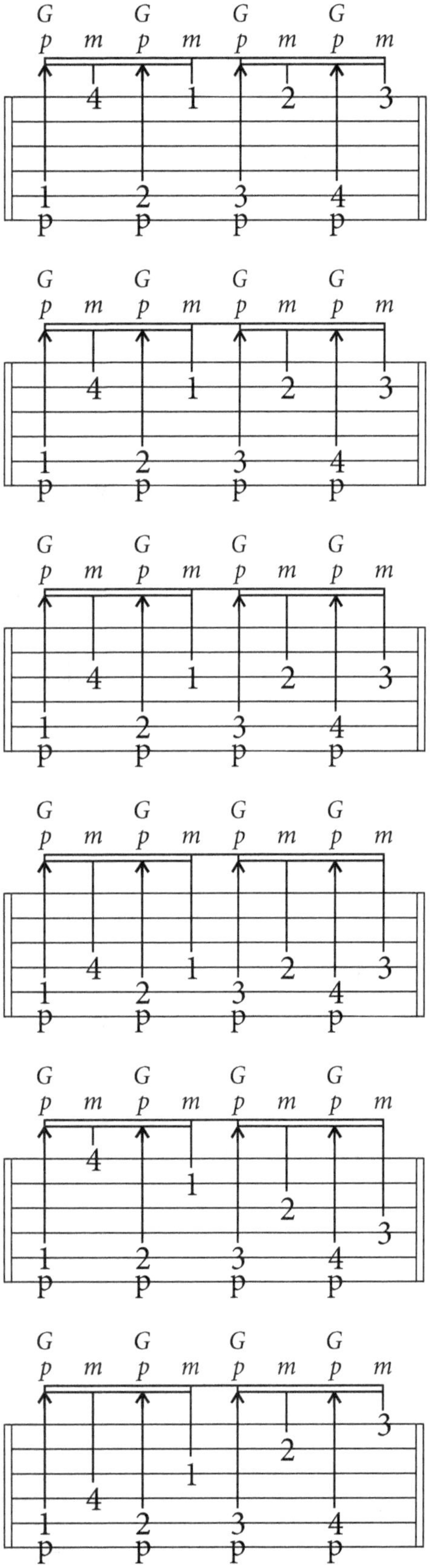

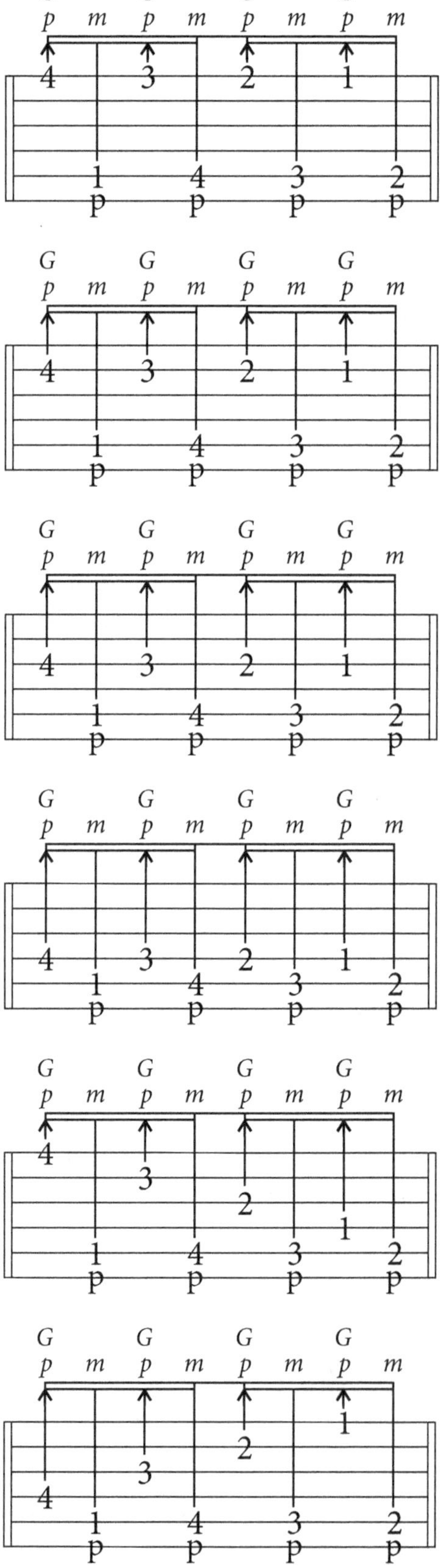

§ IVa

A **B**

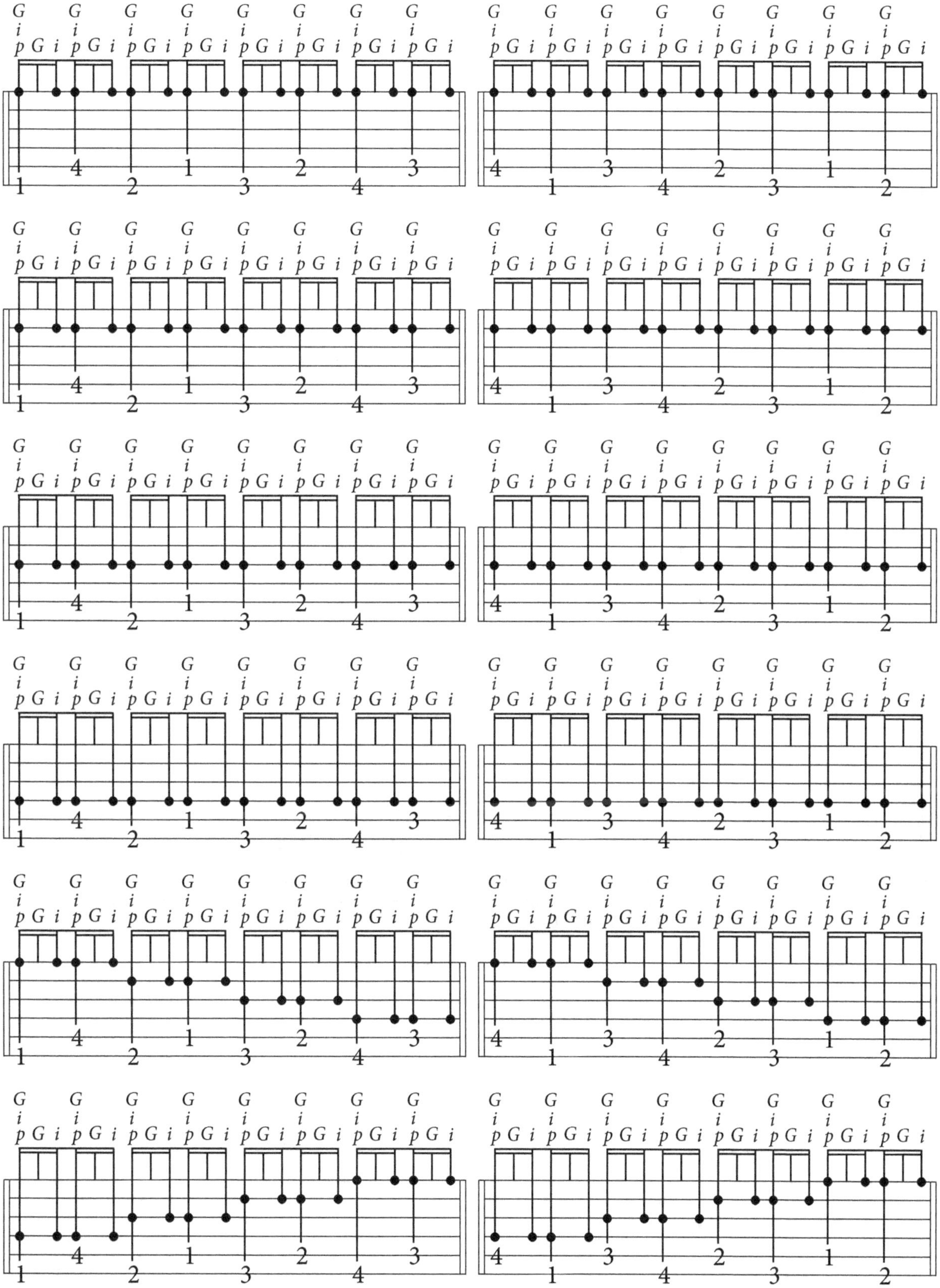

G G G G G G G G
i i i i i i i i
p G i p G i p G i p G i p G i p G i p G i p G i
4 1 2 3
1 2 3 4
G G G G G G G G
i i i i i i i i
p G i p G i p G i p G i p G i p G i p G i p G i
4 3 2 1
1 4 3 2

§ IVb

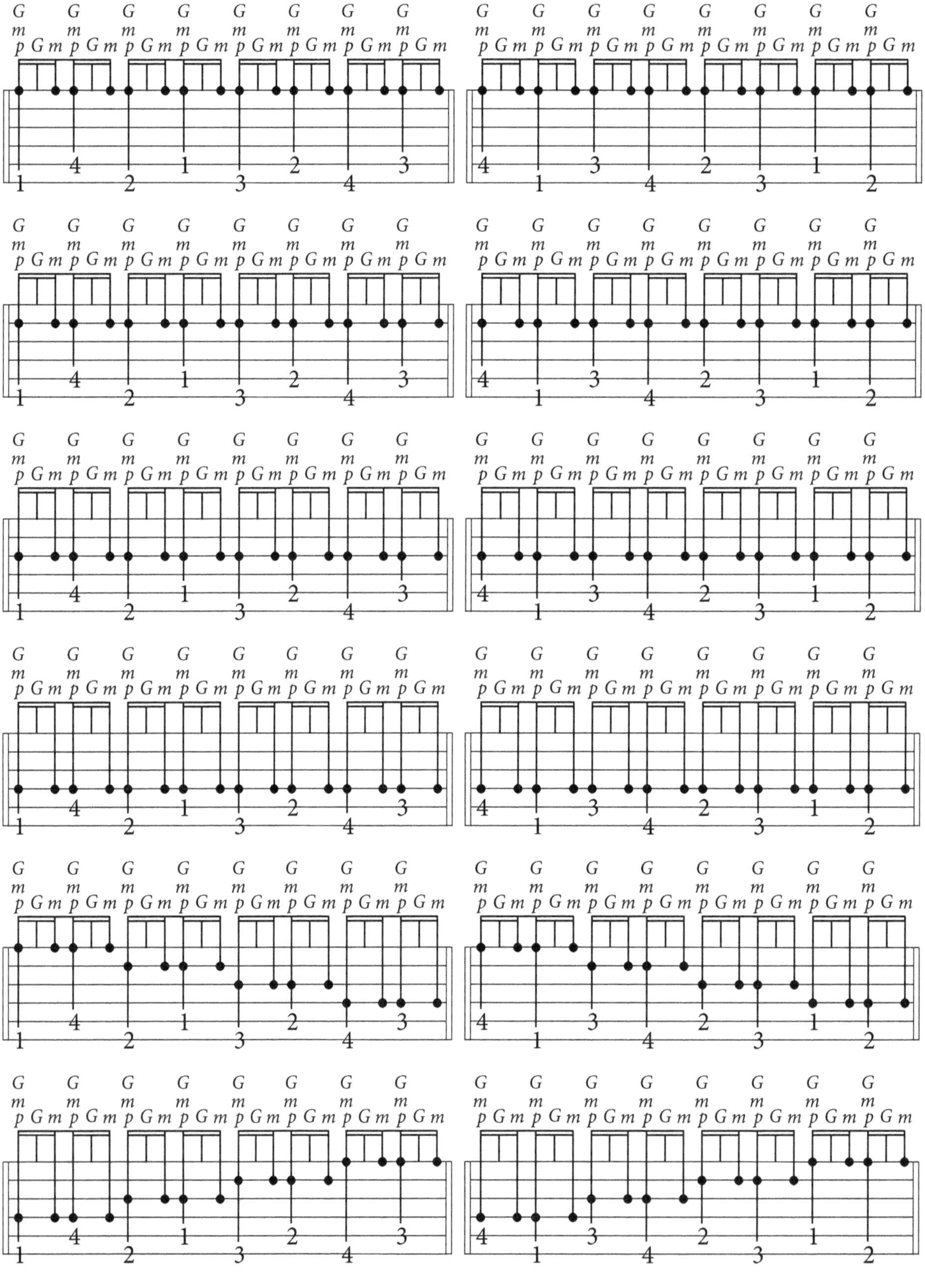

CHAPTER 3
THUMB STROKE IN COMBINATION WITH ACCORDS.

UNIT 1

Combination of Golpe with accords of two notes on ascending and descending rolling Formulas and on scales of two adjacent strings.

§ I Combination of Golpe with accords of two notes on ascending and descending rolling Formulas. The right hand fingers, index (i) and middle finger (m) that play the chords are either on adjacent strings.

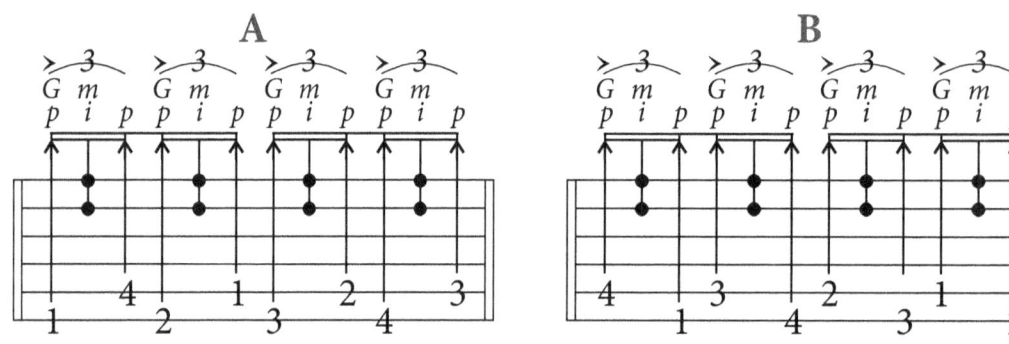

or on remote strings with insertion of one string,

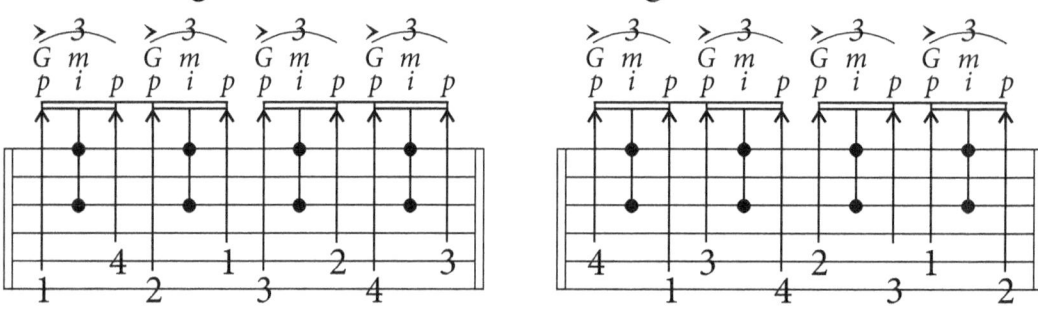

or with insertion of two strings.

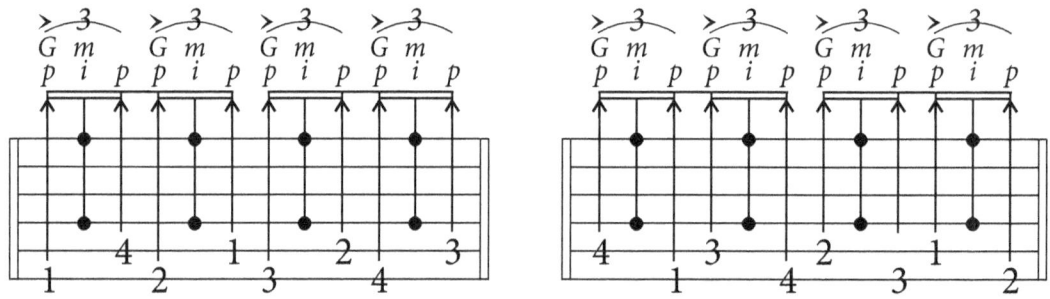

Exercise shaped in triplets. Single Golpe as above or double Golpe as below in § II.

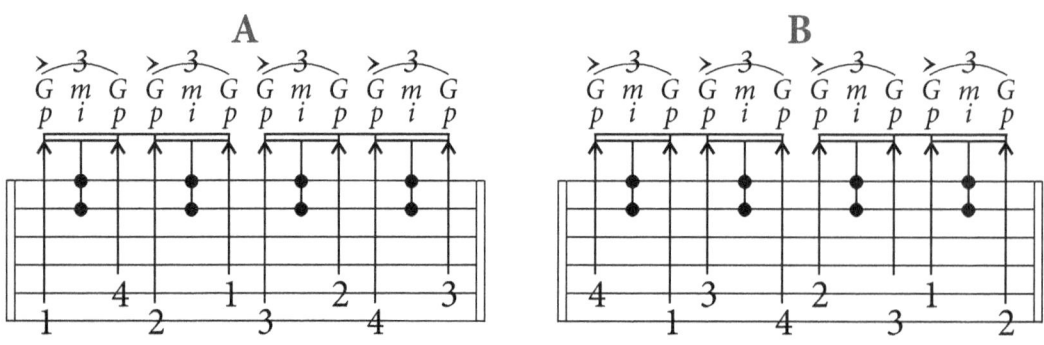

§ III Exercise based on the ascending and descending rolling Formulas with simultaneous stroke of two strings by the fingers (i) and (m) as if it is a chord or if it is an accord of two notes. Single Golpe within the meter.

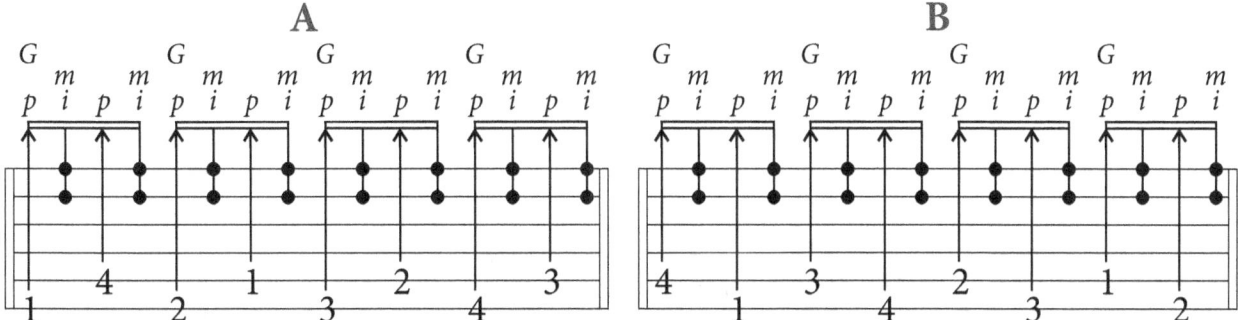

§ IV Same exercise as the previous with double Golpe within the met

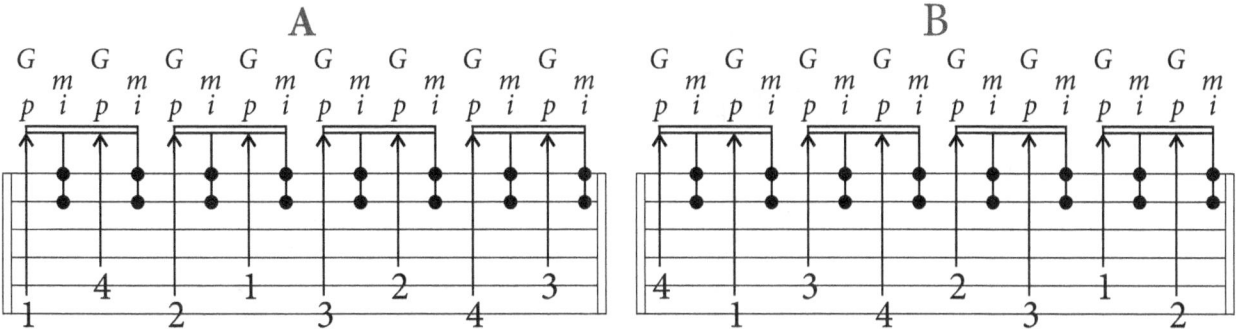

§ V Replacement of the scales of the previous exercises with scales of two adjacent strings.

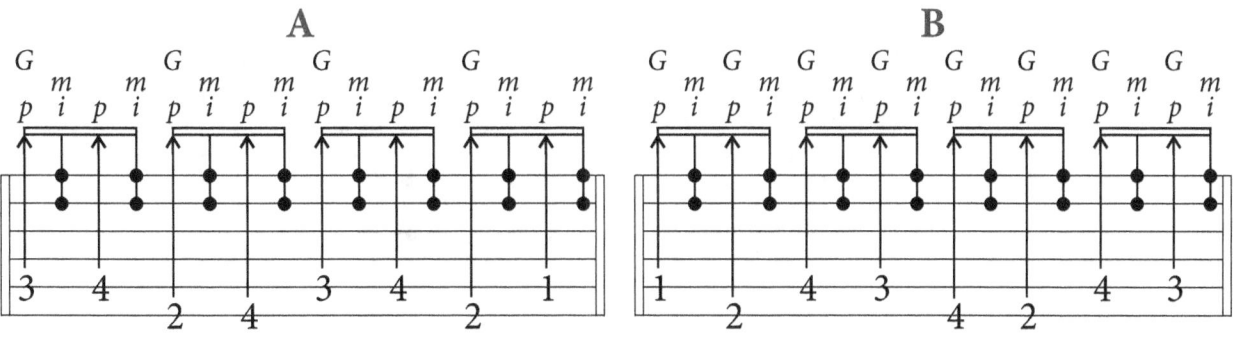

§ I

§ II

§ III

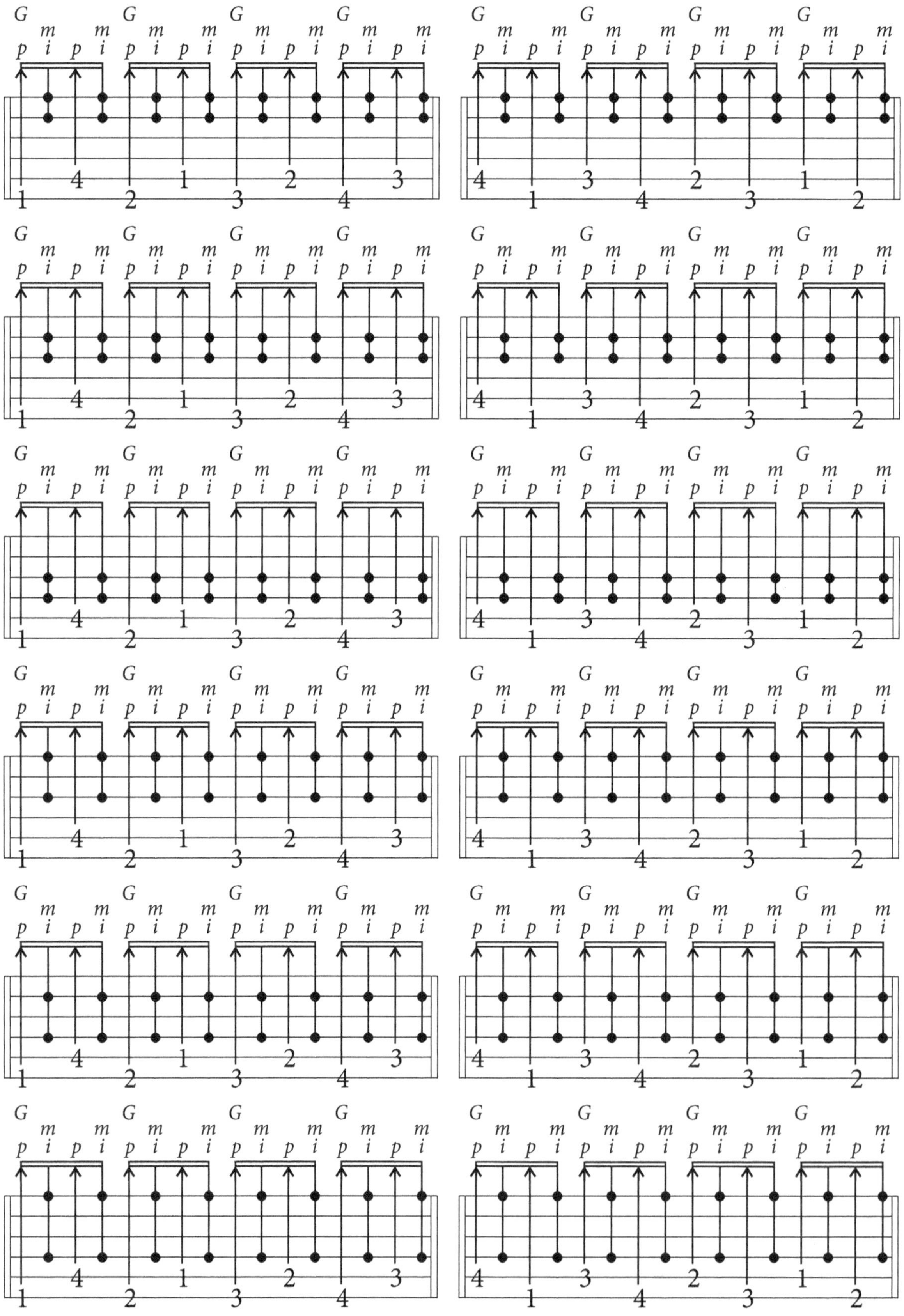

§ IV   A   B

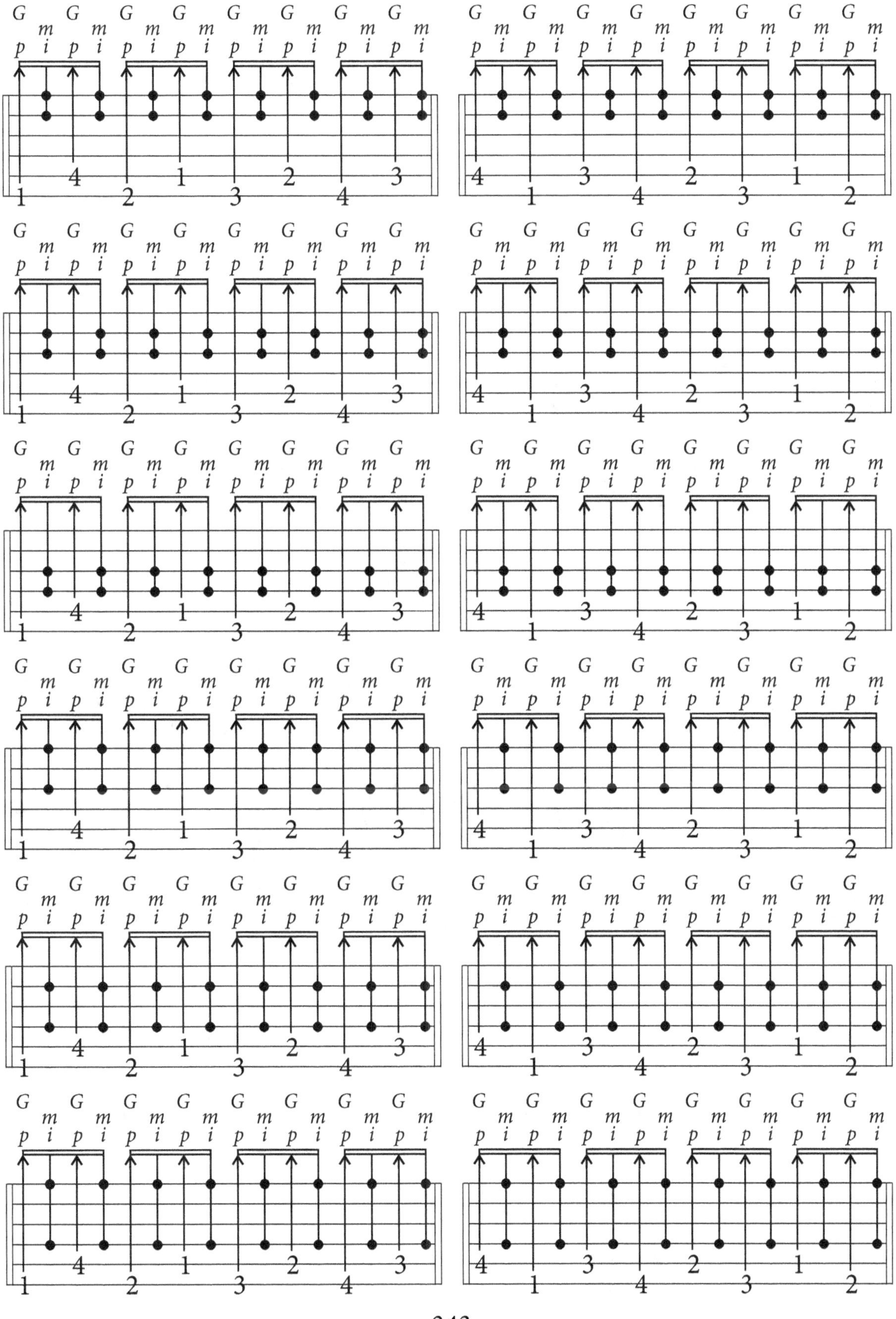

§ V

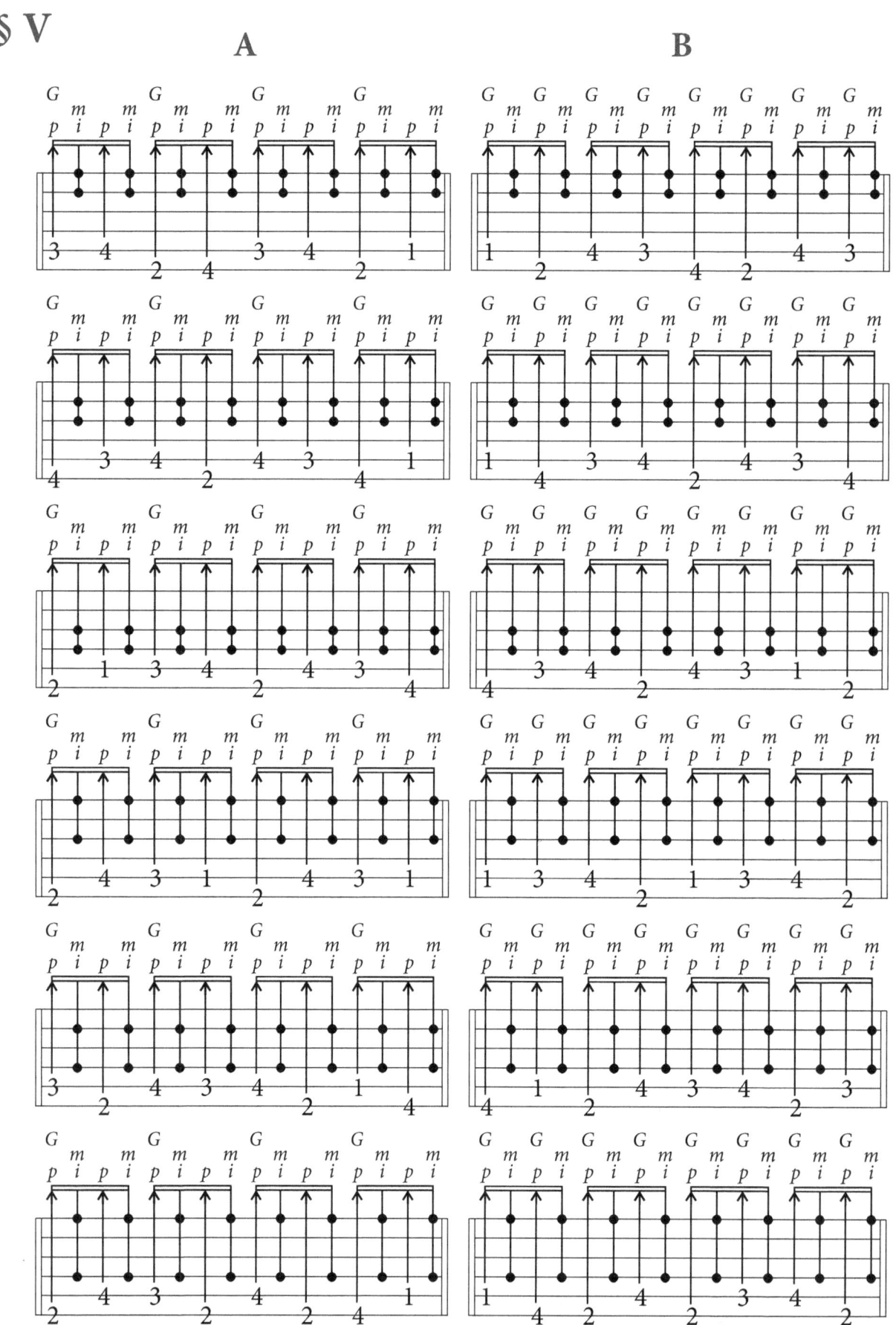

344

UNIT 2

Simultaneous stroke of thumb
with index (i) and middle finger (m)
with Golpe on the rolling (ascending and descending) Formulas
and on scale of two adjacent strings.

§ I Simultaneous stroke of thumb with index (i) and middle finger (m) with Golpe on the ascending rolling Formulas of the left hand. Exercise that refers (in relation to the index and middle finger of the right hand) to one string,

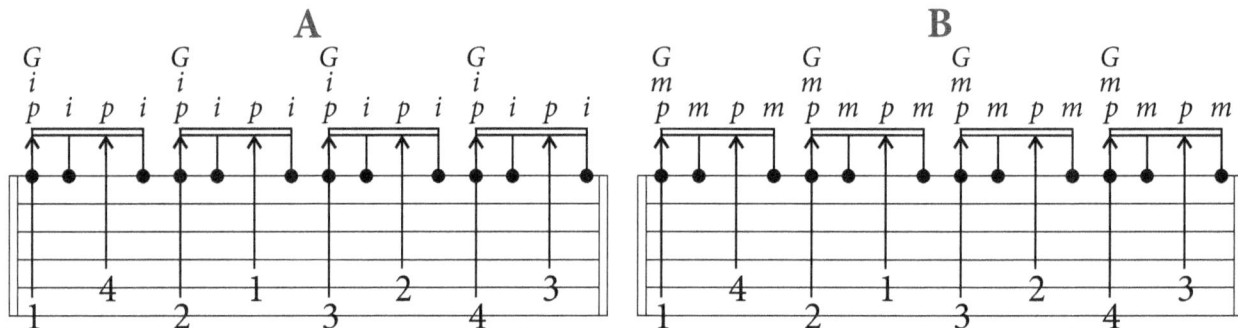

or to more strings, as the index and middle finger of the right hand move from the 1st to the 4th string within the Formula and return from the 4th to the 1st string.

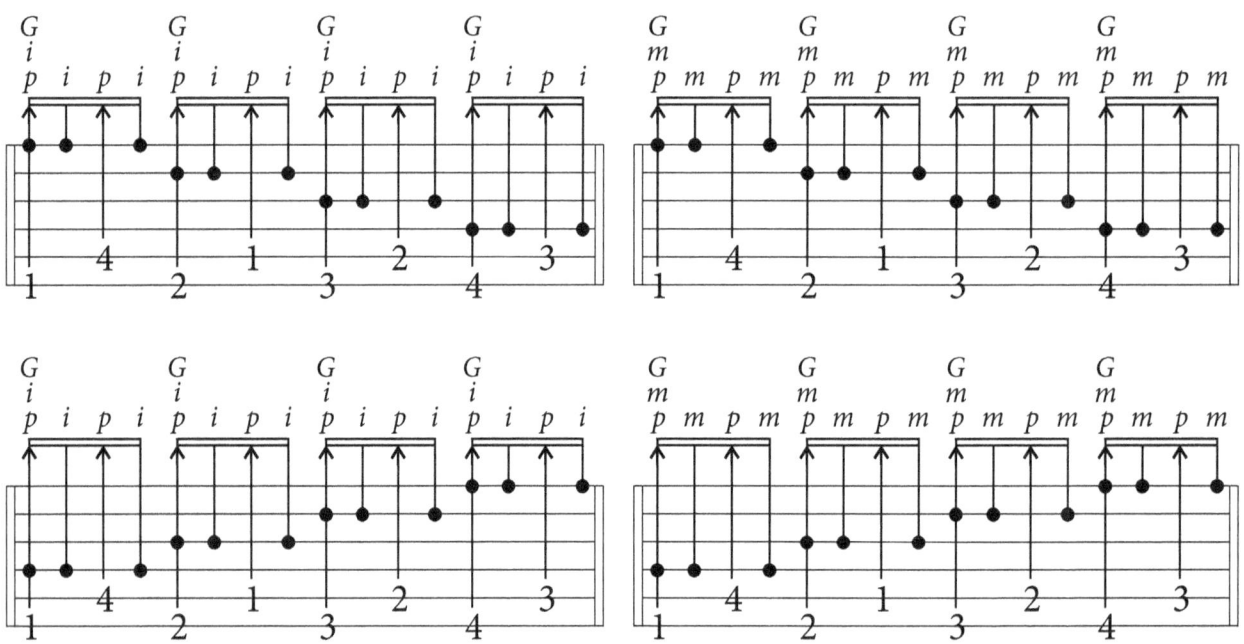

You can also practice with a second Golpe within the meter as the arrow shows:

G
↑

§ II Simultaneous stroke of thumb with index (i) and middle finger (m) with Golpe on the descending rolling Formulas of the left hand. Exercise that refers (in relation to the index and middle finger of the right hand) to one string,

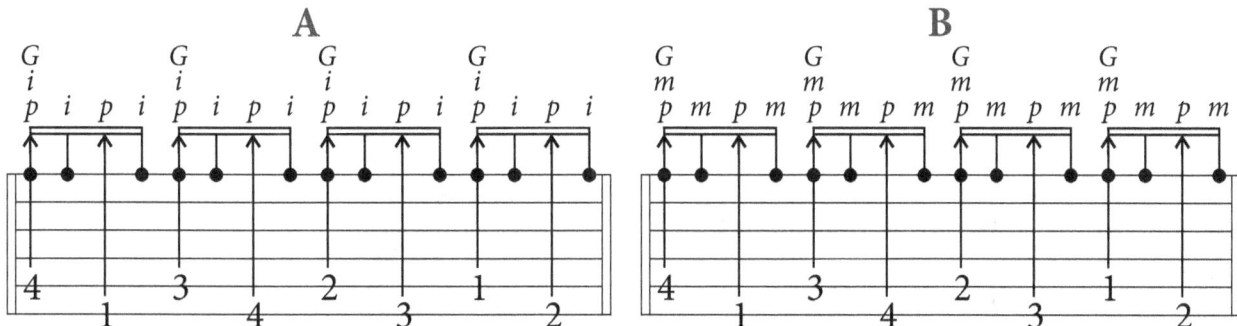

Or to more strings, as the index and middle finger of the right hand move from the 1st to the 4th string within the meter and return from the 4th to the 1st string.

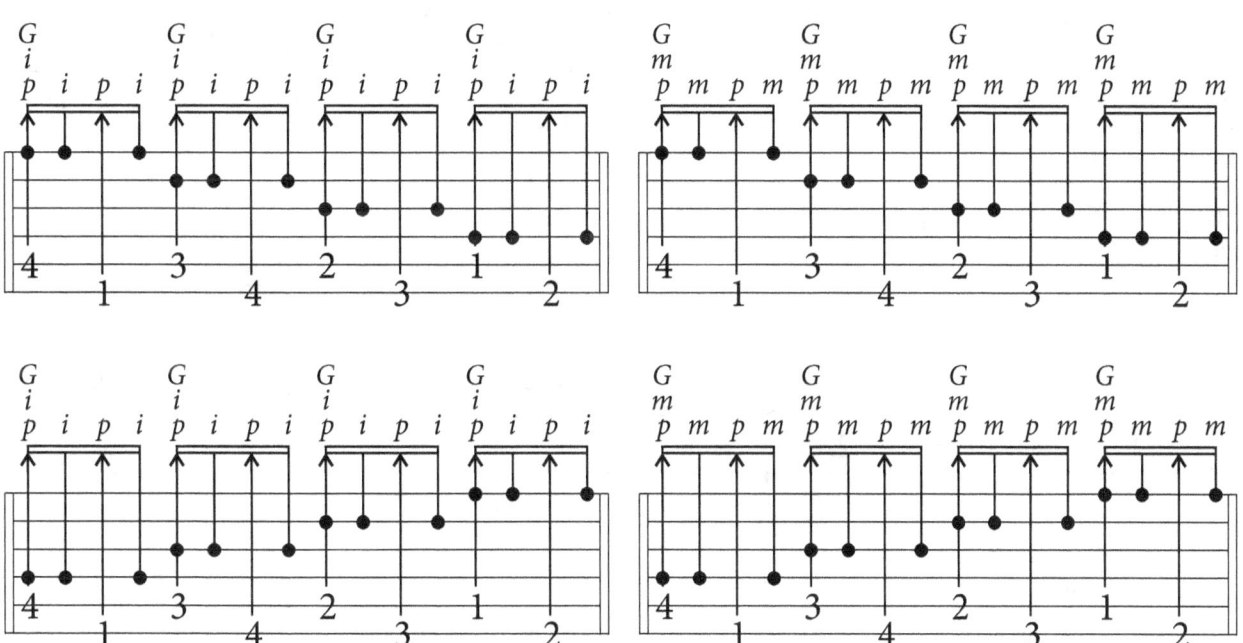

§ **III** Same exercise varied in the fingering of the right hand and with participation of the ring finger.

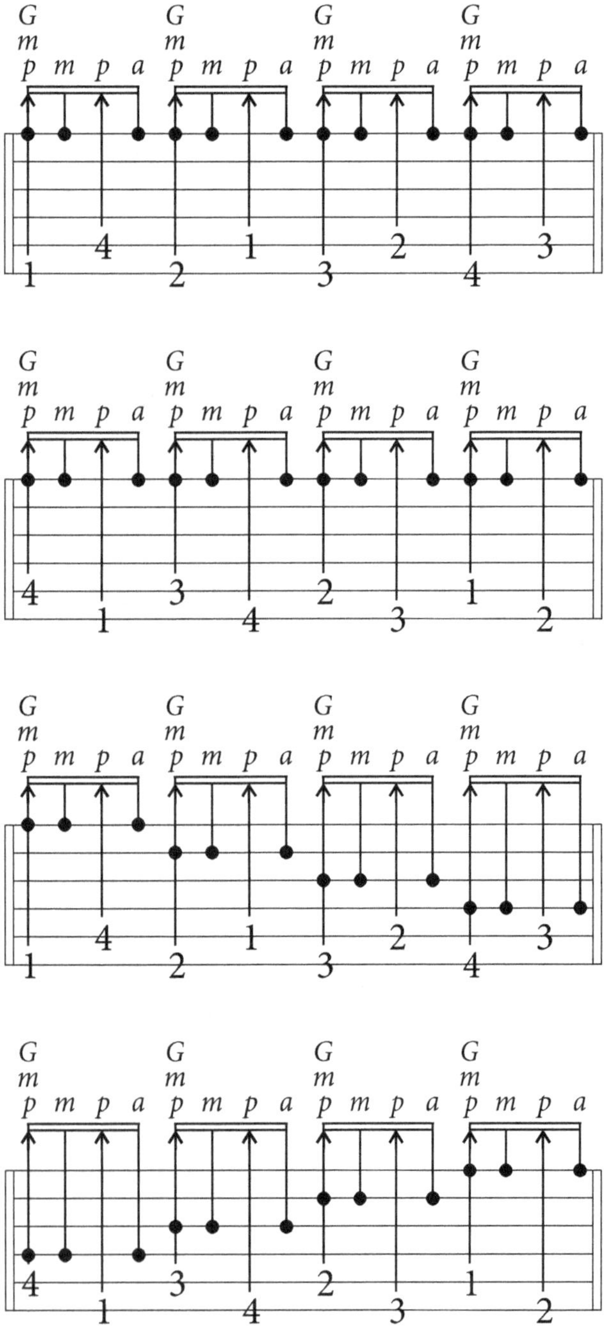

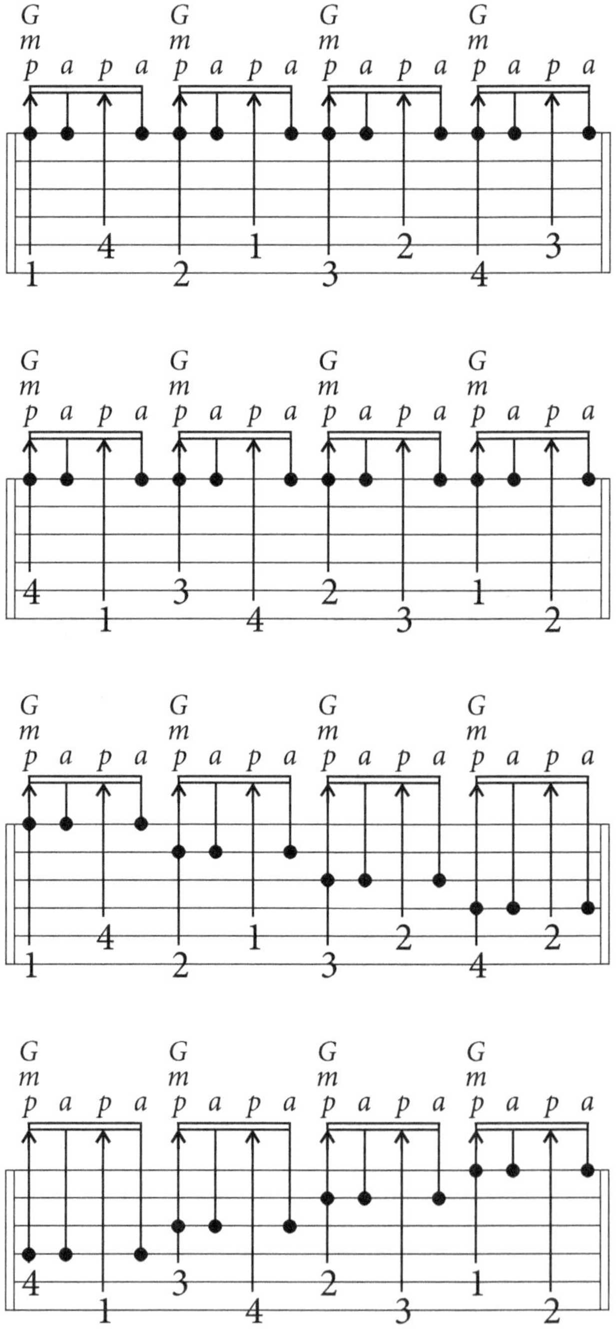

Practice also with a second Golpe within the meter.

§ IV Same exercise on the scales of two adjacent strings.

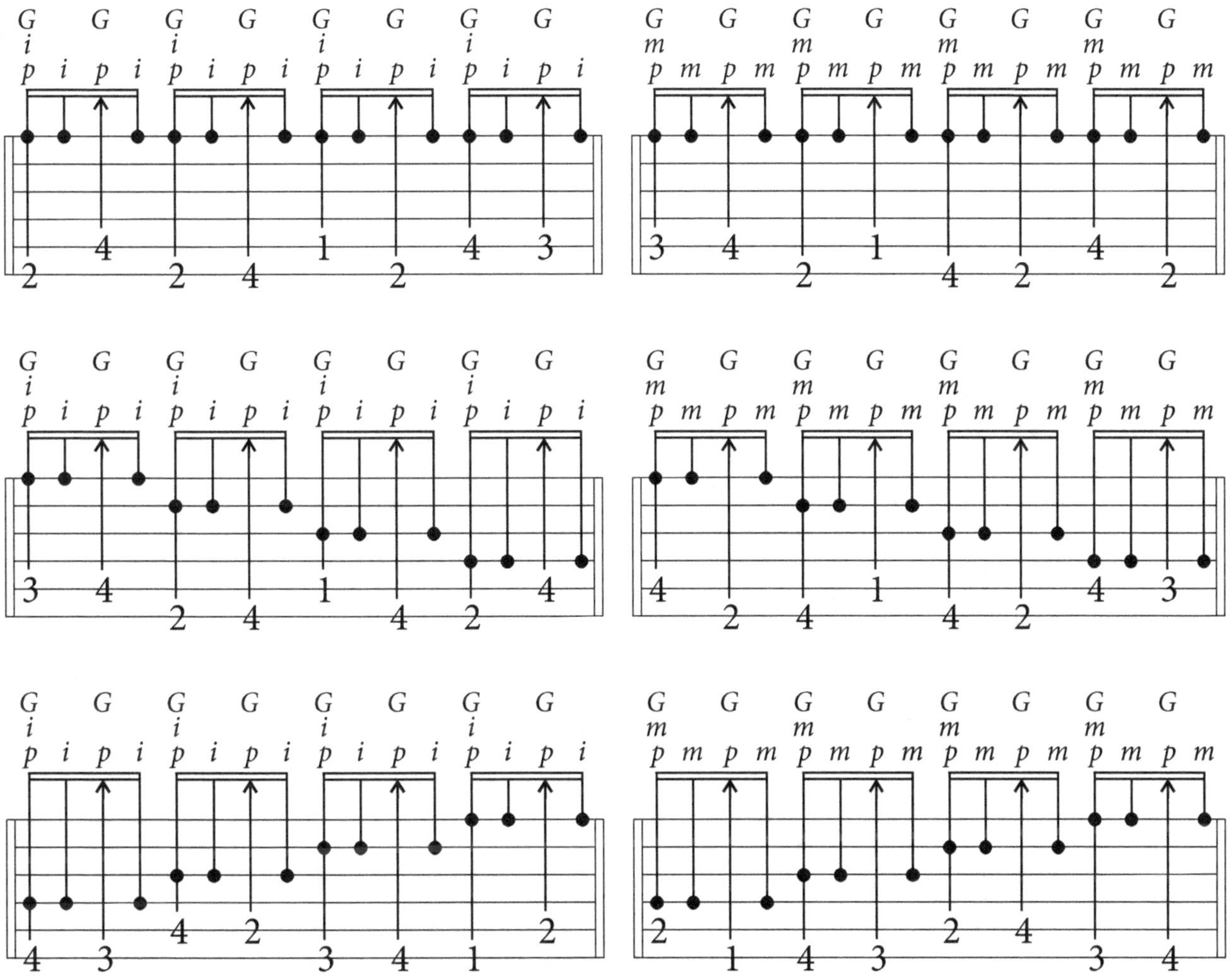

Practice adding in columns A and B a second Golpe as shown above.

§ V Same exercise on the scales of two adjacent strings.

A | B

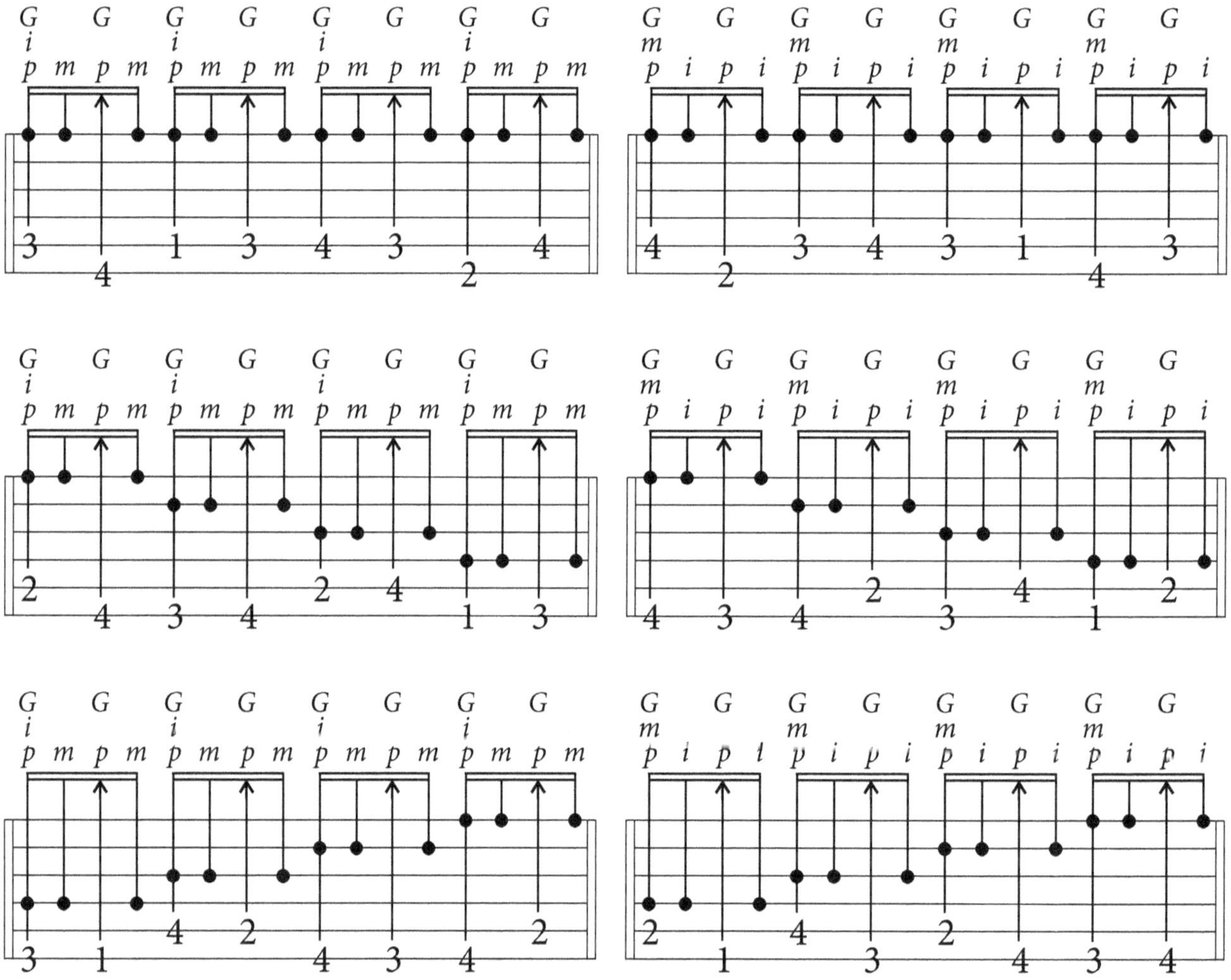

§ VI Double Golpe within the meter with simultaneous stroke of the thumb and index (as well as middle finger) on the ascending rolling Formulas. Exercise with special difficulties.

A   B

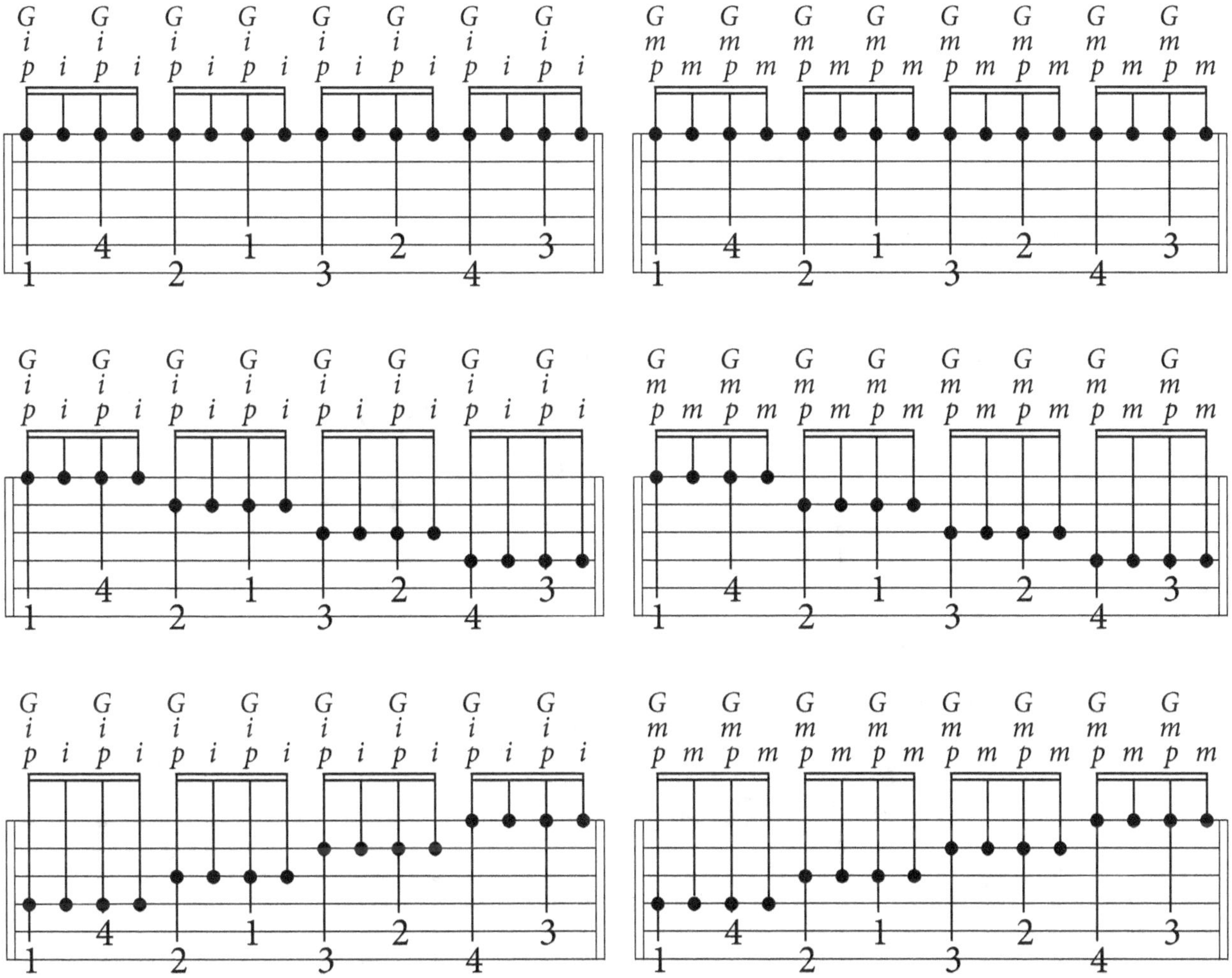

§ **VII** Double Golpe within the meter with simultaneous stroke of the thumb and index (as well as middle) on the descending rolling Formulas. Exercise with special difficulties.

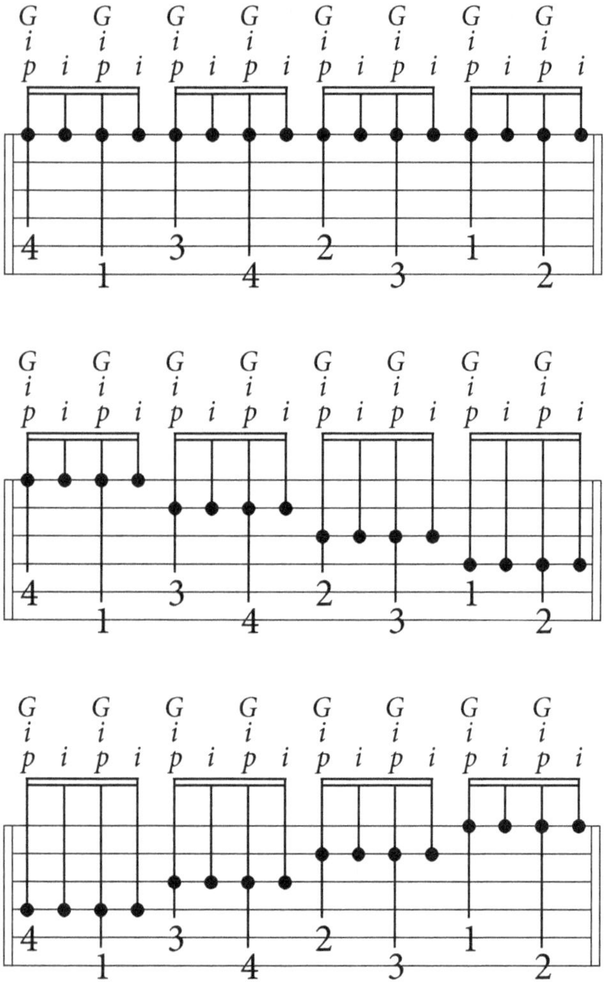

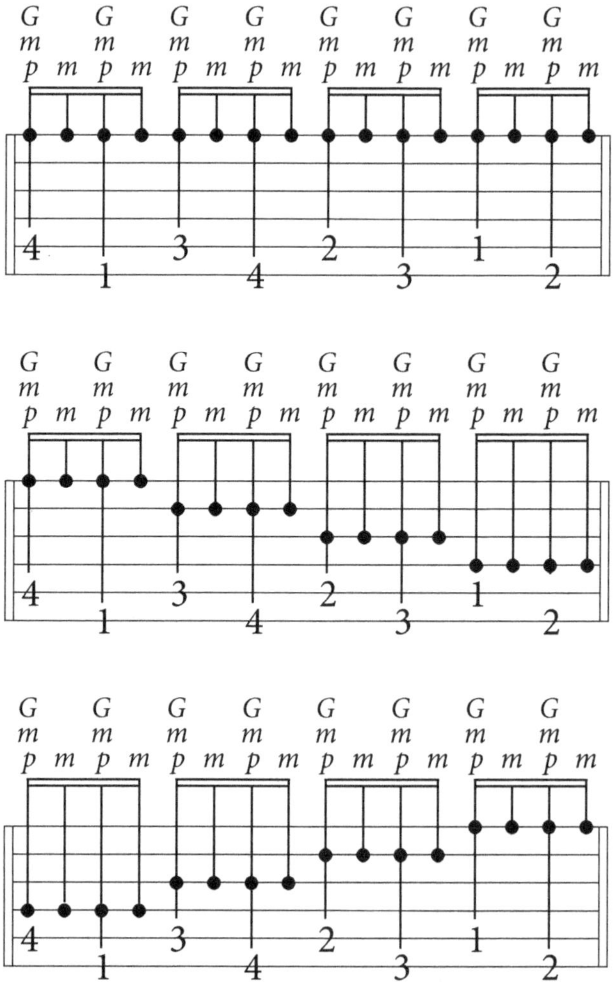

§ VIII Double Golpe within the meter with simultaneous stroke of the thumb with the index (as well as with the middle finger) on the scales of two adjacent strings.

A   B

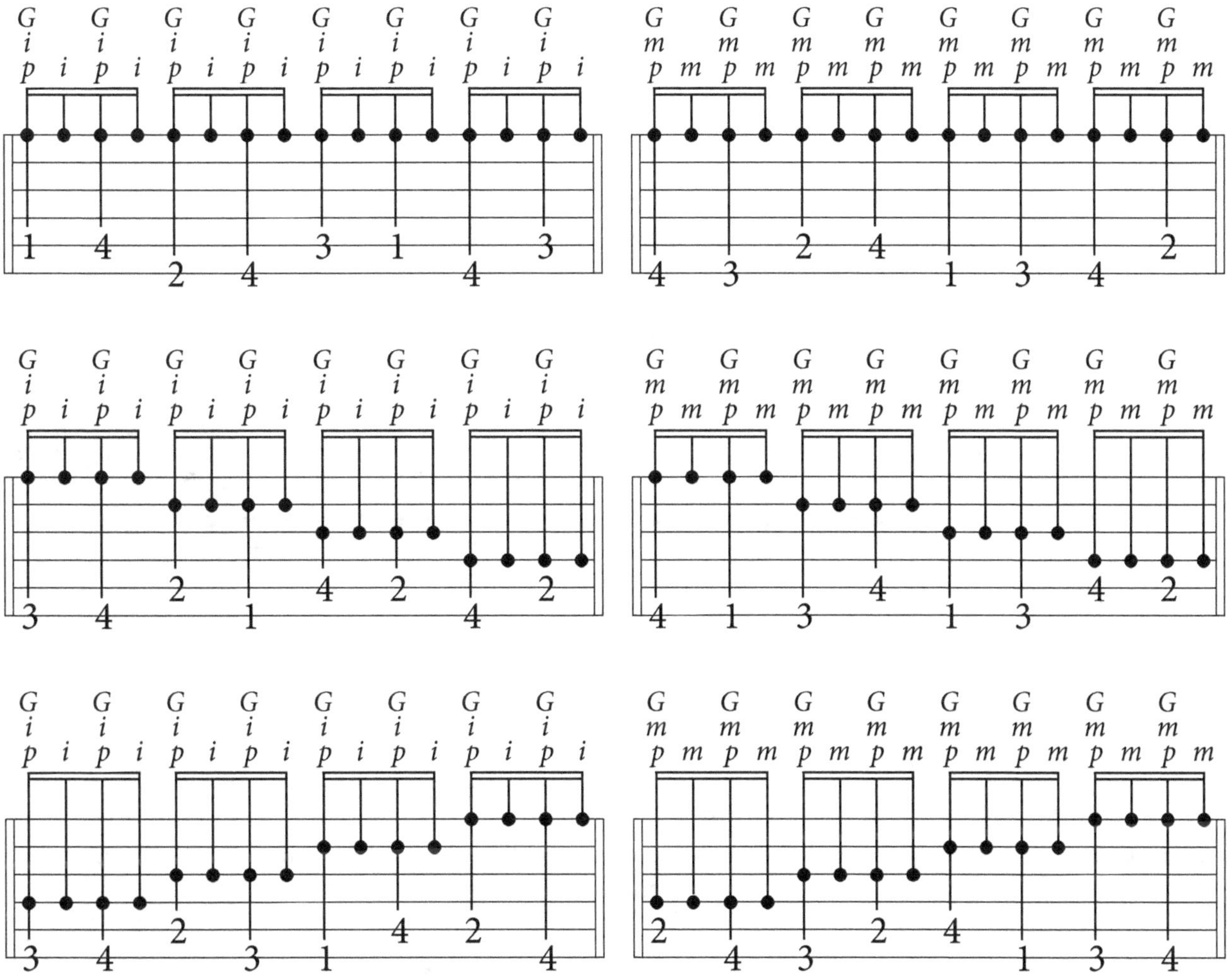

§ **IX** Variation on the previous exercise with movement of the pair of strings on which the scales of two adjacent strings are played and insertion of string or strings.

A

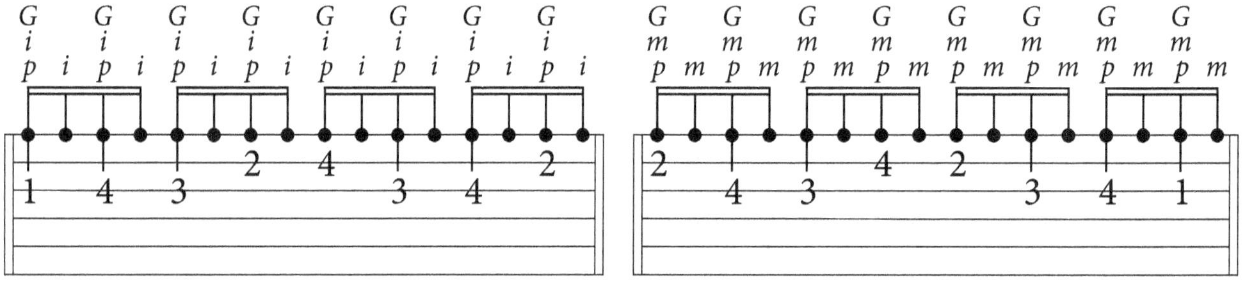

B

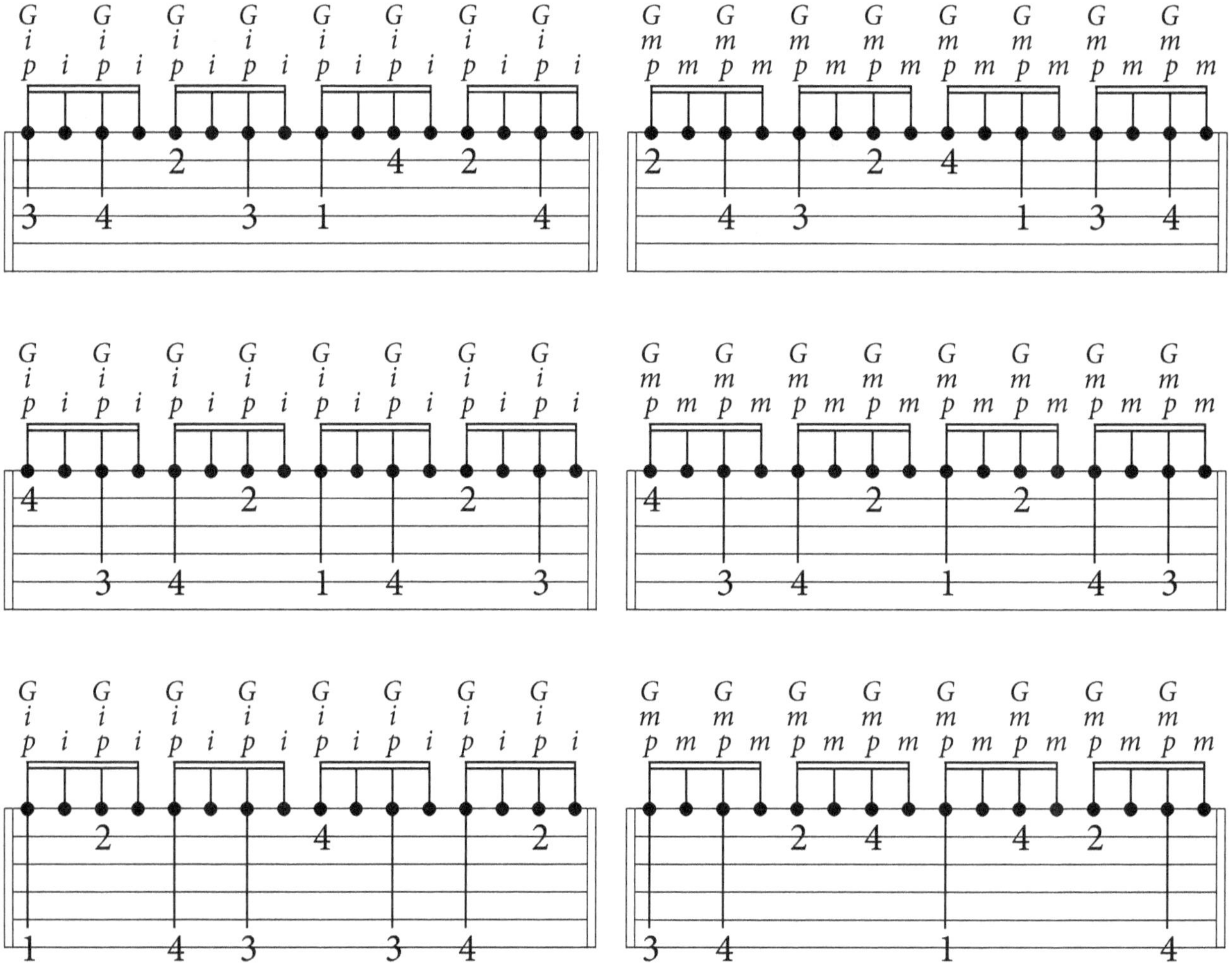

§ X Same mechanism of exercises as in the previous ones with extension of the meter by one note. Use of adjacent strings scales. Participation of the ring finger, too in this paragraph.

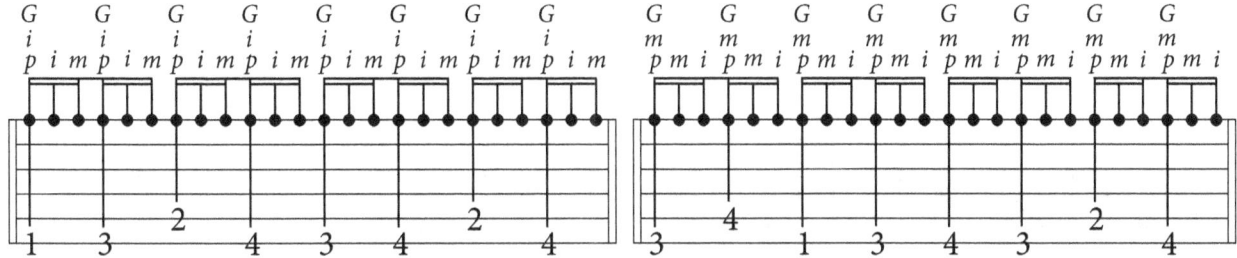

§ XI Accords of two notes with index, middle finger and thumb. Simultaneous performance of these chords with the thumb and Golpe. Movement of the chords on adjacent strings. Insertion of string or strings in different variations.

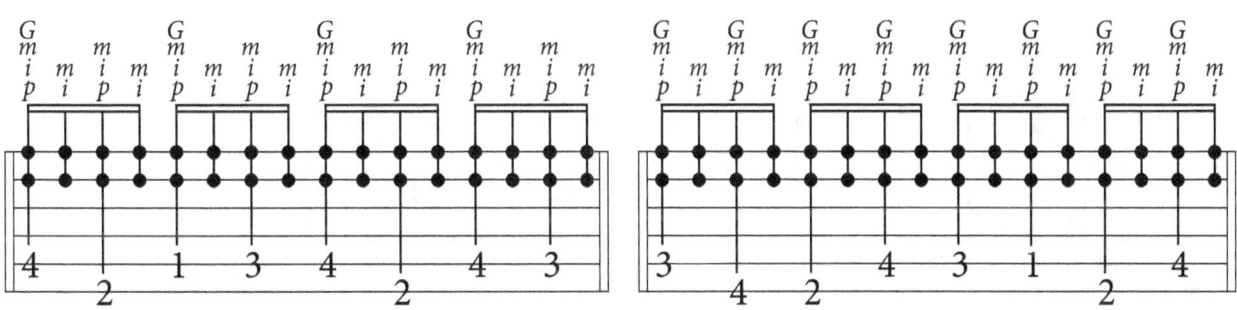

§ I

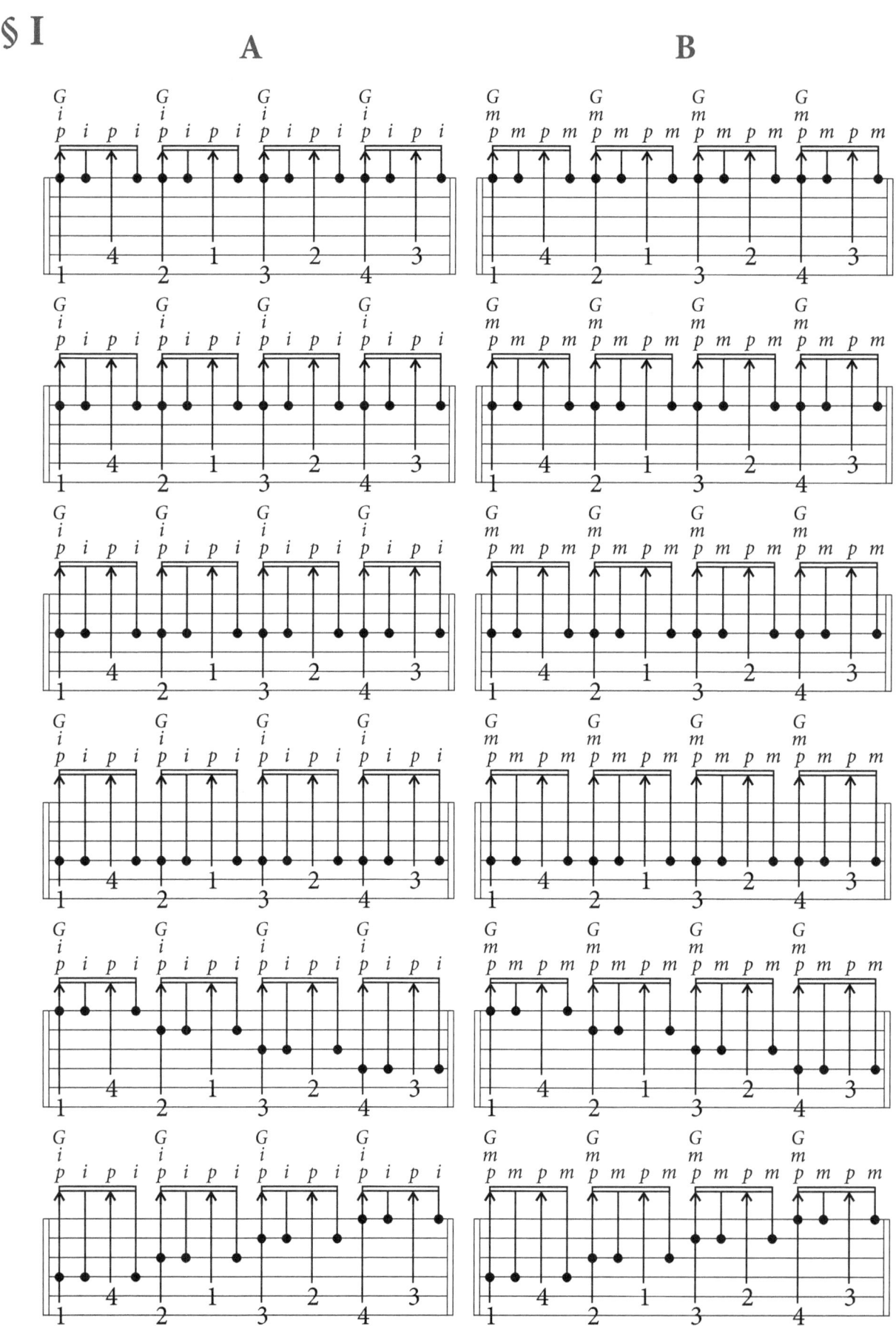

§ II

A

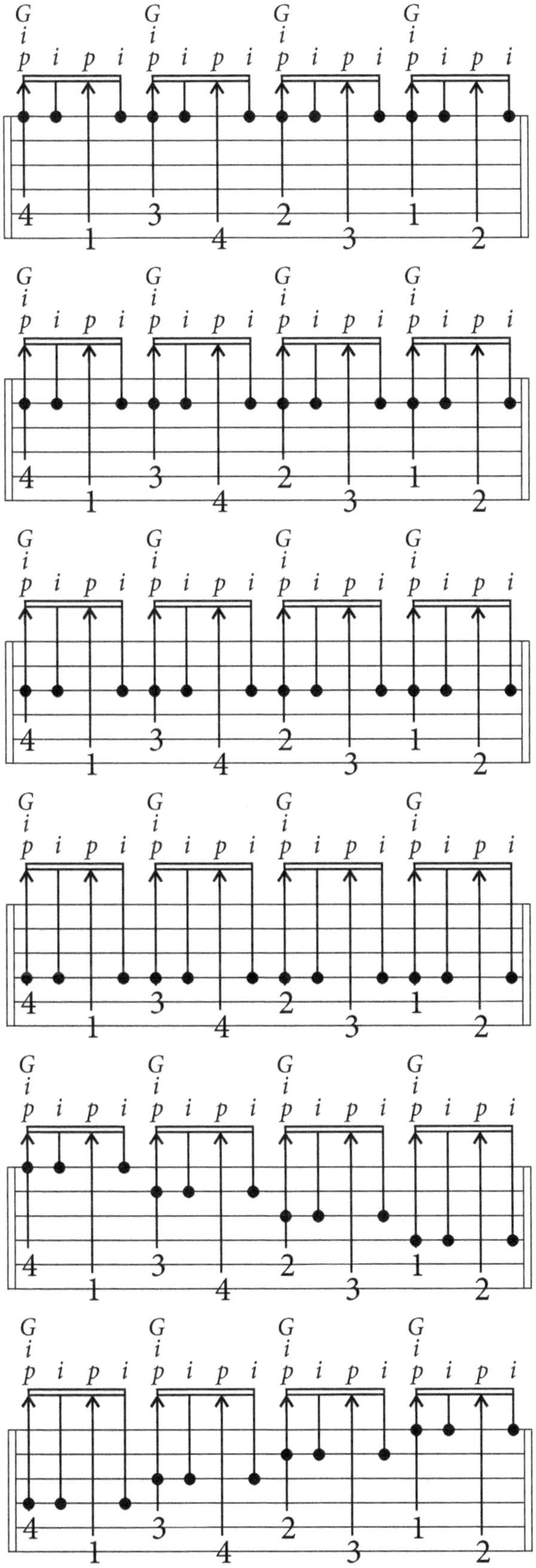

G G G G
i i i i
p i p i p i p i p i p i p i p i
4 1 3 4 2 3 1 2
G G G G
i i i i
p i p i p i p i p i p i p i p i
4 1 3 4 2 3 1 2
G G G G
i i i i
p i p i p i p i p i p i p i p i
4 1 3 4 2 3 1 2
G G G G
i i i i
p i p i p i p i p i p i p i p i
4 1 3 4 2 3 1 2
G G G G
i i i i
p i p i p i p i p i p i p i p i
4 1 3 4 2 3 1 2
G G G G
i i i i
p i p i p i p i p i p i p i p i
4 1 3 4 2 3 1 2

B

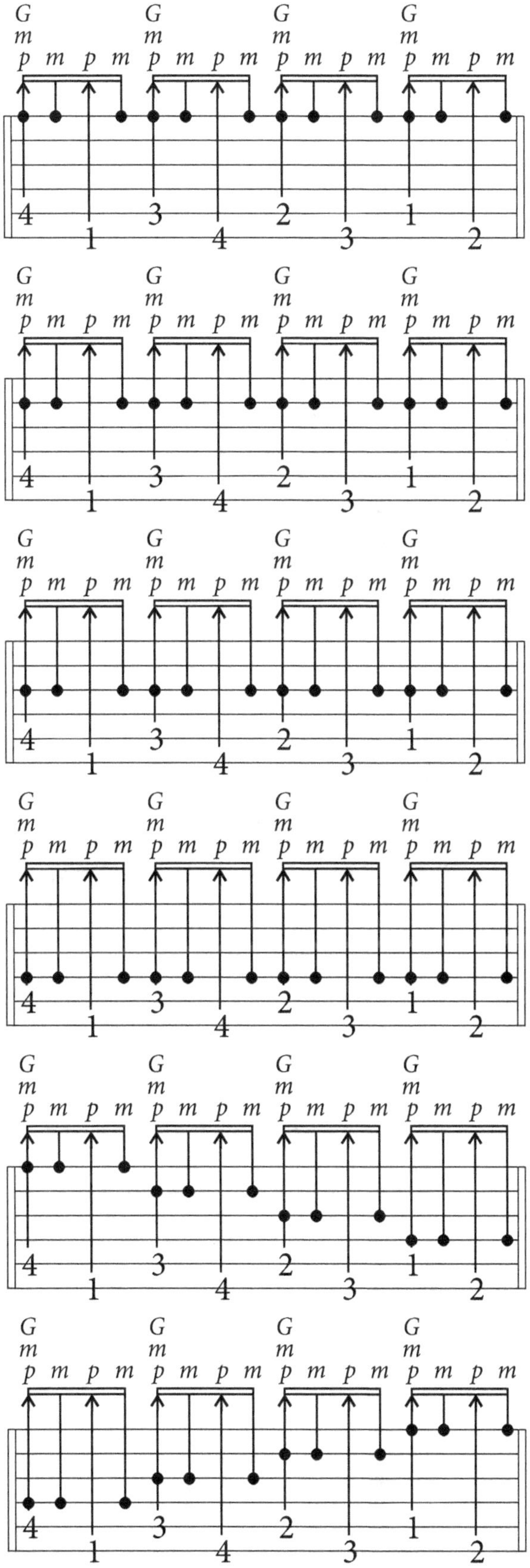

G G G G
m m m m
p m p m p m p m p m p m p m p m
4 1 3 4 2 3 1 2
G G G G
m m m m
p m p m p m p m p m p m p m p m
4 1 3 4 2 3 1 2
G G G G
m m m m
p m p m p m p m p m p m p m p m
4 1 3 4 2 3 1 2
G G G G
m m m m
p m p m p m p m p m p m p m p m
4 1 3 4 2 3 1 2
G G G G
m m m m
p m p m p m p m p m p m p m p m
4 1 3 4 2 3 1 2
G G G G
m m m m
p m p m p m p m p m p m p m p m
4 1 3 4 2 3 1 2

§ III

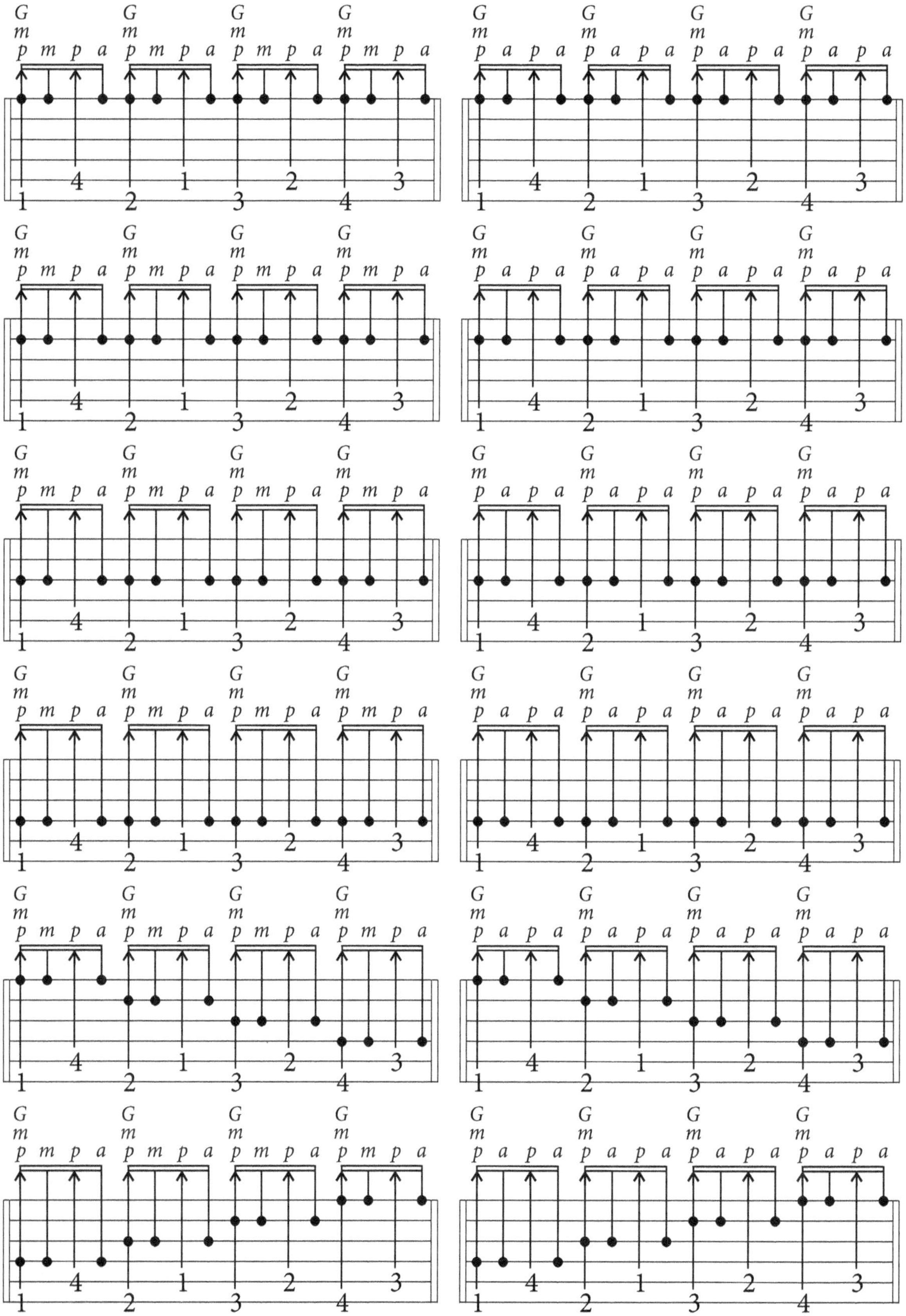

C   D

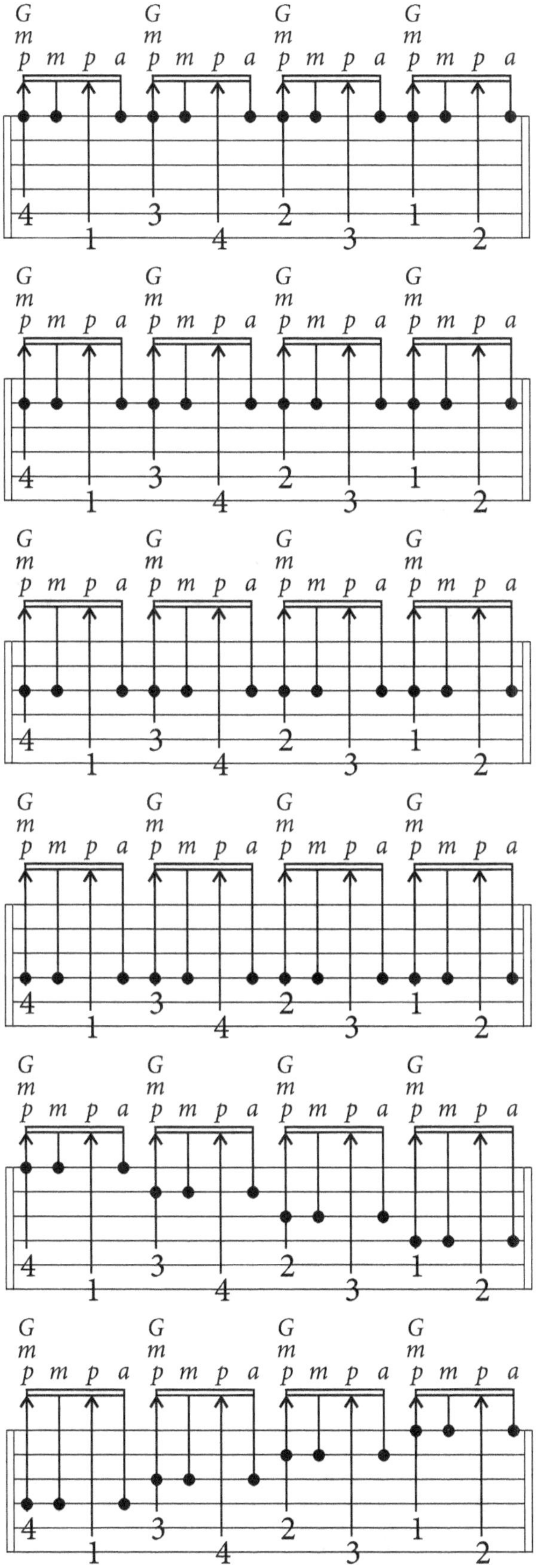

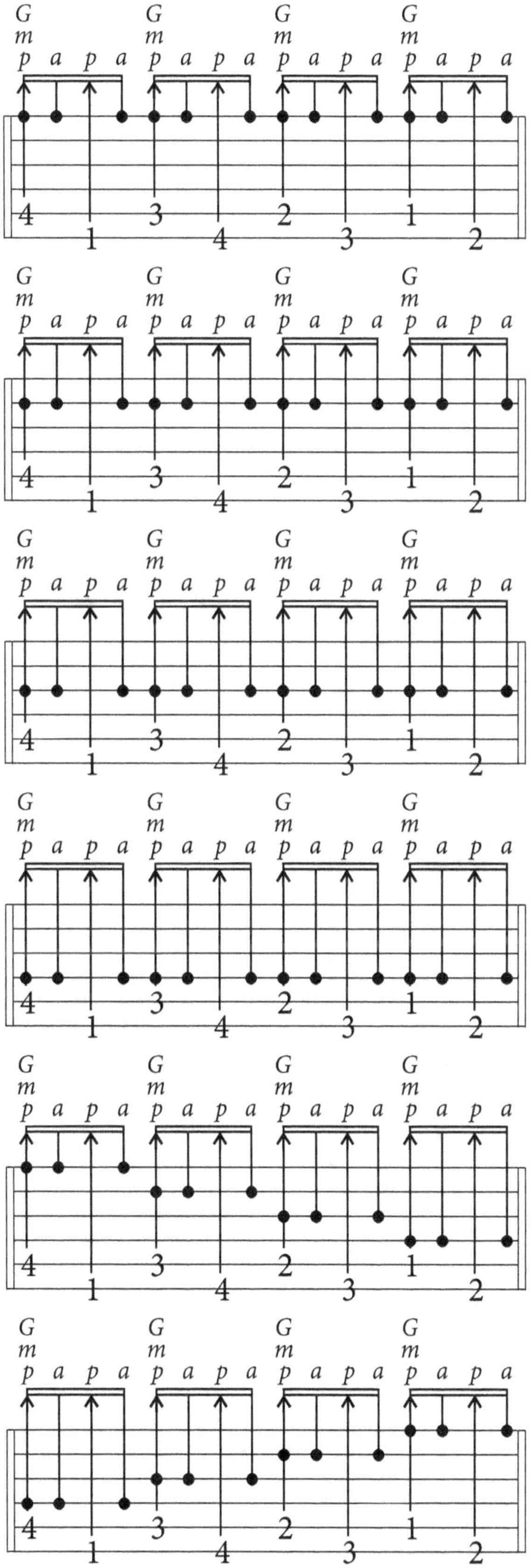

§ IV

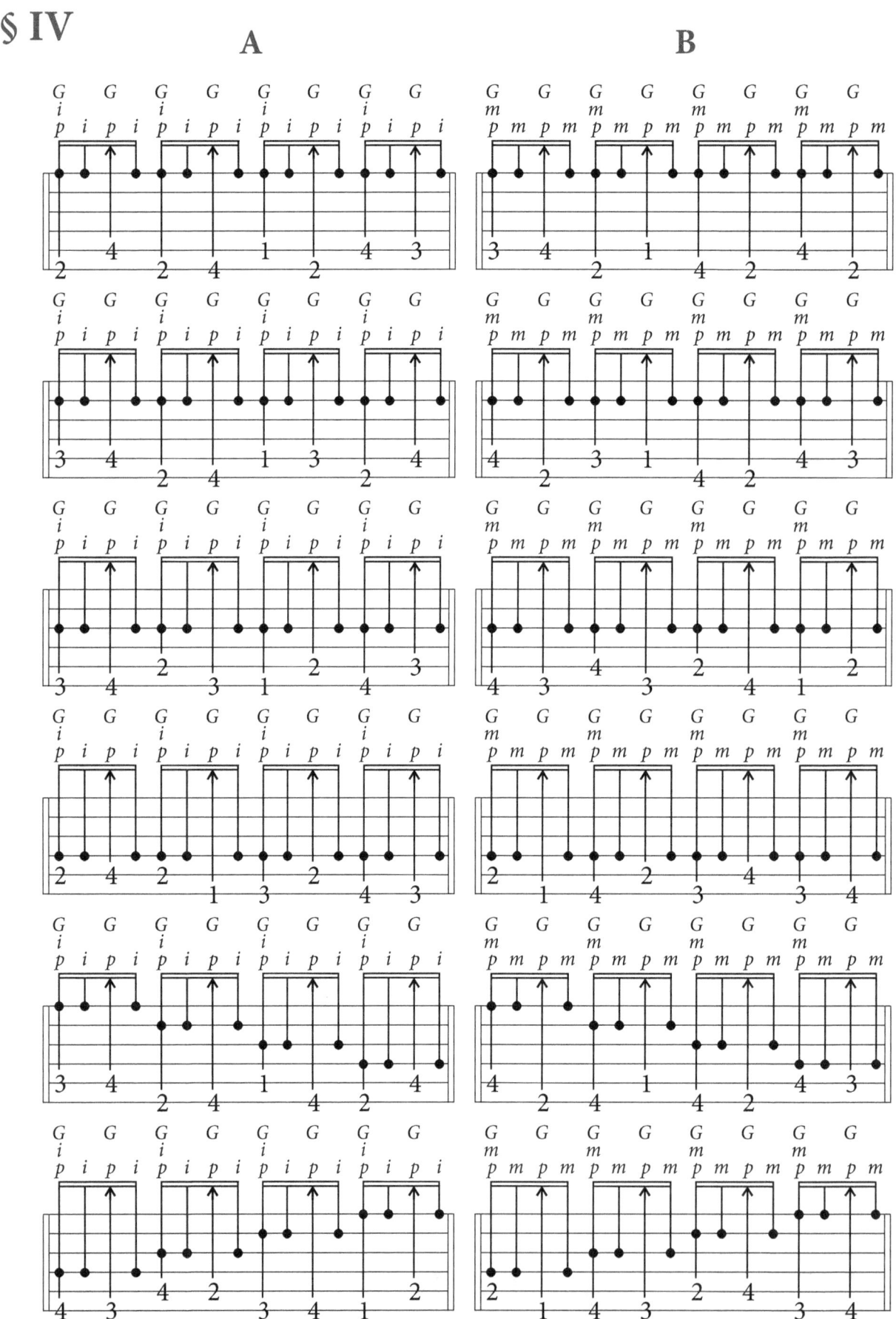

§ V

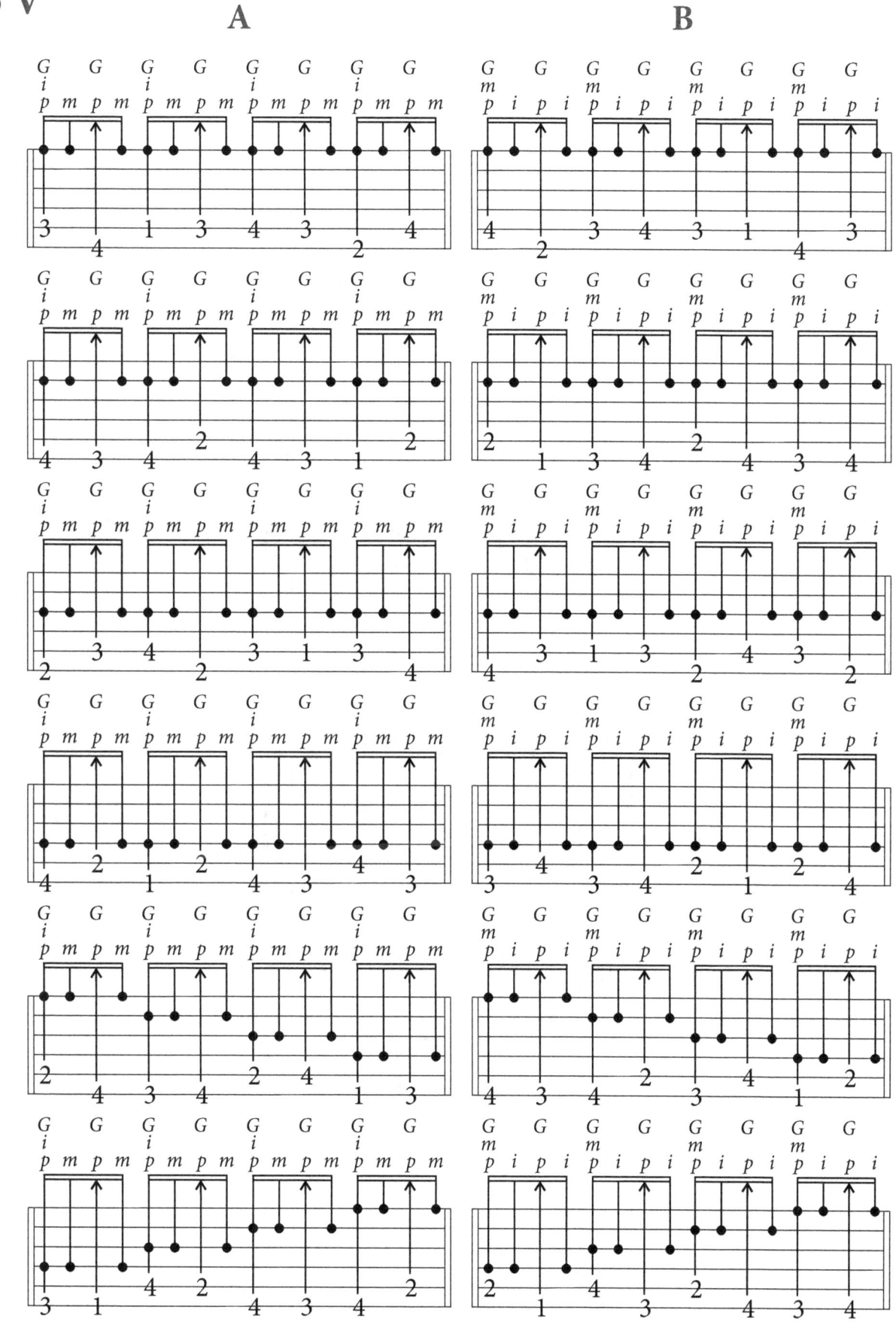

361

C

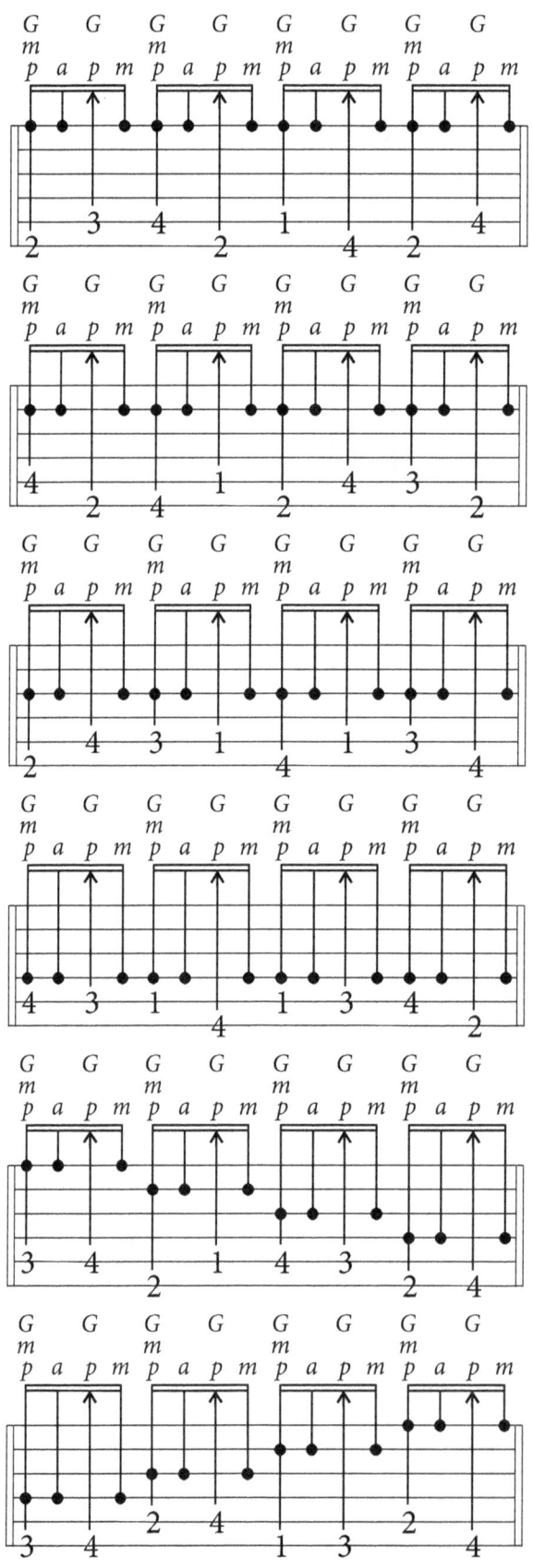

§ VI

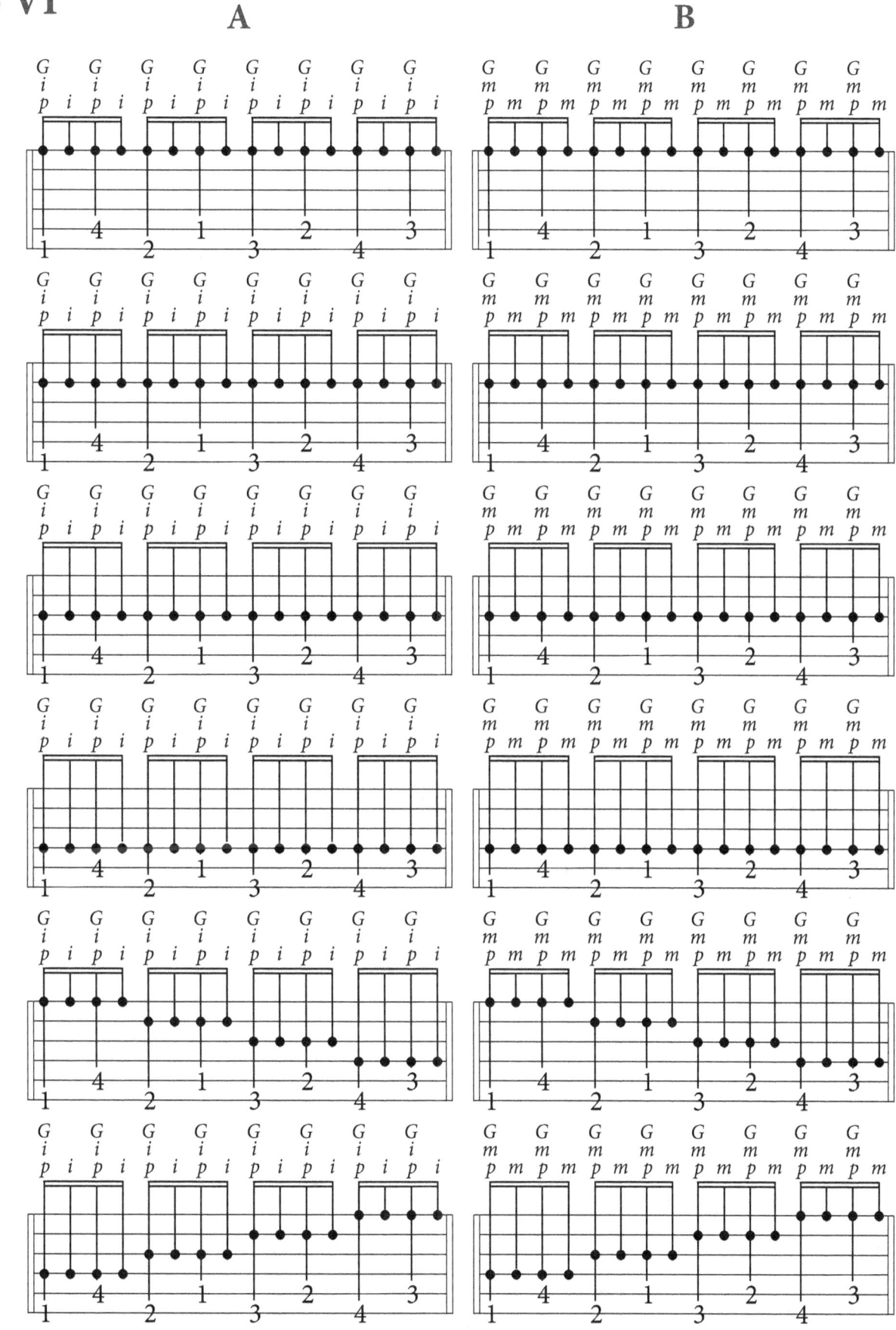

§ VII

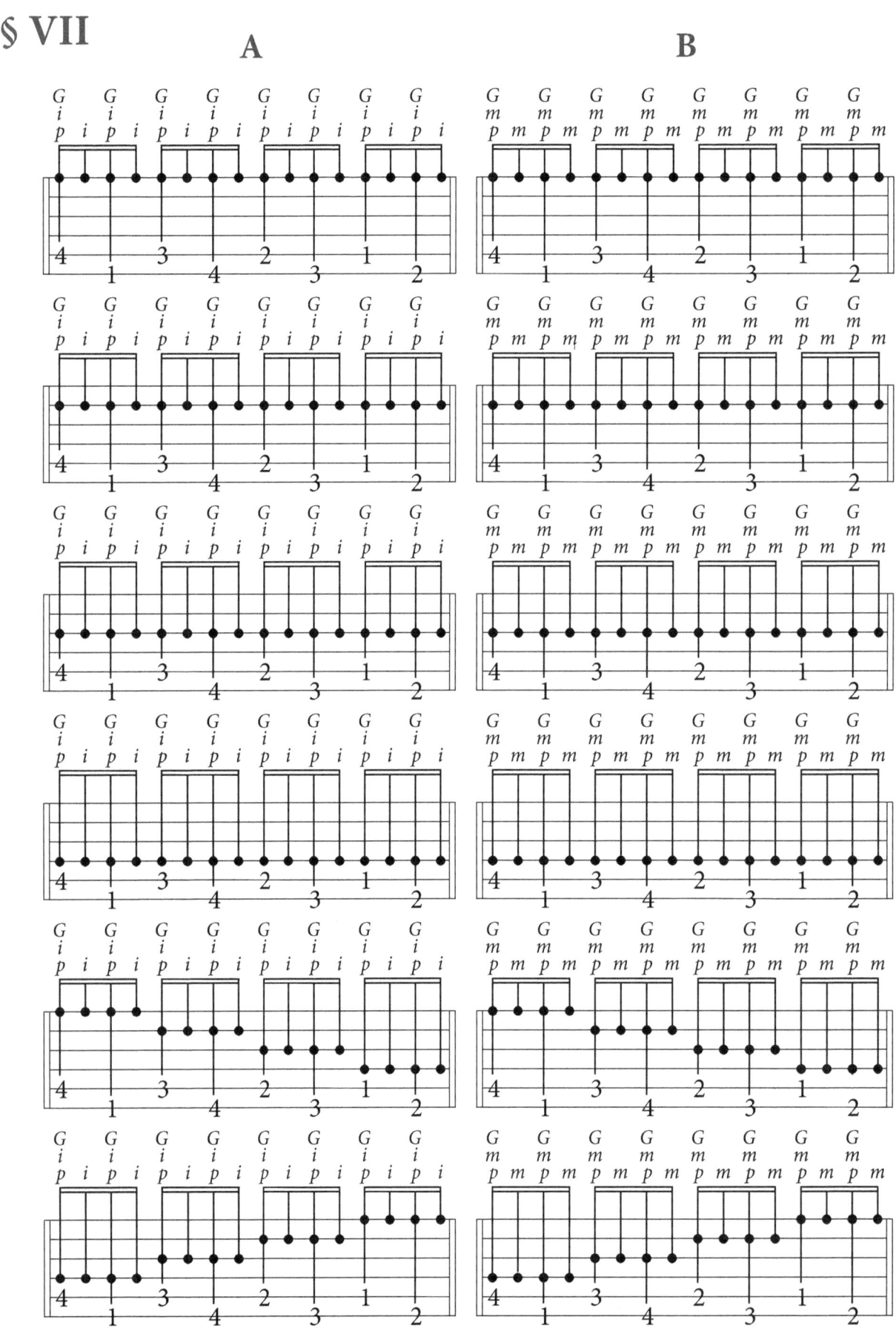

364

§ VIII

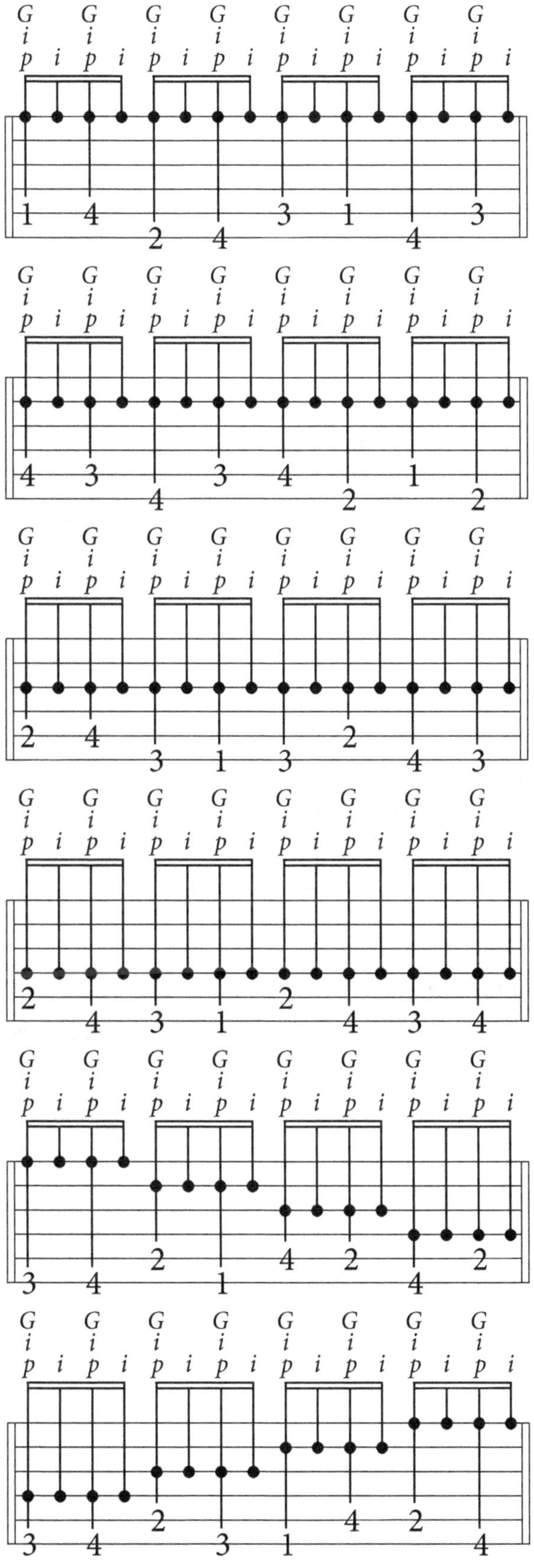

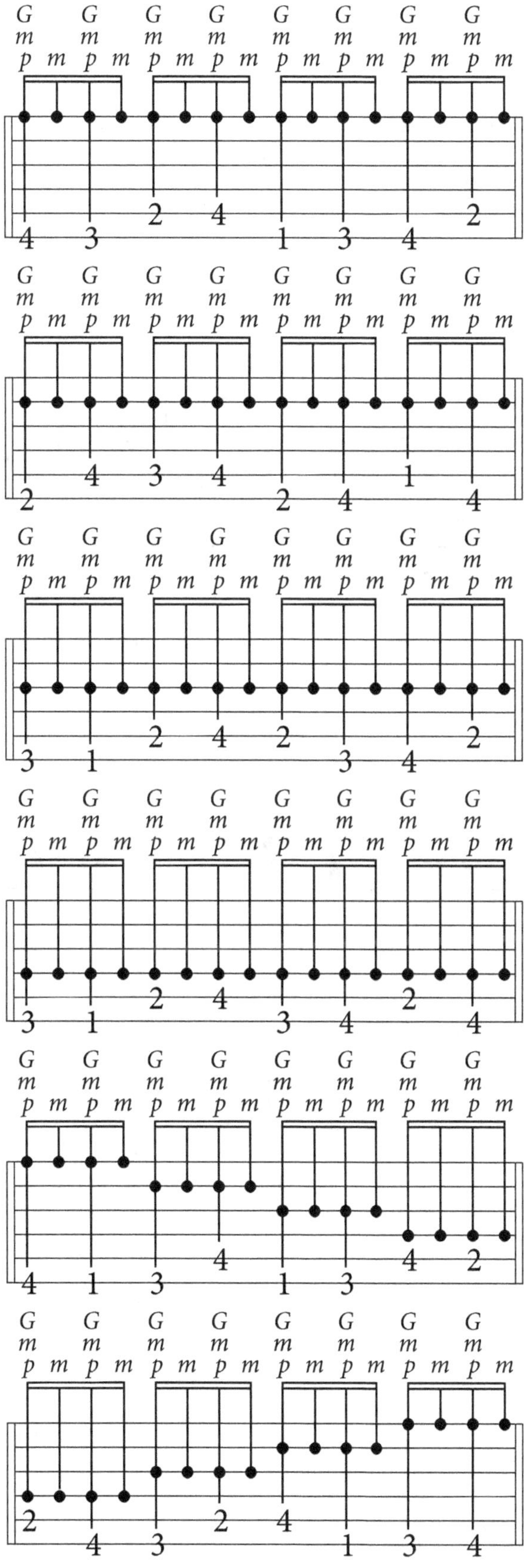

§ IX   A

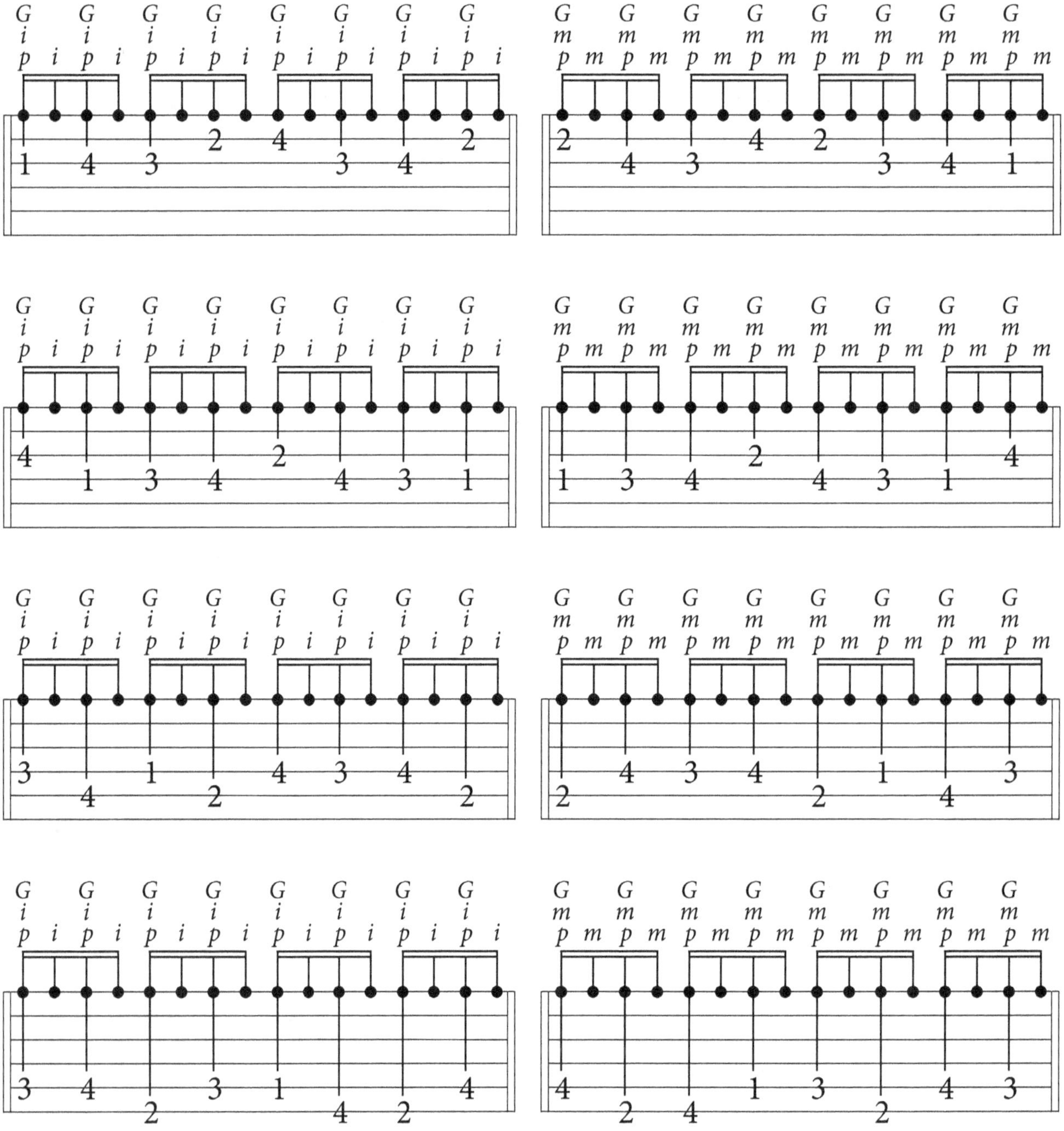

B

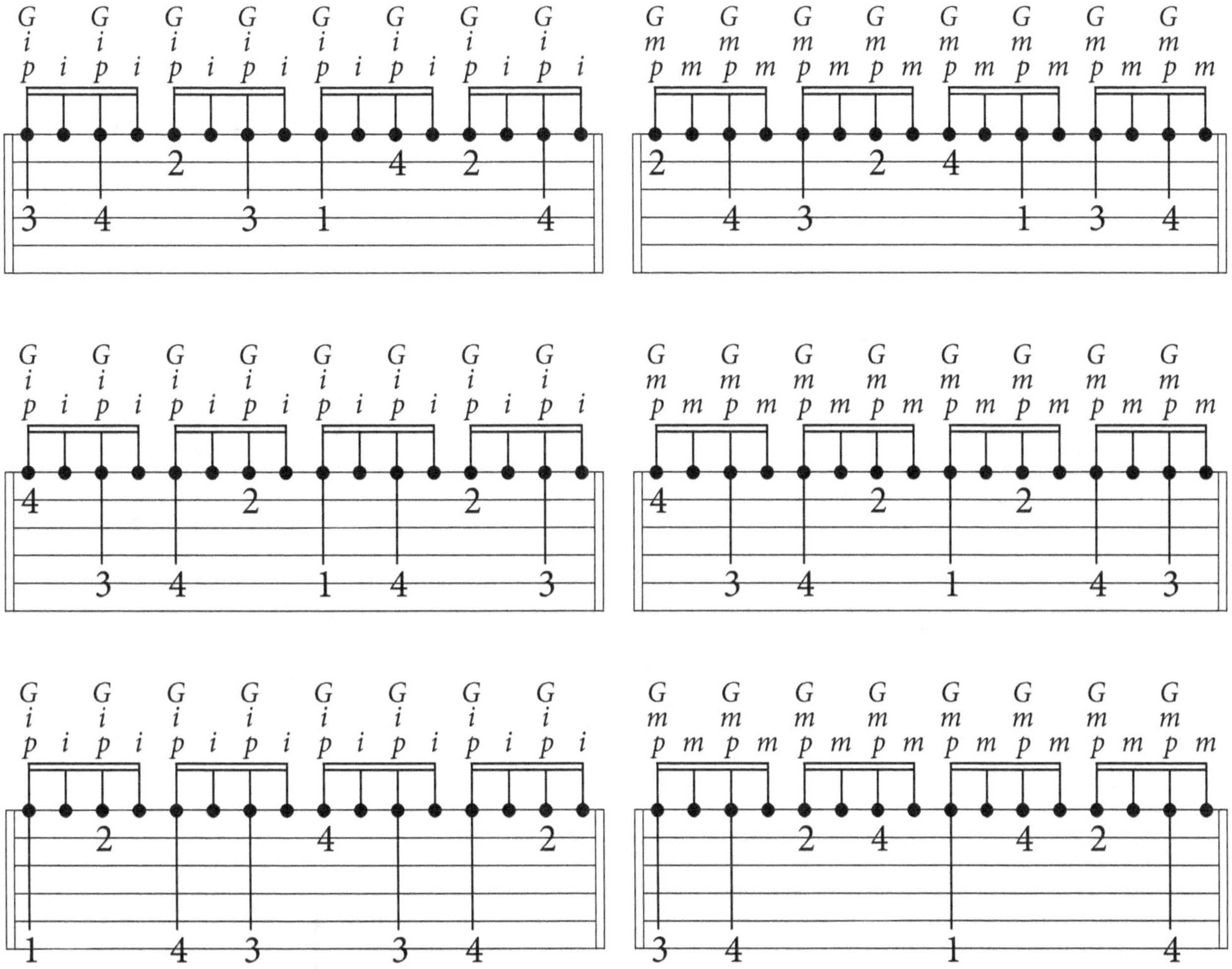

§ X

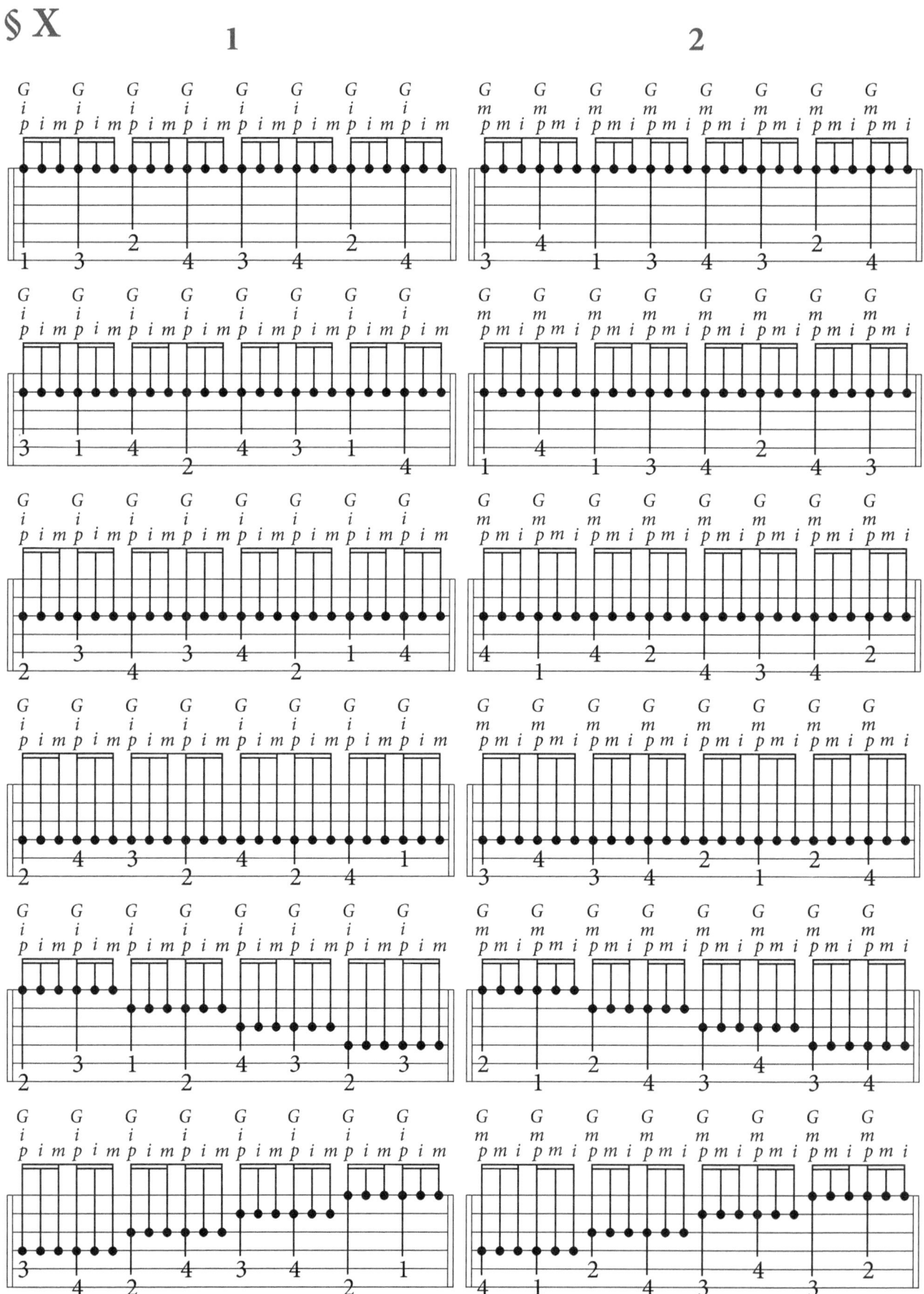

368

3

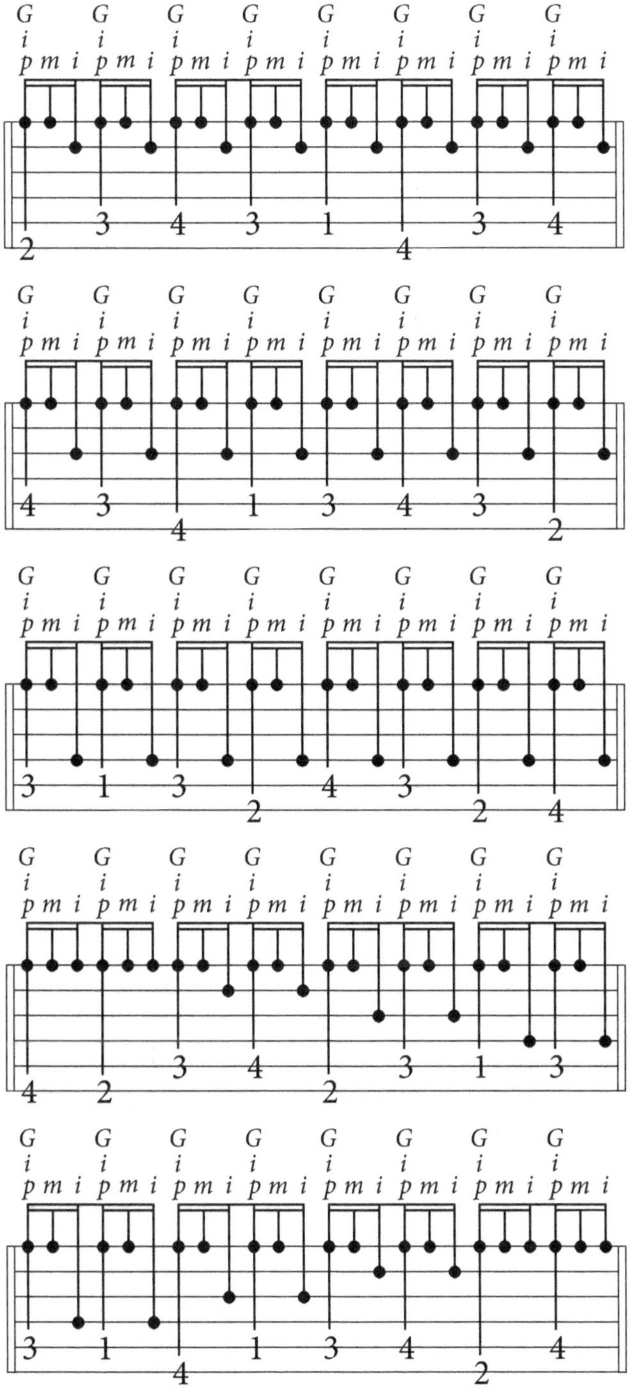
G G G G G G G G
i i i i i i i i
p m i p m i p m i p m i p m i p m i p m i p m i

4

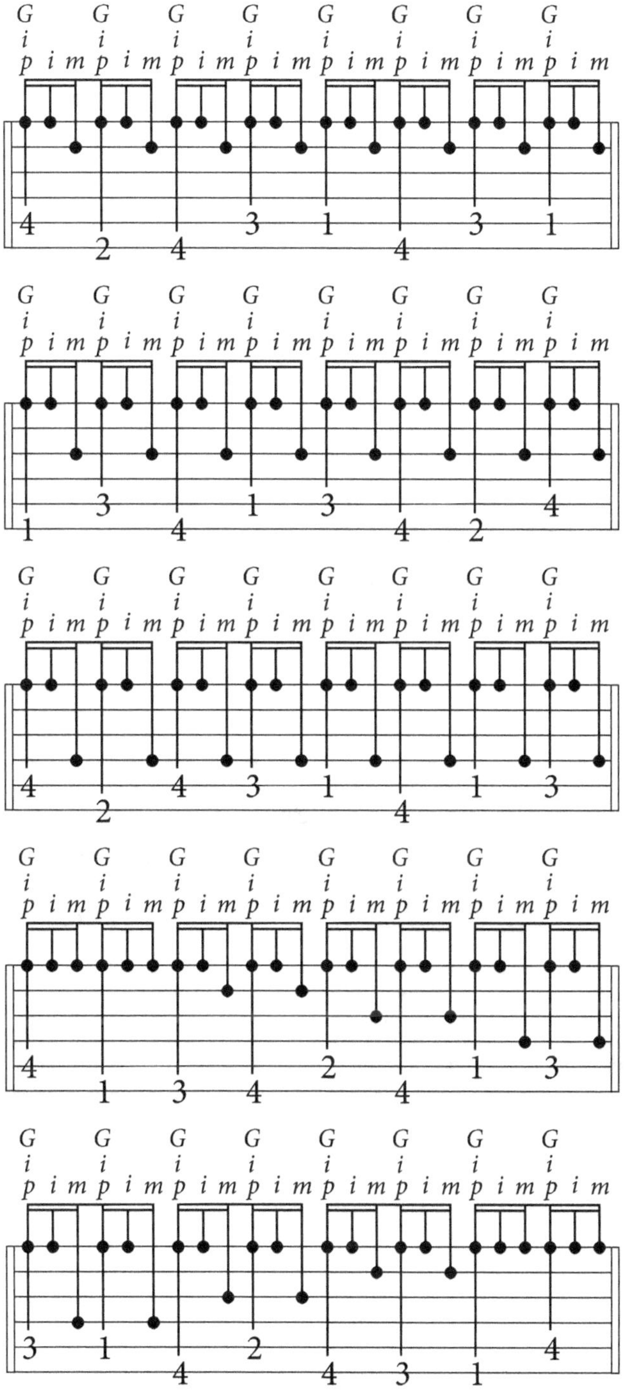
G G G G G G G G
i i i i i i i i
p i m p i m p i m p i m p i m p i m p i m p i m

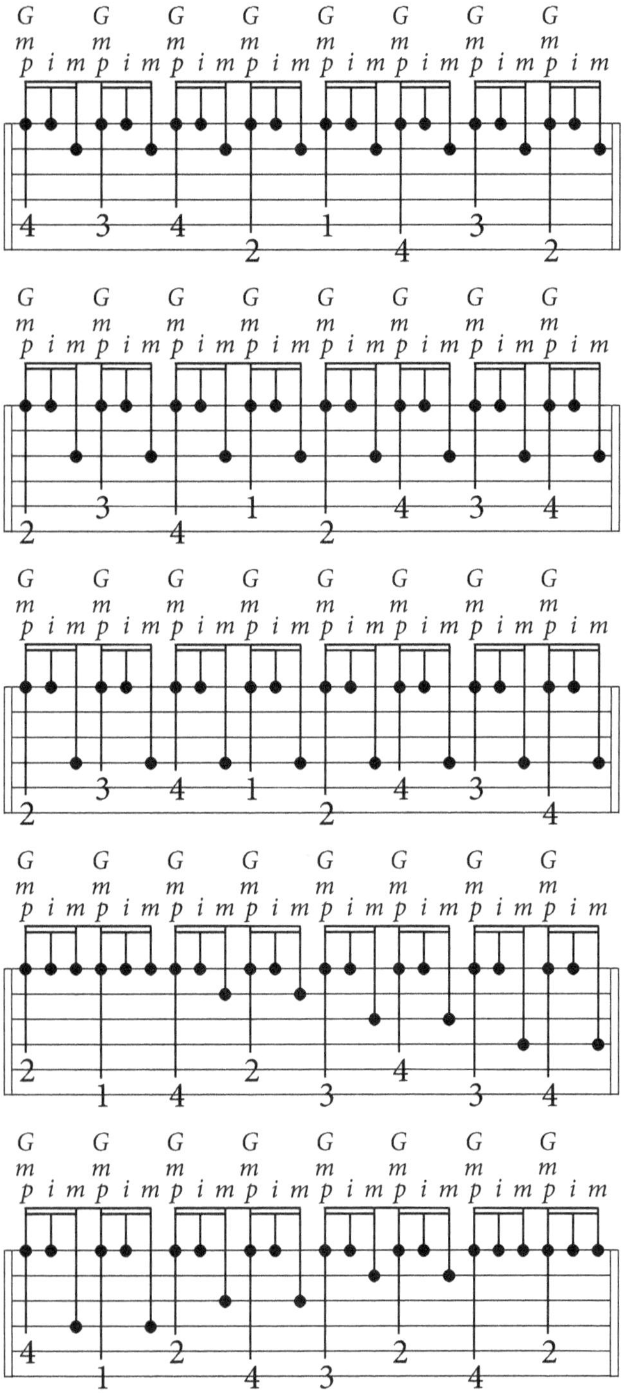

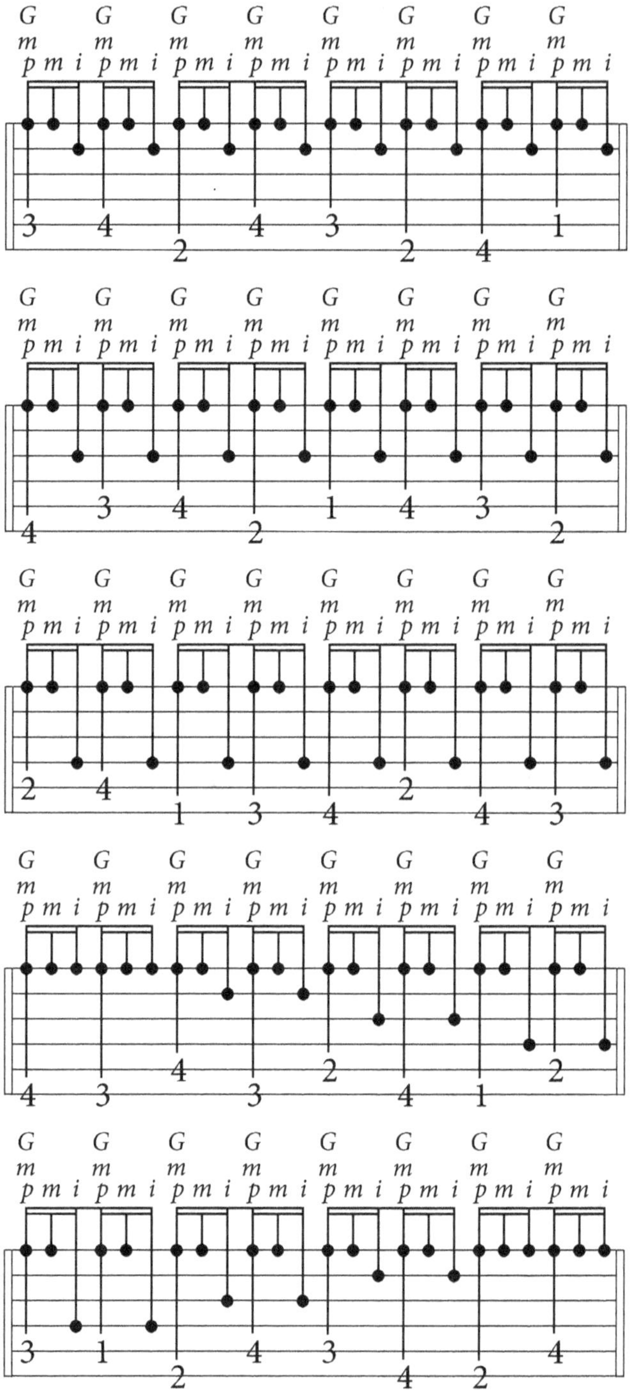

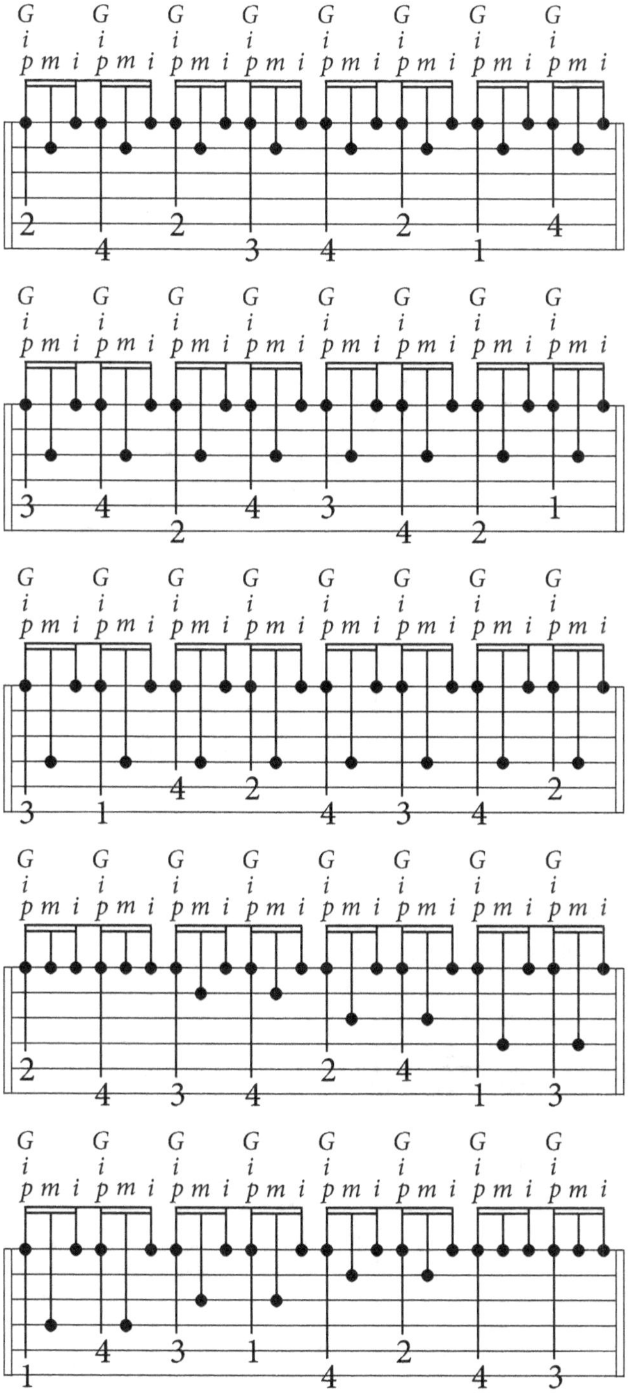

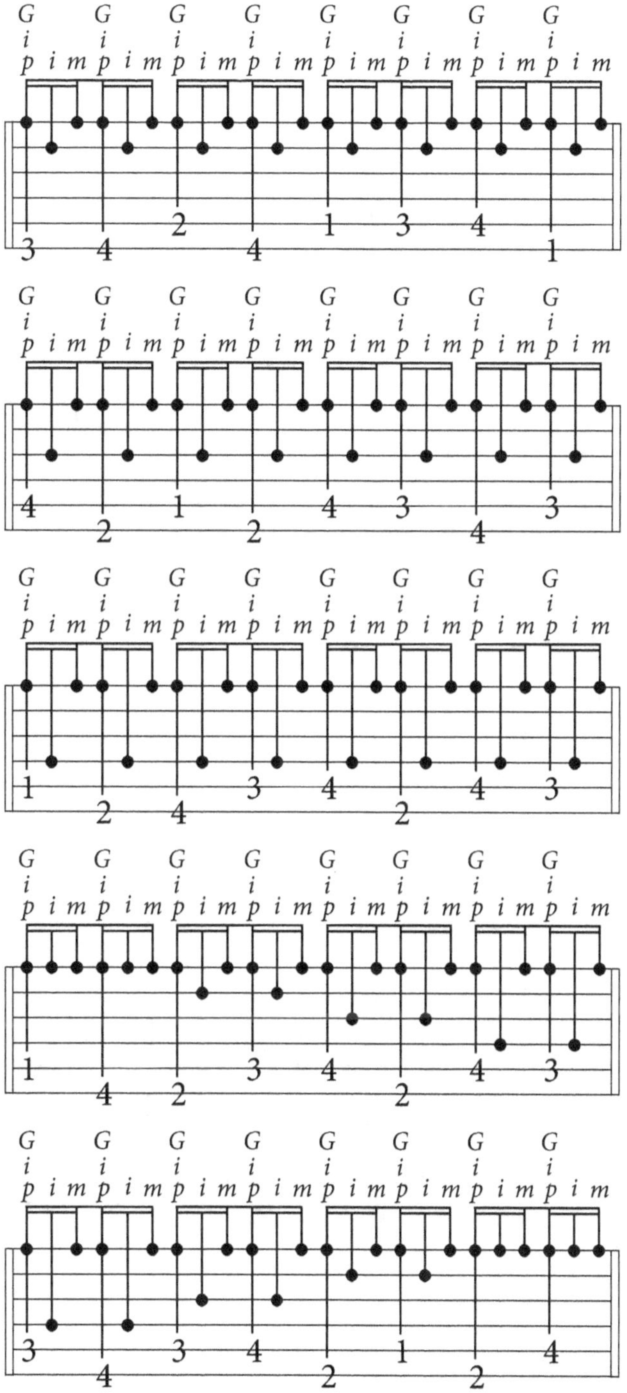

9

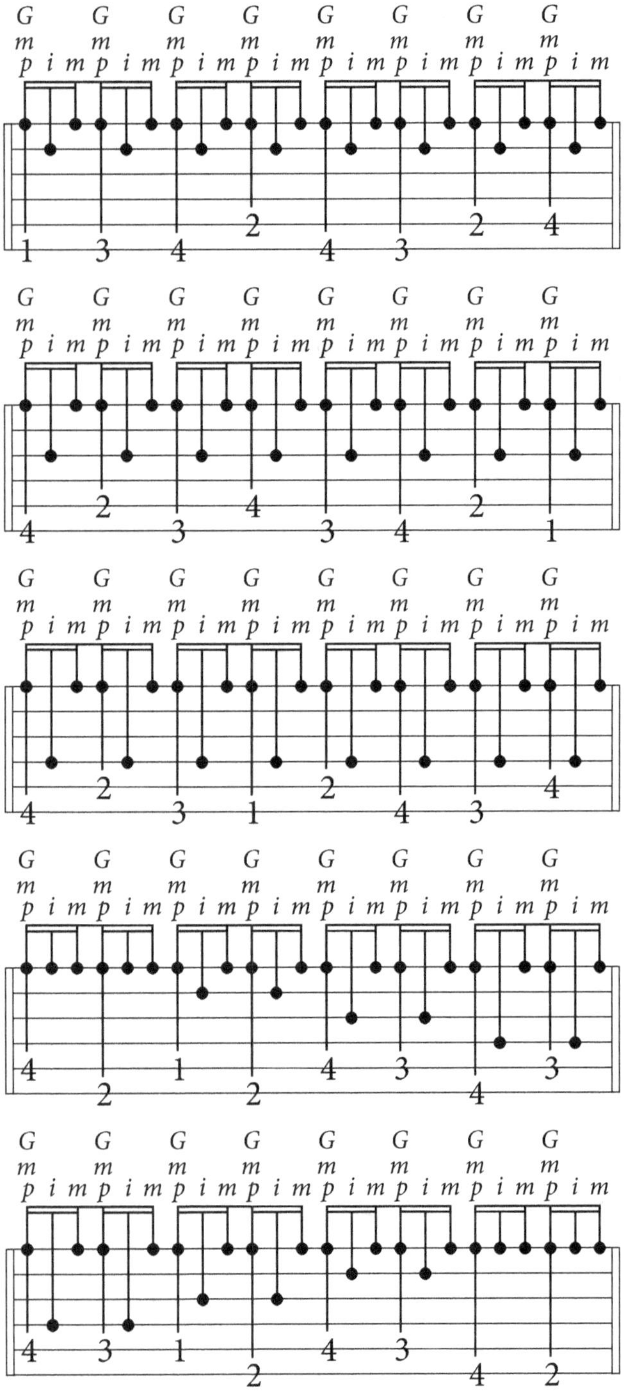
G G G G G G G G
m m m m m m m m
p i m p i m p i m p i m p i m p i m p i m p i m
1 3 4 2 4 3 2 4
4 2 3 4 3 4 2 1
4 2 3 1 2 4 3 4
4 2 1 2 4 3 4 3
4 3 1 2 4 3 4 2

10

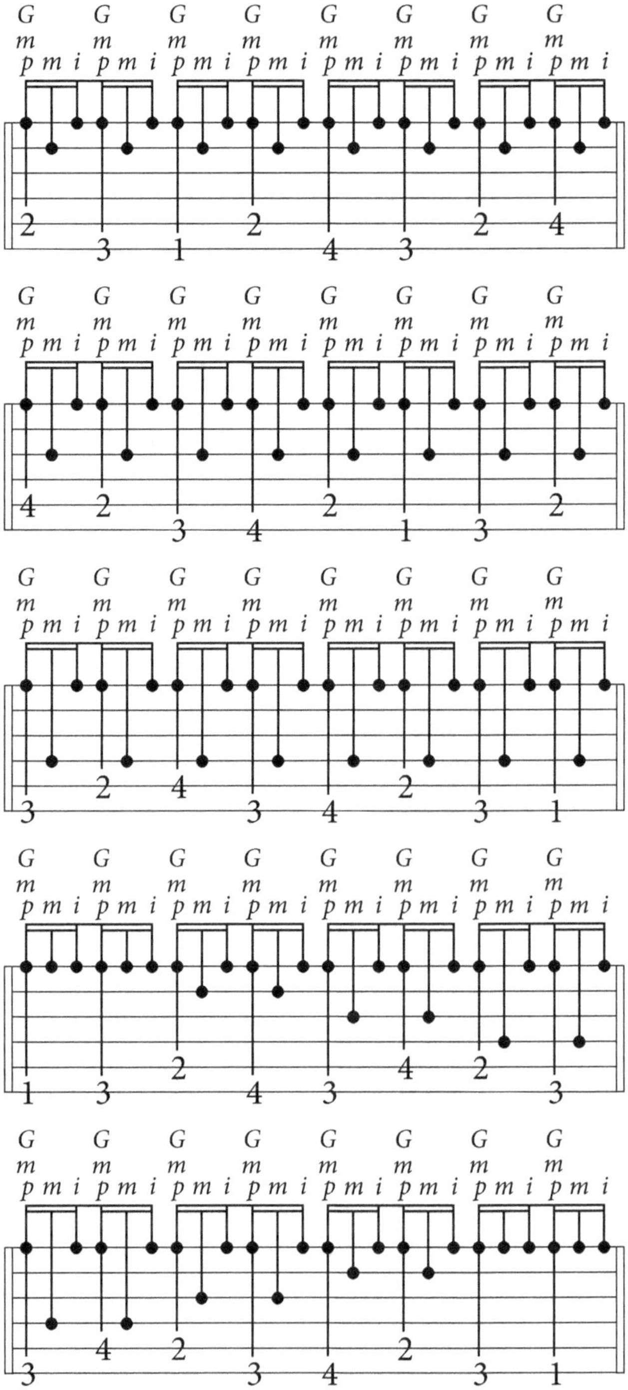
G G G G G G G G
m m m m m m m m
p m i p m i p m i p m i p m i p m i p m i p m i
2 3 1 2 4 3 2 4
4 2 3 4 2 1 3 2
3 2 4 3 4 2 3 1
1 3 2 4 3 4 2 3
3 4 2 3 4 2 3 1

13   **14**

§ XI

A B

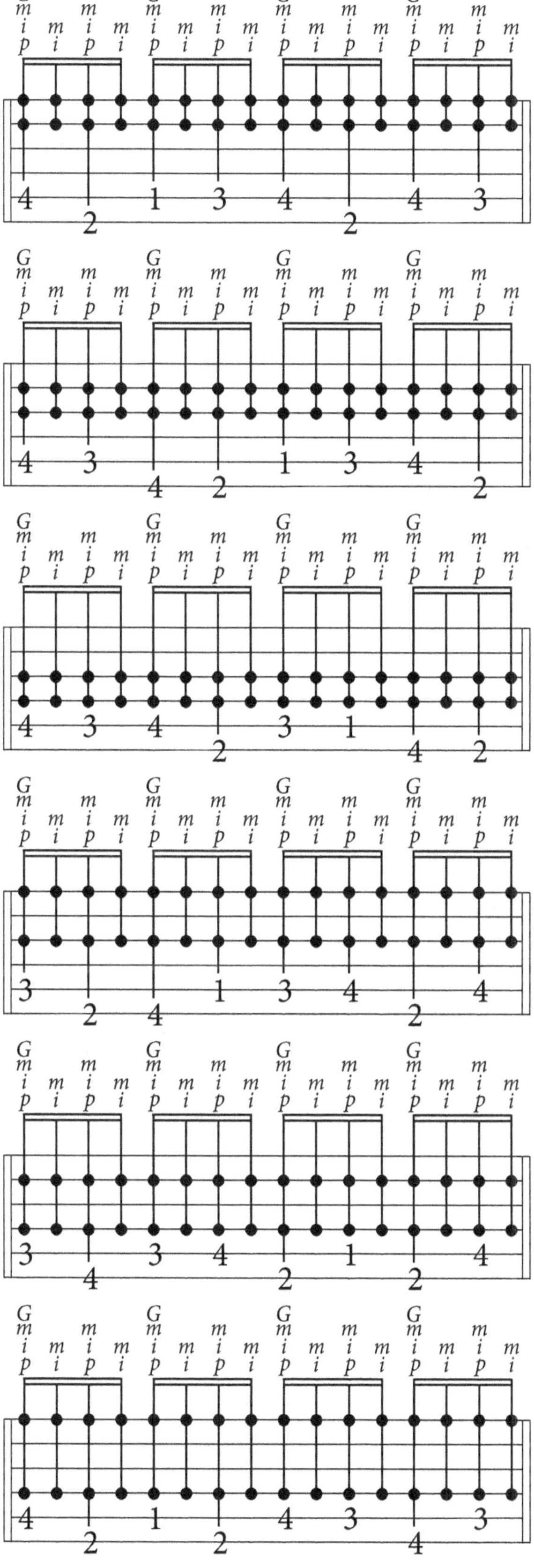

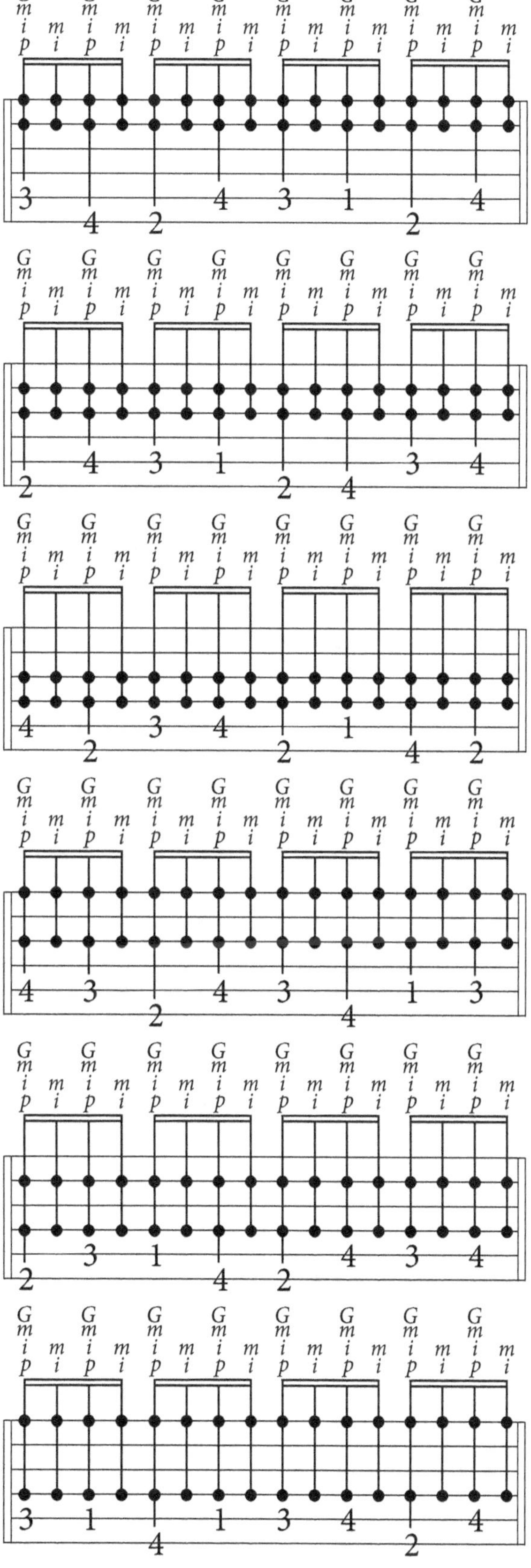

CHAPTER 4

EXERCISES THAT REFER TO THUMB STROKE
WITH GOLPE IN COMBINATION
WITH INDEX AND MIDDLE FINGER.

UNIT 1

Exercises that refer to thumb stroke with Golpe
in combination with index (i) and middle finger (m)
on the various Formulas of the left hand as described below in detail.
Practice with both fingers (i) and (m).
The practice of middle finger (m) in these exercises contributes
in the independence of middle finger from the ring finger.

§ I, § II Thumb stroke together with Golpe on the ascending:
§ I

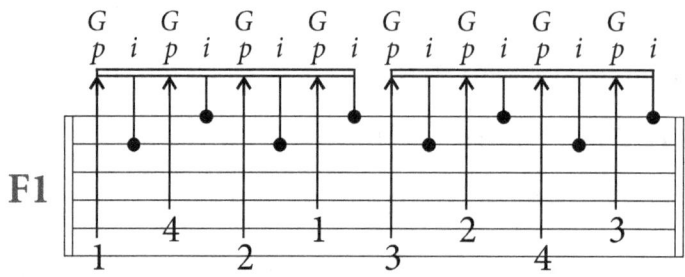

and descending rolling Formulas:
§ II

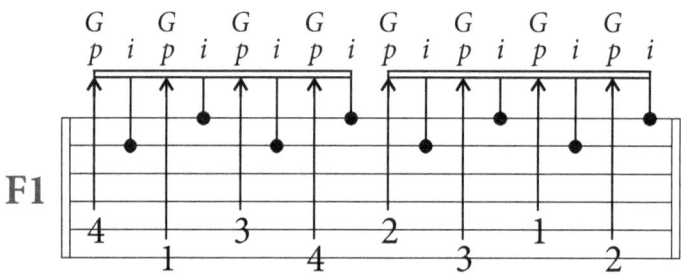

In combination with right hand index. Practice replacing the index with the middle finger on all the variations.

§ III, § IV The previous exercises with reversal of the stroke of index and middle finger. Reversal of arpeggios.
§ III

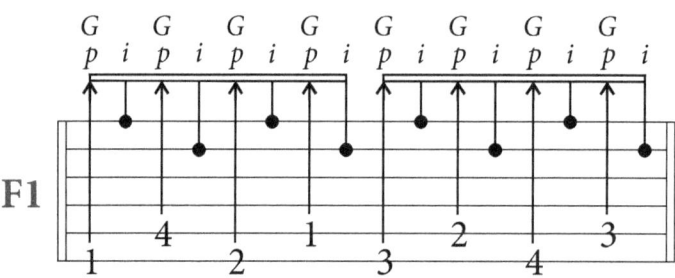

§ IV

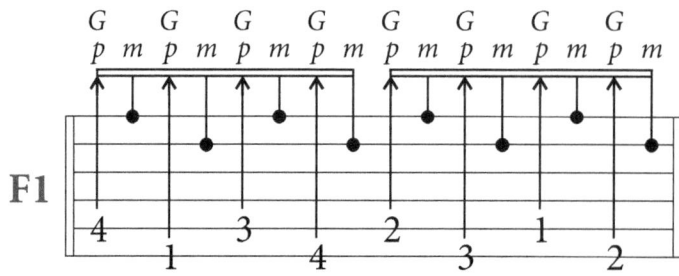

§ I

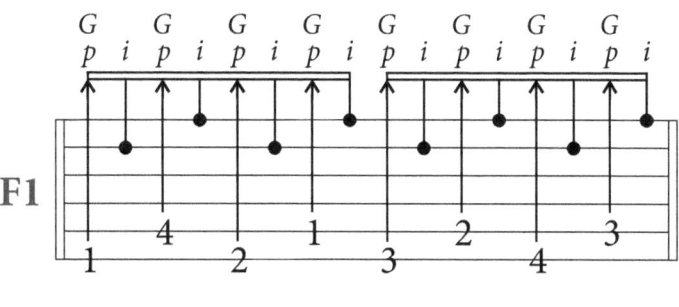

F1

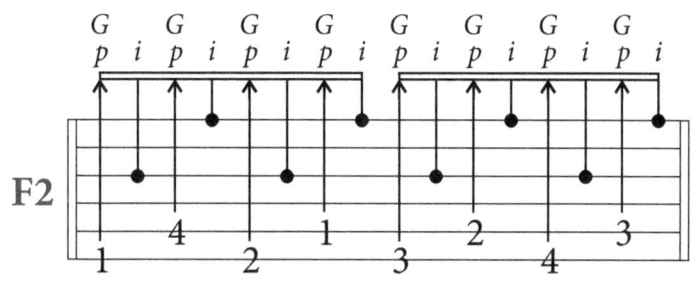

F2

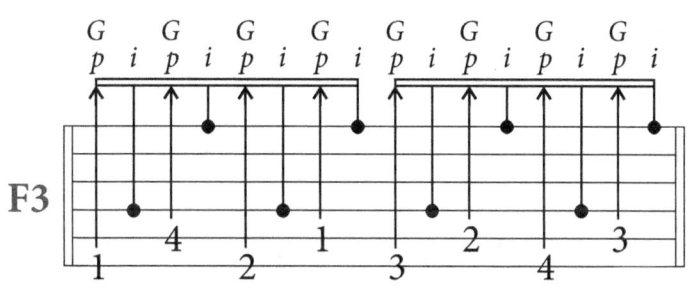

F3

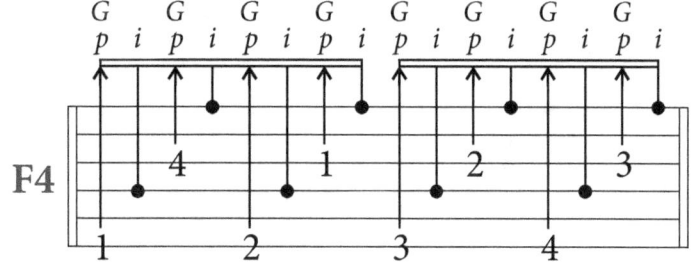

F4

§ II

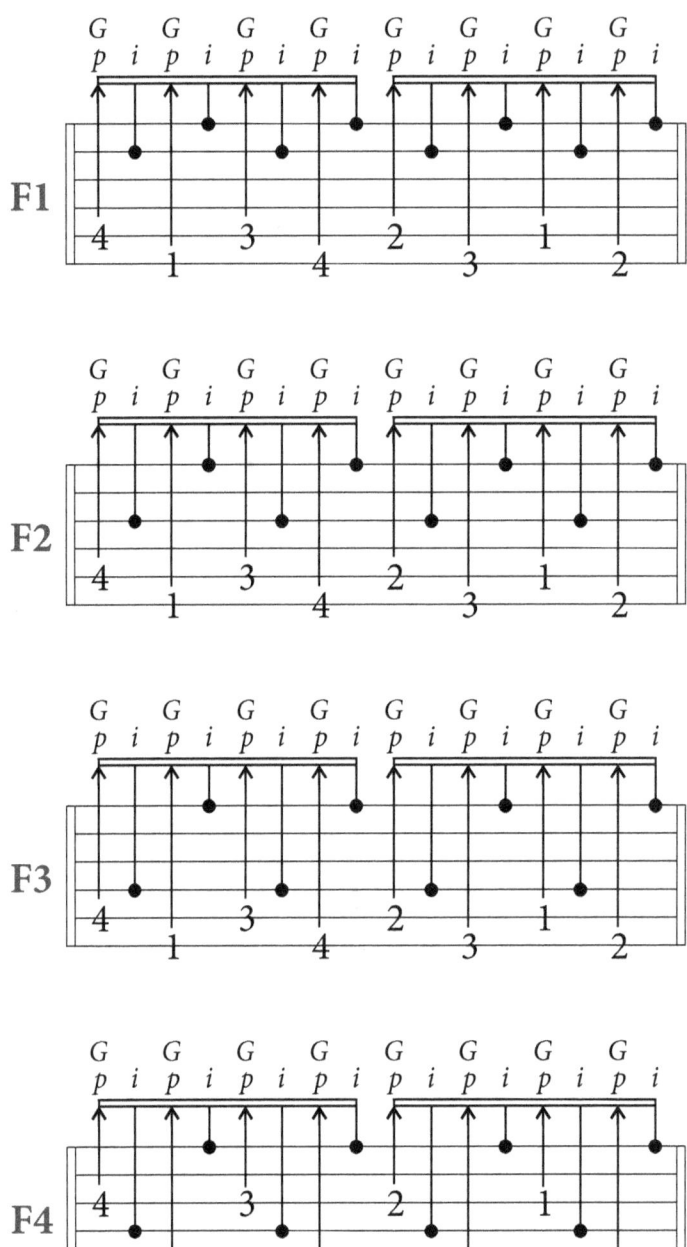

§ III

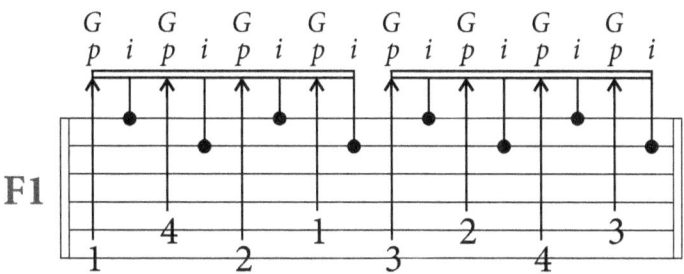
F1

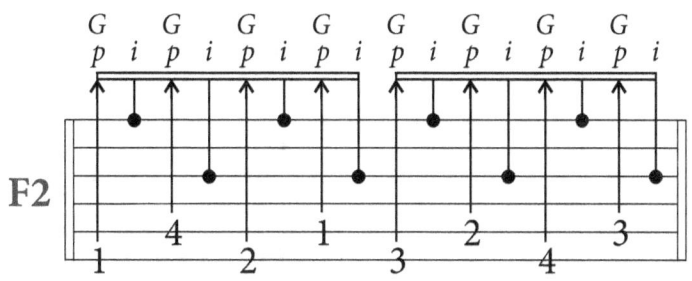
F2

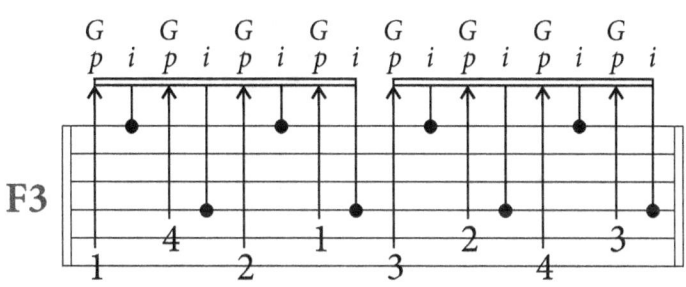
F3

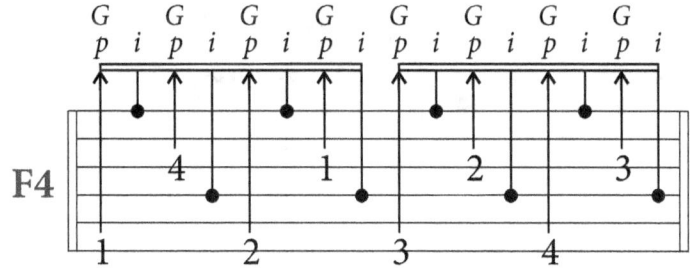
F4

§ IV

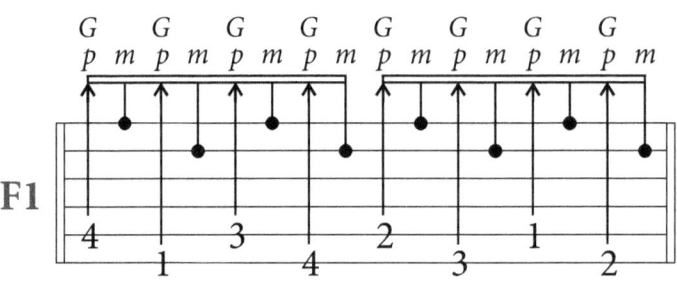

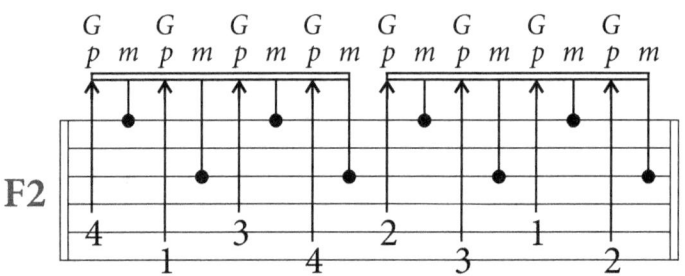

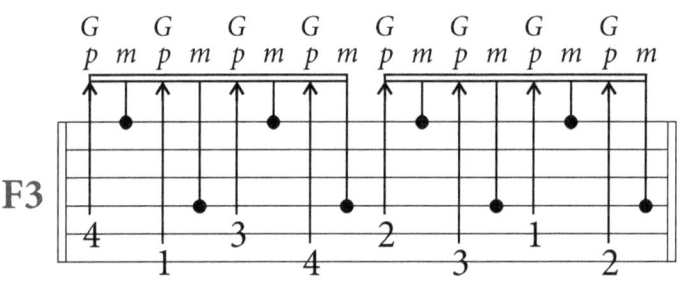

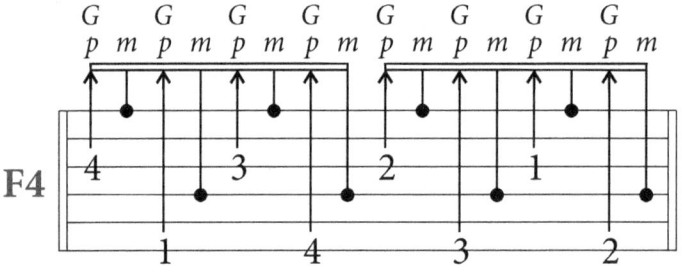

CHAPTER 5

EXERCISES THAT REFER TO THUMB STROKE WITH GOLPE.

UNIT 1

Thumb stroke with Golpe
in combination with index (i) and middle finger (m).
Simple fingering of the left hand. Twelve Formulas.

§ Ia

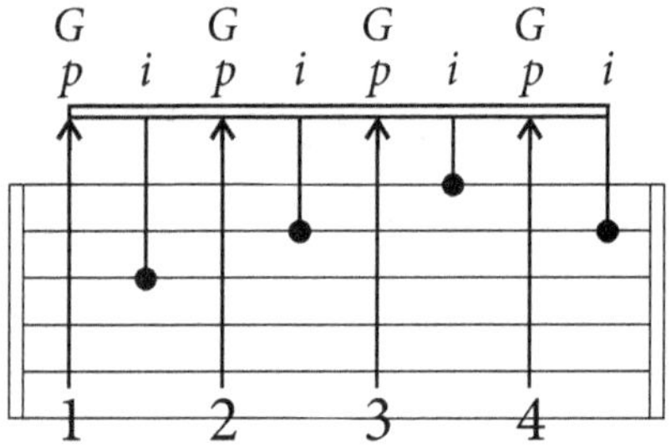

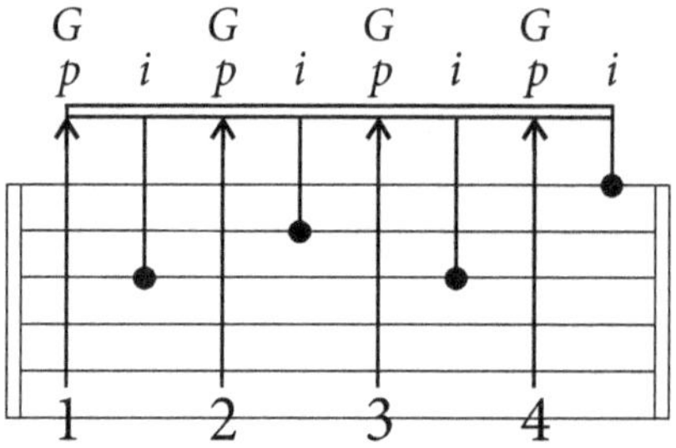

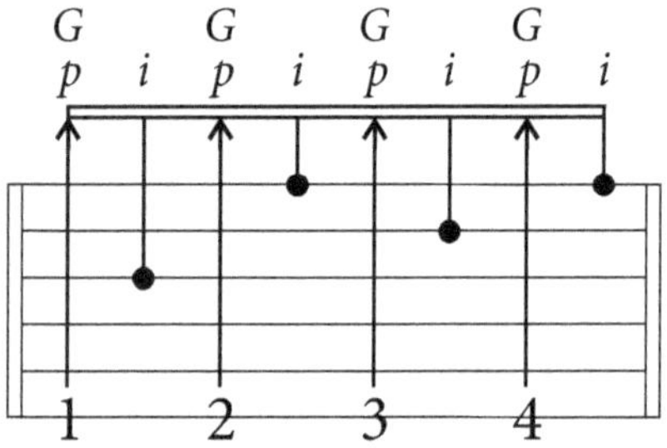

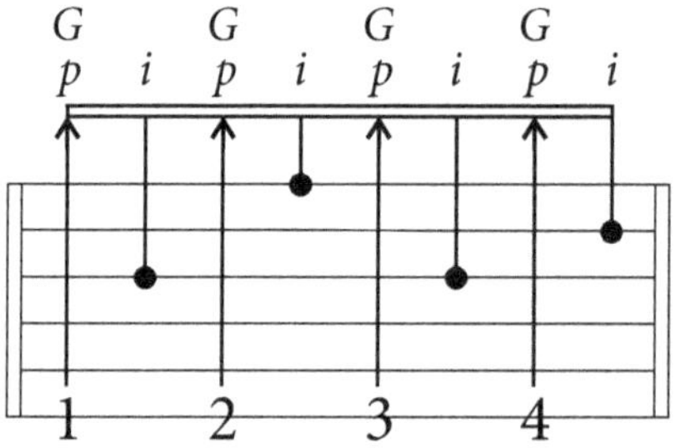

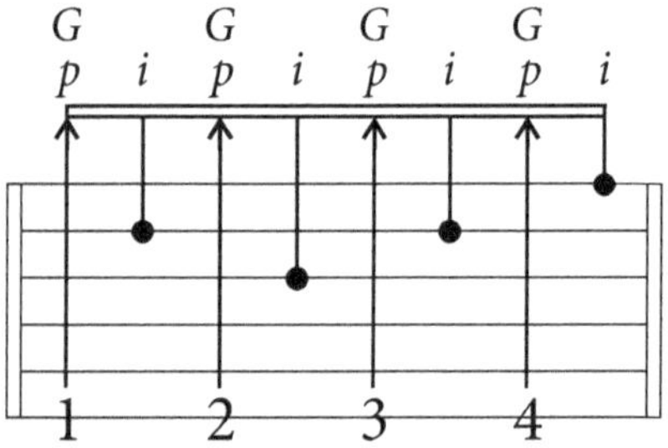

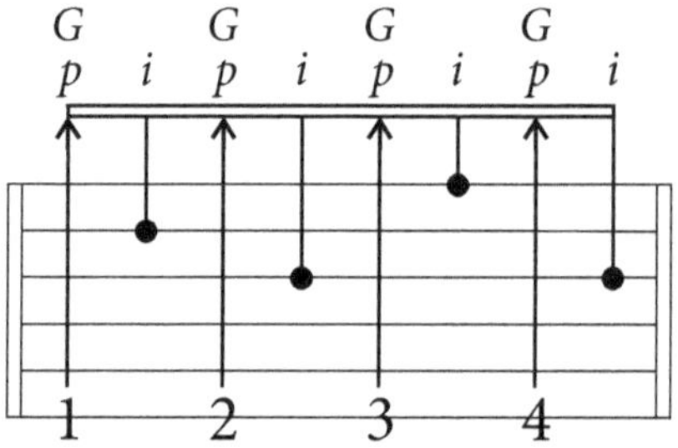

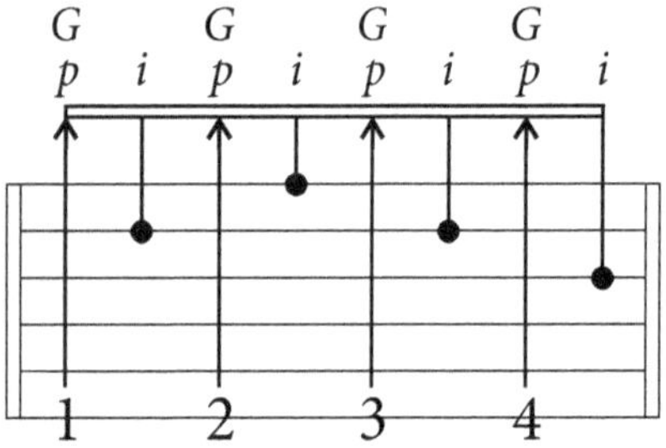

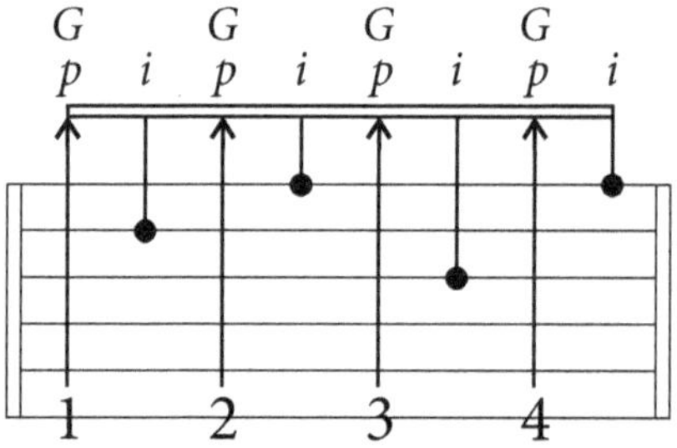

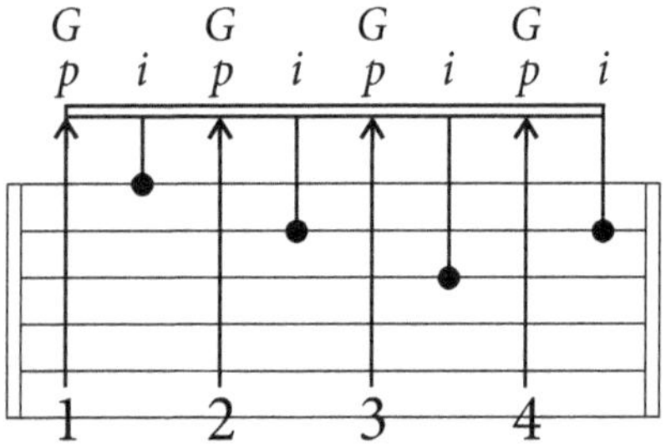

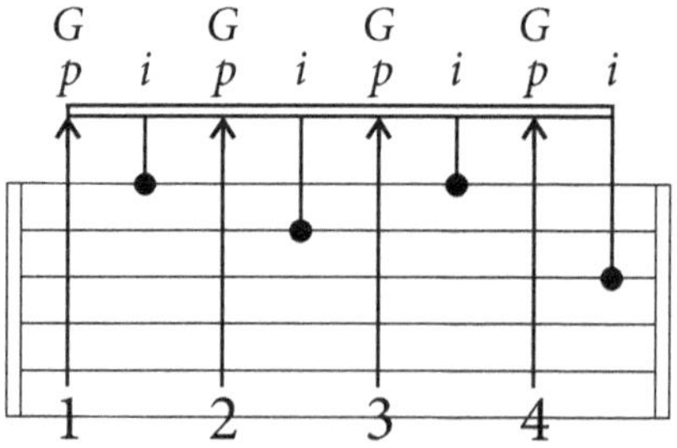

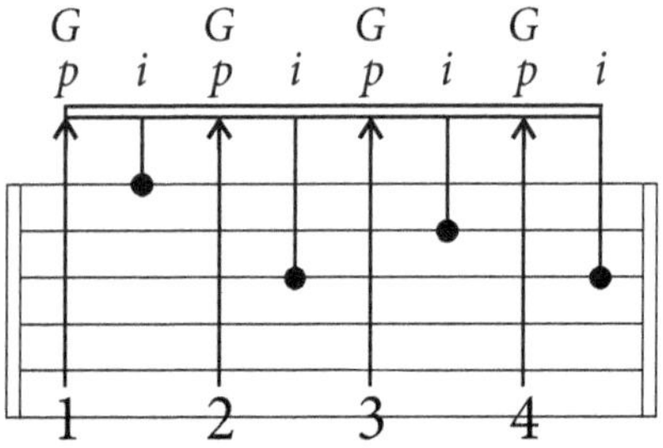

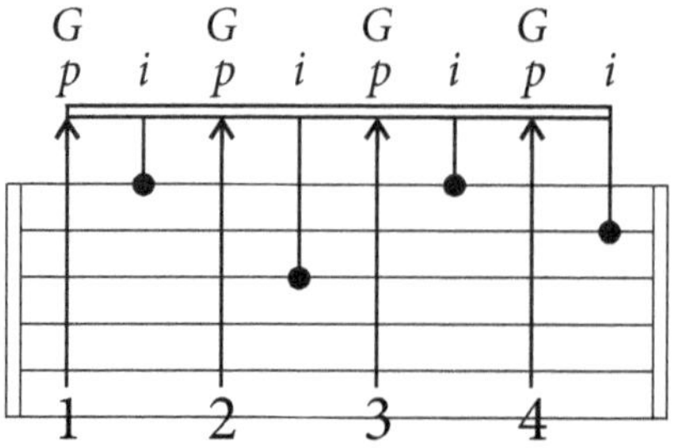

§ Ib

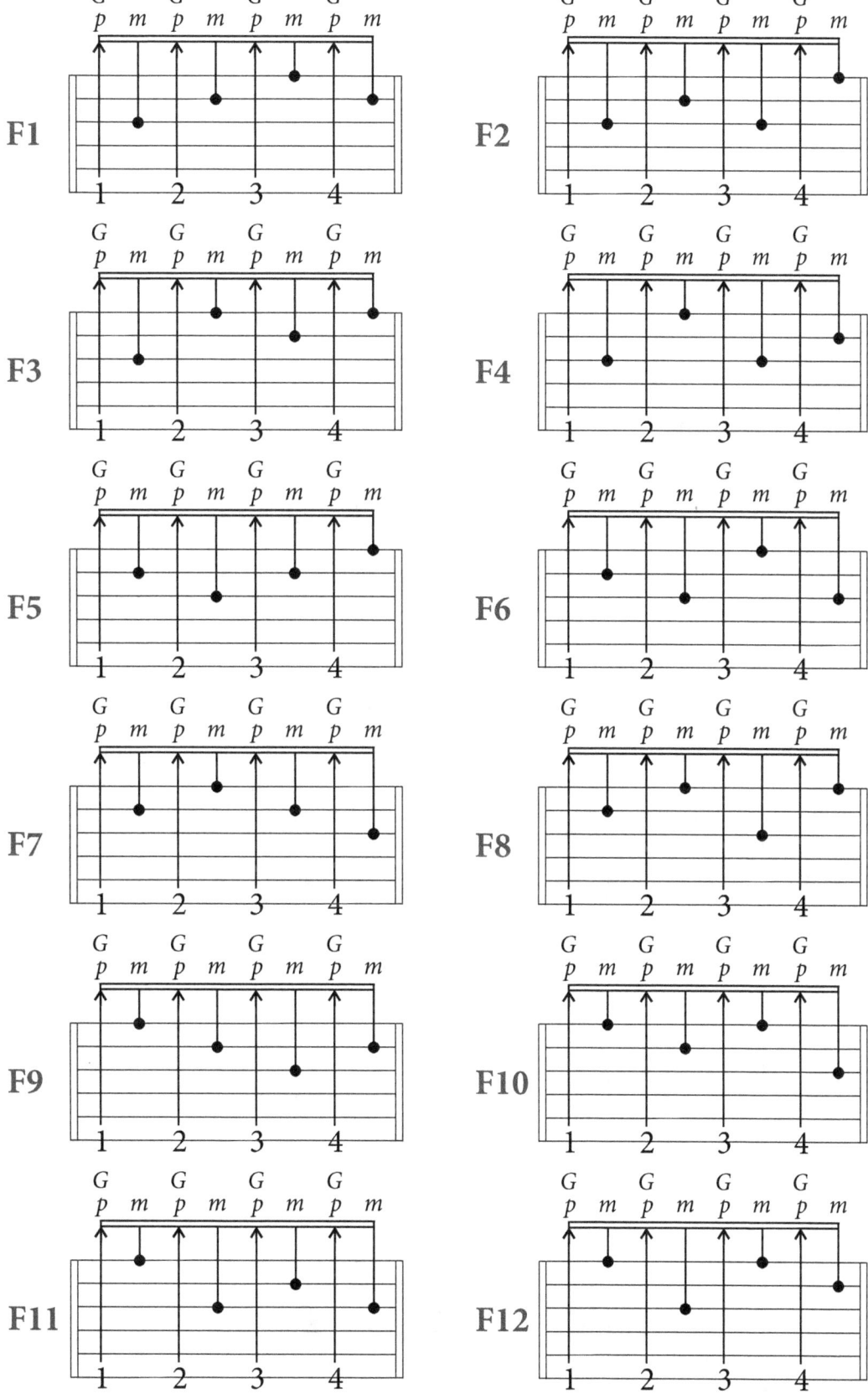

§ IIa

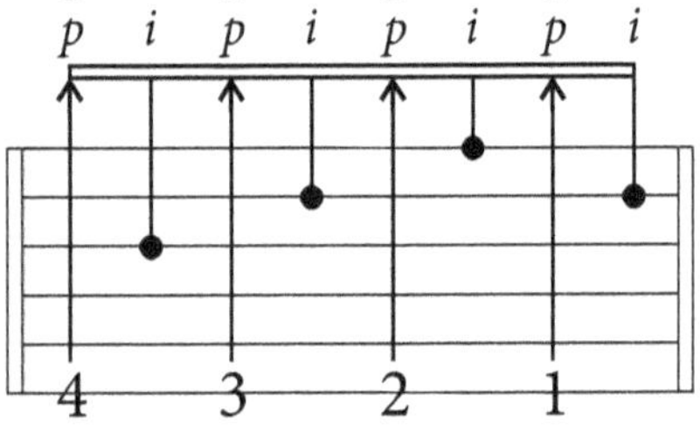

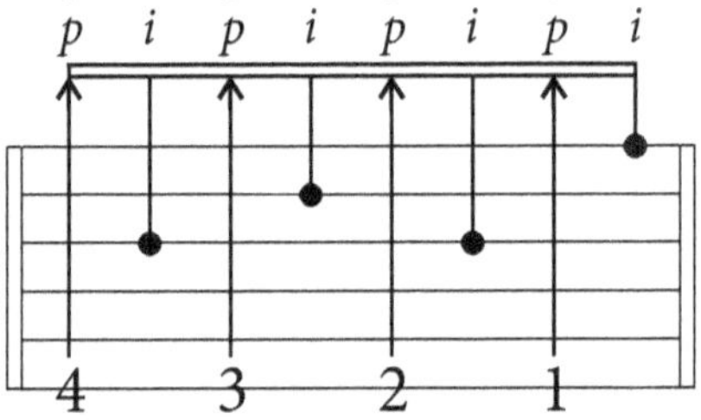

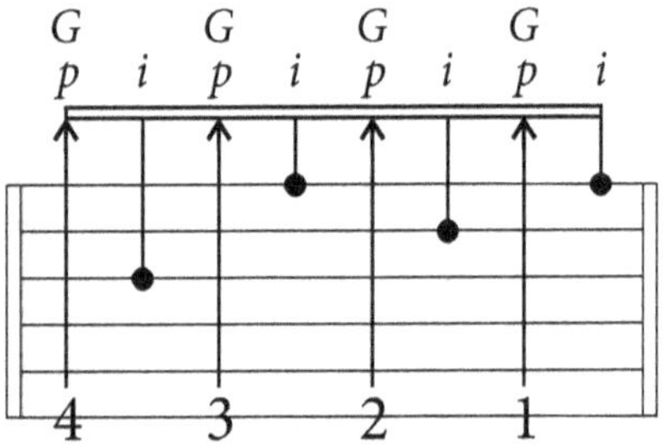

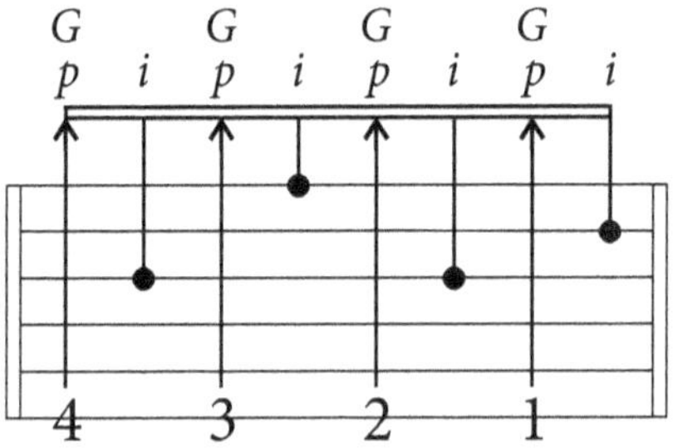

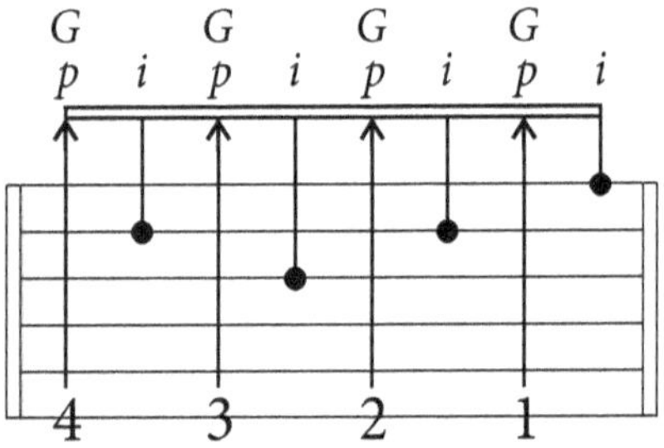

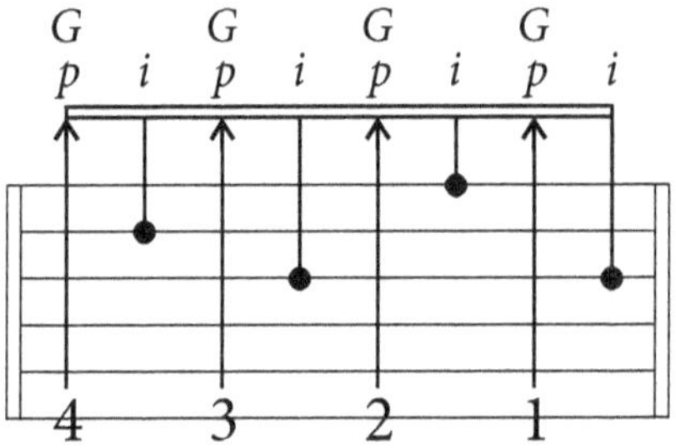

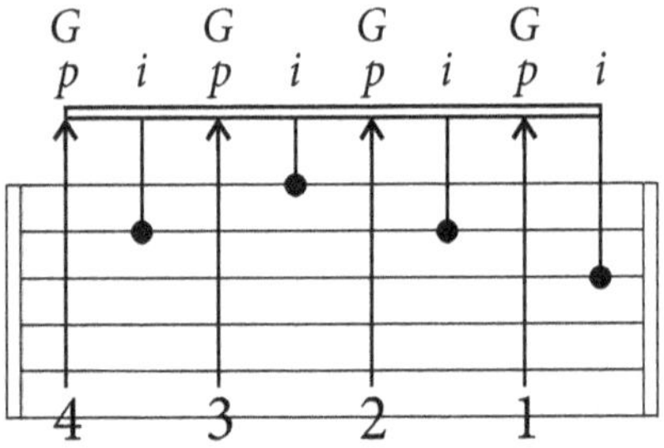

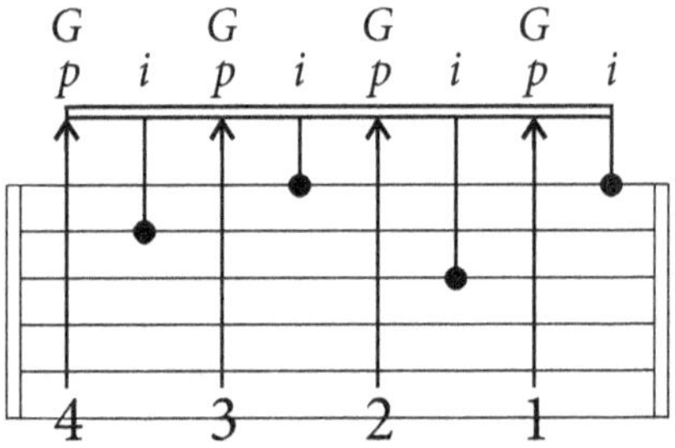

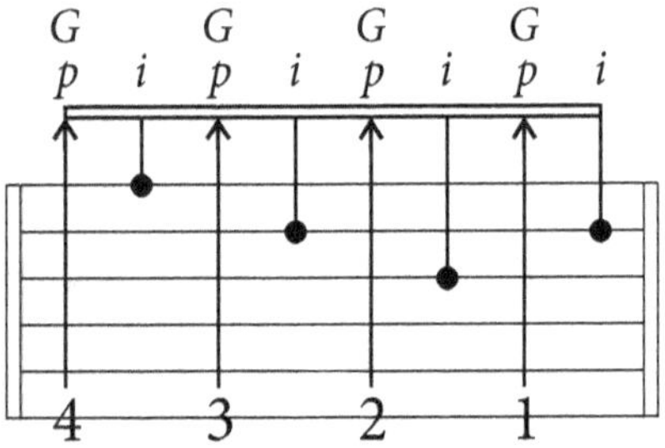

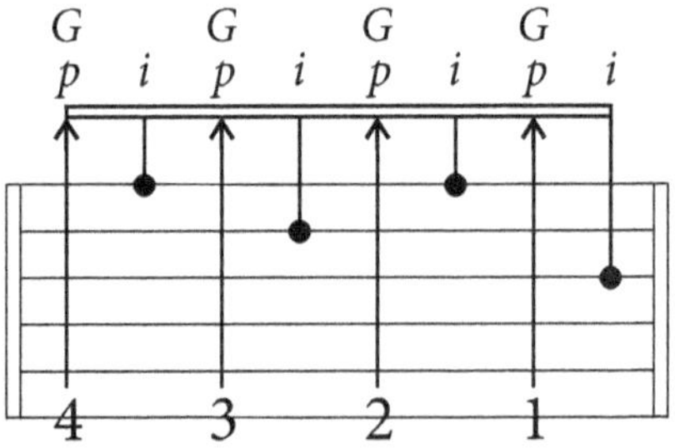

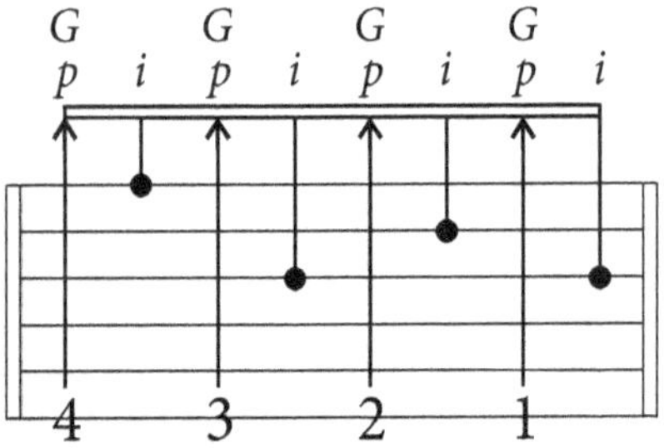

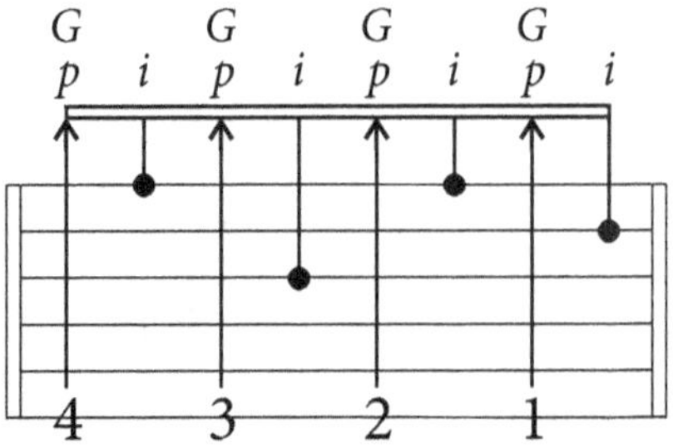

§ IIb

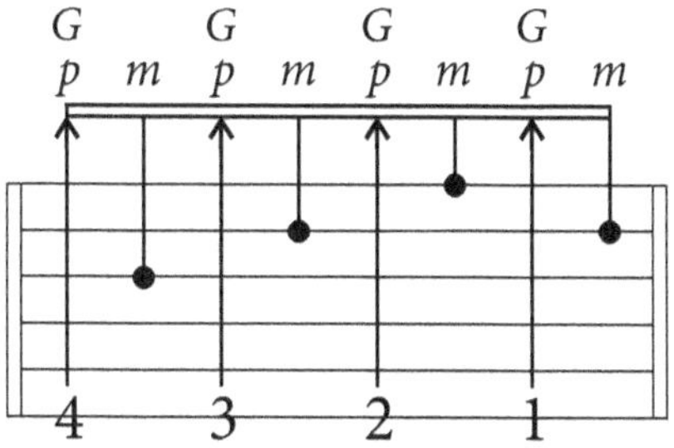

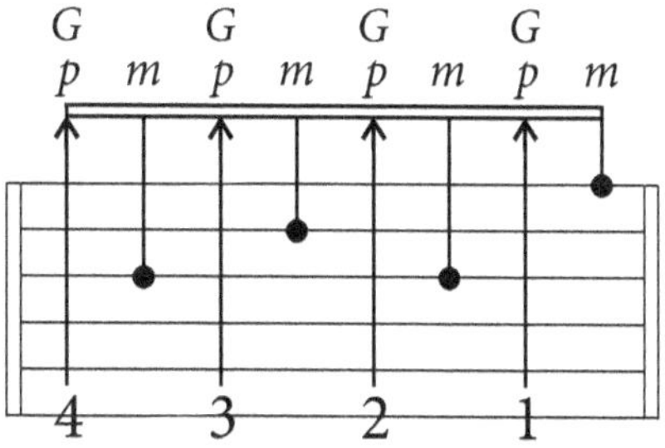

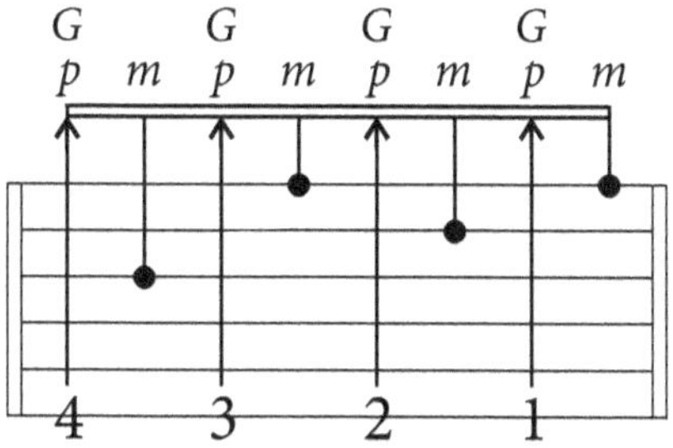

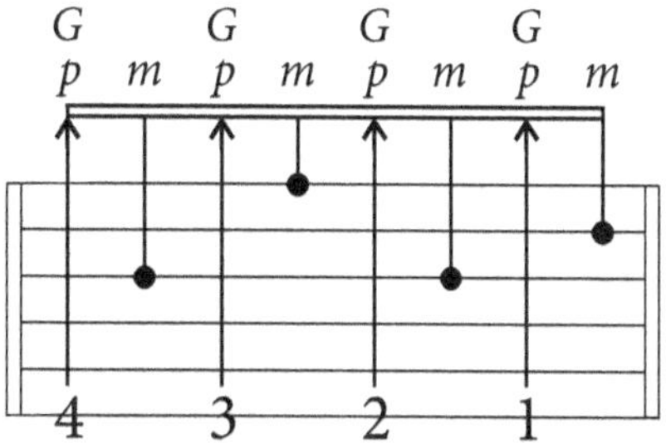

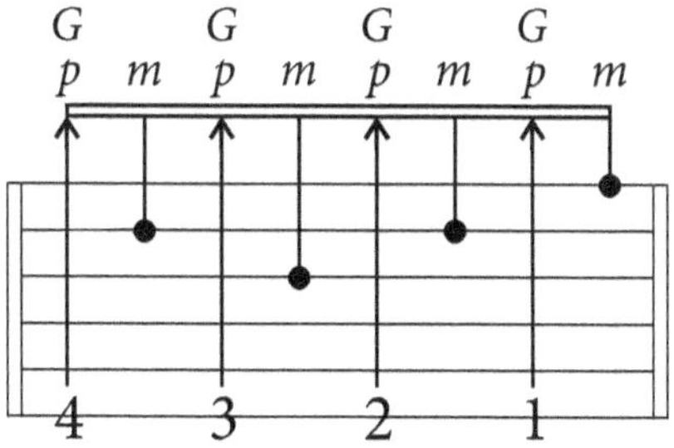

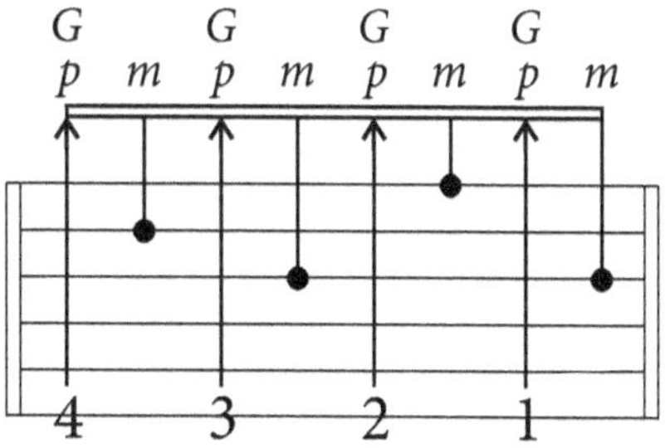

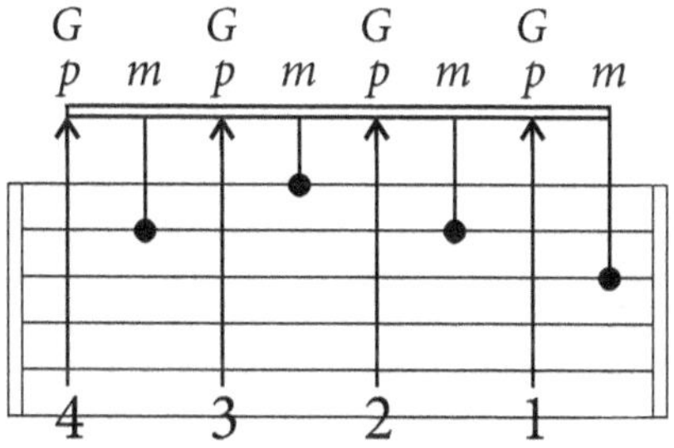

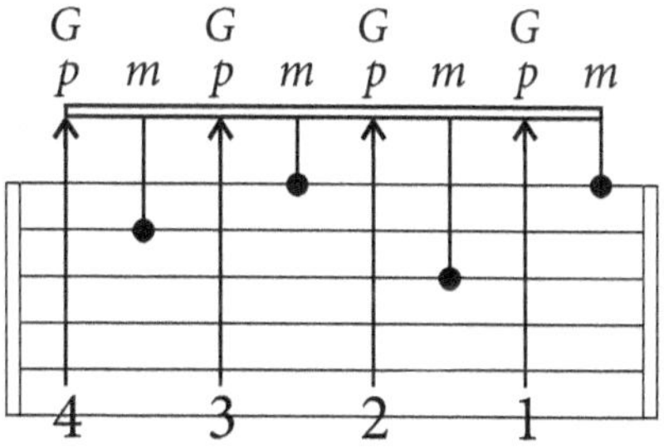

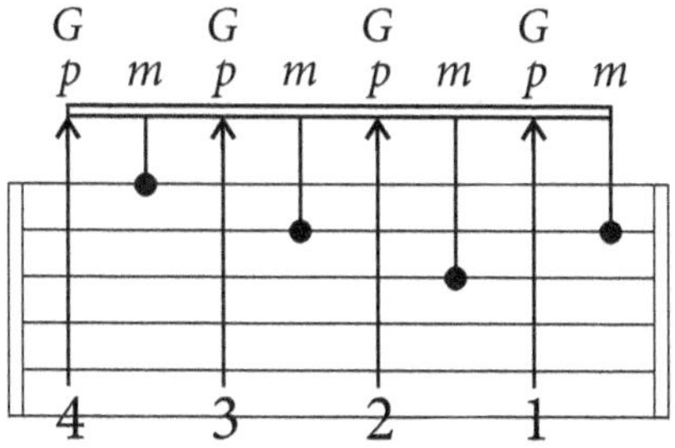

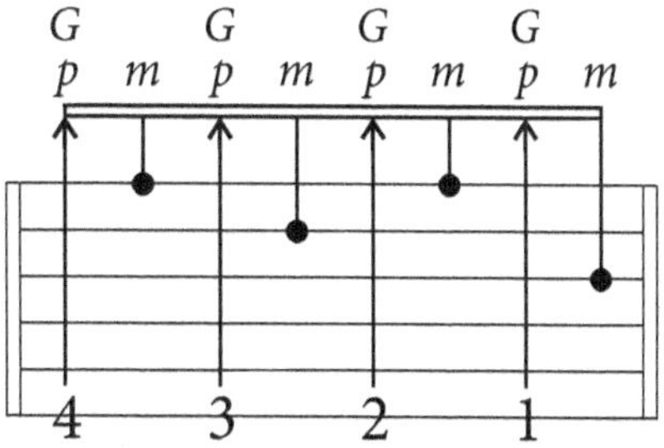

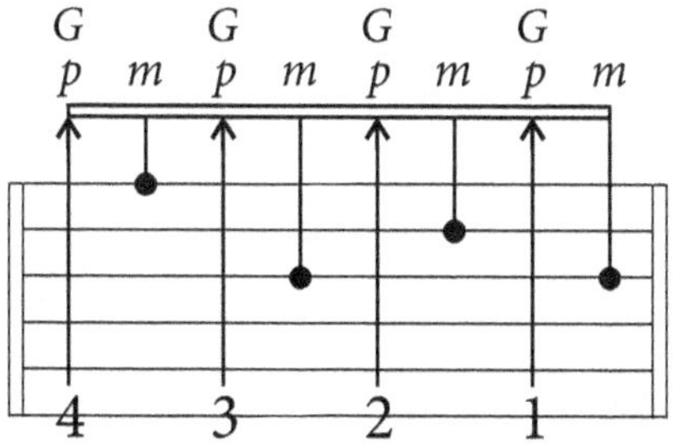

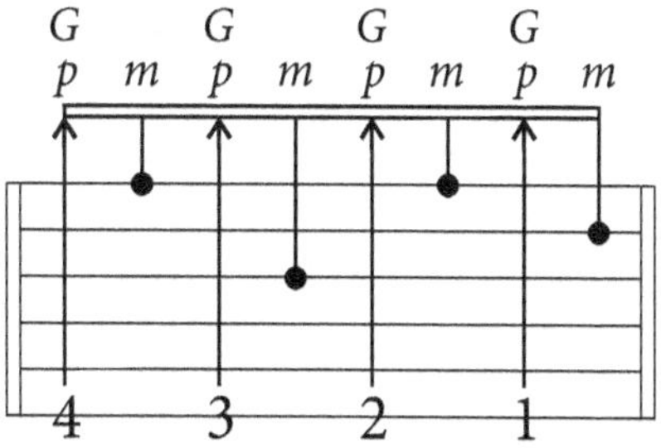

UNIT 2

Exercises for strengthening the thumb.
Thumb stroke on two or three strings simultaneous.

For the strengthening of the thumb stroke place the chromatic scale on the 5th string so that the thumb can strike two strings simultaneously:

§ Ia § Ib

§ IIa § IIb

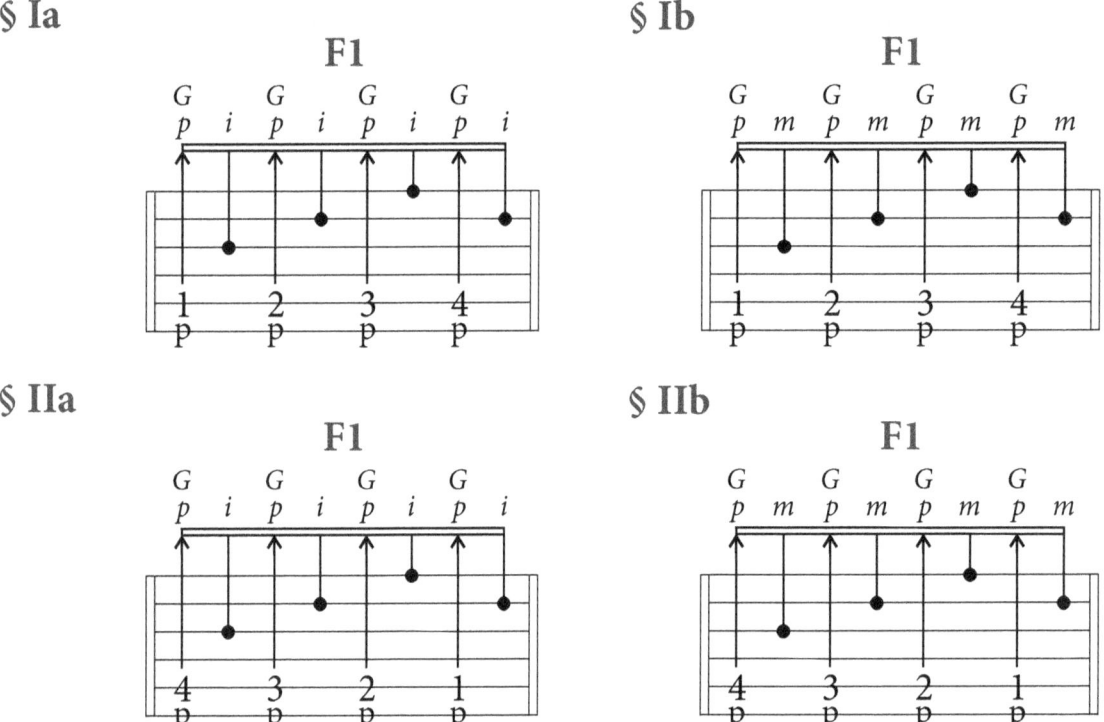

And also on the 4th string so that the thumb can strike three strings simultaneously:

§ IIIa § IIIb

§ IVa § IVb

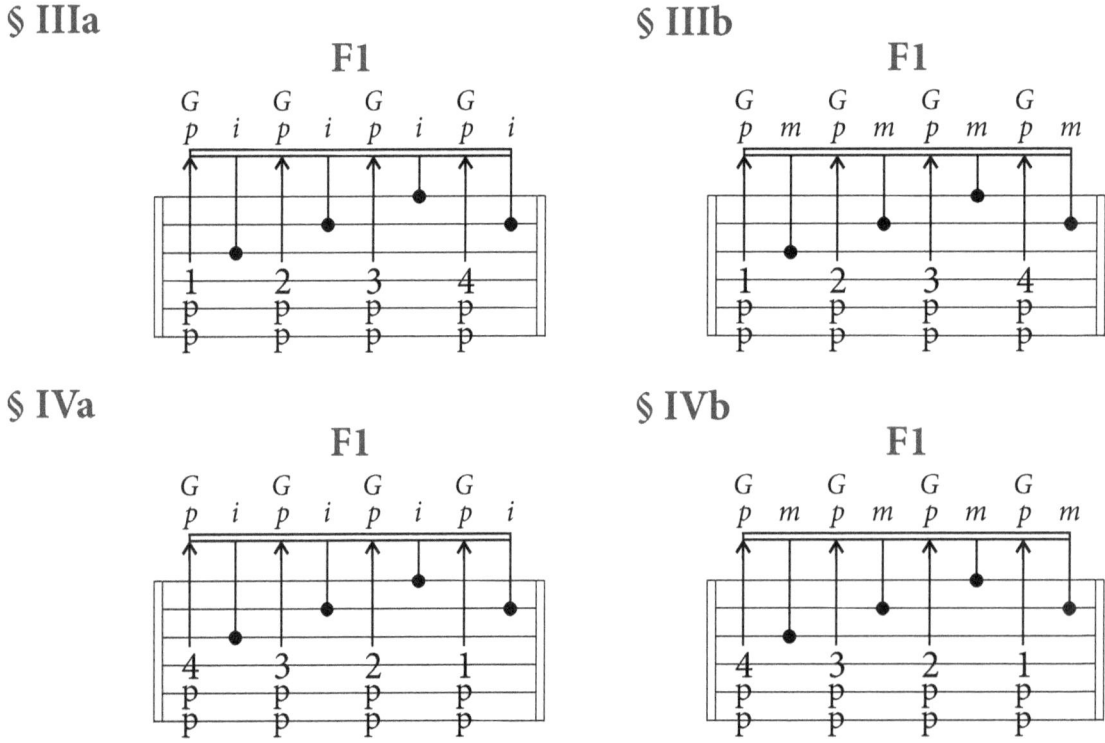

§ Ia

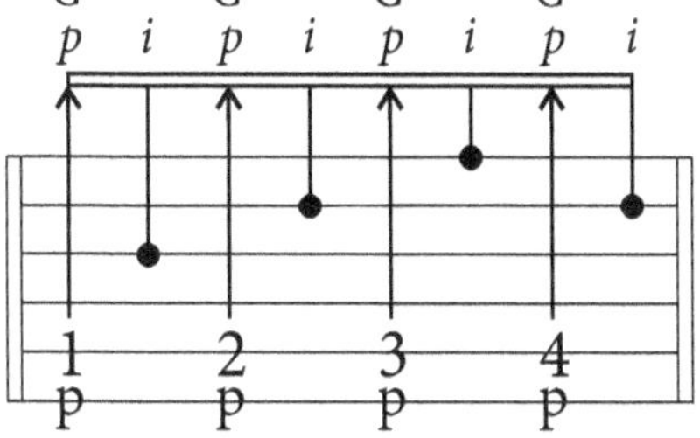

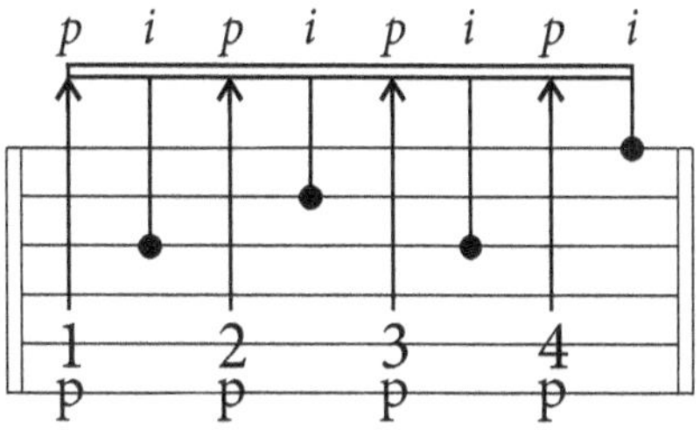

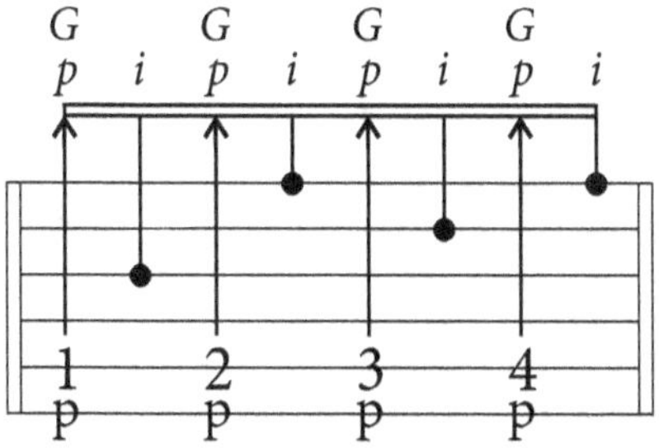

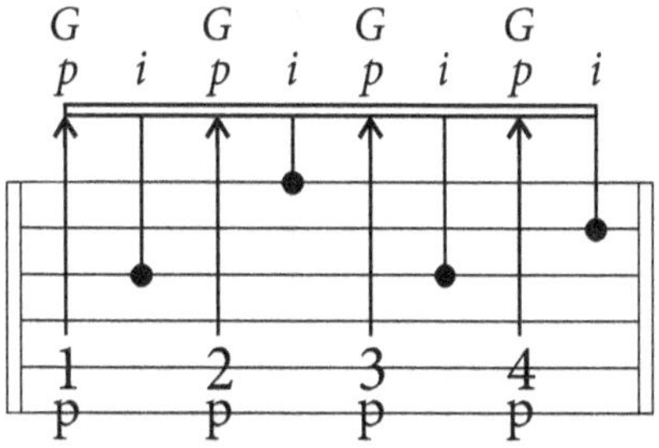

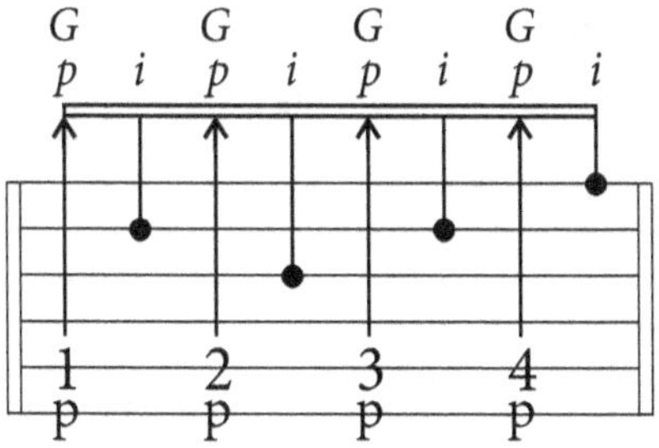

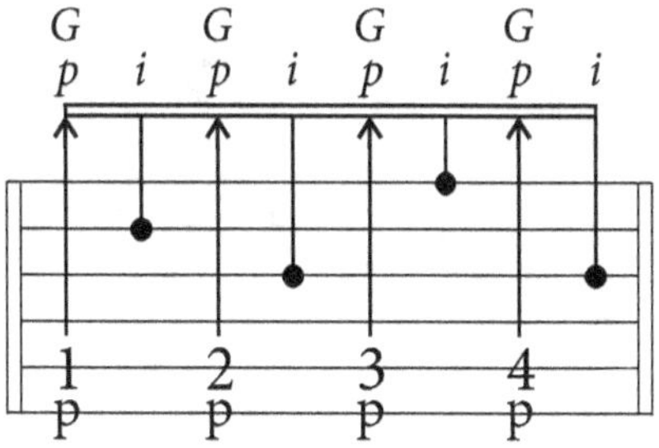

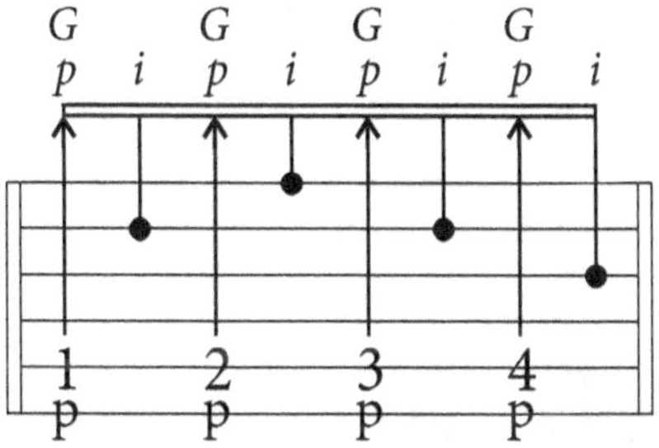

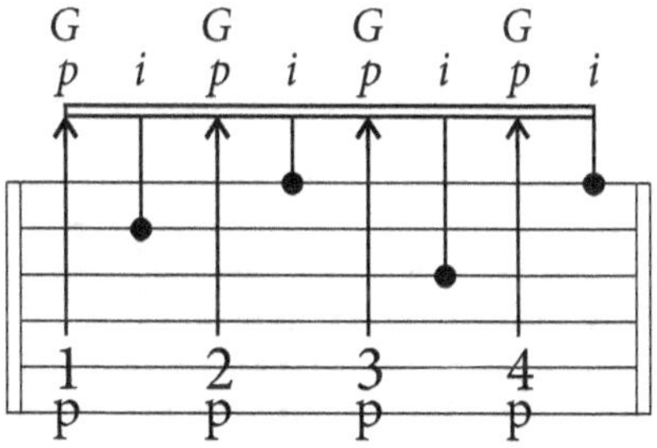

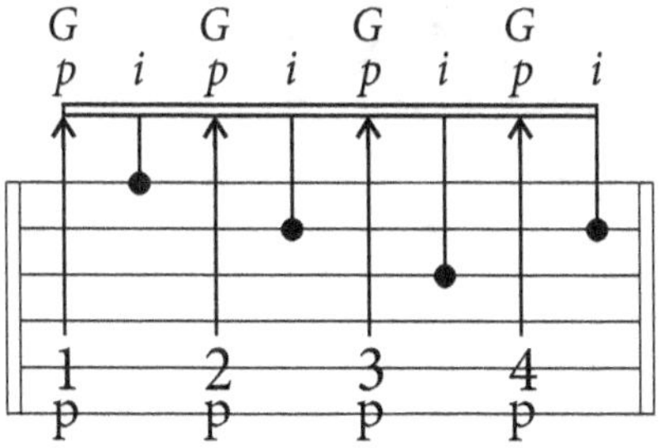

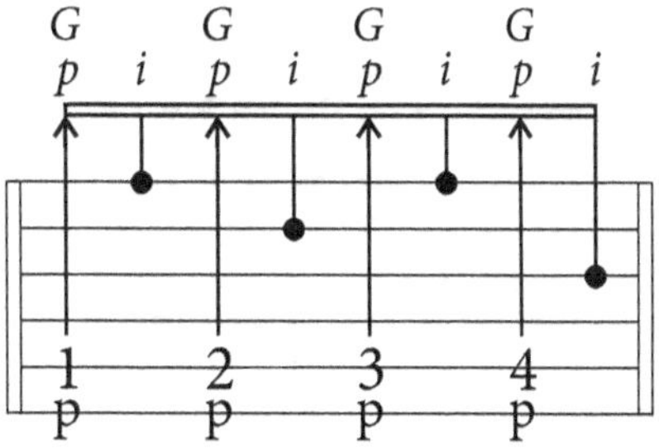

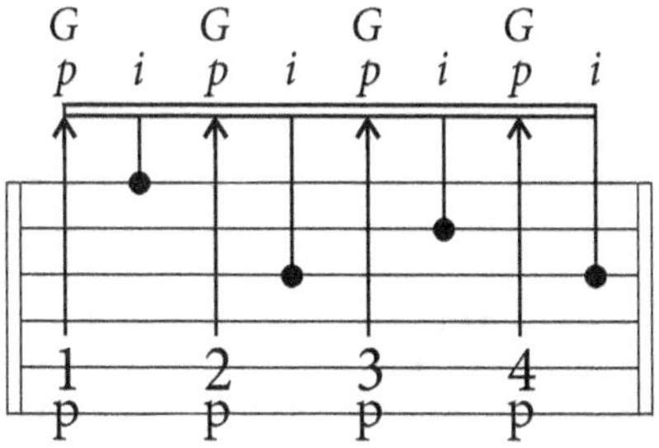

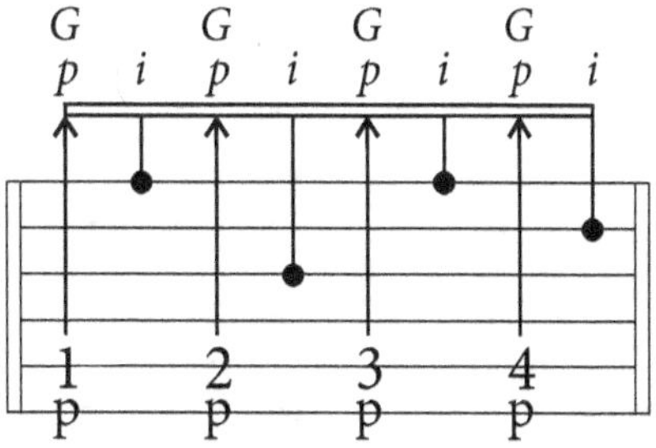

§ Ib

F1　F2

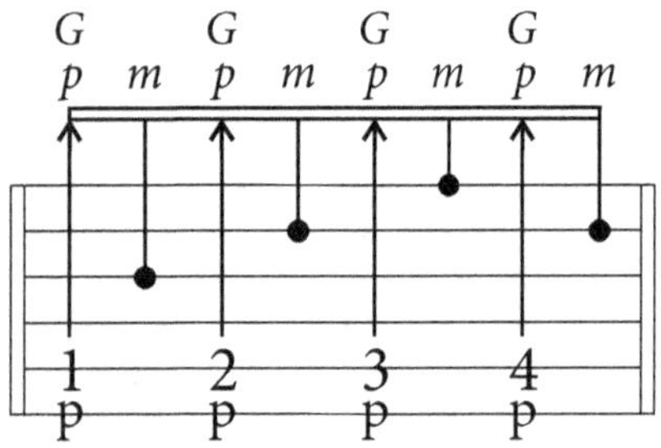

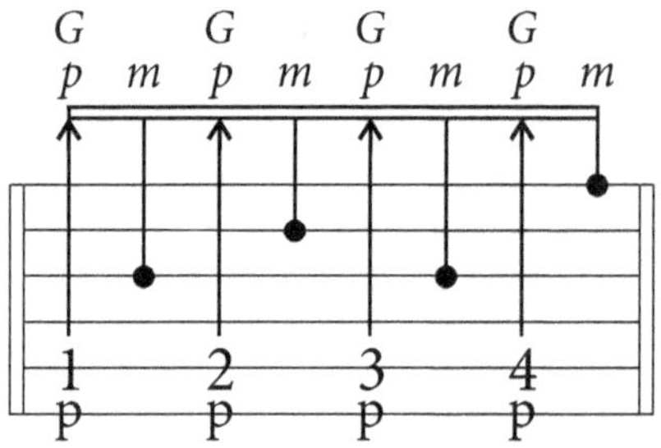

F3 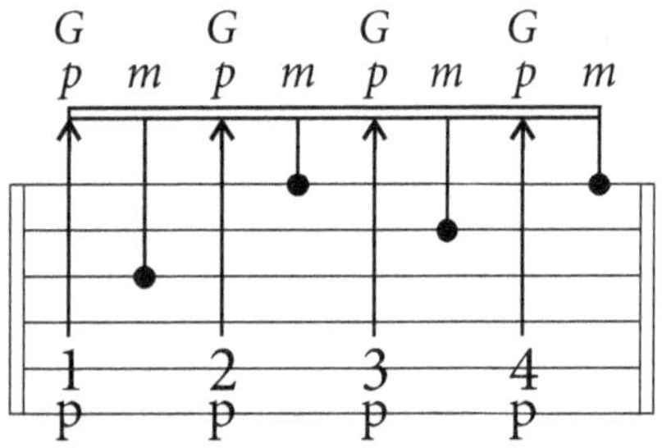　F4

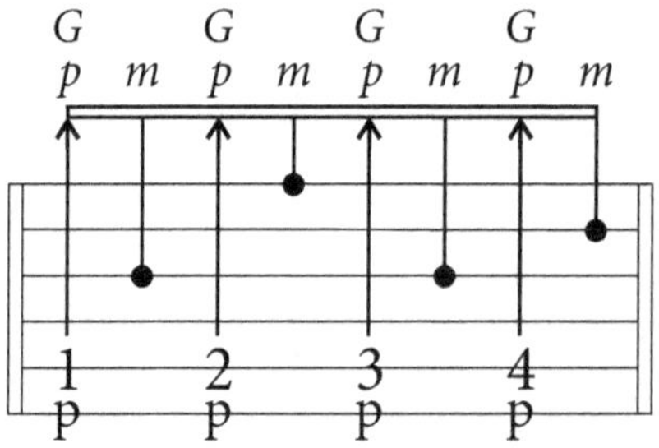

F5 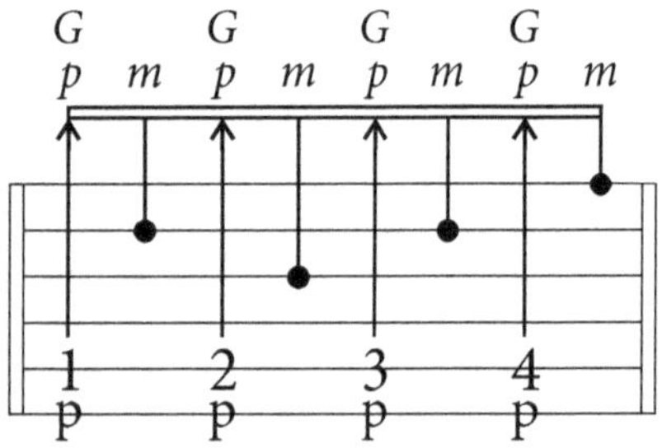　F6

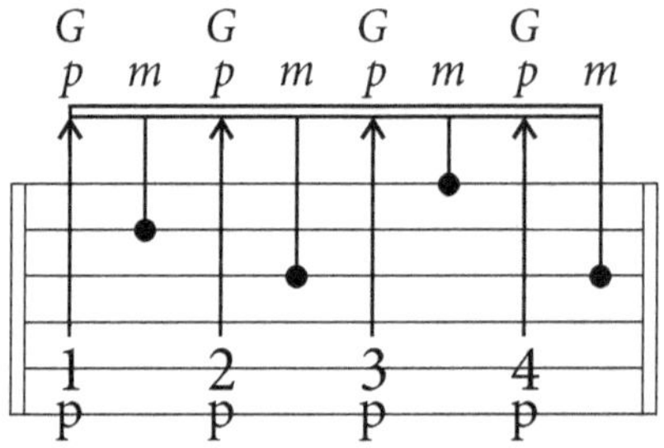

F7 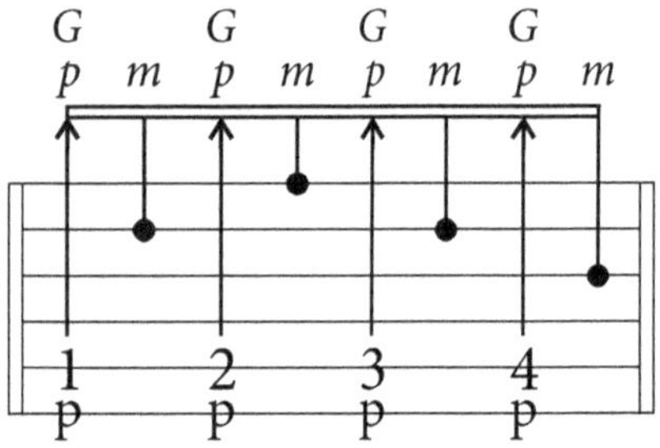　F8

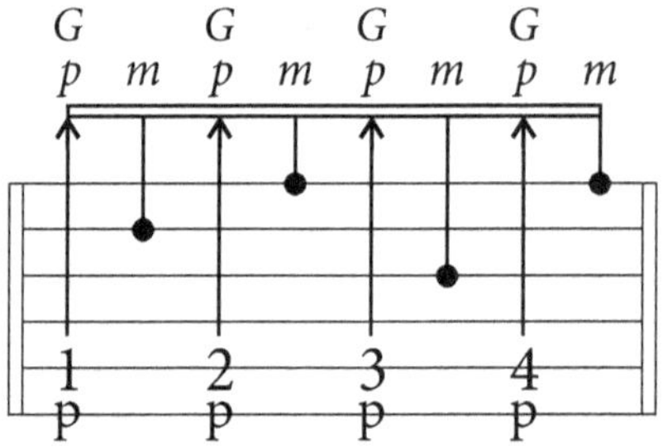

F9 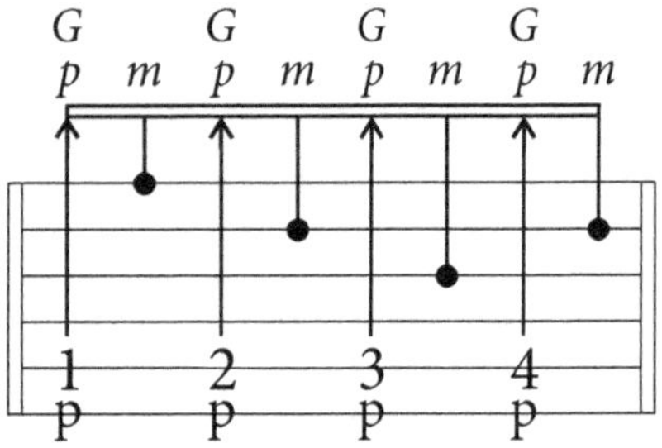　F10

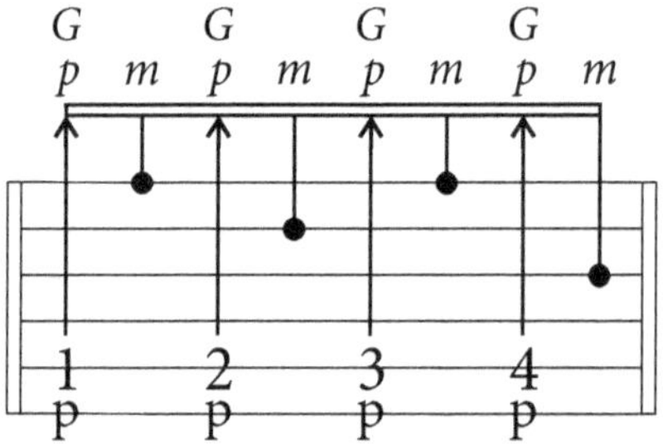

F11 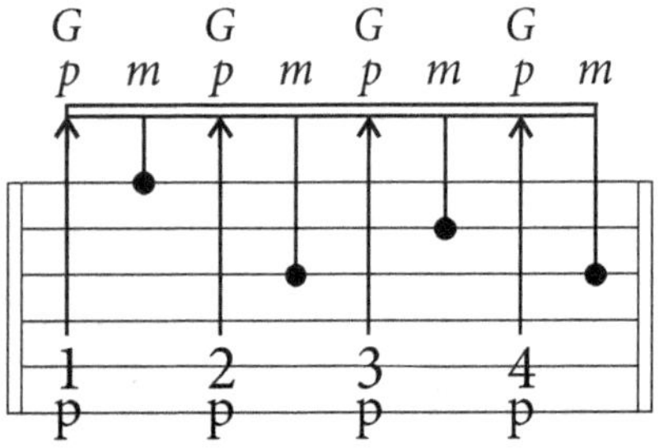　F12

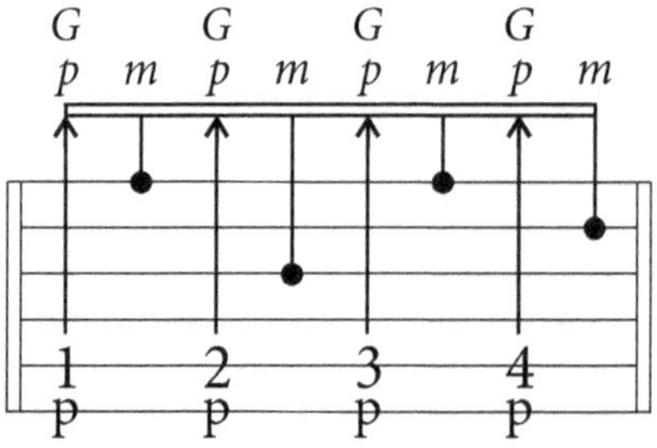

§ IIa

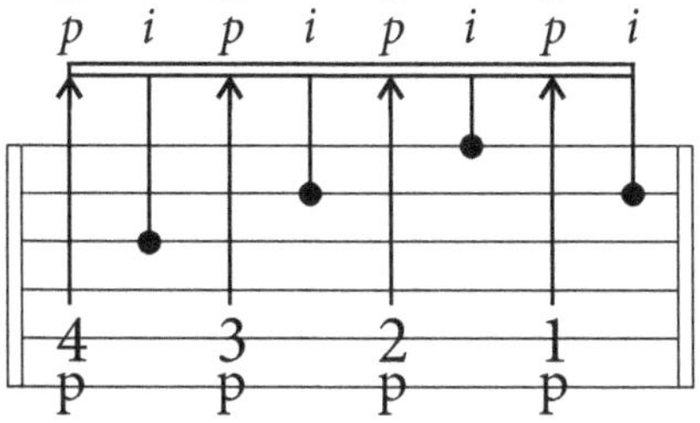

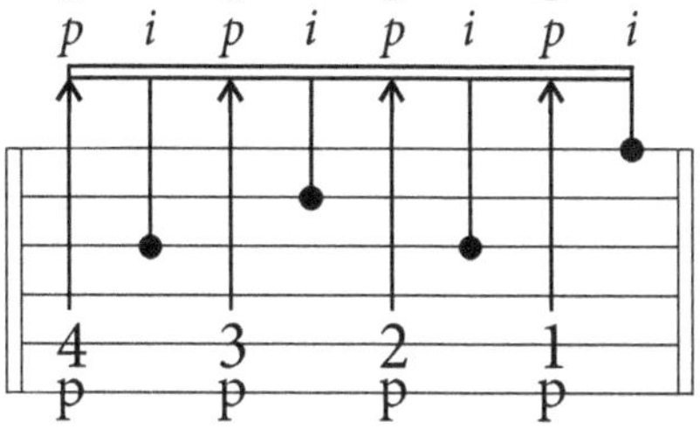

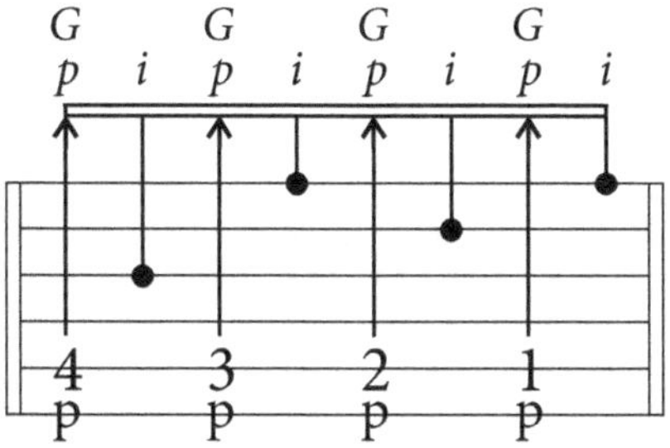

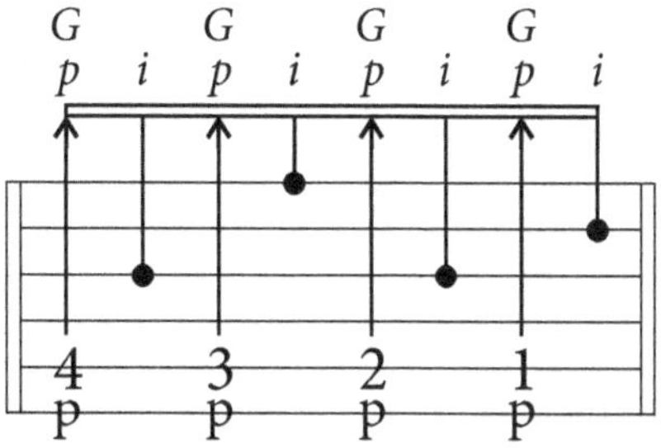

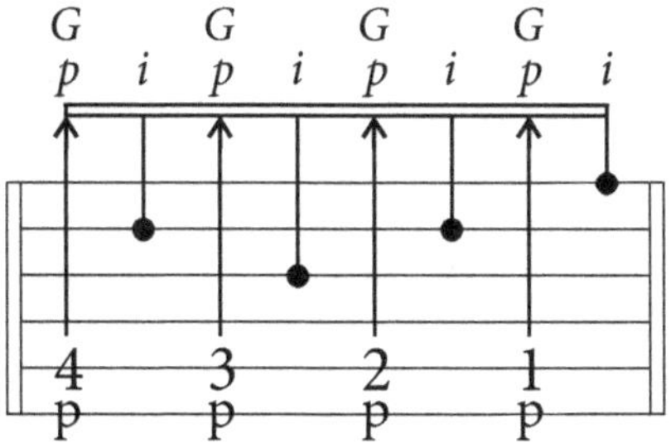

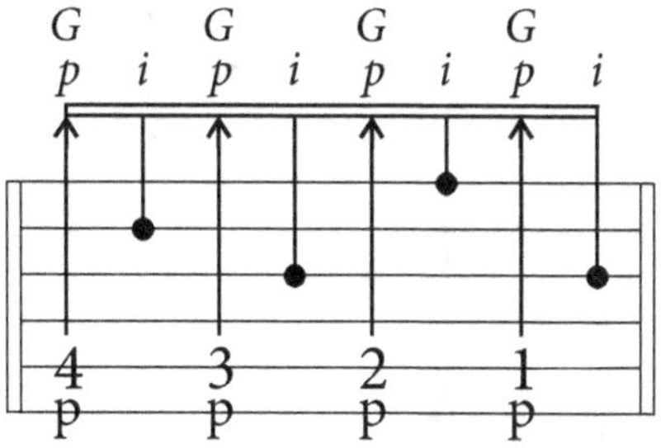

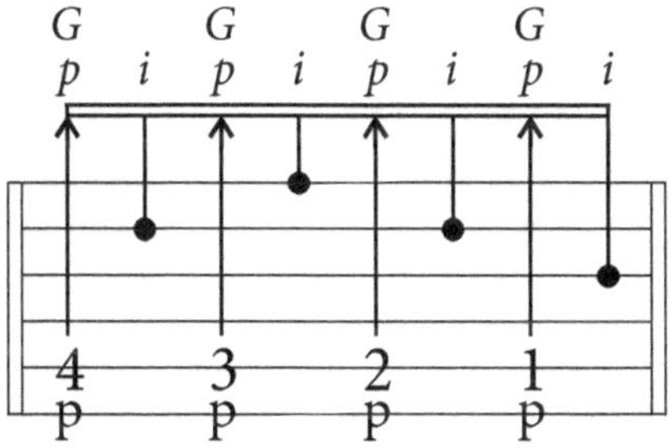

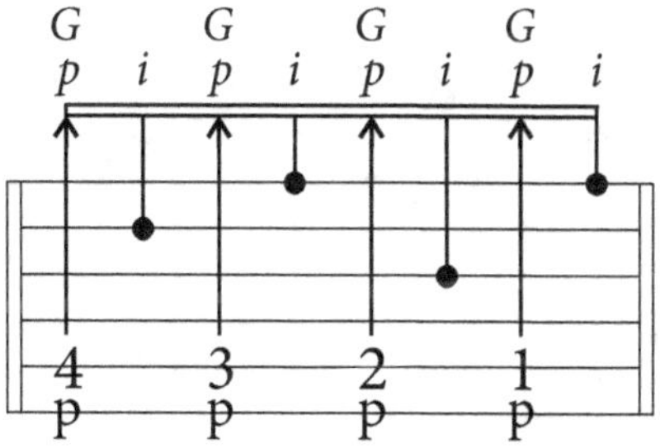

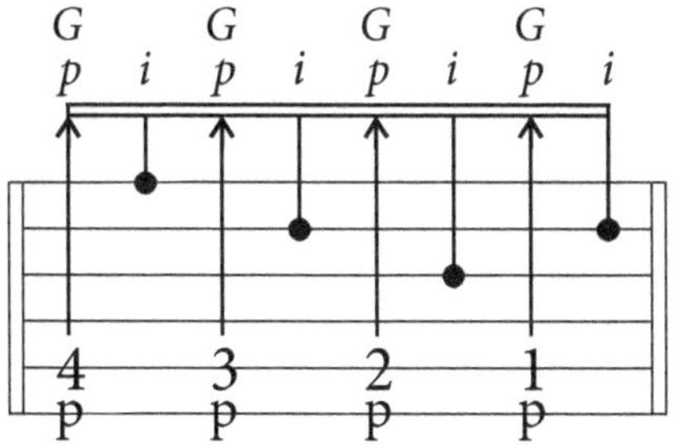

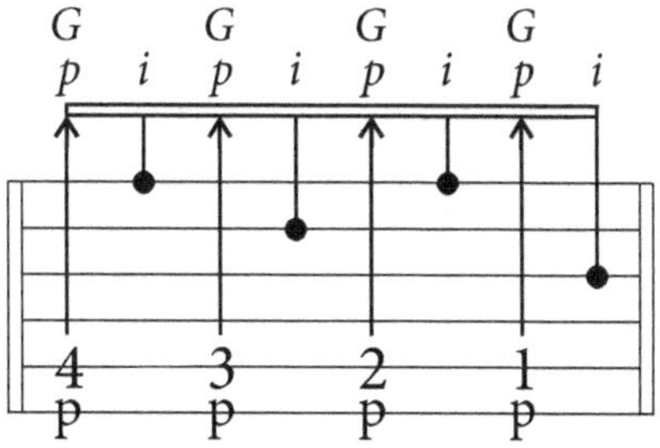

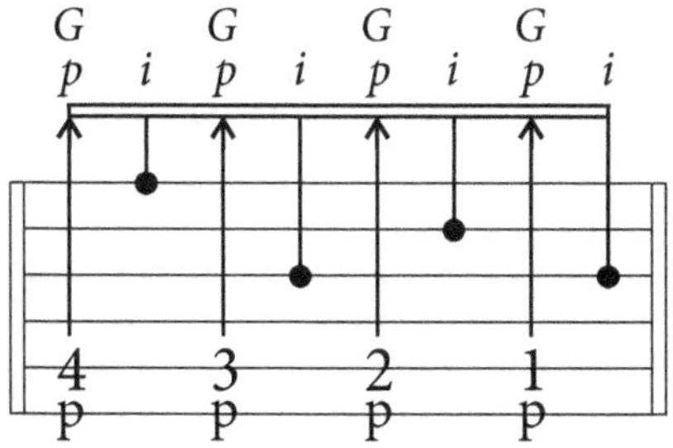

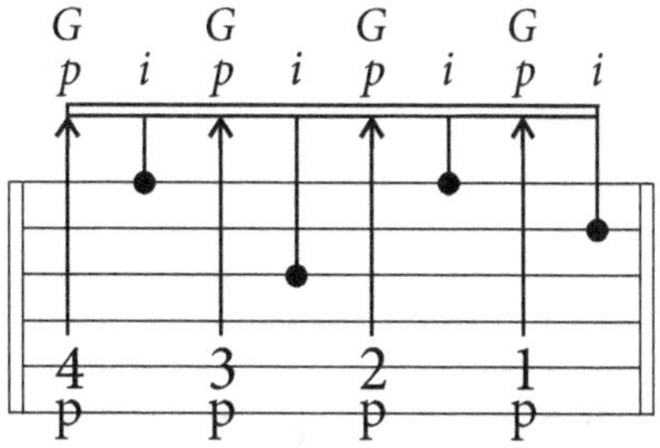

§ IIb

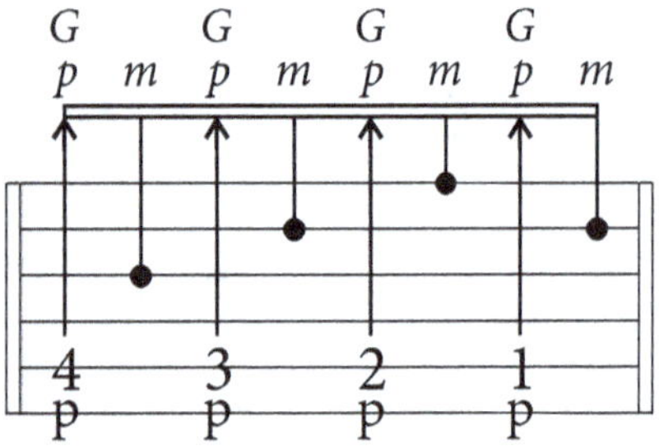

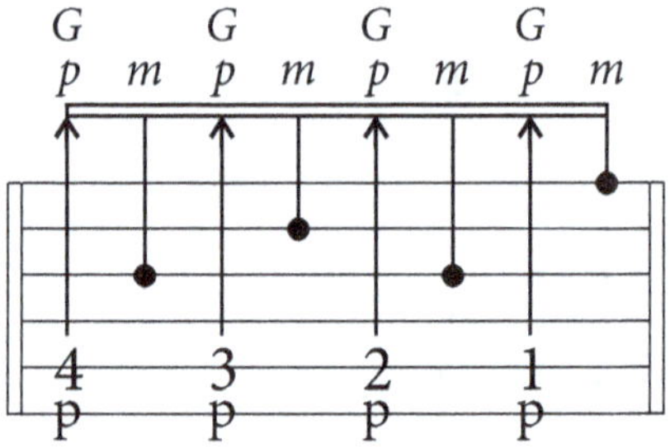

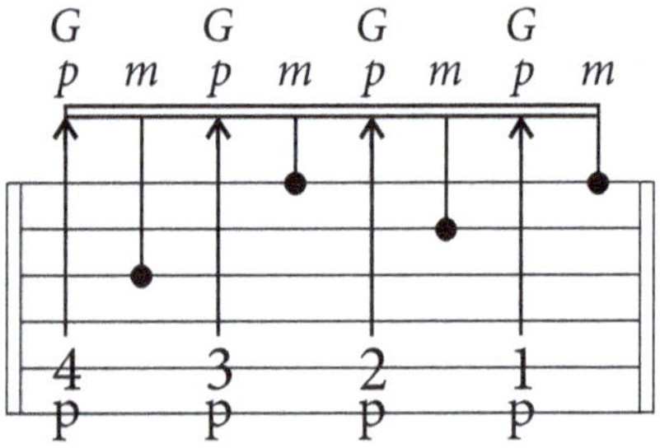

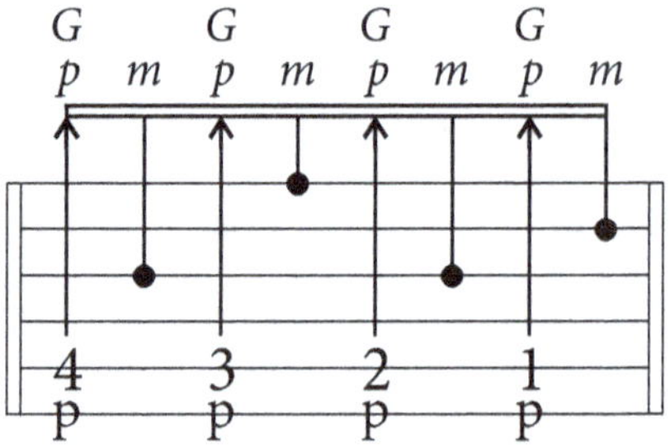

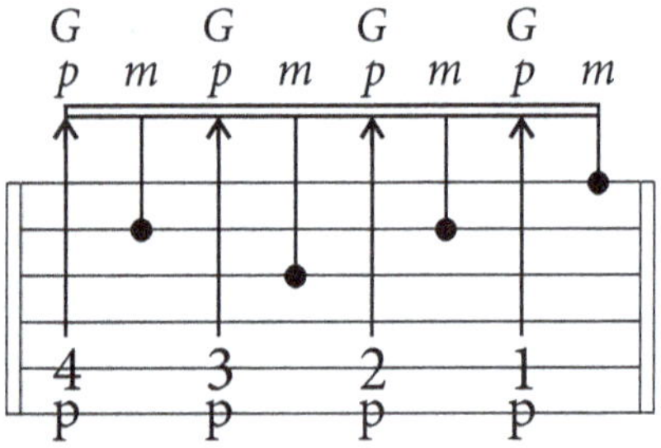

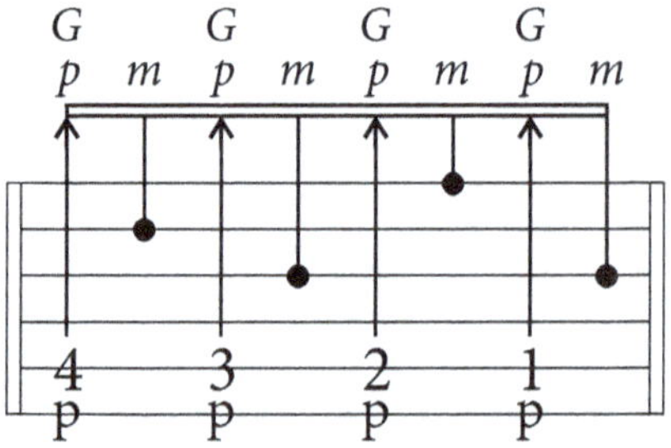

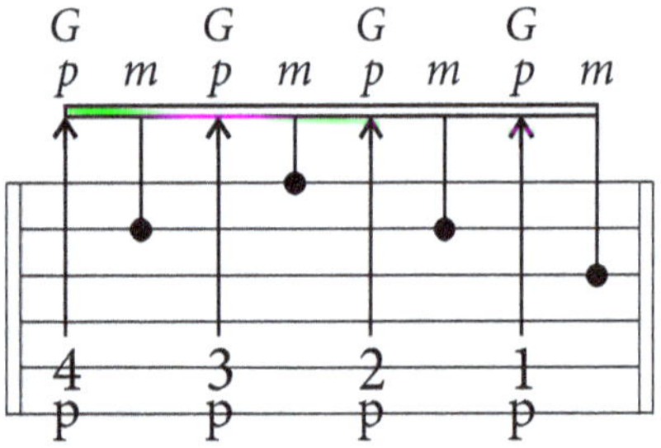

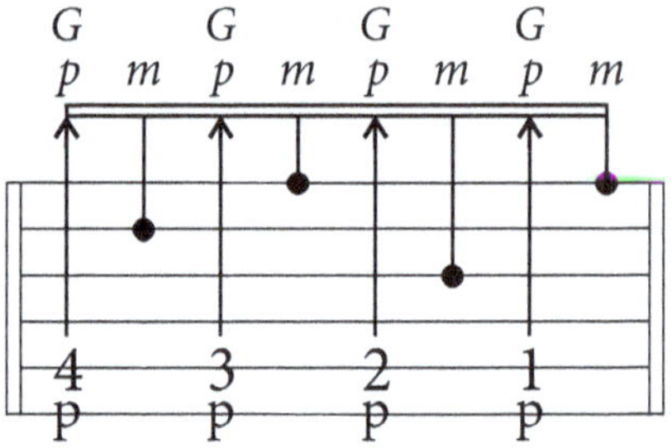

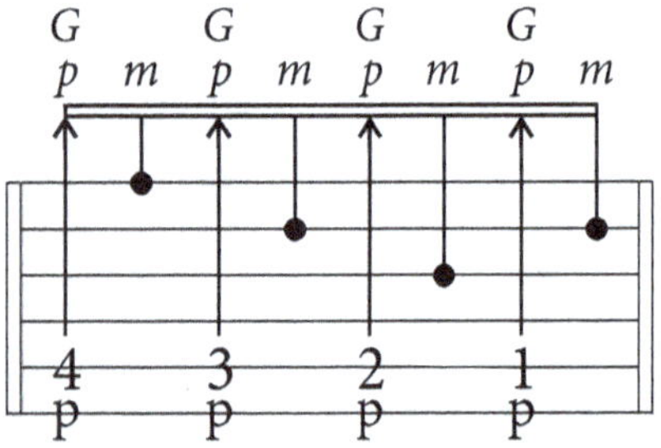

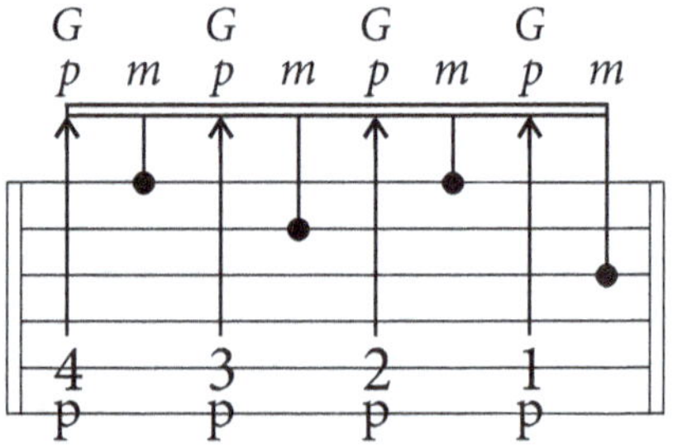

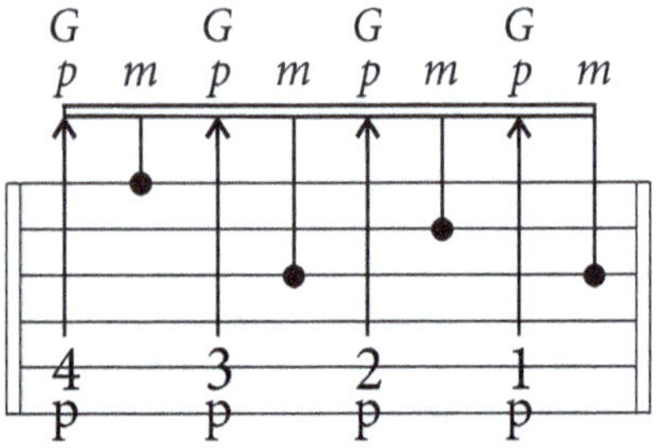

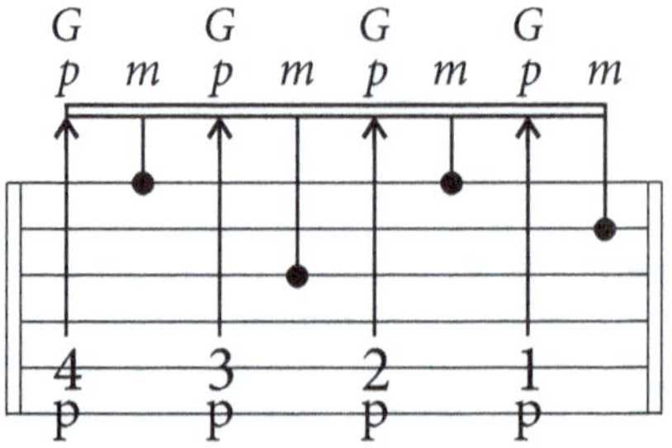

§ IIIa

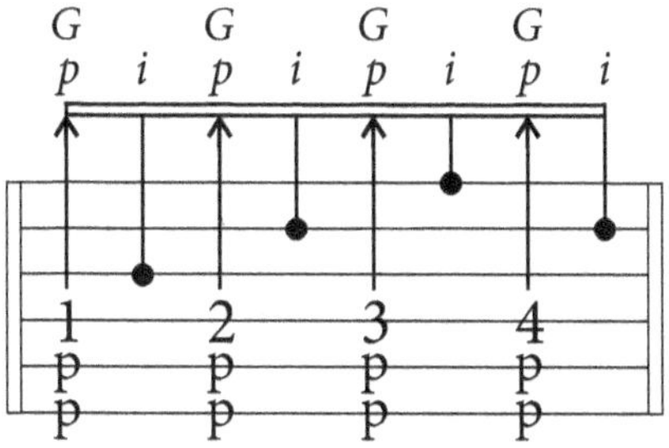

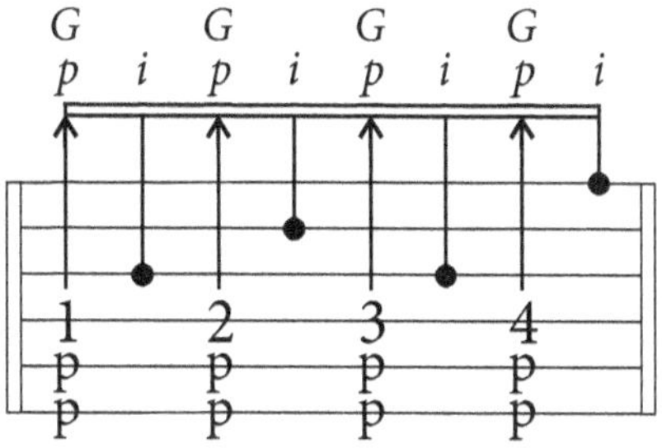

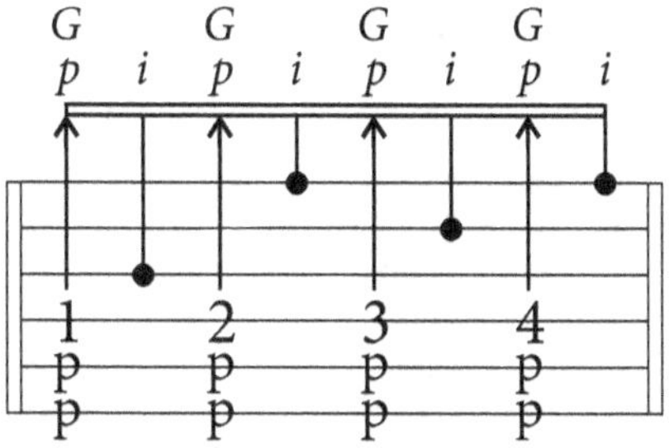

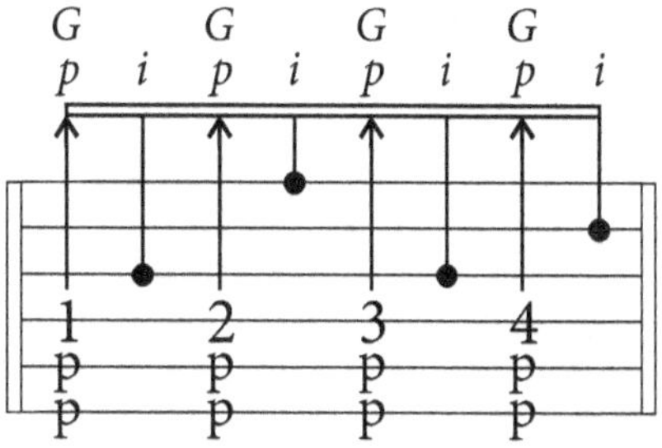

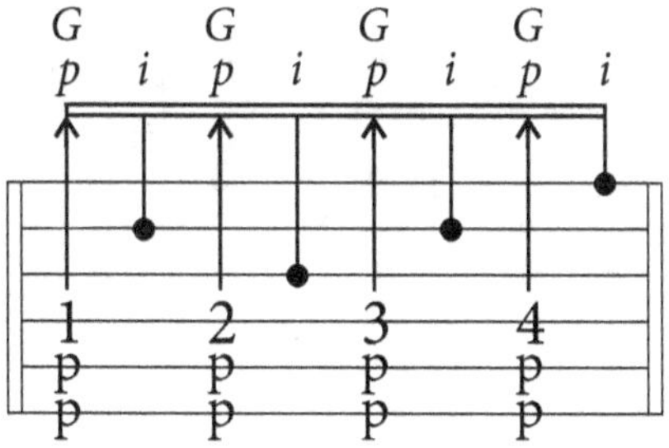

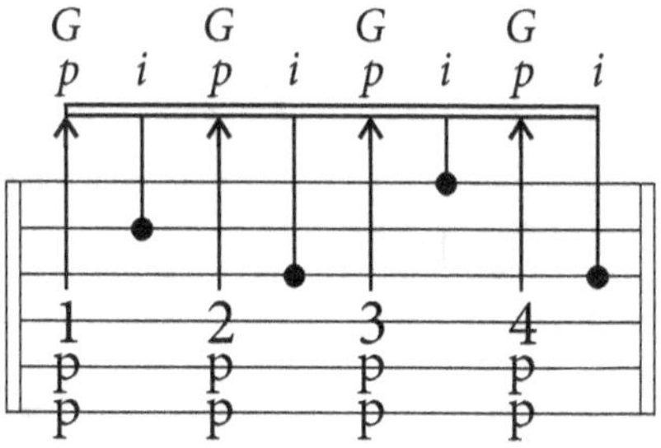

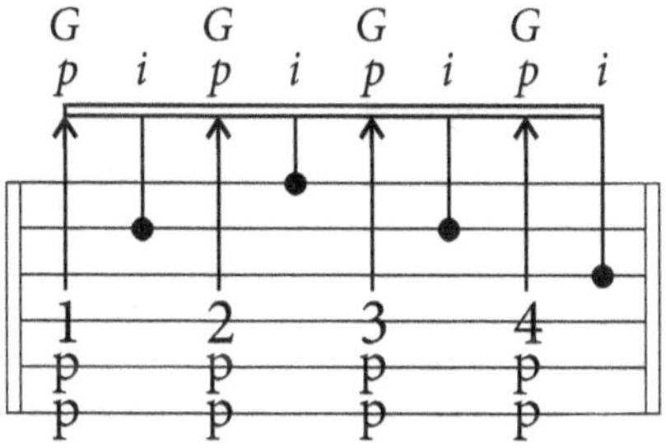

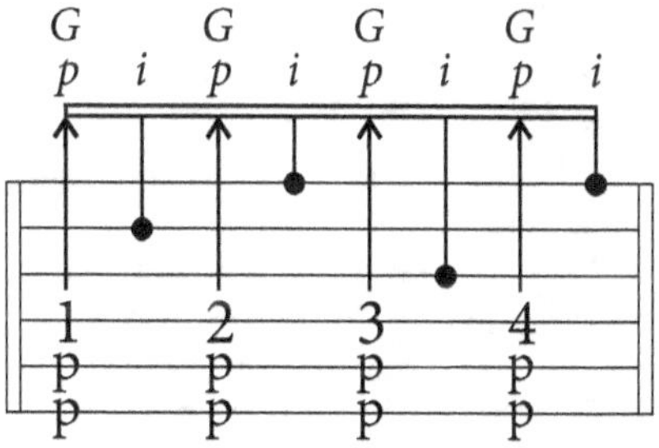

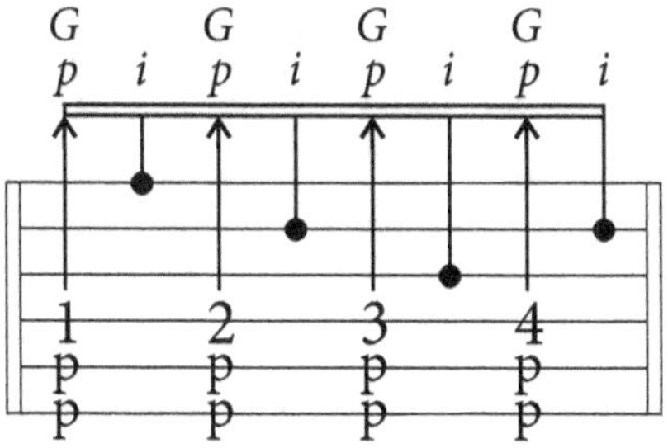

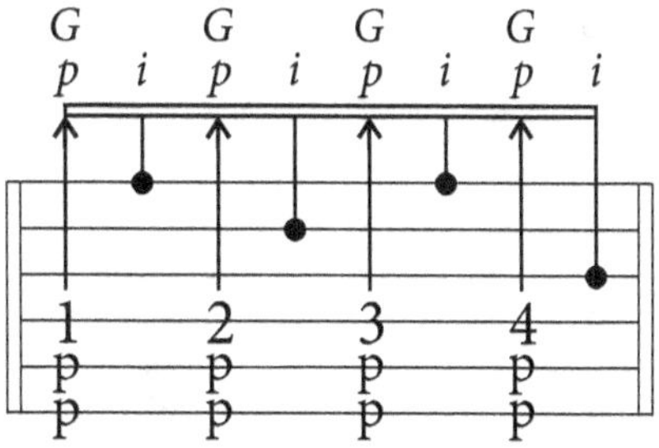

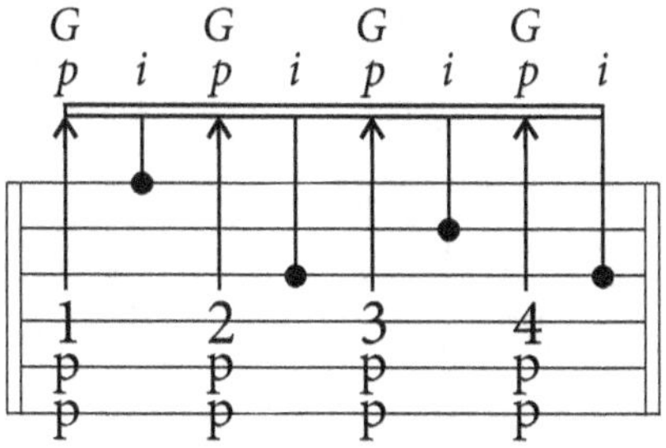

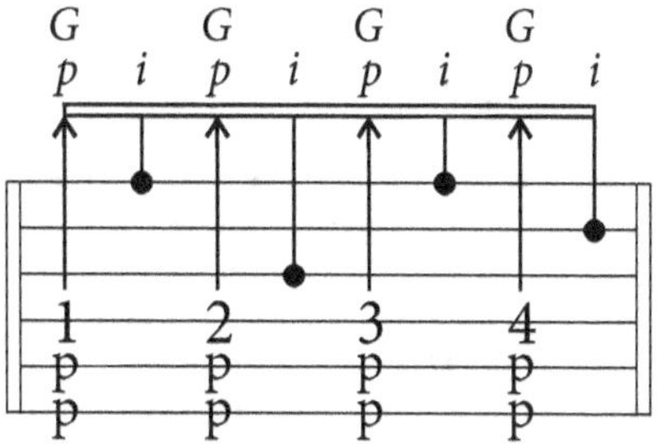

§ IIIb

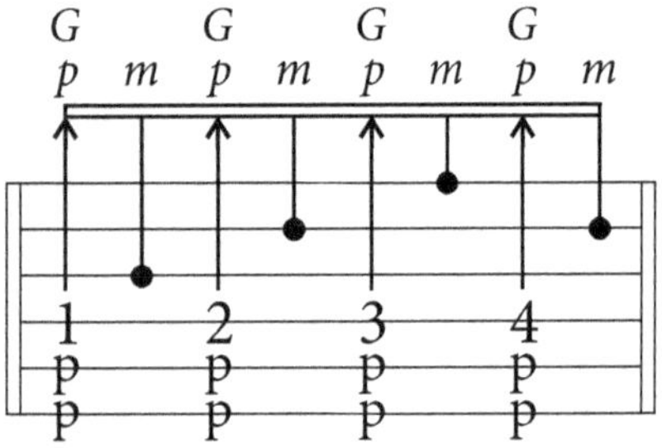

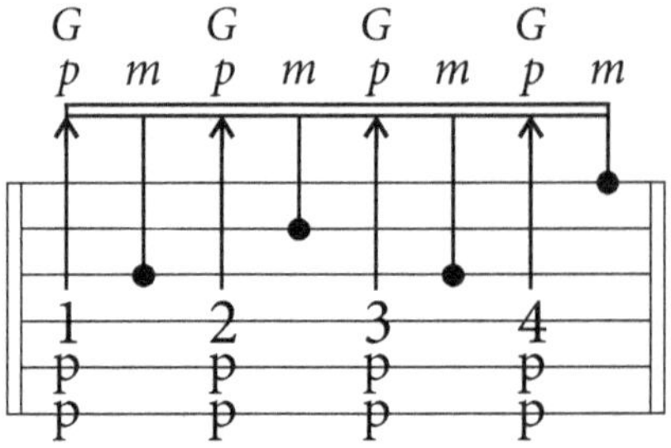

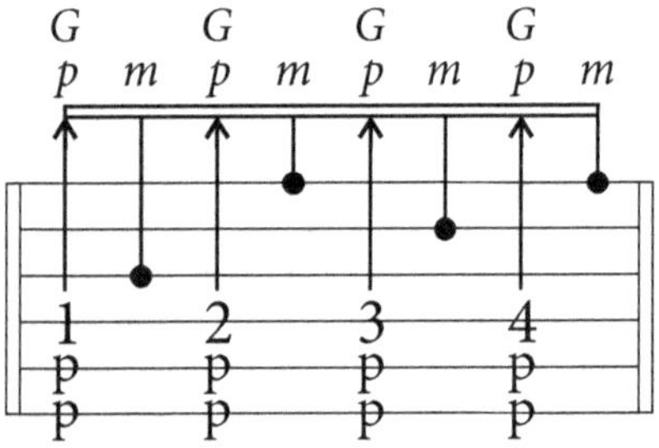

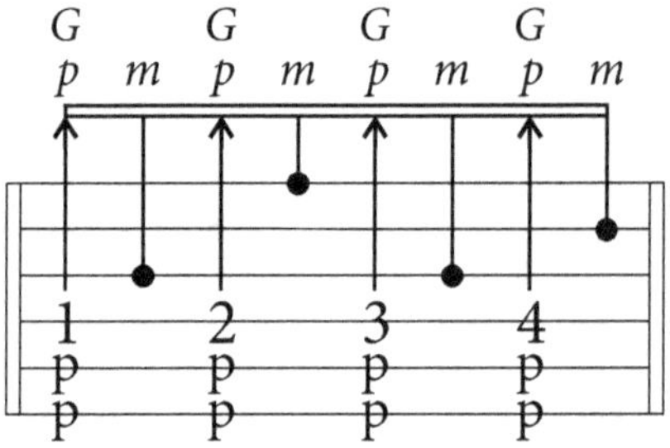

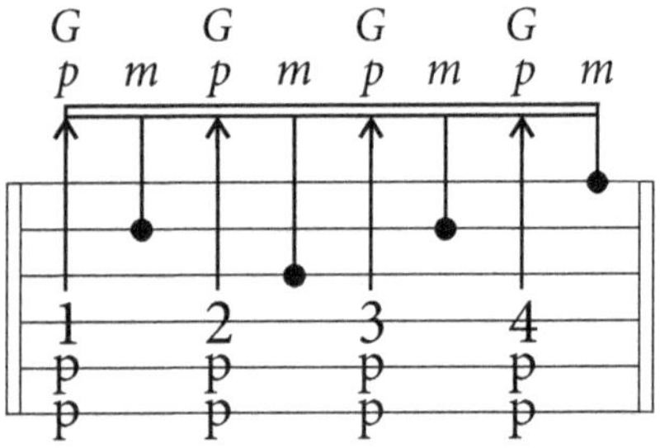

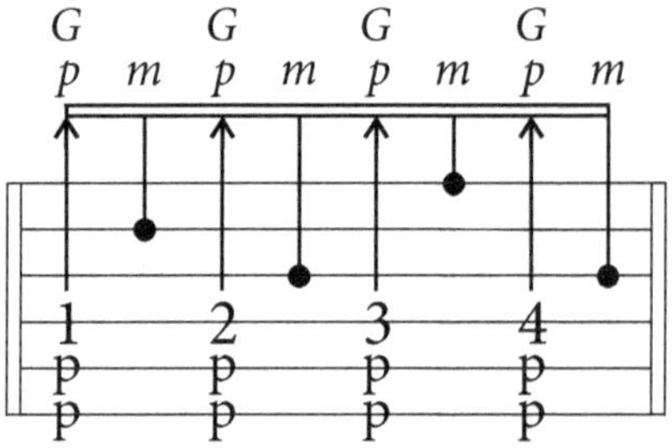

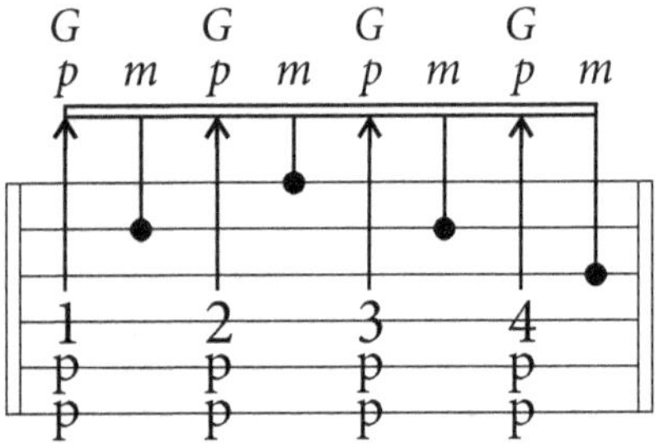

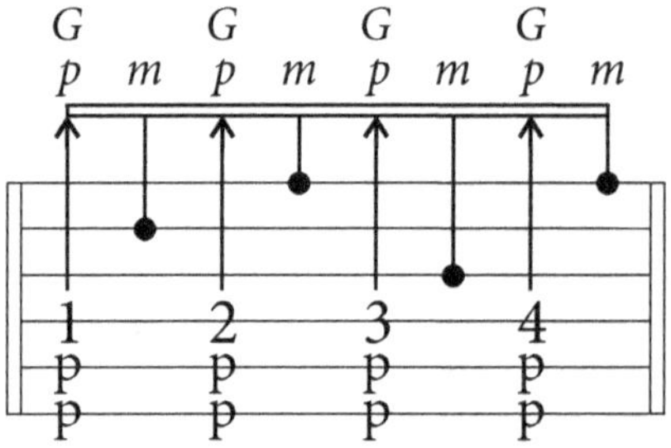

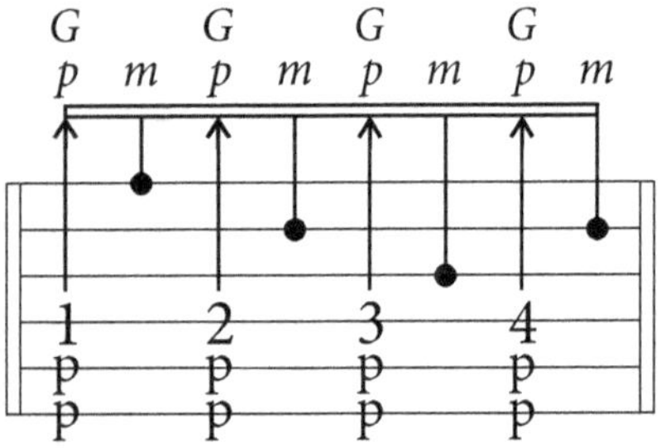

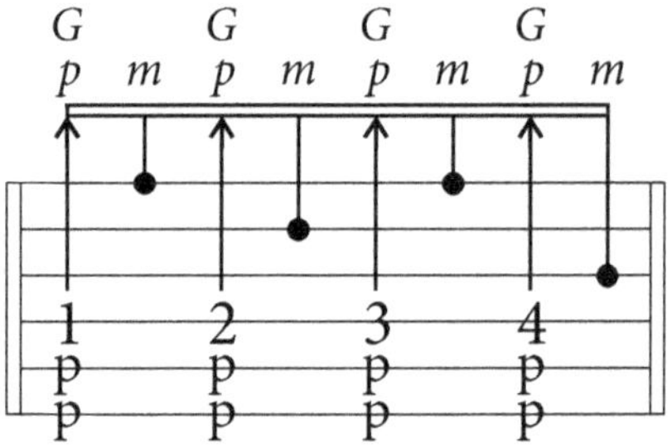

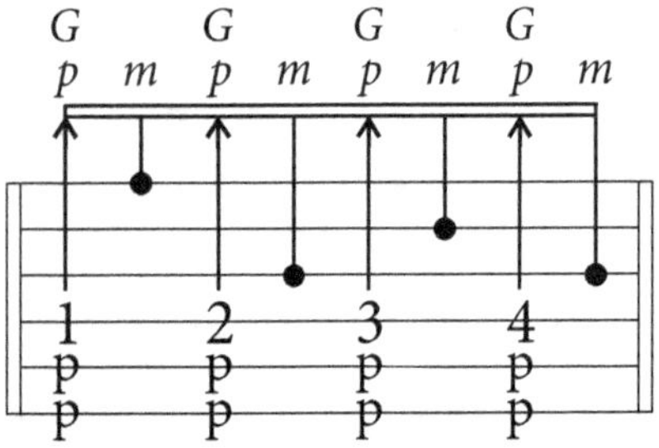

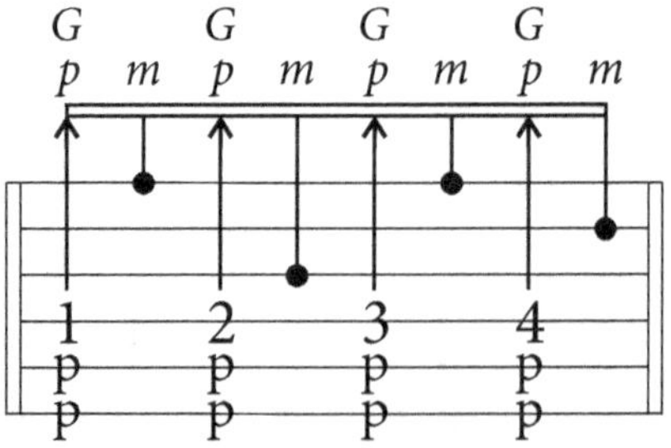

§ IVa

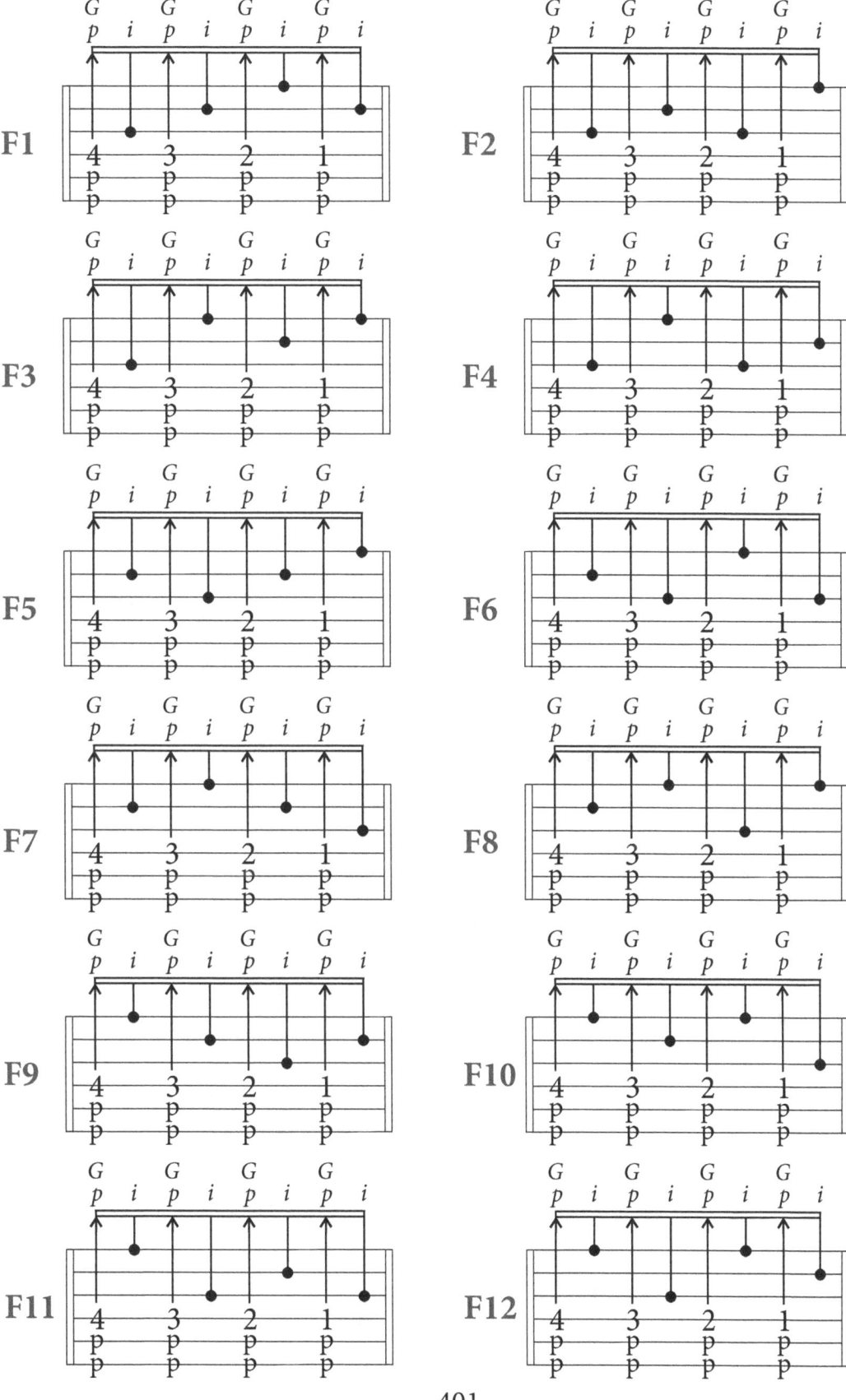

§ IVb

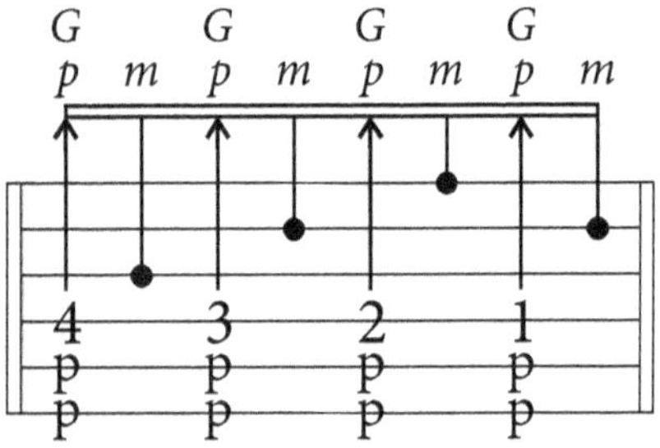

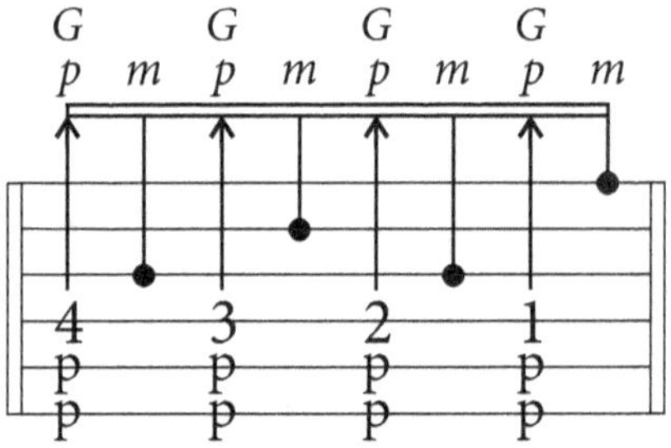

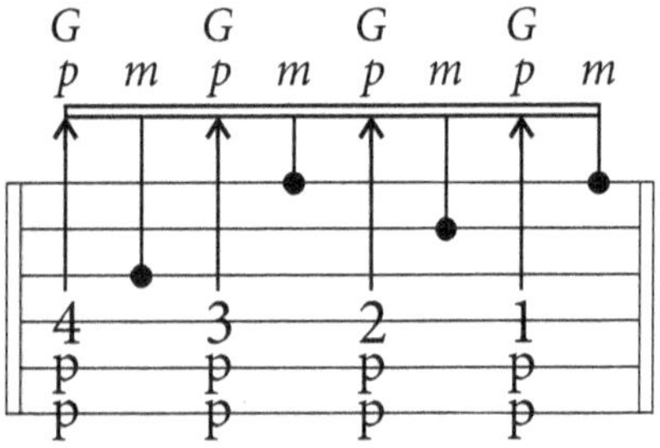

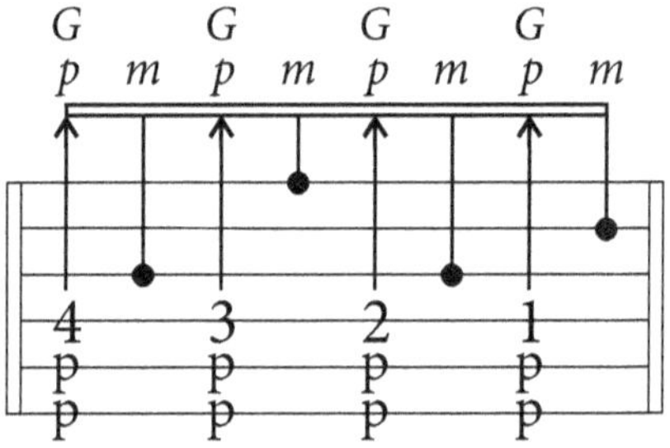

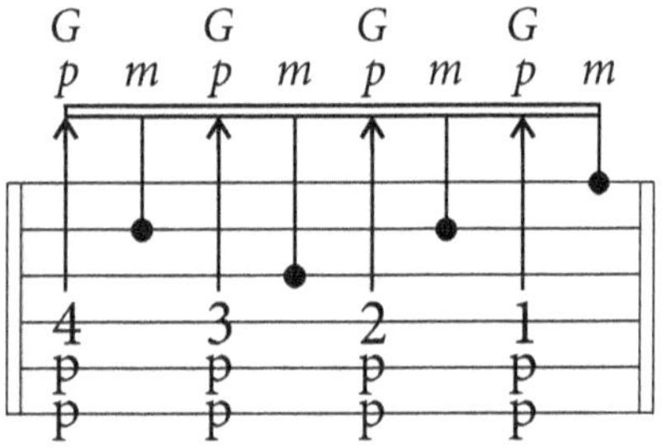

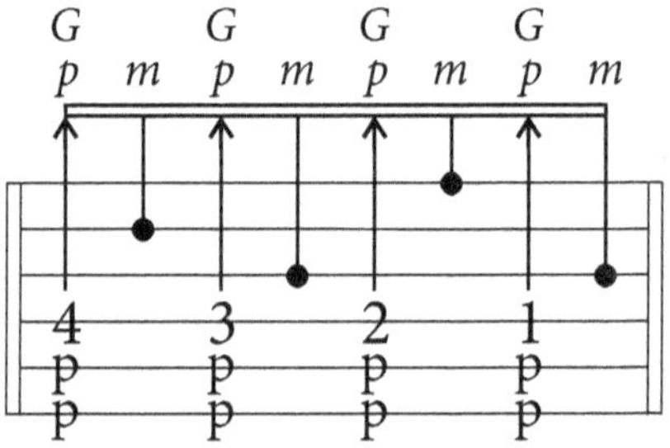

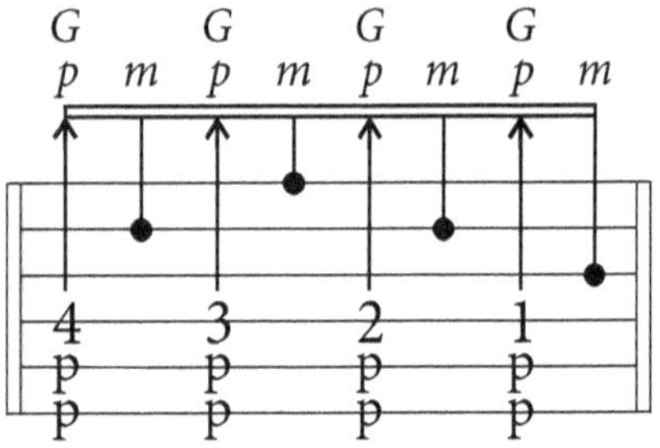

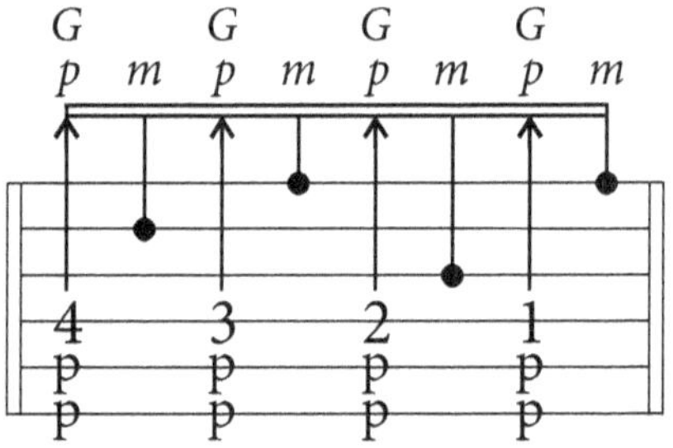

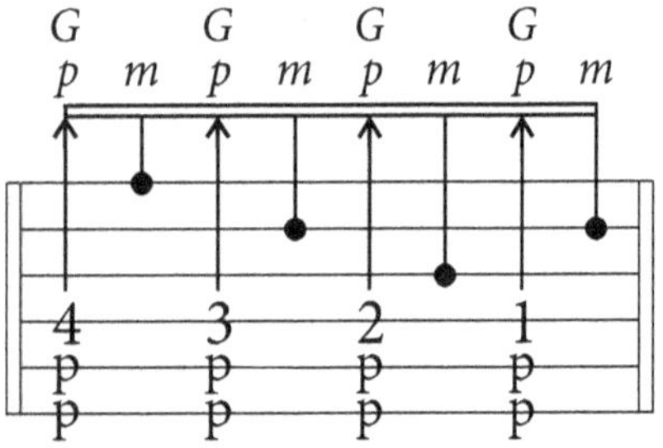

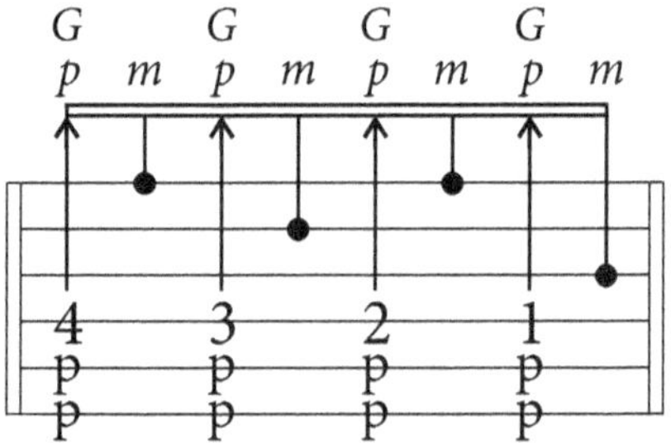

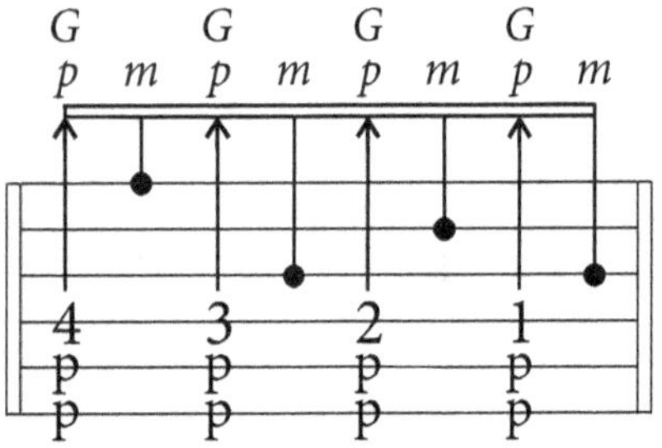

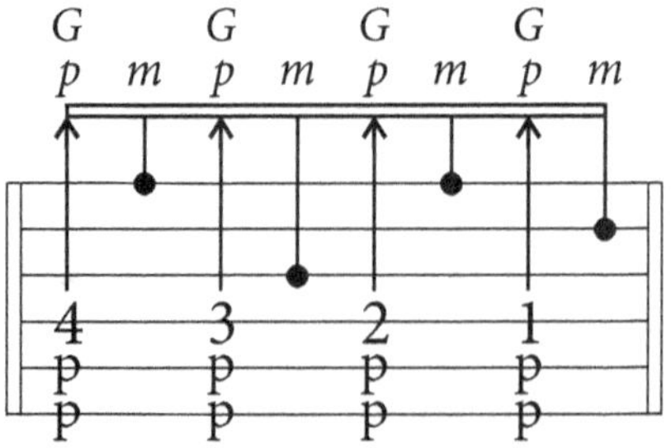

CHAPTER 6
EXERCISES THAT REFER TO THUMB STROKE
WITH GOLPE IN COMBINATION
WITH INDEX AND MIDDLE FINGER
ON VARIOUS FORMULAS.

UNIT 1

Golpe exercises on:
1/. Chromatic scales of one string.
2/. Ascending rolling Formulas.
3/. Descending rolling Formulas.
4/. Scales of two adjacent strings.

§ Ia

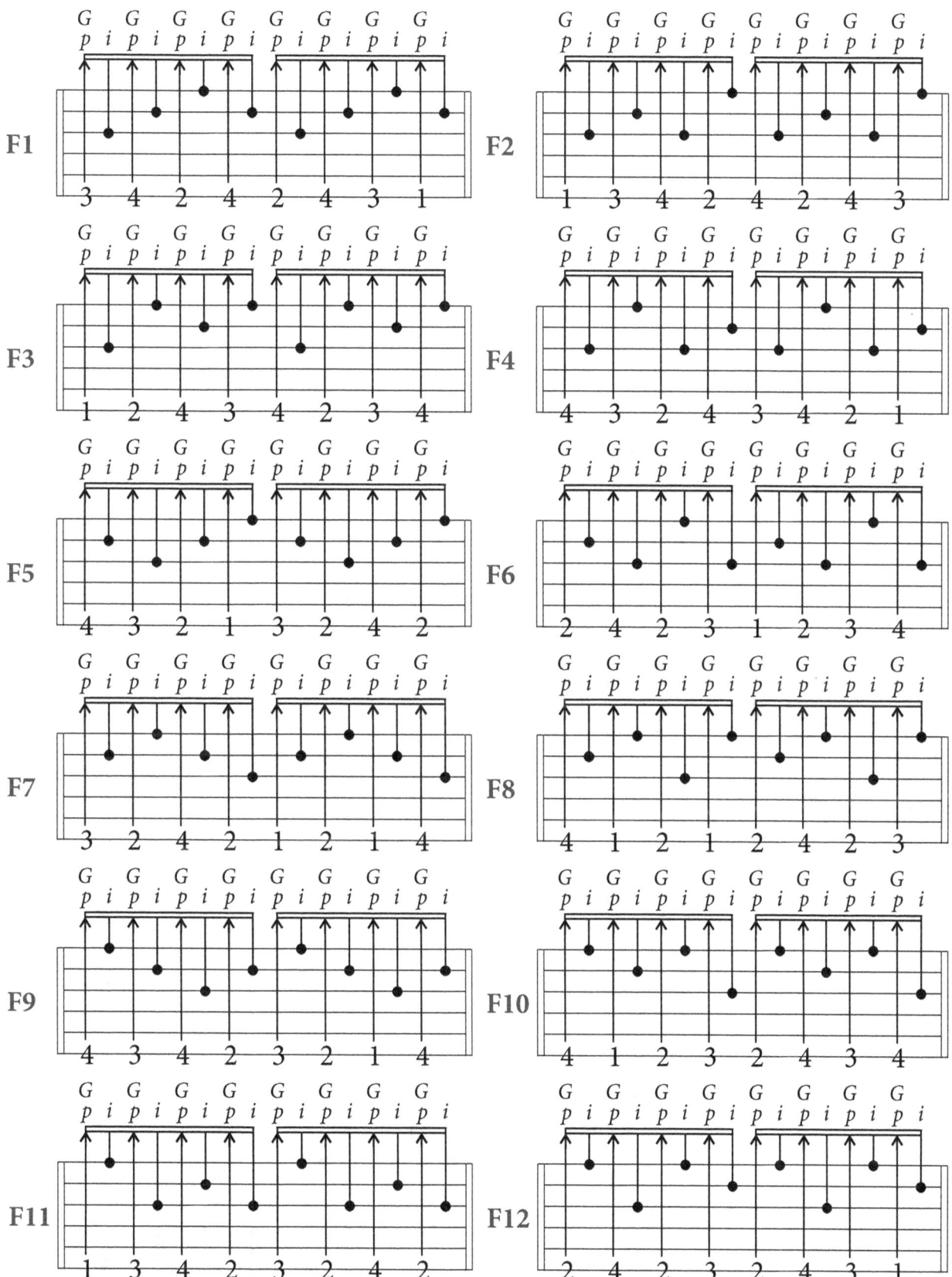

§ Ib

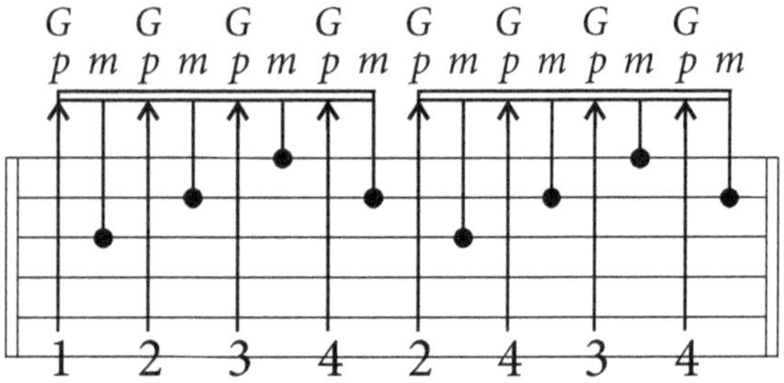

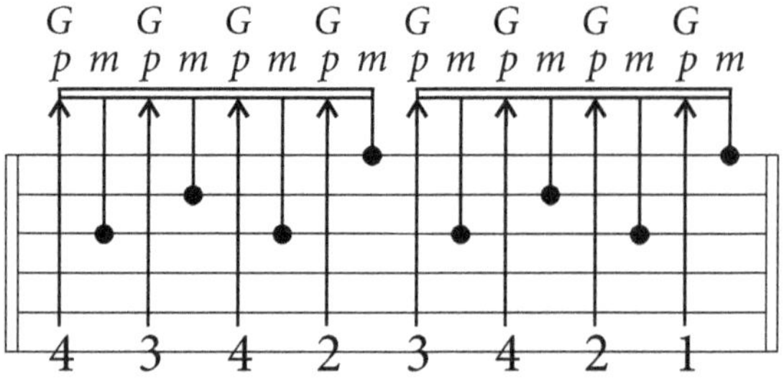

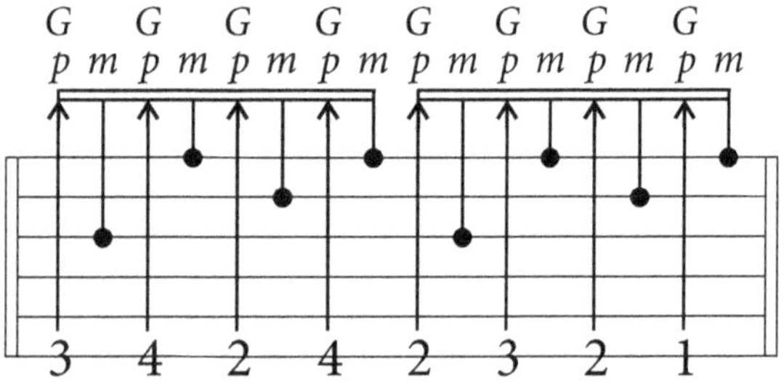

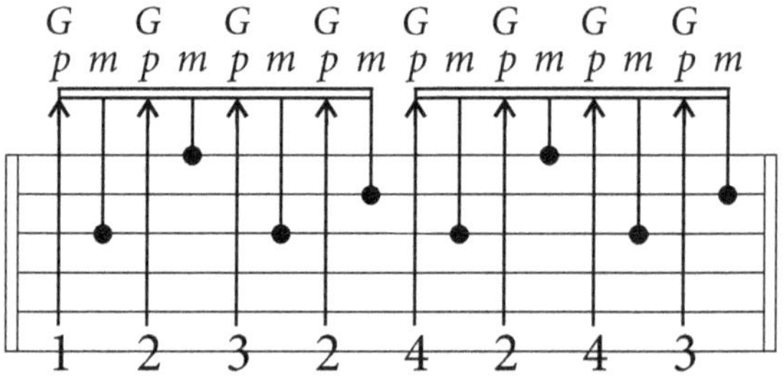

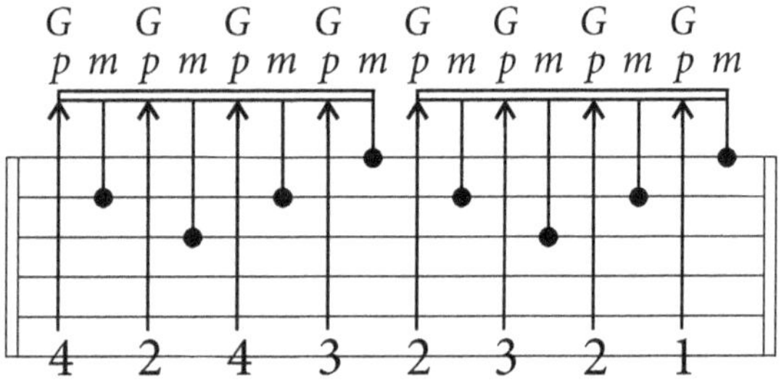

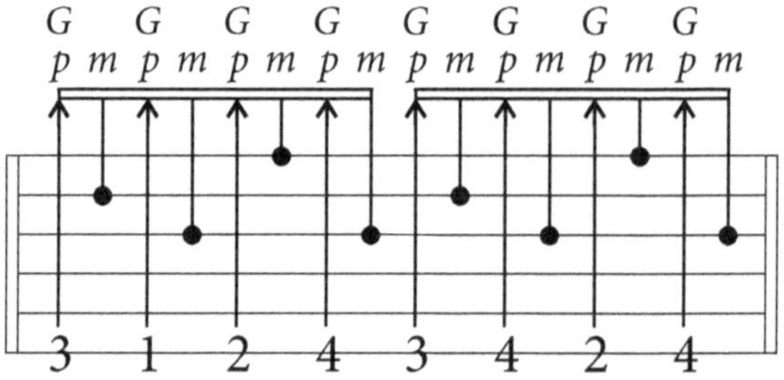

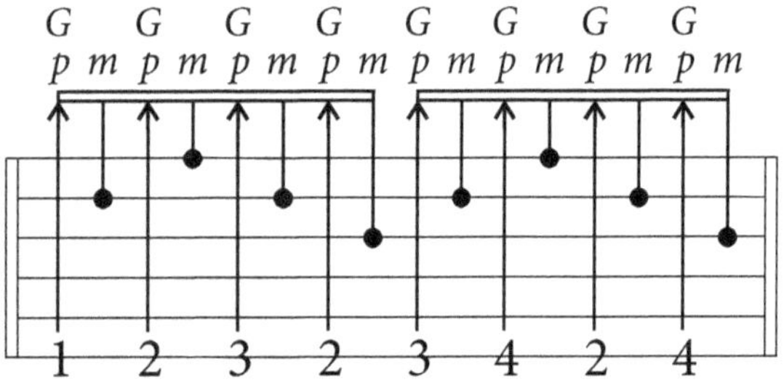

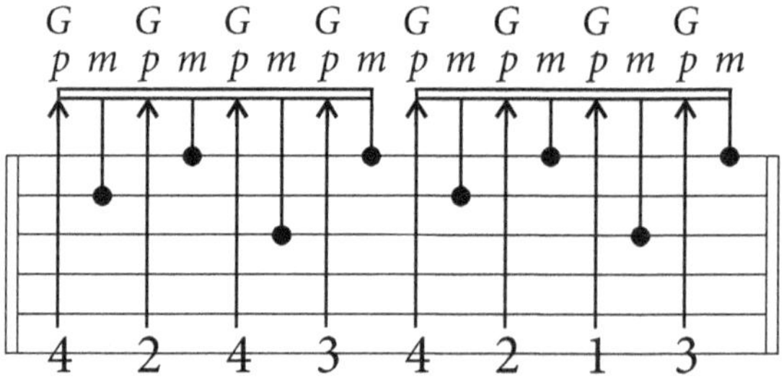

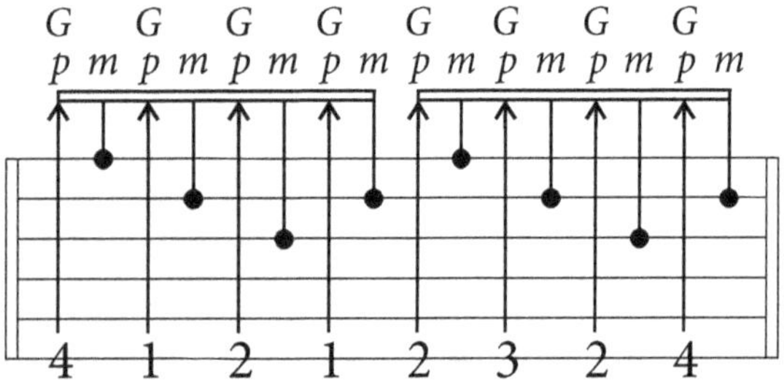

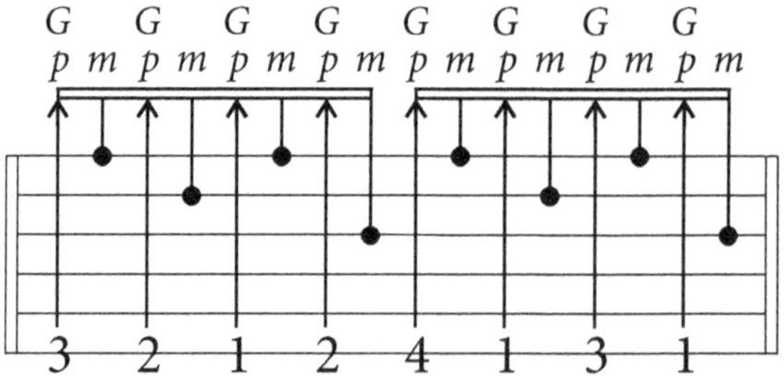

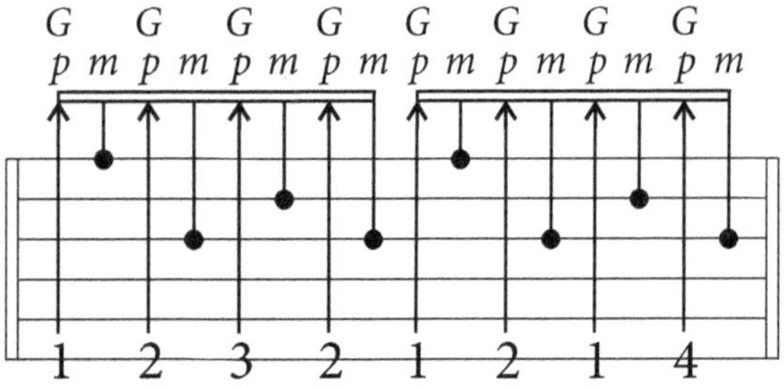

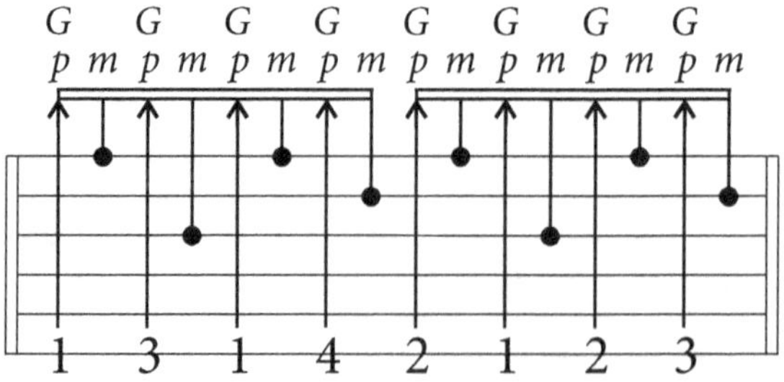

§ IIa

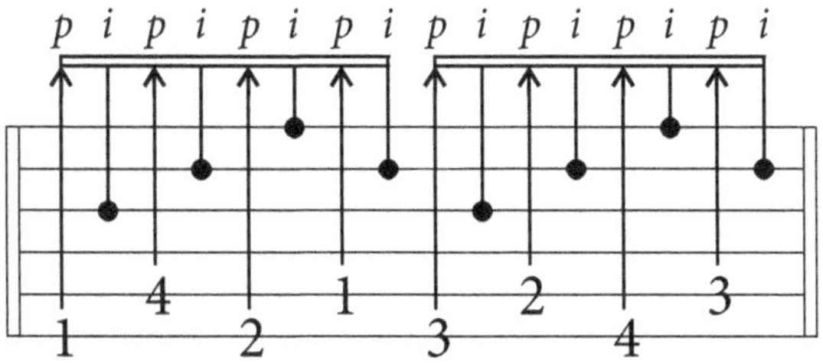
G G G G G G G G
p i p i p i p i p i p i p i p i
4 1 2 3
1 2 3 4

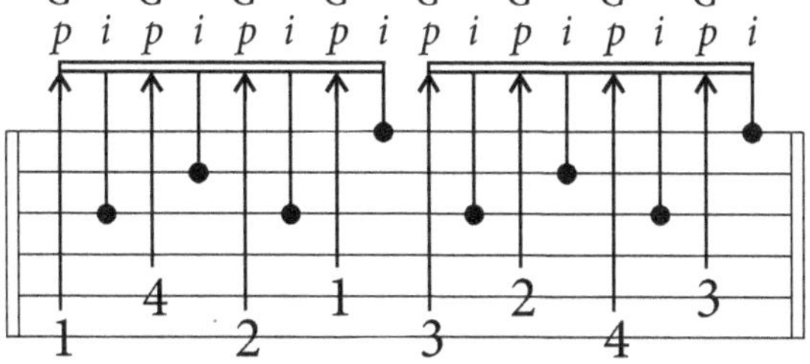
G G G G G G G G
p i p i p i p i p i p i p i p i
4 1 2 3
1 2 3 4

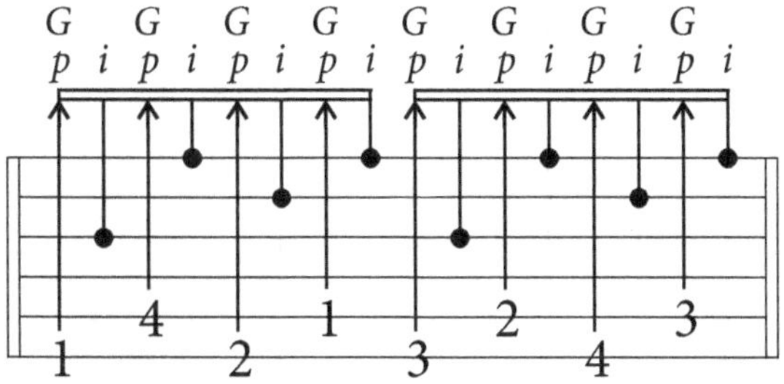
G G G G G G G G
p i p i p i p i p i p i p i p i
4 1 2 3
1 2 3 4

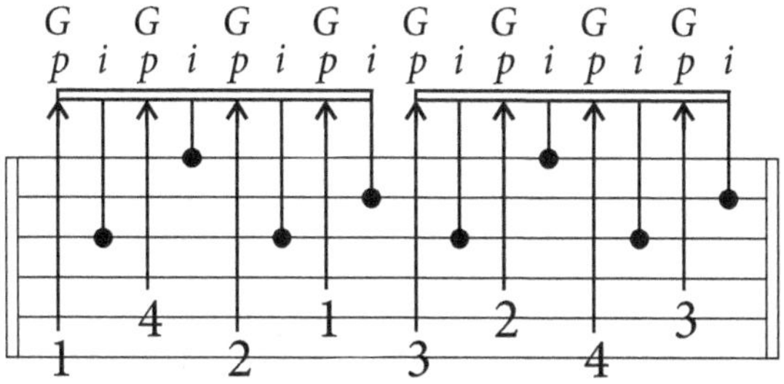
G G G G G G G G
p i p i p i p i p i p i p i p i
4 1 2 3
1 2 3 4

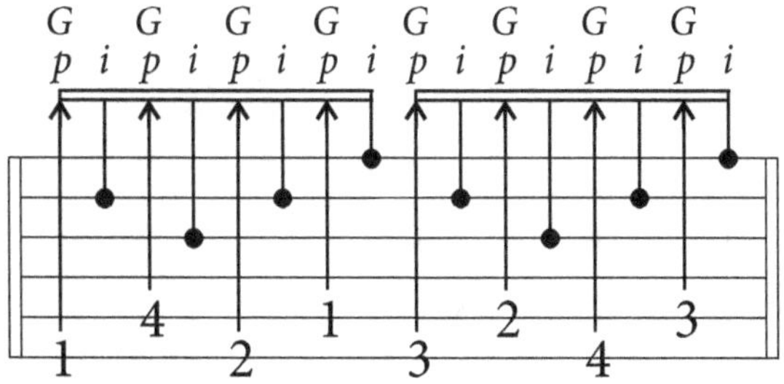
G G G G G G G G
p i p i p i p i p i p i p i p i
4 1 2 3
1 2 3 4

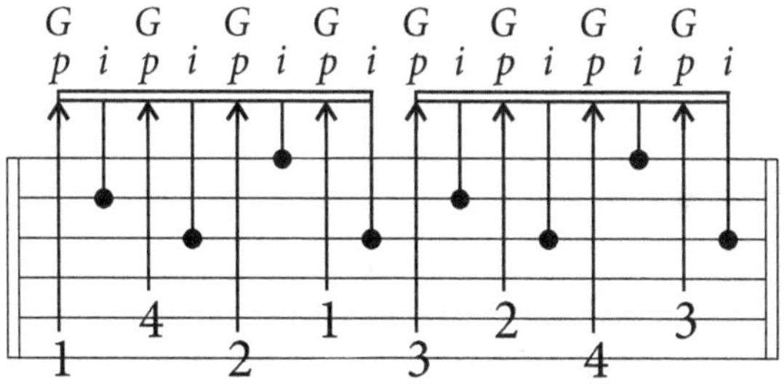
G G G G G G G G
p i p i p i p i p i p i p i p i
4 1 2 3
1 2 3 4

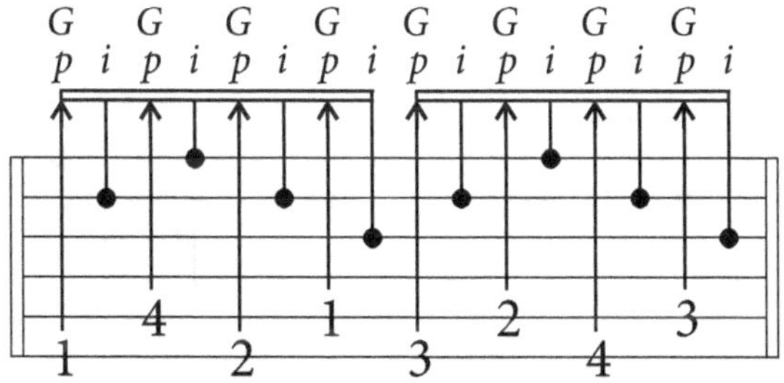
G G G G G G G G
p i p i p i p i p i p i p i p i
4 1 2 3
1 2 3 4

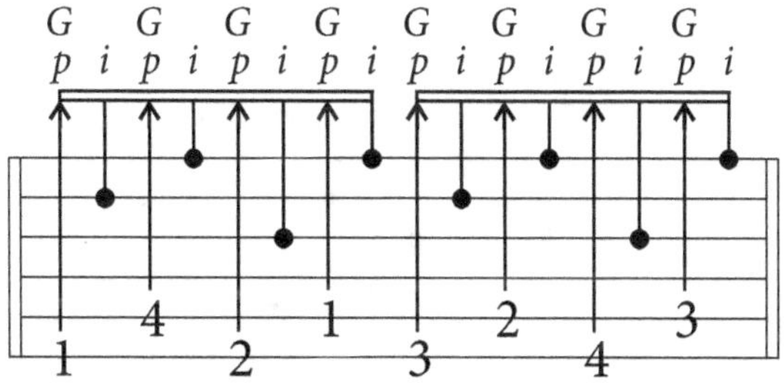
G G G G G G G G
p i p i p i p i p i p i p i p i
4 1 2 3
1 2 3 4

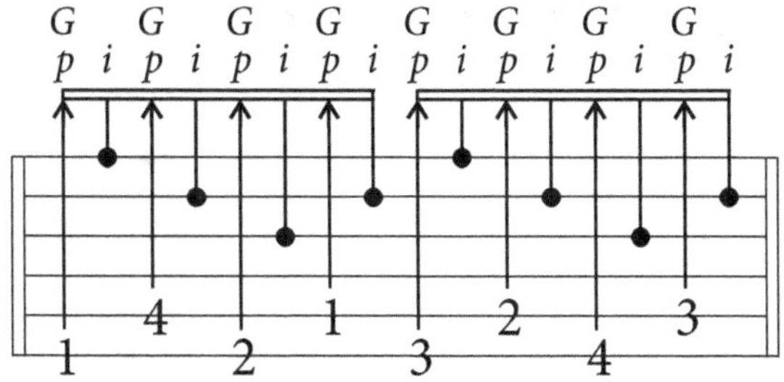
G G G G G G G G
p i p i p i p i p i p i p i p i
4 1 2 3
1 2 3 4

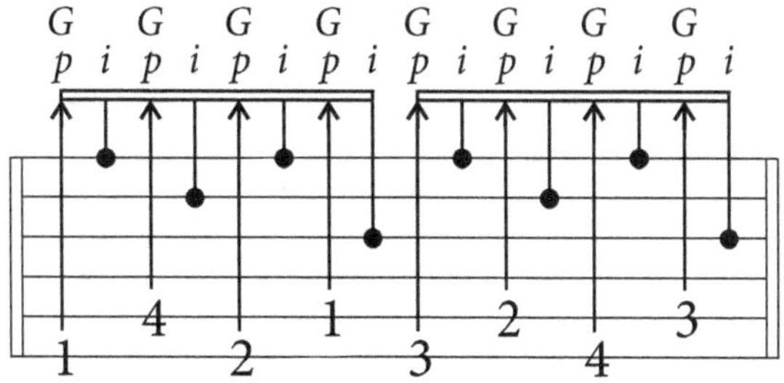
G G G G G G G G
p i p i p i p i p i p i p i p i
4 1 2 3
1 2 3 4

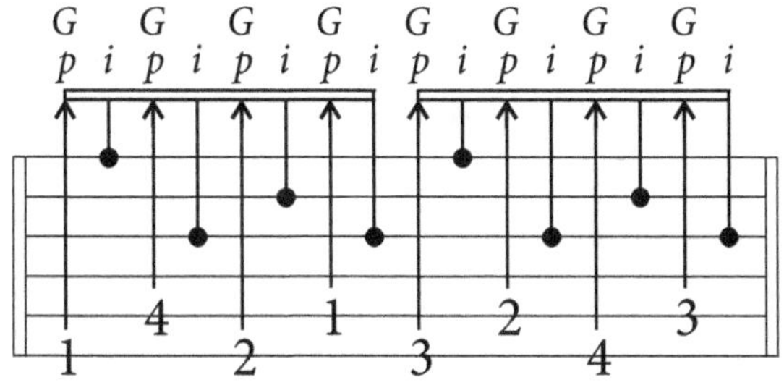
G G G G G G G G
p i p i p i p i p i p i p i p i
4 1 2 3
1 2 3 4

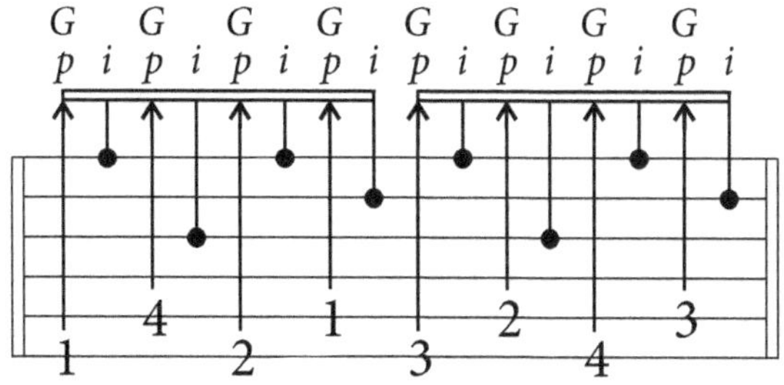
G G G G G G G G
p i p i p i p i p i p i p i p i
4 1 2 3
1 2 3 4

§ IIb

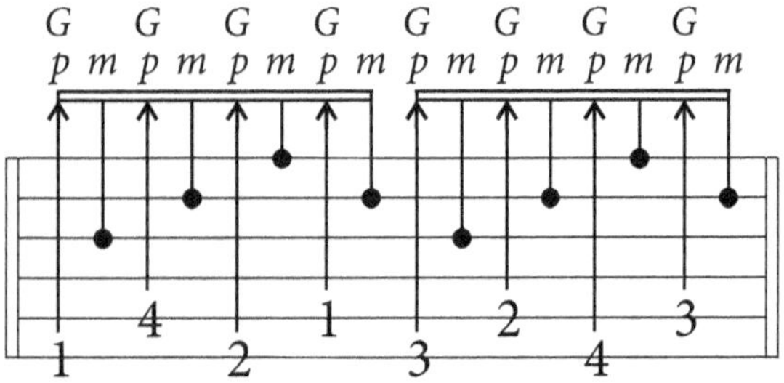

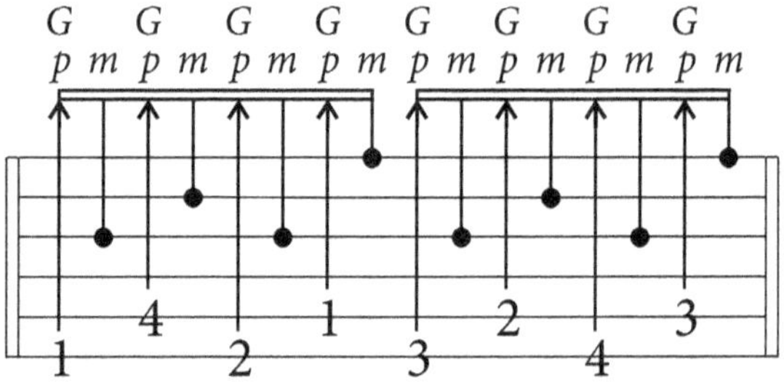

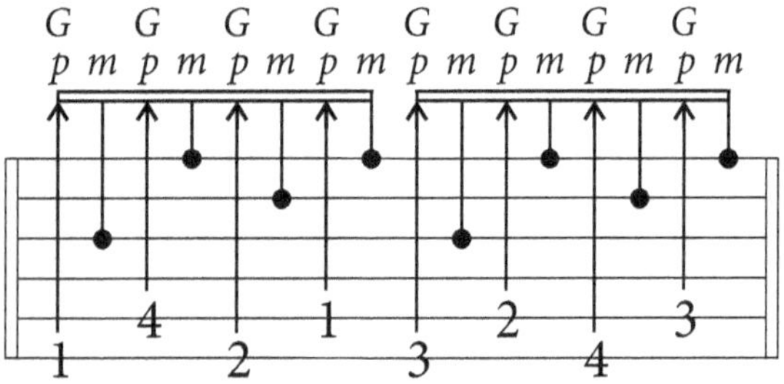

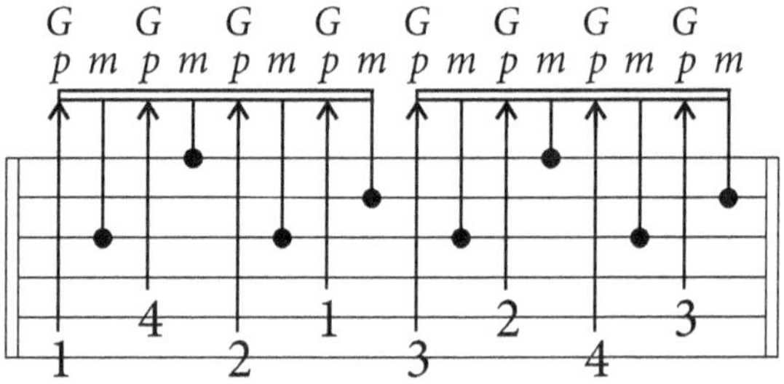

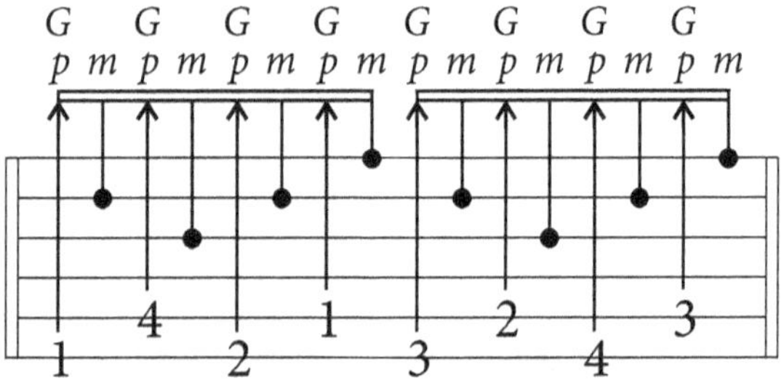

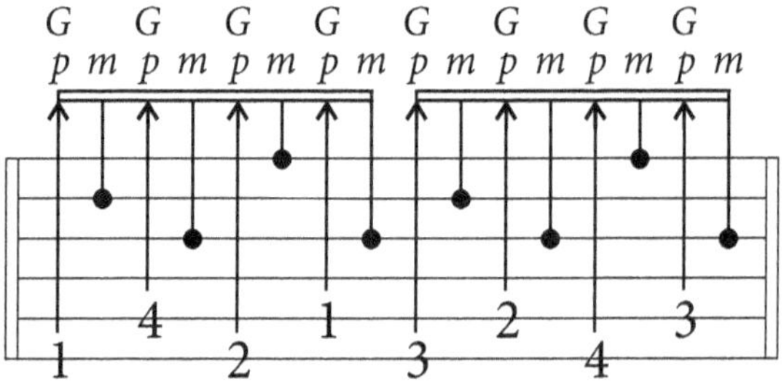

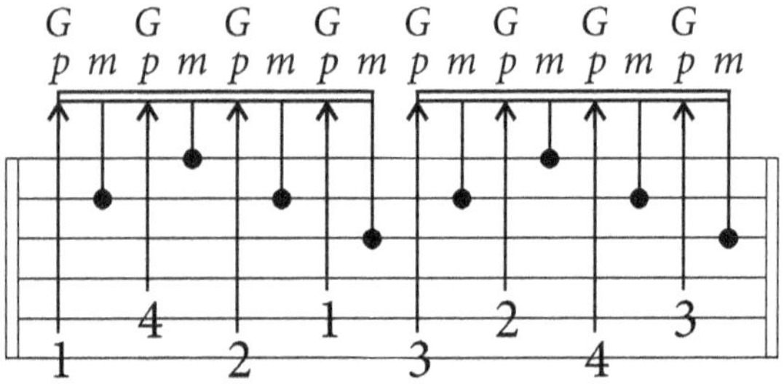

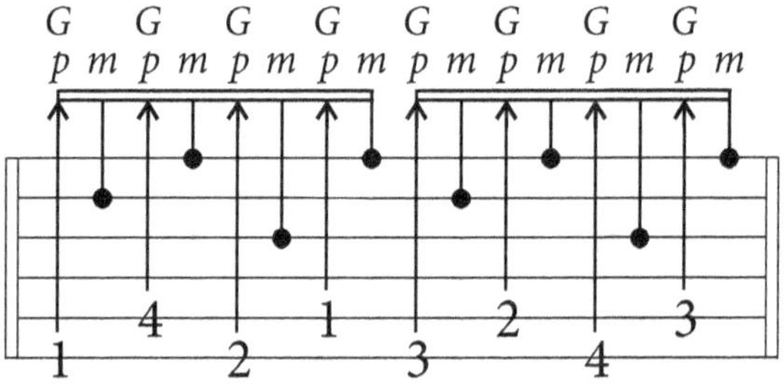

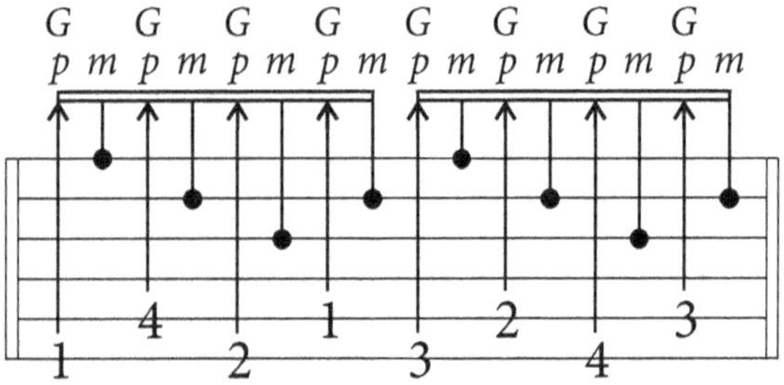

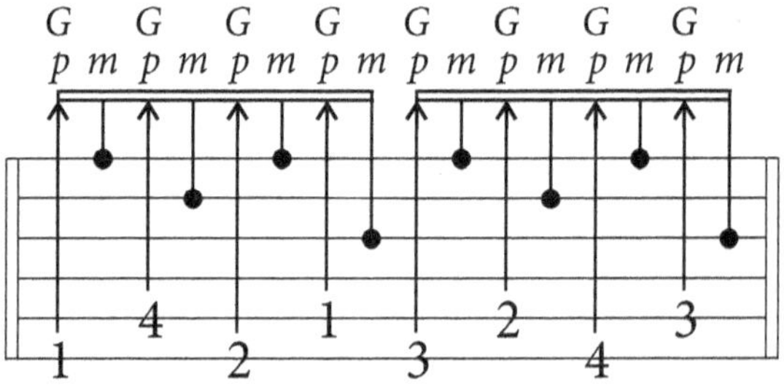

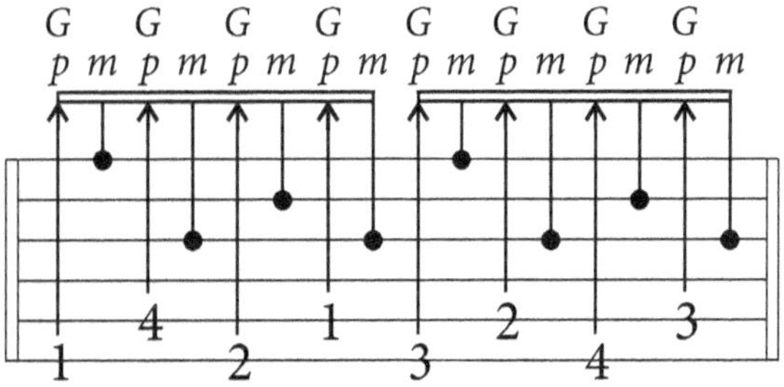

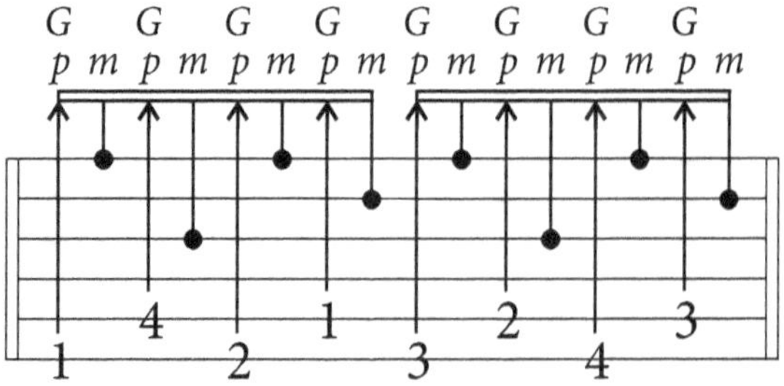

§ IIIa

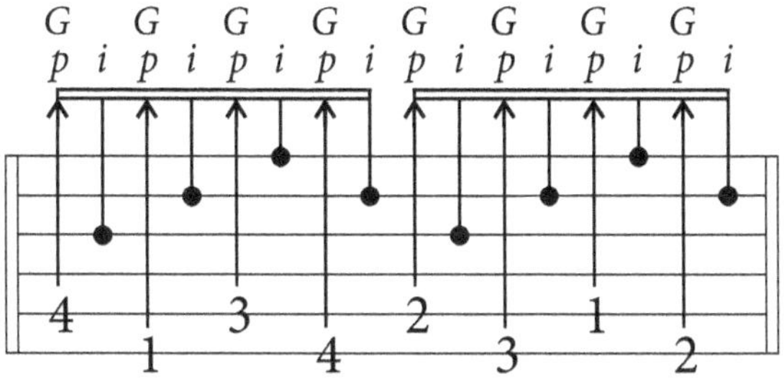

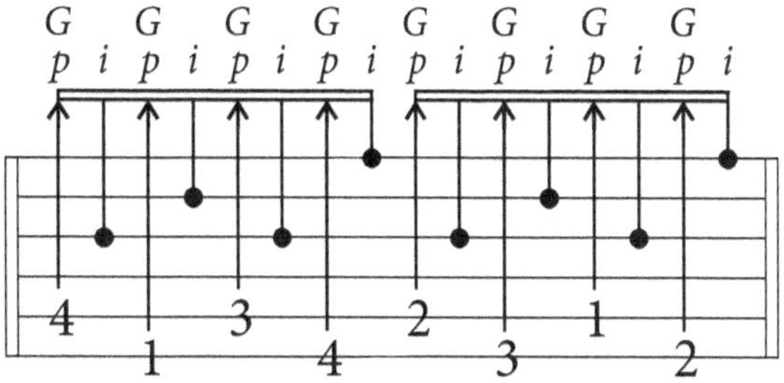

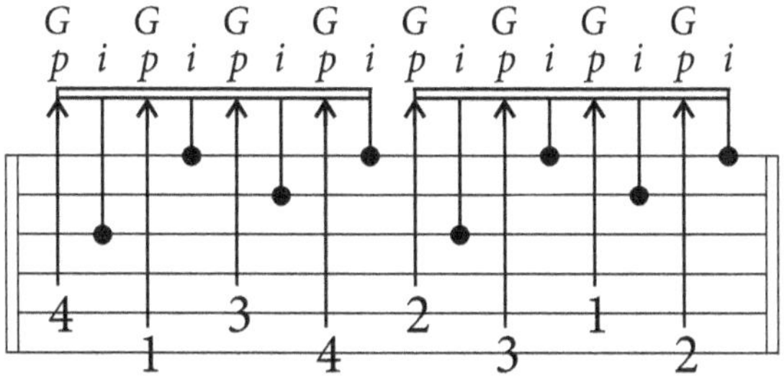

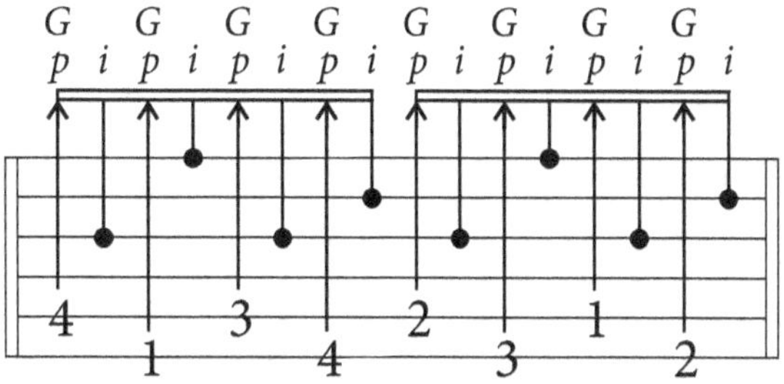

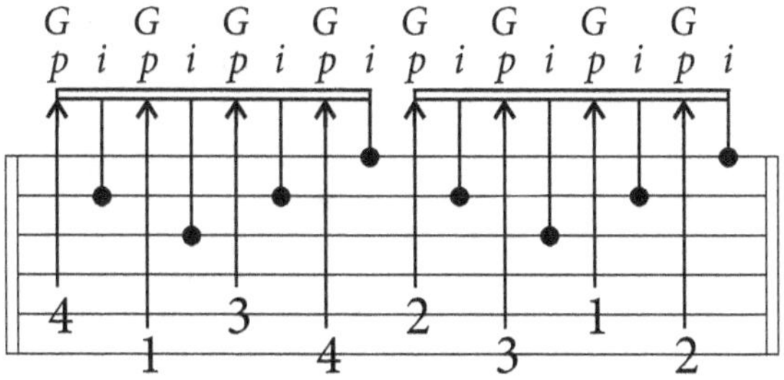

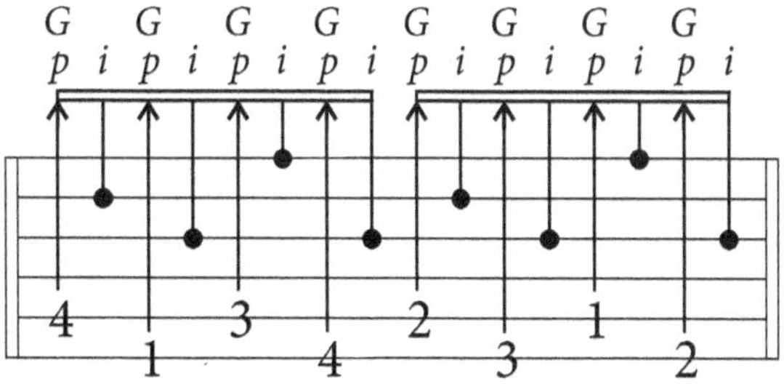

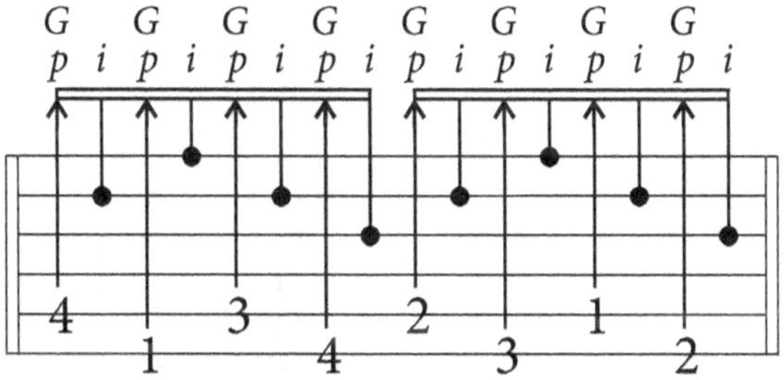

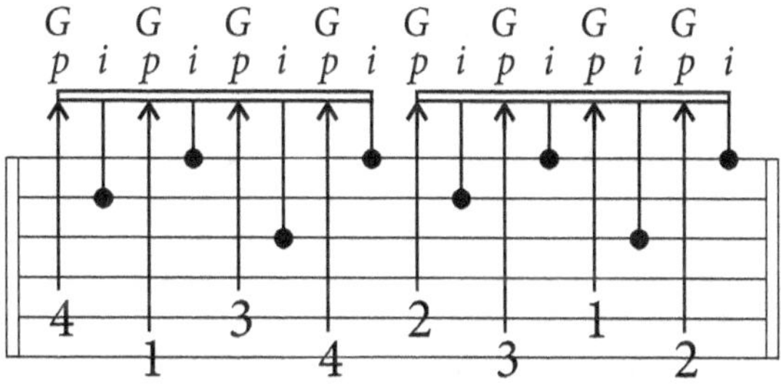

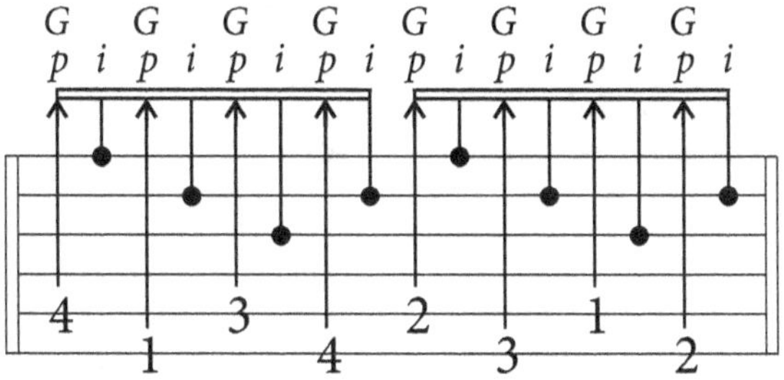

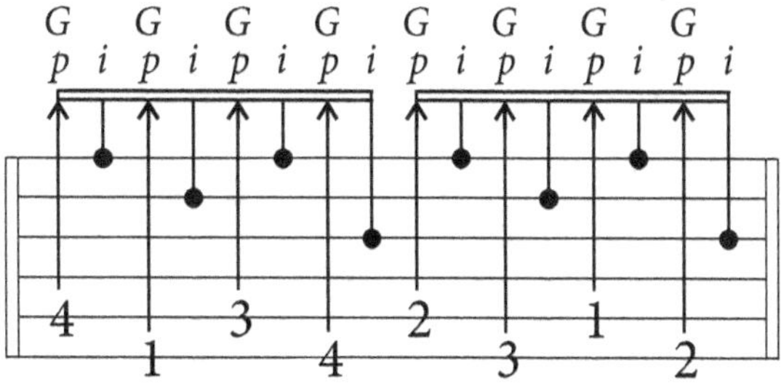

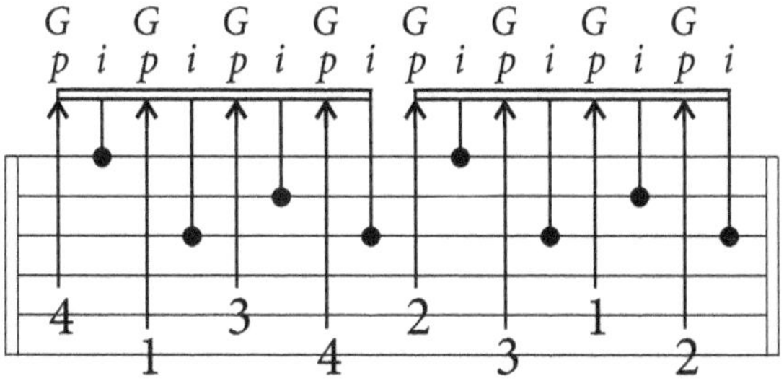

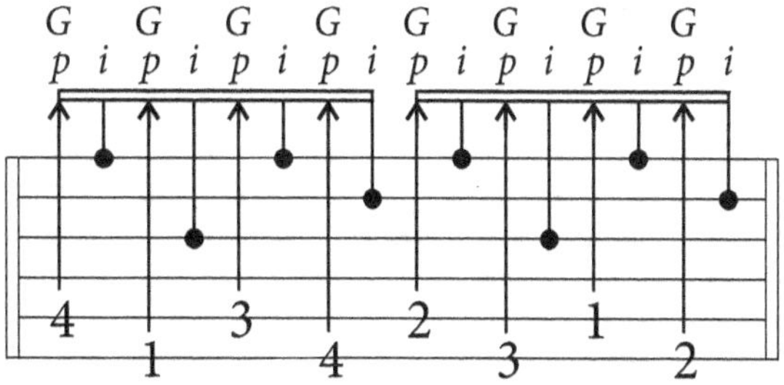

§ IIIb

F1

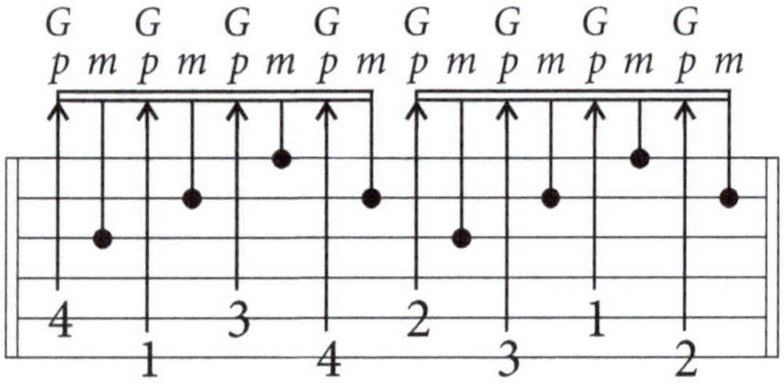

F2

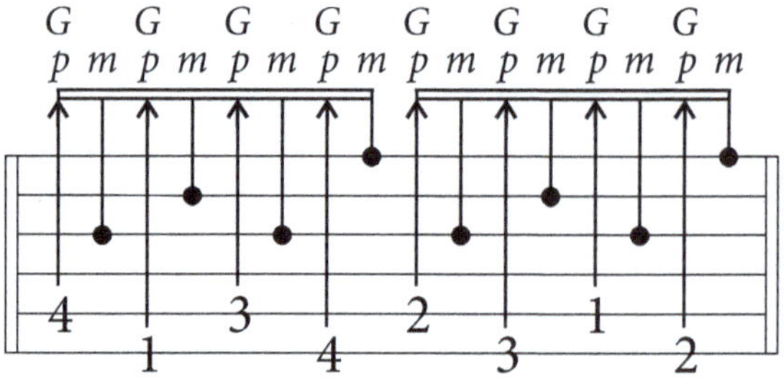

F3

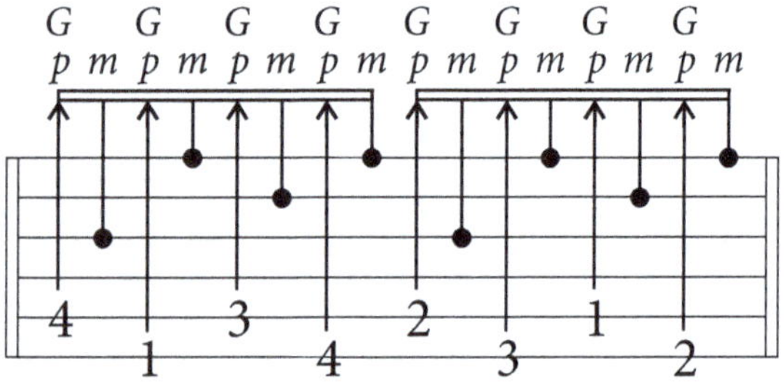

F4

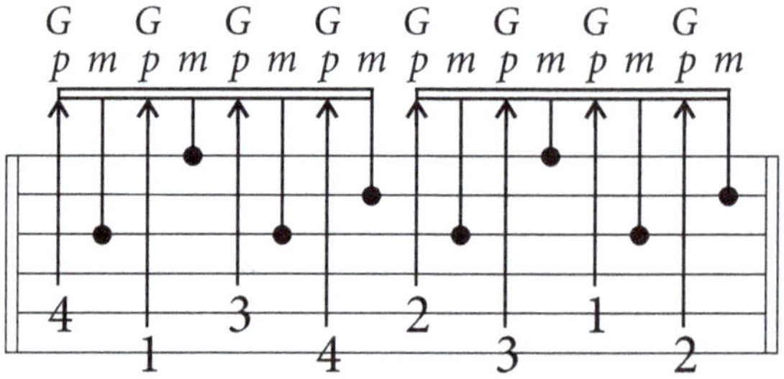

F5

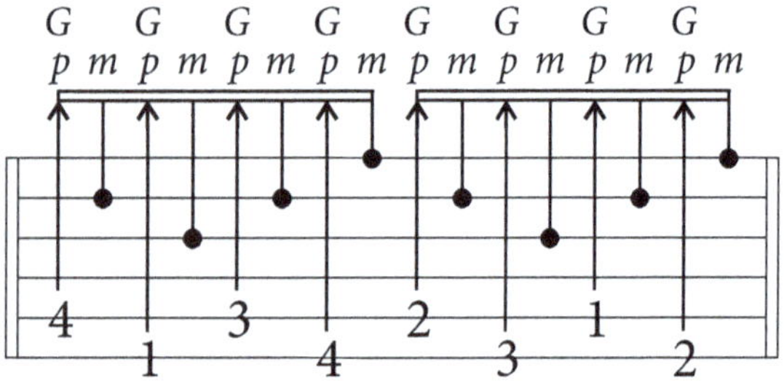

F6

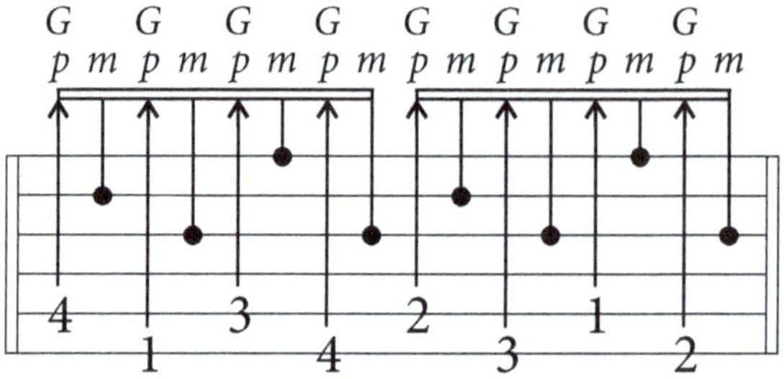

F7

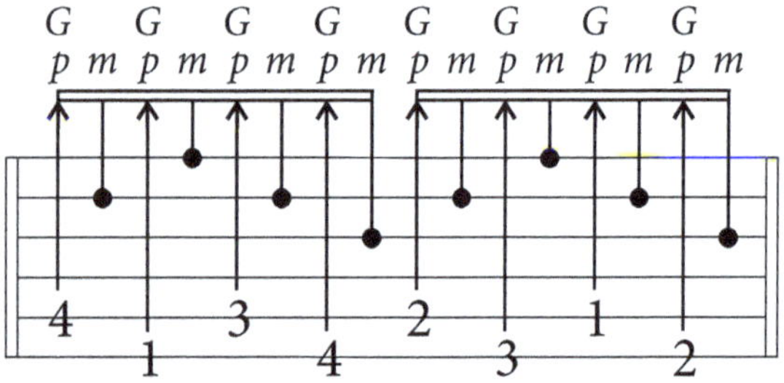

F8

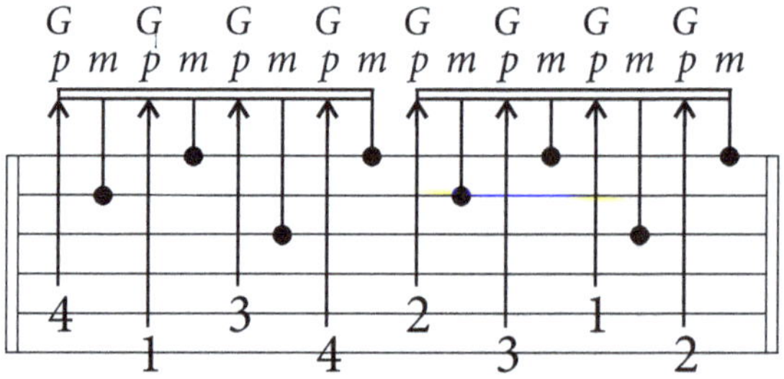

F9

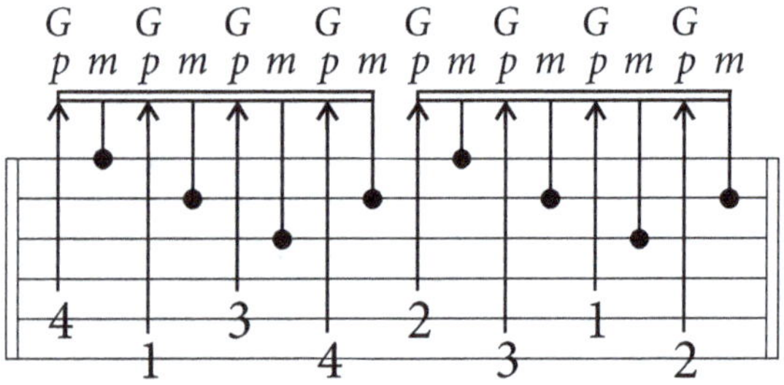

F10

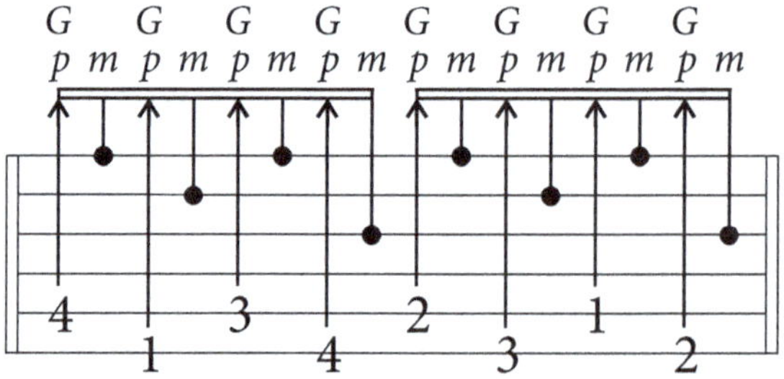

F11

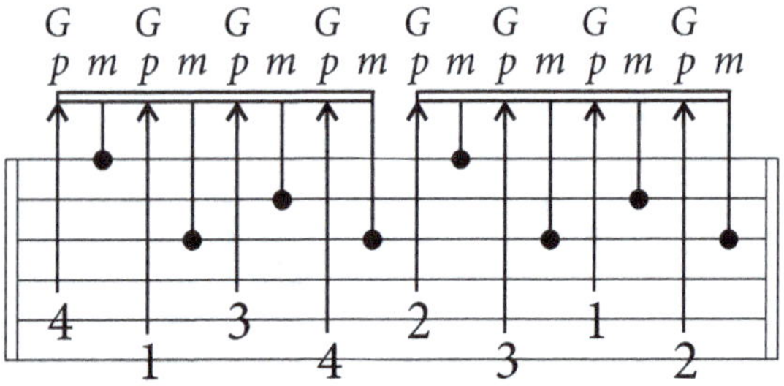

F12

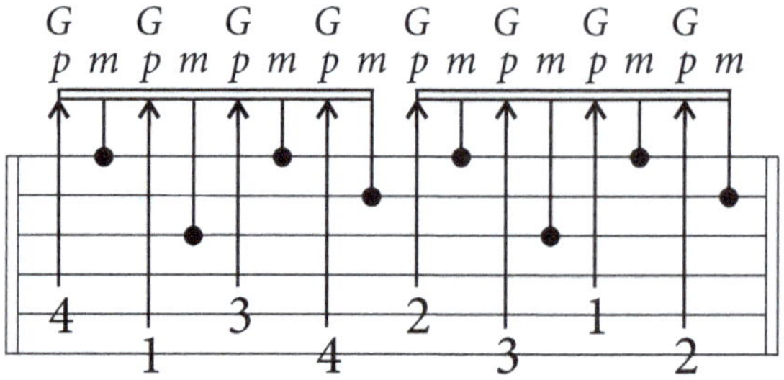

§ IVa

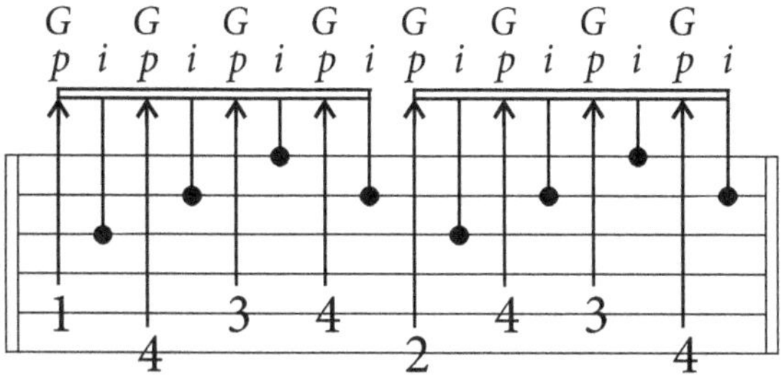

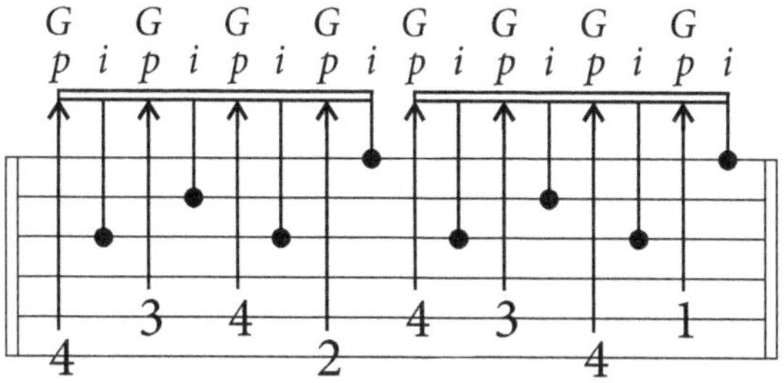

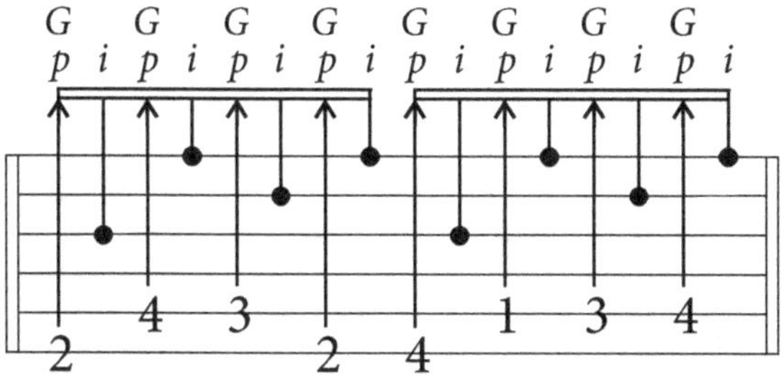

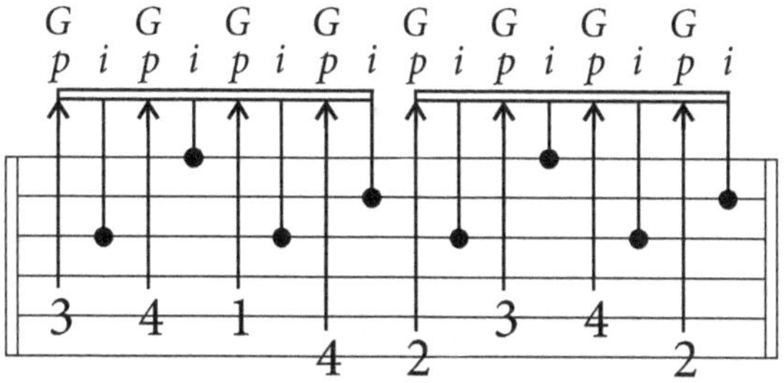

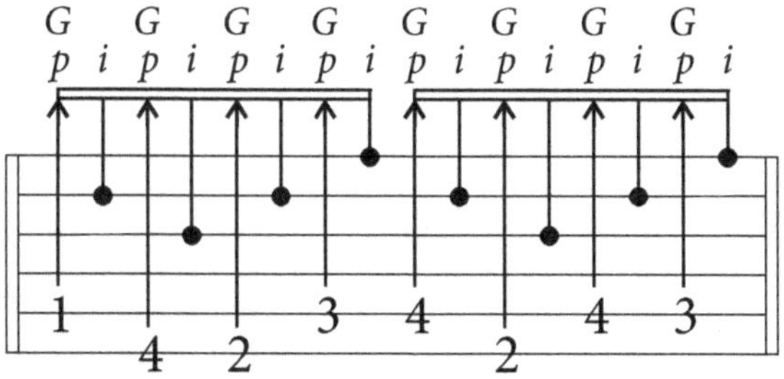

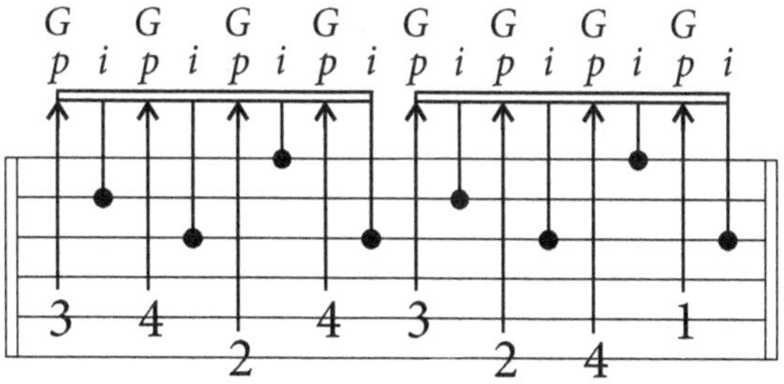

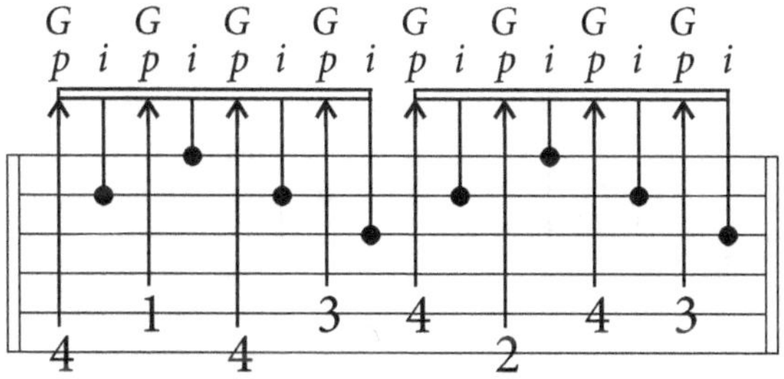

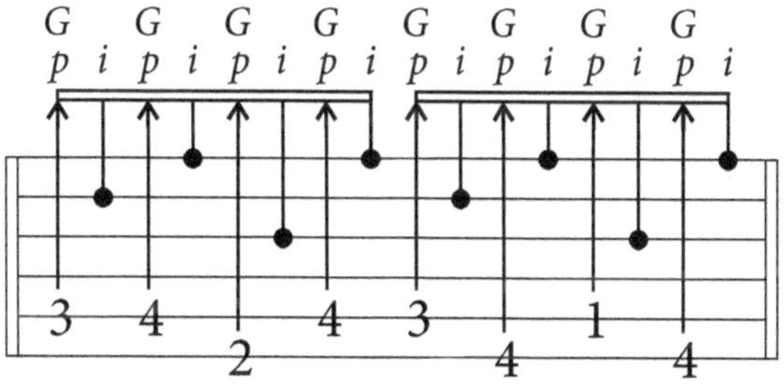

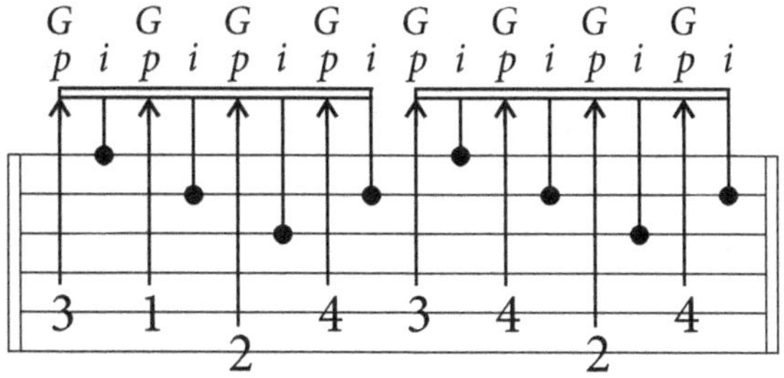

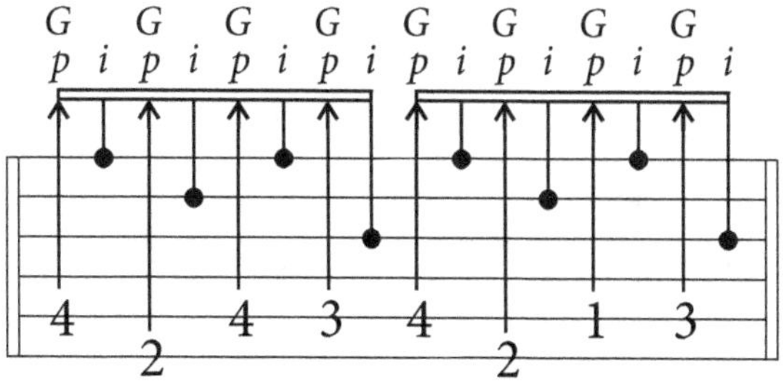

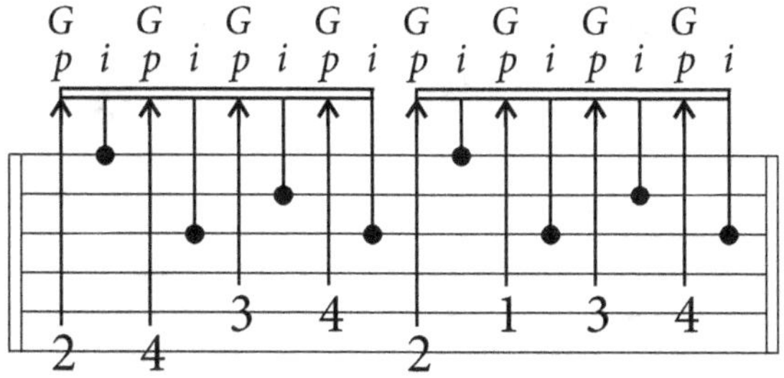

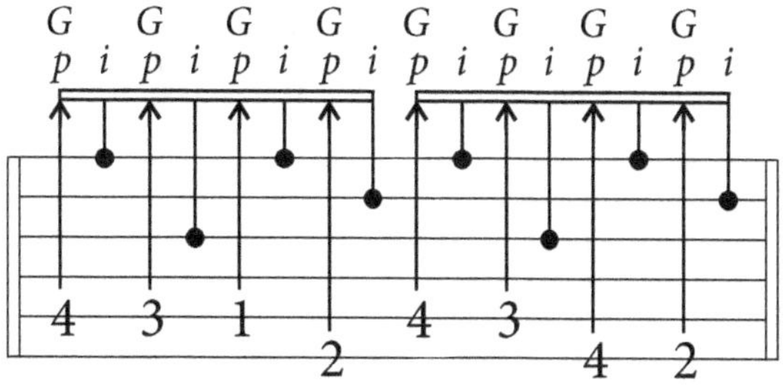

§ IVb

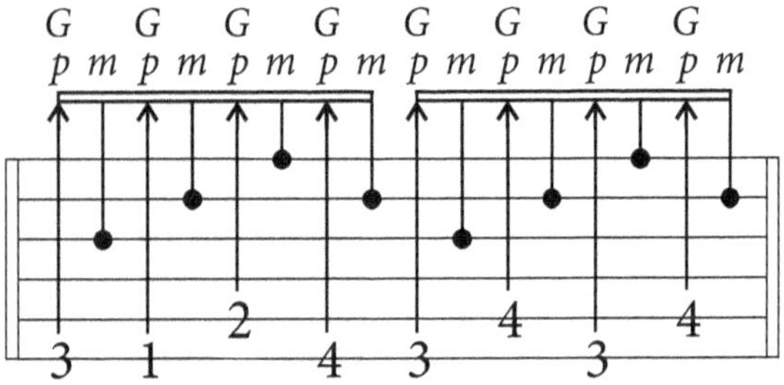

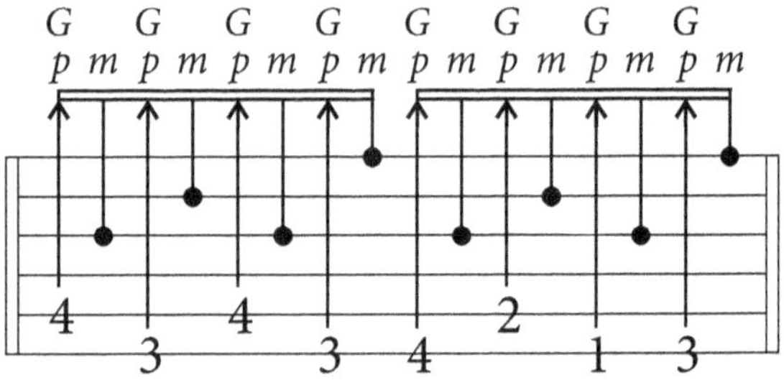

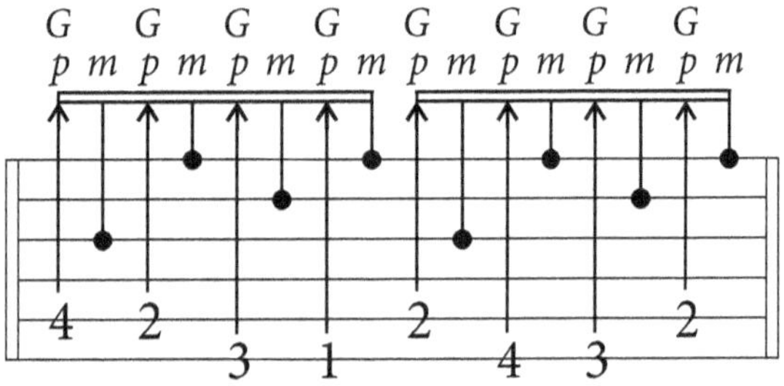

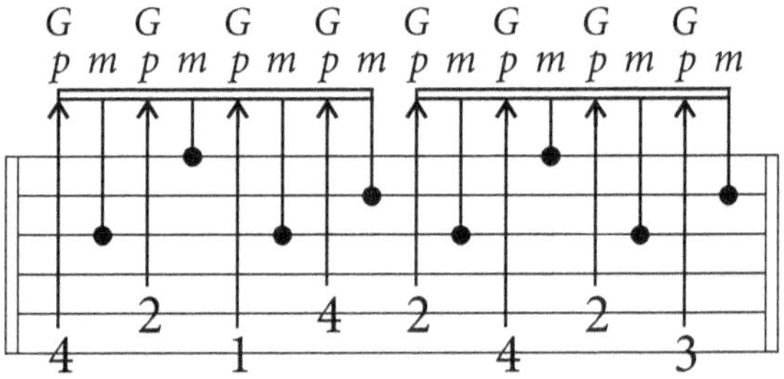

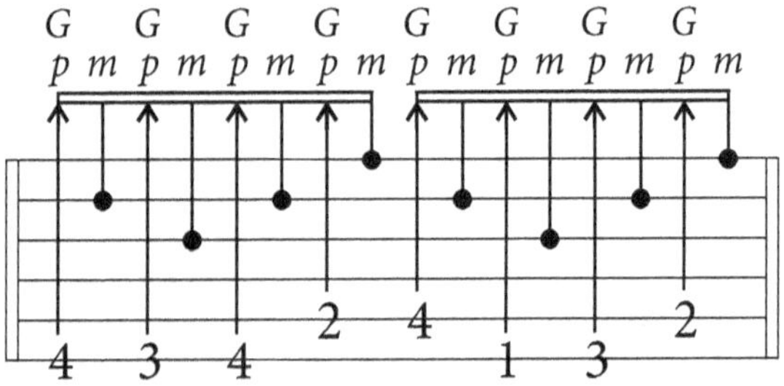

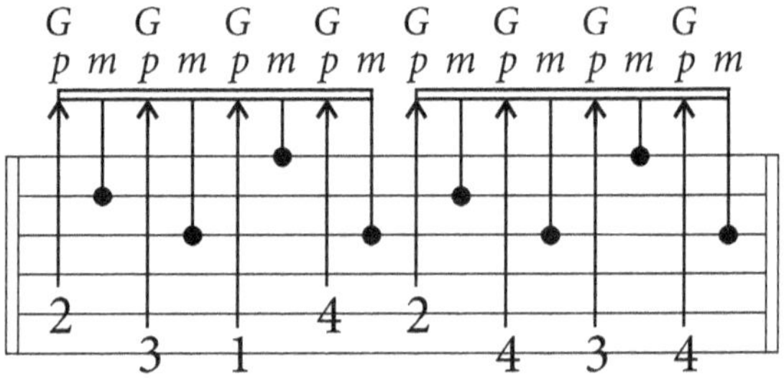

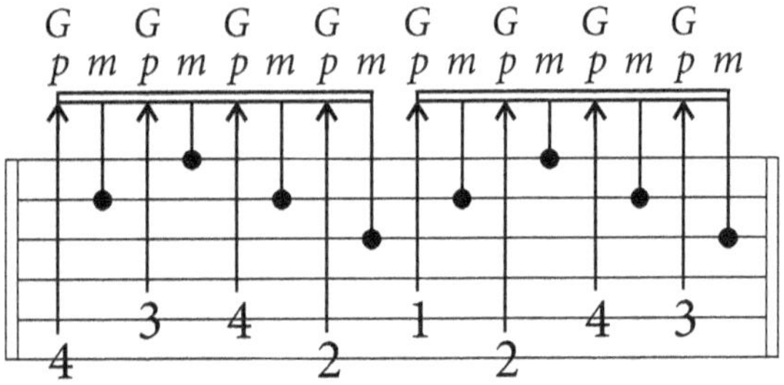

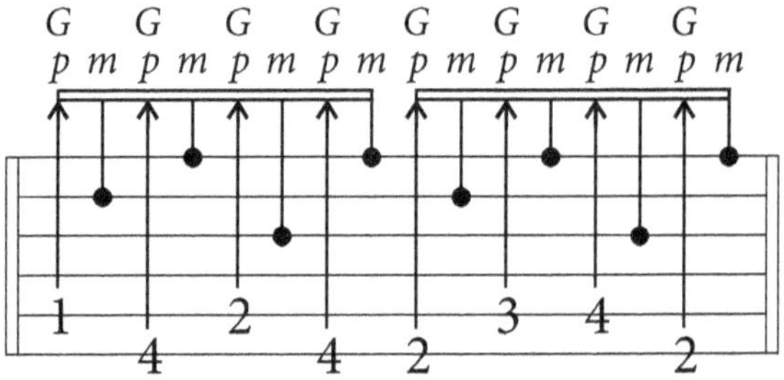

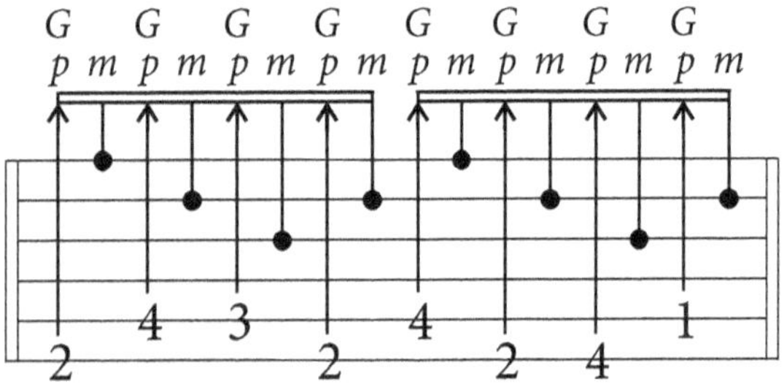

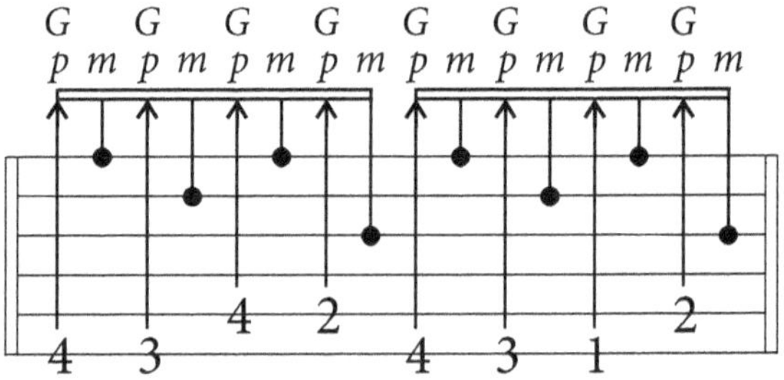

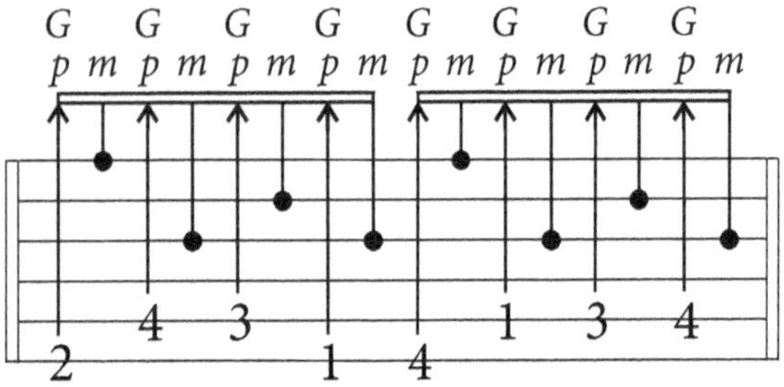

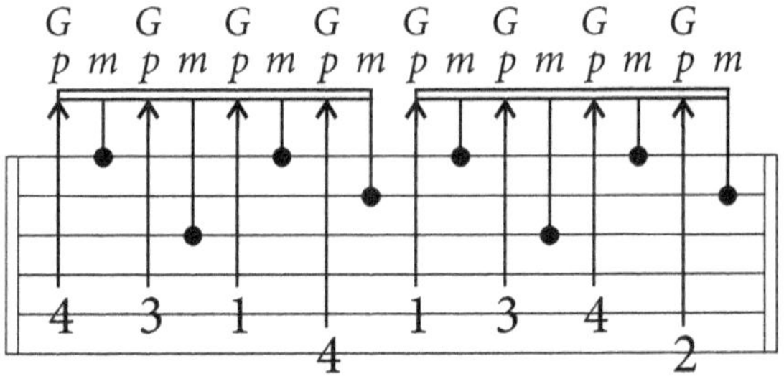

UNIT 2

Simultaneous stroke of thumb with index,
or middle finger with Golpe on:

1/. Chromatic scales of one string.

2/. Ascending rolling Formulas.

3/. Descending rolling Formulas.

4/. Scales of two adjacent strings.

§ Ia
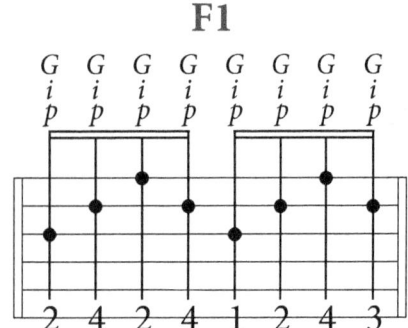

§ Ib
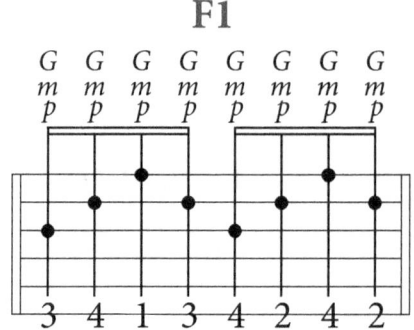

§ IIa
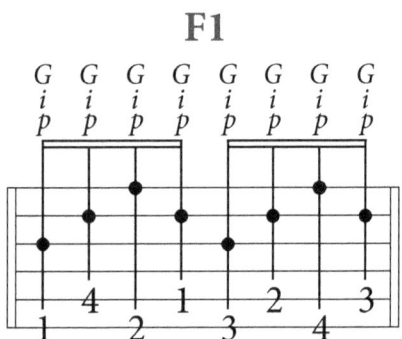

§ IIb
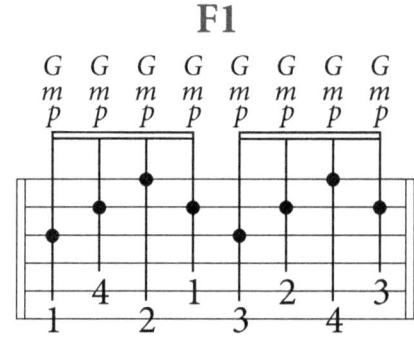

§ IIIa
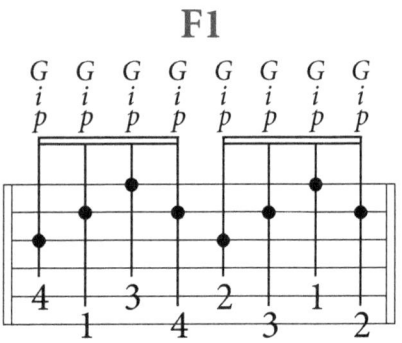

§ IIIb
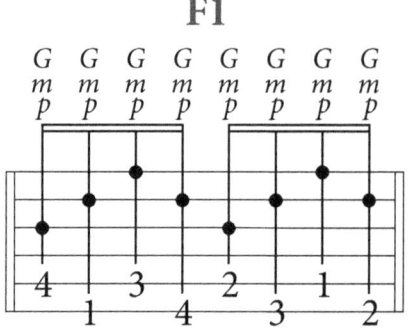

§ IVa
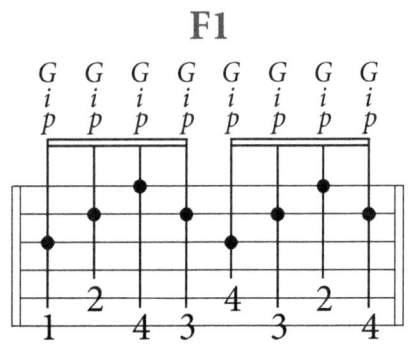

§ IVb
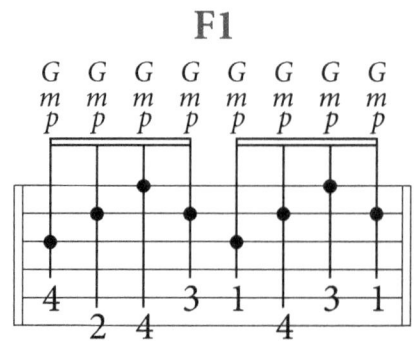

§ Ia

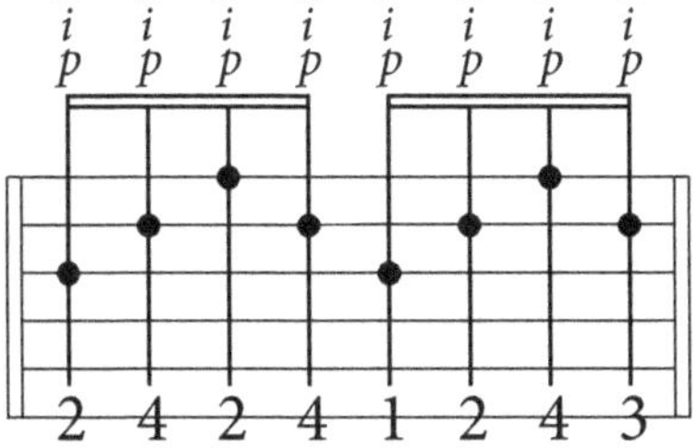

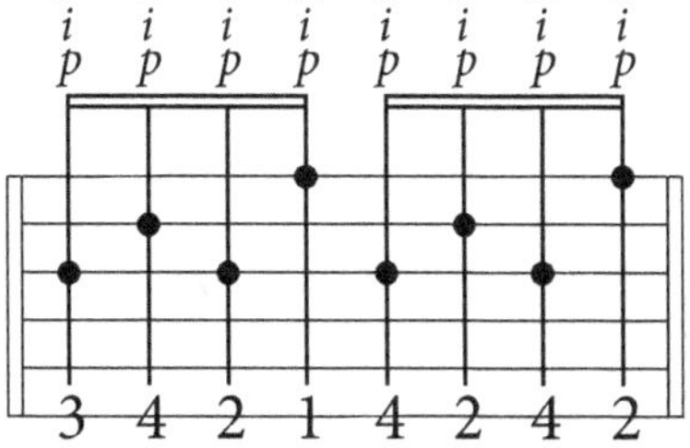

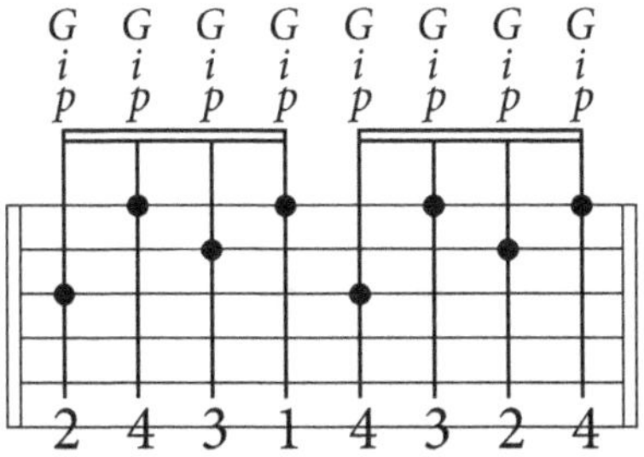

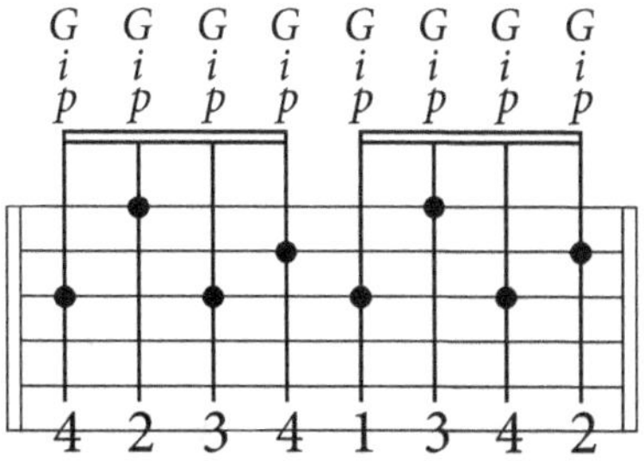

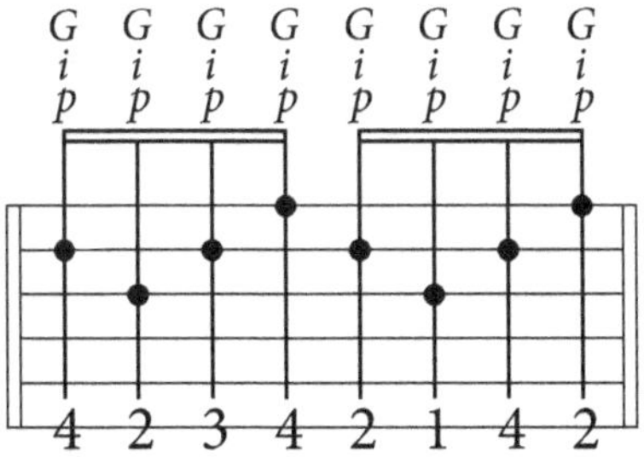

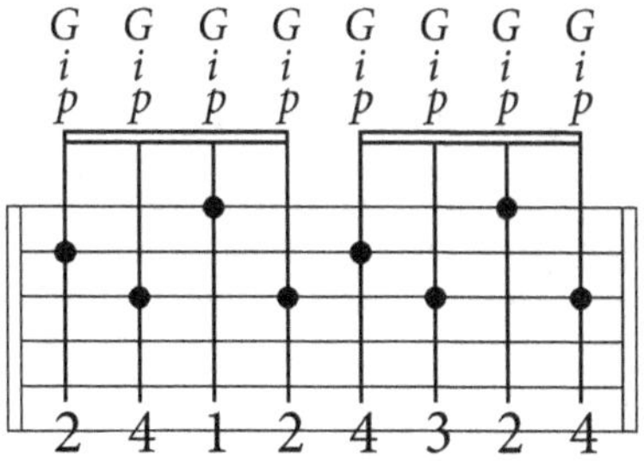

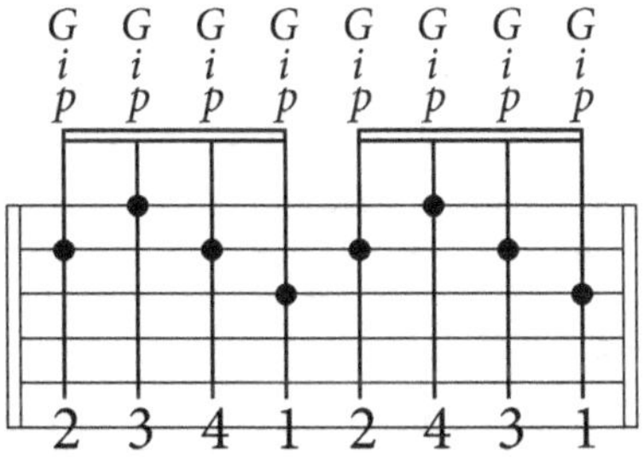

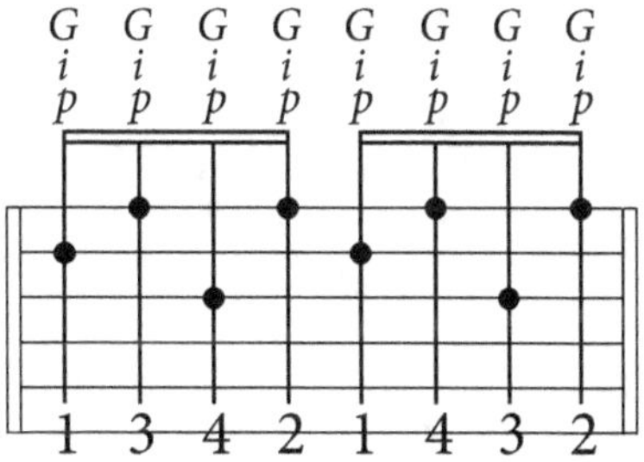

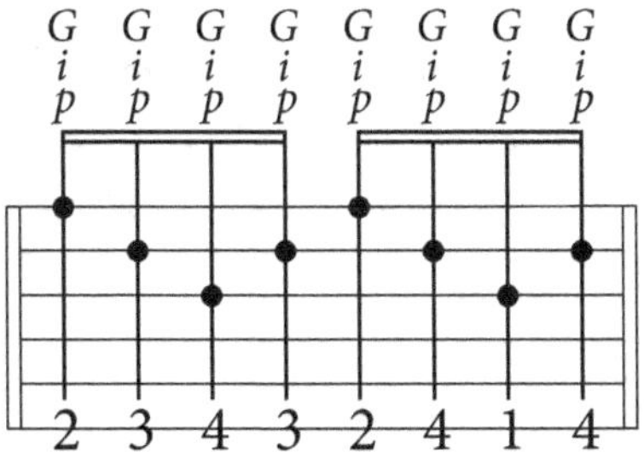

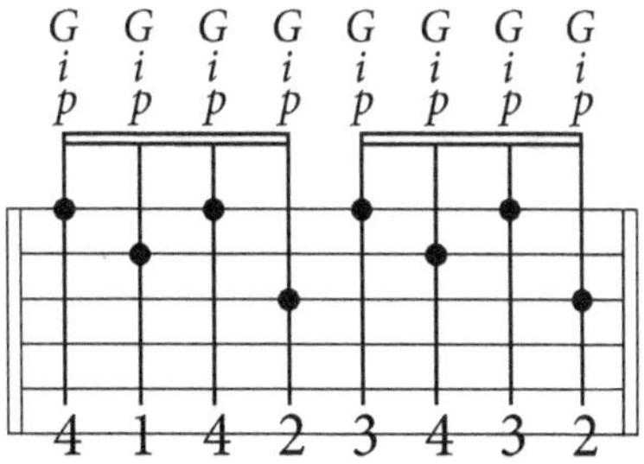

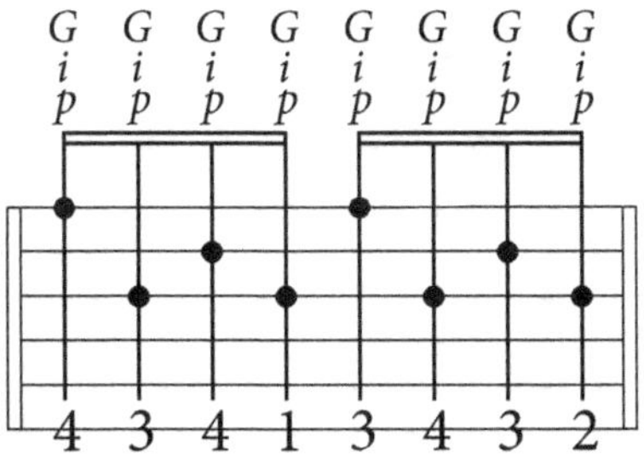

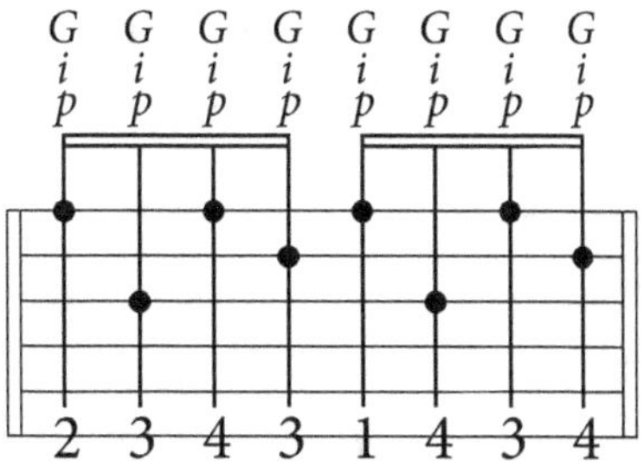

§ Ib

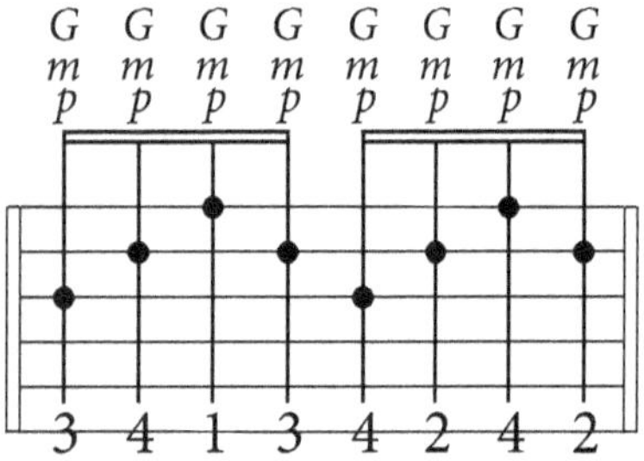

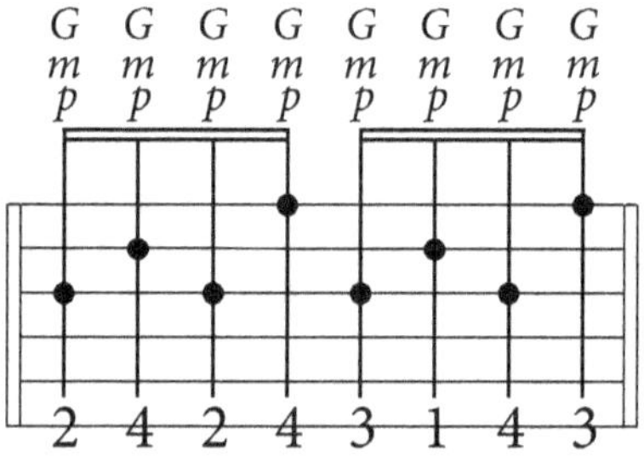

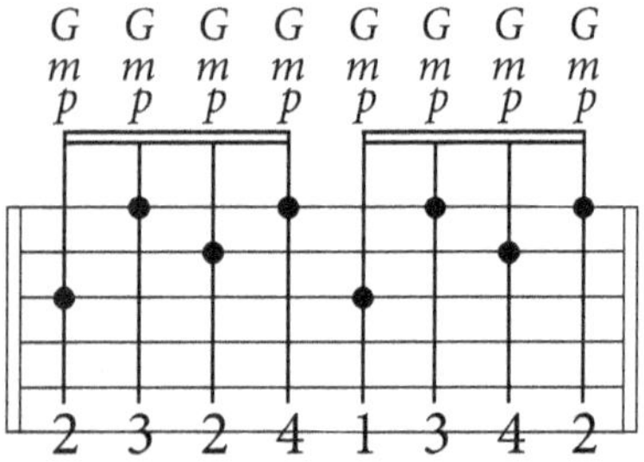

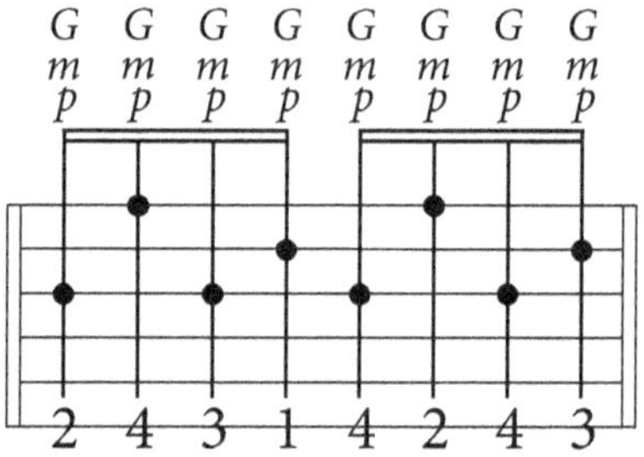

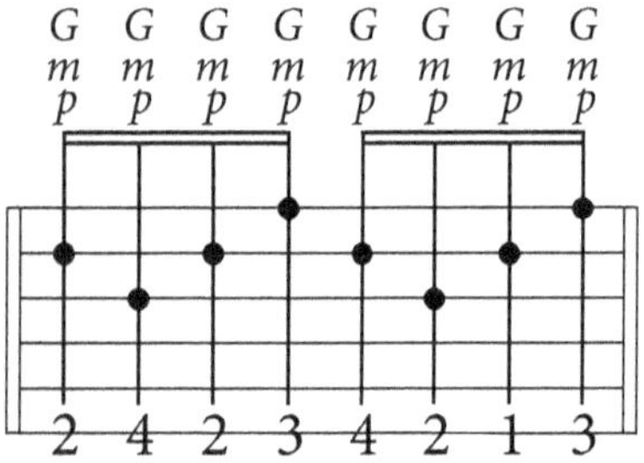

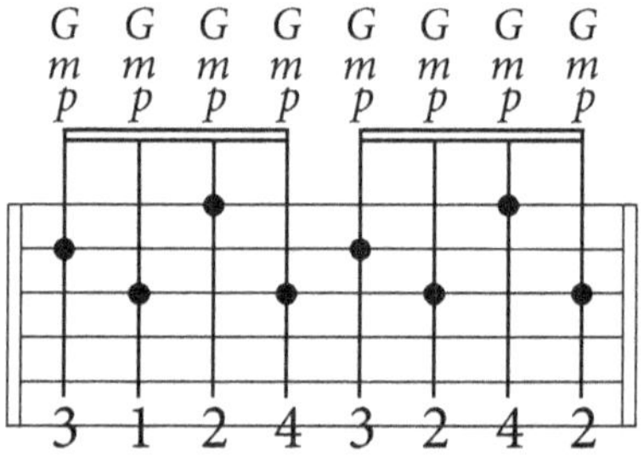

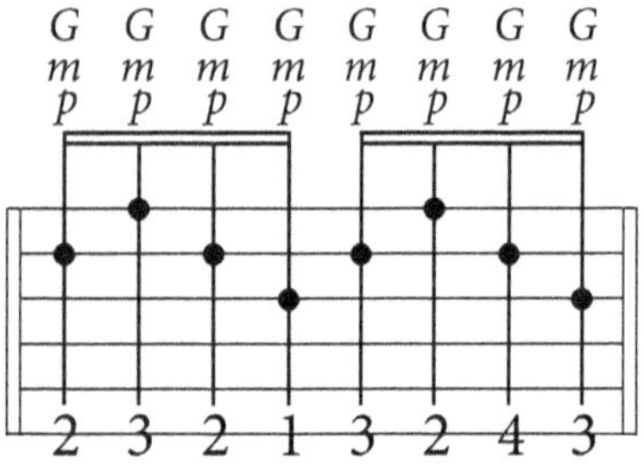

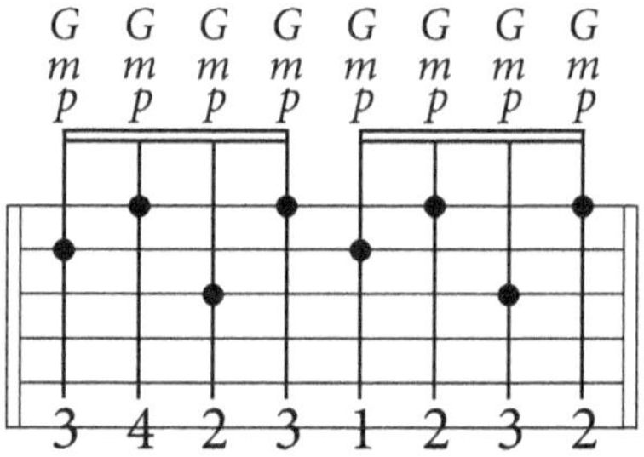

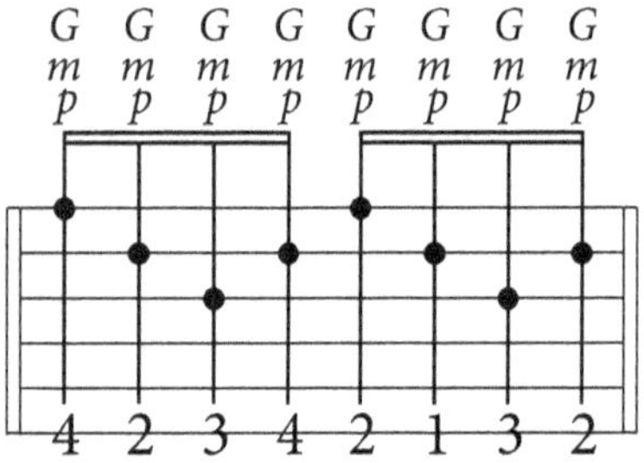

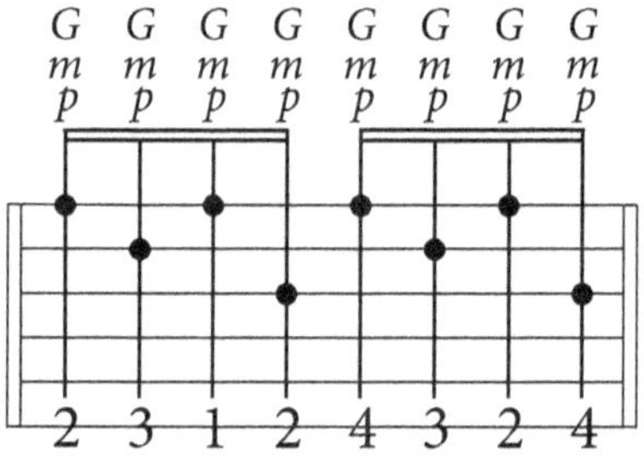

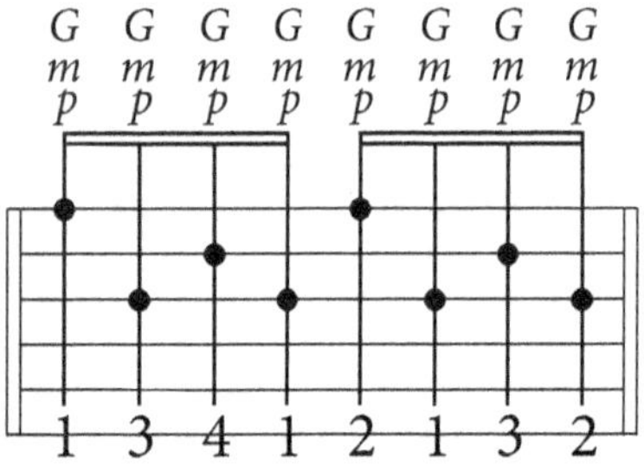

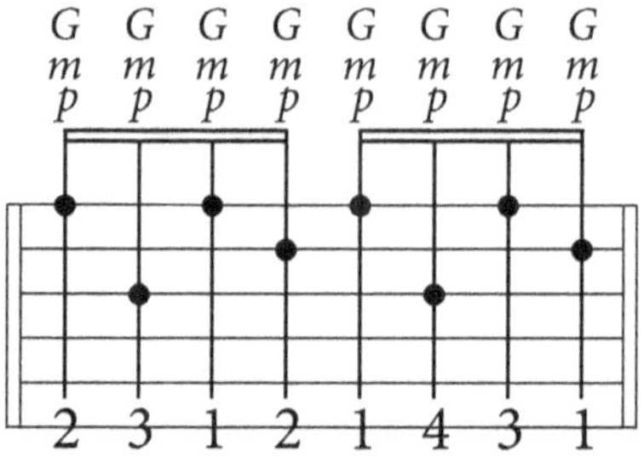

§ IIa

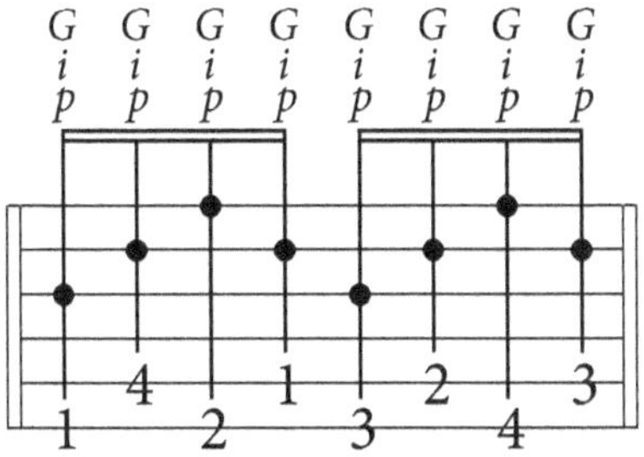

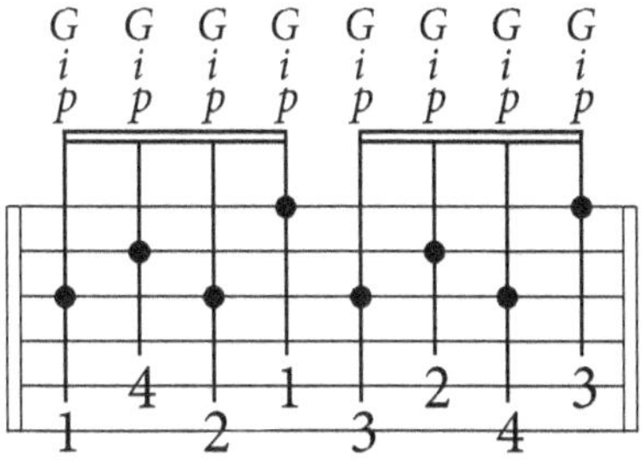

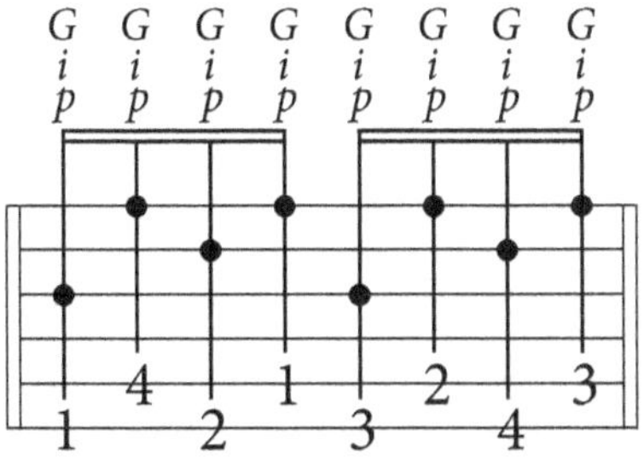

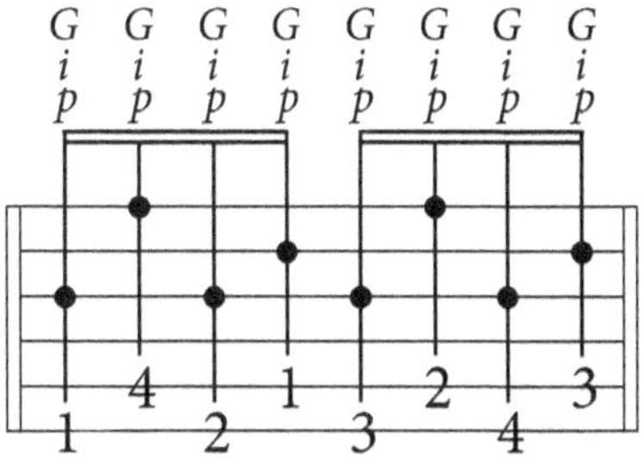

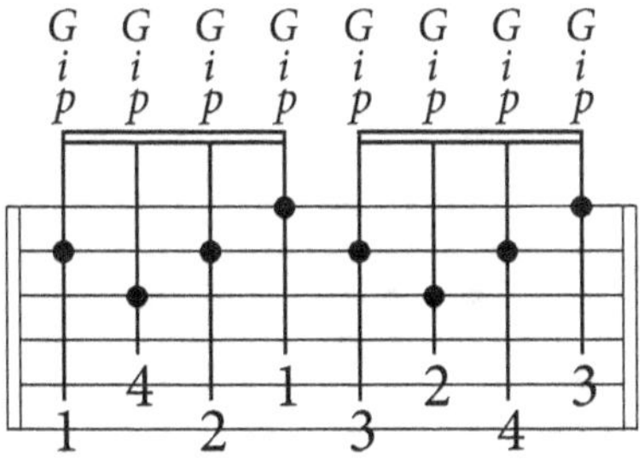

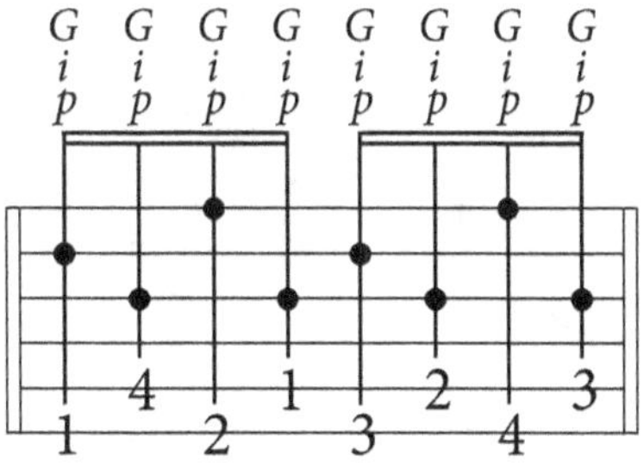

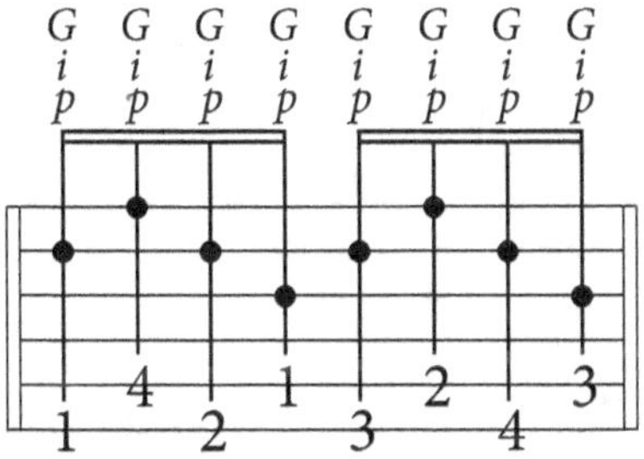

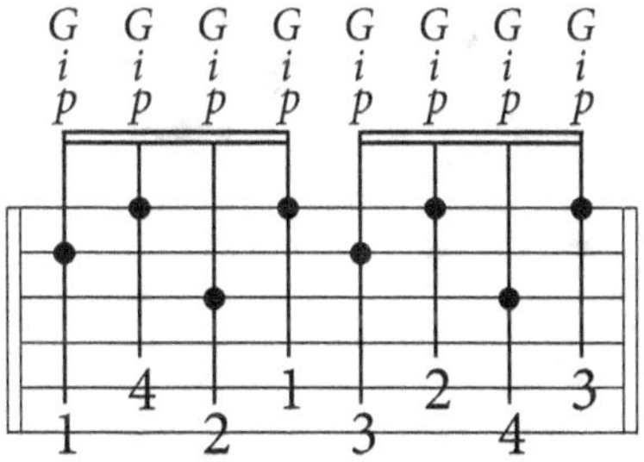

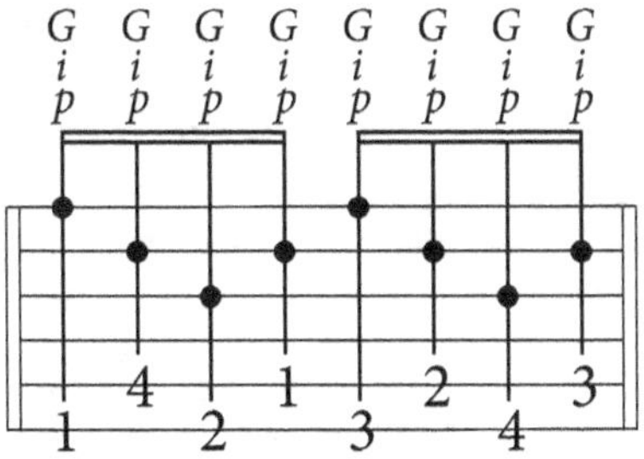

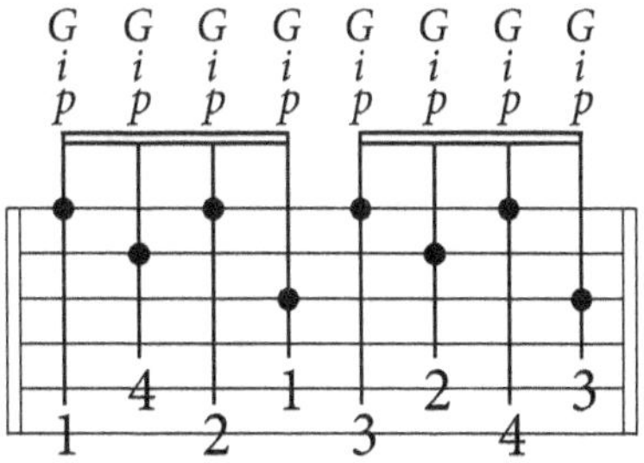

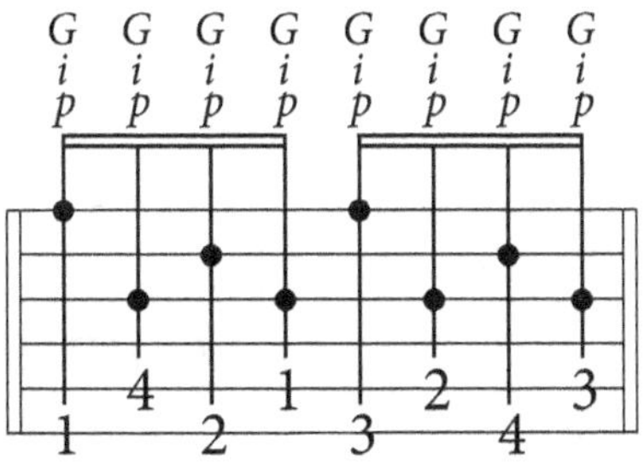

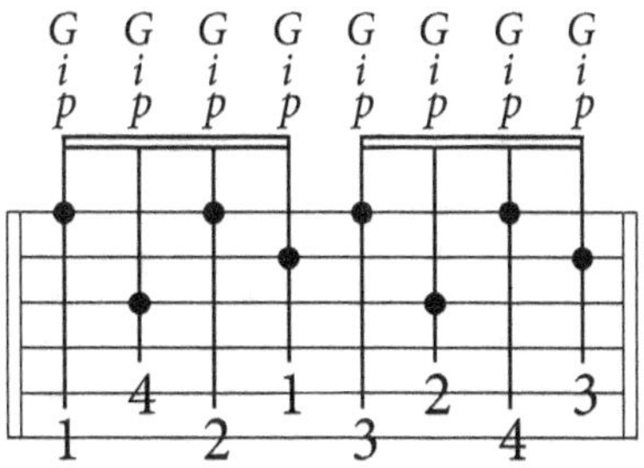

§ IIb

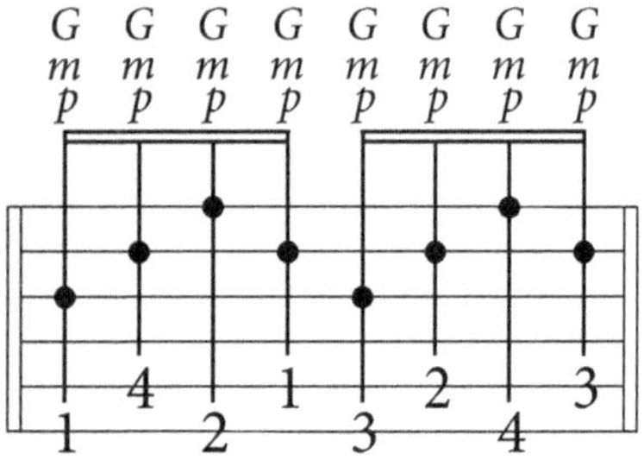

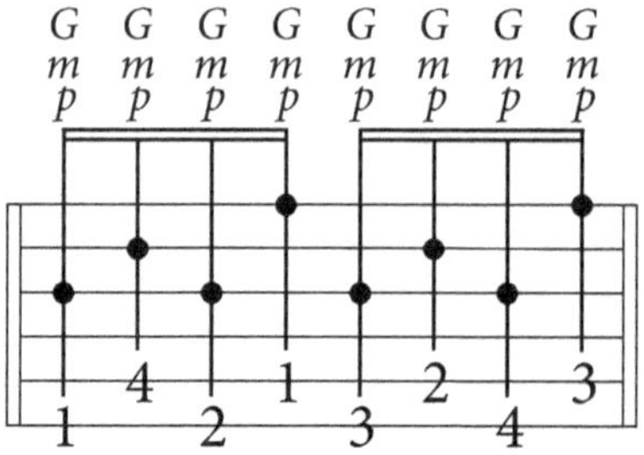

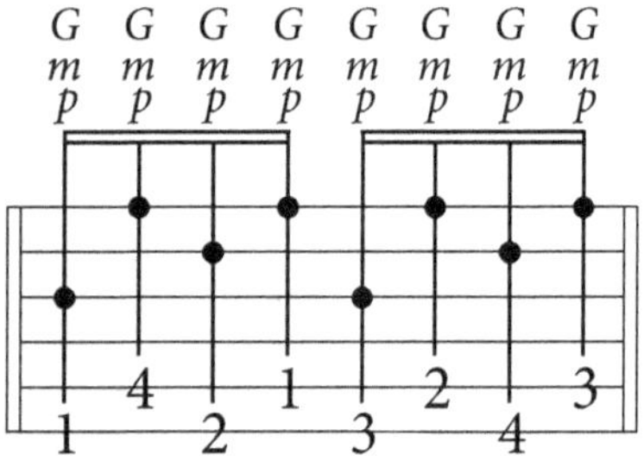

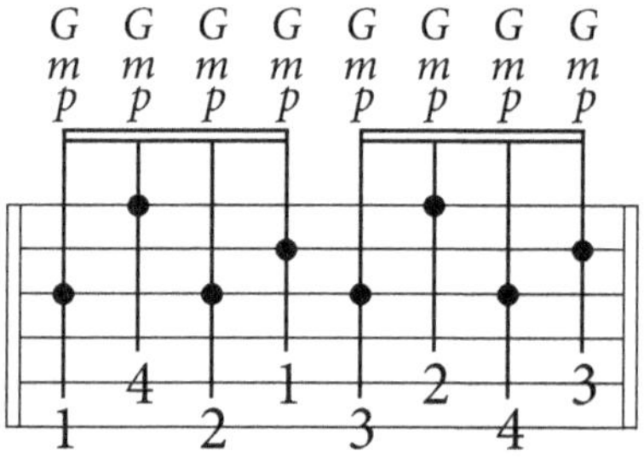

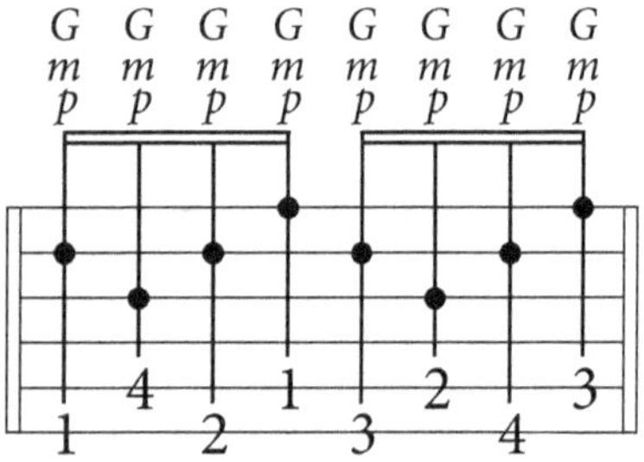

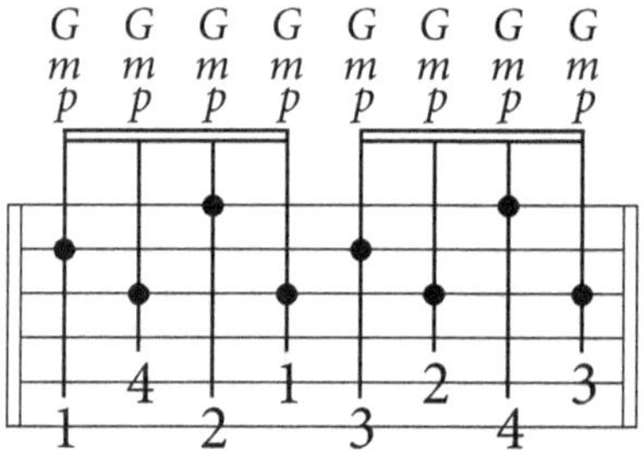

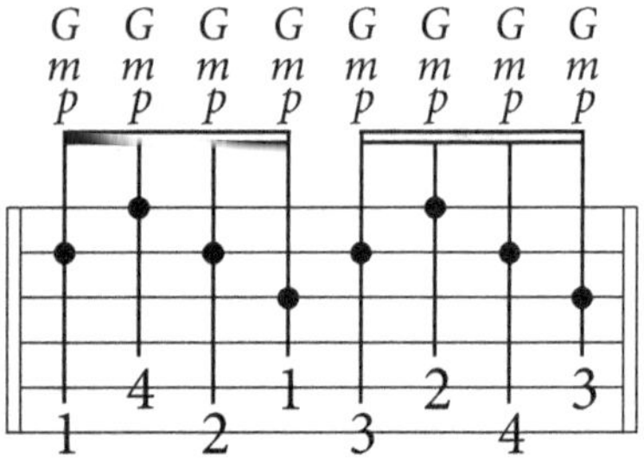

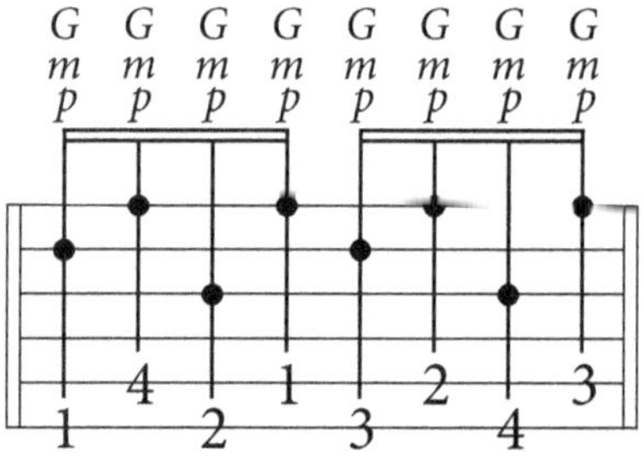

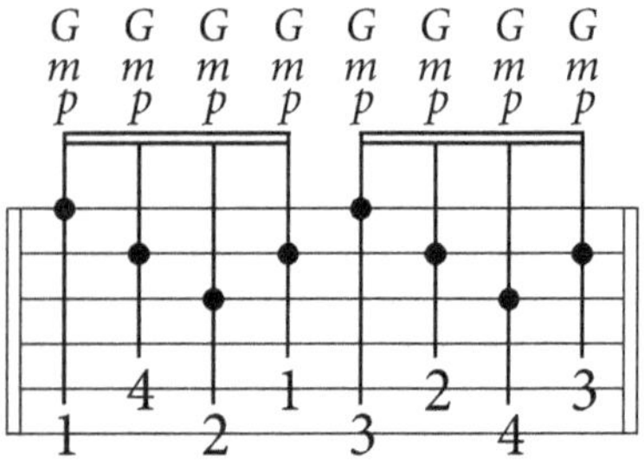

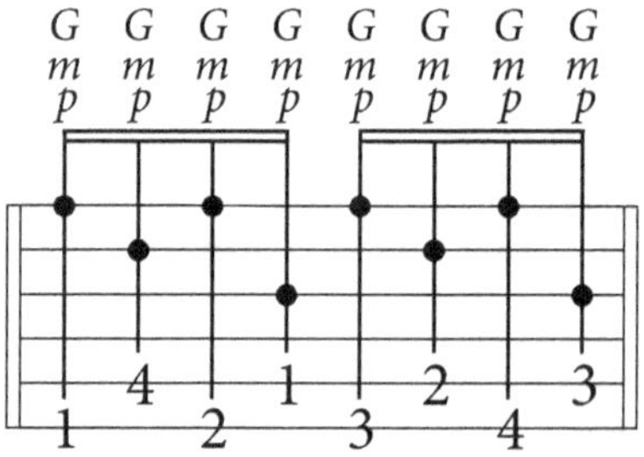

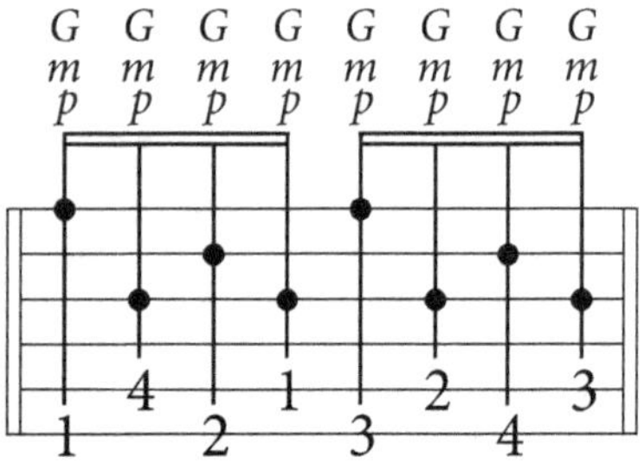

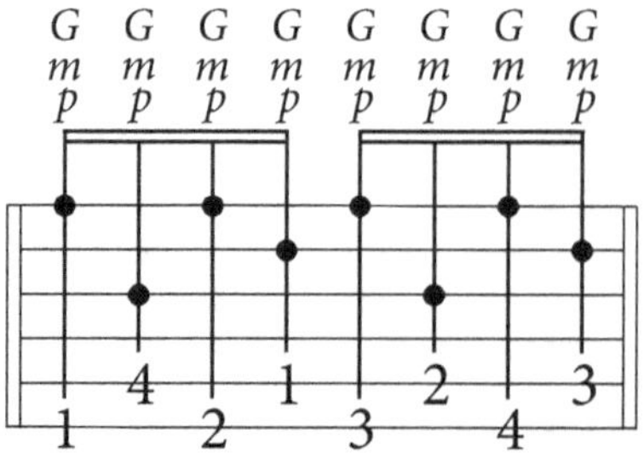

§ IIIa

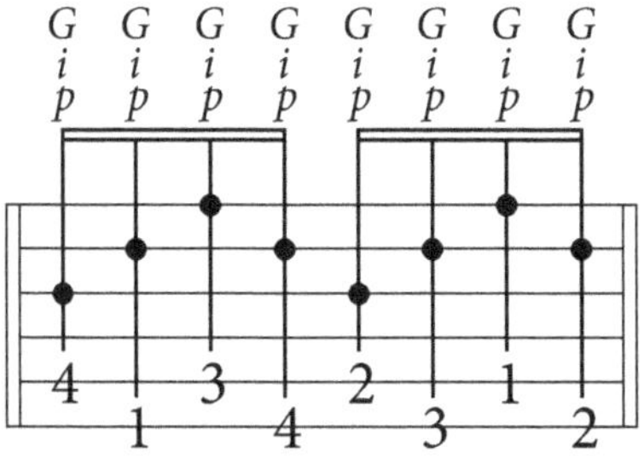

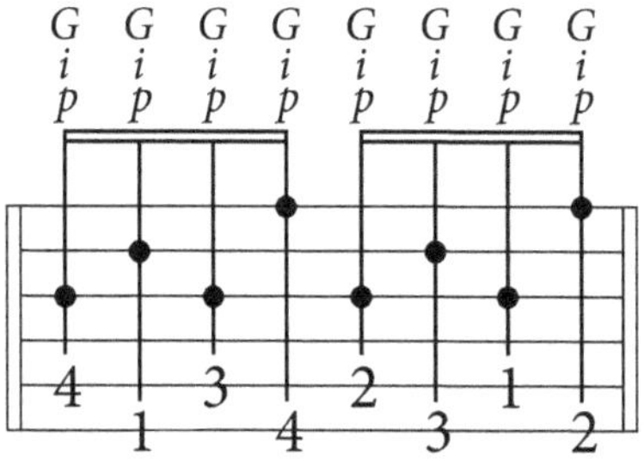

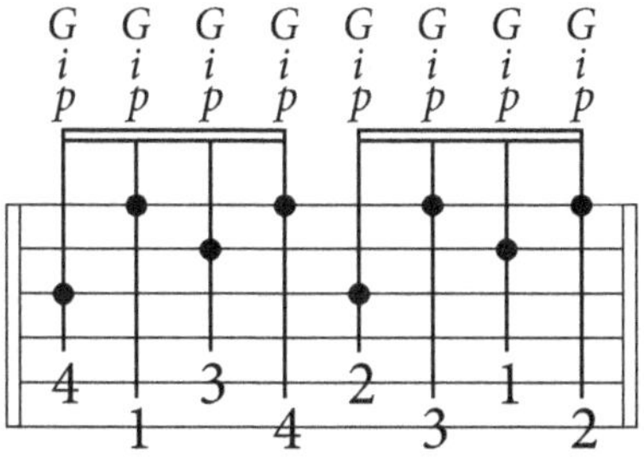

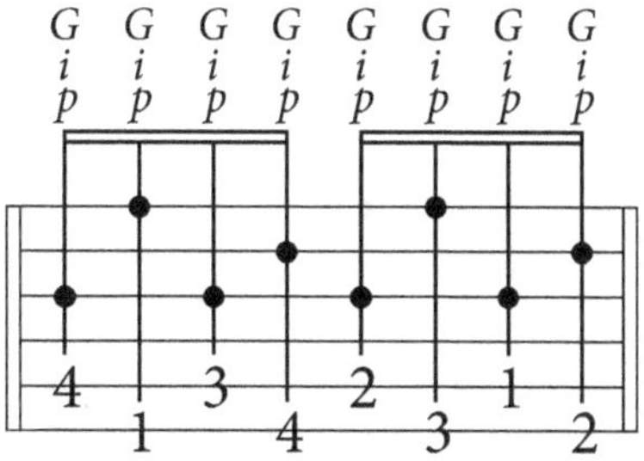

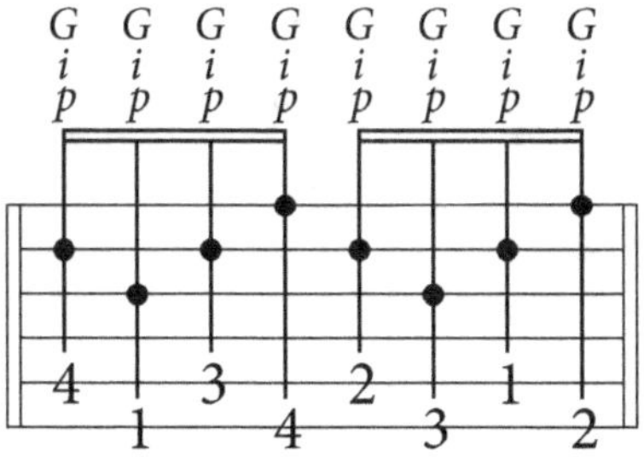

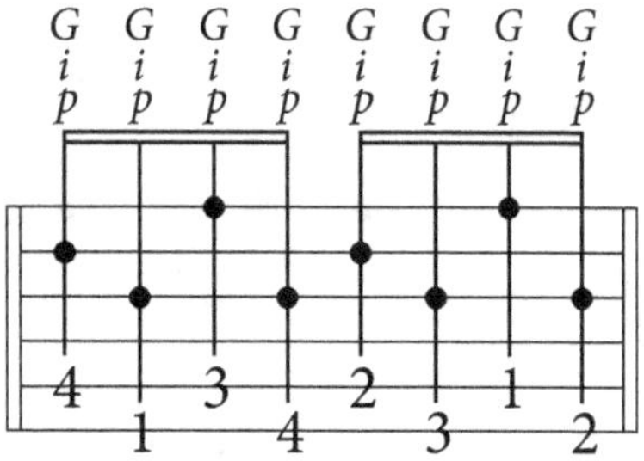

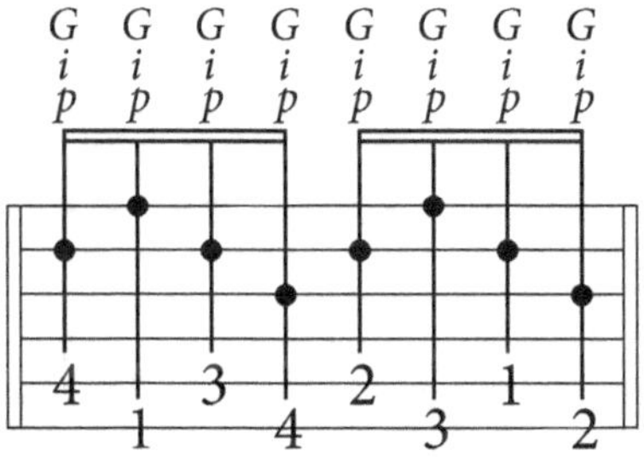

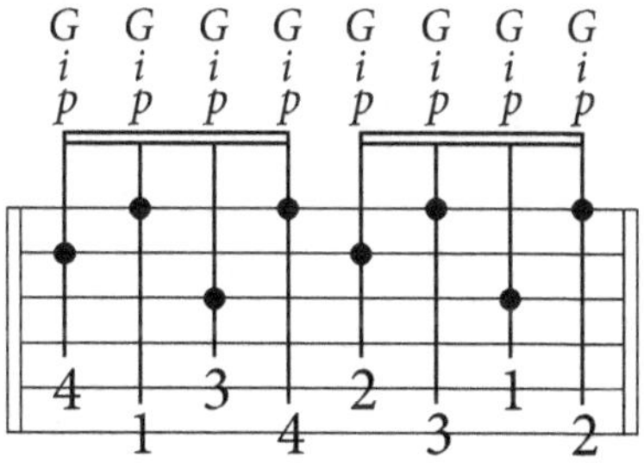

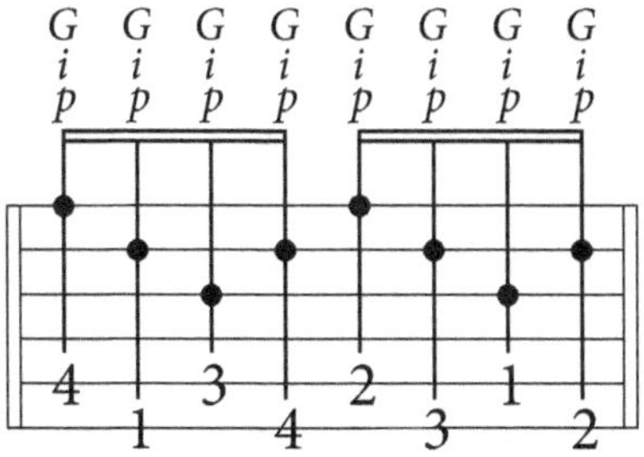

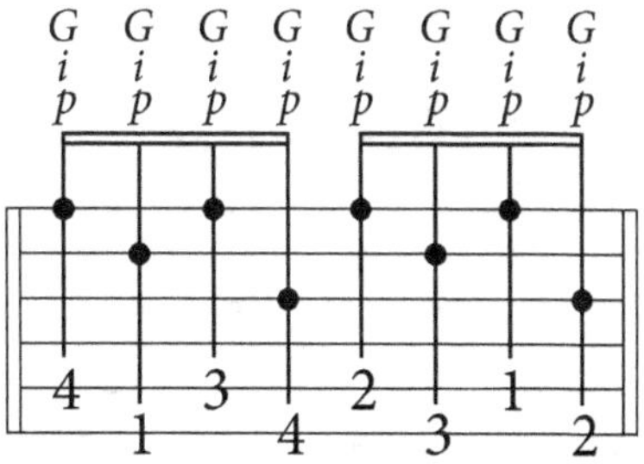

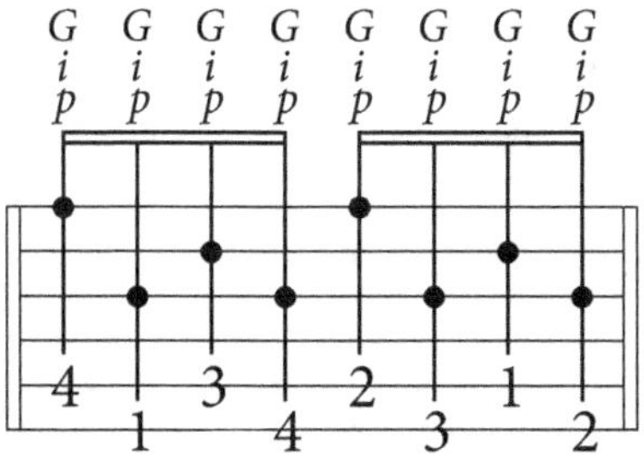

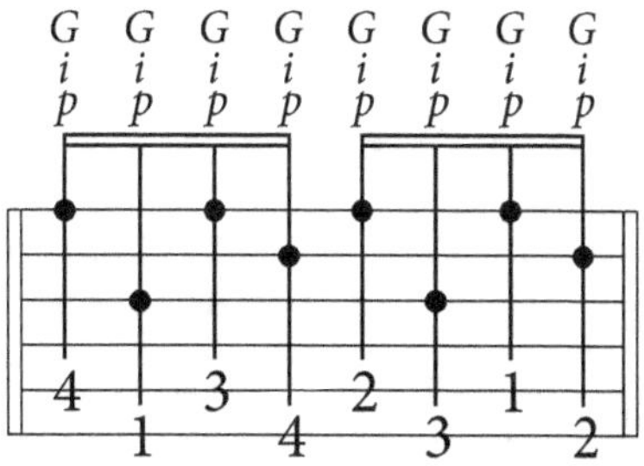

§ IIIb

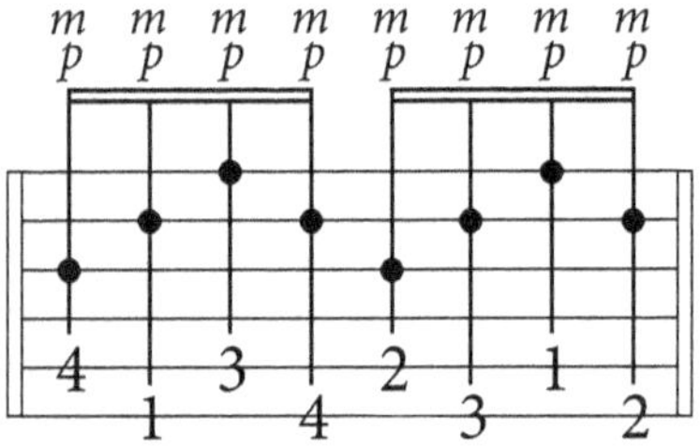

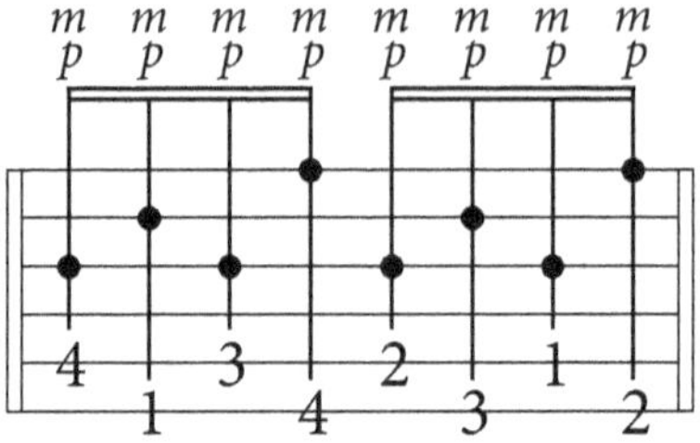

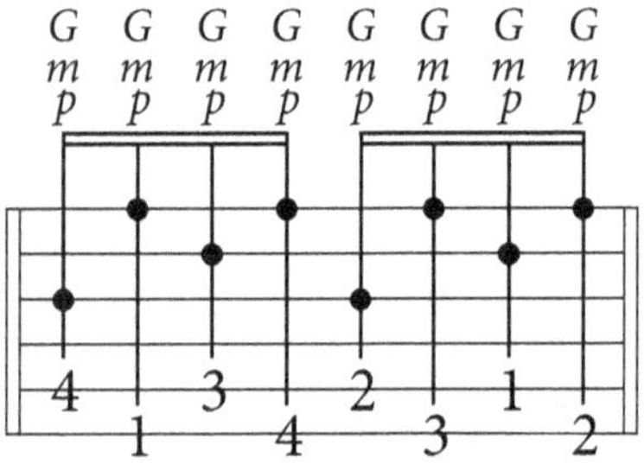

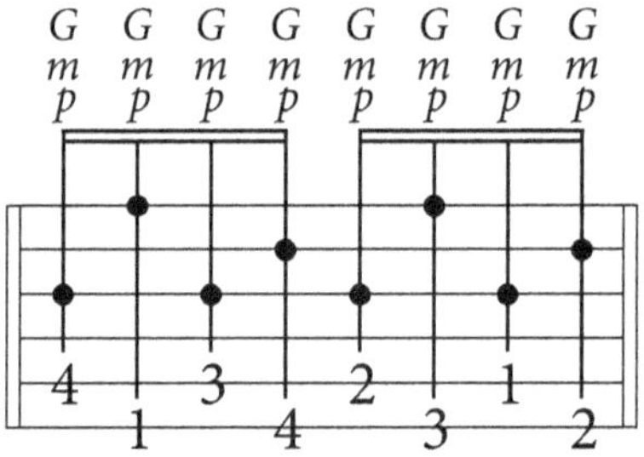

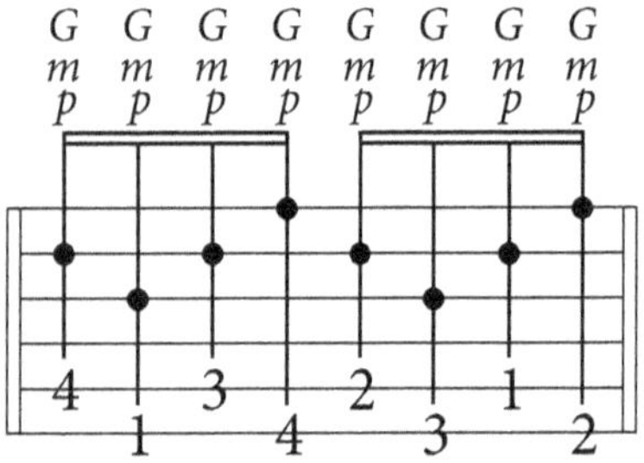

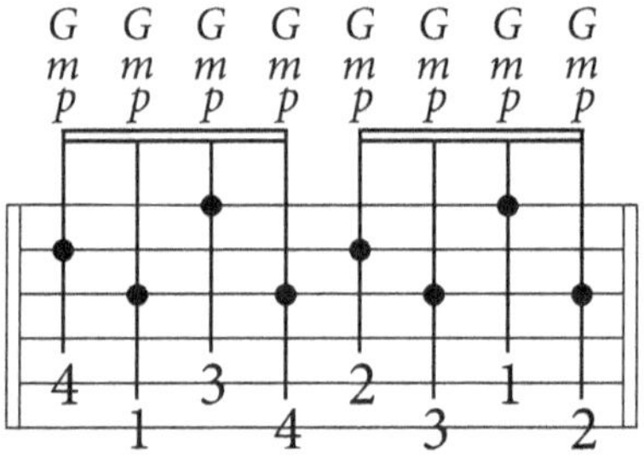

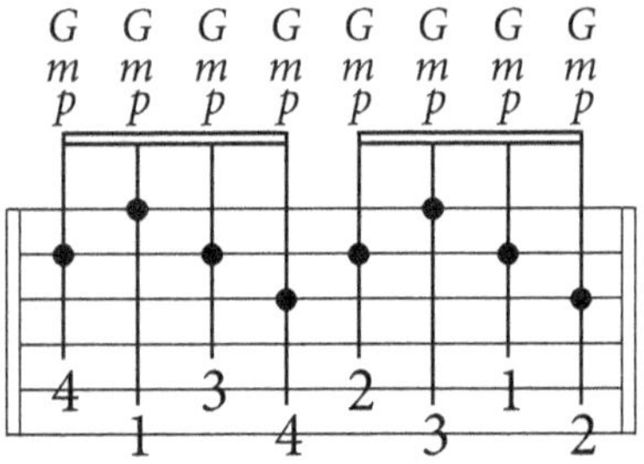

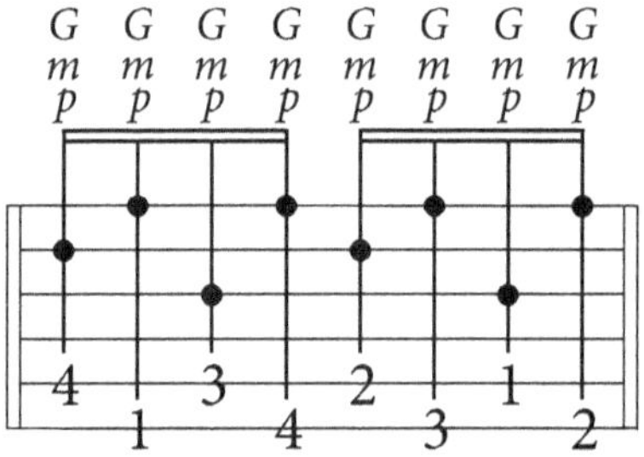

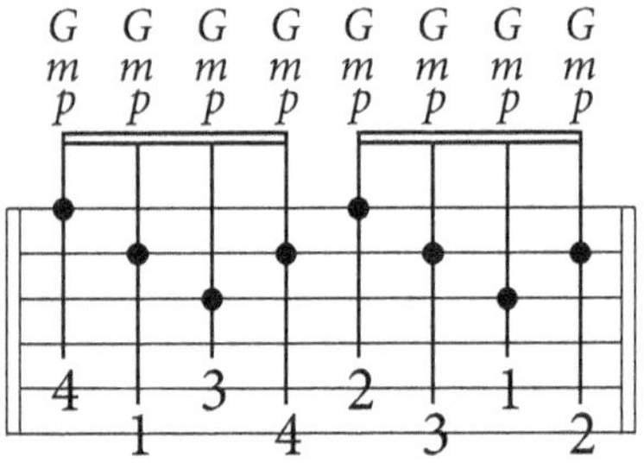

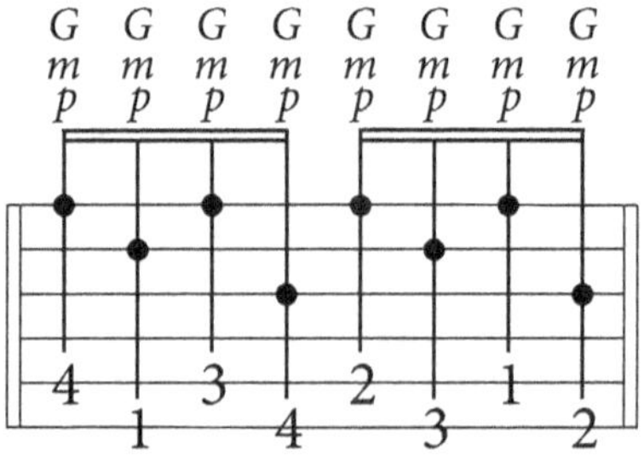

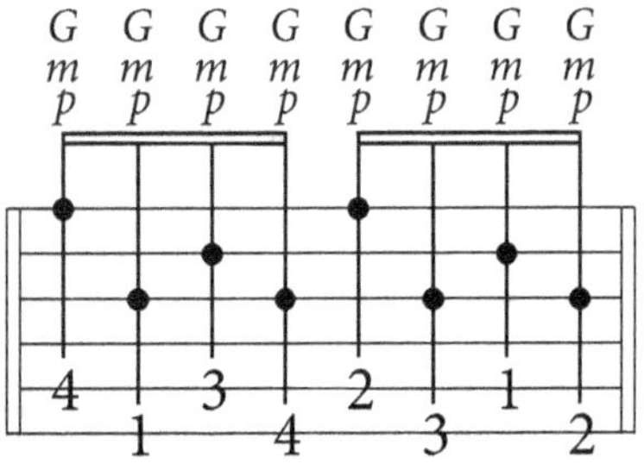

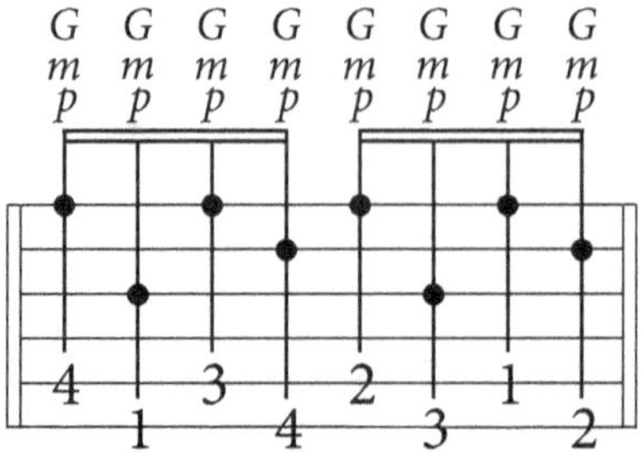

§ IVa

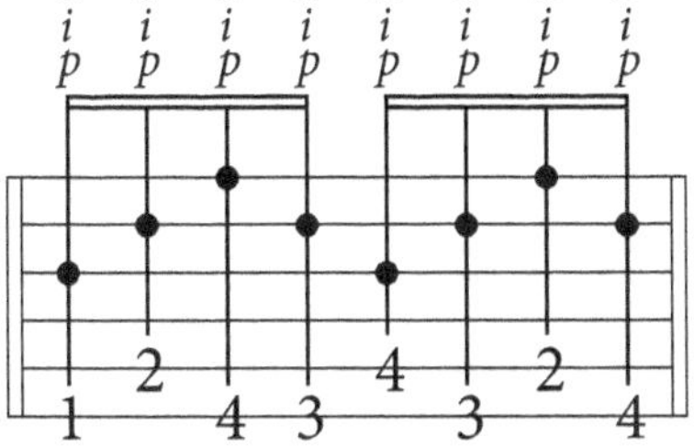

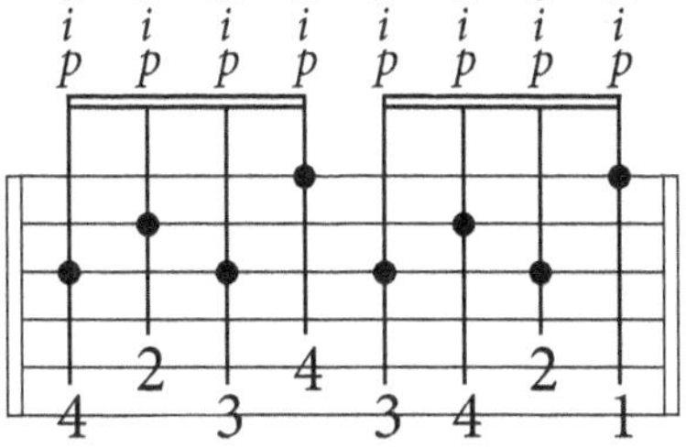

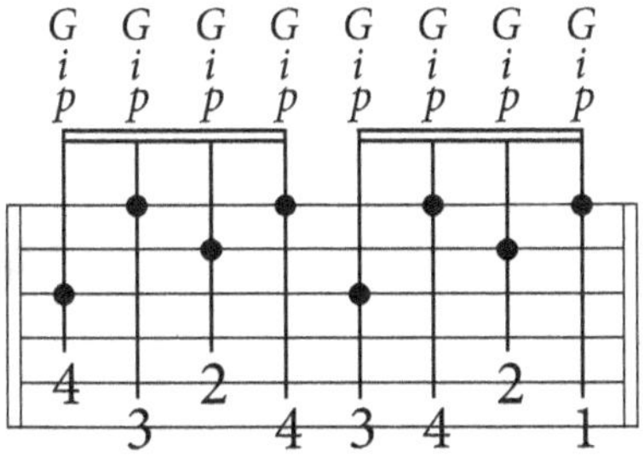

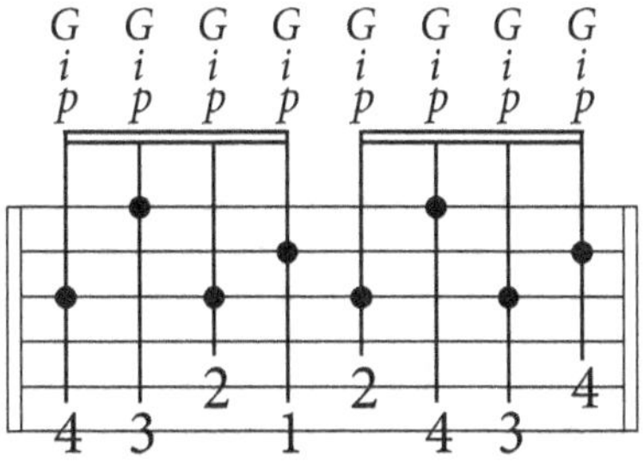

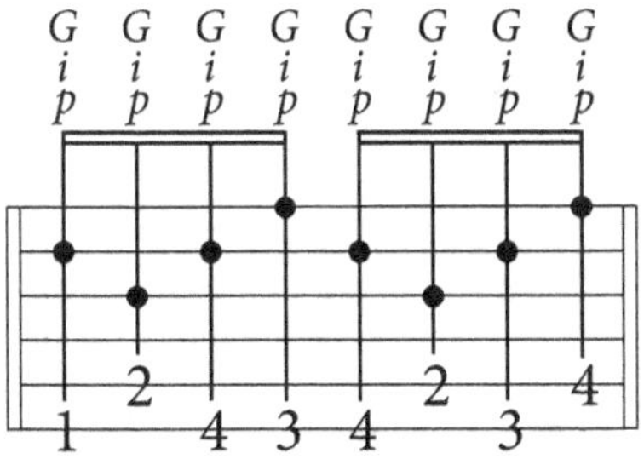

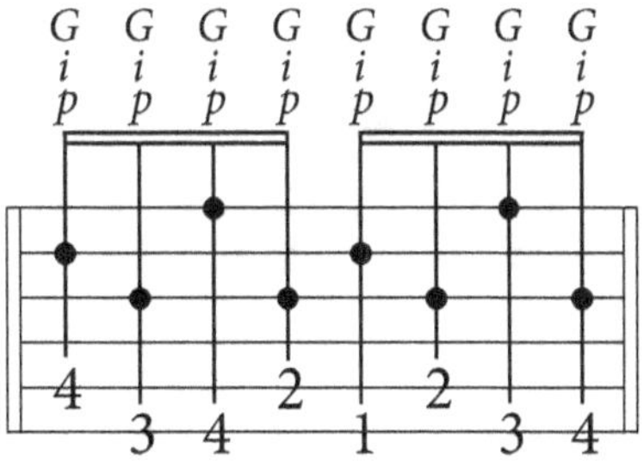

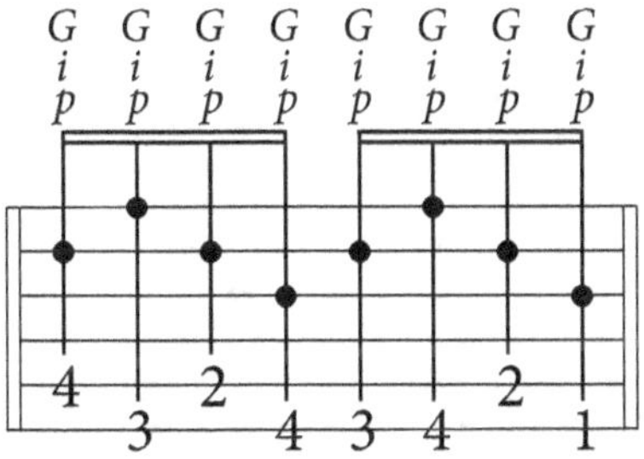

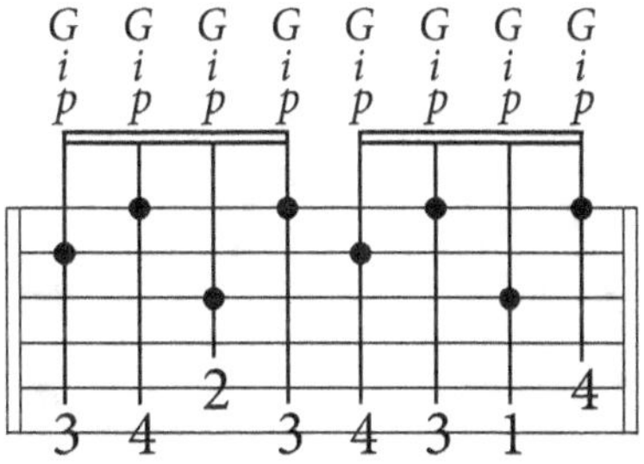

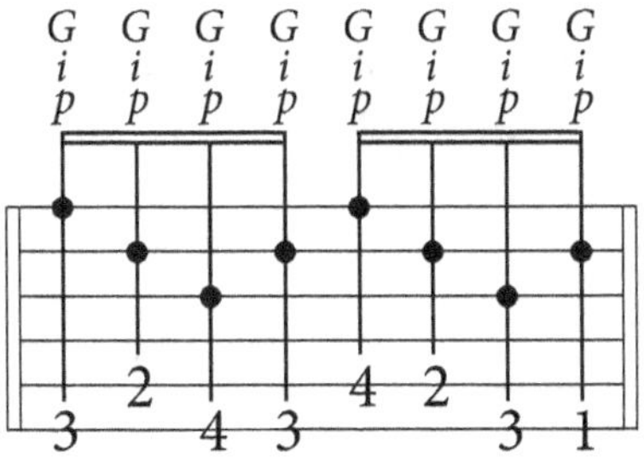

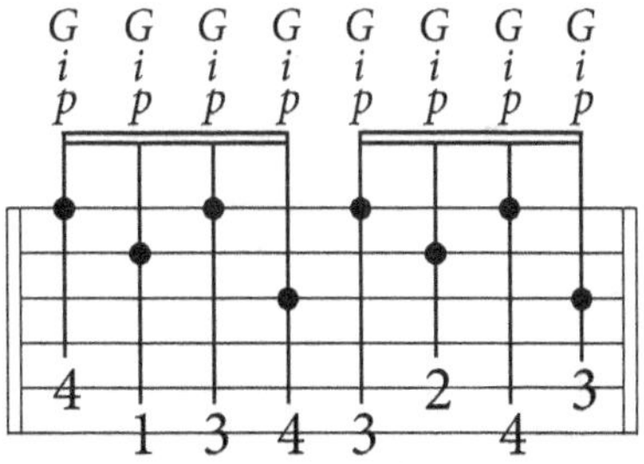

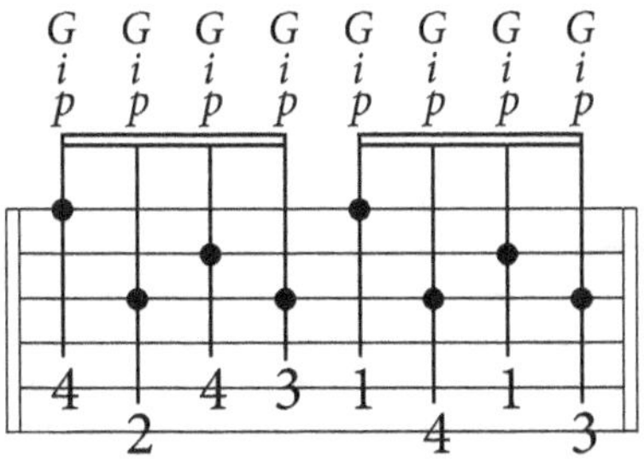

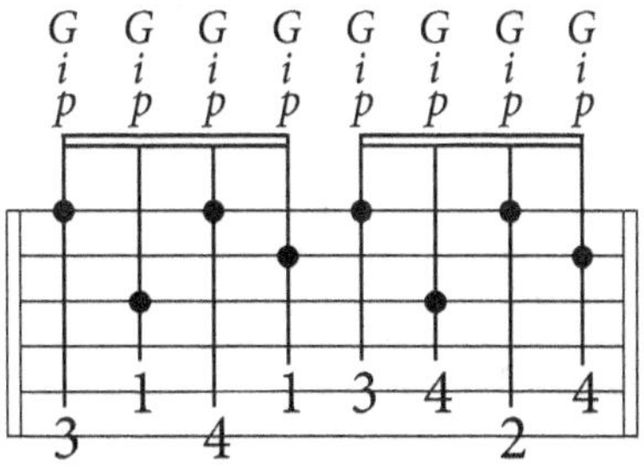

§ IVb

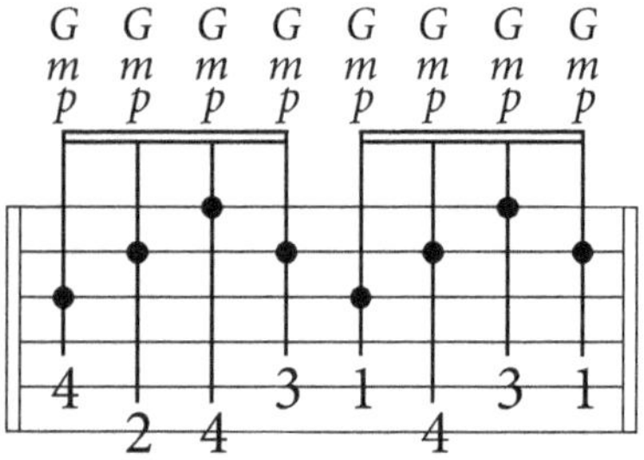

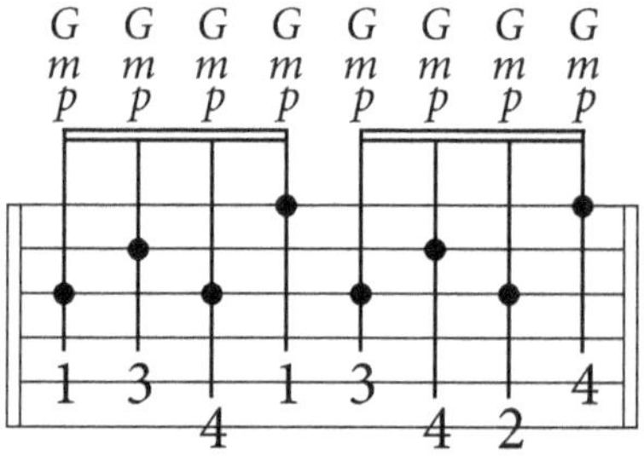

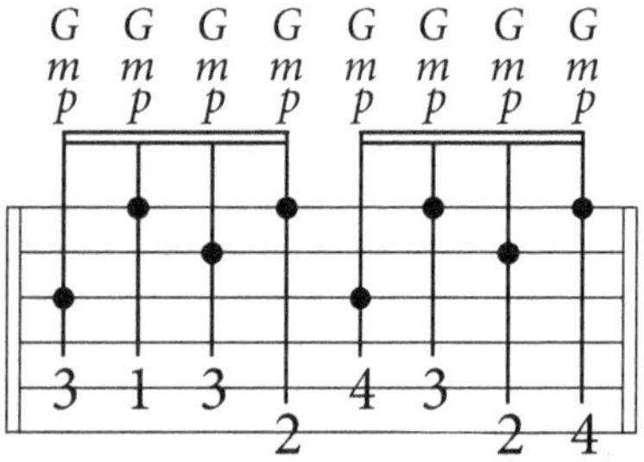

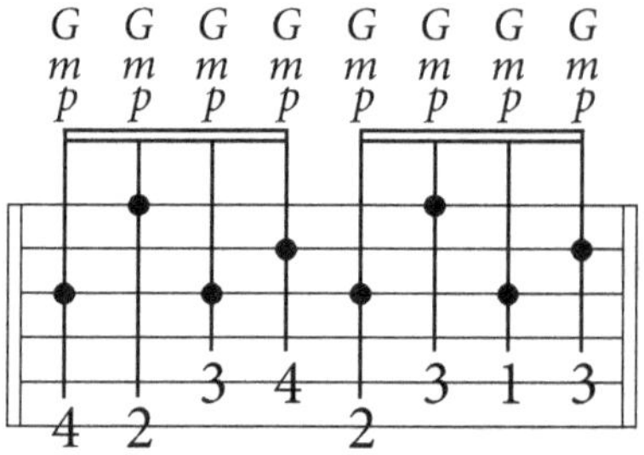

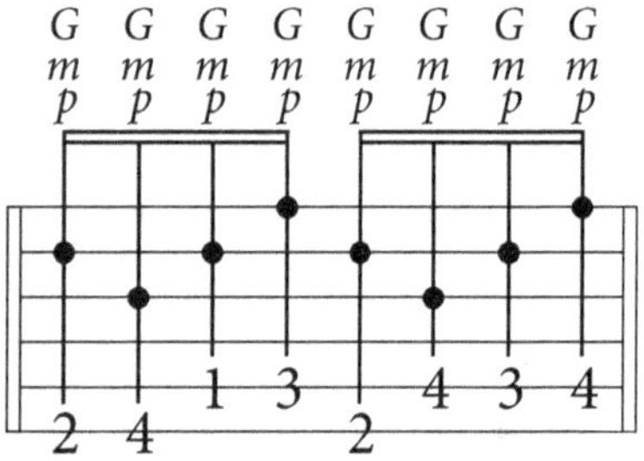

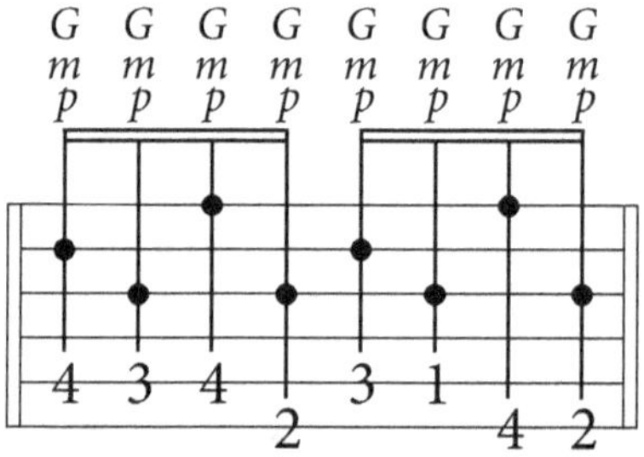

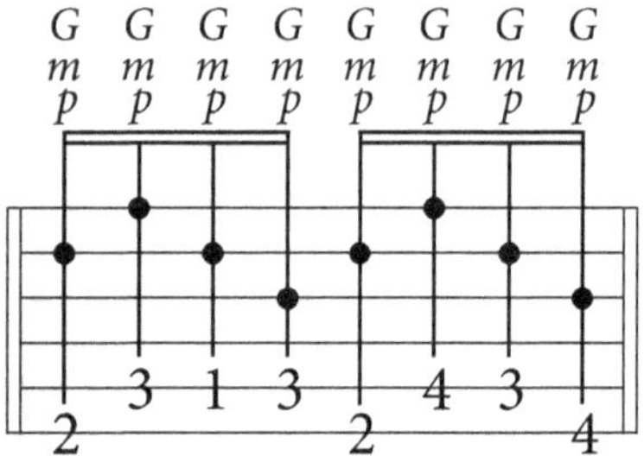

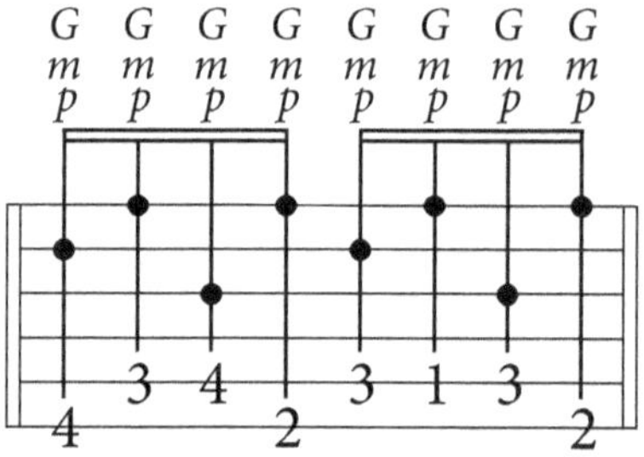

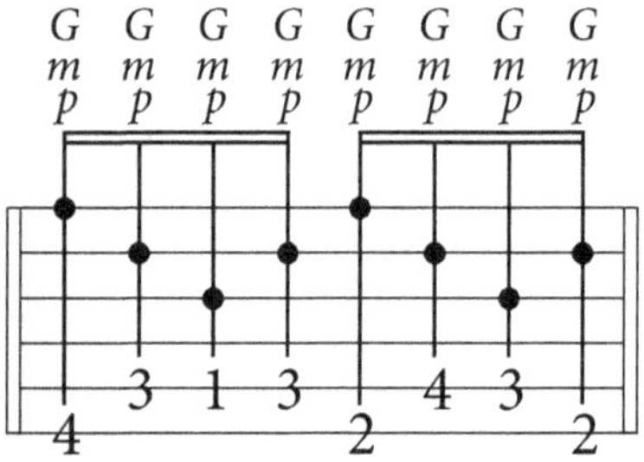

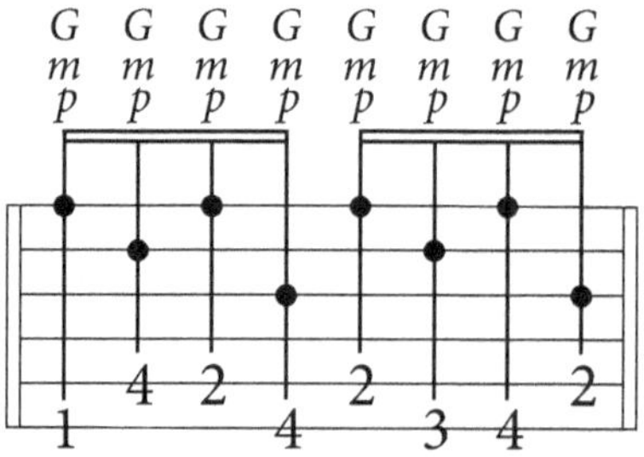

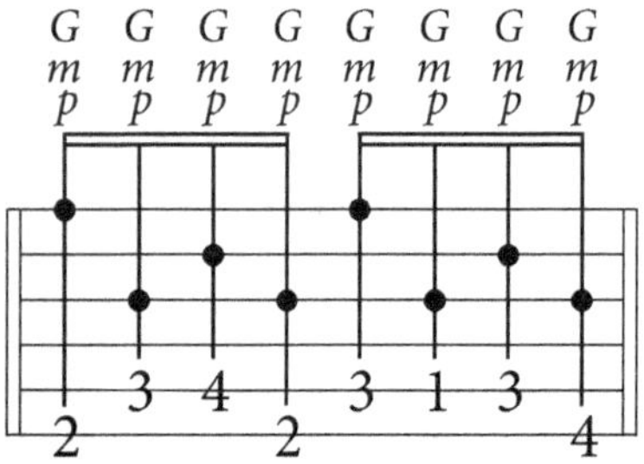

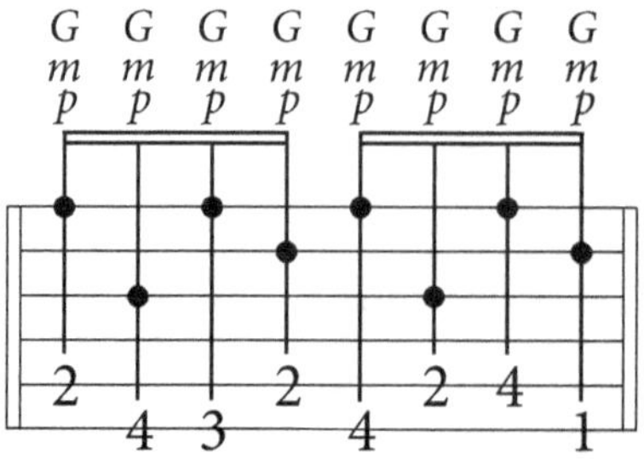

UNIT 3

The exercises of the previous unit
with greater participation of index and middle finger.

Exercises on:

1/. Chromatic scales of one string.

2/. Ascending rolling Formulas.

3/. Descending rolling Formulas.

4/. Scales of two adjacent strings.

§ Ia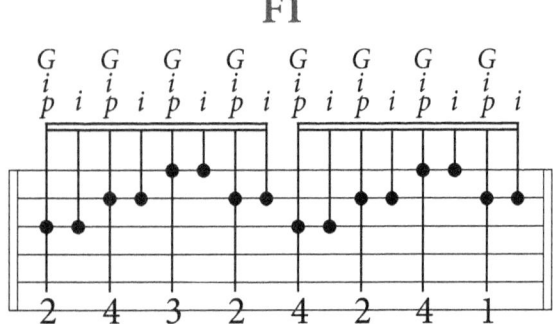

§ Ib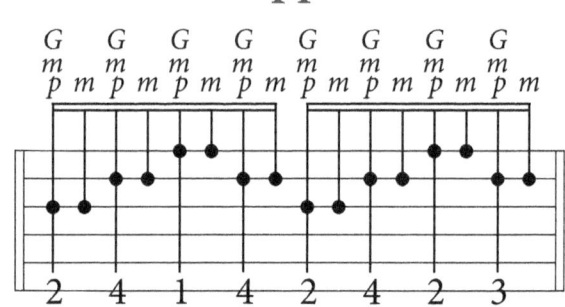

§ IIa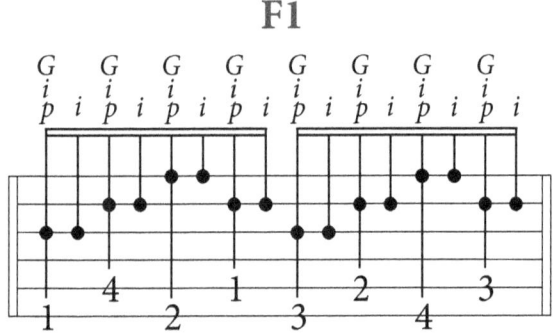

§ IIb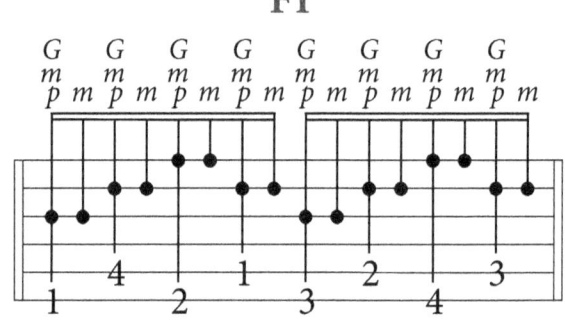

§ IIIa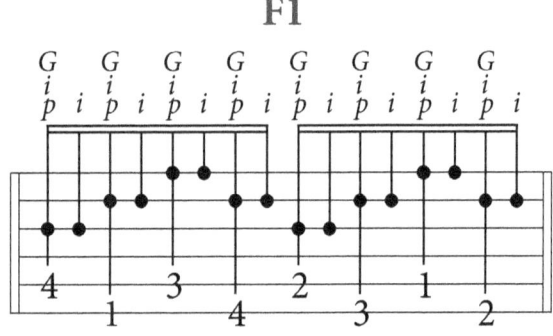

§ IIIb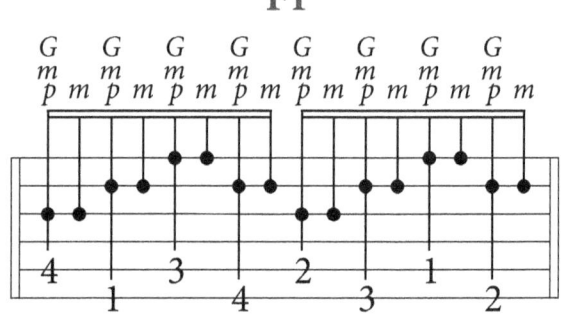

§ IVa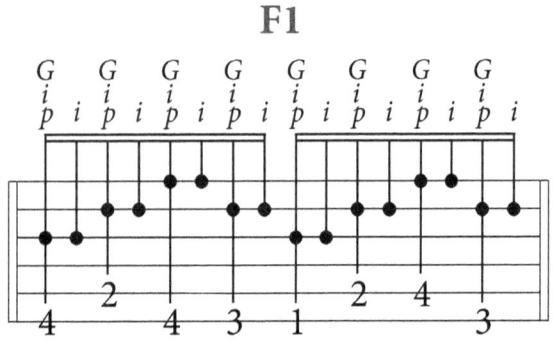

§ IVb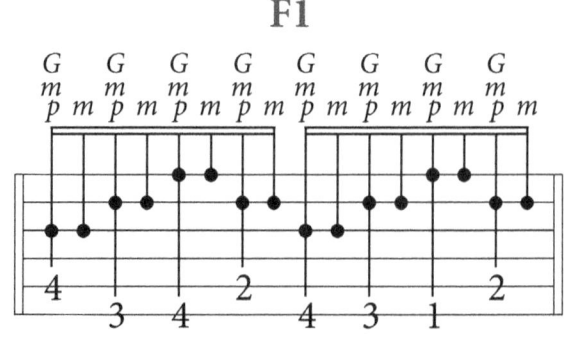

§ Ia

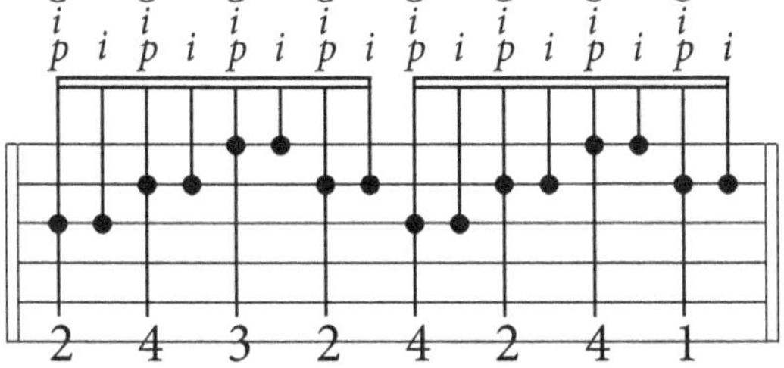

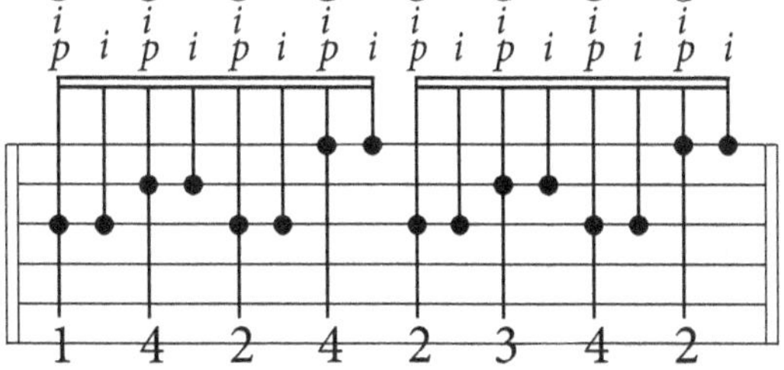

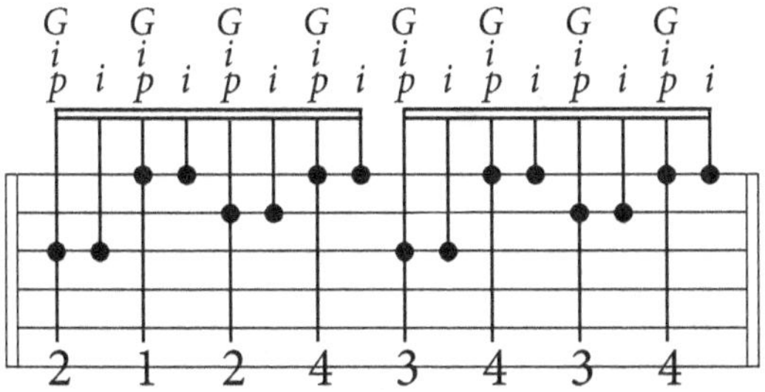

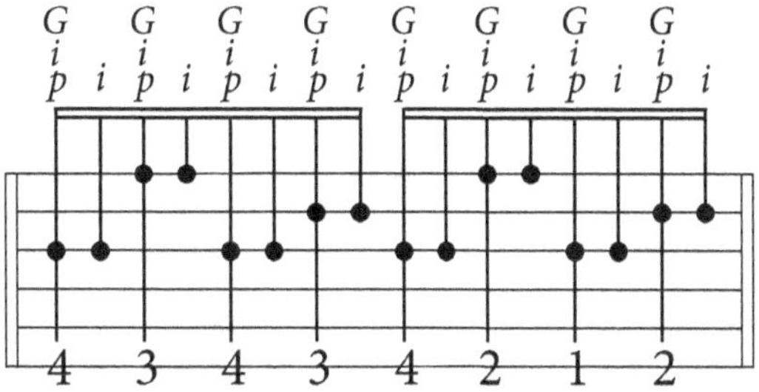

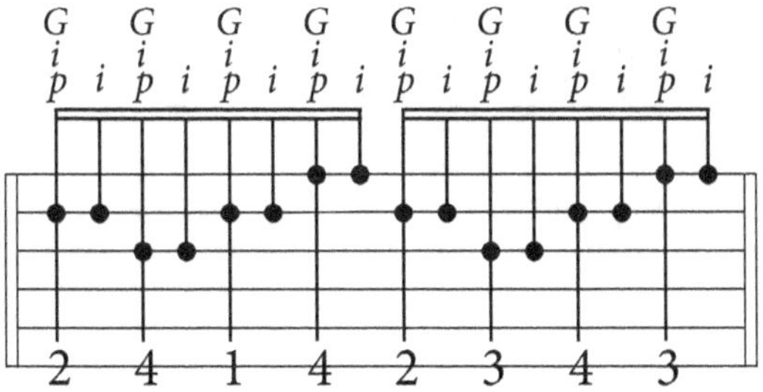

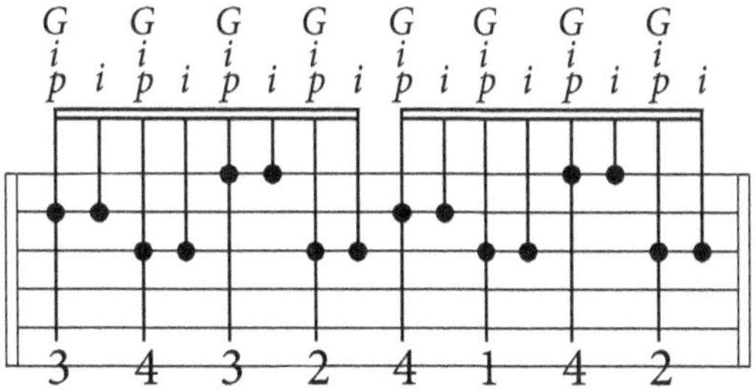

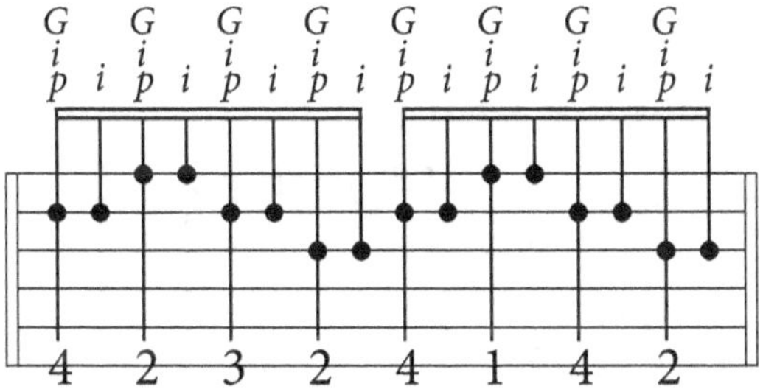

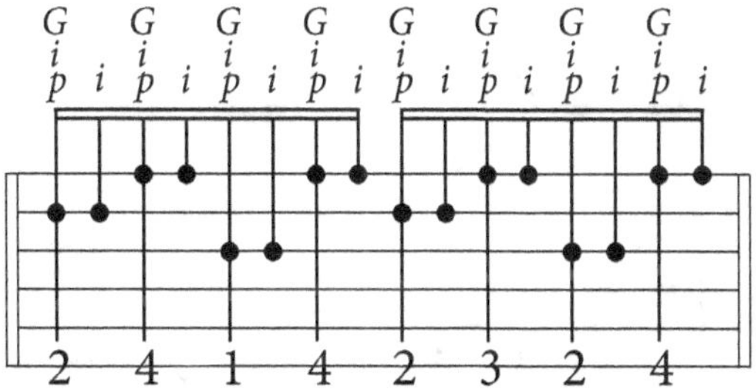

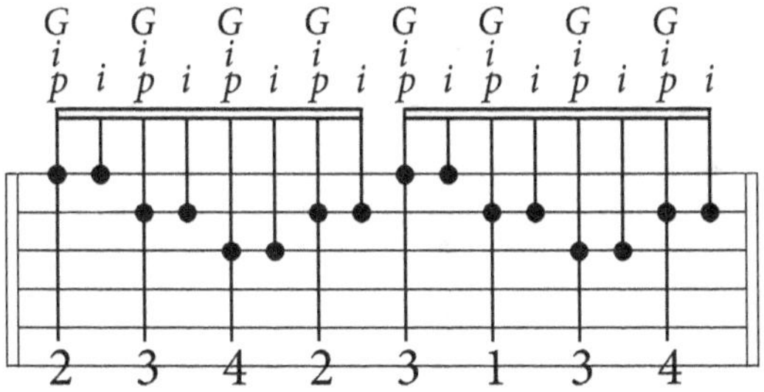

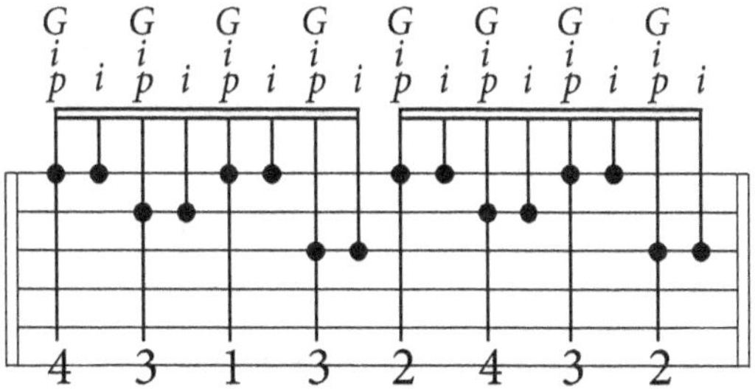

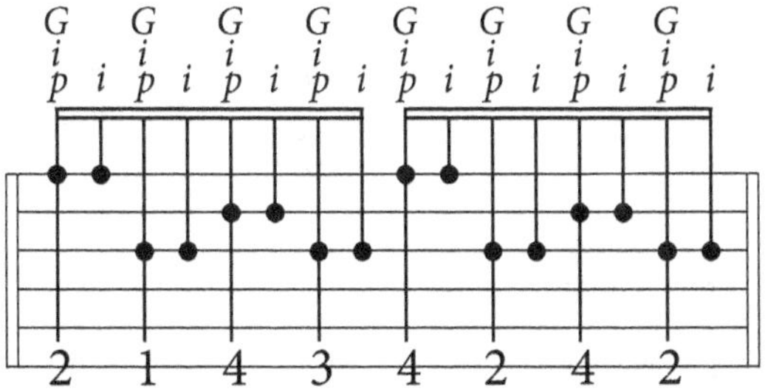

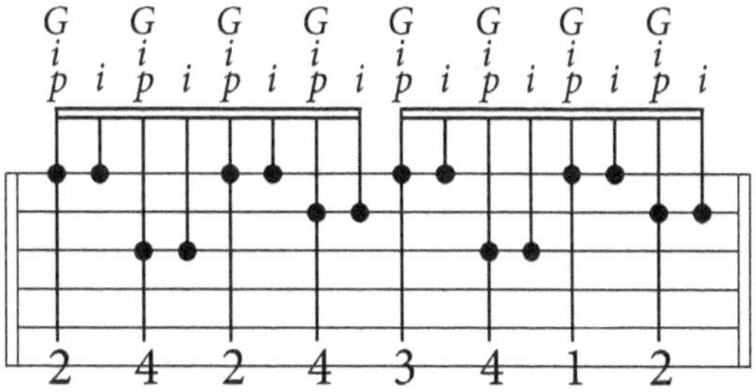

§ Ib

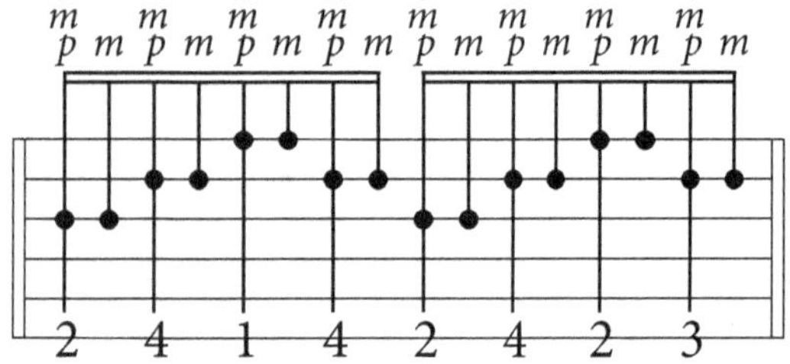

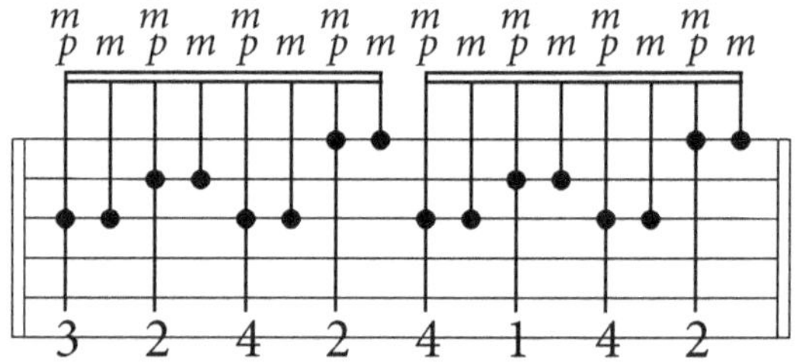

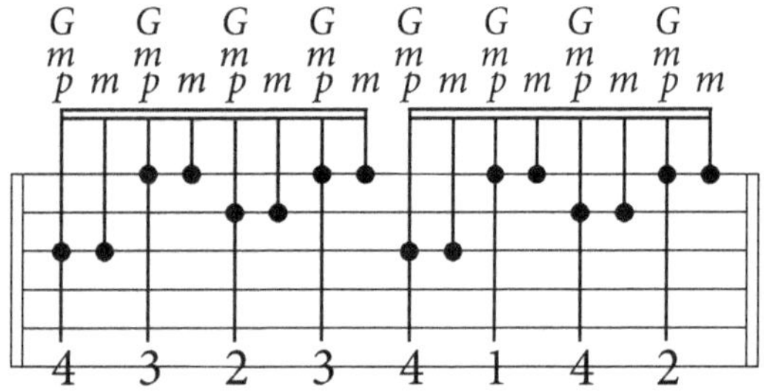

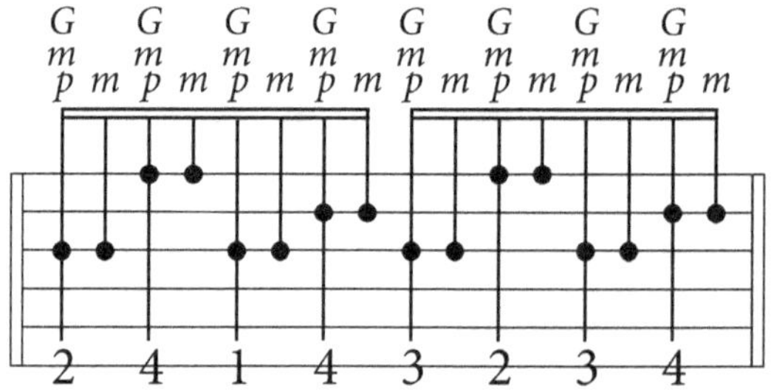

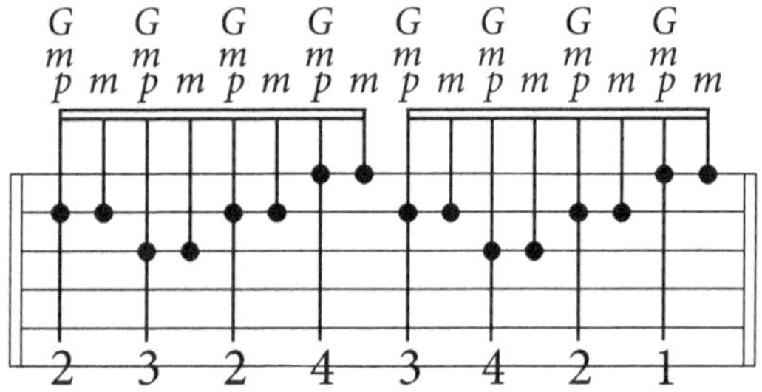

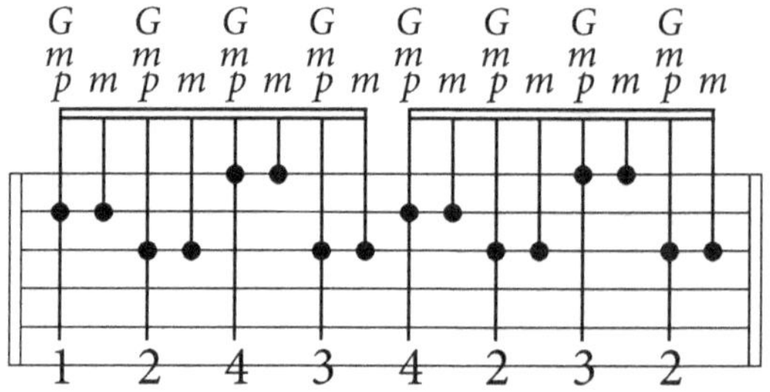

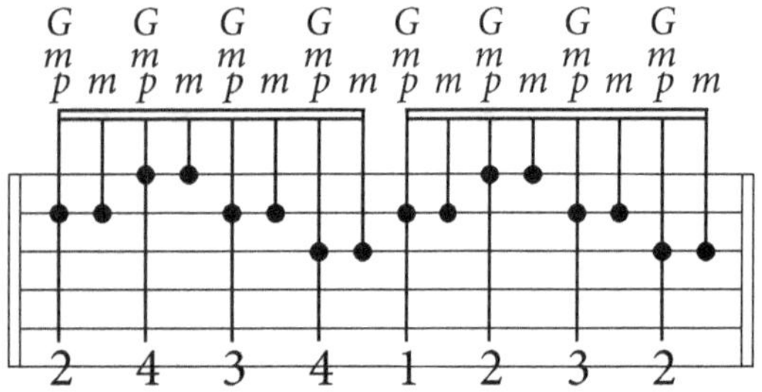

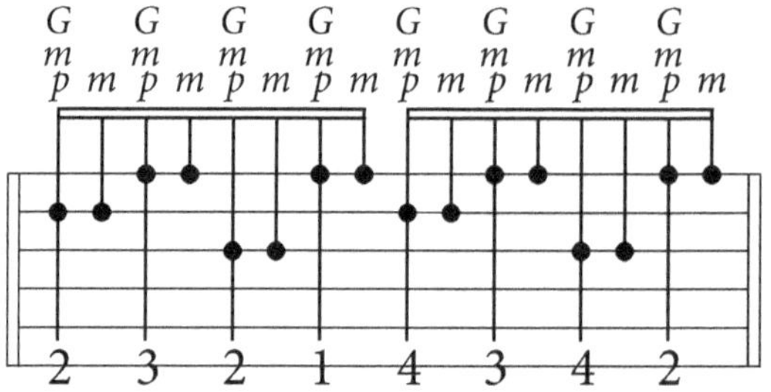

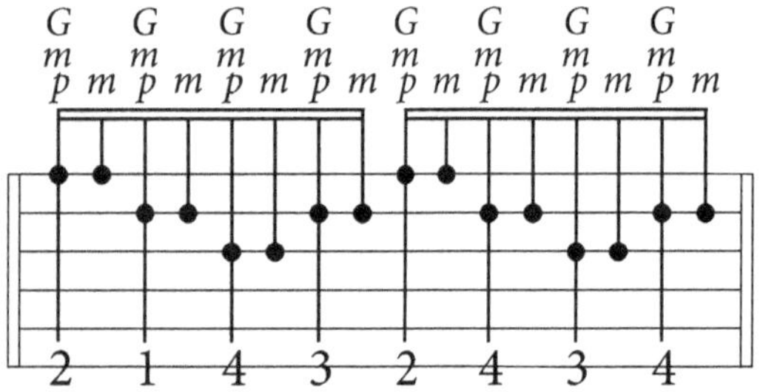

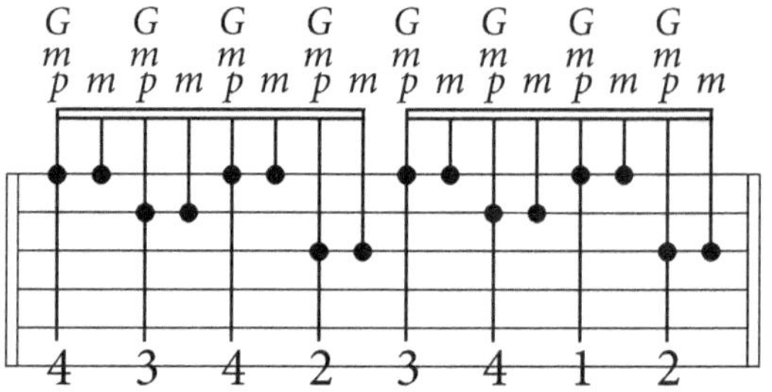

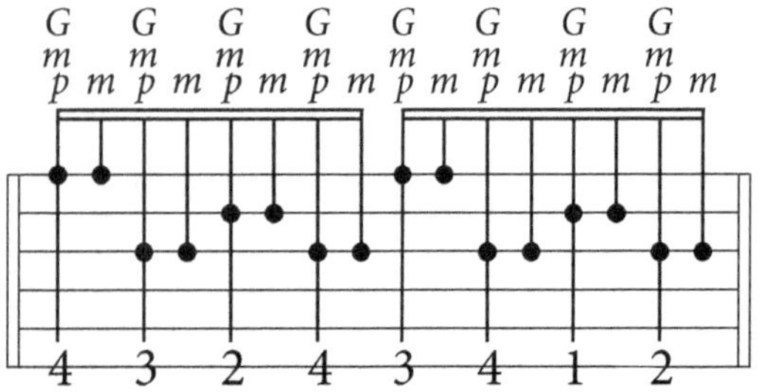

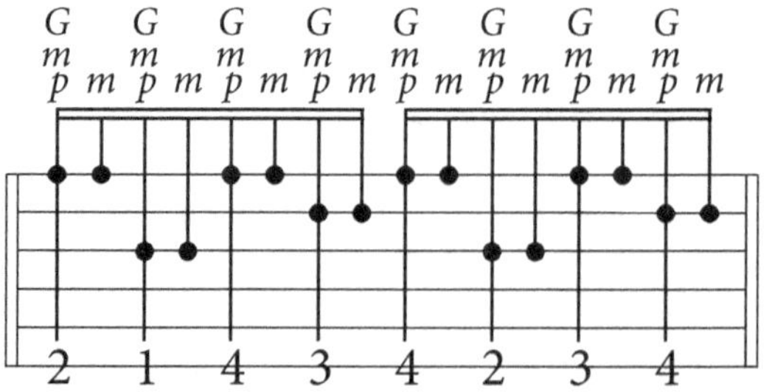

§ IIa

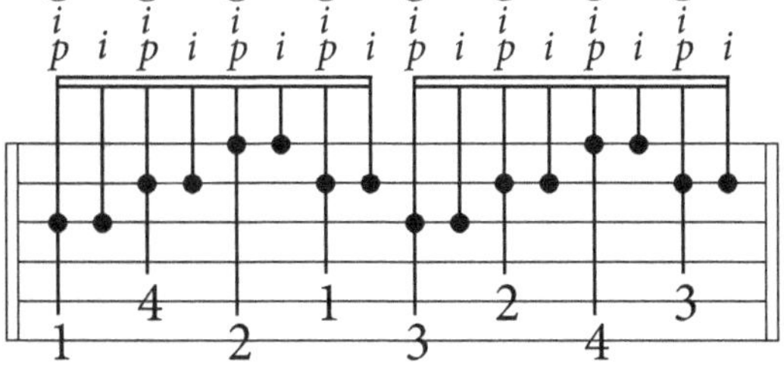

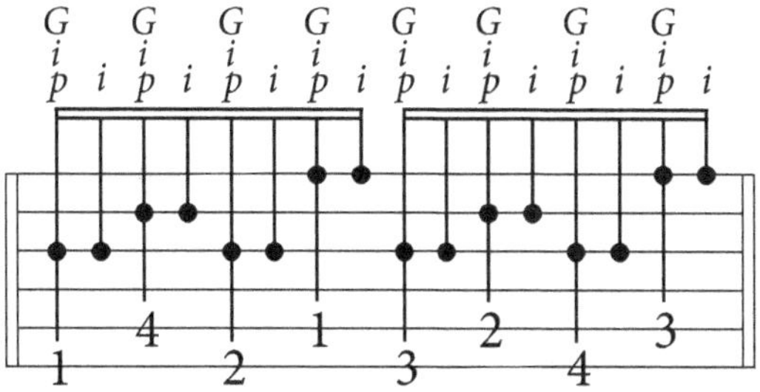

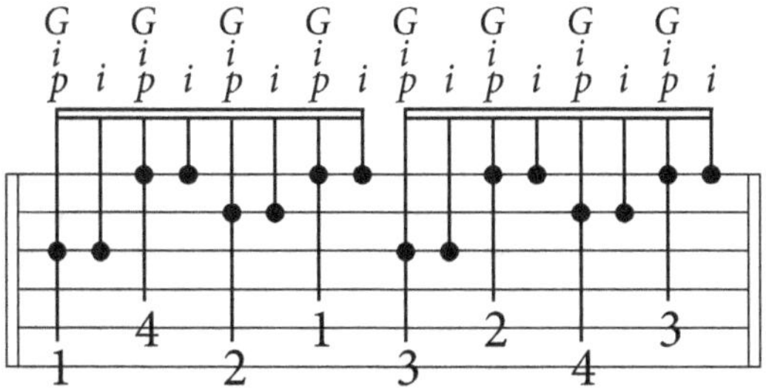

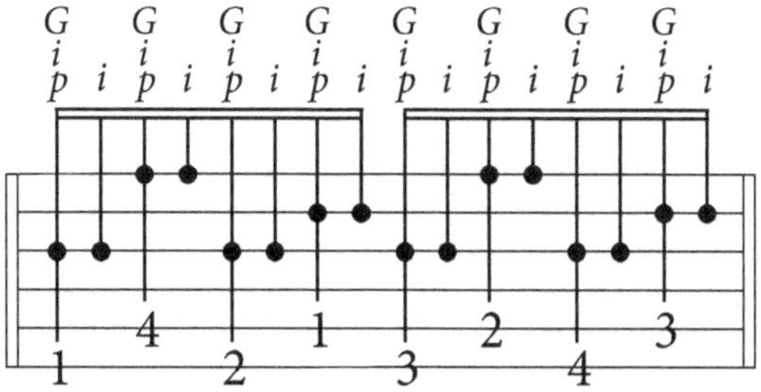

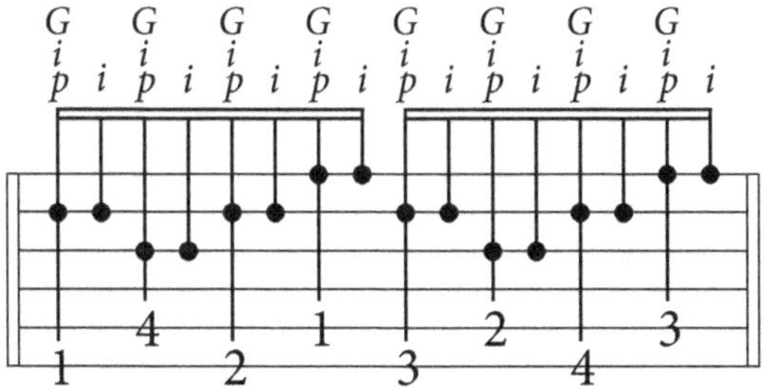

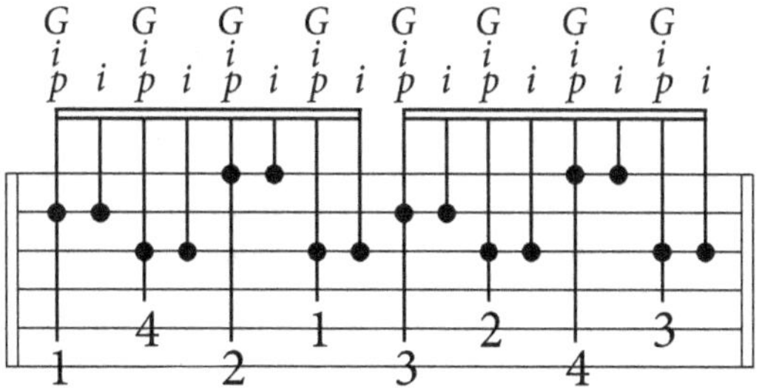

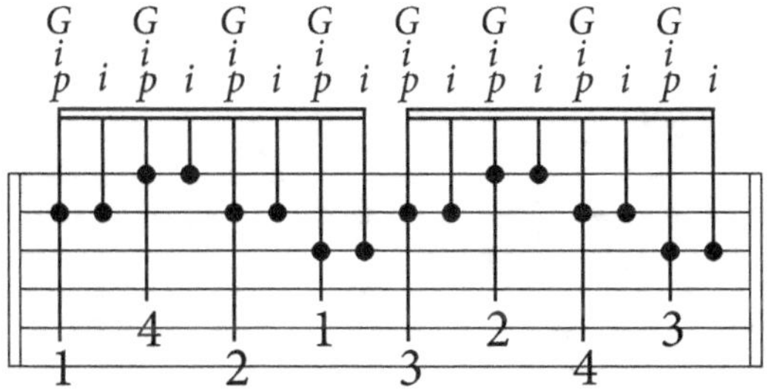

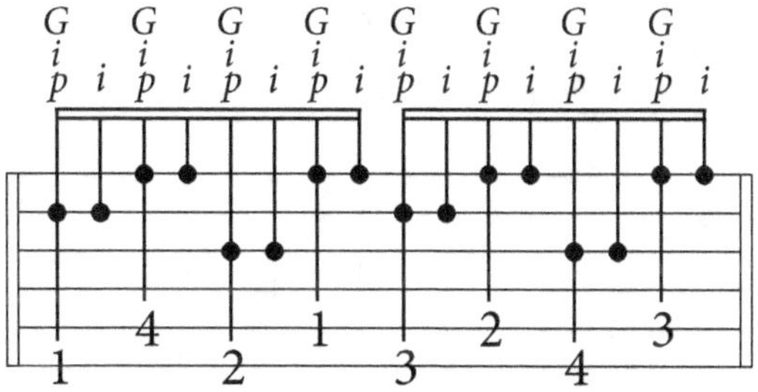

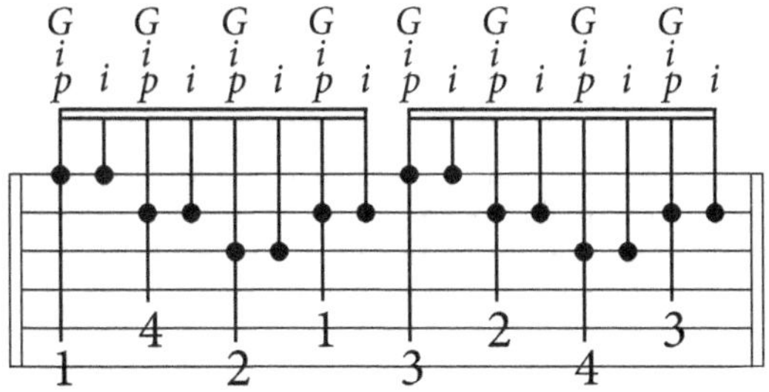

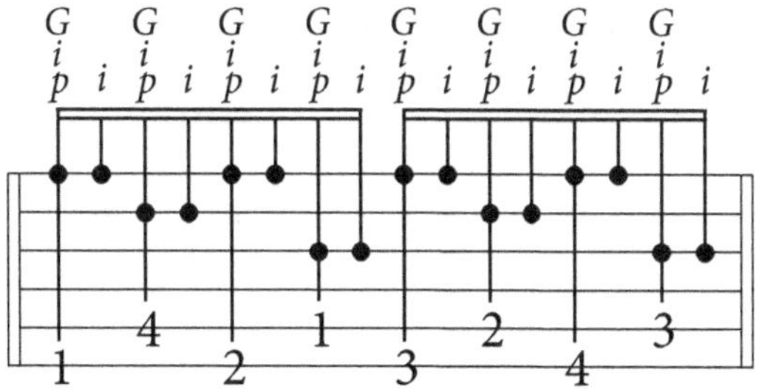

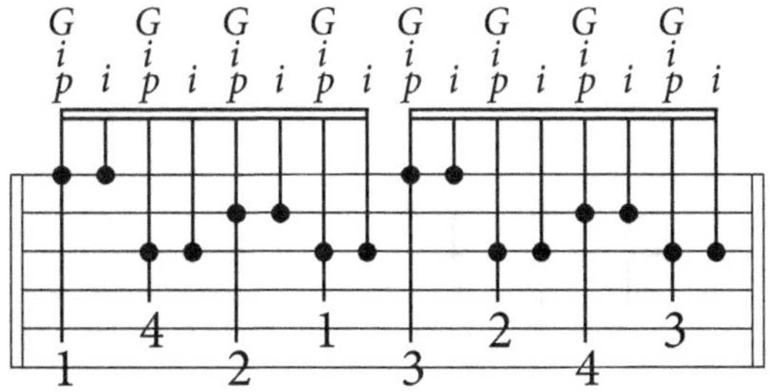

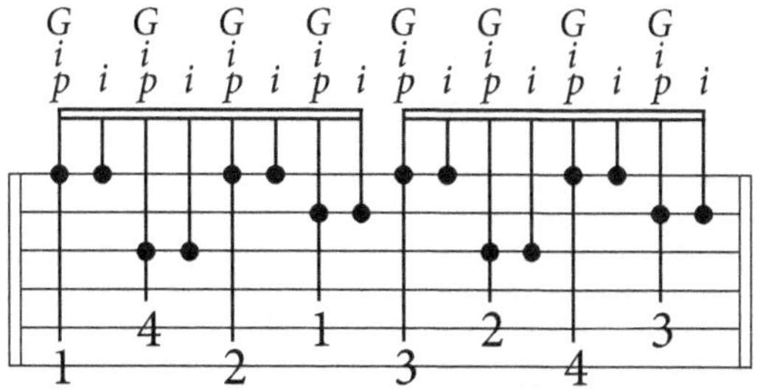

§ IIb

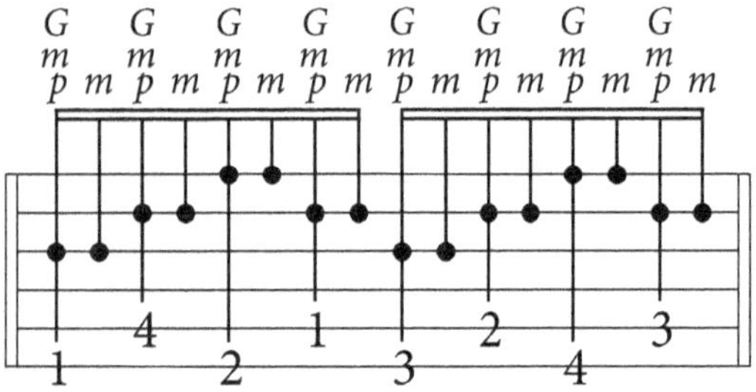

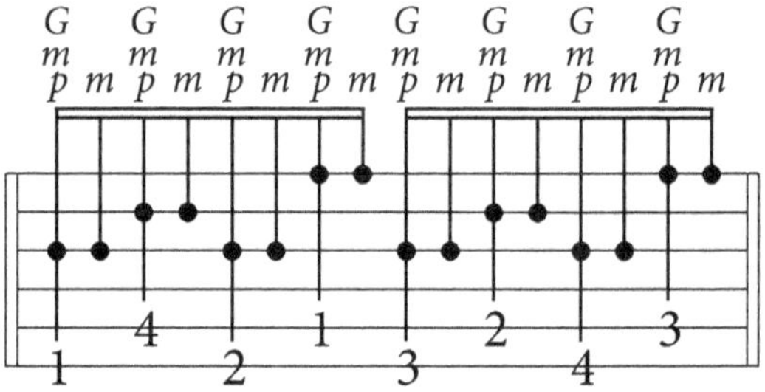

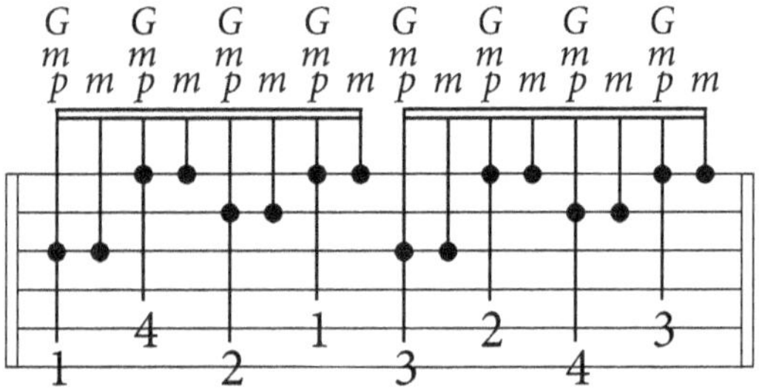

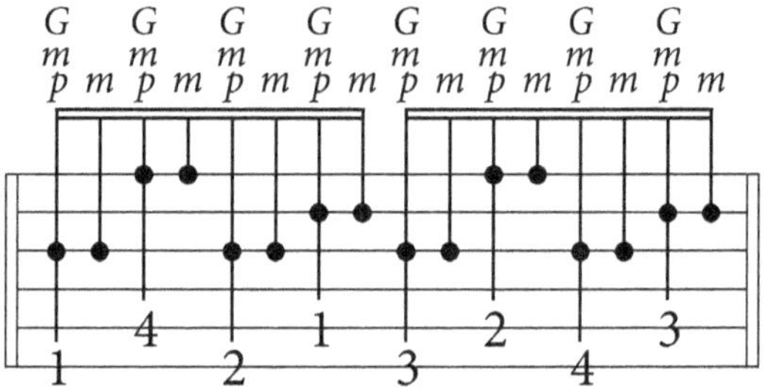

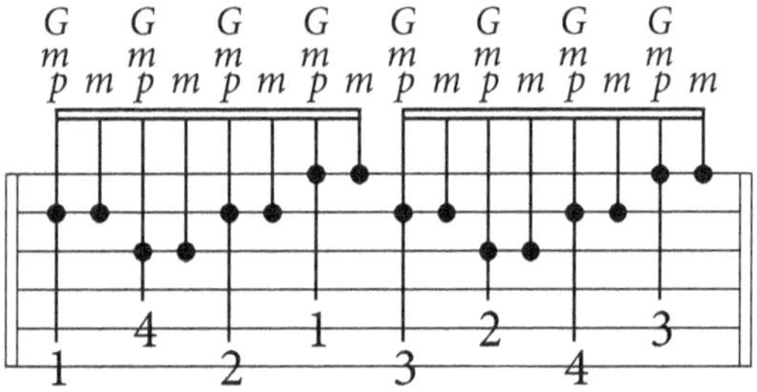

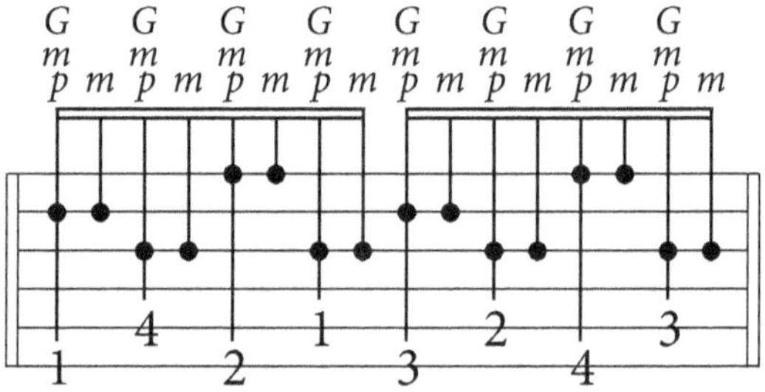

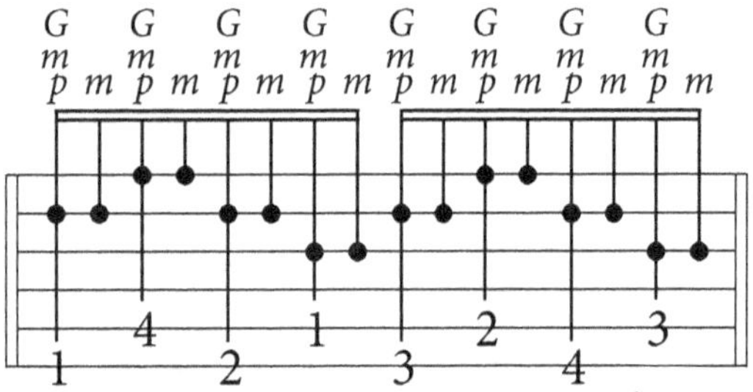

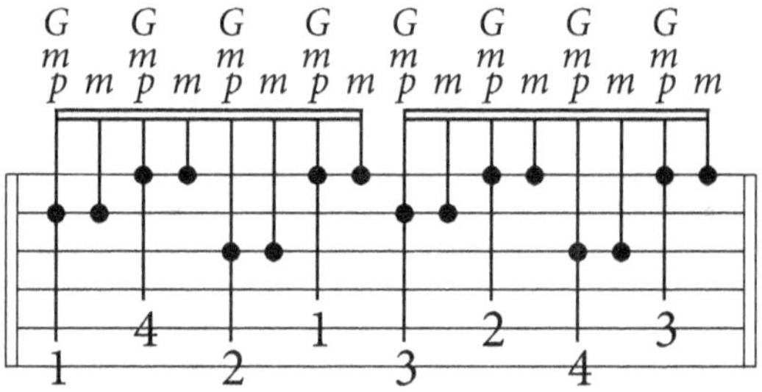

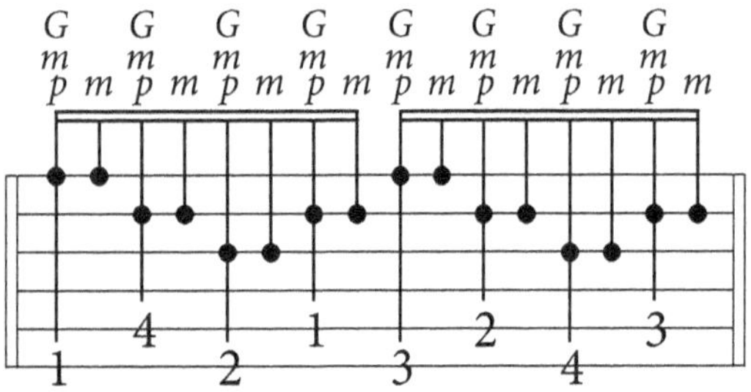

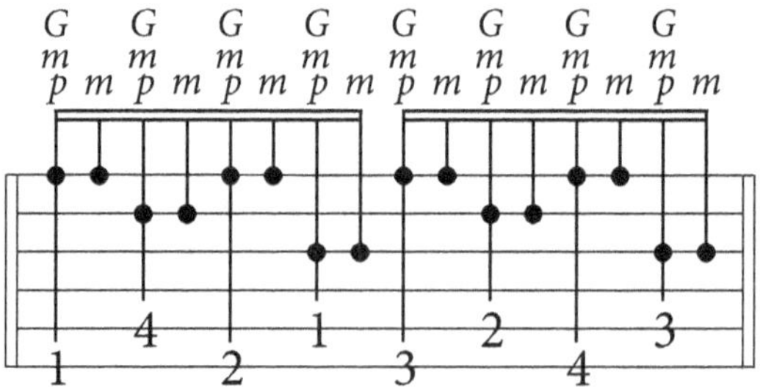

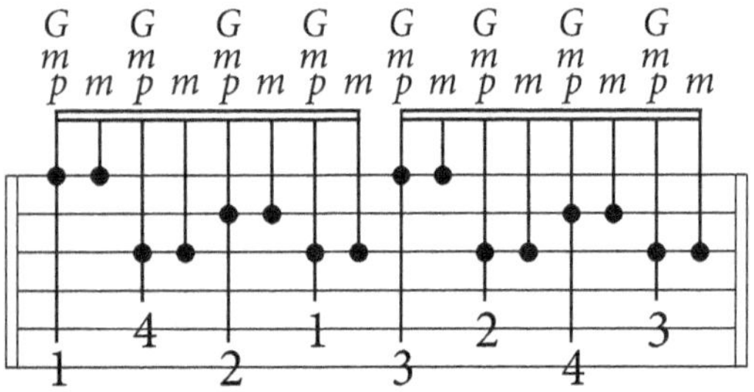

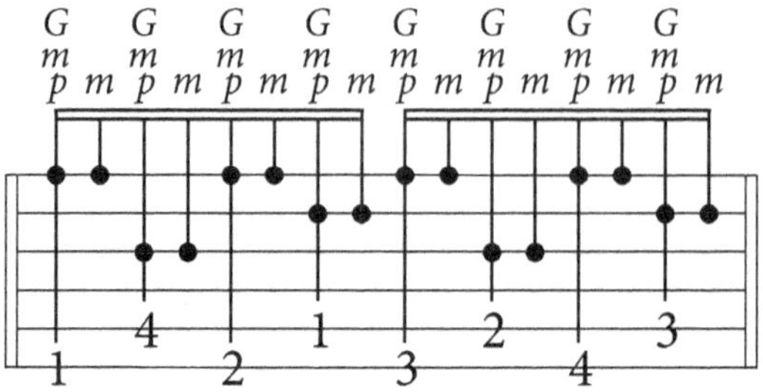

§ IIIa

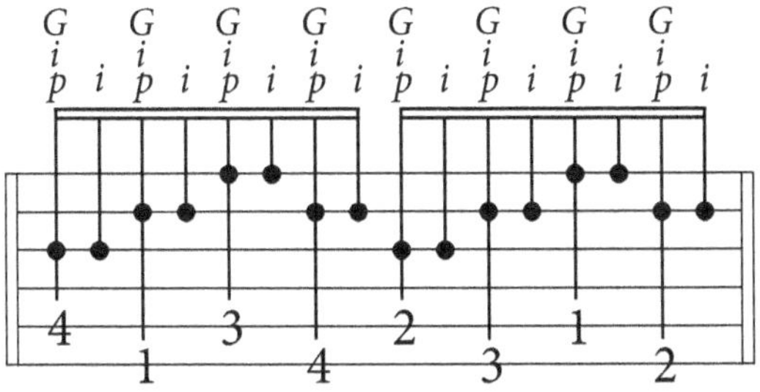

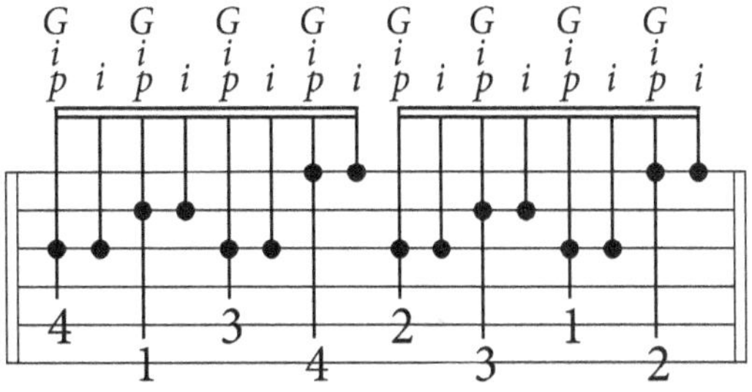

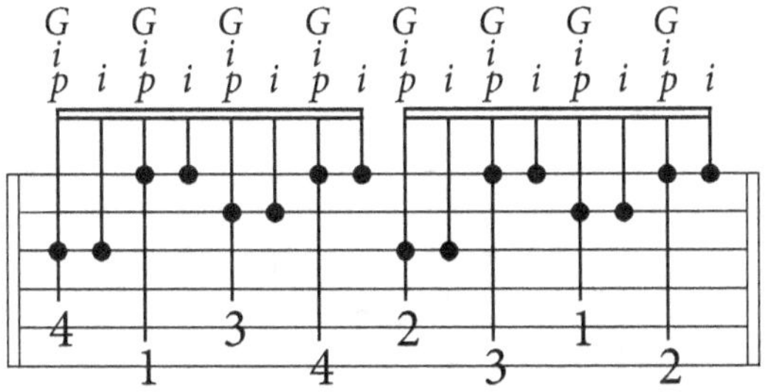

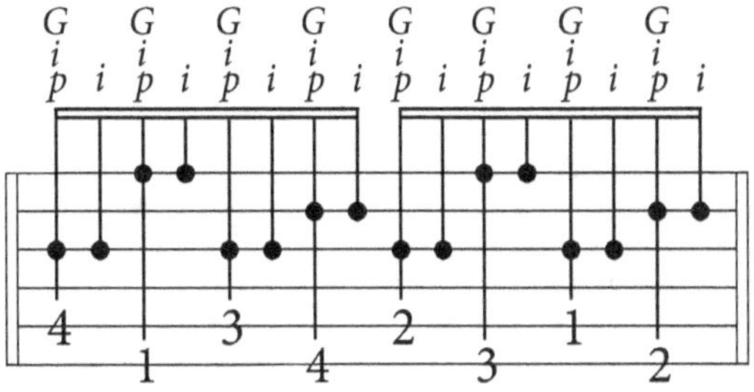

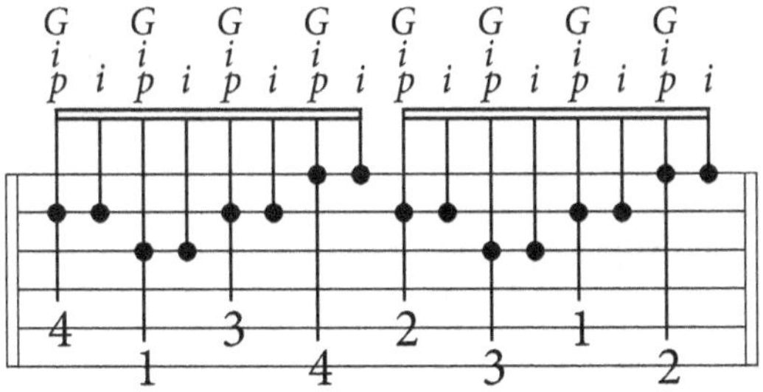

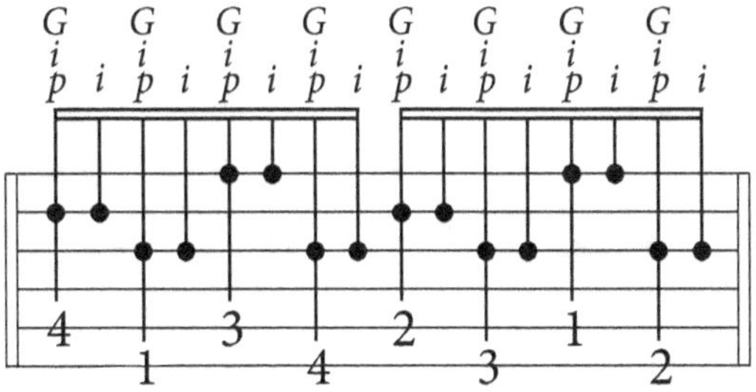

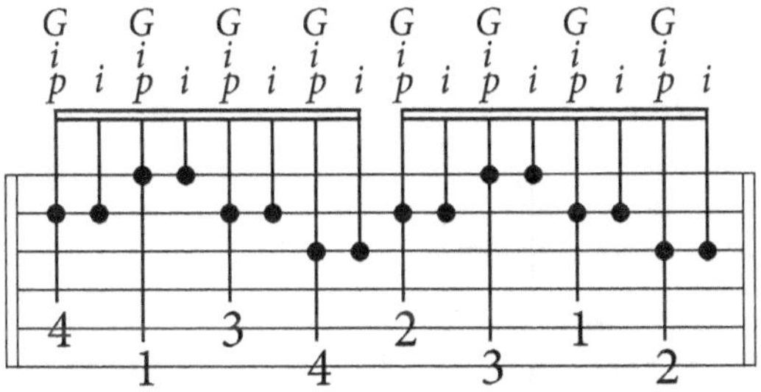

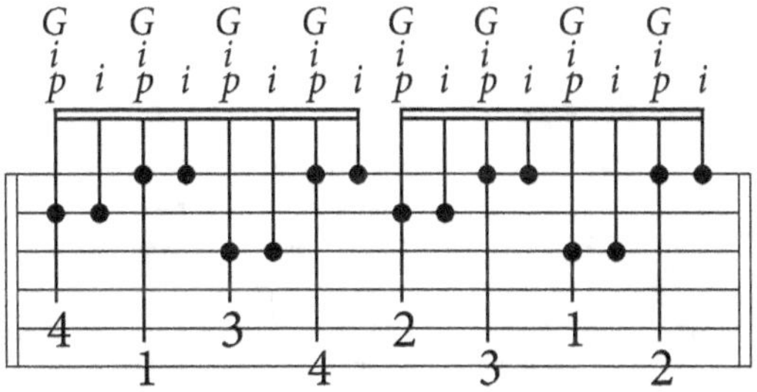

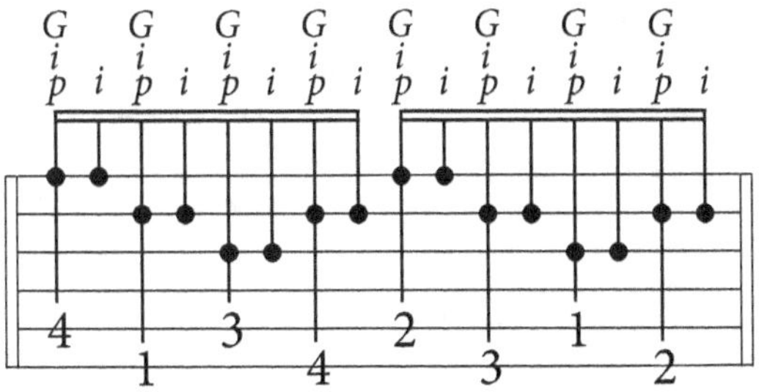

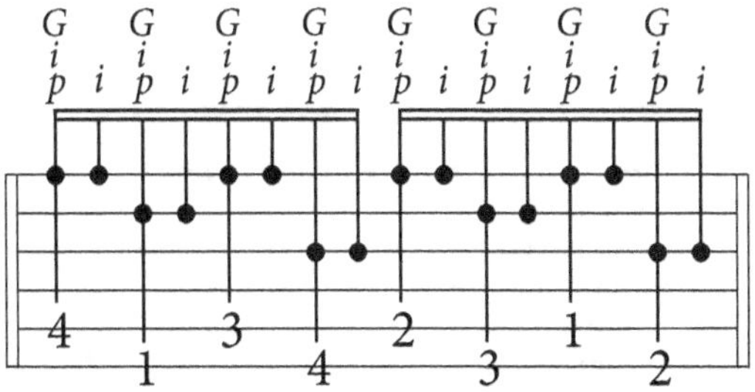

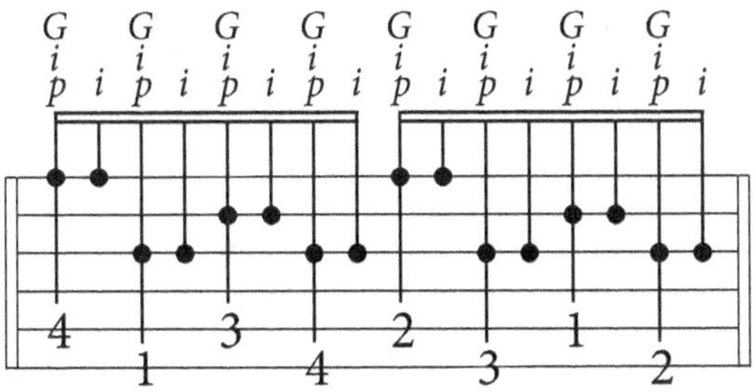

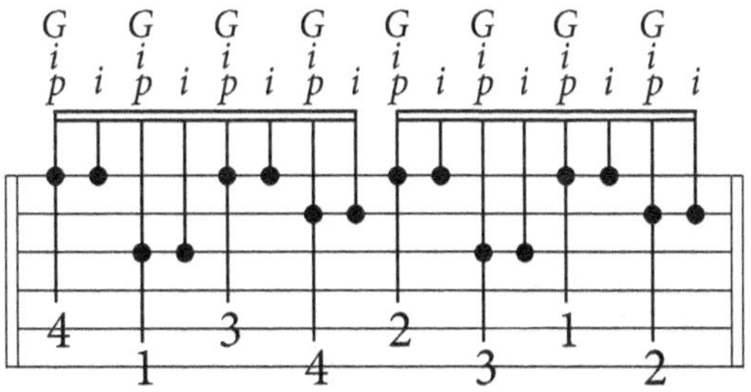

§ IIIb

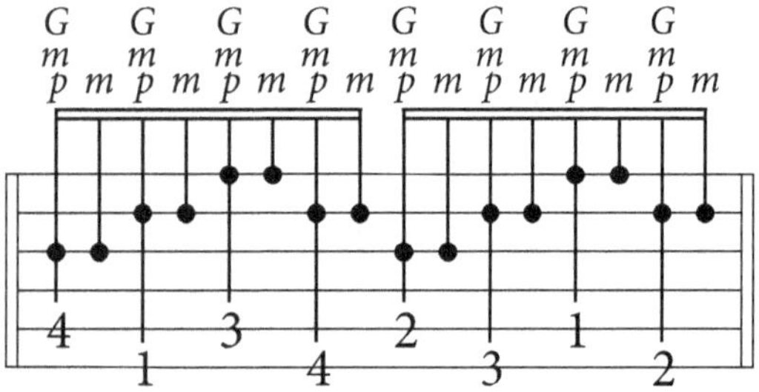

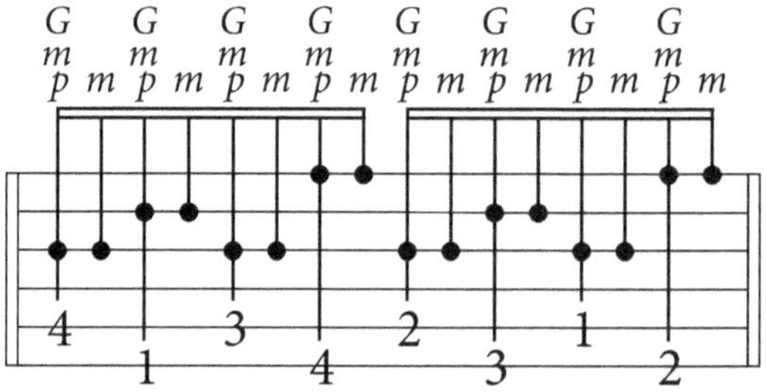

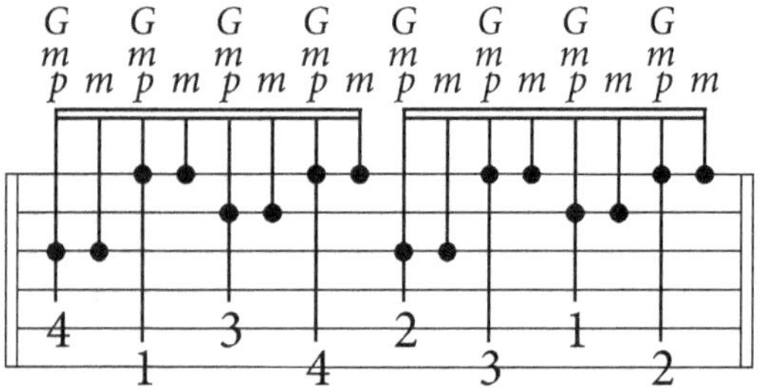

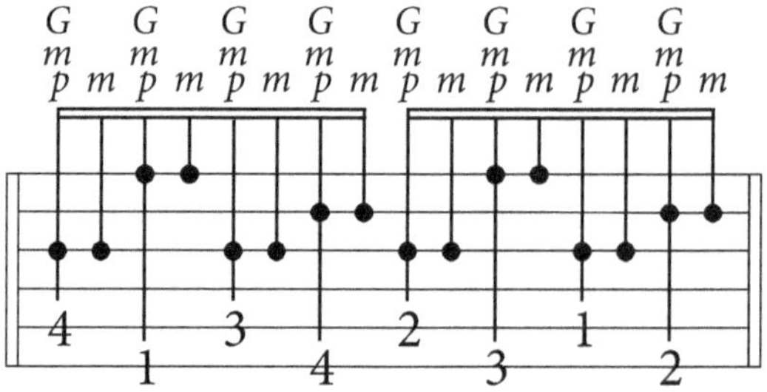

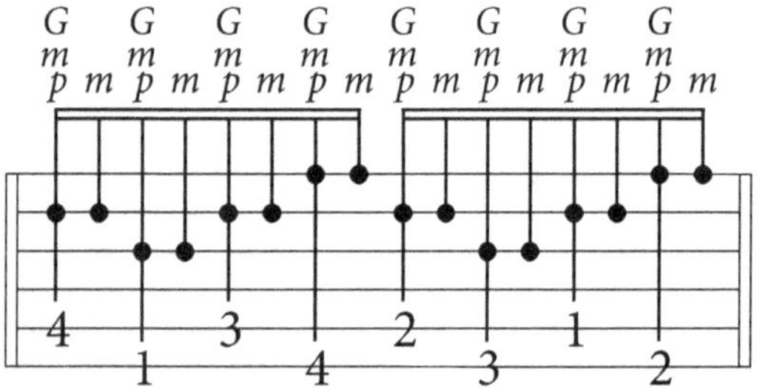

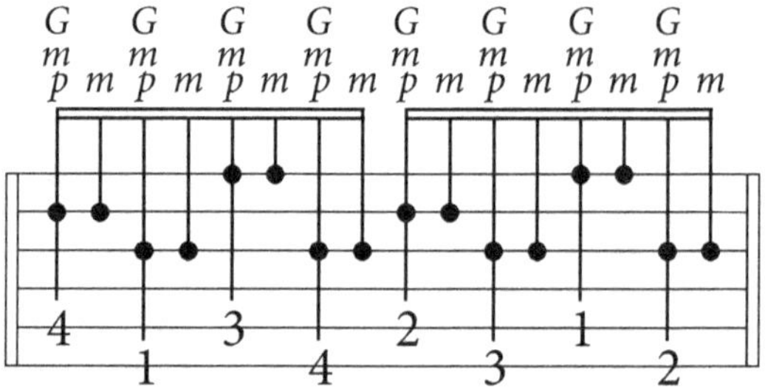

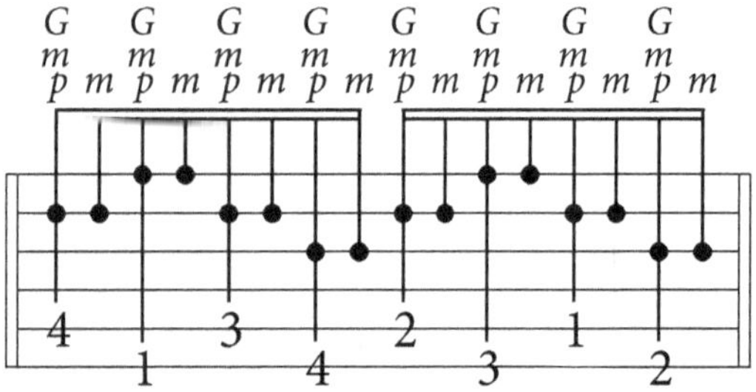

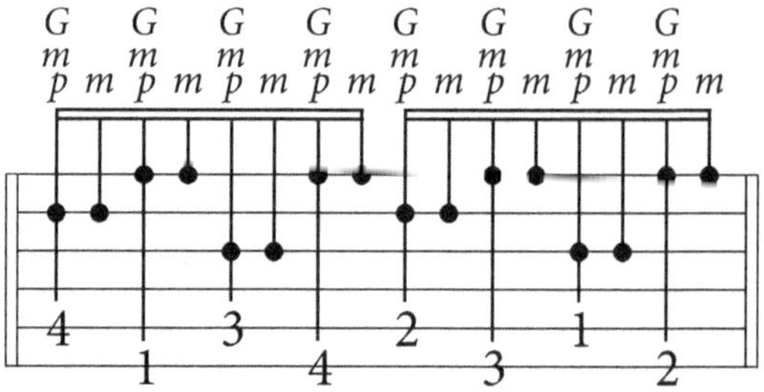

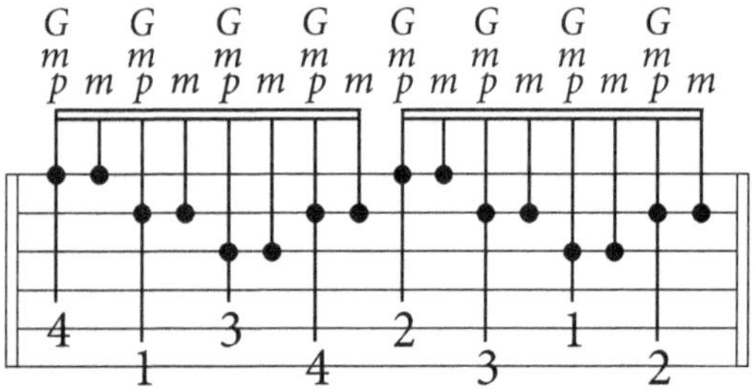

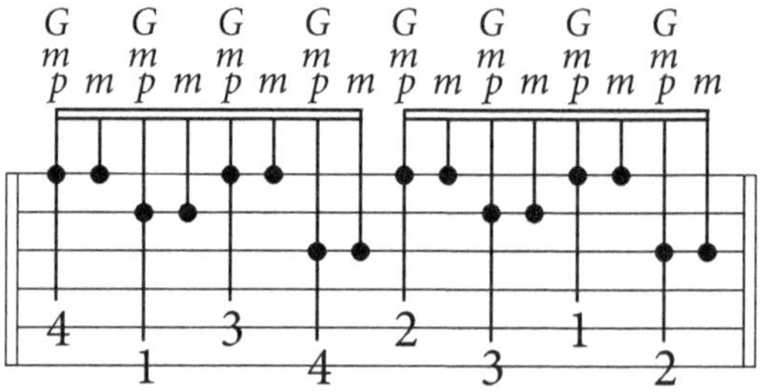

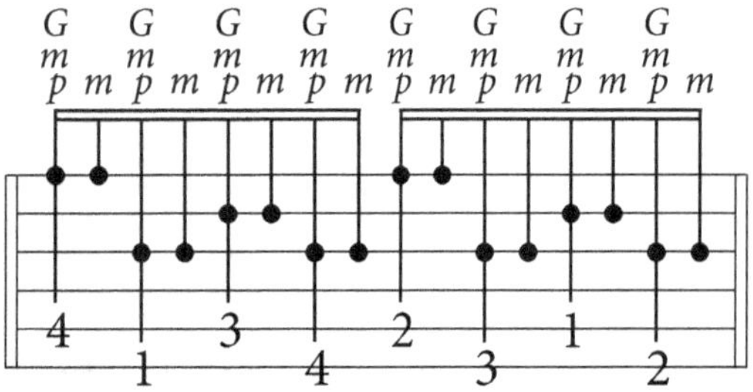

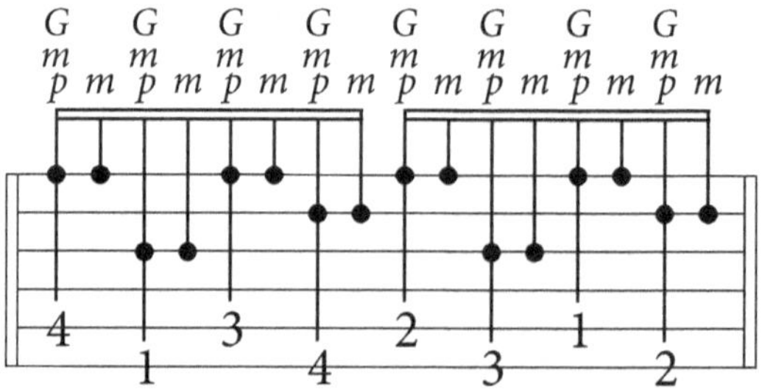

§ IVa

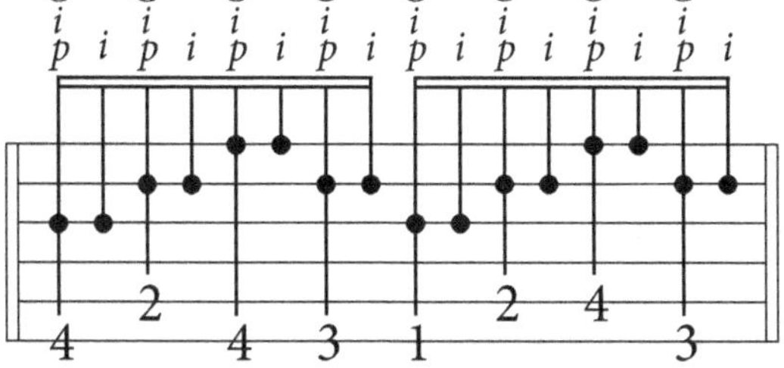

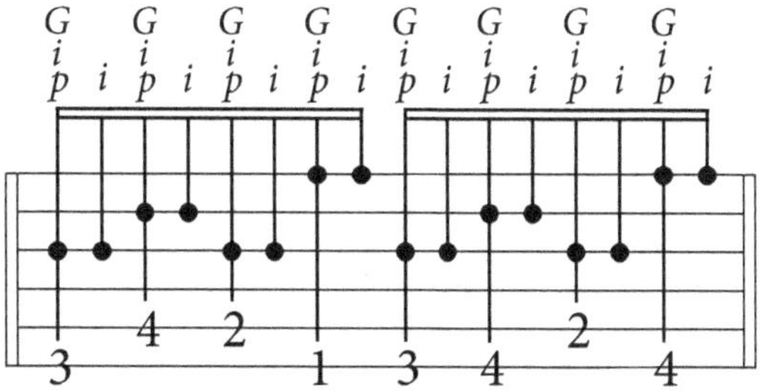

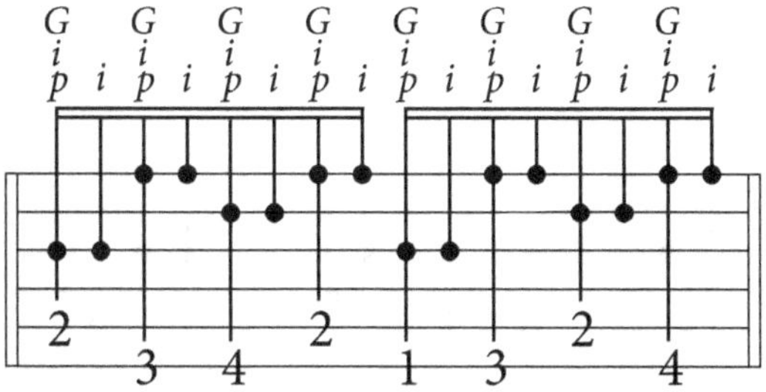

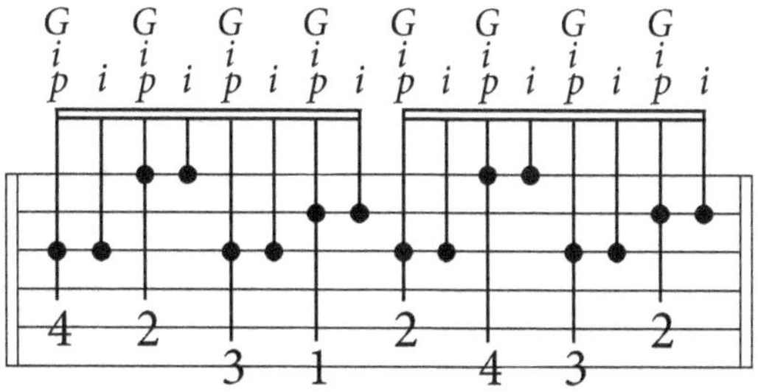

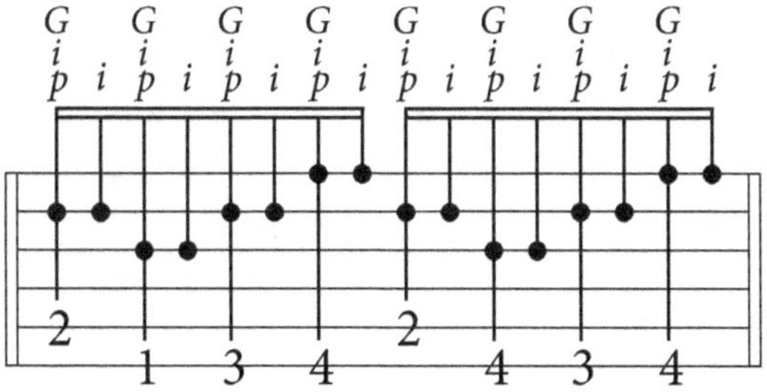

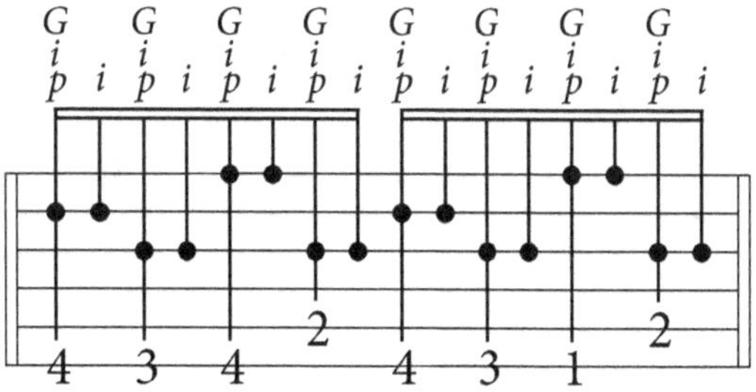

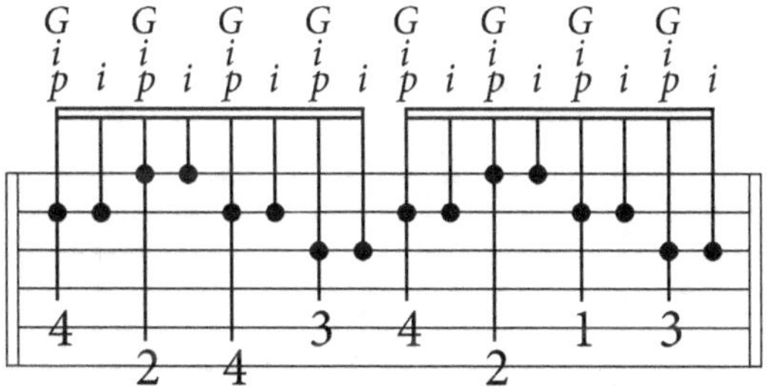

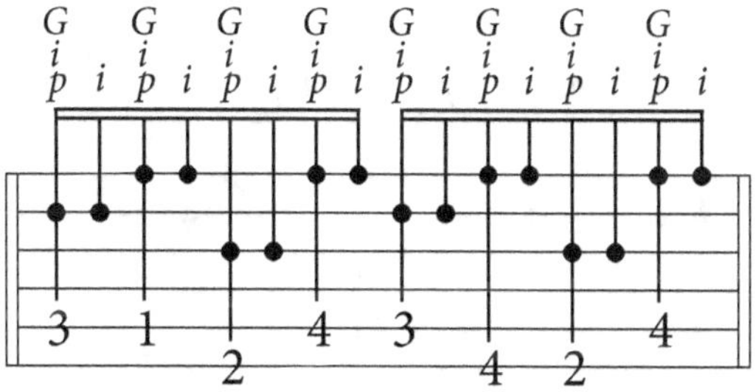

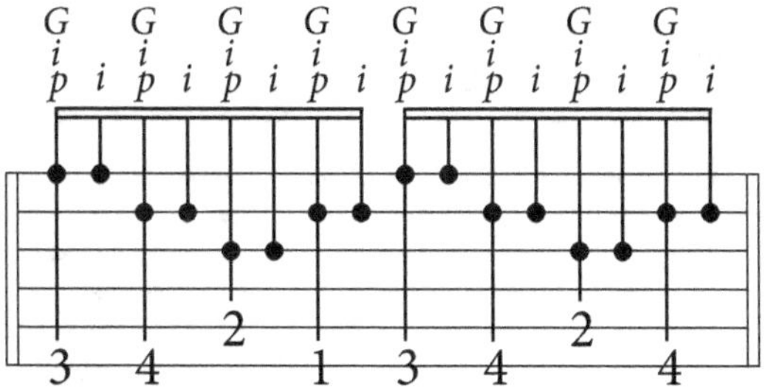

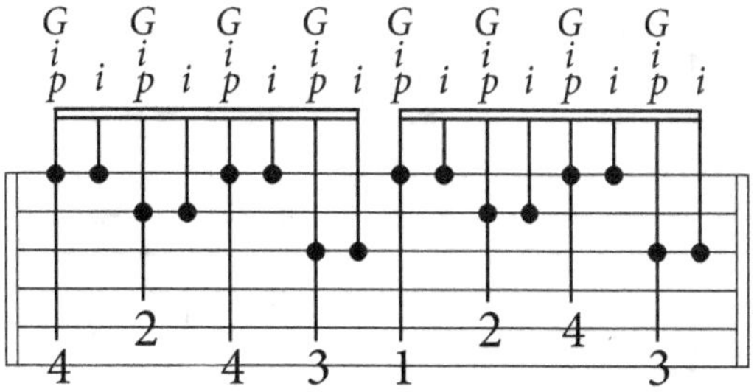

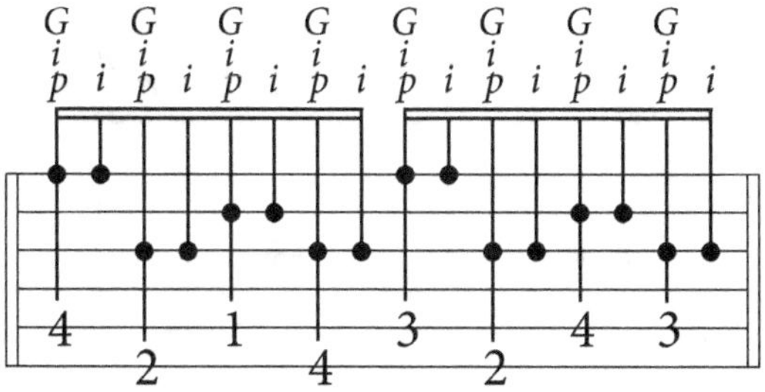

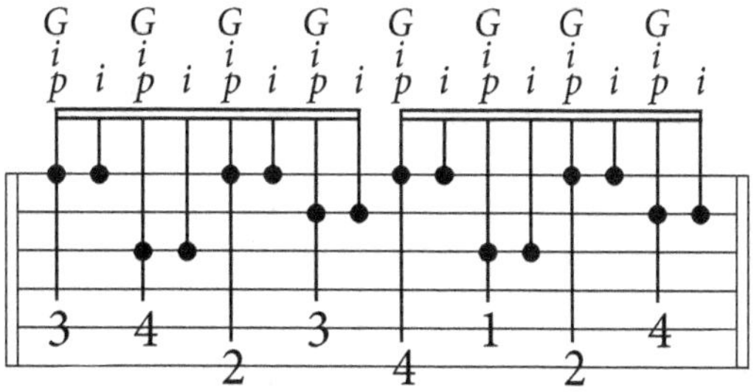

§ IVb

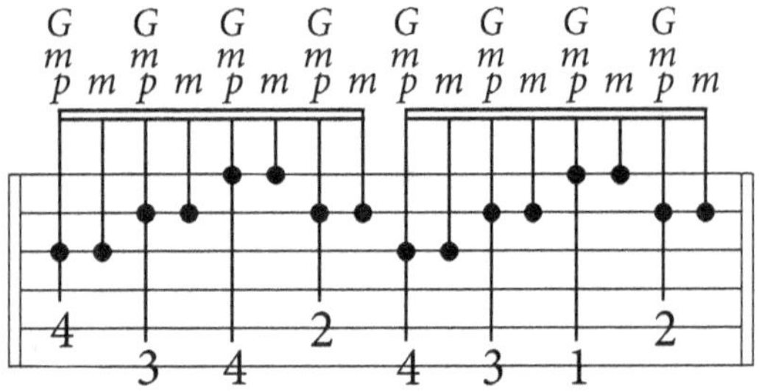

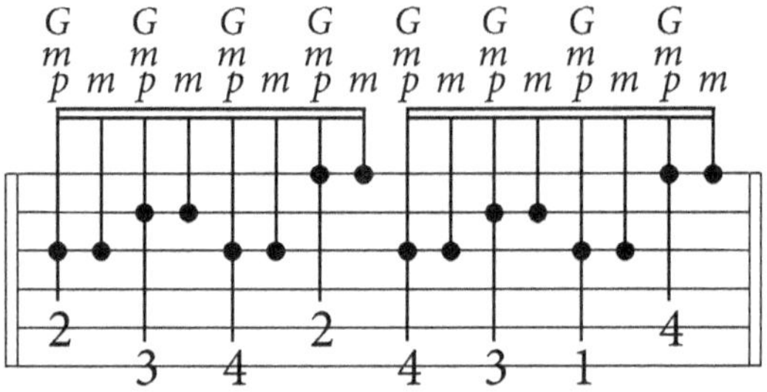

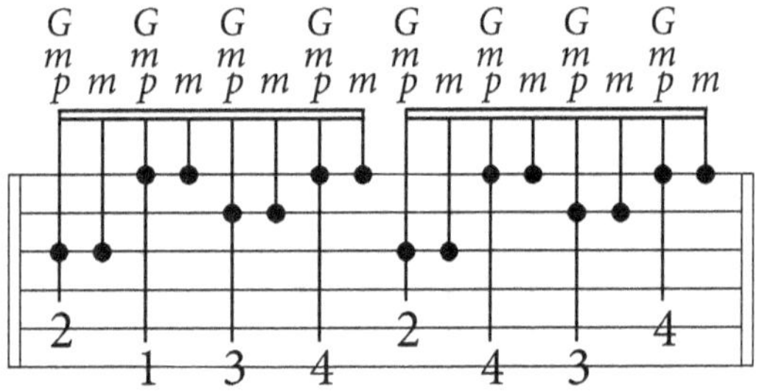

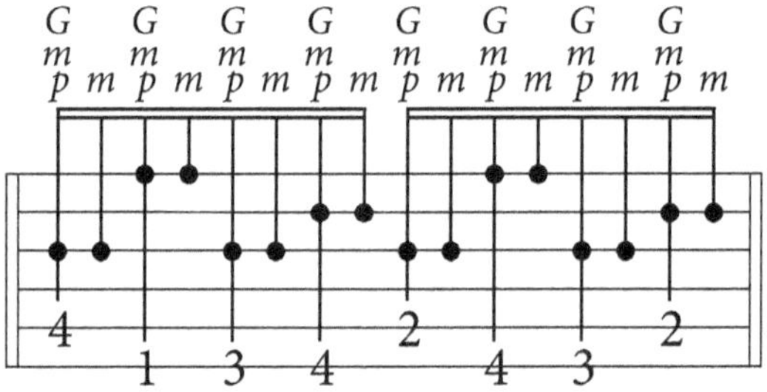

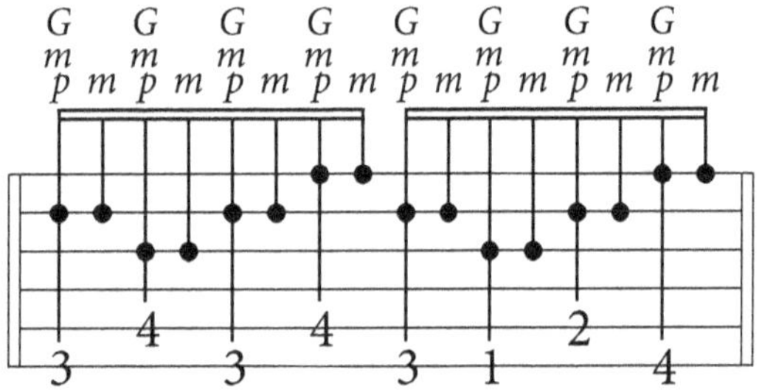

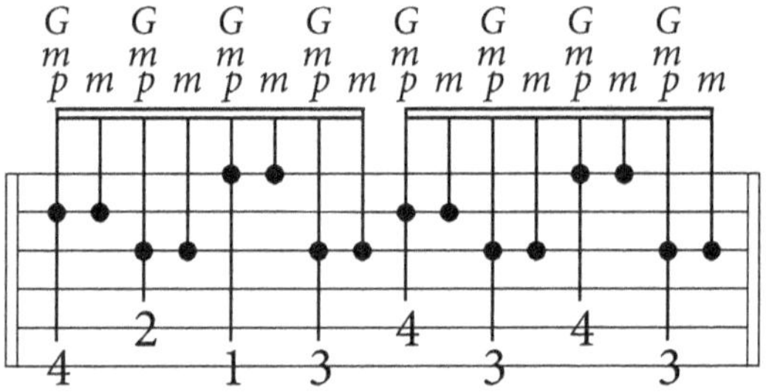

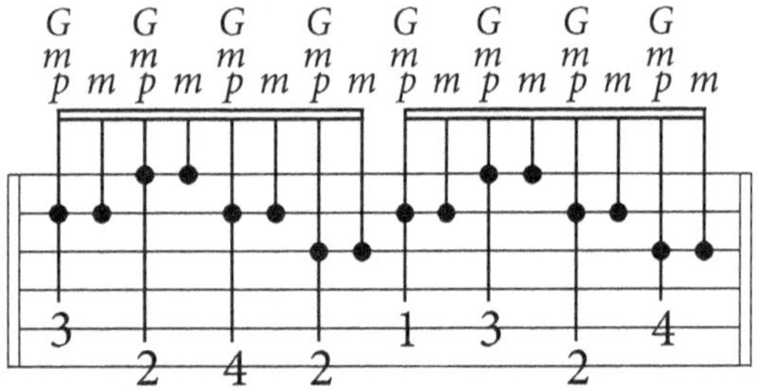

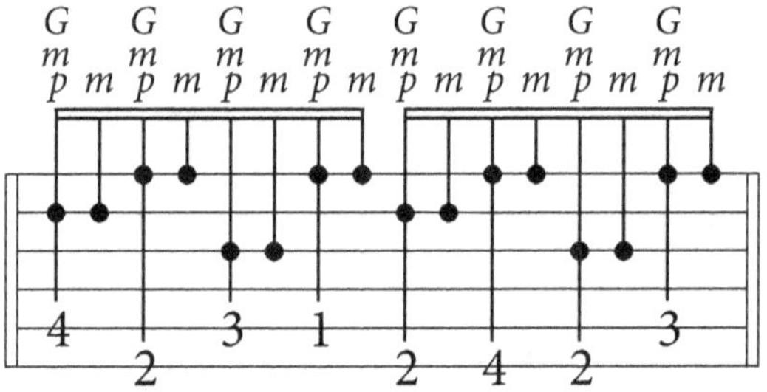

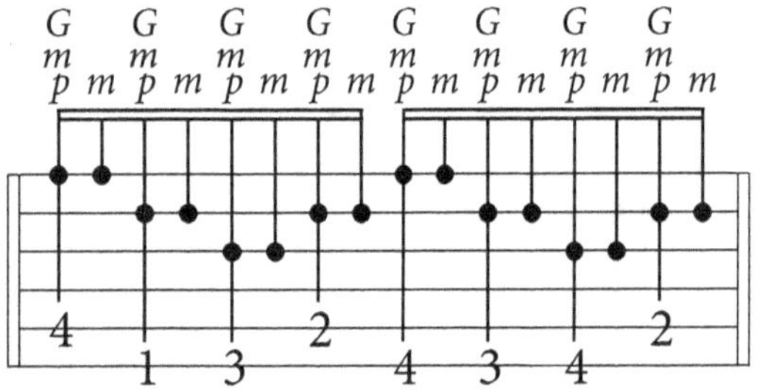

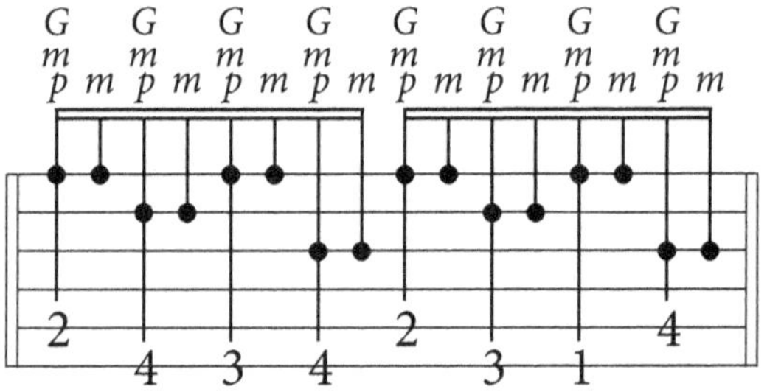

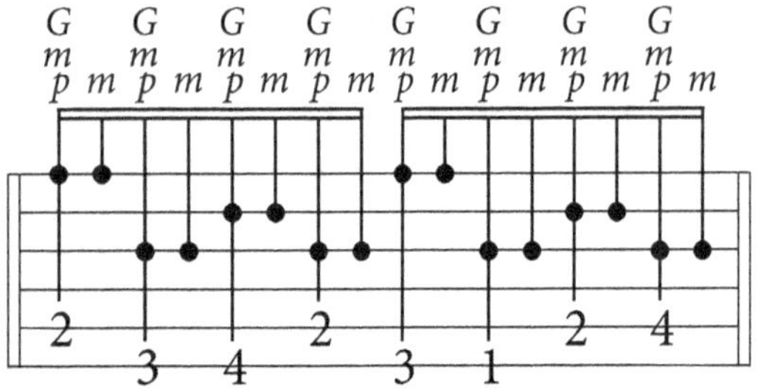

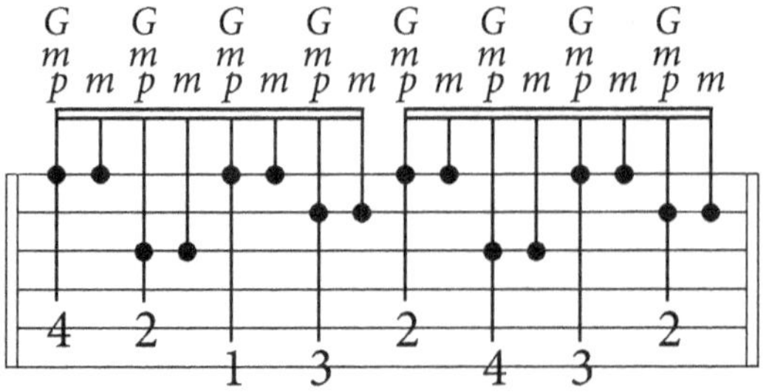

UNIT 4

Thumb stroke on two and three strings
simultaneously with Golpe.

§ Ia
F1

§ Ib
F1

§ IIa
F1

§ IIb
F1

§ Ia

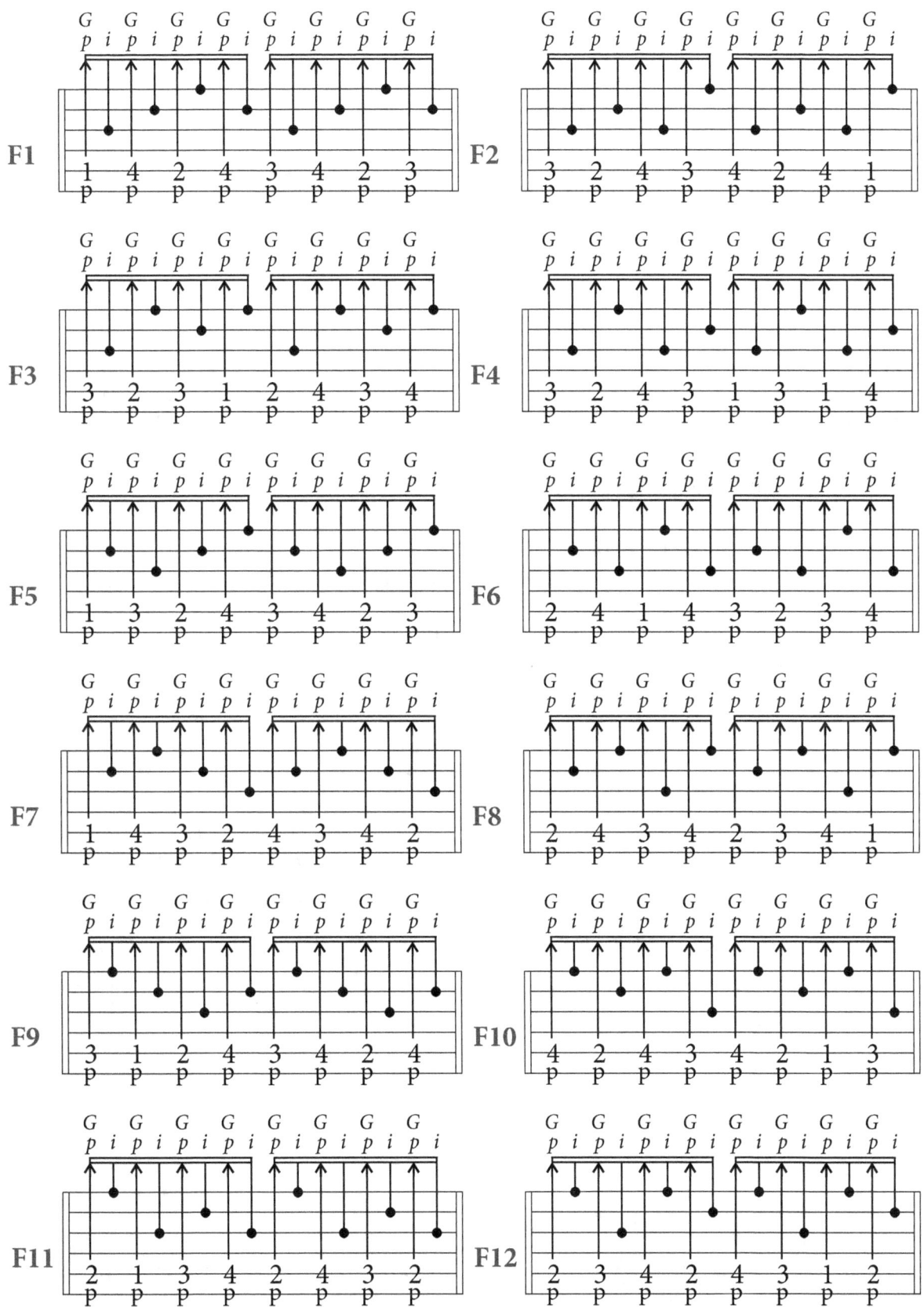

§ Ib

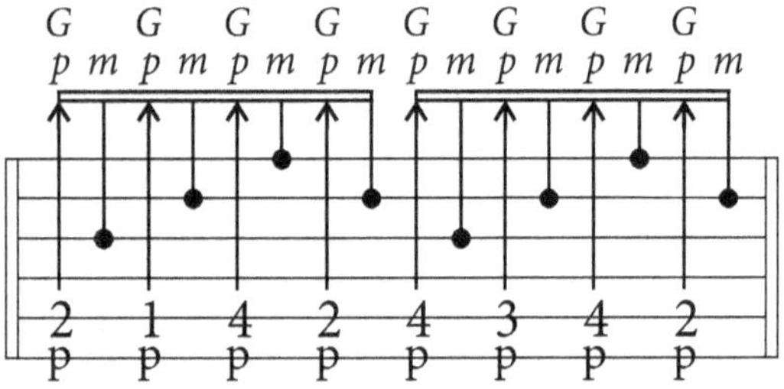

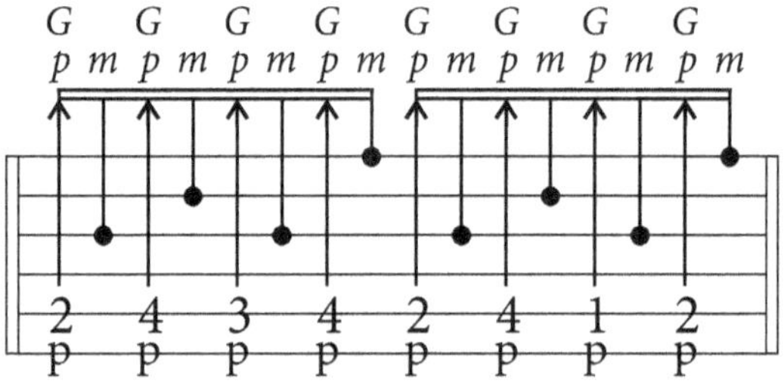

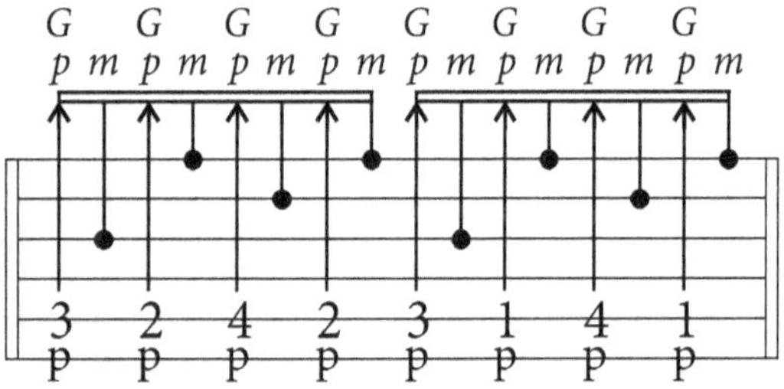

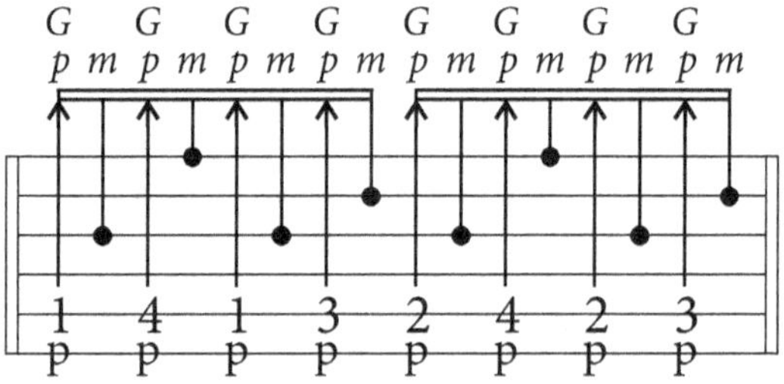

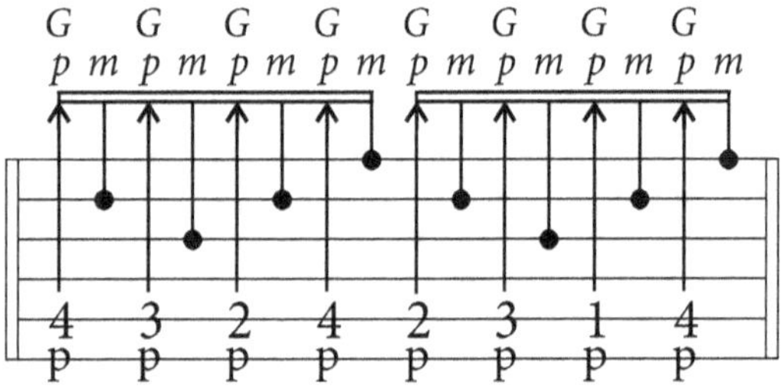

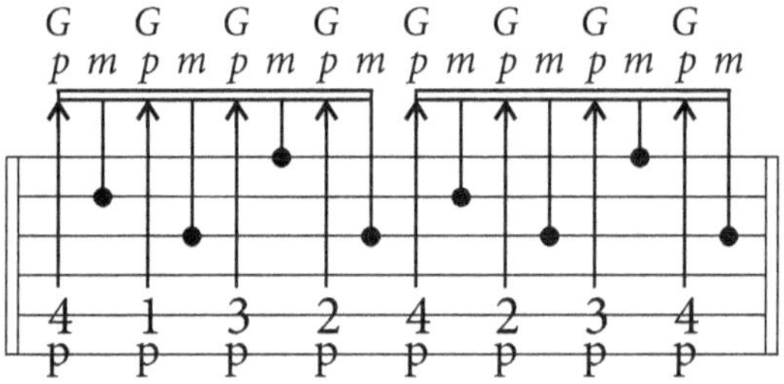

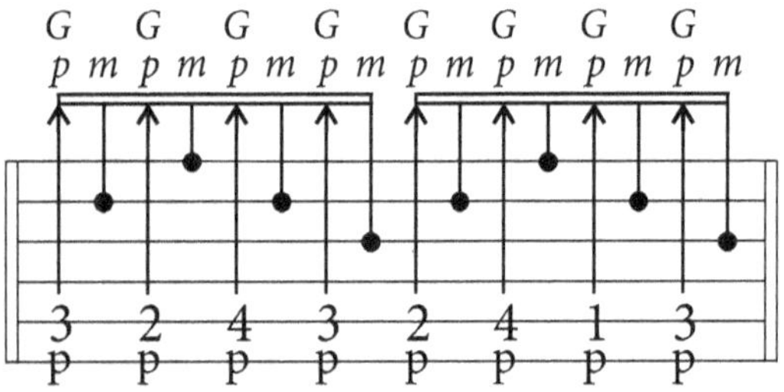

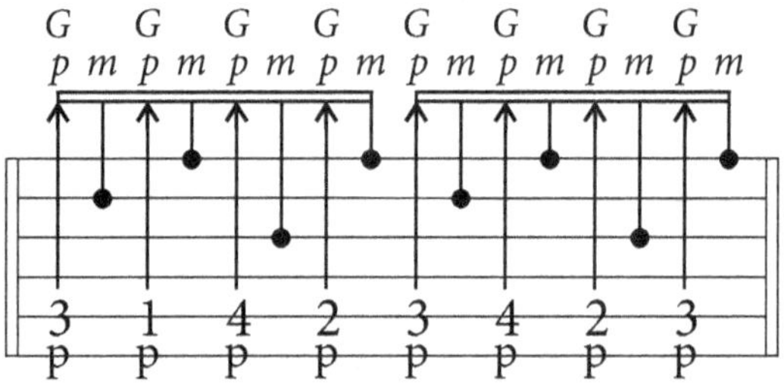

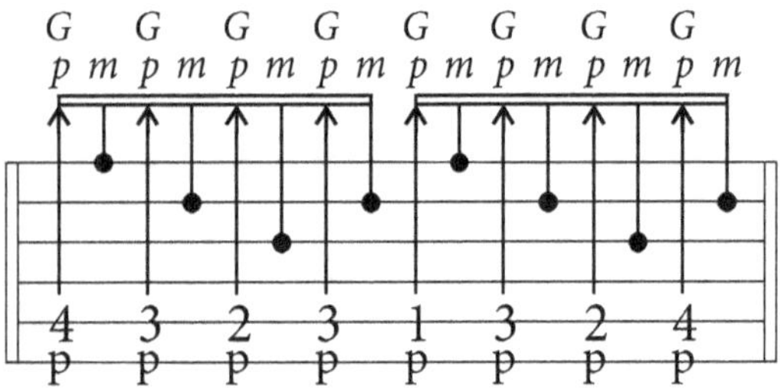

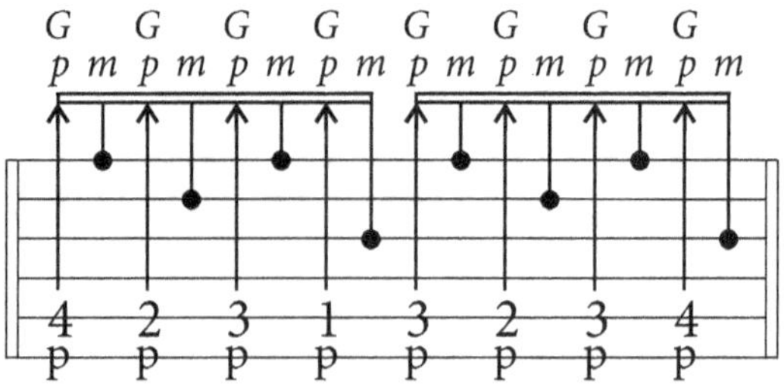

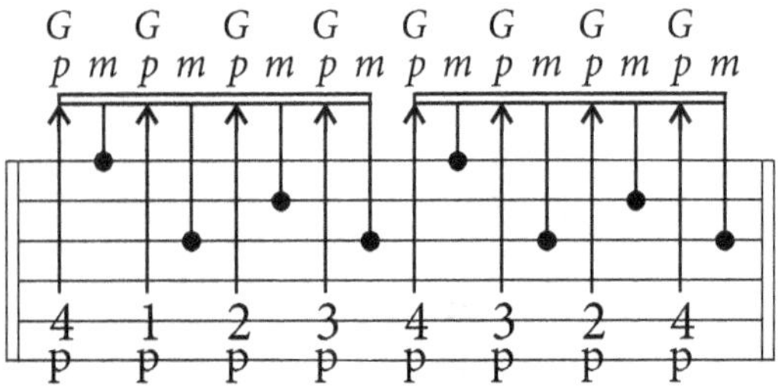

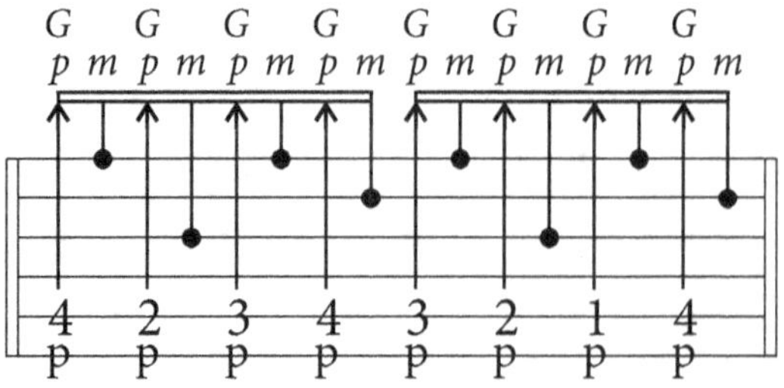

§ IIa

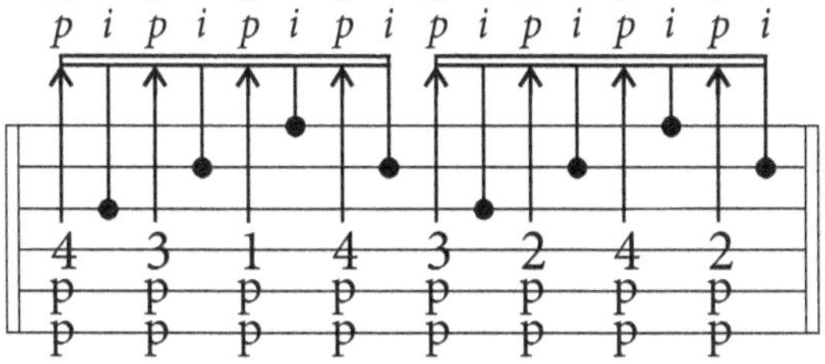

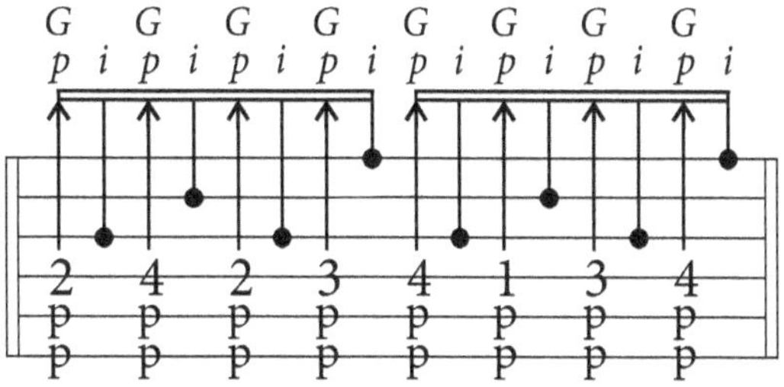

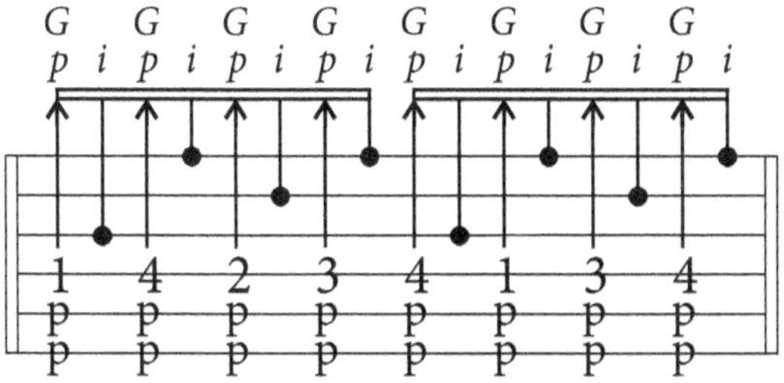

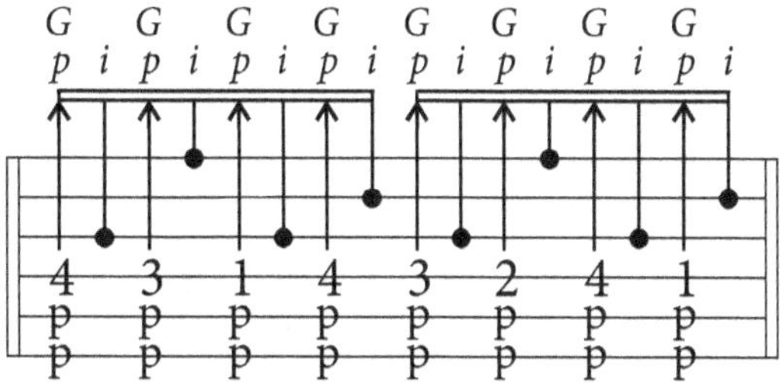

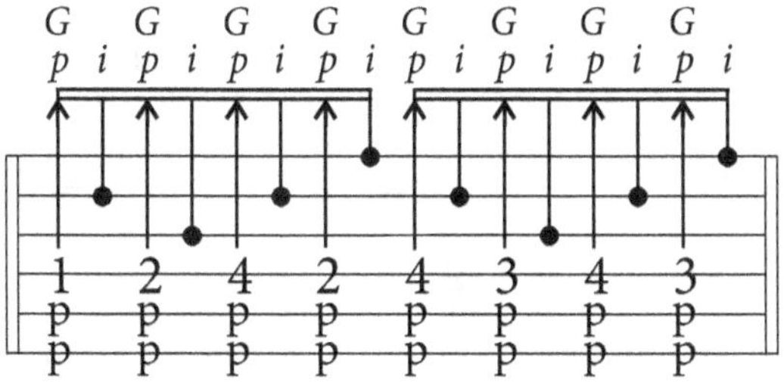

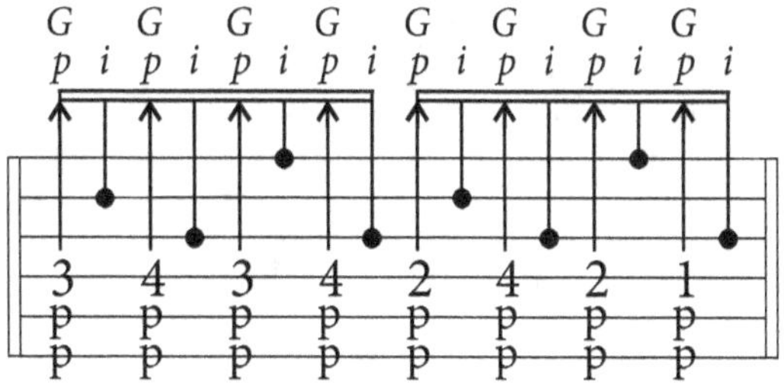

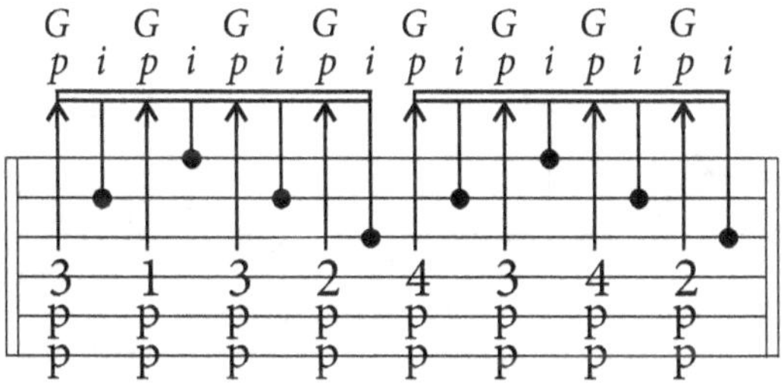

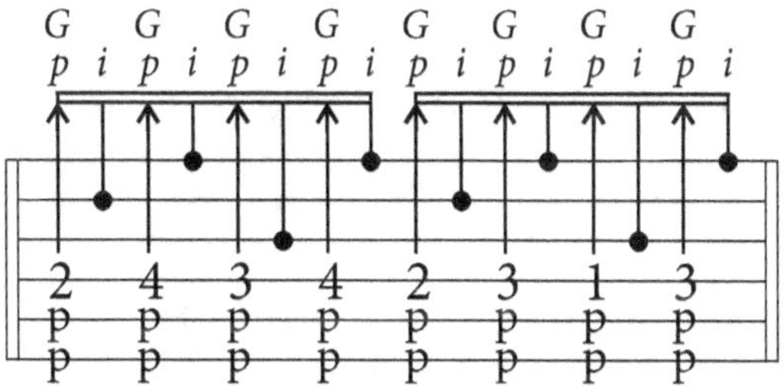

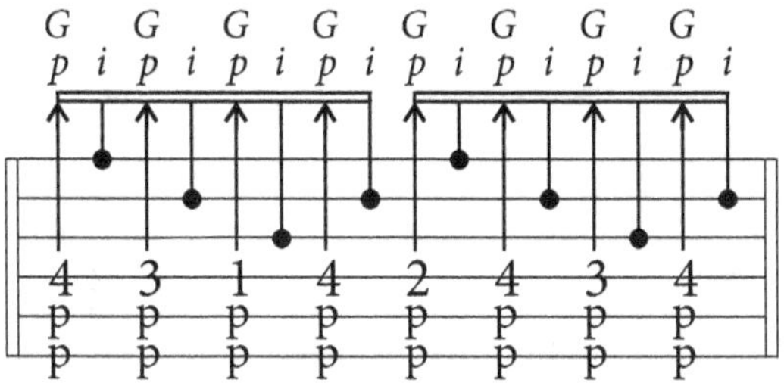

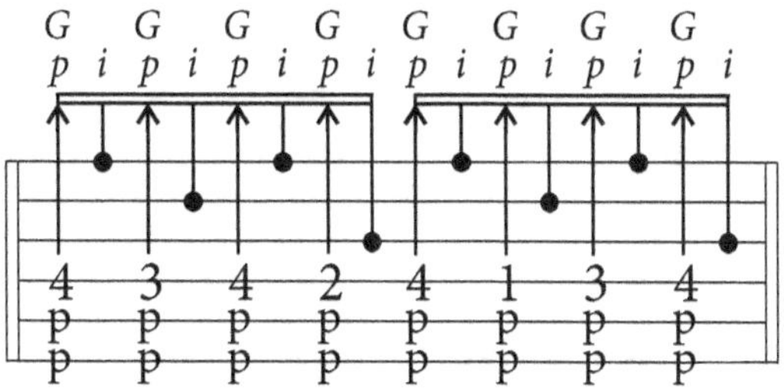

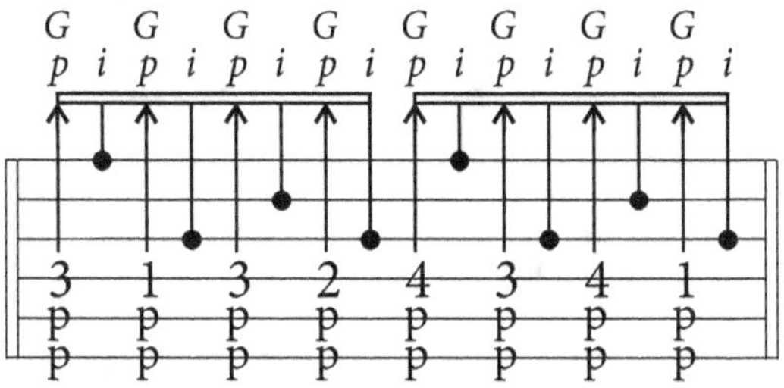

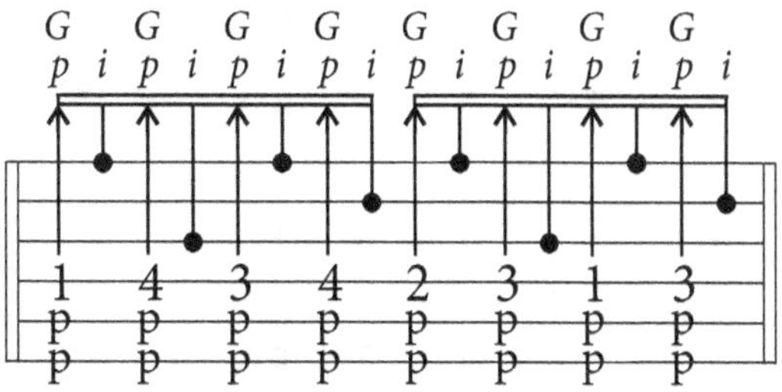

§ IIb

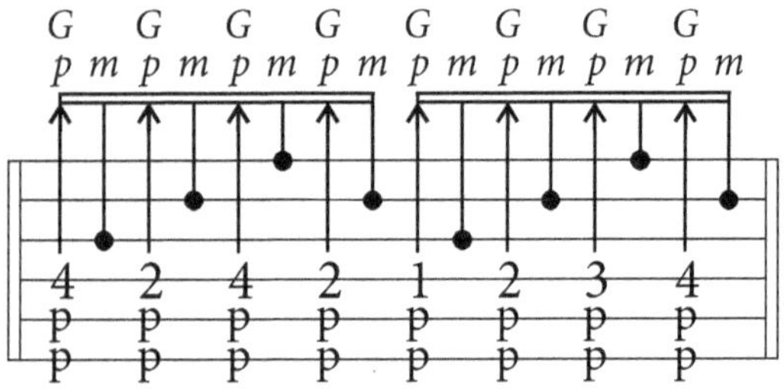

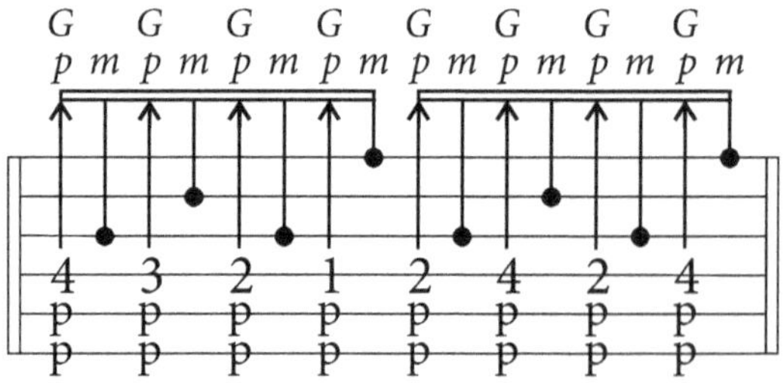

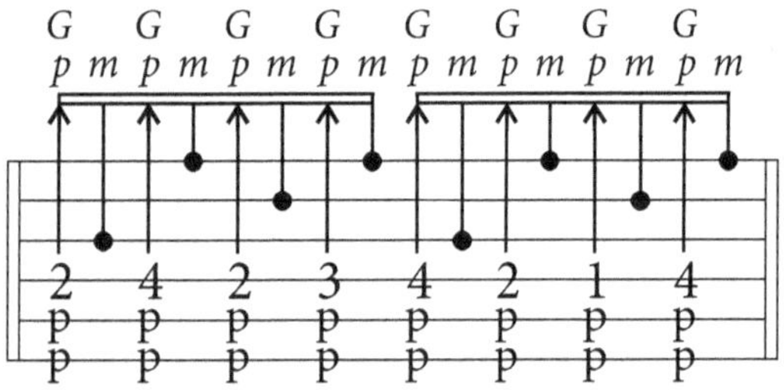

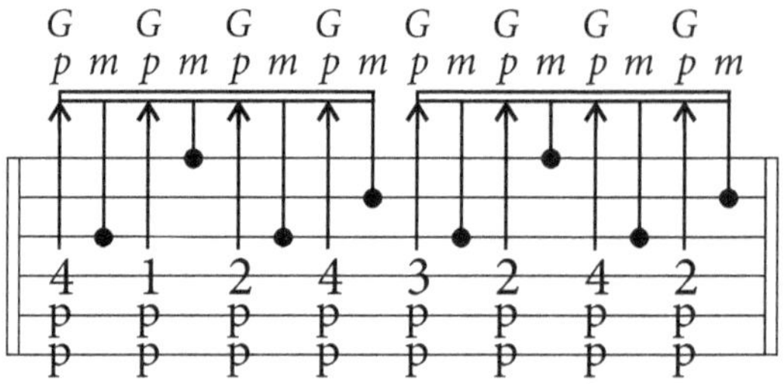

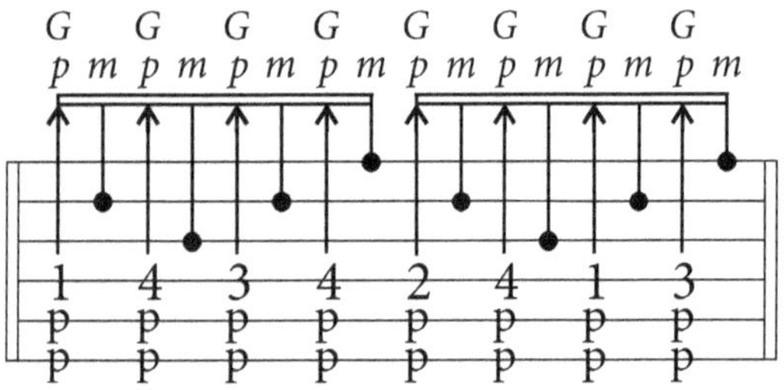

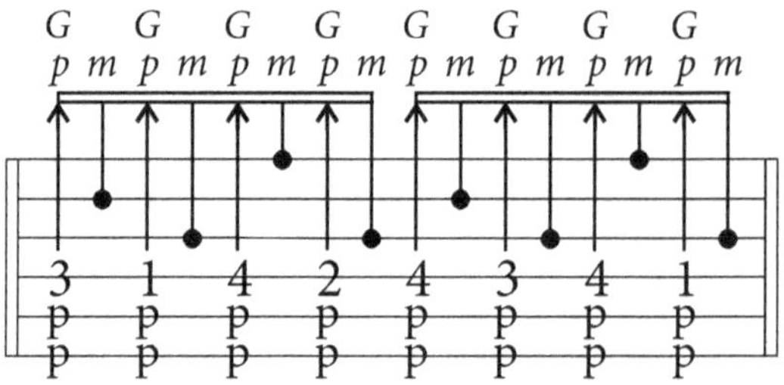

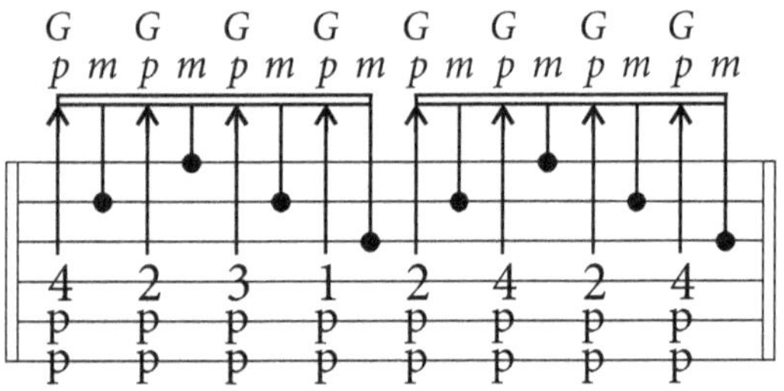

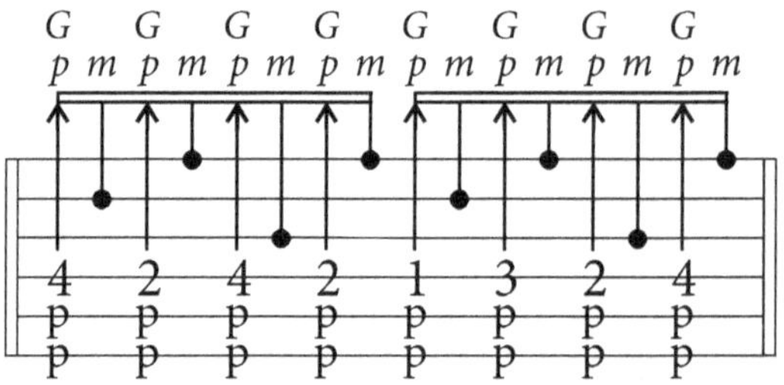

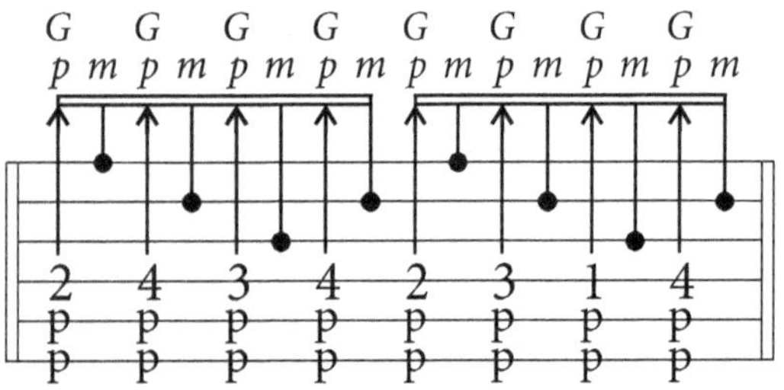

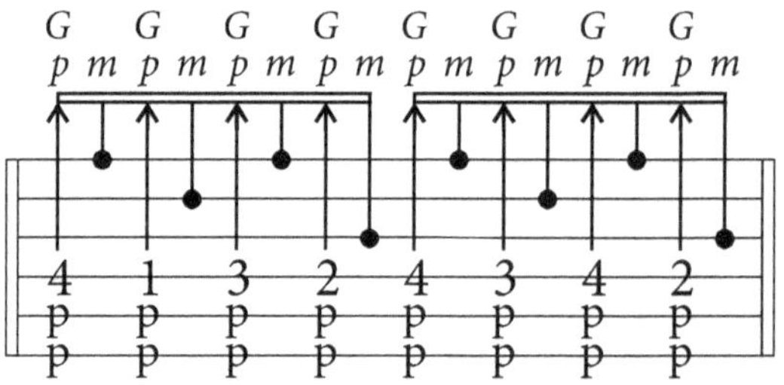

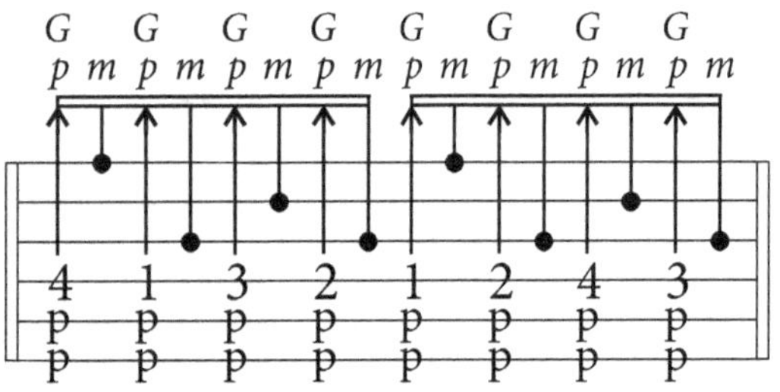

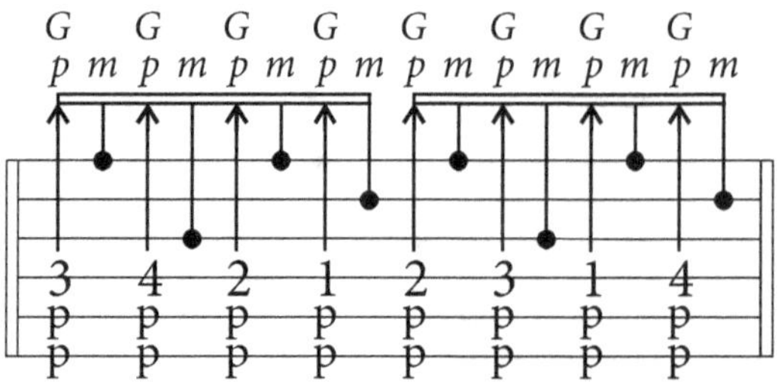

CHAPTER 7

RASGUEADOS AND GOLPE.

The left hand holds a chord of four notes as the following:

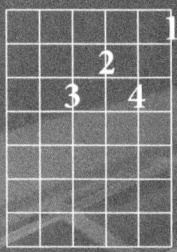

Of course this can be alternated with other chords of four notes.

1A
↑ ↑ ↑

i m i

G			G			G
i	m	i	i	m	i	i	m	i
↑	↑	↑	↑	↑	↑	↑	↑	↑

G	G		G	G		G	G
i	m	i	i	m	i	i	m	i
↑	↑	↑	↑	↑	↑	↑	↑	↑

G G G
i m i
↑ ↑ ↑

m i m

G			G			G
m	i	m	m	i	m	m	i	m
↑	↑	↑	↑	↑	↑	↑	↑	↑

G	G		G	G		G	G
m	i	m	m	i	m	m	i	m
↑	↑	↑	↑	↑	↑	↑	↑	↑

G G G
m i m
↑ ↑ ↑

1B
↑ ↑ ↑

i i m

G *i i m* ↑ ↑ ↑	G *i i m* ↑ ↑ ↑	G *i i m* ↑ ↑ ↑
G G *i i m* ↑ ↑ ↑	G G *i i m* ↑ ↑ ↑	G G *i i m* ↑ ↑ ↑
G G G *i i m* ↑ ↑ ↑		

i mm

G *i m m* ↑ ↑ ↑	G *i m m* ↑ ↑ ↑	G *i m m* ↑ ↑ ↑
G G *i m m* ↑ ↑ ↑	G G *i m m* ↑ ↑ ↑	G G *i m m* ↑ ↑ ↑
G G G *i m m* ↑ ↑ ↑		

1C
↑ ↑ ↑

m i i

G			G			G
m	i	i	m	i	i	m	i	i
↑	↑	↑	↑	↑	↑	↑	↑	↑

G G   G   G   G G
m i i   m i i   m i i
↑ ↑ ↑   ↑ ↑ ↑   ↑ ↑ ↑

G G G
m i i
↑ ↑ ↑

m m i

G			G			G
m	m	i	m	m	i	m	m	i
↑	↑	↑	↑	↑	↑	↑	↑	↑

G G   G G   G G
m m i   m m i   m m i
↑ ↑ ↑   ↑ ↑ ↑   ↑ ↑ ↑

G G G
m m i
↑ ↑ ↑

2

↑ ↑ ↓

i m i

G	G	G G
i m i	*i m i*	*i m i*
↑ ↑ ↓	↑ ↑ ↓	↑ ↑ ↓

m i m

G	G	G G
m i m	*m i m*	*m i m*
↑ ↑ ↓	↑ ↑ ↓	↑ ↑ ↓

i i m

G	G	G G
i i m	*i i m*	*i i m*
↑ ↑ ↓	↑ ↑ ↓	↑ ↑ ↓

i m m

G	G	G G
i m m	*i m m*	*i m m*
↑ ↑ ↓	↑ ↑ ↓	↑ ↑ ↓

m i i

G	G	G G
m i i	*m i i*	*m i i*
↑ ↑ ↓	↑ ↑ ↓	↑ ↑ ↓

m m i

G	G	G G
m m i	*m m i*	*m m i*
↑ ↑ ↓	↑ ↑ ↓	↑ ↑ ↓

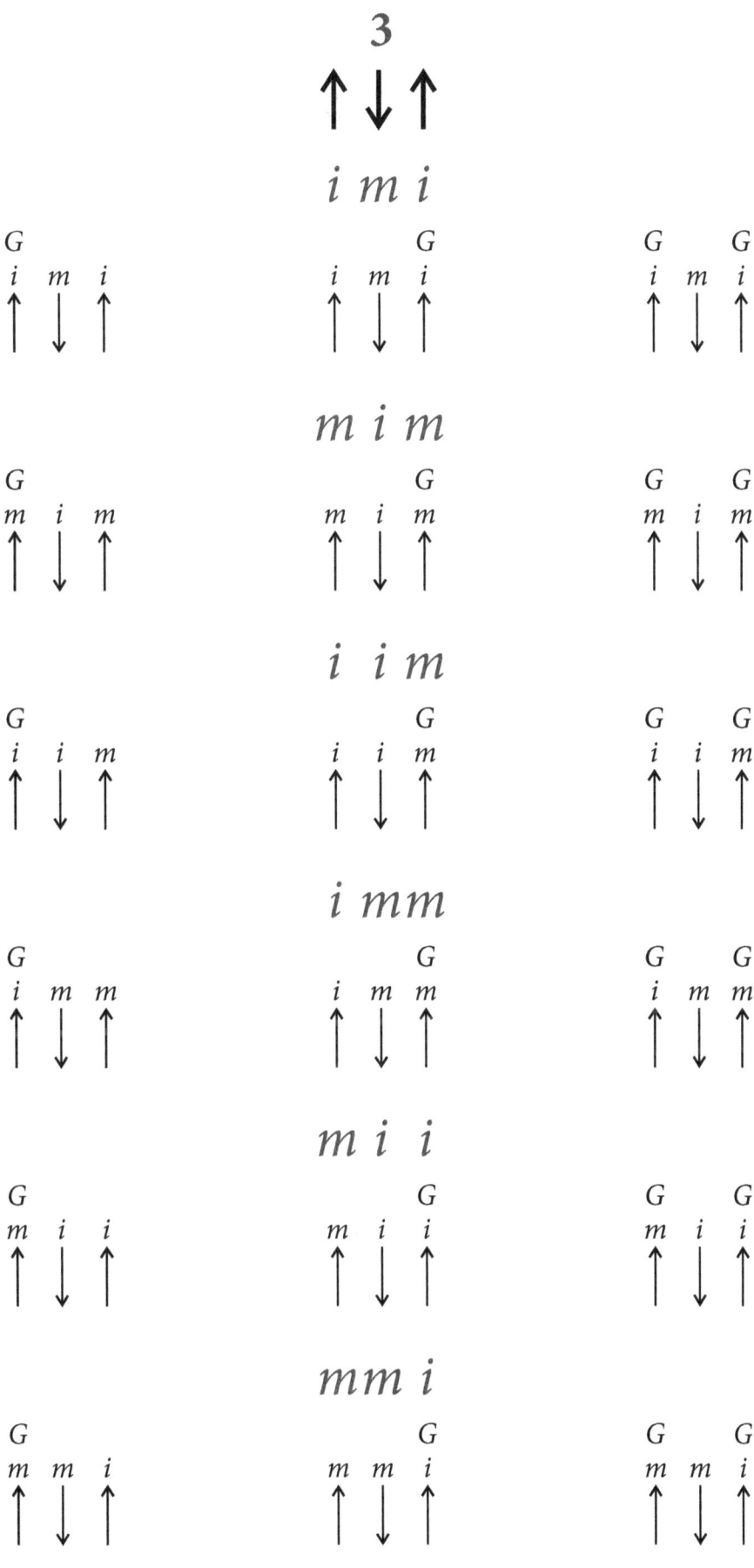

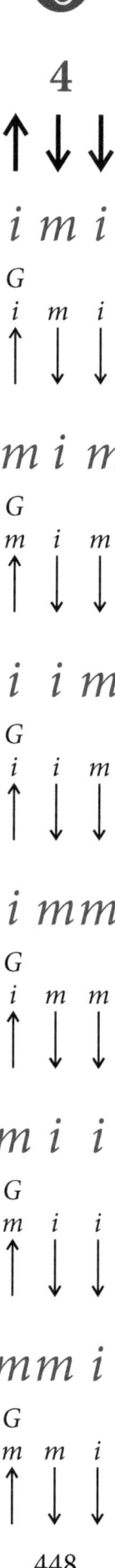

5

↓ ↓ ↑

i m i

       G
i *m* *i*
↓ ↓ ↑

m i m

       G
m *i* *m*
↓ ↓ ↑

i i m

       G
i *i* *m*
↓ ↓ ↑

i mm

       G
i *m* *m*
↓ ↓ ↑

m i i

       G
m *i* *i*
↓ ↓ ↑

mm i

       G
m *m* *i*
↓ ↓ ↑

6

↓ ↑ ↓
i m i

   G
i m i
↓ ↑ ↓

m i m

   G
m i m
↓ ↑ ↓

i i m

   G
i i m
↓ ↑ ↓

i mm

   G
i m m
↓ ↑ ↓

m i i

   G
m i i
↓ ↑ ↓

mm i

   G
m m i
↓ ↑ ↓

About the Author

Angelo started his studies in 1971, at University Of Athens School Of Medicine in obstetrics and gynecology. Along his medical training and about the same time, he began formal studies in classical guitar at National Conservatory of Athens, Greece.

After successfully completing his medical and music studies, he began his career working as an obstetrician at Kalamata County Hospital, where he witnessed the delivery of hundreds of newborns. Later on, he successfully founded a privately owned medical clinic catered to the needs of the local community.

About 25 years ago Angelo's passion for music was rekindled when a family friend living in Spain, vacationing in Kalamata, introduced him to the unique rhythms and sounds of Flamenco.

Certainly, did not take long for him to completely fall head-over-heels with the music traditions of southern Spain communities of Andalusia, Extremadura and Murcia.

Early on, as a beginner, he struggled trying to locate teaching material and sources to augment his limited at that time knowledge of Flamenco guitar techniques and styles. He frantically searched to find books and lessons explaining these special techniques used in Rasgueados, Pulgar (Alzapua), Golpe and Tremolo. Nothing was available, nothing was organized.

Not be able to locate any Flamenco teaching material, Angelo started in the most amateur, coarse way to generate his own specific technique based exercises needed to develop skills and dexterity.

Decades-long research and effort went into this book and accompanied series in order to educate you in the most efficient, convenient and systematic way.

Organized and presented in current form, this material is guaranteed to satisfy the most demanding and widely possible Classical and Flamenco guitar audience committed in learning the most intricate details of these highly specialized guitar techniques.

Having faith that his work, book series and wearable devices will serve you well, Angelo looks forward in meeting and working with each of you, now and in the near future.

www.ingramcontent.com/pod-product-compliance
Lightning Source LLC
Chambersburg PA
CBHW080514020526
44111CB00053B/2689